Communications in Computer and Information Science 1795

Rationale

The CCIS series is devoted to the publication of proceedings of computer science conferences. Its aim is to efficiently disseminate original research results in informatics in printed and electronic form. While the focus is on publication of peer-reviewed full papers presenting mature work, inclusion of reviewed short papers reporting on work in progress is welcome, too. Besides globally relevant meetings with internationally representative program committees guaranteeing a strict peer-reviewing and paper selection process, conferences run by societies or of high regional or national relevance are also considered for publication.

Topics

The topical scope of CCIS spans the entire spectrum of informatics ranging from foundational topics in the theory of computing to information and communications science and technology and a broad variety of interdisciplinary application fields.

Information for Volume Editors and Authors

Publication in CCIS is free of charge. No royalties are paid, however, we offer registered conference participants temporary free access to the online version of the conference proceedings on SpringerLink (http://link.springer.com) by means of an http referrer from the conference website and/or a number of complimentary printed copies, as specified in the official acceptance email of the event.

CCIS proceedings can be published in time for distribution at conferences or as post-proceedings, and delivered in the form of printed books and/or electronically as USBs and/or e-content licenses for accessing proceedings at SpringerLink. Furthermore, CCIS proceedings are included in the CCIS electronic book series hosted in the SpringerLink digital library at http://link.springer.com/bookseries/7899. Conferences publishing in CCIS are allowed to use Online Conference Service (OCS) for managing the whole proceedings lifecycle (from submission and reviewing to preparing for publication) free of charge.

Publication process

The language of publication is exclusively English. Authors publishing in CCIS have to sign the Springer CCIS copyright transfer form, however, they are free to use their material published in CCIS for substantially changed, more elaborate subsequent publications elsewhere. For the preparation of the camera-ready papers/files, authors have to strictly adhere to the Springer CCIS Authors' Instructions and are strongly encouraged to use the CCIS LaTeX style files or templates.

Abstracting/Indexing

CCIS is abstracted/indexed in DBLP, Google Scholar, EI-Compendex, Mathematical Reviews, SCImago, Scopus. CCIS volumes are also submitted for the inclusion in ISI Proceedings.

How to start

To start the evaluation of your proposal for inclusion in the CCIS series, please send an e-mail to ccis@springer.com.

Pierangela Samarati · Marten van Sinderen ·
Sabrina De Capitani di Vimercati ·
Fons Wijnhoven
Editors

E-Business
and Telecommunications

18th International Conference, ICETE 2021
Virtual Event, July 6–9, 2021
Revised Selected Papers

 Springer

Editors
Pierangela Samarati
Università degli Studi di Milano
Milan, Italy

Sabrina De Capitani di Vimercati
Università degli Studi di Milano
Milan, Italy

Marten van Sinderen
University of Twente
Enschede, The Netherlands

Fons Wijnhoven
University of Twente
Enschede, The Netherlands

ISSN 1865-0929   ISSN 1865-0937 (electronic)
Communications in Computer and Information Science
ISBN 978-3-031-36839-4   ISBN 978-3-031-36840-0 (eBook)
https://doi.org/10.1007/978-3-031-36840-0

This Springer imprint is published by the registered company Springer Nature Switzerland AG
The registered company address is: Gewerbestrasse 11, 6330 Cham, Switzerland

Preface

The 18th International Joint Conference on e-Business and Telecommunications, ICETE 2021, combined several conferences, including the 18th International Conference on e-Business, ICE-B 2021, and the 18th International Conference on Security and Cryptography, SECRYPT 2021.

ICE-B 2021 received 34 paper submissions from 19 countries, of which 21% are included in this book and SECRYPT 2021 received 163 paper submissions from 43 countries, of which 6% are included in this book. These events were held online due to Covid-19, on July 6 to 9, 2021.

The papers in this volume have been selected by the event chairs on the basis of comments provided by the program committee members, the assessments by the session chairs, and the program chairs' global view of all papers included in the technical program. The authors of selected papers worked on received reviews and comments to deliver extended versions of their conference papers with at least 30% innovative material.

ICE-B aims at bringing together researchers and practitioners who are interested in e-Business technology and its current applications. The scope of the conference covers low-level technological issues, such as technology platforms, internet of things and web services, but also higher-level issues, such as business processes, business intelligence, value setting and business strategy.

SECRYPT focuses on all aspects of security and privacy. The scope of the conference covers novel research on all theoretical and practical aspects of data protection, privacy, security, and applied cryptography, as well as the application of security technology, the implementation of advanced prototypes and techniques, lessons learned and future directions.

We thank all the authors for their valuable contributions and we very much appreciated the useful and critical comments of the reviewers which have contributed much to the quality and value of what we present to you in this book.

July 2021

Pierangela Samarati
Marten van Sinderen
Sabrina De Capitani di Vimercati
Fons Wijnhoven

Organization

Conference Chair

ICE-B

Marten van Sinderen — University of Twente, The Netherlands

SECRYPT

Pierangela Samarati — Università degli Studi di Milano, Italy

Program Chair

ICE-B

Fons Wijnhoven — University of Twente, The Netherlands

SECRYPT

Sabrina De Capitani di Vimercati — Università degli Studi di Milano, Italy

ICE-B Program Committee

Andreas Ahrens	Hochschule Wismar, University of Applied Sciences, Technology, Business and Design, Germany
Saadat Alhashmi	University of Sharjah, UAE
Salvatore Ammirato	University of Calabria, Italy
Dimitris Apostolou	University of Piraeus, Greece
Alexandros Bousdekis	National Technical University of Athens, Greece
Wojciech Cellary	Poznan University of Economics and Business, Poland
Chun-Liang Chen	National Taiwan University of Arts, Taiwan, Republic of China

Ritesh Chugh	Central Queensland University, Australia
Soon Chun	City University of New York, USA
Dimitris Drossos	Athens University of Economics and Business, Greece
Valerio Frascolla	Intel, Germany
Andreas Gadatsch	Hochschule Bonn-Rhein-Sieg, Germany
Francisco García-Sánchez	University of Murcia, Spain
Pierre Hadaya	University of Quebec at Montreal, Canada
Mark Hwang	Central Michigan University, USA
Dimitrios Katehakis	FORTH, Greece
Carmen Lam	University of Hong Kong, China
Giorgio Leonardi	University of Eastern Piedmont, Italy
Alvin Leung	City University of Hong Kong, China
Olga Levina	TH Brandenburg, Germany
Peter Loos	German Research Center for Artificial Intelligence, Germany
Samaneh Madanian	Auckland University of Technology, New Zealand
José Mata	University of Lausanne, Switzerland
Daniel O'Leary	University of Southern California, USA
Wilma Penzo	University of Bologna, Italy
Charmaine Plessis	University of South Africa, South Africa
Pak-Lok Poon	Central Queensland University, Australia
Ela Pustulka-Hunt	FHNW Olten, Switzerland
Jana-Rebecca Rehse	University of Mannheim, Germany
Gustavo Rossi	Universidad Nacional de La Plata, Argentina
Jarogniew Rykowski	Poznan University of Economics (PUE), Poland
Rong-an Shang	Soochow University, Taiwan, Republic of China
Agostinho Sousa Pinto	Polytechnic Institute of Porto, Portugal
Vesna Spasojevic Brkic	University of Belgrade, Serbia
Riccardo Spinelli	Università degli Studi di Genova, Italy
Emmanouil Stiakakis	University of Macedonia, Greece
Zhaohao Sun	PNG University of Technology, Papua New Guinea
James Thong	Hong Kong University of Science and Technology, China
Ben van Lier	Rotterdam University of Applied Sciences, The Netherlands / Steinbeis University Berlin, Germany
Alfredo Vellido	Universitat Politècnica de Catalunya, Spain
Christian Wolff	University of Luxembourg, Luxembourg
Geraldo Zimbrão	UFRJ, Brazil

SECRYPT Program Committee

Massimiliano Albanese	George Mason University, USA
Cristina Alcaraz	University of Malaga, Spain
Peter Amthor	Technische Universität Ilmenau, Germany
Muhammad Asghar	University of Auckland, New Zealand
Diogo Barradas	University of Waterloo, Canada
Francesco Buccafurri	University of Reggio Calabria, Italy
Ning Cao	Walmart Labs, USA
Xiaochun Cheng	Middlesex University London, UK
Frederic Cuppens	Polytechnique de Montréal, Canada
Nora Cuppens	Polytechnique de Montréal, Canada
Giovanni Di Crescenzo	Perspecta Labs, USA
Roberto Di Pietro	Hamad Bin Khalifa University, Qatar
Mario Di Raimondo	Università of Catania, Italy
Vasiliki Diamantopoulou	University of the Aegean, Greece
Josep Domingo-Ferrer	Rovira i Virgili University, Spain
Ruggero Donida Labati	Università degli Studi di Milano, Italy
Mohammed Erradi	ENSIAS, Mohammed V University in Rabat, Morocco
Csilla Farkas	University of South Carolina, USA
Alberto Ferrante	Università della Svizzera Italiana, Switzerland
Josep-Lluis Ferrer-Gomila	University of the Balearic Islands, Spain
Sara Foresti	Università degli Studi di Milano, Italy
Steven Furnell	University of Nottingham, UK
Joaquin Garcia-Alfaro	Télécom SudParis, France
Angelo Genovese	Università degli Studi di Milano, Italy
Dimitris Gritzalis	Athens University of Economics & Business, Greece
Stefanos Gritzalis	University of Piraeus, Greece
Jinguang Han	Queen's University Belfast, UK
Christophe Huygens	KU Leuven, Belgium
Ghassan Karame	NEC Laboratories, Germany
Sokratis Katsikas	Norwegian University of Science and Technology, Norway
Shinsaku Kiyomoto	KDDI Research Inc., Japan
Albert Levi	Sabanci University, Turkey
Jay Ligatti	University of South Florida, USA
Giovanni Livraga	Università degli Studi di Milano, Italy
Riccardo Longo	University of Trento, Italy
Suryadipta Majumdar	Concordia University, Canada
Yunlong Mao	Nanjing University, China

Evangelos Markatos	ICS, Forth, Greece
Fabio Martinelli	Consiglio Nazionale delle Ricerche, Italy
Sjouke Mauw	University of Luxembourg, Luxembourg
David Megias	Universitat Oberta de Catalunya, Spain
Weizhi Meng	Technical University of Denmark, Denmark
Alessio Merlo	University of Genoa, Italy
Rolf Oppliger	eSECURITY Technologies, Switzerland
Stefano Paraboschi	Università degli Studi di Bergamo, Italy
Gerardo Pelosi	Politecnico di Milano, Italy
Günther Pernul	University of Regensburg, Germany
Yunior Ramirez Cruz	Université du Luxembourg, Luxembourg
Silvio Ranise	Fondazione Bruno Kessler, Italy
Andreas Schaad	Offenburg University of Applied Sciences, Germany
Fabio Scotti	Università degli Studi di Milano, Italy
Kun Sun	George Mason University, USA
Issa Traore	University of Victoria, Canada
Corrado Visaggio	Università degli Studi del Sannio, Italy
Roopa Vishwanathan	New Mexico State University, USA
Cong Wang	City University of Hong Kong, China
Haining Wang	University of Delaware, USA
Lingyu Wang	Concordia University, Canada
Jiawei Yuan	University of Massachusetts Dartmouth, USA
Qiang Zeng	University of South Carolina, USA
Shengzhi Zhang	Boston University Metropolitan College, USA
Yongjun Zhao	Nanyang Technological University, Singapore

SECRYPT Additional Reviewers

Matteo Acclavio	University of Luxembourg, Luxembourg
Iftakhar Ahmad	University of South Carolina, USA
Sebastien Andreina	NEC Laboratories Europe GmbH, Germany
Yahya Benkaouz	Mohammed V University of Rabat, Morocco
Stefano Berlato	University of Genoa, Italy
Samira Briongos	NEC Laboratories Europe, Germany
Rosangela Casolare	University of Molise, Italy
El Mostapha Chakir	Henceforth, Morocco
Vincenzo De Angelis	University of Reggio Calabria, Italy
Pengbin Feng	George Mason University, USA
Mahdi Hashemi	George Mason University, USA
Ke He	University of Auckland, New Zealand

Qinwen Hu	University of Auckland, New Zealand
Emanuela Marasco	George Mason University, USA
Umberto Morelli	FBK, Italy
Oleksii Osliak	CNR, Italy
Gaurav Panwar	New Mexico State University, USA
Marco Pernpruner	Fondazione Bruno Kessler and University of Genoa, Italy
Konstantinos Rantos	International Hellenic University, Greece
Federico Savasta	University of Catania, Italy
Giada Sciarretta	Fondazione Bruno Kessler, Italy
Qiyang Song	Tsinghua University, China
Ioannis Stylios	University of the Aegean, Greece
Alessandro Tomasi	Fondazione Bruno Kessler, Italy
Hien Truong	NEC Laboratories Europe, Germany
Siva Likitha Valluru	University of South Carolina, USA
Junzhe Wang	University of South Carolina, USA
Shu Wang	George Mason University, USA
Chuxiong Wu	University of South Carolina, USA
Semen Yurkov	University of Luxembourg, Luxembourg
Rachid Zennou	ENSIAS Mohammed V University of Rabat, Morocco
Fei Zuo	University of South Carolina, USA

ICE-B Invited Speakers

| Jan vom Brocke | University of Liechtenstein, Liechtenstein |
| Florian Matthes | Technische Universität München, Germany |

SECRYPT Invited Speakers

Ravi Sandhu	University of Texas San Antonio, USA
V. S. Subrahmanian	Dartmouth College, USA
Jaideep Vaidya	Rutgers Business School, USA

Contents

e-Business

The Digital Content Formation Labor Costs for Electronic Libraries and Examples of the Formation of Virtual Exhibitions

Nikolay Kalenov (ID), Gennadiy Savin (ID), Irina Sobolevskaya(✉) (ID),
and Alexander Sotnikov (ID)

Joint Supercomputer Center of the Russian Academy of Sciences — Branch of Federal State
Institution "Scientific Research Institute for System Analysis of the Russian Academy of
Sciences" (JSCC RAS — Branch of SRISA), Leninsky av. 32 a, 119334 Moscow, Russia
{nkalenov,ins,asotnikov}@jscc.ru

Abstract. Scientific digital libraries are characterized by high requirements for the quality of digital copies of printed scientific sources, since any ambiguity or contamination within chemical formulas or mathematical expressions can lead to erroneous perception or misunderstanding of the meaning. Special requirements for digital copies are also imposed when digitizing rare editions and archival documents that are of scientific and historical value not only in their content, and in the notes of scientists in the margins of a book or archival document. Requirements for the quality of digitized materials determine the significant labor intensity of preparation; it is necessary to evaluate it when planning work on filling scientific libraries. The article presents a labor cost calculation methodology for creating integrated digital content for the digital library "Scientific Heritage of Russia" (DL SHR). The content of the DL SHR contains rare (out of print, hard-to find) books, 3D-museum objects and archival documents, which make digital copies of these materials very labour intensive. This needs to be assessed when planning the content filling for DL SHR. The developed technique includes the decomposition of the entire technological process into a number of operations performed by specialists of a certain profile (archivists, librarians, editors, scanners, etc.). Each phase is divided into several operations, and for every operation the time spent on this type of work is estimated. A unit of DL SHR content can be an archival document, a page of a book, a whole book, a biography of a scientist, etc. The assessment of the time period is carried out either according to published standards, or, in their absence, based on analysis of the experience of performing the operation when forming the content of the DL SHR. The article provides data on the calculation of time costs for individual operations of the formation of digital objects and their collections in relation to DL SHR, taking into account Russian standards and 15 years of experience.

Keywords: Scientific heritage · Digital library · Russian scientists · Information system · Network technologies · Virtual exhibitions · Museum objects · Digitization · Scientific digital library · Digitalization · Digital books · 3D-models · Technology · Labor contribution · Span time

© The Author(s), under exclusive license to Springer Nature Switzerland AG 2023
P. Samarati et al. (Eds.): ICETE 2021, CCIS 1795, pp. 3–28, 2023.
https://doi.org/10.1007/978-3-031-36840-0_1

1 Introduction

The creation of digital libraries is one of the most rapidly developing field in computer science. In the world today there is a huge collection of scientific information a huge number of collections of scientific information resources called digital libraries. These digital libraries contain different thematic and types of management, use different approaches to the formation of their funds (content). It should be noted that although the term "digital library" is used in a great number of publications, a single clear definition of it has not yet been given. Not referring to the term that was discussed 20 or more years ago, we will give several definitions related to modern times [1].

In some publications [2–4] the term "digital library" is defined as an information system that allows you to keep secure and give full play to various types of digital documents (text, visual, audio, video, etc.), localized in the system itself, as well as available to it through telecommunication networks.

Presently scientific publications [5–7] indicate that "Digital libraries" (DL) are forms of complex distributed information systems, providing new opportunities for working with heterogeneous information. DL are considered as the basis for creating a global distributed repository of knowledge. Actually, the authors of these articles point out that does not exist a single generally accepted definition of the digital libraries.

Here are some definitions [8] of the term "digital library":

Digital libraries are organized collections of information resources and associated tools for creating, archiving, sharing, searching, and using information that can be accessed electronically [9].

A digital library is a library in which collections are stored in digital formats (as opposed to print, microform, or other media) and accessible by computers. The digital content may be stored locally, or accessed remotely via computer networks. A digital library is a type of information retrieval system [10]. A digital library, digital repository, or digital collection, is an online database of digital objects that can include text, still images, audio, video, digital documents, or other digital media formats. Objects can consist of digitized content like print or photographs, as well as originally produced digital content like word processor files or social media posts. In addition to storing content, digital libraries provide means for organizing, searching, and retrieving the content contained in the collection [11].

Without going into the discussion of the above definitions, we note that, no matter how the term "digital libraries" is interpreted, a special technology is needed to implement in practice an "access network", "information system" or "ordered collection". Provision of information resources to users is what unites the traditional and digital libraries. Both libraries should create a reference apparatus that allows a user to find what interests him among the resources that the libraries provide. For traditional libraries, these are various kinds of catalogs (including electronic ones) with search elements that have developed in many years of library practice. For digital libraries (in the broad sense of this term) - metadata bases with a search interface of varying complexity [12, 13]. A significant difference between electronic libraries from traditional ones is that the latter use ready-made primary information - printed publications published by other organizations. The formation of electronic libraries is often associated with the need for purposeful digitization of certain publications. First of all, this is typical for scientific DL, formed according to narrow thematic or other fixed principles. These include Jubilothèque UPMC's scientific digital library [14], the digital library of theses formed by the RSL [15]; Electronic Library of the Boris Yeltsin Presidential Library, dedicated to the issues of Russian statehood [16]; DL "Scientific heritage of Russia" [17], The National Science Digital Library [18], DL "German National Library of Science and Technology" [19], individual scientific institutes, see for example [20–22], etc.

Creation and maintenance of digital libraries is labor intensive. Some labor related to the DL ontology (the choice of the database structure, the definition of classes of objects included in the DL and their relationships, metadata profiles and information presentation formats) or the creation or adaptation of the software shell [23].

DL maintenance is constantly required and the amount of work involved in its maintenance is not so much related to technical support, but rather to the creation of content. But with the formation of content, including both digital objects themselves and their metadata, which ensure the quality of search.

The subject of this article is the assessment of permanent labor contributions to support digital libraries using the example of the Digital Library "Scientific Heritage of Russia" [24–28].

The digital library "Scientific Heritage of Russia" (DL SHR) [17] has been operating in Ethernet mode since 2010 (Fig. 1).

Fig. 1. The digital library "Scientific Heritage of Russia". Home page.

The main goal of the DL SHR is to create, preserve, and provide access to accurate and reliable information about outstanding scientists who have contributed to the development of Russian science and scientific achievements. The DL SHR contains biographical information about scientists, the major publications (bibliography and scanned full texts), archival information and museum objects related to them. The library includes text information, digitized prints, archival documents, photographs and films, 3D models of museum items [1] (Fig. 2).

To date, the DL SHR provides information on more than 6100 scientists who worked in Russia from the 18th to the first quarter of the 20th centuries; about 25,000 books published during this period have been digitized and available to users.

DL SHR.

Table 1 presents data on the fields of knowledge of the number of scientists reflected in the DL SHR, working in a certain period, and the number of digitized publications, they are authors [29].

Fig. 2. The digital library "Scientific Heritage of Russia" collections list.

Table 1. Data on the fields of knowledge of the number of scientists reflected in the DL SHR, working in a certain period, and the number of digitized publications, they are authors [1].

Science Name	Number of Scientists	Number of Digitized Publications
Astronomy	98	374
Biology	142	1590
Mathematics	102	556
Medicine	77	240
Mechanics	40	753
Earth sciences	166	1878
Technics	21	491
PHysics	79	1592
CHemistry	65	1269
PHilosophy	203	1865
Social sciences, humanity, religion	1523	5851

The DL SHR is based on the principle of distributed data with centralized editorial processing, content downloading and technology support. More than 20 libraries, institutes and museums prepare information for DL SHR according to uniform rules.

The task of content providers the selection of materials in accordance with the principles, the formation of metadata about the inclusion of objects in the DL SHR (personalities, publications, archival documents, museum items, photographs, multimedia materials), the digitization of publications and information processing in accordance with the rules of the system (for DL SHR adopted, according to which the scanned text is not recognized, with the exception of the Table of contents, the transfer of processed materials to the editorial group.

The editorial team performs the following functions:

- makes the final decision on the inclusion of publications proposed by providers in the digital library;
- metadata validation;

– prepares the editions that have passed the control for loading into the software shell of the demo part of the digital library.

The object-oriented approach chosen in the design of the DL SHR, the use of distributed data preparation technology, the reflection in the DL SHR of various digital objects of scientific purpose and positive experience of many years of its operation allows to consider the DL SHR as a prototype of the Common Digital Space of Scientific Knowledge (CDSSK) [30]. The creation of the CDSSK is the most important challenge for the development of a system (that will provide scientific, educational and cultural informational support and preserve scientific data and knowledge) for scientific educational and cultural (informational) support and preservation of scientific data and knowledge.

In this regard it is important to build a labor input model for the CDSK on the basis of the DLSHR operating experience. The model is built on examples of the most labor-intensive processes, which are the digitization of printed publications (the formation of electronic books) and the creation of 3D models of museum objects.

2 Shaping the Book Content of the Digital Library "Scientific Heritage of Russia"

The DL SHR content is determined according to the principle "from person to publication". Therefore, to include a book in the DL SHR content, it is necessary to enter information about its author first. Accordingly, the information about scientists who were instrumental in the development of Russian science is entered into the DL SHR at the first stage [1].

To determine the scientific interests of the selected person, a universal hierarchical classification (K) of knowledge areas is used. This classification is adopted to systematize the entire flow of scientific and technical information.

In accordance with the DL SHR metadata standards bibliographical data related to scientists, their scientific interests in terms of classification, and a bibliography of their main works are entered into the library.

Librarians perform this work. It includes four stages:

– the search for sources of scientist biographical data;
– the compilation of a detailed biography;
– the selection of bibliography;
– the input of data into the DL SHR technological block.

Let's denote the average time spent on the implementation of each stage, respectively, through t_p^1, t_p^2, t_p^3.

Suppose the information is entered into the system, then the scientific technological processes carried out in the preparation of the publication for inclusion in the DL SHR are presented in Fig. 3. And Table 2 [1, 25].

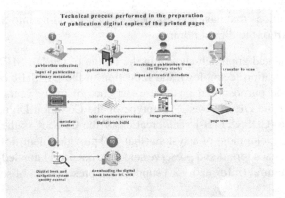

Fig. 3. Technological processes carried out in the preparation of the publication for inclusion in the DL SHR.

Table 2. Technological processes carried out in the preparation of the publication for inclusion in the DL SHR [1].

Stage number	Project scope	By whom	Accounting unit	Time
1	Selection of the publication proposed for inclusion in the digital library; Input into the technological block of primary metadata of the publication including connections with persons	Librarian (organization - participant of the project)	Book	t_k^1
2	Application consideration	Editorial team member	Book	t_k^2
3	Getting the book from the library stock; the introduction of extended metadata of publications (including the serialization of the book to classification K)	Librarian (organization - participant of the project)	Book	t_k^3
4	Sending for scanning, preparing a book for scanning	Librarian (organization - participant of the project)	Book	t_k^4
5	Page Scanning	Scanner-Operator	Page	t_s^1
6	Image processing	Technical Specialist	Page	t_s^2

(continued)

Table 2. (*continued*)

Stage number	Project scope	By whom	Accounting unit	Time
7	Table of contents processing; digital book build	Technical Specialist	Book	t_k^5
8	Book metadata quality control	Editor	Book	t_k^6
9	Page metadata and navigation system quality control	Editor	Page	t_s^3
10	Downloading the digital book into the DL SHR (link start-up between the book layout and metadata)	Technical Specialist	Book	t_k^7

Thus, if a book of N pages is entered into the DL SHR the total span time T_B for its inclusion in the Library will be [1]:

$$T_B = \sum_{i=1}^{7} t_k^i + N \cdot \sum_{i=1}^{3} t_s^i \qquad (1)$$

Generating information on the scientist that is reflected in the DL SHR includes three times intervals.

To implement the **first stage** (time interval t_p^1), it is necessary to perform the following operations:

- selection of authoritative publications (primary documents);
- obtaining information about the scientist, ordering Items from a library;
- delivery from storage;
- issuing to the user (in this case, to the employee compiling the biography of the scientist);
- compiling a biography of the scientist based on information from the publications received;
- returning the publications to the funds.

The time spent on the selection of publications can be estimated using the norm "Implementation of thematic information; search and selection of documents ". Analysis of the data of the DL SHR shows that on average, when compiling a biography of a scientist, from 2 to 3 sources are used) is 15 min.

Technological operations of library related to the issuance and acceptance of editions of the funds are normalized per edition and total 13 min. Let us estimate that operations last about 30 min (considering that 2 items are to be loaned) [1].

To estimate the time spent on compiling a biography of a scientist, we will use the rule "writing an abstract: studying and analyzing the document for which the abstract is being prepared; writing a text ", equating conditionally compiling a biography to compiling an abstract of selected publications). This rate per one author's sheet (40,000 characters) is 5920 min. An analysis of the data reflected in the DL SHR shows that the volume of the text of a scientist's biography ranges from 1000 to 31000 characters and is, on average, about 6000 characters, or 15% of the printed sheet. Thus, the standard time for compiling a biography of a scientist and entering it into the system is 888 min, the total time for completing the first stage of forming data about a scientist is $t_p^1 = 15 + 30 + 888 = 933$ min.

The span time on the implementation of the **second stage** (the formation of a bibliographic list of the scientist's publications) can be estimated on the basis of the norm for compiling a bibliographic index, which is 13500 min per author's sheet. The volume of the bibliography of the first year of his activity - the average number of publications by one scientist has increased several times over the last century in his scientific activity. Analysis of the data entered in the DL SHR shows that the bibliographic list of one scientist, on average, is 2200 characters, or 5.5% of the author's sheet. According to the norms, it takes 742 min to compose it.

Entering structured data about a scientist can be interpreted as the operation "typing on the keyboard information about the reader: last name, first name, patronymic, characterizing his characteristics (education, specialty, other information." According to the norms, 6 min are given for this operation.

Thus, the total time spent on creating digital library information about one scientist $(T_P = t_p^1 + t_p^2 + t_p^3)$ is 1681 min or (rounded up) 28 h of work of a librarian.

When assessing the labor costs of librarians t_k^1, t_k^3 and t_k^4, we will use, together with the already considered norms for the selection of literature, the norms for "forming a bibliographic record for documents in a language (descriptive cataloging)" (18 min per document), "indexing (meaningful cataloging)" (18) and "entering computer basic information about the document (author, title) in a specialized program" (5 min), "preparing documents for microfilming and scanning documents" (5 min), "transferring documents for microfilming and scanning" (16 min). The results are as follows:

$$t_k^1 + t_k^3 + t_k^4 = 75\,\text{min}$$

Consider the processes (indicated as stages in Table 1) performed by the staff of the editorial team, scanners and technicians. As a basis, we will take the experience of the DL SHR database provisioning and the norms for scanning documents in a non-contact method (this is the technology used in the DL SHR), presented in [31].

The results are as follows (stage 2 in Table 1), an employee of the editorial group decides to enter the input into the digital library of books proposed by the project participants. To do so an item is checked according to the following parameters:

- compliance with the system journal of the library;
- compliance with copyright rules;
- detection of duplication of bibliographic record rules. Then a unique number is then assigned to the e-book (ID). If the item (book) cannot be registered, a note is made a

mark is made indicating the reason for such a decision. The rate for one employee is 30 books per shift. Based on this, we get

$$t_k^2 = 16\,\text{min}$$

The rate per operator for page scanning (step 5) is 800 pages per shift. It means that

$$t_s^1 = 0.6\,\text{min}$$

The main task of the **6th stage** (image processing) is to check and edit the graphic images of the digital pages. It includes three technological processes:

- automatic scan processing by a special program - automatic processing;
- manual correction.

As a result of the first process, typical scanning defects are corrected to an acceptable level.

The second process involves:

- checking the sequential display of pages (page numbering should be sequential, search for pages missed during scanning);
- checking the quality of scanning (the degree of readability of the text, at least 98% of the information presented on the page must be readable);
- Checking the quality of automatic processing of scanned pages (correct page cropping, geometric correction of text, text bends and distortions);
- the simplest editing of scanned pages (cropping, removing extraneous elements).

As part of the third process, the pages are manually processed in one of the graphic editors. This stage is provided for the most complex editions, many formulas, Tables, illustrations, etc. It includes:

- geometric correction of text, text bends and distortions;
- removal of extraneous elements on the pages of electronic books (operator's fingers, stripes, shadows, and other extraneous elements);
- color correction.

The rate per operator during this stage is 800 pages per shift. Thus

$$t_s^2 = 0.6\,\text{min}$$

The main tasks of the **7th stage** are:

- formation of the Table of contents of the book (recognition and editing of text or its manual input);
- layout of an e-book in a special program based on prepared high-quality graphic formed pages and a generated Table of contents;
- creation of the most accurate navigation system of the digital book.

In the process of creating a navigation system, the technician must ensure:

- the correctness of typing, titles, notes and other parts of the navigation system;
- the correctness of the electronic links and the navigation system;
- completeness of the e-book: sequential number of pages, order of sections.

The day's work for one specialist is 5 e-books per shift

$$t_k^5 = 96 \, \text{min}$$

Stage 8 (book metadata quality control) includes:

- checking the correspondence of the author name, the title, the output data to those on the cove page;
- checking the formatting of records - spelling, punctuation, accepted word abbreviations in bibliographic data;
- checking the compliance of the information entered in the fields "type of publication", "language", "pages", the original. The "pages" field is verified strictly according to the electronic version of the book and includes the total number of files in the digital version, prepared for uploading to the site, checking for the presence of appropriate indexes;
- checking the formatting of the bibliographic description (according to standards).

The day's work for one specialist is 10 e-books per shift, from which follows:

$$t_k^6 = 48 \, \text{min}$$

At **stage 9** (page metadata and navigation system quality control), the issuing editor checks the layout of the e-book on the production server. The work of the editor includes the analysis of graphic images of the pages and checking the navigation system. It includes:

- checking the sequential display of pages;
- checking the quality of scanning (the degree of readability of the text, at least 99% of the information presented on the page must be readable);
- checking the quality of processing of scanned pages (correct page cropping, geometric text correction, absence of text bends and other distortions, absence of "extraneous elements" - stripes, shadows, operator fingerprints, etc.);
- checking links for their opening;
- checking links for compliance with the chapters and contents of the book.

When certain shortcomings are identified, the corresponding information is transmitted to the operator of the 6th stage. The norm for these works is 1200 pages per shift, based on this, we get

$$t_s^3 = 0.4 \, \text{min}$$

At the **final stage**, the issuing editor publishes the book and metadata on the e-library portal and checks the availability of the downloaded information. The production rate for one specialist is 50 e-books per shift,

$$t_k = 9.6 \, \text{min}$$

Substituting the obtained values into formula (1), we find that the average time spent on digitizing and including one book of N pages in the digital library will be (in min)

$$T_B = 244.6 + 1.6 \cdot N \tag{2}$$

Library workers from this time spend.
$T_L = 75$ min.
Editors

$$T_R = 64 + 0.4 \cdot N$$

Technical specialists

$$T_c = 105.6 + 0.6 \cdot N$$

Scanning operators

$$T_0 = 0.6 \cdot N$$

To prepare and enter into DL the first book of a scientist that was not previously presented in the DL, 200 pages in volume will take about 38 h, including ~ 29.5 h of work of library specialists, ~ 2.5 h of work of an editor, ~ 2 h of work of an operator-scanner, ~ 4 h of work of a technical specialist. By introducing another book by the same author, the processing time will be reduced the work needs of librarians will be reduced to one and a half hours, and the total preparation time for a book will be about 10 h [1].

3 Shaping Archival Content of the Digital Library "Scientific Heritage of Russia"

Suppose the personal data is entered into the system. Then the technological processes that is carried out in order to prepare the publication for inclusion in the DL SHR are presented in Table 3. We understand an archival document as a paper document. Digitizing a photo and video archive requires much more labour than digitizing paper documents [32].

Table 3. Technological processes carried out in the preparation of the archival record for inclusion in the DL SHR [32].

Stage number	Project scope	By whom	Accounting unit	Time
1	Selection and input the archival record proposed for inclusion in the digital library;	Registrar	Archival record	t_k^1

(*continued*)

Table 3. (*continued*)

Stage number	Project scope	By whom	Accounting unit	Time
2	Application consideration	Editorial team member	Archival record	t_k^2
3	Getting and introduction the archival record from the Archive;	Registrar	Archival record	t_k^3
4	Sending for scanning, preparing archival record for scanning	Registrar	Archival record	t_k^4
5	Archival record Scanning	Scanner-Operator	Archival record page	t_s^1
6	Image processing	Technical Specialist	Archival record page	t_s^2
7	Archival record metadata quality control	Editor	Archival record	t_k^5
8	Page metadata and navigation system quality control	Editor	Archival record page	t_s^3
9	Downloading the digital archival record into the DL SHR	Technical Specialist	Archival record	t_k^6

Thus, if an archival record of N pages is entered into the DL SHR then total span time T_A for its inclusion in the Library will be [1]:

$$T_A = \sum_{i=1}^{6} t_k^i + N \cdot \sum_{i=1}^{3} t_s^i \qquad (3)$$

When assessing the labor costs of registrars t_k^1, t_k^3 and t_k^4, we will use considered norms for archival documents digitization (42 min per document), "indexing (meaningful cataloging)" (7 min per document) and "entering computer basic information about the document (author, title, etc.) in a specialized program" (6 min). The results are as follows:

$$t_k^1 + t_k^3 + t_k^4 = 55 \, \text{min}$$

We will take the experience in provisioning as a basis for DL SHR database provisioning and the norms for scanning documents in a non-contact method (this is the technology used in the DL SHR), presented in [33, 34].

The rate for one employee is 45 archival records per shift. Based on this, we get

$$t_k^2 = 10 \, \text{min}$$

The rate per operator for page scanning (step 5) is 200 pages per shift. It means that

$$t_s^1 = 0.15 \, \text{min}$$

The main task of the **6th stage** (image processing) is to check and edit the graphic images of the digital pages.

The rate per operator during this stage is 200 pages per shift. Thus

$$t_s^2 = 0.15 \, \text{min}$$

Stage 7 (archival record metadata quality control).

The day's work for one specialist is 10 archival records per shift, it therefore follows:

$$t_k^6 = 32 \, \text{min}$$

At **stage 8** (page with metadata and navigation system quality control), the issuing editor checks the layout of the archival record on the production server.

When certain defects are identified, the corresponding information is transmitted to the operator of the 6th stage. The norm for these works is 800 pages per shift, based on this, we get

$$t_s^3 = 0.3 \, \text{min}$$

At the **final stage**, the issuing editor publishes the archival record and metadata on the e-library portal and checks the availability of the downloaded information. The production rate for one specialist is 100 archival records per shift,

$$t_k = 19.2 \, \text{min}$$

Substituting the obtained values into formula (1), we find that the average time spent on digitizing and including one archival record of N pages in the digital library will be (in min)

$$T_A = 116.2 + 0.6 \cdot N$$

Registrar workers from this time spend

$$T_R = 55 \, \text{min}$$

Editors

$$T_E = 57 + 0.3 \cdot N$$

Technical specialists

$$T_T = 87.5 + 0.15 \cdot N$$

Scanning operators

$$T_0 = 0.15 \cdot N$$

To prepare and enter into Digital Library (DL) the archival record of a scientist that was not previously presented in the DL, 100 archival in volume will take about 27 h, including ~ 20.5 h of work of registrar specialists, ~ 2 h of work of an editor, ~ 1.5 h of work of an operator- scanner, ~ 3 h of work of a technical specialist. By introducing another archival record by the same person, the processing time will be reduced the work needs of registrars will be reduced to one hour, and the total preparation time for a archival record will be about 7 h [32].

4 Shaping 3D-Content of the Digital Library "Scientific Heritage of Russia"

Along with digital publications DL SHR contains multimedia content and, in particular, 3D-models of museum objects. These objects can be associated with a specific person (or several persons) or they can be combined into an independent collection dedicated, among other things, to a certain research area or event. The estimated staff time required for creation of 3D-model (one object) and of digitals collections that include several objects will be discussed below.

Various methods are used to visualize a three-dimensional object [35]. These methods can be based on SfM-technologies [36–38], software and technological solutions used, in particular, in laser and optical 3D-scanning, photogrammetry methods [39].

Museum objects digitization is performed on specialized equipment. To convert books, maps, manuscripts, various graphic images into digital form, planetary, flatbed or other types of scanners are used, which differ in resolution, the ability to scan various types of images, and other properties.

In the DL SHR project, digitization is performed by the following types of scanning systems:

- scanning complex based on the MINOLTA PS7000 planetary scanner;
- scanning complex based on PlanScan S-600 color planetary scanner;
- scanning complex based on Powerscan D14000 A0–20/25 color scanner;
- scanning complex based on PlanScan A2-VC-B color scanner;
- to digitize information stored on microfiches, a scanning complex based on the Kodak ABR 3000 DSV microfiche scanner is used.
- a 3D digitization complex based on the Rekam T-50 rotary platform and a Canon EOS600D digital camera is used to digitize museum information.

The files obtained as a result of digitization are transferred to the digital resource layout group. At this stage, as a rule, from a set of individual images, after appropriate processing, the creation (layout) of a digital resource is carried out. As a result of layout, we get an e-book, a virtual 3D image of an object, a digitized copy of a movie or a photograph in a certain format.

At the final stage, the digital resource is placed on the technological server for preparing the digital content of the electronic library, or directly on the site of the interdisciplinary collection.

Optical 3D-scanners are used to quickly digitize various small and medium-sized objects, like a digitized set or the entire "field of view" of the scanner at the same time. To digitize geometry and capture texture in low light, special white or blue lamps are used as light sources. One of the disadvantages of optical 3D-scanners is the impossibility of constructing objects with a reflective or light-absorbing structure [40].

Laser 3D-scanners provide greater accuracy and detail when digitizing objects compared to optical 3D-scanners. For precise spatial reference of the laser to the scanned object, it is necessary to use special markers that are attached in close proximity to the object or directly on the exposure object. In addition, the main disadvantage of the scanner is the impossibility of transferring the texture of the object. Nevertheless, 3D-laser scanners solve satisfactorily the task of constructing the most detailed surface of the scanned object (without the need to visualize the texture and).

Unlike 3D-scanning technologies, the photogrammetry method [41, 42] allows you to build a high-quality 3D-model with the transfer of the texture and color of the object. However, computationally, building 3D-models from a set of images using the photogrammetry method is a rather laborious task. For example, the processing of 124 photographs on one of the nodes of the MVS-10P cluster [43] installed at the MSC RAS took 41 h of calculations [33].

For the formation of digital 3D-models in the DL SHR there was a model of interactive animation technology [33]. This technology does not imply the construction of a full-fledged 3D-model based on a programmatic change (scrolling) of a fixed view of an object (frames) using standard interactive display programs that simulate a change in the point of view of the original object. To create such an interactive cartoon, you need a set of pre-prepared scenes that will be separate exposition frames.

Before proceeding with the formation of digital 3D-models of museum objects in order to include them in the electronic library, it is necessary to carry out certain preparatory work performed by the staff of the museum, which owns the modeled object.

This work includes:

- Selection of an object for digitization with the documentation preparation;
- Inspection of the object for preservation with the preparation of a protocol of inspection or entry into the register of museum items;
- Issuance of an object for digitization.

The standard time T_0, desired for this type of work is, on average, 130 min per object.

After this preparatory work is completed, the main cycle of work begins on the creation of a digital 3D-model of the museum object. The technological processes carried out in the preparation of a digital 3D-model of a museum object for inclusion in the DL SHR are shown in (Fig. 4).

This cycle of work includes the following main stages:

1. Preparing for digitizing. It means setting up an object at the shooting location, adjusting lighting, etc.
2. Digitization of the object. To carry out this work, a special complex based on a specialized rotary platform and a digital camera. The end result of this stage is an array of data, files with photographs of the object taken from 120 angles;
3. Processing of the data set obtained at the first stage. At this stage, the background on which the image was taken is removed from each photo. This is done using a software module specially designed for this stage;

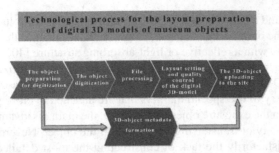

Fig. 4. The technological processes carried out in the preparation of a digital 3D-model of a museum object for inclusion in the DL SHR.

4. Layout and quality control of the digital resource image. The result of this phase is digital 3D-images of museum items.
5. Description of the museum item, the digital 3D-model of which is included in the digital library. The museum staff did this work.
6. Loading the generated model into the DL SHR.

Lets $T_1, T_2, T_3, T_4, T_5, T_6$- time intervals required for processing one museum object at stages 1–6, respectively.

Table 4 shows the technological processes carried out in the creation of museum 3D-objects for inclusion in the DL SHR [44].

Table 4. The technological processes carried out in the creation of museum 3D-objects for inclusion in the DL SHR [29].

Stage number	Project scope	By whom	Accounting unit	Time
1	Preparing for digitizing	Museum employee	Museum object	T_1
2	Digitization of the object	Technical Specialist	Folder containing 120 jpg files for each object photographed	T_2
3	Processing of the data set obtained at the first stage	Technical Specialist	obtained files	T_3
4	Layout and quality control of the digital resource image	Technical Specialist	Digital 3D-object	T_4
5	Description of the museum item, the digital 3D-model of which is included in the digital library	Museum employee	Digital 3D-object	T_5

(*continued*)

Table 4. (*continued*)

Stage number	Project scope	By whom	Accounting unit	Time
6	Loading the generated model into the DL SHR	Technical Specialist	Digital 3D-object	T_6

Thus, if there are M digital museum 3D-objects are introduced into the DL SHR then the average time T_{av} for the inclusion of this volume of digital resources in the DL SHR is:

$$T_{av} = M \cdot \sum_{i=0}^{6} T_i$$

After several objects have been digitized, they can be combined into one or more collections. Let T_k be the average time required to form and describe a collection. Then the total time T is total for the formation of a digital collection of museum 3D objects is:

$$T = T_{av} + T_k$$

The following are the numerical values of the average time spent on the formation of digital 3D-models of museum items based on the experience of creating content in the DL SHR. In the process of replenishing the digital library content, more than 100 3D-models of museum items were prepared, combined into several collections. Among them is a digital 3D-collection of models of fruits by I.V. Michurin, stored in the State Biological Museum named after K. A. Timiryazev (GBMT), digital 3D-collection of anthropological reconstructions by M.M. Gerasimov, stored in the GBMT and the State Darwin Museums.

The average time values $T_1, T_2, T_3, T_4, T_5, T_6$ are given below, based on the experience of formation, including these collections.

To implement the first stage (preparation of the object for digitization, interval T_1), an average of 45 min is required.

To implement the second stage (digitization of the selected content, interval T_2), on average, 20 min per object.

To implement the third stage (processing the files obtained as a result of digitization, time interval T_3), an average of 290 min per object is required.

To implement the fourth stage (layout and quality control of the image of a digital resource, time interval T_4), on average, 25 min per object is required.

To implement the fifth stage (description of a digital 3D-object, time interval T_5), an average of 15 min is required per object.

To implement the sixth stage (loading a 3D-object into the DL SHR, time interval T_6), on average, 35 min are required per object.

Thus, the total time spent on presenting one digital 3D-model of a museum object in the DL SHR is:

$$T = 45 + 20 + 290 + 25 + 15 + 35 + 130 = 560 \, \text{min}$$

To generate at least 40 digital 3D-models of museum objects (time T_k), an average of 180 min is required.

When forming a digital 3D-collection of anthropological reconstructions, M.M. Gerasimov was created and uploaded to the site http://acadlib.ru/, integrated with the DL SHR, 50 works by M.M. Gerasimov. The total time taken to create this collection was:

$$T_{Ger} = 415 \cdot 50 + 180 = 28180 \, \text{min}$$

That's about 470 h.

5   Some Examples of Using Suggested Technology

One of the areas of application suggested information technology is the formation of virtual exhibitions on the basis of the resources of the DL SHR. Virtual exhibitions provide to users with heterogeneous information, jointed according to certain criteria. These can be exhibitions dedicated to an individual scientist, any event, natural phenomenon, etc.

Despite the fact that each virtual exhibition is unique in its content, the following main types of sections can be distinguished in the formation of such exhibitions in the DL SHR environment:

- the main thematic section;
- interactive section;
- biographical section;
- section of video materials;
- section of photographic documents;
- library;
- section "Collection of 3D-objects";
- reviews section;
- contacts.

A virtual exhibition can contain general information about a particular field of science, scientific information both at the level of a children's encyclopedia, and more detailed information [36]. Virtual exhibitions allow you to combine the resources of each thematic subspace, making, among other things, an emphasis on one or another audience.

A practical example of using a virtual exhibition in the processes of school education is the exhibition "The Garden of Life", realized on the platform of the DL SHR [45], posted in the public domain at http://3d.acadlib.ru.

"The Garden of Life" exhibition is dedicated to the life and scientific work of the rare Russian scholar biologist and plant breeder Ivan Vladimirovich Michurin (1855–1935) (Fig. 5).

Ivan Michurin was the author of many varieties of fruit and berry crops. Honorary member of the American scientific society "Breeders", honorary member of the USSR Academy of Sciences. He developed methods of fruit and berry plants selection by the method of distant hybridization.

Fig. 5. The home page of the exhibition site "The Garden of Life".

The information presented at this exhibition is primarily targeted at secondary school students.

The exhibition thematically divided into two parts: biographical - "Ivan Michurin - who is he?" and socio-political - "The fruits and roots of Michurin biology".

The biographical section is built in the genre of an interactive interview game. First, the user is given curious facts or well-established judgments about Michurin and asked to choose the correct statement. Then the user's choice is refuted or confirmed by documents, photographs or museum items.

The section "The Fruits and Roots of Michurin's Biology" refers to the history of science in the part related to conflicts in the second third of the twentieth century between groups of Soviet scientists who support and refute genetics, also divided into two parts. Visitors to the exhibition are told what was the essence of the conflict between the opposing sides, and on the basis of facts they explain that I.V. Michurin had nothing to do with these events.

The virtual exhibition also includes the following sections:

– Photo gallery. This section contains photographic documents from the funds of the Russian State Archive of film and photo document (RSAFPD) and the State Biological Museum named after K. A. Timiryazev (SBMT) (Figs. 6, 7).

– Video materials. This section contains digitized films fragments from the RSAFPD and SBMT collections which contain include documentary footage showing Ivan Michurin at work in his garden, fragments of his speeches at various symposiums on botany and genetics.

– Collection 360. This section presents digitized museum items from the SBMT collection. These objects are high-quality digital 3D-models of fruits grown by Ivan Michurin; in addition, each model is supplied with a description.

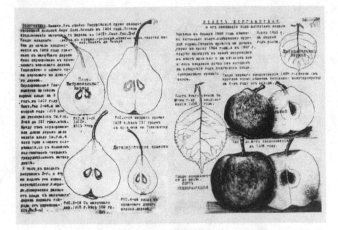

Fig. 6. A page from the diary of Ivan Michurin.

Fig. 7. Ivan. Michurin in his garden. Michurinsk (The town (before 1932 named Kozlov) where Ivan Michurin was born.). Early 1930s. RGAKFD. Arch. No. 2–111567".

– Library. This section contains publications on the exhibition subject that are included into the DL SHR. There are 18 books in the library. Including the four-book set by Ivan Michurin, as well as "Selected works" in Russian and Chinese (Fig. 8).

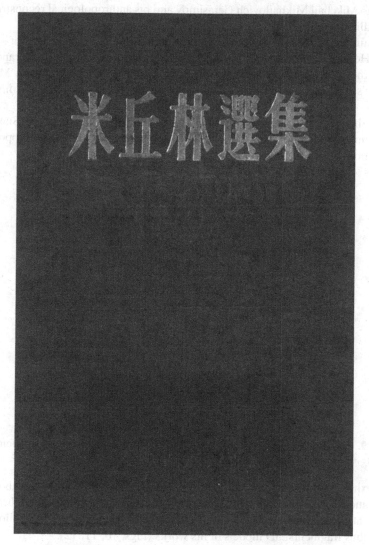

Fig. 8. I.V. Michurin. "Selected works" in Chinese.

– Reviews. This section was created for feedback from visitors of the virtual exhibition. Here you can make various reports on the exhibition subject (after obligatory registration) and exchange opinions with other exhibition visitors;

– Contacts. This section contains the contacts of the administrator of the virtual
exhibition for communication with him.

The second example of a virtual exhibition was being created on the technological
platform of the DL SHR named "Forensical sculpture reconstruction". This exhibition is
dedicated to Mikchail Mikhailovich Gerasimov and his anthropological reconstructions
(http://acadlib.ru/).

Mikchail Gerasimov was an anthropologist, archaeologist, sculptor, doctor scientist
(history). He is the author of the method for restoring the external appearance of a
person on the basis of skeletal remains - the so-called "Gerasimov method". Mikchail
Gerasimov's works are exhibited in many biological, anthropological and historical
museums.

This exhibition was created jointly with SBMT, RSAFPD and the State Darwin Museum. Within the framework of the project, more than 50 anthropological
reconstructions by M.M. Gerasimov (Fig. 9).

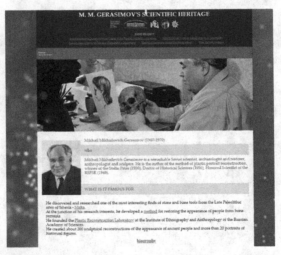

Fig. 9. The home page of the exhibition site "Forensical sculpture reconstruction".

This exhibition presents the Mikchail Gerasimov biography, literature about him;
his publications, archival documents related to Mikchail. Gerasimov, the anthropology
development history documents connected with Mikchail Gerasimov's, his bibliography,
digitized films fragments, 3D models of his works (Figs. 10, 11, 12).

Fig. 10. Mikhail Gerasimov at work.

Fig. 11. A Neanderthal youth from Le Moustier (France). 1954. M.M. Gerasimov reconstruction.

Using the technology of creation natural science virtual exhibitions, it is possible to solve the problem of providing and popularizing scientific information to schoolchildren and students.

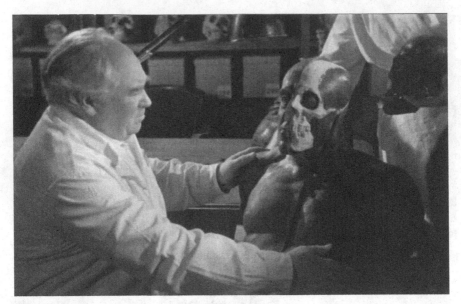

Fig. 12. In the Laboratory of Plastic Reconstruction. The musculature modelling of the Ivan the Terrible torso. 1964.

6 Conclusions

Along with publications related to individual scientists, publications related to various scientific events – conferences, symposiums, significant dates - are introduced into the DL SHR. These publications are usually combined into collections or special issues of journals. Accordingly, the decision to digitize such publications is usually made not in relation to individual articles, but to the issue as a whole.

In this case, the technology of these materials processing for inclusion in the DL is somewhat different from the technology of processing books. Since Journals issues are not linked to individual scientists, but to event data, the information preparing requires significantly less costs than the formation of the scientist biography.

Using the results obtained, it is possible to solve the problem of optimizing the time spent on creating digital copies of printed materials and museum objects using methods of paralleling technological processes performed by library or museum specialists (preparation of object metadata) and technical specialists (digitization of materials and quality control).

The research is carried out by Joint SuperComputer Center of the Russian Academy of Sciences – Branch of Federal State Institution "Scientific Research Institute for System Analysis of the Russian Academy of Sciences" within the framework of a state assignment 0580–2022-0014.

References

1. Kalenov, N., Savin, G., Sobolevskaya, I., Sotnikov, A.: Some estimates of labor contribution for creating digital libraries. In: Proceedings of the 18th International Conference on e-Business, ICE-B 2021, pp, 59–66 (2021). https://doi.org/10.5220/0010512500590066
2. Antopol'skij, A.B., Majstrovich, T.V.: Elektronnye Biblioteki: principy sozdaniya. Liberiya-Bibinform, pp. 288 (2007)
3. Jupp, B.: The Internet library of early journals. ASLIB Proc. **49**(6), 153–158 (1997)
4. Schwartz, C.: Digital libraries: an overview. J. Acad. Librarianship. **26**(6), 385–393 (2000)
5. Bogdanova, I.F., Bogdanova, N.F.: Elektronnye biblioteki: istoriya i sovremennost'. In Informacionnoe obshchestvo: obrazovanie, nauka, kul'tura i tekhnologii budushchego. Vypusk **1**, 133–153 (2017)
6. Mahajan, A.K., Hogarth, D.K.: Taking control of your digital library how modern citation managers do more than just referencing. Chest **144**(6), 1930–1933 (2013)
7. Parn, E.A., Edwards, D.: Vision and advocacy of optoelectronic technology developments in the AECO sector. Built Environ. Proj. Asset Manage. SI. **7**(3), 330–348 (2017)
8. https://dic.academic.ru/dic.nsf/fin_enc/31885 (2022). Accessed 26 Apr 2022
9. https://www.encyclopedia.com/literature-and-arts/journalism-and-publishing/libraries-books-and-printing/digital-libraries (2022). Accessed 24 April 2022
10. https://www.newworldencyclopedia.org/entry/Digital_library (2022). Accessed 24 Apr 2022
11. https://ru.wikipedia.org/wiki/Elektronnaya_biblioteka (2022). Accessed 24 Apr 2022
12. Carstensen, L.W.: Desk-top scanning for cartographic digitization and spatial-analysis. Photogram. Eng. Remote Sens. **57**(11), 1437–1446 (1991)
13. Chen, J., Lu, Q.: A method for automatic analysis table of contents in Chinese books. Libr. Hi Tech. **33**(3), 424–438 (2015)
14. http://documentation.sorbonne-universites.fr/en/resources/digital-libraries/jubilotheque-upmcs-scientific-digital-library.html (2024). Accessed 24 Feb 2024
15. https://www.prlib.ru/collections (2022). Accessed 24 Apr 2022
16. https://diss.rsl.ru/ (2022). Accessed 24 Apr 2022
17. http://heritage1.jscc.ru/ (2022). Accessed 24 Apr 2022
18. https://nsdl.oercommons.org/ (2022). Accessed 24 Apr 2022
19. https://www.tib.eu/de/ (2022). Accessed 24 Apr 2022
20. http://i.uran.ru/nasledie/ (2022). Accessed 24 Apr 2022
21. https://iphlib.ru/library (2022). Accessed 24 Apr 2022
22. http://library.iea.ras.ru/index.html (2022). Accessed 24 Apr 2022
23. Kozlova, T., Zambrzhitskaia, E., Simakov, D., Balbarin, Y.: Algorithms for calculating the cost in the conditions of digitalization of industrial production. In: International Scientific Conference Digital Transformation on Manufacturing, Infrastructure and Service, vol. 497, pp. 012078 (2019).
24. Kirillov, S.A., Malinin, A.I., Kirillov, S.A.: Metodika obrabotki otskanirovannyh izobrazhenij v proekte elektronnoj biblioteki "Nauchnoe nasledie Rossii". In: Informacionnoe obespechenie nauki: novye tekhnologii, pp. 99–107 (2009)
25. Kalenov, N.E., Savin, G.I., Serebryakov, V.A., Sotnikov, A.N.: Principy postroeniya i formirovaniya elektronnoj biblioteki "Nauchnoe nasledie Rossii". In: Programmnye produkty i sistemy 2012, vol. 4, no. 100, pp. 30–40 (2012)
26. Kalenov, N.E.: Upravlenie tekhnologiej napolneniya elektronnoj biblioteki "Nauchnoe nasledie Rossii". In: Elektronnye biblioteki: perspektivnye metody i tekhnologii, elektronnye kollekcii: trudy XVI Vserossijskaya nauchnaya konferenciya RCDL, pp. 357–361 (2014)
27. Sotnikov A.N., Kirillov S.A.: Tekhnologiya podgotovki elektronnyh izdanij dlya elektronnoj biblioteki "Nauchnoe nasledie Rossii". In: Informacionnoe obespechenie nauki: novye tekhnologii, pp. 178–190 (2015)

28. Zabrovskaya, I.E., Kirillov, S.A., Kondrat'eva, E.A., Pruglo, O.A., Sotnikov, A.N.: Voprosy formirovaniya fondov elektronnoj biblioteki "Nauchnoe nasledie Rossii". In: Informacionnoe obespechenie nauki: novye tekhnologii, pp. 184–191 (2017)

29. Kalenov, N., Sobolevskaya, I., Sotnikov, A.: Archival and museum information as a component of the common digital space of scientific knowledge. In: Proceedings of the 10th International Conference on Data Science, Technology and Applications, DATA 2021, pp. 144–149 (2021). https://doi.org/10.5220/0010512401440149

30. Antopol'skij, A.B., Kalenov, N.E., Serebryakov, V.A., Sotnikov, A.N.: O edinom cifrovom prostranstve nauchnyh znanij. Vestnik Rossijskoj akademii 89(7), 728–735 (2019)

31. YUmasheva, Y.U.: Metodicheskie rekomendacii po elektronnomu kopirovaniyu arhivnyh dokumentov i upravleniyu poluchennym informacionnym massivom. VNIIDAD, p. 125 (2012)

32. Kalenov, N., Sobolevskaya, I., Sotnikov, A.: The role of the common digital space of scientific knowledge in the educational technology development. In: 15th International Multi-Conference on Society, Cybernetics and Informatics, IMSCI 2021, pp. 35–38 (2021)

33. Sobolevskaya, I.N., Sotnikov, A.N.: Principles of 3D Web-collections visualization. In: Proceedings of the 3rd International Conference on Computer-Human Interaction Research and Applications, pp. 145–151 (2019)

34. Hipsley, CA., Aguilar, R., Black, JR., Hocknull SA.: High-throughput microCT scanning of small specimens: preparation, packing, parameters and post-processing. Sci. Rep. 10(1), 13863 (2020)

35. Kalenov, N.E., Kirillov, S.A., Sobolevskaya, I.N., Sotnikov, A.N.: Vizualizaciya cifrovyh 3d- ob"ektov pri formirovanii virtual'nyh vystavok. Elektronnye biblioteki. 23(4), 418–432 (2020)

36. Wróżyński, R., Pyszny, K., Sojka, M., Przybyła, C., Murat-Błażejewska, S.: Ground volume assessment using "Structure from Motion" photogrammetry with a smartphone and a compact camera. Open Geosciences. 9, 281–294 (2017)

37. Scopigno, R.: Digital fabrication techniques for cultural heritage: a survey. Comput. Graph. Forum. 36, 6–21 (2017)

38. Garstki, K.: Virtual representation: the production of 3D digital artifacts. Archaeol. Method Theory. 24, 726–750 (2017)

39. Guidi, G., Malik, U.S., Micoli, L.L.: Optimal lateral displacement in automatic close-range photogrammetry. Sensors 20(21), 6280 (2020)

40. Medina, J.J, Maley, J.M., Sannapareddy, S.S., Medina, N.N., Gilman C.M., McCormack, J.E.: A rapid and cost-effective pipeline for digitization of museum specimens with 3D photogrammetry. PLOS ONE 15(8), e0236417 (2020)

41. Lobanov, A.N.: Fotogrammetriya. Nedra, 552 (1984)

42. Gill, F., Myurrej, U., Rajt, M.: Prakticheskaya optimizaciya. Mir. 509 (1985)

43. http://new.jscc.ru/resources/hpc/#item1587 (2022). Accessed 24 Apr 2022

44. Wuttke, U., Spiecker, C., Neuroth, H.: PARTHENOS - a digital research infrastructure for eHumanities and eHeritage. Bibliothek forschung und praxis. 43(1), 11–20 (2019)

45. Munster, S.: Digital heritage as a scholarly field-topics, researchers, and perspectives from a bibliometric point of view. Acm J. Comput. Cult. Heritage. 2019. 12(3), 12 (2019)

An Analysis of Cultural Content on Short Video Platforms: Cultural Protection Perspective

Lifu Li[✉], Kyeong Kang, and Osama Sohaib

Faculty of Engineering and Information Technology,
University of Technology Sydney, Sydney, Australia
{Lifu.Li,Kyeong.Kang,Osama.Sohaib}@uts.edu.au

Abstract. This study analyses the relationship between ethnic minority groups' (EMGs) short video content and online viewers' watching interest based on the short video platform background. It considers China's short video interactive environment and divides the cultural content into the cultural vision unit and cultural audition unit according to the sensory marketing theory. Through testing numerous EMG video content based on the covariance analysis method, the paper presents the relationships between short cultural video content and online viewers' watching interest. Meanwhile, because of the differences among Chinese EMGs, this paper divides them into seven main groups and promotes the multi-group analysis, aiming to present specific results for each major group. The research findings can guide EMG video producers to improve their video content and contribute to Chinese EMG cultural protection and cultural diversity.

Keywords: Short video platform · Ethnic minority group users · Cultural content · Online viewers' watching interest · Sensory marketing theory

1 Introduction

The short video platform is a kind of digital media platform that consists of user-generated content based on the video hosting service [1]. With the improvement of Web 3.0, the short video platform industry is becoming a prevalent global industry with numerous online users attracted by electronic word-of-mouth [2, 3]. Unlike professionally generated content on traditional social media platforms, short video platform users have more opportunities to present their personalised content without strict requirements for format and style [4, 5]. As a social networking platform, online users can produce and upload short videos in less than 60 s, and the video content can include personal daily life, landscape and cultural content [1]. In China, popular short video platforms, i.e. the TikTok platform launched by ByteDance, have successfully attracted more than 500 million active users in three years [6]. Its development speed is much faster than conventional social media. In the first quarter of 2018, the TikTok platform has become the most downloaded app, with 45.8 million downloads worldwide [7]. The main reason for the popularity of short video platforms is the diversity of short video creation and the uncertainty of video content [8, 9]. The features, such as a variety of video content and a 60-s time limit, are comfortable for platform users to spread information quickly, as well as for ethnic minority group (EMG) users to spread cultural content [10].

Regarding the short video content uploaded on short video platforms, some are related to Chinese EMGs' culture and play significant roles in online viewers' watching interest, such as costumes from the Yi group, EMG language from the Chaoxian group, and folk dances from the Dai group, which has not attracted enough attention by existing studies [10, 11]. To be specific, in addition to the major group Han, 55 EMGs distribute in China, and most of them have their original history, language and writing system, which is different from the major group [12]. According to China's national education policy, all EMG generations can accept bilingual education at their local schools, allowing them to inherit their original language and learn traditional culture [12, 13]. This kind of policy is beneficial for EMGs to control various cultural knowledge and apply it in their short video content. Meanwhile, considering their particular living environment and unique cultural background, EMGs' living environment and cultural background have specific characteristics [14]. This means that, compared with the major group, EMG short video producers with distinctive cultural preferences would produce unique short video content while using short video platforms. Furthermore, most EMG residents, such as the Bai group, the Shui group and the Hui group, live in China's western areas, with about 64% of Chinese territory, and the level of economic development is relatively low [15, 16]. Many younger EMG generations have decided to abandon their original environment and move from western to eastern regions because China's first wave of urbanisation developed in eastern areas [17]. During this process, more and more younger EMG generations have accepted the mainstream culture, causing the Chinese EMG culture faces the risk of disappearing.

To increase the influence of Chinese EMG culture and attract more users' attention, this research analyses what kinds of short video content created by EMG producers can attract online viewers' watching attention on short video platforms. Research results are helpful for EMG short video producers to create more engaging content and enhance their influence quickly, which is beneficial to protecting EMG culture directly. Based on the sensory marketing theory, the sensations affecting consumers' attitudes and behaviours include haptics, olfaction, audition, taste, and vision [18]. Due to the limitation of online short video communication, EMG short video producers have to pay more attention to the vision and audition parts rather than other sensations. Thus, through analysing existing short video content uploaded by EMG producers on short video platforms, such as costumes, folk songs and EMG language, this study divides them into the vision and audition parts, and the first research question is as follows: *What kinds of EMG short video content are related to cultural vision and cultural audition separately?*

Different EMGs have different characteristics, indicating that a detailed classification of EMGs is required in this study. These unique cultural symbols could make a particular group stand out among competitors and attract the attention of online viewers on short video platforms [11]. Referring to the EMG cultural division proposed by Ma (2008), the research classifies 55 EMGs into seven main groups. Specifically, the main group 1 includes Tibetan, Yugu, Menba, Luoba and Tu, because most of them use a similar writing system and believe in Tibetan Buddhism [19]. Meanwhile, influenced by the living environment and cultural backgrounds, these seven main groups' specific cultural preferences might be presented in their short video content. For instance, Tibetan Buddhism is prevalent in the main group 1, and the main group 4 residents prefer to display their folk dances and folk songs [20, 21]. Hence, different main groups can produce unique cultural content on short video platforms. The second question of this paper is as follows: *What kinds of short video content are conducive to a particular EMG to attract viewers' watching interest on short video platforms?*

In addition to these research questions proposed by the prior research [11], this study considers the living environment of EMGs and designs specific cultural protection methods based on the technical advantages of short video platforms. Although existing scholars have applied digital technology and developed policy strategies to protect EMG culture [22–27], few of them have discovered the considerable influence of short video platforms and protect EMG by spreading culture on short video platforms. Unlike prior EMG cultural protection methods, encouraging EMGs to spread cultural content on short video platforms has no strict capital, sites, and labour resources requirements. It can enhance EMG's cultural influence in a short period, which is worthwhile for this study to explore. In light of this, the third research question is as follows: *What kinds of cultural protection methods can be designed based on the development of EMG short video content?*

The paper significantly contributes to theoretical and practical implicants. Firstly, this study explores the cultural content produced by EMG users on short video platforms, which existing scholars ignore. Secondly, to systematically analyse EMG cultural content on short video platforms, this paper divides various cultural content into vision and audition aspects according to the sensory marketing theory, benefiting to explore the relationship between EMG cultural content and online viewers' watching interests. Meanwhile, based on the research results, suitable cultural protection suggestions can be presented, assisting EMG short video producers in designing appropriate cultural content and enhancing EMG cultural influence. As cultural short video content becomes more and more popular, EMG culture can be spread and protected, potentially improving their living conditions.

The rest of the paper is structured as follows. Firstly, prior studies about EMG cultural content, cultural protection and sensory marketing theory have been reviewed, and the relationships between cultural content and viewers' watching interest are analysed. Then, based on the sensory marketing model, the research model is established, and several hypotheses have been presented. Next, the methodology of this study is described, including the process of data collection, data analysis and research results. The key findings, implications, and future studies are discussed in the final part.

2 Literature Review

2.1 EMG Cultural Content

Most previous studies focus on ordinary users on social media platforms, and they divide these online users according to their gender, age, educational background and platforms using experience [28–31]. Although the EMG population is vast and increasingly more Chinese EMG individuals begin to use short video platforms, few types of research distinguish EMGs from the major group and focus on their particular cultural features. Meanwhile, some prior studies divide the short video content based on entertainment, politics, and business aspects [30, 32], and others utilise the content analysis method and summarise some specific content categories, including gaming, sports, and news [33, 34]. However, there has been no study of the classification of cultural video content uploaded by Chinese EMG users [11]. In light of this, it is meaningful for this paper to explore the cultural context created and uploaded by EMG producers on short video platforms and discuss how the cultural content affects online viewers' watching interest.

Table 1. Seven main EMGs based on their religion and geophagy [15, 19].

Main group	Language and writing	Religion	Marriage	Living area	Ethnic characteristics
Group 1 (Tibetan, Yugu, Menba, Luoba, Tu)	Independent	Tibetan Buddhism	Inter-ethnic marriage	Western areas (Xizang and Qinghai province)	Religious culture, painting (Thang-ga)
Group 2 (Hui, Sala, Dongxiang, Baoan)	Mandarin	Islam	Inter-ethnic marriage	Scattering throughout the country, and some of them living in Ningxia province	Food culture (kebab, hand-pulled noodles)
Group 3 (Man, Hezhe, Xibo)	Mandarin	No obvious religious beliefs	High marriage rate with Han group	Scattering throughout the country, and some of them living in north areas	Costume (chi-pao)
Group 4 (Mongolian, Elunchun, Ewenke, Dawoer)	Mandarin	Multiple religious beliefs	High marriage rate with Han group	North area (Inner Mongolia autonomous region)	Folk Song, sports (wrestling)
Group 5 (Chaoxian)	Independent	No obvious religious beliefs	Low marriage rate with Han group (10%)	North-eastern areas (Jilin province)	Language

(*continued*)

Table 1. (*continued*)

Main group	Language and writing	Religion	Marriage	Living area	Ethnic characteristics
Group 6 (Uyghur, Kazakh, Uzbek, Tajik, Kirgiz, Tatar, Russian)	Independent	Most believe in Islam	Inter-ethnic marriage	North-western areas (Xinjiang province)	Religious culture, local landscape
Group 7 (Miao, Yi, Lisu, Wa, She, Gaoshan, Lahu, Shui, Naxi, Jingpo, Mulao, Zhuang, Buyi, Dong, Yao, Bai, Tujia, Hani, Dai, Li, Qiang, Bulang, Maonan, Gelao, Achang, Pumi, Nu, Deang, Jing, Dulong, Jinuo)	Mandarin	Multiple religious beliefs	High marriage rate with Han group	Southwest areas (Yunnan, Sichuan, Guangxi province)	Handmade goods, folk dance, folk song

To comprehensively analyse the video content posted by EMGs, the paper draws on Ma (2008) and Li's research (2012) and divides 55 EMGs into seven main groups, improving the efficiency of data collection. As Table 1 shows, the division is based on their language, religion, marriage, living area, and group characteristics [15, 19]. For instance, most residents from the main group 2, such as the Hui group, the Sala group, the Dongxiang group and the Baoan group, have the same religious belief as Islam [35]. Most of the residents from the main group 6, including Uyghur, Kazakh, Uzbek, Tajik, Kirgiz, Tatar, and Russian, prefer to use their group language and cannot accept marriage the residents from the Han group [19]. Therefore, cultural vision and audition content analysis should be distinguished based on seven different main groups. However, because of the large population of Chinese EMG residents and the complex classification of EMGs, existing studies tend to choose one or two EMGs as their research targets, such as the handwork research from the Li group and the language research from the Chaoxian group [12, 25, 36]. Due to the different cultural environments, the research results from these particular groups cannot be directly applied to other EMGs. Thus, considering this existing problem, the paper refers to Ma's (2008) and Li's study results (2012) and divides 55 EMGs into seven main groups based on their languages, customs, religions, and residential environment, which will be explained in the methodology section.

2.2 Cultural Protection in China's Environment

Existing scholars related to EMG cultural protection focus on digital technologies, such as AI technology, 3D model and VR technology [22–25], which needs numerous financial and technical supports and cannot be applied in less-developed areas. In addition to the digital technical strategies, many researchers pay much attention to the cooperation with official departments and guide them to establish various policies to guide young EMG residents to inherit traditional culture [26, 27]. Still, this cultural protection method needs local governments and residents' long-term participation. Compared with previous cultural protection methods, it is more suitable to utilise the considerable influence of short video platforms and spread EMG culture through creating various cultural short videos.

Unlike traditional social media platforms, various functions on short video platforms, such as the thumb up, group chat and online store functions, benefit Chinese EMG short video producers to display their cultural content and promote an online business [6, 37]. With the number of short video clicks increasing, the EMG cultural content will be spread constantly, and the traffic income of Chinese EMG video producers will increase simultaneously. Therefore, the cultural protection method based on the short video platforms would not only give full play to the advantages of Chinese EMG culture but also increase their income.

2.3 Sensory Marketing Model

As the sensory marketing model created by Krishna (2012) presents, viewers' watching interest can be influenced by haptics, olfaction, audition, taste, and visual aspects. However, given the limitation of the short video platform function, EMG video producers cannot communicate with online users face to face, which results in them having to focus on the part of the cultural audition and cultural vision content, as Fig. 1 shows. According to the users' continuance intention theory based on the uses and gratification research [38, 39], the number of likes can reflect users' enjoyment of watching short videos. Meanwhile, unlike average short video content, the short video content created by EMG users has unique cultural features and specific attractive to online viewers. By presenting the cultural audition and cultural vision content, Chinese EMG video producers could provide online viewers with hedonic gratification and attract more viewers' watching attention in the sharing process [11]. Thus, the cultural content produced by EMG users would have a positive relationship with online viewers' watching interest.

Furthermore, considering different EMGs have different cultural characteristics [19], this study designs the EMG background as a moderating factor to moderate the relationship between cultural content and online viewers' watching interest, which is helpful in exploring additional findings and discuss managerial implications. Specifically, different from other main groups, the main group 1 users are more familiar with Tibetan Buddhism knowledge and have the ability to display religious products, such as Thangka and Butter Sculpture [40]. This could result in online viewers focusing on the short video

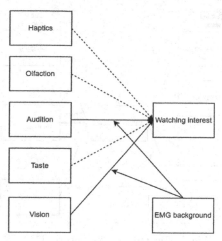

Fig. 1. The relationships between cultural sensations and users' watching intention in short video platforms based on different EMGs.

producers from the main group 1 while they browse religious content. Therefore, it is significant for this study to design video producers' EMG background as a moderating factor and promote the multi-group analysis.

3 Research Model

Based on the sensory marketing theory, the paper classifies various cultural content into *Cultural vision* and *Cultural audition* units. Specifically, as Fig. 2 shows, the *Cultural vision* unit includes costume, handwork, folk dance and landscape, and the *Cultural audition* unit includes language, custom introduction and folk song. Meanwhile, this paper designs the EMG background as the moderating factor to moderate the relationship between cultural content and viewers' watching interest. The results will be presented in the key finding section through multi-group analysis.

3.1 Cultural Vision Unit

Based on the sensory marketing model [18] and the use and gratification research [38, 39], the research framework established in Fig. 2 shows the relationship between cultural sensations created by EMG producers and viewers' watching interest on short video platforms. Firstly, in addition to the appearance of the characters on the screen, the character's clothing can give a deep impression to online viewers [41]. Specifically, most Chinese EMGs have unique costumes with various styles and beautiful colours [15], which can be presented in their short video content and provide online viewers with an attractive cultural vision. For instance, during major festivals, the Miao girls wear their costumes made by the Miao silver to present their beauty and potentially display their family status [42]. The unique cultural costumes can be delivered through the short video function and utilised to attract online viewers' watching interest. Thus,

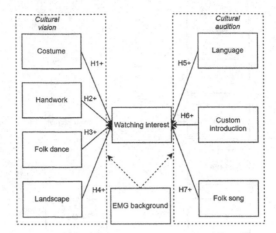

Fig. 2. The research framework [11].

some EMGs can wear their beautiful costumes while creating short videos, which could make them stand out and attract online viewers' watching interest. The paper proposes that:

Hypothesis 1: Costume in EMG short videos positively correlates with viewers' watching intention on the short video platform.

In addition to costumes in EMG short video content, cultural handworks, such as silver ornament from the main group 7, are attractive to online viewers [42]. Some Chinese EMGs are skilful at handwork that is a type of tangible cultural heritage. For instance, the EMG residents living in the Xiangxi area have a rich heritage of wood carvings, such as woodcarving grid doors and window patterns with a long history [43]. Given its unique cultural significance, wood carving considerably influences the art market. Thus, cultural handwork from Chinese EMGs would also have the advantage of attracting online viewers' attention, and they can be applied to short video content. The paper proposes that:

Hypothesis 2: Handwork in EMG short video positively correlates with viewers' watching intention on the short video platform.

Unlike costume and handwork, folk dance belongs to an intangible cultural heritage, which is attractive to Chinese online viewers. In detail, influenced by the social and cultural atmosphere, many Uighur residents from the main group 6 have cheerful personalities and are naturally skilful at folk dances, although most of them have not accepted professional dance training [44]. In recent years, various folk dances with ethnic characteristics have been recorded in short videos and uploaded to the short video platform, attracting numerous viewers' watching interest. Hence, the paper proposes that:

Hypothesis 3: Folk dance in EMG short video positively correlates with viewers' watching intention on the short video platform.

Most Chinese EMG residents' living environment is far from urban pollution, providing tourists with picturesque landscapes and places of interest, such as beautiful autumnal colours in the Kanas area and highland scape in the Jiuzhaigou area [45]. All of these attractive landscapes have been recorded and uploaded by some Chinese EMG video producers on the short video platform, which could alleviate the city dwellers' visual fatigue and positively affect online viewers' watching interest [46]. In light of this, the landscape visual content produced by EMGs could positively affect online users' watching intention, and the paper proposes that:

Hypothesis 4: Landscape in EMG short video positively correlates with viewers' watching intention on the short video platform.

3.2 Cultural Audition Unit

Most EMGs from group 1, group 5 and group 6 have their original language and writing systems that are different from the major group Han. For example, influenced by Korean waves, including Korean TV programs and idol groups, more and more younger Chinese generations are attracted by Korean culture and prefer to choose the Korean language as their second language [47, 48]. Within this cultural environment, some of the short video producers from the Chaoxian group (Korean) utilise this opportunity and design a series of language course videos to enhance their online social influence. Therefore, based on the impact of EMG language, the paper proposes:

Hypothesis 5: Language in EMG short video positively correlates with users' watching intention on the short video platform.

To assist online viewers in understanding EMG culture, different kinds of customs, including traditional religions, festivals and etiquettes, have been introduced and explained by Chinese EMG video producers. Specifically, some of the Chinese EMGs have their original religion, such as Tibetan Buddhism and Islamism, which is reflected in their daily customs. In Tibetan culture, OM MANI PADME HUM is usually carved in some stones, placed on prayer wheels, and recited every day by all Tibetans [49], providing outsiders with a sharp mental shock. For the main group 4, the Mongolia Naadam Festival has the particular social and cultural backgrounds, and it can connect viewers from different groups [50]. Considering the influence of EMG customs, it has a positive relationship with online viewers' watching interest, and thus the paper supposes:

Hypothesis 6: Custom introduction in EMG short video positively correlates with users' watching intention on the short video platform.

In addition to EMG language, EMG individuals from the main group 1 show the talent for traditional music, such as Mongolians' famous grassland songs [51]. Compared with the mainstream songs, these folk songs show Mongolians' unique regional characteristics and reflect their ethnic history and religious beliefs, having a particular acoustical appeal to the online audience [51]. Therefore, folk songs produced by Chinese EMGs positively affect online viewers' watching intention, and the study supposes:

Hypothesis 7: Folk song in EMG short video positively correlates with users' watching intention on the short video platform.

4 Methodology

4.1 Research Setting

To collect and analyse EMG cultural content, nine Chinese college students have been organised as a research team based on the research requirements. The research chooses them because they can distinguish the EMG language from the Chinese language and have extensive academic experience in the use of short video platforms, such as TikTok and Kuaishou platforms. Meanwhile, this study requires the research team members to read the related literature about Chinese EMGs, i.e. *Types of the Ethnic Relationships in Modern China* written by Ma (2008) and *Illustration of 56 ethnic groups in China written* by Li (2018), which is helpful for them to learn the basic knowledge of Chinese EMGs and understand various ethnic characteristics. Due to the situation of the COVID-19 pandemic, the study decides to promote a distance-training for this team through the Zoom platform. After this process, the research team promotes online observation based on the content analysis method [52] and categorises various EMG video content based on the research model from July 2020 to August 2020.

4.2 Research Measurement

The research members are not fixed and focus on one specific EMG but rotate every three days to ensure objectivity in content collection and scoring [53]. This research provides the research team with a particular content categorisation and scoring criteria Table based on the research model, conducing to improve the statistics' accuracy. As Table 2 shows, the research team can refer to the scoring criteria Table based on specific examples of EMG short videos on the TikTok platform [53]. Considering the number of questions and the number of research team members, the paper refers to the Likert 7 point scale [43] to increase the score's accuracy. The range is from the lowest score $=$ 2 to the highest score $= 7$, and 1 point means there is no related content in this EMG short video content. Due to the paper format's limitation, the paper only provides the screenshot of EMG short video content in Table 2, assisting readers in understanding.

In addition to the necessary information about the EMG video producers, including producers' gender and group, the study requires the research team to record the number of like that can be utilised to evaluate short video viewers' watching interest of these EMG short video content. In order to reflect the relevance between EMG cultural content and online viewers' watching interest, the research divides these different numbers of likes into seven dimensions, from the lowest 1 to the highest 7. Meanwhile, team members should set the video release time within 24 h during the statistical process because the

Table 2. The scoring criteria of EMG short video content.

Types of content	The example of the lowest score (2 points)	The example of the highest score (7 points)
Costume	(Simply costume from the Miao)	(Luxurious dressed from the Miao)
Handwork	(Simple handwork, paper folding)	(Professional painting, Thang-ga)
Folk dance	(Simple dance)	(Professional Uighur dance)
Landscape	(Common architecture landscape)	(Beautiful landscape in Tibet)
Language	(Simple communication)	(Professional language teaching)

(continued)

Table 2. (*continued*)

Custom introduction	(Simple introduction to the Man's traditional wedding)	(Comprehensive introduction to the Man culture)
Folk song	(Simple song)	(Professional instrument display)

length of post time directly impacts the number of likes. Hence, limiting the video release time is necessary. Furthermore, according to the score of EMG cultural content uploaded by the research team, the paper utilises the covariance analysis method to explore the relationship between various Chinese EMG short video content and online viewers' watching interest.

4.3 Data Collection

After defining the content categories of Chinese EMG short videos and creating essential scoring criteria, from July 2020 to August 2020, the research group has recorded and scored 1007 EMG short videos from the TikTok platform. Among the content recorded (Table 3), more than 43% of video data is from the group 7, and only 5.96% of the data recorded is from the group 3. This is because the main group 7 include 31 EMGs. Meanwhile, according to the gender distribution (Table 4), except for both females and males or no one shown in the short video, more than 54% of the characters in short videos are females, and only 25% are males. Through comparison of gender distribution, the statistical results are similar among these seven groups. This claims that, for all EMGs, females in short videos are more popular than males on the short video platform.

Moreover, according to the data collection results (Table 5), most EMG short video producers prefer to show their local landscape because they live in remote areas where the environment is different from urban areas and has particular attraction for online viewers.

Table 3. EMG short videos distribution (n = 1007) [11].

Group ID	Number	Relative frequency
Group 1	136	13.51%
Group 2	74	7.35%
Group 3	60	5.96%
Group 4	87	8.64%
Group 5	84	8.34%
Group 6	131	13.01%
Group 7	435	43.20%

Table 4. EMG short video producers' gender distribution (n = 1007).

Gender	Total	Group 1	Group 2	Group 3	Group 4	Group 5	Group 6	Group 7
Female	545	77	44	36	39	38	60	251
	54.12%	56.62%	59.46%	60%	44.83%	45.24%	45.80%	57.70%
Male	261	41	21	21	26	14	45	93
	25.92%	30.15%	28.38%	35%	29.89%	16.67%	34.35%	21.38%
Both	201	18	9	3	22	32	26	91
	19.96%	13.24%	12.16%	5%	25.29%	38.10%	19.85%	20.92%

Meanwhile, group 3 and the group 4 rarely use their original languages because they have a very high marriage rate with the Han group and gradually accept the mainstream culture and speak the Mandarin language [19]. Few video producers show the content related to handwork and folk dances, although Chinese EMGs widely adopt both customs and folk songs as their video content. This might be because folk dances and folk songs have a marked difference in the skilful difficulty.

4.4 Data Analysis

To research the relationship between EMG cultural video content and online viewers' watching interest, the study requires team members to score the attractiveness of the video content based on the number of likes in each video. Specifically, the research sorts 1007 EMG short videos by the number of likes and evenly divides all like numbers into seven levels in order of less to more. The number of recorded videos in each level is the same. As the table of ratings shows (Table 6), the amount of 0 to 29 likes is equal to the lowest score of 1 point, and the amount of 1476 to 121000 likes is equal to the highest score of 7 points. Based on the comparison of the number of likes (Table 7), the group 7 is the most popular among short video viewers. Still, the videos created by the group 2 are not attractive to viewers. This might be because most of the inhabitants of the group 7 live with the Han group and have more similar living habits and cultural backgrounds

Table 5. EMG short video producers' gender distribution (n = 1007).

Group ID	Custom	Handwork	Folk dance	Landscape	EMG language	Custom explanation	Folk song
G1	82	24	39	104	31	59	72
n=136	60.29%	17.65%	28.68%	76.47%	22.79%	43.38%	52.94%
G2	32	11	6	36	8	23	21
n=74	43.24%	14.86%	8.11%	48.65%	10.81%	31.08%	28.38%
G3	34	11	26	34	4	33	37
n=60	56.67%	18.33%	43.33%	56.67%	6.67%	55.00%	61.67%
G4	62	36	49	55	23	36	45
n=87	71.26%	41.38%	56.32%	63.22%	26.44%	41.38%	51.72%
G5	43	28	27	56	29	33	37
n=84	51.19%	33.33%	32.14%	66.67%	34.52%	39.29%	44.05%
G6	90	20	60	92	37	40	78
n=131	68.70%	15.27%	45.80%	70.23%	28.24%	30.53%	59.54%
G7	354	157	189	299	222	268	297
n=435	81.38%	36.09%	43.45%	68.74%	51.03%	61.61%	68.28%

to the Han than other groups. Hence, the cultural content created by the main group 7 is easier to be accepted by online viewers.

Table 6. The rating of the number of likes.

Score (1 = the lowest score, 7 = the highest score)	The number of likes
1 point	0–29
2 points	30–74
3 points	75–142
4 points	143–257
5 points	258–504
6 points	506–1462
7 points	1476–121000

This research utilises the covariance analysis method (Fig. 3) to analyse the relationships between various EMG video content and online viewers' watching interest based on these seven groups' cultural content. Following the formula of covariance, the EMG cultural content score is set to X, and the score of the likes is set to Y. After the calculation, the covariance of the relationships has been present in Table 8. For all Chinese EMGs, in addition to the EMG language content, others have a positive relationship with viewers' watching interest, from 0.581 to 0.822. Specifically, as Table 8 shows, the calculation results will change significantly while comparing different groups specifically. For instance, all kinds of content created by the group 1 short video producers are

Table 7. The popularity rank of each group.

Rank	Group ID	Average Score (Users' watching interest)
1	G7	4.4
2	G1	4
3	G4	3.99
4	G5	3.63
5	G6	3.60
6	G3	3.48
7	G2	3.04

beneficial for attracting online viewers' watching interest, between 0.122 and 1.924, but most of the video content uploaded by the group 5 negatively correlates with viewers' watching attention, between -0.847 and -2.06.

$$Cov(X, Y) = E[(X - \mu_x)(Y - \mu_y)]$$

Fig. 3. The covariance analysis formula.

Table 8. The covariance analysis of video content and users' watching interest [11].

Group ID	Costume	Handwork	Folk dance	Landscape	Language	Custom	Folk song
G1	0.439	1.386	1.924	0.395	0.122	0.402	0.584
G2	−0.65	0.545	0.1	0.317	−3.321	2.273	−0.3
G3	0.867	1.136	−0.412	0.237	0.667	2.188	0.079
G4	0.96	1.214	1.432	0.754	−0.237	0.965	0.995
G5	−0.919	1.016	−2.06	0.409	−0.847	0.234	−1.456
G6	0.882	2.437	1.012	0.784	−1.33	1.905	0.321
G7	0.43	0.54	0.572	0.556	−0.065	0.365	0.602
All	0.687	0.822	0.666	0.625	−0.281	0.679	0.581

5 Discussion and Implication

5.1 Key Findings

Through the comparison among the covariance analysis of all Chinese EMGs and every main group, the data analysis results in Table 9 show the strengths and weaknesses of each main group, answering the first and second research questions. Firstly, in the costume part, group 3, group 4, and group 6 have more advantages than the other groups. This means online viewers on the short video platform tend to follow the video producers from these three groups who wear and present their unique EMG customs. In contrast, the costumes shown by group 2 and group 5 do not positively impact online viewers' watching interest. Secondly, handwork requires EMG video-makers to acquire specific skills, such as silverware manufacturing from the Miao group, Korean group food-making, and the Dulong group's exceptional hunting skills. No matter which group it is, skilful handwork has a significant appeal to online viewers. Thirdly, the audience on the TikTok platform has strict requirements for folk dance. In China, most folk dances are combined with the culture of villages. In order to cater to people's new aesthetic, in recent years, many dancers from the Han group have continued to innovate and improve folk dance performances [54]. This may explain why online viewers are not particularly interested in ordinary folk dances. Nevertheless, group 4 and group 6 still show a significant advantage in dance performance, and their covariances scores are 1.432 and 1.012, respectively. Fourthly, there is a positive relationship between the landscape display and the viewers' watching intention in every EMG. This is because most EMG video producers are from China's western areas, and the natural scenery in western areas, such as Xinjiang province and Xizang province, is much more beautiful than in eastern areas where most Chinese residents live [55]. This could lead many users to expect to see a different view in these EMG short videos.

In addition to cultural vision, cultural audition content designed by EMGs also has a strong relationship with short video viewers' watching interest, as Table 9 presents. Firstly, 91.51% of residents in China are from the Han group [56], which means most online users are familiar with Mandarin and might not be interested in the EMG language. Although the data result of EMG language content could recommend EMG video producers not to display EMG language in their short video content, this recommendation is unbeneficial for EMG language heritage. Secondly, online viewers have an intense curiosity about EMG customs related to group 2, group 3, and group 6, and the covariances scored are 2.273, 2.188, and 1.905 separately, which are much higher than the covariance of whole EMGs that is 0.679. However, considering the analysis result of EMG language, the video producers who promote custom explanations are best to use Mandarin rather than their original language. Thirdly, compared with the outcome of folk dance, online viewers on the TikTok platform have a higher acceptance of folk songs, especially the folk songs shared by group 4. This might be based on the efforts of many Mongolian singers, such as Tenger, whose song named 'Mongolian' earned him numerous honours and fame across the country [51]. Therefore, celebrities of each EMG have a potential relationship with the cultural prevalence of that group.

Finally, following the third research question, this study claims specific cultural strengths and weaknesses for each major group and provides suitable cultural protection strategies. For instance, as Table 10 states, short video producers from group 1 should focus on handwork and landscape content instead of language, and the producers from group 2 should pay more attention to handwork, landscape and custom introduction rather than costume and language. Thus, to enhance EMG's cultural popularity and promote cultural protection, EMG short video producers and related departments need to play their strengths and attract viewers' watching interest.

Table 9. The summary of all results.

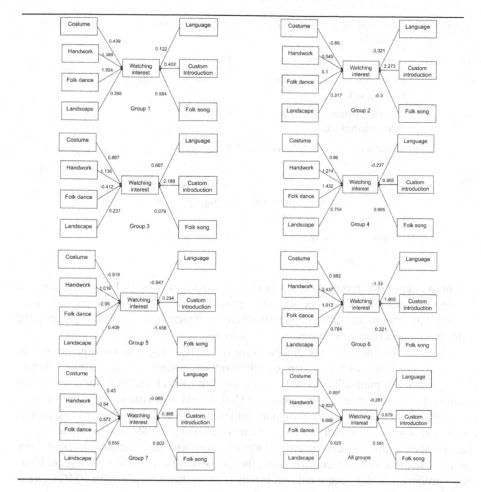

5.2 Theoretical and Practical Implications

This study makes several significant theoretical and practical contributions. Firstly, this research establishes the research framework based on the sensory marketing model created by Krishna (2012) and divides EMG cultural content based on cultural vision content and cultural audition content. Although existing studies have proved that audition and vision can influence viewers' attitudes to regular short video content, it has not analysed whether EMG vision and audition content would affect viewers' watching interest. In order to spread EMG culture on SMPs, this paper promotes the classification of EMG short video content on the TikTok platform. Meanwhile, based on different Chinese EMGs' cultural backgrounds, it also explores what specific content effectively attracts online viewers' watching interest on short video platforms. Therefore, this study focuses on the relationship between specific EMG cultural content and online viewers'

Table 10. Cultural protection strategies for each group.

Group ID	Cultural strengths for EMG producers	Cultural weaknesses for EMG producers
G1	Handwork, landscape	Language
G2	Handwork, landscape, custom introduction	Costume, language
G3	Costume, handwork, landscape, custom introduction	Language
G4	Costume, handwork, folk dance, landscape, folk song	Language
G5	Handwork, landscape	Costume, language
G6	Costume, handwork, fork dance, landscape, custom introduction	Language
G7	Handwork, landscape	Language

watching interest and promotes comparisons among seven main EMG cultural content. The research results could be beneficial to provide EMG video producers with some valuable suggestions and guide them to improve their video content. In this process, the EMG culture in China will be spread and inherited.

Moreover, TikTok is an essential platform for EMGs to spread a unique group culture. In recent years, as the concept of urbanisation prevails in China, many younger EMG generations gradually accept the modern culture, which results in some traditional cultures facing the danger of disappearance [57]. Faced with issues, prior studies focus on technical, financial and policy support, which needs numerous financial and human resources. Based on the short video platform's advantages, EMG video producers can improve their cultural video content and attract online viewers' watching interest. With the increase in viewers' watching interest, they are willing to build trust with these EMG video producers and purchase cultural products from them, which helps EMGs spread their unique culture and enhance their income.

5.3 Limitations and Future Study

Some drawbacks related to this research should be discussed. Firstly, the data results will be subjectively influenced by the research members in the grading process, although the research team members take responsibility for data collection and scoring for each EMG video content. Hence, future studies should organise more team members to promote the grading work, reducing the impact of subjectivity. Secondly, the paper divides content classification into seven categories according to the cultural vision and the cultural audition based on the sensory marketing theory. However, with the deepening of research, content classification can be more specific. Furthermore, the relationships between online viewers' watching interest and Chinese EMG short video content are not limited to the research framework. Other significant relationships should be focused on, like the relationship between online viewers' purchasing interest and Chinese EMG short video content, which needs future studies to promote deep analysis based on existing literature. Finally, the data analysis based on the covariance analysis method has specific limitations, and this study needs to test the measurement model, including its reliability, convergent validity and discriminant validity. To examine hypotheses in the research model and explore online viewers' watching interest, future studies will apply the variance-based structural equation modelling and partial least squares path modelling on SmartPLS 3.0, which is helpful to comprehensively examine the path coefficient and provide a deep understanding of the research model.

6 Conclusion

Given the urbanisation developments in China, more and more EMG generations tend to accept the mainstream culture and ignore their actual cultural knowledge, causing numerous traditional EMG cultures to face the danger of disappearance. Considering the positive relationship between cultural content and viewers' watching interest, this paper focuses on the short video produced by EMGs and designs particular strategies to protect EMG culture and enhance its influence, which is different from the prior research [11]. Specifically, given the research framework and data analysis results, this study presents what cultural content is more attractive to online viewers and what plays a negative role. Through the covariance analysis of each group, the paper provides specific recommendations for them to improve their cultural content and enhance their cultural influence. For instance, the group 3, the group 4 and the group 6 show a significant advantage in costume, indicating they can display their group clothes in their short videos. As viewers' watching interest is satisfied, more and more EMG cultural content will be presented on short video platforms, and EMG culture will be accepted and protected potentially.

References

1. Kaye, D.B.V., Chen, X., Zeng, J.: The co-evolution of two Chinese mobile short video apps: parallel platformization of Douyin and TikTok. Mob. Media Commun. 9(2), 229–253 (2021)
2. Xie, X.-Z., et al.: Does customer co-creation value lead to electronic word-of-mouth? :an empirical study on the short-video platform industry. Soc. Sci. J. 56(3), 401–416 (2019)
3. Mou, J.B.: Study on social media marketing campaign strategy-TikTok and Instagram. Massachusetts Institute of Technology (2020)
4. Wang, Y.-H., Gu, T.-J., Wang, S.-Y.: Causes and characteristics of short video platform internet community taking the TikTok short video application as an example. In: 2019 IEEE International Conference on Consumer Electronics-Taiwan (ICCE-TW). IEEE (2019)
5. Li, L., Kang, K.: Analyzing shopping behavior of the middle-aged users in Tiktok live streaming platform (2020)
6. Zhou, Q.: Understanding user behaviors of creative practice on short video sharing platforms– a case study of TikTok and Bilibili. University of Cincinnati (2019)
7. Omar, B., Dequan, W.: Watch, share or create: the influence of personality traits and user motivation on tiktok mobile video usage. Int. J. Interact. Mobile. Technol. (iJIM) 14(04), 121–137 (2020)

8. Bresnick, E.: Intensified play: cinematic study of TikTok mobile app. Research Gate (2019). https://www.researchgate.net/publication/335570557_Intensified_Play_Cinematic_study_of_TikTok_mobile_app. Accessed 5 Jan 2020

9. Li, L., Kang, K., Sohaib, O.: Investigating factors affecting Chinese tertiary students' online-startup motivation based on the COM-B behaviour changing theory. Journal of Entrepreneurship in Emerging Economies (2021)

10. Li, L., Kang, K.: Why ethnic minority groups' online-startups are booming in China's tight cultural ecosystem? Journal of Entrepreneurship in Emerging Economies (2021)

11. Li, L., Kang, K.: Exploring the relationships between cultural content and viewers' watching interest: a study of Tiktok videos produced by Chinese ethnic minority groups. In: 18th International Conference on e-Business. SCITEPRESS-Science and Technology Publications (2021)

12. Xiong, W., Jacob, W.J., Ye, H.: Minority language issues in Chinese higher education: policy reforms and practice among the Korean and Mongol ethnic groups. Front. Educ. China **11**(4), 455–482 (2016)

13. Rong, M.: Bilingual education for China's ethnic minorities. Chin. Educ. Soc. **40**(2), 9–25 (2007)

14. Postiglione, G.A.: The education of ethnic minority groups in China. In: The Routledge international companion to multicultural education, pp. 521–531. Routledge (2009)

15. Li, X.: Illustration of 56 ethnic groups in China (2012). CNPolitics.org

16. Yang, S., Ding, S., D'Alessandro, S.: Are all Chinese shoppers the same? Evidence of differences in values, decision making and shopping motivations between the Han majority and other minorities in China. J. Retail. Consum. Serv. **44**, 24–34 (2018)

17. Schneider, A., Mertes, C.: Expansion and growth in Chinese cities, 1978–2010. Environ. Res. Lett. **9**(2), 024008 (2014)

18. Krishna, A.: An integrative review of sensory marketing: engaging the senses to affect perception, judgment and behavior. J. Consum. Psychol. **22**(3), 332–351 (2012)

19. Ma, R.: Types of the Ethnic Relationships in Modern China. Society **28**(1), 1–23 (2008)

20. Powers, J.,: Introduction to Tibetan Buddhism. Shambhala Publications, Boulder (2007)

21. Pawan, S., Dawut, R., Kurban, S.: Uyghur meshrep culture and its social function. Fourth World J. **15**(2), 81–90 (2017)

22. Wu, X., et al.: Research on digital protection of brocade technique based on action recognition. In: Proceedings - 2017 4th International Conference on Information Science and Control Engineering (ICISCE) (2017)

23. Wu, X., Wei, G., Chunjie, J., Ping, W., Xinye, S.: Application of gesture recognition interaction to digital virtual reconstruction of Yunnan bronze drum. In: Deng, K., Yu, Z., Patnaik, S., Wang, J. (eds.) Recent Developments in Mechatronics and Intelligent Robotics. Advances in Intelligent Systems and Computing, vol. 856, pp. 1003–1012. Springer, Cham (2019). https://doi.org/10.1007/978-3-030-00214-5_123

24. Wu, X., et al.: Research on the new way of digital protection and inheritance of the Dai paper-cut. In: 2017 2nd IEEE International Conference on Computational Intelligence and Applications (ICCIA) (2017)

25. Lei, W., et al.: Virtual digital promotion and communication of Yi Costume in Yunnan. in Proceedings - 2017 4th International Conference on Information Science and Control Engineering (ICISCE) (2017)

26. Long, Y., et al.: The development status and protection of traditional Qiang ethnic minority villages. In: AIP Conference Proceedings (2018)

27. Li, G., Zhang, B.: Identification of landscape character types for trans-regional integration in the Wuling Mountain multi-ethnic area of southwest China. Landsc. Urban Plan. **162**, 25–35 (2017)

28. Mao, M., et al.: Testing ageing theory among later middle-aged and older users using social media. In: CSCW 2017 - Companion of the 2017 ACM Conference on Computer Supported Cooperative Work and Social Computing (2017)
29. Chen, H., Maynard, S.B., Ahmad, A.: A comparison of information security curricula in China and the USA. In: Proceedings of the 11th Australian Information Security Management Conference, ISM 2013 (2014)
30. Han, M.C., Kim, Y.: How culture and friends affect acceptance of social media commerce and purchase intentions: a comparative study of consumers in the U.S. and China. J. Int. Consum. Marketing. 30(5), 326–335 (2018)
31. Abdul Molok, N.N., et al.: Information security awareness through the use of social media. In: 2014 the 5th International Conference on Information and Communication Technology for the Muslim World (ICT4M) (2014)
32. Zhang, Z.: Infrastructuralization of Tik Tok: transformation, power relationships, and platformization of video entertainment in China. Media Cult. Soc. 43(2), 0163443720939452 (2020)
33. Zimmer, F., Scheibe, K.: What drives streamers? Users' characteristics and motivations on social live streaming services. In: Proceedings of the 52nd Hawaii International Conference on System Sciences (2019)
34. Friedlander, M.B.: Streamer motives and user-generated content on social live-streaming services (2017)
35. Man, K.: Islamic Menhuan system, patrilineal family, and gender relations of Dongxiang people in Gansu, China. Gender and Family in East Asia, pp. 177–92 (2014)
36. Oranratmanee, R.: Cultural geography of vernacular architecture in a cross-cultural context: houses of the dai ethnic minority in South China. J. Cult. Geogr. 37(1), 67–87 (2020)
37. Liu, G.-F., et al.: Research on the influence of social media short video marketing on consumer brand attitude. Adv. Soc. Sci. Educ. Humanit. Res. 336, 784–789 (2019)
38. Li, H., et al.: Modeling hedonic is continuance through the uses and gratifications theory: an empirical study in online games. Comput. Hum. Behav. 48, 261–272 (2015)
39. Katz, E.: Utilization of mass communication by the individual. The uses of mass communications: Current perspectives on gratifications research, pp. 19–32 (1974)
40. Cooke, S.: Butterfingers: Resculpting religion at a Tibetan Buddhist monastery. Provincial China. 2(1), 38 (2010)
41. El Khoury, E., Senac, C., Joly, P.: Face-and-clothing based people clustering in video content. In: Proceedings of the International Conference on Multimedia Information Retrieval (2010)
42. Liu, J.: Analysis of "Miao Silver" Market Opportunities. In: 2nd International Conference on Civil, Materials and Environmental Sciences. Atlantis Press (2015)
43. Baishan, L.: Cultural implication of woodcarving grid door and window patterns in Xiangxi minority group. Design Res. 5, 18 (2012)
44. Wong, C.-F.: Uyghur folk singing and the rural musical place in Northwest China. In: Leung, B.-W. (ed.) Traditional Musics in the Modern World: Transmission, Evolution, and Challenges. Landscapes: the Arts, Aesthetics, and Education, vol. 24, pp. 141–155. Springer, Cham (2018). https://doi.org/10.1007/978-3-319-91599-9_10
45. Yang, J., Ryan, C., Zhang, L.: External entrepreneurs/investors and guanxi: hostels in a tourism area, Xinjiang, China. Int. J. Contemp. Hospitality Manag. 26, 49 (2014)
46. Yang, J., Ryan, C., Zhang, L.: Ethnic minority tourism in China-Han perspectives of Tuva figures in a landscape. Tour. Manage. 36, 45–56 (2013)
47. Ahn, J.: The new Korean Wave in China: Chinese users' use of Korean popular culture via the Internet. Int. J. Contents 10(3), 47–54 (2014)
48. Jang, G., Paik, W.K.: Korean wave as tool for Korea's new cultural diplomacy. Adv. Appl. Sociol. 2(03), 196 (2012)

49. Campbell, J.: Traveller in space: gender, identity and Tibetan Buddhism. Bloomsbury Publishing (2018)
50. Liuhong, Z., Gang, G.: The comparative study of the development of of sports tourism project between Xinjiang and inner Mongolia Naadam festivals. In: 2011 International Conference on Future Computer Science and Education. IEEE (2011)
51. Henochowicz, A.: Blue heaven, parched land: Mongolian folksong and the Chinese State. Grad. J. Asia-Pacific Stud. **6**(1), 37–50 (2008)
52. Neuendorf, K.A., Kumar, A.: Content analysis. The International Encyclopedia of Political Communication, pp. 1–10 (2015)
53. Krippendorff, K.: Content analysis: an introduction to its methodology. SAGE Publications (2018)
54. Chou, E.S.: Folk dance in China: the dance pioneer Dai Ailian, 1916–2006. In: Congress on Research in Dance. Cambridge University Press (2016)
55. Wang, L., Chen, L.: Spatiotemporal dataset on Chinese population distribution and its driving factors from 1949 to 2013. Scientific data **3**(1), 1–16 (2016)
56. The sixth nationwide population census. National Bureau of Statistics (2010)
57. Xu, W., et al.: Digital inheritance of the traditional Dulong culture in Yunnan based on gesture interaction. In: Advances in Intelligent Systems and Computing, pp. 231–239 (2019)

Technology Transfer and Valuation Methods in Use by University Technology Transfer Offices

A. Rocha[1]([✉]) [ID], F. Romero[2] [ID], R. M. Lima[2] [ID], M. Amorim[3] [ID], and M. Cruz-Cunha[4] [ID]

[1] Polytechnic Institute of Cávado and Ave, Barcelos, Portugal
arocha@ipca.pt
[2] Algoritmi Research Center, Department of Production and Systems, School of Engineering, University of Minho, Braga, Portugal
[3] GOVCOPP Governance Competitiveness and Public Policies, University of Aveiro, Aveiro, Portugal
[4] 2Ai Artificial Intelligence Laboratory, Polytechnic Institute of Cávado and Ave, Barcelos, Portugal

Abstract. Valuing research deliverables implies the assessment of knowledge, skills, and solutions that can create benefits for a wide scope of stakeholders, including researchers, research units, universities, businesses, and the larger society. Investing in early-stage technology or technology that is novel and has an inventive step can imply a high-risk investment. High-quality information and advice are needed, and valuation methods are required, to support decision making regarding intellectual property rights protection, define a technology value proposition, devise a roadmap to bring technology into the market, and support negotiations with potential licensees. To provide information and evidence regarding the main technology valuation methods in use by Portuguese University Technology Transfer Offices (TTOs), qualitative and quantitative data have been collected by surveying and interviewing eight Portuguese University TTOs. From the data it was possible to conclude that pre-defined rating/ranking methods and models are the most frequently used valuation methods, followed by market valuation approaches. Previous agreements and discounted cash-flow projections are mainly used when a spin-off firm is under consideration or when there is a manifestation of interest from a potential investor. Royalty standards are used to prepare licensing negotiations, and Real Options, Monte Carlo simulation, rules of thumb, and Auctions are not being used.

Keywords: Technology transfer · Technology valuation and licensing · University and industry relation

1 Introduction

University technology transfer refers to the process of exchanging technical solutions, knowledge, and skills between universities and businesses, with the aim of exploring valuable tangible and intangible assets creating utility for those who benefit from their application [1].

P. Samarati et al. (Eds.): ICETE 2021, CCIS 1795, pp. 51–66, 2023.
https://doi.org/10.1007/978-3-031-36840-0_3

Technology Transfer Offices (TTOs) act as mediators in the valorization process, by reviewing and assessing invention disclosures in close collaboration with researchers, to define a protection strategy for Intellectual Property Rights (IPR), and to devise a plan to bring scientific and technological research results to the marketplace and the wider society. These possible valorization routes include licensing, selling IPR, establishing research and cooperation agreements, and the creation of a spin-off company or a joint venture.

Throughout this process technical and market assessments are carried out to support IPR decisions, define a technology value proposition, and support negotiations to reach a balanced deal to transfer valuable assets that are novel, have industrial applicability, and involve an inventive step.

Technology transfer creates utility beyond the opportunity of making money, either for universities or businesses, it can lead to the development of new projects and competitive advantages, including the development of new solutions not owned by other companies, updating and improving products, services, or manufacturing processes, or by reducing costs of industrialization and commercialization [2].

To further expand our knowledge regarding valuation processes supporting technology transfer, this article provides information and evidence on what are the main technology valuation methods in use by Portuguese University Technology Transfer Offices.

2 Methodology

This study is integrated into a larger research project [3–5] for the study of management of research, and valorization of technology, which involved an extensive literature review and the collection of complementary information by employing a semi-structured survey and interviewing the heads of staff of eight Portuguese University Technology Transfer Offices (TTOs).

The eight TTOs are linked to eight Portuguese Universities:

(a) TecMinho, University of Minho;
(b) UPIN, University of Porto;
(c) UATEC, University of Aveiro;
(d) DITS, University of Coimbra;
(e) Innovation and Development Office, University of Beira Interior;
(f) RIA, Research and Innovation Accelerator, University Nova of Lisboa;
(g) Technology Transfer Office, University of Évora;
(h) CRIA, University of Algarve;

This sample was purposefully chosen due to the high regional and national influence of the universities, and the experience and ability of the TTOs to provide data that would expand the understanding of technology transfer processes. Five out of the eight universities appear regularly in world rankings of the top 1000 universities [6].

The semi-structured survey was focused on technology valuation methods. A Likert scale has been used to classify the frequency of each method. The higher the value the higher the frequency of use, on a scale between 1 and 5. Since the sample is constrained to Portuguese universities, a descriptive analysis was adopted to process the data, and a content analysis of the interviews has been performed to gain further insights on which to base the conclusion regarding the frequency of use of different technology valuation methods in use by Portuguese University technology transfer offices.

3   Technology and Technology Transfer Offices

It is usual to equate a patent with one technology, but these days such cases are rare. Usually, multiple patents or multiple technical and knowledge solutions are required to obtain a technology and multiple technologies are responsible for a product, so it is prudent to obtain technology from other sources rather than investing time and resources to get a complete product or to find the perfect solution [7].

Technology transfer corresponds to the process of transferring technical solutions and scientific and technological knowledge from one organization to another, intending to take advantage of and exploit research results in favor of the development of the state of the art, science, economy, and the society.

Technology transfer processes are often carried out by inventors or by technology transfer offices or companies.

Technology transfer offices promote the use of R&D results through the assessment and protection of industrial property rights and through the dissemination of information, the negotiation of transfer agreements, and the provision of support services to create spin-off companies (start-up companies created to exploit research results coming out from one organization), they also administer and monitor licensing contracts, the transfer of materials, and the administration of equity participation, collecting and sharing the revenue from technology transfer agreements [8].

The closer the technology transfer offices are to the researchers, the more efficient they tend to be in establishing a relationship of mutual cooperation [9], which is important to encourage researchers to provide regular information about their research activities and results [10].

The disclosure of research results triggers the valuation process, to determine its economic value, define its commercialization strategy, and combine its unique characteristics with the needs and interests of organizations that can take advantage of its use. The acquisition of technology and its transformation into new or improved products and processes allows organizations to acquire competitive advantages, either by offering solutions not owned by other companies, by updating and improving their range of products and services or to answer to specific customer needs or market trends. The acquisition of intellectual property rights also makes it possible to offer better or differentiated solutions or at a more competitive production and distribution costs.

4   Valorization Routes

Possible valorization routes include licensing, selling intellectual property rights, the establishment of research and cooperation agreements, and the participation in the share capital of companies through the creation of spin-offs or the establishment of joint ventures.

A licensing agreement gives access to knowledge and technology that would otherwise be difficult to obtain, given the time, costs, and possibility of obtaining a technology with the same or similar applications.

To license a technology a contract is established in which the technology owner agrees not to enforce its industrial property rights against one or more organizations wanting to exploit the technology, and the licensee may be granted the right to exclude others to use the licensed asset. A licensing agreement creates contractual rights, duties, and obligations between the owner and the licensing entity, which govern their relationship in a legally binding manner [11].

The technology owner can grant exclusive licenses for use (purpose and application) and territorial exploitation or, alternatively, grant non-exclusive licenses for any scope of use or territory where protection has been enforced, the owner, in either case, can reserve for himself the right of exploitation, provided that this possibility is defined in the technology transfer agreement.

Selling the technology should also be considered as an option, when the new technical and knowledge solution is peripheral to the organization's activities and is not necessary for the development of new knowledge and technology, and when there is no interest on the part of the organization and the R&D team in creating a company to explore the technology.

The creation of a spin-off is an adequate option when we have the proof-of-concept of a full commercial product based on new technology and when it is considered that licensing is an unprofitable option given the value of the invention and the strength of the protection or when are having difficulties on getting profitable business proposals to license the technology.

Another way of valuing the R&D results is through the establishment of Cooperation Research And Development Agreement (CRADAS), Material Transfer Agreements (MTAs) (and non-disclosure agreements (NDAs), which allow the owner to maintain the control of technology and at the same time access resources, knowledge and technology from RTD (Research, Technology, and Development) partners to continue or develop new R&D projects.

After reviewing the valorization options, for the disclosed technical solution, we have to decide whether or not we should pursue the protection of intellectual property rights. But, in either case, we must assess its patentability to make decisions regarding the best way to protect the invention and make a profit from it.

The good use of information available in patent directories can reduce the costs and time of R&D projects and give us information about changes that have occurred in the field of the invention and information about patents with the same purpose of the invention if they exist [12].

A patent is a good option to guarantee the exploitation of intellectual property rights of a new technical solution and to protect future revenue [13]. An industrial secret can also be a good option when the claims of the invention do not prevent others from circumventing the invention to obtain similar results or when the field of invention moves so fast that patents may become irrelevant, and when it is very difficult to detect patent infringements, such as the case, of inventions applicable to production methods, where the use of the invention in the final product is not evident [14, 15]. The industrial secret can even outlast the temporal protection of a patent, but there are no guarantees that this may happen, it also has the advantage of using the invention in different countries without paying fees to enforce territorial rights.

5   Transferring the Technology

To transfer technology, we have to find an opportunity to combine the characteristics and advantages of the technology with the needs and interests of organizations.

Finding organizations that are willing to replace, update or diversify their product range is the opportunity we are looking for, and the better the technology is aligned or tailor-made to one organization the higher the odds of licensing it [14, 16].

In determining the attractiveness and commercial potential of an invention we must assess how it fits within the technological space of potential licensees to look for an alignment between the characteristics of the technology and the capabilities and resources held by companies [17]. During this analysis we must strive to (1) identify which technologies have to be integrated with the technical solution to obtain an entire commercial product; (2) analyze the possibility of combining the technology with existing products and systems; (3) Determine which knowledge has to be transferred to companies and whether they are able to use them; (4) Analyze the possibility of producing the technology on a large scale and its robustness to function in different environments [18].

The development of full products and their demonstration on the ground reduces the licensee's perception of risk, but in addition to the risks and costs associated with technology development, there are also risks and costs in the introduction of new industrial products [17]. The ideal is to find licensees who have a positive attitude towards risk. Smaller companies are more likely to adopt technology in the early stages of development, where the risk is higher, or technologies that have disruptive characteristics, which allow for the development of next-generation products based on different scientific and engineering domains [19]. Larger companies, as they have more pre-established commitments, are less flexible in adopting new technology and tend to prefer solutions of an incremental nature, which add something new to a pre-existing invention or that change its design [17, 20]. But regardless of the company's maturity and size, technology adoption is dependent on its strategic orientation.

As growth through the development of new products and processes is more important for companies that are characterized by a pioneering attitude in the introduction of new technologies and business opportunities, these companies are preferred technology licensees that we should look for [17]. Nevertheless, the technology can also be useful to companies that want to remain competitive or that want to compete with companies already installed in the market. We must therefore pay particular attention to existing and overlapping patents in terms of results and who owns them, in order to direct the invention to companies that may require new technology to accompany pioneering ones. We must also observe the rate of growth of patents and articles in a given area, and who has developed them which are the organizations that are applying them, to identify developers and users, and figure out the importance of different subclasses of patents for the industry.

When looking for avenues for technology licensing we must also consider the technology readiness level and its complexity of application and use. Larger companies generally have more resources and a greater financial capacity to move the technology forward and to deal with its complexity, if the technology is ready for market and industrialization, then it must be, not the size of the company, but the number of consumers in the market targeted by the invention that must dictate the companies we should look for [17].

A good licensee is one that has a significant current market share and a credible brand, but it is not always possible to license the technology to the companies that we consider the most suitable for developing and commercializing the invention, because companies may not be interested in the invention or at that time may not be part of their development strategy to have it.

Once we have clarified which companies, we want to work with. we must devote serious efforts in marketing the technology value proposition.

6   Technology Value Proposition

The size and quality of the researchers and technology transfer offices network of contacts play a critical role in technology transfer [21]. Inventors predominantly reach agreements through contracts with large companies, technology transfer professionals tend to establish a greater number of agreements with small or medium-sized companies. Smaller companies have fewer resources to invest in technological surveillance activities, being more receptive to information disseminated by technology transfer offices, so investing in direct marketing to small companies may generate greater gains compared to marketing actions aimed at large companies [22]. Nevertheless, the greatest number of successful cases in technology licensing occur when technologies are developed for companies or with the participation of companies [23, 24].

Technology transfer offices also use informal contact networks to obtain support, to assess the technology technical and market potential, to identify further resources for new development stages, to get access to financial resources, and to support the creation of spin-off companies. These informal networks made up of different economic, technological, state, and business agents, are contacted whenever the technology justifies it, whether before or after obtaining intellectual property rights.

Based on the information obtained through informal networks of contact, market studies, and the technology transfer office assessment and information provided by the inventors, a technology value proposition is formulated to market the technology.

Technology transfer offices use multiple communication channels to convey the technology value proposition, which must consist, of a brief presentation that identifies the potential consumers, identifies the existing problems. Quantifying them and presenting the reasons why people need the solution, and the solution must be described in quantifiable economic and social benefits for the target audience.

The value proposition should be based on what we know about the overt or hidden problems or desires of end consumers. The value proposition must objectively describe the problem or trend, mentioning how it can be overcome or solved through our offer at a reasonable cost considering its benefits [25].

7 Valuation Methods

7.1 Technology Assessment Methods

Determining the value of an invention involves a high degree of uncertainty, to manage this uncertainty assessment methods are used aimed at minimizing the potential costs with patent protection and leading fair negotiations with potential licensees.

To assess invention disclosures quick evaluation methods, based on checklists and brief assessment reports are used to understand the technology, its market, and potential for profit. At a later stage, more in-depth assessment methods are used including the projection of discounted cash flows.

Among the assessment practices, which assume greater importance to understand the technology, are [26]:

(a) Analysis and description of the technology readiness level, its attributes, claims, and the identification of all its potential applications.
(b) Characterization of further development stages and the definition of an action plan to gather the necessary resources to bring the technology to market;
(c) Assessing the possibility of the patent being redesigned (at what cost, time, and technical and legal risks);
(d) Analysis of the technology's competitive and differentiating advantages.

At this stage of understanding the technology, we want to get as much information as possible to clarify the tasks needed to get the technology proof-of-concept (if not yet attained) and to determine the most promising applications, with a stronger bond between the technology and its market.

Market research is the starting point for analyzing the relationship between technology, its applications, and its market, identifying end-consumers and their needs, and identifying competing companies and solutions. The information gained with the market study allows, on one hand, to make decisions about which applications can be better accepted and, on the other hand, it allows to define the value proposition and to define a marketing strategy to attract the interest of potential licensees.

To obtain data on the invention and its market potential, there are several methods with different levels of depth that can be applied at different moments in the evaluation process.

The most common approaches for technology assessment are [3, 27–29]: (1) Predefined models and evaluation matrices; (2) TEC algorithm; (3) Economic value assessment; (4) Market value assessment; (5) Valuation based on technology costs; (6) Valuation rules of thumbs; (7) Real Options and Monte Carlo simulation; (8) Valuing through patent auctions.

Pre-defined Models and Evaluation Matrices. Methods based on pre-defined evaluation models make the evaluation process faster and facilitate the evaluation of multiple dimensions of the invention. among these instruments are:

(a) EPO IPscore, from the European Patent Office, is a tool to evaluate patents, technologies, and projects. "This tool can be used to (1) evaluate patent portfolios, individual patent applications, and granted patents; (2) analyze complex patented technologies;

(3) assess research projects before filing a patent application. EPO IPscore has 32 factors grouped in four categories (legal status, technology, Market conditions, and finance), and the results are presented in a ranking radar graph" [3, 45].

(b) IPR Valuation checklist, from the UK Intellectual property Office, including sixty questions to support determining the value of IPR and discussions with potential licensees [3, 46].

(c) COAP – Commercial Opportunities Appraisal Process, from the Warwick University, in which ten evaluation criteria are scored (1) Uniqueness of the technology; (2) Technology readiness level; (3) Market value; (4) Anticipated profit margins; (5) Intensity of competition; (6) Technology competitive; (7) Ease of access to market; (8) Customer conservatism; (9) Team commitment; (10) Team commercial experience [3].

(d) Quicklook Commercialization Assessment, developed by the University of Texas, consists of a four-step procedure (1) Market characterization; (Identification of end-users and potential licensees; (3) Contact experts and companies; (4) Prepare a valorization report. This report is structured in nine steps: (1) Technology Description; (2) Benefits; (3) Commercial Markets; (4) Market Interest; (5) Technology readiness; (6) Protection strategy and status; (7) Competing technologies and companies; (8) Barriers to market entry; (9) Recommendations [3].

(e) Checklist of 100 criteria to value a and license a technology, by Tom Arnold and Tim Headley, presented by (Razgaities, 2007) [28]. This checklist includes an assessment in nine categories: (1) Intrinsic quality; (2) Protections and threats of protection; (3) Market; (4) Competitiveness; (5) Value brought to the table by the licensee; (6) Finance; (7) Risk; (8) Legal issues; (9) Government regulatory considerations [3].

Pre-defined models and evaluation matrices designed to rate, rank, and describe technologies and their markets are being used by more than half of the Portuguese Technology Transfer Offices.

7.2 TEC Algorithm

TEC algorithm, developed by the University of North Carolina, aims to find the strongest T-P-M (Technology-Product-Market) connections. A market study is carried out to verify whether the product concepts derived from the technology are viable and have the potential to be licensed and valued [33].

TEC algorithm is started by idealizing multiple product concepts for the technology and them on the analysis of the strongest bonds between the Technology, the Product, and its Market (TPM analysis), to determine which product alternatives have the strongest linkages to gain value from the technology.

This analysis leads us to study the following components [30, 31]:

(1) Technology: Its potential (whether the technology provides better performance, is easier to use, reduces costs, or is easier to access) and its unique characteristics (claims that define the technology).

(2) The products or processes: When describing application attributes, it is important to state the essential properties of the commercial object that differentiates it, creating value for consumers. This differentiation can result from unique attributes and from

attributes that have a greater weight in relation to attributes of other alternatives (if any).

(3) The market: The market corresponds to a large area of business in a given economic sector and may contain several market segments.

(4) Market segments: Market segments correspond to homogeneous groups of consumers who share similar needs, motivations, and perceptions. We can segment the market into two major dimensions: (1) Consumer market segments, where we must consider: (a) The geographical area and population size; (b) Demographics: age group, gender, income, occupation, education, religion, ethnicity, household size; (c) Psychography: lifestyle, behaviour patterns, beliefs, values and attitudes towards self, family and society. (2) Institutional market segments, where we must consider: (a) Demographic variables: industrial sectors, company size, location; (b) Operational variables: technologies offered and degree of technology use; (c) Procurement variables: the centralization or decentralization of procurement; the acquisition criteria, such as quality, price, or differentiation; if companies are conservative, followers or innovative; (d) Specialization variables: the concentration of efforts on specific applications or multiple applications; (e) Personal variables: the similarities between the technology its buyer and sellers; the attitude towards risk and loyalty to suppliers or brands. Segmentation by institutional markets is particularly useful to analyze and identify potential licensees.

(5) Consumers: They are the potential buyers of the product or process within a sector or market segment that shares well-defined characteristics.

(6) Needs: These are what drive consumers to choose a particular product or process. Knowing the consumer and their needs, especially those not completely satisfied, their attitudes, and their motivations are the key element for the commercialization of products or processes derived from technology.

The analysis and study of these concepts are useful to identify the strongest bonds between the technology, the product, and its market, to focus marketing and commercialization efforts.

7.3 Economic Value Assessment

The economic approach consists of forecasting the technology profits to derive financial metrics, such as return on investment, payback period, internal rate of return, and net-present value, considering specific hurdle rates, that in some cases can be as high as 30% due to investment risk [3, 27].

The economic approach uses the discounted cash-flow method to deal with and license technology [3, 32, 33]. Discounted cash flows are important to prepare for negotiations to reach a fair deal and to have a basis on which the technology transfer payments structure can be defined. They are also relevant when the deal involves a single lump sum payment or when the creation of a firm is under consideration, providing a basis for equity participation [3, 34].

The interview results let us know that half of the interviewees use discounted cash flows and some do subcontract these when a potential licensee shows interest in licensing the technology. When negotiations come, it is useful to have one or more scenarios based on a cash-flow projection to support discussions "We are currently negotiating with a company where we are going to see three scenarios, we have the best and then we have two other alternative scenarios. We usually try to outline several scenarios, in the negotiation, we only talk about one scenario, but we have two other scenarios up our sleeve to put on top of the table." DITS.

Cash flow projections are also useful to support the creation of a spin-off company "When researchers are interested in setting up a company, we estimate for five years to assess expected net profit, that is going to support the company business plan and potential return for investors." UATEC. They are also valuable to work on a basis of credibility "We provide the study to companies to work on a basis of credibility and they give the value they give, good or bad, but so far the experience I have is that companies use those numbers but then they can make a detour from them, as to negotiate the deal." GAAPI.

The discounted cash flow method is used according to Kemmerer and Jiaquing [32], by more than half of the entities that license the technology.

Market Value Assessment. The market approach consists in the analysis of market information, including the analysis of competitive alternatives and in the observation of comparable agreements and standard payments practiced in the industrial sector. This approach is very frequently used alongside ranking and rating methods.

The analysis of previous licensing agreements and payment values practiced in the industry, known as royalty standards, may provide guidance to define and defend the payments' structure and their value during the negotiation of a licensing agreement [3, 7, 35–38]. The search for comparable agreements and royalty standards is an effort that usually pays-off [28], although the specificity of each technology may not call for standard agreements, we should not expect to find an agreement that meets all the wanted specifications. Nevertheless, it is important for the TTOs to build and maintain a portfolio of reference agreements that can be used if needed [9].

Comparable agreements and royalty standards are used by more than half of the Portuguese technology transfer offices. UPIN testimony is an explicit example of the use of previous licensing agreements and royalty standards – "We do establish a range for royalties, we do it based on previous agreements that we know, but it all depends on the company we are dealing with and then it is a process of negotiation between what we are offered, which is the minimum, and what we want, which can be the maximum. Industry royalty standard varies a lot, it has to do with the implementation time of the technology in that sector and not only with the sector itself, it has to do with the costs that the company will have to develop that technology or if it is already a ready-made solution, therefore, according to the risk that the company will have, we also have to adjust our royalties. The information about royalty standards is always useful to give us a reference in terms of the minimum and maximum values we were talking about. We also use other models. We have a database where we have agreements that we already had the opportunity to analyze and from which we rely upon. We also have other databases where we can get these useful agreements."

Keeping a database of agreements is, according to Dodds and Somersalo [9], an important part of the work of a technology transfer manager – "Producing and analyzing licensing agreements is a big part of the work of a technology transfer manager. In this sense, it is important to establish a portfolio of reference agreements that can be used when necessary."

Publications with licensing agreements and royalty are a good source of agreements that we can turn to. The most well-known and continuously updated database is the US Securities and Exchange Commission (SEC) «Royaltystat», which is based on the Edgar Archive – Edgar is an archive of the North American Administration that gathers quarterly reports of all activities and economic and financial results of companies listed on the New York Stock Exchange.

By subscribing to the «Royaltystat» database at the following URL: http://www.roy altystat.com/, subscribers have access to the most recent agreements and statistical data on the structure of payments and royalties, being able to make searches through several queries and the SIC classification – Standard Industrial Classification.

The analysis of comparable license agreements and the observation of royalties standards can provide us with useful information, but it is still a very limited approach given the unique structure of each license agreement, hence the importance of not using this approach in isolation, we must combine it with other valuation methods always paying attention to the technology readiness level and performing a market assessment and, for example, using the TEC Algorithm, to identify the competitive advantages and the appropriate price for the technology to be transferred.

Valuation Based on Technology Costs. The cost approach quantifies the costs of obtaining the technology, it can be particularly valuable to determine if it is worth licensing a technology instead of further developing it, or to consider the creation of a spin-off company to value the investment done or to be done.

Evaluation based on development costs is rarely a base on which firms negotiate licensing agreements [3, 28, 39]. Companies are interested in obtaining technology easily and more cheaply than it would cost if they were to develop it by themselves, and the cost of creating a technology may have little to do with its market value [17].

Portuguese Technology Transfer offices frequently try to determine how much did it cost to develop the technology – "We calculate the development costs and estimate their market value, if they are incompatible it is because the business does not make sense, if they are compatible, we assume the market value, therefore, the development costs serve to verify if it makes sense to go ahead with a project." INOV.

The market value of the technology is the appropriate metric to define the price of the invention – "It is always the market value that determines the value of the technology, regardless of all the costs that the University had during the research until the discovery and further development, we are not going to show how much we spent, we always make our calculations based on «this is what you will earn». Our objective is always to put technologies on the market with better or worse deals. From the moment a company is involved, and new phases of development are needed, we try to articulate with the company a way to co-finance these costs either by the company or through an incentive scheme, if these costs have already occurred, have already occurred, our objective is to try to place our product on the market and from there to create added value, not only economically but also for society." UPIN.

Valuation Rules of Thumb. The 25% rule splits the value of a technology into four parts, according to Razgaities [3, 28]: (1) the technology creation, (2) the steps required for industrial manufacturing, (3) the manufacturing itself, and (4) the technology sales by itself or within a larger product or platform. Each part represents a quarter of the technology value, the creation of the technology is just one of four parts (25%) through which value is created. if the technology is ready for manufacturing, a value of 33% or higher may be defined, this argument is that the technology has already reached a portion of the manufacturing process, so the manufacturing itself and the sales are the next two big steps ahead, so the technology is two-thirds of the way. In the case of software, values can ascend to 50%, if the technology is ready for sales.

The 25% rule is frequently applied to the EBIT – Earnings before interests and taxes [3, 32], and the licensee pays a fee equivalent to 25% of the technology contribution to the operational results gained by the solution that embeds the technology.

The use of rules of thumb is not a frequent practice among Portuguese Technology transfer offices.

Real Options and Monte Carlo Simulation. The real options method is used to assess multiple assumptions in a cash-flow projection, each assumption having different degrees of uncertainty for which risk-adjusted hurdle rates must be defined. This is a time-consuming approach, but it may bring a more complete analysis to determine the investment return [3, 40, 41]. Authors like Speser [3, 17] refer to real options as unnecessarily complicated, not providing an accurate and precise assessment of technology value, real options can be better used in planning R&D or developing IP strategies, and not to prepare negotiations. The Monte Carlo allows to account for risk in quantitative analysis and decision making and multiple scenarios are generated to simulate the potential investment return.

The real options and Monte Carlo simulation are not being used by any of the Portuguese Technology Transfer Offices.

Valuation Through Auctions. Patent auctions can be used to transfer technology by interacting with multiple investors in a bidding process [3]. Patent auctions are gaining increasing importance in technology transfer processes [3, 42]. Auctions can be a practical way of making value out of patents, provided they are of high quality [43]. Auctions are particularly relevant to transfer inventive solutions that otherwise would fall in absence of payments of patent fees. Planning auction events requires considerable organization and advertising, and it is not likely to have several bids for a technology [44]. Portuguese Technology Transfer Offices never used auctions to transfer technology.

8   Conclusion

Technology assessment methods are useful to understand the invention, identify resources and skills, understand the risk associated with the investment, support the invention's marketing strategy, and above all prepare and guide the negotiation process.

At an initial stage, preparatory to filing a patent application, patent databases are used to determine the novelty, inventive step, and industrial applicability, and predefined evaluation models and matrices, are used to make a quick assessment of the technology market and commercialization potential.

At a later stage, usually when there is a manifestation of interest from a company arises or to make a presentation to a potential investor, Portuguese technology transfer offices, tend to look for comparable agreements (if any), to the observation of royalty standards, and cash-flow projections can be done to support the negotiation process or the creation of a new spin-off company.

Transversal to these two phases, contacts are developed with industry and with formal or informal networks of partners to obtain advice, financing, or access to technical and market information, or to facilitate access to equipment and materials external to the institution. The resources gained through the interaction with formal and informal networks are also used to further invest in the technology to get its proof of concept and/or proof of market.

The application of technology assessment methods can serve as a baseline to design a balanced agreement that both parties consider equitable in the division of potential gains, to bring the technology into its industrialization stage and market.

Rules of thumb are not being used, since there are doubts regarding its reliability and because every agreement is unique, values can vary according to the rights granted, the technology development stage, manufacturing and distribution requirements, and other constraints. Real options and Monte Carlo simulation are also not in use, technology transfer professionals prefer valuation methods that are simpler and faster to assess the technology value.

To reinforce these conclusions, and to better understand how technology transfer offices use different valuation practices and methods, one avenue of research would be to expand this study to include technology transfer offices from Portuguese universities and also from other countries within the European Union. Furthermore, the study of the value created by licensing agreements should be explored in search of a possible correlation between technology licensing and its impact on research teams and technology transfer offices performance and financial profitability. These research lines would create the opportunity to better understand the application of technology valuation methods and the overall impact of university-industry relations on the outcomes of research teams and technology transfer offices.

Acknowledgment. This work was funded by national funds, through the FCT – Fundação para a Ciência e Tecnologia and FCT/MCTES in the scope of projects UIDB/05549/2020 and UIDB/00319/2020.

References

1. HERA: Higher education and research act 2017. UK Public General Acts. 2017 c. 29. Part 3. Research and innovation functions. Section 93 (2017). https://www.legislation.gov.uk/ukpga/2017/29/section/93/enacted

2. Hockaday, T.: University Technology Transfer: What It Is and How to Do It. Johns Hopkins University Press (2020). ISBN-13: 978-1421437057
3. Rocha, A., Romero, F., Cunha, M., Lima, R., Amorim, M.: A preliminary analysis of the use of valuation methods by technology transfer offices. In: Proceedings of the 18th International Conference on e-Business - ICE-B, pp. 136–143 (2021). https://doi.org/10.5220/0010599901360143. ISBN 978-989-758-527-2; ISSN 2184-772X
4. Rocha, A.: Gestão de projetos de Investigação, Desenvolvimento e Inovação: Práticas e definição de um modelo para a valorização de tecnologia. Escola de Engenharia, Departamento de Produção e Sistemas, Universidade do Minho, Tese de Doutoramento em Engenharia Industrial e de Sistemas (2018)
5. Rocha, A., Lima, R., Marlene, A., Romero, F.: Payment types included on technology licensing agreements and earnings distribution among Portuguese universities. Tékhne - Review of Applied Management Studies. Elsevier. SOURCE-WORK-ID: cv-prod-id-687275 (2017). https://doi.org/10.1016/j.tekhne.2017.11.001. Part of ISSN: 1645-9911
6. CWUR: Center for World University Rankings (2019). https://cwur.org/2018-19.php
7. WIPO/ITC: Exchanging value: negotiating technology licensing agreements. A training Manual. World Intellectual Property Organization (2005)
8. COM: 182 final. Improving knowledge transfer between research institutions and industry across Europe: embracing open innovation. Voluntary guidelines for universities and other research institutions to improve their links with industry across Europe. Comunicação da Comissão das Comunidades Europeias. SEC, 2007, p. 449 (2007)
9. Dodds, J., Somersalo, S.: Practical considerations for the establishment of a technology transfer office. In: Krattiger, A., Mahoney, R.T., Nelsen, L., et al. (eds.) Intellectual Property Management in Health and Agricultural Innovation: A Handbook of Best Practices. MIHR, Oxford, U.K., and PIPRA, Davis, U.S.A. (2007)
10. Sante, D.: The role of the inventor in the technology transfer process. In: Krattiger, A., Mahoney, R.T., Nelsen, L., et al. (eds.).Intellectual Property Management in Health and Agricultural Innovation: A Handbook of Best Practices. MIHR: Oxford, U.K. and PIPRA (2007)
11. Thalhammen-Reyero: Transfer and valuation of biomedical intellectual property. Chapter 22. In: Taxation and Valuation of Technology: Theory, Practice and the Law. Horvath and Chiidikoff Editors (2008)
12. Smith, H.: What innovation is – How companies develop operating systems for innovation. CSC White Paper. European Office of Technology and Innovation (2005)
13. Howell, S.: Financing innovation: evidence from R&D grants. Am. Econ. Rev. 107(4), 1136–1164 (2017). https://doi.org/10.1257/aer.20150808
14. Dolfsma, W.: Patent strategizing. J. Intellect. Capital 12(2). Emerald Group Publishing Limited (2011). https://doi.org/10.1108/14691931111123377
15. Nelsen, L.: The rise of intellectual property protection in the American University. Sci. Mag. 279(5356), 1460–1461 (1998). https://doi.org/10.1126/science.279.5356.1460
16. Gatignon, H., Robertson, Fein, A.: Incumbent defence strategies against new product entry. Int. J. Res. Market. 14(2), 163–176 (1997)
17. Speser, S.: The Art & Transfer of Technology Transfer. John Wiley & Sons Inc, Hoboken, New Jersey (2006)
18. Rocha, A.: Avaliação e licenciamento de tecnologia em Universidades. Dissertação de Mestrado em Engenharia Industrial, na área da Avaliação e Gestão de Projetos e da Inovação. University of Minho. SOURCE-WORK-ID: cv-prod-id-687537 (2009)
19. Shane, S.: Encouraging university entrepreneurship? the effect of the Bayh-Dole act on university patenting in the United States. J. Bus. Ventur. 19(1), 127–151 (2004)
20. Thursby, J., Jensen, R., Thursby, M.: Objectives, characteristics and outcomes of university licensing: a survey of major U.S Universities. J. Technol. Trans. 26, 59–72 (2001)

21. Kolchinsky, P.: The entrepreneur's guide to a biotech startup. Evelexa.com (2004)
22. Ramakrishnan, V., Chen, J., Balakrishnan, K.: Effective strategies for marketing biomedical inventions: lessons learnt from NIH license leads. J. Med. Mark. **5**(4), 342–352. Henry Stewart Publications 1745–7904 (2005)
23. Harmon, B., Ardishvili, A., Cardozo, R., Elder, T., Leuthold, J., Parshall, J.: Mapping the university technology transfer process. J. Bus. Ventur. **12**(6) (1997)
24. Hsu, D., Shen, Y., Yuan, B., Chou, C.: Toward successful commercialization of university technology: performance drivers of university technology transfer in Taiwan. Technol. Forecast. Soc. Change **92** (2015). https://doi.org/10.1016/j.techfore.2014.11.002
25. CONNECT Sweden: How to succeed in market and sales: advice to start-ups (2004)
26. Rocha, A.: Gestão de projetos de investigação, desenvolvimento e inovação: práticas e definição de um modelo de integração para a valorização de tecnologia. Tese de Doutoramento em Engenharia Industrial e de Sistemas. Universidade do Minho (2018). http://hdl.handle.net/1822/58967
27. Razgaitis, R.: Pricing the intellectual property of early-stage technologies: a primer of basic valuation tools and considerations. In: Krattiger, A., Mahoney, R.T., Nelsen, L., et al. (eds.) Intellectual Property Management in Health and Agricultural Innovation: A Handbook of Best Practices. MIHR, Oxford, U.K., and PIPRA, Davis, U.S.A (2007)
28. Razgaities, R.: Valuation and Princing of Technology-Based Intellectual Property. John Wiley & Sons Inc, Hoboken, New Jersey (2003)
29. Schiltz, E.: How can high-growth business opportunities for a cutting-edge technology be discovered? Master degree in management from the NOVA – School of Business and Economics. University Nova of Lisbon (2019)
30. Cruz, E.: Criar uma empresa de sucesso. Edições Sílabo, Lda, Lisboa (2006)
31. Schenck, B.: Marketing das PMEs. Porto Editora, lda, Porto (2005)
32. Kemmerer, J., Jiaquing, E.: Profitibility and royalty rates across industries: some preliminary evidence. J. Acad. Bus. Econ. (2008)
33. Degnan, S., Horton, C.: A survey of licensed royalties. Les Nouvelles, pp. 91–96 (1997)
34. Wirz, C., Rabie, M., Tanami, M., Hajjar, L., Gardner, J., Little, D.: Invention disclosure system using blockchain. Customer: Dave Knuteson, Milestone 3. CSCI E-599 – Harvard Extension School (2019)
35. Nabulsi, B., Belt, E.: The patent is dead; long live the royalties! In: VIVO – The business and Medicine Report. Informa Business information Inc. (2015)
36. Stevens, A.: Intellectual property valuation manual for academic institutions. WIPO – World Intellectual Property Organization (2016). https://www.wipo.int/meetings/en/doc_details.jsp?doc_id=332588
37. Pressman, L., Planting, M., Yuskavage, R., Okubo, S., Moylan, C., Bond, J.: The Economic Contribution of University/Nonprofit Inventions in the United States. Association of University Technology Managers and Biotechnology Innovation Organization (2017)
38. Heiden, V., Petit, N.: Patent Trespass and the Royalty Gap: Exploring the Nature and Impact of "Patent Holdout". Hoover Institution Working Group on Intellectual Property, Innovation, and Prosperity. Stanford University (2017)
39. Lagrost, C., Martin, D., Dubois, C., Quazzotti, S.: Intellectual property valuation: how to approach the selection of an appropriate valuation method. J. Intellect. Cap. **11**(4), 481–503 (2010)
40. Soares, I., Moreira, J., Pinho, C., Couto, J.: Decisões de Investimento. Análise Financeira de Projectos. Edições Sílabo. Lisboa (2007)
41. Lazzolino, G., Migliano, G.: The valuation of a patent through the real options approach: a tutorial. J. Bus. Valuation Econ. Loss Anal. **10**(1) (2015)
42. Jarosz, J., Heider, R., Bazelon, C., Bieri, C., Hess, P.: Patent auctions: how far have we come? Patent Auctions. Les Nouvelles, September 2010

43. EPO: Patents up for auctions. European Patent Office (2008)
44. Dakin, K.J., Lindsey, J.: Technology transfer - financing and commercializing the high-tech product or service from research to roll out. J. Technol. Transfer **16**(3), 62 (1991)

Webography

45. EPO IPScore. https://www.epo.org/searching-for-patents/business/ipscore.html. May 2022
46. IPR Valuation checklist, from the UK Intellectual property Office. https://www.gov.uk/guidance/valuing-your-intellectual-property. May 2022

Improved Protection of User Data Through the Use of a Traceable Anonymous One Time Password

Mukuka Kangwa(✉) (iD), Charles S. Lubobya, and Jackson Phiri (iD)

University of Zambia, Great East Campus, Lusaka, Zambia
mukukakangwa@yahoo.com

Abstract. The rapid embracing of technology in the delivery of commerce services by various service providers often results in the user surrendering their Personally Identifiable Information (PII) to the service providers thereby subjecting user data to possible online leakage and consequently putting the safety of the user at risk. This paper is proposing enhancing the protection of user PII using a traceable One Time Password (OTP) derived from the RFC 6238 Time-based One Time Password (TOTP) standard. The approach was complemented with the use of a one-way hardware based data protector that was deliberately designed to only allow data to flow in one direction to prevent online hackers having access to user data stored by service providers. Tests were conducted on the developed solution determine its effectiveness. Accessories and tools such as Arduino microcontrollers, python programming language, Arduino IDE (programming platform) and the Proteus Simulation software. Results obtained from the experiments conducted demonstrate that the user data was being protected successfully as access from online was restricted as desired.

Keywords: Personally identifiable information · Data privacy · One time Password · Data protection · Time-based one time password · Firmware and TOR

1 Background

In the recent past there has been a rapid adoption of Information Communication Technology (ICT) in the delivery of consumer services. Among the most famous include eBay and Amazon e-commerce platforms. Those offering online electronic services often require those who want to use their platforms to provide personal data such as names, Phone numbers, emails addresses and so on before they could grant them access to their platforms for online commerce [1]. This approach has led to gigantic amounts personal data being collected and aggregated by a number of service providers who end up storing it online and hence making that data susceptible to online leakage [2]. Personal data in wrong hands can expose the owner of the information to high risk such as financial fraud being perpetrated using their credentials as well as against them. Even though several solutions have been designed and employed to address this challenge, the problem persists [3]. A number of incidents have been reported where massive amounts

P. Samarati et al. (Eds.): ICETE 2021, CCIS 1795, pp. 67–83, 2023.
https://doi.org/10.1007/978-3-031-36840-0_4

of personal data has fallen into wrong hands thereby breaching user privacy [4]. Data exposed to the internet, be it on the edge equipment like phones and tablets, or in the cloud like Amazon or Microsoft cloud services, is at risk hence the need to provide more effective data fortification approaches [5].

2 Similar Works

Frank and Michael patented an approach that would help enhance the protection of personal user data. Their model proposed having a Trusted Party that would provide static Identities (ID) to users. Block chain technology was to be used to store and protect the personal data. The diagram shown in Fig. 1 below gives a summary of how the model is to operate; the user, having previously registered with the ID service provider, obtains an ID from the digital ID provider and submits it to the e-commerce platform service provider as proof of identification. The e-commerce platform provider confirms with the ID provider if the user can be trusted as being a traceable person through the ID service providers, if need arose. The response the ID provider returns determines whether or not a service will be offered to the user. Further, an offline escrow was to be used for storing the personal data to be accessed via legally approved means. Pseudonymization was preferred over anonymization to make it possible to trace a user when there is need [2]. Pseudonymization transform data in a manner that makes the resulting data traceable to the original owner using extra information that is normally held by the data handlers such as Banks and Mobile Network Operators. Anonymization, on the other hand, transforms data in a manner that it makes it impossible to trace back the anonymized data to the original owner regardless of extra information available. It is a one-way data transformation.

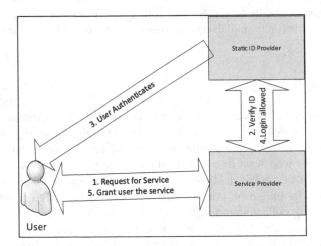

Fig. 1. Static ID Provider Concept.

The use of static electronic IDs is not sufficient for guaranteeing privacy to the users as a static ID can be profiled and the user patterns studied thereby compromising the privacy of the user [1]. In addition, the use of Block chain technology might not be feasible as the technology is currently resource intensive [6]. A global solution utilizing this technology would require huge amounts of computing resources for the proof of works to be used to effectively prevent data from being leaked or modified or even being deleted. The Block chain technology requires some modifications to make it resource friendly.

Further, Block chain technology has an inherent scalability challenge due to its design. The model proposed by Frank and Michael seeks to solve a global problem by providing access that is global hence scalability is very key to accommodate everyone who desires to adopt the proposed solution. Block chain also faces some privacy and security issues which need resolving. Employing the solution to address the challenge of privacy might partly address one problem and yet introduce more issues[6].

Block chain technology experiences time lag due to its design; when one node generates a transaction, a number of other nodes need to confirm and reach consensus before a transaction can be completed leading to transactions delaying to complete [7]. Further, its complexity makes the cost of building and maintaining it prohibitive. Cheaper ways of developing the technology need to be sought if it is to be widely adopted. Perhaps it can be built as a shared online service where costs can be shared [8].

E-commerce platforms keep client information online so that they can easily authenticate the users before granting them access to any service. A lot of user data is being held in the cloud by various service providers hence making that data susceptible to leakage [9]. Attacks have been orchestrated against e-commerce platforms such as e-bay who suffered a Distributed Denial of Service (DDoS) attack in which their databases holding user personal date were scanned and customer data was uncovered [10]. The attack was probable as the databases were reachable through the internet.

Fanghan and team proposed a model that would give data owners the control to decide who to grant access. The use of a cloud server was proposed to store some of the user data. The user encrypts their data before sharing and decides who can be given access by sharing their decryption keys with only the approved users [9]. Even though the data is encrypted, if the key shared finds itself in wrong hands, then the encrypted data, if accessed can be decrypted. In addition, it means several users can be granted access to the data hence increasing points of possible data leak. In fact, despite being encrypted, data is most likely to be in plain text when being processed, for example in response to a request for data, hence making it vulnerable to leakage [11].

Locher et'al, proposed the use of a distributed ledger to protect data [12]. The distributed ledger owes its security to the requirement of consensus being reached before any transaction is approved and considered as completed. This approach results in delayed transaction confirmation as well as huge resources being required to make the technology operational [6].

Peter et'al recognizes the General Data Protection Regulation (GDPR) as one way of addressing the widespread internet users' privacy challenges. The European Union proposed the GDPR as a way of protecting the privacy of individuals by promoting pseudonymization of personal data in conjunction with existing data security practices [13]. The proposed additional measures indicate that the existing techniques are no longer adequate hence the data leakages and privacy violations that are experienced every now and then. Peter et'al defined pseudonymization as transforming data in such a way that the resulting information cannot be associated with the original owner without the need for additional date. The authors proposed that Pseudonymization techniques be used by various data processors such as mobile operators to protect user privacy. These included data scrambling or obfuscation, blurring, masking, tokenization and encryption [13].

Sergio et'al are of the view that the advancement in technology has resulted in the need for more effective techniques to offer security and privacy to personal and other sensitive information. They contend that existing solutions might not be adequate to meet the required levels of privacy and security required by regulations such as the European GDPR [14]. Methods such as pseudonymization and anonymization were proposed. Pseudonymization was favored over anonymization as they intended to use their solution for the protection of Health data for children.

The team further proposed conjoining pseudonymization with other security techniques such as hashing of pseudo IDs and encryption of pseudonymized data [14].

There is need to ensure that only pseudonymized data is made online while raw identifying data is kept offline. Furthermore, necessary internal controls must also be put in place to ensure data is not leaked by internal parties.

3   Design of Proposed Solution

The best way to protect information from leakage is to make it isolated [15]. The proposed design in Fig. 3 below seeks to achieve that.

The use of a Trusted Third Party to hold personal user data demands that other service providers demanding KYC confirm with the KYC Agency if the requesting party is genuine. The KYC agency provides assurance without sharing the PII of the requesting party. This enables the requesting party to have access to services without sharing and hence risking their PII to leakage.

The Solution is designed on two principles; first being that the user will utilize Random Pseudo IDs and the second being that the user data with identifying information will be kept off the internet. The diagram in Fig. 2 below gives a summary of the user's presence online.

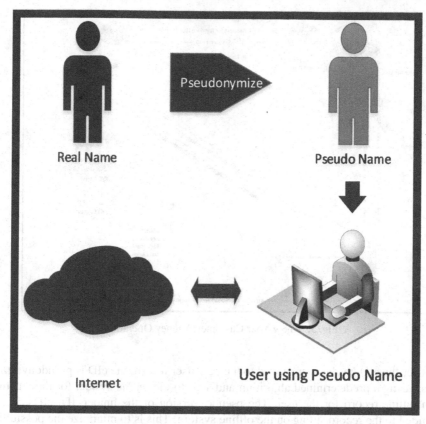

Fig. 2. Use of Pseudo ID while Online.

The solution will operate as outlined below:

The user will first register with the KYC Agency in their country of residence by submitting their PII such as their National IDs, Residential address, Contact details like phone numbers and email addresses.

Once the user has satisfied requirements for registration with the KYC Agency, the KYC Agency creates a record with full Identifying Information of the user and appends a universally unique ID on the record. The data is kept on the "Offline" system that is not accessible from the internet as depicted in Fig. 3 below.

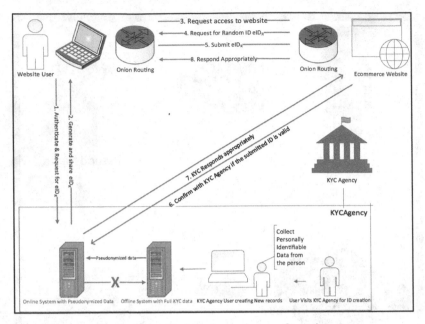

Fig. 3. Know Your Customer Agency Operation.

After the eID has been appended to the new user record, the eID is pseudonymized (eIDs) using a predetermined algorithm and sent to the online system for the creation of an online record for the user. The pseudo version of the unique ID, eIDs, is not appended to the record sitting on the offline system. This is to minimize the possibility of associating offline data to online pseudo IDs if they are leaked.

The only communication between the Offline system and only system will be the automatic transmission of the Pseudo ID, eIDs, to the online system. The transmission will be determined by the firmware sitting on the microcontrollers. When the online system receives the pseudo ID, eIDs, it will automatically create a record with the eIDs as the primary key. Figure 4 below gives a detailed flow of the registration process.

The Data protector ((Restricted Memory System) that will safeguard the PII will connect the offline system to the online system and operate as follows:

Data exchange between the two systems will only flow in one direction as depicted in Fig. 5 below. The aim of this restriction is to ensure that no one is able to access the PII from the Internet. This is to reduce the possibility of a hacker accessing the PII without needing physical access to the system hosting the sensitive data [1].

Furthermore, despite data being able to flow towards the online system from the offline system, to prevent huge amounts of data from being sent using the offline system, there is a bandwidth restriction imposed between the two systems. If, for example, 10gigabyte of data was to be sent from the offline system to the online system via a serial connection of 9600bps, it would take more than 100 days to complete the transfer. Sending of pseudo IDs would take few milliseconds as they only constitute few kilobytes per unique record created at any given time. The slow rate of data transfer would be a

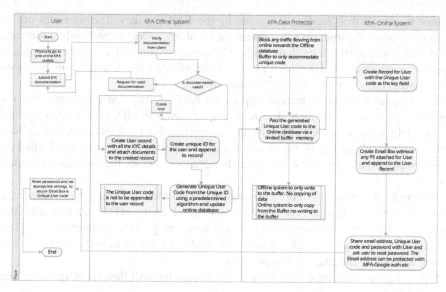

Fig. 4. User Registration with KPA [15].

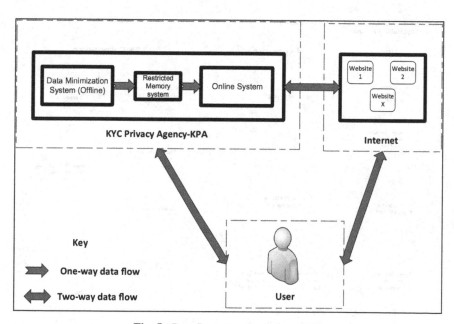

Fig. 5. Data Protector Operations [15].

deterrent to a hacker. Moreover, the system would periodically reset the connection between the two hence disrupt any exploitive data transfer in session.

The user will either access the KYC Agency to generate a universally unique random ID, eIDr, or first access an ecommerce site or request to transact. The site will request the user to submit their random ID issued by the KYC Agency. The sites will not be allowed to collect PII from users to prevent data leakage prevalent with online services.

The user will need to Logon to the KYC Agency system via a website or app and request a unique random ID. The KYC will authenticate the users using an enhanced TOTP system based on the RFC 6238 standard.

User Logons on to the Website or App for the KYC Agency. Once authenticated, the user generates Random ID eIDr. The KYC system sends the ID, *eIDr*, to Anonymous email or is displayed on an App. Then the user enters the eIDr on the website. The website verifies with KYC Agency if they issued the eIDr supplied by the user. Depending on the feedback of the Agency, the website either grants or denies the user access to their services.

To protect the user from being profiled based on their location, sites visited, the identity of the device they are using and so on, Onion Routing (TOR) can be used. TOR masks any identifying data about the user and hence help maintain their privacy [16]. The data hidden includes identifying information about the devices being used the client thereby addressing the challenge of profiling.

Figure 6 gives a pictorial view of how the transaction will flow from the beginning to the end.

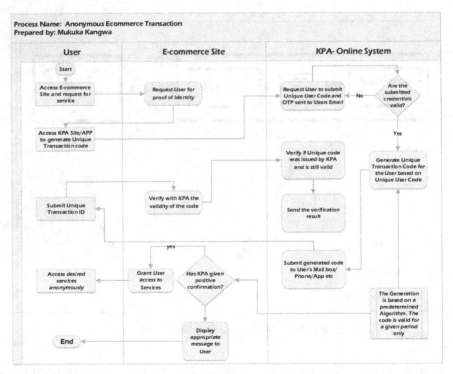

Fig. 6. Anonymous Ecommerce Transaction [15].

The KYC Agency system will host the mail boxes for the users and will periodically destroy emails containing random IDs after the predetermined validity period elapses.

Proposed Universally Unique electronic ID (eID).
The following format of the universally unique ID is being proposed:

The eID will comprise 10 digits representing the unique ID for the person being created on the system and 3 digits representing the country the person is a citizen of as shown below:

X X X. X X X X X X X X X X.

The 10 digits for the universally unique portion of the ID is to accommodate for the growth of population for counties like China and India. The 3 digits for country is to accommodate the number of existing countries in the world and the new countries that might image. The first Citizen to be registered for example would have the eID shown below:

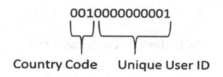

Country Code   Unique User ID

4 Experiment Approach

Only the RMS was built as other components such as ecommerce sites could be built using existing solutions.

The Data protector (RMS) was put together using the following; two Arduino UNO microcontrollers, copper cables, serial ports, serial monitors, python programming language, Arduino UNO IDE and Proteus Simulation software.

Serial communication was preferred over parallel communication in building the RMS to ensure that data flows in one direction only. Two way communication would require two cables physically connected between the two devices. To enforce one-way communication, one cable was disconnected. This would ensure that even if the online component attempted to communicate to the offline component, the communication would fail.

Two microcontrollers were employed instead of one. This was to control the security of the system as hardware is susceptible to hardware Trojans. These viruses can be embedded into the hardware when being manufactured to deliberately leak information later. For the Trojans to be activated, one would need access to the hardware either physically or remotely [17]. One Arduino UNO connecting the offline side was configured as a Master while the one facing the online system was configured as a slave as shown in the circuit in Fig. 7 below. Even if the Arduino facing the online system was compromised, the hacker would not be able to breach the entire connection as they would need physical access to the Master Arduino to change configurations and enable two-way communication thus making it impossible to achieve without having physical access. The diagram below shows how the experiment was setup.

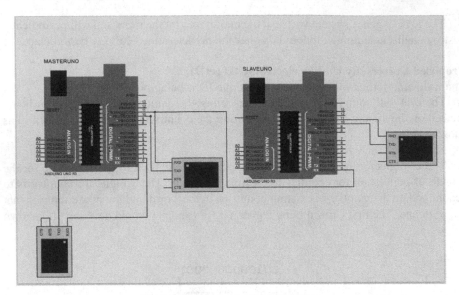

Fig. 7. Hardware Configuration [15].

Tests were conducted as follow: Data was sent from the offline system to the online system via the RMS. Data was also sent from the online system to the offline system. Six scenarios were tested. In scenario 1 and 2, both the Transmitting and receiving PINs were physically connected while in Scenario 3 and 4, the cable connecting Transmitting PIN for the Master Arduino to the receiving PIN of the Slave Arduino was disconnected. In scenario 5 and 6, the receiving PIN of the Master Arduino connected to the Transmitting PIN of the slave Arduino was disconnected. The Bandwidth between the two Arduinos was set at 9600bps. Figure 8 below gives focused view on how the microcontrollers were connected to achieve the desired design.

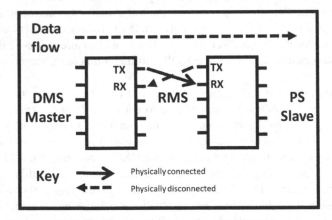

Fig. 8. Physical Configuration of RMS [15].

5   Generation of Random IDS

The generation of Random IDs was done via the use of a modified TOTP as opposed to the standard RFC6238 proposed by the Internet Engineering Task Force (IETF). The approach used is the modification of the method proposed by the standard. The standard is used to generate One Time Passwords (OTP) that are time sensitive using the Unix epoch time as one of the variables in the generation of the passwords [18]. Our objective was to make the random OTP act as an identifier when need arise without comprising the privacy of the user involved. The approach is to generate the password as proposed by the standard then modify the resulting password by passing it through a function that modifies it with an ID for that particular user as shown in Fig. 9 below.

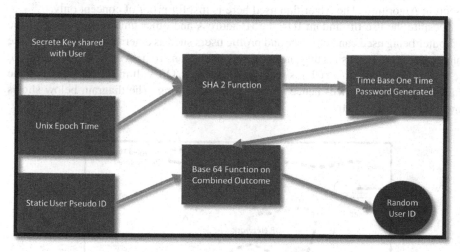

Fig. 9. Generation of Random IDs (User OTP) [19].

To the user the ID is random but the system can perform a reverse operation to generate an ID for the user of the random ID if need arise.

Example of Random ID Generated.
Using the standard TOTP generated using RFC 6238 was: ***054465.***
    Convert to decimal (054465) = 1010100010001100101.
    The Unique offline ID for the user was 001(country ID). 0010000001 (Unique User ID).
    The ID is Decimal. We convert it to Hexadecimal we get 254A47A81 (Pseudo ID for user to be stored online).
    The Pseudo ID, eIDs, for the User is 254A47A81 (0010010000001).
    Appending the Pseudo ID to the standard TOTP 054465 (1010100010001100101 Base 10).
Results in: 0010010000001101010001000110010.

    Converting to Base 64

Results in: BQ3DHgeMF4D2Jo + 1F.

Random User ID, eIDr, is: BQ3DHgeMF4D2Jo + 1F.

The Random ID will keep changing whenever the user generates one as one of the inputs is Unix epoch time which is continuously changing. However, the Unique user ID part will remain static hence when need arise, it will be possible to trace back to the original user ID that generated and used that Random ID if fraud is committed. This will need to be done with the help of the KYC Agency.

Another benefit with this approach is that, it will be possible to trace who generated which Random ID at any given time without keeping voluminous records of logs indicating the Random ID generated by who at what time and so on. By just examining the Random ID, the Unique user ID can be deciphered by the KYC agency who will have a secrete Algorithm. The Algorithm used here is just for proof of concept only.

Despite the use of random IDs, the IP address and other unique properties of the computer being used can help trace and profile users such as determining where they are connecting from, what sites they are accessing and so on. To help address this challenge the use of Onion Routing (OR) is recommended [20]. OR will mask the source of the requests to access services hence prevent online profiling. The diagram below shows how OR works (Fig. 10).

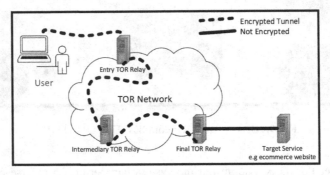

Fig. 10. How a TOR Network Works.

By masking the actual of the requests, the user is shielded from being identified online not only in terms of user name but also other profiling elements such as sites visited, services accessed, from where and so on. This helps further enhance user privacy.

6 Results and Discussion

Table 1 provides a summary of Results based on Experiments conducted.

Table 1. Experiment Results.

No	Test |Scenario	Connections/Setup	Results	Result
1	Normal connection-Two way communication	1. Connection transmitting data from Master to Slave in place 2. Connection sending data from Slave to Master in place	Data can be sent successfully both ways	Fail
2	Have one connection removed (remove TX-RX-Master-Slave)	1. The cable sending data from the Master to the Slave is removed 2. The cable sending data from the Slave towards the Master remains connected	1. Data sent from Master didn't reach the slave despite the other connection being intact) 2. Data sent from the slave direction did not reach the Master	Fail
3	Have one connection removed (remove RX-TX-Master-Slave)	1. The cable sending data from the Master to the Slave remains connected 2. The cable sending data from the Slave towards the Master is disconnected	1. Data sent from Master successfully reached the slave 2. Data sent from the Slave didn't reach the Master	Pass
4	Amount of data Transmittable	Speed set at 9600	Sending 10GB estimated at more than 100days	Pass
5	Generation of Random IDs	Use system based on RFC6238 Result further processed using user ID	Generate OTPs with embeded Unqiue user ID	Possible
6	Decipher user ID	Use reverse of functional to process TOTP using user ID	Should be able to generate User identifier only known to the KYC urgency	Possible

In Test 1 data was successfully sent both ways with the transmitting and receiving PINs connected correctly on both the Master and Slave Arduino. That is, data was able to flow from the offline system holding PII to the online system susceptible to online hacking. This was a fail as the objective was to ensure that data could only flow in one direction. That is, from the offline system towards the online system. In this scenario data successfully flowed in both directions hence the RMS cannot protect PII by preventing access by users connecting from the Internet. It is vital that data does not flow from the online system to the offline system even if bandwidth is restricted as malware can be created as a very small payload and yet cause serious damage to data once deployed into the system storing PII. The test results for the first scenario make the configuration undesirable.

In the Scenario covered by test 2 with transmitting PIN on the Master Arduino not connected to the receiving PIN on the Slave Arduino while the receiving PIN on the Master Arduino remained connected to the transmitting PIN of the Slave Arduino, data could not flow in any direction as shown in the diagram below (Fig. 11).

In the scenario depicted in test 3, with the transmitting PIN of the Master Arduino connected to the transmitting PIN of the receiving Arduino, while the receiving PIN.

While the receiving PIN is disconnected from the transmitting PIN of the Slave Arduino, data was sent successfully from the Master Slave Arduino connecting the offline system towards the Slave Arduino connecting the Online system but data could not be sent from Slave Arduino connecting the online system towards the Master Arduino connecting the offline system. The diagram in Fig. 12 below shows the tests and results.

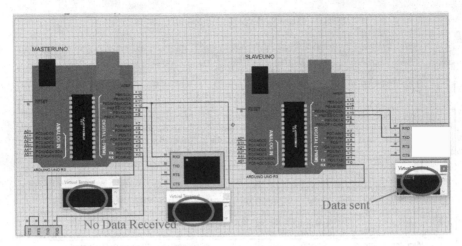

Fig. 11. Test 2 Result.

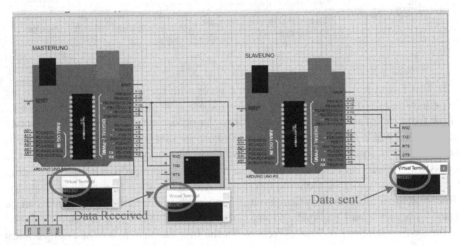

Fig. 12. Test 3 Results.

Test 3 was successful as data could only flow in one direction. That is, data could only flow from the offline system towards the online system. This was the desired config-uration as it would prevent hackers successfully accessing PII data sitting on the offline database. It would also prevent malware from being introduced from the online system to the offline system. This result shows that it is possible to keep sensitive data "offline" while allowing real-time connection between the offline system and online system for the creation of corresponding records for the user to access online services anonymously once created on the KYC system. Figure 13 below shows the data monitored on the serial port.

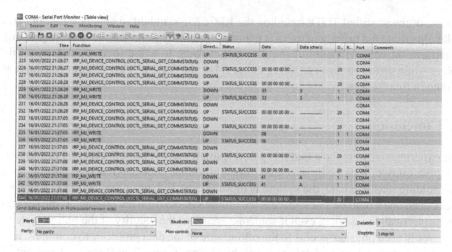

Fig. 13. Serial Data Monitored on Serial Port.

The restriction of the bandwidth between the offline and online system to 9600 bps ensured that only minimal data could pass across at any given time. The valid data transmissions across the two systems are short bursts of few characters. The restriction helps prevent theft of sensitive PII by both internal and external parties.

The diagram below gives a feel of how long it would take to transmit given amount of data IF some disgruntled internal staff attempted and succeed to hack the system from inside (Fig. 14).

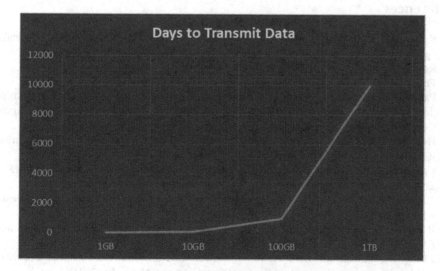

Fig. 14. Data Transmission Duration.

For this solution to be effective, online data must be anonymous so that if the records are leaked, no identifying information would be part of the leaked records. Furthermore, the use of the modified TOTP based on the RFC6238 standard to generate random IDs will help ensure the privacy of users is maintained and at the same time make it possible to retrieve the actual identity of the user if they were to abuse their anonymity while online while saving storage space by getting rid of the need to store voluminous amount of data in form of logs.

7 Conclusion

The experiment results show that it is possible to protect PII from hackers by preventing any possibility of data being accessed. Since no online user can reach the offline system holding sensitive data, the system is more secure. Enhanced protection is achieved because no one would be able to access the offline system from the internet as the separation is physical. In addition, even if someone breached the security of the online system, they would need physical access to the offline side of the data protector to configure it to accept and allow transfer of data towards the offline system. The Restricted amount of data that can be sent via the data protector is a huge deterrent to would-be data criminals as the time it would take would render the exercise futile. Furthermore, the use of the modified RFC6238 for the generation of random IDs makes it possible for the user to maintain their privacy while at the same time provide a possibility to trace a fraudster hiding behind being anonymous whenever need arise. The modification further removes the need for the storage of huge amounts of data in form of logs detailing the Random IDs generated by whom and when and so on. The use of TOR can further help achieve enhanced privacy for users.

References

1. Kangwa, M., Lubobya, C.S., Phiri, J.: Prevention of personally identifiable information leakage in E-commerce via offline data minimisation and pseudonymisation. Int. J. Innov. Sci. Res. Technol. **6**(1), 209–212 (2021)
2. Frank A Cona, M.D.P.: Digital Identity, Personal Dato, US 2019 / 0333054 A1 (2019)
3. Pawar, H.R., Harkut, D.G.: Classical and quantum cryptography for image encryption decryption. In: Proceedings of 2018 3rd IEEE International Conference on Research in Intelligent Computing in Engineering RICE 2018, pp. 1–4 (2018)
4. Hauer, B.: Data and information leakage prevention within the scope of information security. IEEE Access **3**, 2554–2565 (2015)
5. Coppolino, L., D'Antonio, S., Mazzeo, G., Romano, L.: A comprehensive survey of hardware-assisted security: from the edge to the cloud. Int. Things **6**, 100055 (2019)
6. Tan, C.D., Min, F., Wang, M., Zhang, H.R., Zhang, Z.H.: Discovering patterns with weak-wildcard gaps. IEEE Access **4**, 4922–4932 (2016)
7. Il-Agure, Z., Belsam, A., Yun-ke, C.: The semantics of anomalies in IoT integrated BlockChain network, pp. 144–146. IEEE (2019)
8. Zhang, P., Alkubati, M., Bao, Y., Yu, G.: Research advances on blockchain-as-a-service: architectures, applications and challenges. Digit. Commun. Networks (2021)
9. Ye, F., Dong, X., Shen, J., Cao, Z., Zhao, W.: A verifiable dynamic multi-user searchable encryption scheme without trusted third parties. In: Proceedings of the International Conference on Parallel and Distributed Systems - ICPADS, vol. 2019, pp. 896–900, December 2019

10. Innab, N., Alamri, A.: The impact of DDoS on E-commerce. In: 21st Saudi Computer Society National Computer Conference, NCC 2018, pp. 1–4 (2018)
11. Zhan, J., Fan, X., Cai, L., Gao, Y., Zhuang, J.: TPTVer: a trusted third party based trusted verifier for multi-layered outsourced big data system in cloud environment. China Commun. **15**(2), 122–137 (2018)
12. Locher, T., Obermeier, S., Pignolet, Y.A.: When can a distributed ledger replace a trusted third party?. In: 2018 IEEE International Conference on Internet of Things (iThings) and IEEE Green Computing and Communications (GreenCom) and IEEE Cyber, Physical and Social Computing (CPSCom) and IEEE Smart Data (SmartData), pp. 1069–1077 (2018)
13. Štarchoň, P., Pikulík, T.: GDPR principles in data protection encourage pseudonymization through most popular and full-personalized devices - mobile phones. Procedia Comput. Sci. **151**(2018), 303–312 (2019)
14. Ribeiro, S.L., Nakamura, E.T.: Privacy protection with pseudonymization and anonymization in a health IoT system: Results from OCARIoT. In: Proceedings of 2019 IEEE 19th International Conference on Bioinformatics and Bioengineering BIBE 2019, pp. 904–908 (2019)
15. Kangwa, M., Lubobya, C., Phiri, J.: Enhanced protection of ecommerce users personal data and privacy using the trusted third party model. In: Proceedings of the 18th International Conference on e-Business - ICE-B, pp. 116–126 (2021)
16. Jardine, E., Lindner, A.M., Owenson, G.: The potential harms of the Tor anonymity network cluster disproportionately in free countries. Proc. Natl. Acad. Sci. U. S. A. **117**(50), 31716–31721 (2020)
17. Ali, S.S., Chakraborty, R.S., Mukhopadhyay, D., Bhunia, S.: Multi-level attacks: an emerging security concern for cryptographic hardware. In: Proceedings of Design, Automation and Test in Europe DATE, pp. 1176–1179 (2011)
18. M'Raihi, D., Machani, S., Pei, M., Rydell, J.: Internet Engineering Task Force (IETF): Request for Comments: 6238 (2011)
19. Kangwa, M., Lubobya, C.S., Phiri, J.: Protection of personally identifiable Information and Privacy via the use of Hardware and Software, vol. 0958 (2021)
20. Winter, P.: Enhancing Censorship Resistance in the Tor Anonymity Network Enhancing Censorship Resistance in the Tor Anonymity Network, Karlstad University (2014)

Gamified Self-paced E-Learning: Two Iterations of an Educational Design Experiment

Anke Schüll$^{(\boxtimes)}$ (iD) and Laura Brocksieper

University of Siegen, Kohlbettstr. 15, 57076 Siegen, Germany
anke.schuell@uni-siegen.de

Abstract. This paper contributes to research on gamified learning by providing lessons learned from a gamified, self-paced, digital distant learning environment on business information systems. It expands previous research by reporting on a second iteration of an educational design experiment in S/4 HANA. Design elements were composed into a playful layout and associations with a non-learning-context were included, in order to create a more relaxed learning experience. Mistakes were allowed, to keep the students' attention high and to make achievements more rewarding. A mixed media approach was applied to enrich students' learning experience and to avoid monotony. This paper contributes to the body of knowledge by providing lessons learned from a radical conversion of a traditional face-to-face course into a digital distant learning environment using elements of gamification, self-paced learning, and learning from mistakes.

Keywords: Gamification · Digital distant learning · Educational design experiment

1 Introduction

Within universities, students are expected to learn autonomously and in a self-organized manner [3] to prepare them for lifelong learning [6]. E-learning has become the "new normal" due to the pandemic, a development which could promote the preparation for lifelong learning: in e-learning environments, students take a more active role within their learning process and face higher requirements regarding self-organization, self-assessment, and self-motivation [10]. Digital learning enables students to take control of what they want to learn and when [2]. This comes with more challenges related to self-management: students' ability to master their own learning progress becomes a key predictor of academic success [2].

This paper reports on two iterations of an evolutionary experimental approach to solving a practical and complex educational problem. The term "educational design experiment" has been coined to describe this approach [12, 13]. The practical and complex educational problem to be solved in the first iteration was transforming an Enterprise Resource Planning (ERP)-training into a gamified hands-on training which is accessible online [22]. This hands-on training accompanied a lecture on business information systems (BIS). The target audience consists of first semester students. Most of these

© The Author(s), under exclusive license to Springer Nature Switzerland AG 2023
P. Samarati et al. (Eds.): ICETE 2021, CCIS 1795, pp. 84–102, 2023.
https://doi.org/10.1007/978-3-031-36840-0_5

students were novices to the topic. The second iteration improved the learning environment based on the students' feedback and their suggestions and changed the underlying system from the SAP ERP system to S/4 HANA. Both systems, the SAP ERP System and S/4 HANA, were hosted by the SAP Academic Competence Center (SAP ACC) for Europe, the Middle East and Africa. Hosting, tutorials and support for these systems were provided by the SAP UCC.

2   Gamified, Self-paced-Learning

Educational design research is focused on the systematic analysis, design and development of solutions for complex problems in educational practice grounded on research [16]. It aims to contribute to the body of knowledge about the characteristics of these educational interventions and the process of designing and developing them [16]. Solving a problem in educational practice, putting knowledge to use in an innovative way, and/or increasing the robustness and systematic nature of design practice could be reasons to conduct an educational design experiment [13].

The goal of the educational design experiment presented in this paper was to create an e-learning environment that supports students in achieving their learning goals through distance learning, without compromising the scope or scale of the content. Extended experience with hands-on ERP-trainings and insight from recent literature were used in an innovative way within this gamified, self-paced learning experiment.

Allowing mistakes to happen during the learning process, while at the same time providing corrective feedback, can improve learning success [24]. Constructive interaction with students about their mistakes can accelerate learning, provide a deeper understanding of underlying concepts and improve students' ability to transfer their knowledge to new tasks [14]. A study in a medical context confirmed that students who were confronted with mistakes during their learning process could react better in a critical situation than those without this experience [14]. Even though there are seldom lives at stake when working in business information systems, tremendous costs could result from mistakes made within a company. Realizing the consequences of errors during academic courses could raise students' awareness for data quality and provide them with the confidence to handle mistakes if necessary.

Self-regulated learning requires students to set goals, plan ahead, and to monitor and reflect on their learning process [7]. It encourages students to take the initiative [15]. They have to select and use learning strategies to achieve assigned learning goals [28] and consciously take actions to generate information or improve their academic skills [15]. Self-paced e-learning platforms allow students to interact with a learning system anywhere, anytime and at their own individual pace [25]. Using these platforms for self-regulated learning means that students need to organize and track their own learning progress [1]. This requires an autonomy, which is particularly challenging for students who are unfamiliar with self-regulated learning [3]. Even though it requires a higher level of effort, self-regulated learning is crucial for academic performance and for lifelong learning [7].

Increasing individual engagement is the main goal of gamification [25]. The potential of gamification to support learning, particularly in an e-learning context, has been recognized by the academic literature [2]. Gamified learning environments aim to achieve learning goals by stimulating students' interest in their learning activity, creating a fun environment, and triggering their engagement [6]. Playful elements can support the learning process and increase students' perseverance and resilience [1], arouse their interest, and have a positive effect on their motivation. Students may perceive a gamified lecture as more motivating and interesting, even if it is more time-consuming [5].

Previous studies on gamified ERP system training pointed towards improved achievements of learning goals [1], more fun and an intensified flow experience [6]. Flow describes a psychological state in which a person is totally absorbed in an activity [4]. Achieving this state of deep concentration on a learning activity within a digital distant learning environment could be crucial for the learning experience. Flow thus plays a major role in online learning behavior [7].

Positive emotions like hope, enjoyment or pride have a beneficial impact on motivation and persistence in achieving learning goals, while negative emotions like boredom, anxiety, or anger have the opposite effect [7]. Gamification, which involves the use of playful elements in a more serious, less playful context [4] could be the key to trigger positive emotions and to increase engagement and participation in learning activities.

A gamified design strategy aims to change the learning activity into a more playful, game-like activity [6]. To achieve this, different design elements were combined to spark the students' interest and to avoid monotony. Students should have as much control as possible over their learning process, which includes making mistakes and learning from them. Therefore, elements of gamification, self-paced learning, and learning from mistakes were combined in this educational design experiment to enrich students' learning experience.

2.1 First Iteration: Gamified Hands-on Training on Business Information Systems Within the SAP ERP System

The hands-on training presented here deals with logistic processes, material and information flows and their execution within the SAP ERP system. Business processes related to procurement, manufacturing, stock management, sales and support are the topic of this course [22]. Different scenarios evolve around the production and distribution of bicycles. Following the supply chain from procurement to customer interactions provides students with a sound impression of business process integration. Complexity increases with every step and the dependencies between the activities located in different departments become clear: A sales order triggers the manufacturing of a bike, which is only possible if semi-finished products are available and the raw materials are in stock. If not, then semi-finished products must be produced, and/or raw materials must be procured. Students have to deal with every single step of the business process, always keeping a close eye on their stock levels.

Students are responsible for managing their own master data (e.g., materials, bills of materials, suppliers, and customers). The bill of material is multi-layered and contains raw materials, semi-finished, and finished products. Starting from the procurement of raw materials in different variations, the students proceed to the production of semi-finished products. Interdependencies between the demand resulting from the manufacturing process and the procurement of required materials become obvious. Safety stocks and a production plan are introduced to trigger the demand to manufacture bicycles. The secondary demand for semi-finished products and raw materials is derived from this. All secondary demands must be covered, to enable production of the bikes.

The self-paced, digital, distant learning environment presented in this paper covers the content of the course in a playful way [20]. The roadmap of the course was designed as a game board. It visualizes the content and the different scenarios involved in the course (Fig. 1). Scenario-based learning is a concept based on storytelling, on placing students in a story and letting them take on an active role that is similar to a role they might have to perform in real life or in future [9]. As the scenarios are about the production and distribution of bicycles, the background of the game board reflected the context with a picture of spokes. The game board was accessible online, outside the learning management system used at our university. The purpose of using surroundings that are not related to learning, was to help create a learning environment that doesn't look and feel like "learning". To go along with the topic, some videos were shot in the landscape on local bicycle routes, to trigger associations with leisure activities. The purpose of this was to make the learning process more relaxed [22].

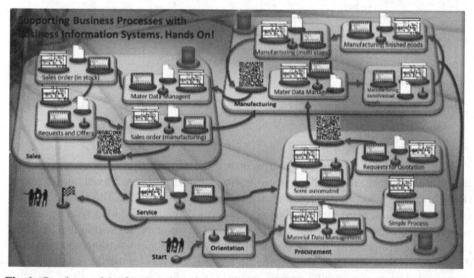

Fig. 1. Roadmap of the first iteration of a gamified, self-paced learning environment on business information systems [22].

The students have access to the learning environment anywhere and anytime, and can progress at their own pace from start to finish. The design elements of the roadmap are largely self-explanatory. Arrows guide students through the roadmap. Each mission is described by four elements: a mini video explaining the goals of the scenario, a process diagram, data sheets and screencasts. QR codes link to mini quizzes, and flashing blue lights link to a troubleshooting file.

Process instances should be executed in the SAP ERP system. Each sub-process is connected with other sub-processes: Sales with manufacturing, manufacturing with procurement, support with sales and procurement. The complexity increases the further students proceed along the roadmap. The process diagram in Fig. 2, a service request, shows the last process to be executed along the roadmap. It builds on processes students have executed before, thus triggering a repetition of activities conducted previously in the case study. One of the bicycles previously delivered to the customer has a broken gearshift, one of the raw materials according to the bicycle's bill of materials. This gearshift needs to be replaced. If no gearshift is in stock, which is highly probable, this will trigger another instance of the procurement process. Only afterwards can the bike be repaired and the service notification closed.

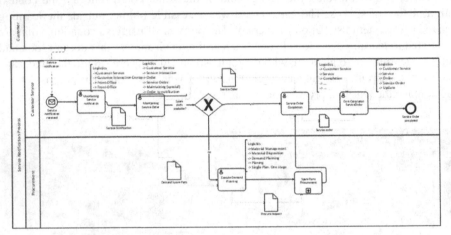

Fig. 2. Business process diagram of the service process according to BPMN 2.0 [20].

The goals and the context of each scenario are explained in mini videos shot in the local landscape. Process diagrams following Business Process Model and Notation (BPMN 2.0) [23] were provided for each process (e.g. Figure 2). The missions to be completed are described by these business process diagrams. A video was embedded within each process model explaining the process and the activities within it. The menu path to the corresponding transaction in the SAP ERP system were included into the diagram as comments. Data sheets provide a compact overview of the data elements necessary to process a specific process instance. Specific data elements (e.g., supplier ID or sales order number) should be noted on these data sheets. Students report when they complete a scenario (a mission within the ERP system) by uploading these data sheets in the learning management system used in our institution, where this upload is rewarded with a badge. Badges can have a positive effect in learning activities [8], as they show the accomplishments of the students and trigger competitive behaviour.

Mistakes can happen at any point in the scenarios. In preparation for real life, these mistakes have consequences: some steps won't work or won't work properly. If mistakes go unnoticed, they will influence activities further along the process, and they will have an impact. These mistakes can be used to improve the learning outcome. There are three aspects which are important for effectively learning from mistakes [14]: that students make the mistakes themselves, that they receive corrective feedback which reminds them of the context in which the mistake was made [14], and that they are assisted in fixing the mistake and reflecting on it [14]. As the frustration level varies from person to person and mistakes can be taken emotionally, feedback needs to be careful and constructive [10]. Delays between a mistake and the feedback can lead to frustration, can overwhelm students in need of support and can have a negative impact on the learning process [11]. Tutors and lecturers provide corrective feedback in the courses. There are troubleshooting files linked to the flashing blue lights to provide corrective feedback outside of the courses. The troubleshooting files contain an overview of typical error messages, explanations of their causes, and hints on how to fix the problem. These troubleshooting files provide support anywhere and anytime, thus empowering the students to correct mistakes by themselves, and helping them to preserve their sense of control.

Social interaction between students and instructors can improve students' self-efficacy, but is more feasible in small courses than in large online courses [3]. Especially when working with the concept of "learning from mistakes", interaction with students is important. Therefore, courses had a limited supervision ratio before the concept turned towards online courses. This ratio was adopted for the digital concept, keeping the group size to a maximum of thirty students. Tutors and lecturers observed their progress within the scenarios. All activities within the system remained undocumented to avoid influencing student behavior. To evaluate the students' perception of the self-paced, digital distant learning platform, an anonymous online survey was conducted at the end of the course. Access to the survey was linked into the platform at the end.

Two hypotheses were evaluated: That self-paced learning has a positive effect on learning efficiency (H_1) and that mistakes have a positive impact on learning efficiency (H_2). Participation was voluntary, without incentives. As most students are of about the same age, and as their gender is not relevant for the analysis, no demographic data was requested. 31% of the 231 students who passed the course in the autumn semester of 2020/21 participated in the survey. 25 of the 72 data sets were incomplete and dismissed from further analysis. As these 47 data sets cover 20% of the participants, their analysis was expected to provide valuable insights, even though the data size is poor [4]. SmartPLS [19] was used to analyse the data.

The first hypothesis posited that self-paced learning has a positive effect on learning efficiency. This hypothesis was supported by the data set. The hands-on training allows the students to become actively involved. A positive correlation of self-paced learning with learning efficiency is in line with the previous literature and was further confirmed by the comments given on the questionnaire: *"Working within the environment was a lot of fun! [...] I would have liked a slightly higher level of difficulty and a little more control. I learned a lot from this project and would always recommend and wish for more of this kind of learning in my studies"* [22]. Another student commented on a positive effect on the learning process: *"It helped me to understand what an ERP system is and, most importantly, it helped make my studies more practical and easier to understand"* [22].

The hypothesis that learning efficiency could be improved by handling mistakes constructively during the learning process was not reflected by the data sets. Literature points towards a negative effect on the learning process if corrective feedback is delayed too long. The fact that long delays could overwhelm learners who need support [11] could be part of the explanation of why the hypothesis had to be dismissed. Students have different frustration levels and not all students perceive mistakes as beneficial for their learning process. One student commented: *"In general, the videos, data sheets, etc. make working with SAP very easy. However, it becomes frustrating when you receive error messages that do not appear in the videos and often leave you sitting in front of the computer at a loss. With a little help from the tutor, however, you can also handle these, and therefore this is not a big problem"* [22]. Another student had a similar comment: *"The work was sometimes really fun, but when errors appeared and it took time until they could be fixed or subsequent errors occurred, it was sometimes really annoying. That also spoiled the fun a bit"* [22]. One student expressed a preference for a higher degree of control and the freedom to work more independently and to make more mistakes: *"In my opinion, watching the videos made it a little too easy to work on the project. At one point or another, I would have liked to take more control to maneuver through the process in the system, so that I could make my own mistakes and learn from them"* [22] (Fig. 3).

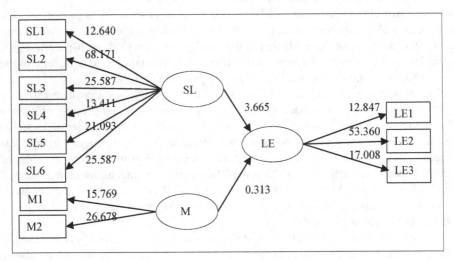

Fig. 3. Path coefficients for the inner and outer loadings; LE – Learning efficiency (items LE1 to LE3), SL – self paced learning (items SL1 to SL6), M – learning from mistakes (items M1 and M2).

Even though the first hypothesis was supported by the data set and the second hypothesis was not, we were able to verify that a hands-on-training within an SAP ERP system could be transformed into a gamified self-paced e-learning environment. Including playful elements improved students' motivation, engagement and persistence. To make achievement more rewarding, errors, mistakes and wrong turns were part of the challenge. The student feedback provided encouragement to continue on this path *"It was a little hard for me to get into at first, but now I don't want to get out. It's a pity it's over, it was really fun"* [22].

2.2   Second Iteration: Gamified Hands-on Training on Business Information Systems in SAP S/4 HANA

While face-to-face courses were not recommended in the autumn semester of 2020/21, the autumn semester of 2021/22 did allow face-to-face courses with the students. A hybrid concept was agreed on to grant the flexibility to change from digital distant learning courses to face-to-face courses and the other way around if necessary. The courses were accompanied by the asynchronous self-paced learning platform.

The feedback from the first iteration indicated several improvements, but the concept as such seemed suitable to the purpose. It was necessary to change the ERP system to SAP S4/HANA [21], which required a change in the scenarios and processes. New videos, data sheets, process models and screencasts were necessary. Screencasts now show the corresponding process diagram, to underline the connection of each step in the S/4 HANA system with the activities in the process.

In the previous autumn semester, all students needed to install a graphical user interface (GUI) and to connect it to the server. This was the first barrier students needed to overcome before they could start working on the content of the course. This semester, switching to S/4 HANA allowed them to access the system without installing a GUI. Access is provided via SAP Fiori. Every single transaction/app can now be addressed by a URL. This allowed us to change the business process diagrams. Instead of long comments listing the navigation path through the menu to reach the transaction in the ERP System corresponding to an activity, now the URL could be connected with the activity. Clicking the activity in the business process diagram thus opens the app in SAP Fiori that is associated with it.

In the first iteration, several students commented on a confusing layout. In this iteration, therefore, the scenarios were arranged into three columns, each representing a domain of the supply chain: source, make and deliver, and service (Fig. 4). The spokes

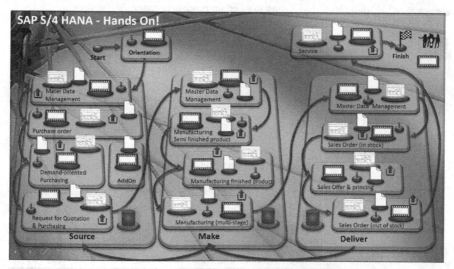

Fig. 4. Roadmap of the second iteration of a gamified self-paced learning environment on business information systems [21].

in the background remained to visualize the context, which is producing bikes. Master data management is the first task to be conducted within each process domain, therefore it is placed at the top of each column. Due to limited resources, quizzes had to be omitted from this iteration.

The design elements of the gamified self-paced, digital distant learning environments are largely self-explanatory (Table 1). Each panel contains a business process diagram.

Table 1. Design Elements of the Roadmap.

Icon	Function
	Each panel corresponds to a domain or a scenario within the domain of the supply chain (source, make or deliver), providing visual clues to the structure of the case study.
	Each mission describes a scenario within the case study that can only be conducted after completing all preliminary scenarios. Each mission is described by five elements:
	1. Introductory videos which explain the goal of the scenario and its relation to the other scenarios.
	2. Business Process Diagrams (BPMN 2.0) plus videos explaining the process. Each activity within the process is linked with the URL of the corresponding transaction in SAP Fiori.
	3. Data Sheets are compact collections of the data belonging to a certain process instance.
	4. Screencasts provide explanations on executing the activities of a process in S/4 HANA.
	5. Upload link to the learning management system.
	Troubleshooting Portal/Pin-board.
	Arrows lead the way along the roadmap, from start to finish . These are marked in different colors. While the blue arrows lead forward, the red arrows lead backwards (repeating previous steps).

Process instances in S/4 HANA are missions to be completed on every panel within a process domain. Data sheets list the necessary data to be entered and contain text fields in which students note their progress. Data sheets fulfill two purposes: providing a compact collection of data entries and providing text fields to be filled out by the students. The data sheets are uploaded in the learning content management system used within our university. In the previous iteration, students had to navigate through the folder structure of the learning management system to upload their data sheets. A new icon was introduced in this. The icon is connected with the corresponding folder in the learning management system to make it easier for students to upload their data sheets.

Badges are granted in this learning management system, if this mission and all previous missions were completed successfully. In addition to acting as a reward, badges are used to segue to the next steps and to encourage students to proceed (Fig. 5).

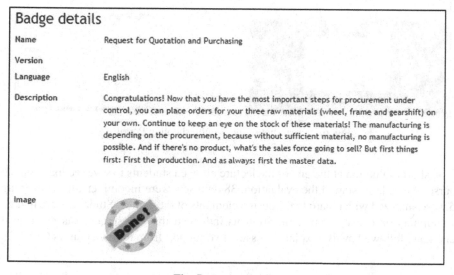

Fig. 5. Badge details.

Students can and will make mistakes when working on the scenarios. In both face-to-face and online courses, support was close at hand without a long delay. Tutors and lecturers provided support during these courses, or via e-mail. A troubleshooting platform was also established to enable students to help themselves and avoid frustration due to long delays. Some errors are rather typical and occur frequently. Predefined solutions are accessible on this platform for these well-known errors. In the first iteration, a text file served this purpose. Students had to scroll through it until they found "their" error description. This second iteration worked with an online open access platform, a troubleshooting portal designed as a pin-board. Access to the portal was password protected.

Students don't always remember the texts of error message, but will often recognize the messages on sight. Instead of text descriptions of error messages, screenshots gave the students visual clues. Under each screenshot was a short description of the situation.

Causes for these errors were explained, with instructions on how to fix the problem. The goal of this is to empower students to help themselves. The layout of the troubleshooting portal reflected the process domains of the roadmap: source, make, deliver, and service (Fig. 6). For mistakes not listed in these domains, the "inbox" allowed students to upload error messages. With each new mistake reported on this pin-board, the collection of solutions grows, covering a broader range of potential issues. This platform also provided hints on insufficient or ambiguous explanations.

Fig. 6. Screenshot of the Troubleshooting Portal.

A short evaluation at the end of the lecture allowed students to give feedback on the course. 93 students started the evaluation, 38 data sets were incomplete, the remaining 55 were analyzed with regard to the design elements of the course. Students were invited to comment on every component. Students indicated that the screencasts were most beneficial, followed by live explanations and live support from tutors/lecturers (Table 2).

Table 2. "What elements of the course did you benefit from most?" (multiple selections possible, N = 55).

Beneficial element	Mentions
Live explanations and live support by my tutors/lecturers	22
Screencasts	37
Troubleshooting portal/pin-board	4
Process diagrams	9

One student commented: *"The tutors were very helpful, that's why I asked them for help and am very content with that."* Another explained *"Helped most. Especially when you had unexplainable problems/error messages"*. Another student explained *"Very helpful, because you did not have to wait for answers, but could ask immediately when something was unclear."*

The screencasts were rated at the top of the list. One student elaborated: *"The screencasts were very helpful, because it wasn't always obvious how to get to a certain command button. The screencasts made the process easier and they explained more than the data sheets, so you could comprehend what's happening."* Students gave suggestions for changes: *"I might prefer it if there were short videos for single activities, so you could find instructions, e.g. for procurement, without searching through the videos. Because the whole process was covered, I was tempted to simply follow the video instructions, without thinking about the task further. When one video told me to finish the rest of the process on my own, I felt a touch of panic because I couldn't remember how. [...] But in the end it became easier, because I was familiar with the functionality and could indeed fulfill the tasks almost completely on my own."*

The troubleshooting pin-board wasn't mentioned too often, but one student commented that he had found his problems there two times, and another commented: *"Helpful for problems that occur often. An option to quickly find a solution from home."*

The business process diagrams showed the process logic of procurement, manufacturing and sales order management. They were visible in each screencast. One student commented *"The process diagrams helped me to understand which actions were necessary."*

As problem management within this distance learning setting was a major concern, students were asked where they looked for assistance when a problem occurred (Table 3).

Table 3. "If a problem occurred, where did you look for assistance?" (multiple selections possible, $N = 55$).

Beneficial element	Mentions
My tutors/lecturer during the live courses (face-to-face or online)	28
My tutor/lecturer via e-mail	34
Other students	21
Troubleshooting pin-board	10
Own research (internet)	14

Some students elaborated on the assistance provided by tutors and lecturers during live courses: *"Very helpful, when you get stuck somewhere, especially with the videoconferences"*. Another commented: *"I attended at the time of the course to get assistance. I always received help and they never "gave up""*. One student voiced a preference for requesting assistance via e-mail *"because it seemed easier to present the problem this way"*. Several students commented that they had tried to resolve issues on their own when they were stuck, and had found the solution themselves.

This autumn semester started with a hybrid concept, allowing students to choose between face-to-face or online courses. Both were accompanied by the self-paced e-learning environment. The students were assigned to a specific course, but could be reassigned on request. At the beginning, about a third of the students chose online groups. During the course of the semester, more students opted for a reassignment to online groups. One student commented on this *"I liked the fact that you could choose between hybrid or fully digital. During the coronavirus restrictions, I realized that I learn more intensively and remember more information with asynchronous learning, because I can motivate myself more, when I am in the mood for the course and am not bound to certain time slots on a schedule."*

The evaluation invited students to summarize their impression. One student commented that the videos should cover all activities of the processes and could be more extensive. Another commented *"Sometimes the videos didn't help, because problems occurred that weren't in the videos. Then I had so solve them myself."* The feeling of being overwhelmed at the beginning, but gaining confidence with every step, was a pattern described by several students. One student commented *"I found the platform intimidating at the beginning, because each wrong click could lead to an error (at least in my mind). Somewhere in the middle of the "source" unit it suddenly got easier, and I could comprehend processes and sequences."* One student wrote: *"With every part that was completed, my ambition to finish increased."* Another described: *"After initial desperation it was fun to work with S/4 HANA at the end."* Fun was mentioned several times. *"Sometimes it was difficult and complicated, but it was fun."* Another commented *"The whole thing was fun and helped us to learn and understand BPMN diagrams. While working on it, it felt a bit like I was completing a real and important, well-paid task."* Another student commented *"Gives an interesting impression on how a business information system works and is used. The videos were very helpful and made you aware of how single processes have an impact on business activities."* Another voiced some expectations about the relevance of the content *"Very interesting and it felt like the content could be useful for life later on, no matter the profession. Digitalization is the future, therefore learning how to work with these programs is very important."*

3   Lessons Learned

Early research on distant learning has identified four categories of influences on distance learning outcomes [26], which will guide the discussion in the next paragraphs:

- Technology characteristics,
- instructor characteristics,
- course characteristics, and
- student characteristics. Demographics, past experience with the technology and individual learning style could also be relevant [27].

The gamified, self-paced digital distant learning environment presented in this paper is accessible online. No technical skills are required to use the learning environment or to access the S/4 HANA system. A mixed media approached was used to avoid monotony. Playful elements were integrated to keep students interested and to encourage them to proceed. Each design element links to a specific perspective of the scenarios: data sheets to the data perspective, process diagrams to the process perspective, screencasts to the IT perspective. A human perspective could be a possible extension for the next iterations. Dicheva et al. (2015) extracted different educational gamification design principles from the literature [5], several of which were put to use in this e-learning environment (Table 4). Scenario-based learning is built around a story in which students take an active role [9]. This story could be more intriguing. In the next iteration, story-telling will be taken into consideration in particular, and the options to make mistakes will be modified.

Table 4. Educational gamification design principles [5] and their coverage within this self-paced e-learning environment.

Design Element	Coverage
Goals	Mini videos introducing into the scenarios
Challenges and quests	Each scenario corresponds to a mission, challenge or quest
Customization	-
Progress to mastery	Developing skills in SAP S/4 HANA, improved understanding of business processes and business information systems
Feedback	Badges and corrective feedback
Competition and cooperation	Students are rewarded with badges, there is no cooperation
Accrual grading	Accumulation of badges
Visible status	Due to privacy issues, lists are anonymous
Access/unlocking content	All content is available anytime, but the functionality of the S/4 HANA system can only be put to proper use after all previous steps have been completed properly
Freedom of choice	As the missions are bound to the business information system, the freedom of choice is limited
Allowing students to choose their own sub-goals within the larger task	Currently, the goals are defined in the scenarios. Extending the freedom to choose sub-goals might be an option for another iteration
Freedom to fail	Struggling, taking wrong turns, and learning from mistakes are some of the core concepts of this case study. These mistakes need to be fixed, but do not result in penalties or negative consequences
Storytelling	Process instances are described in a rather matter of fact way. The storytelling could be more intriguing, which could be an issue for the next iteration
New identities and/or roles, onboarding, or time restrictions	No option yet

The potential of gamification to shape gamers' behavior in a specific direction has led to the rapid adoption of this strategy in various domains, ranging from marketing, to health to sustainability [5]. The majority of case studies on gamified e-learning come from the computer science/IT domain [5]. This could be explained at least in part by a positive attitude of instructors towards IT and the technological skills, that come with the profession as lecturers on the domain. Teaching style and control over technology can influence distance learning outcomes, but they can also be the subject of self-paced e-learning, as a recent study on the adoption of self-paced e-learning for faculty members revealed [17]. Dicheva et al. (2018) referred to the lack of appropriate tools to support course gamification as a major barrier [6]. This should be extended to another major limitation: time. The gamified, self-paced e-learning environment presented here was implemented without any funding, therefore the implementation was limited to on-board resources. Due to the lack of financial means, it was necessary to improvise. The roadmap is an html-document created with an office software program. A BPMN diagram tool was used, along with a free-to-use pin-board for troubleshooting and the learning management system of our university for rewarding students with badges. The videos were shot using a smartphone or a compact camera. Video editing was conducted with the tools at hand. It took a considerable amount of time to figure out a concept, to evaluate the tools at hand and to decide on what could be used, to figure out how to do so, and of course to produce the different elements. Within this case study the most restricting factor was time.

The number of students in the course is rather high, and due to the distance enforced by the situation most students learned from home. The content of the hands-on course, business processes and their support through business information systems, was suitable for a digital transformation. Playful elements were combined with associations with leisure activities to keep the students' interest and concentration high. When evaluating the first iteration, students reported incidents of entering a flow state. Within this non-playful context, this is an encouraging sign that this approach is a beneficial one. There were no comments indicating this for the second iteration, but several students in the first and the second iteration mentioned "fun". Frustration wasn't mentioned at all when evaluating the second iteration. "Intimidating", "complex" and "difficult" were mentioned, but never "frustration". This indicates an appropriate level of difficulty. The confusion that was mentioned in the first iteration changed into an impression of complexity in the second iterations. Rearranging the layout into three columns seemed to have improved comprehensibility.

Due to the circumstances, students became very familiar with digital distant learning. The learning environment required no technical skills and initial reluctance to work with S/4 HANA was worked out with the support of tutors and lecturers in the courses. The students were never left alone with the task, which proved a very important element of the course concept. Therefore, this approach is highly recommended. Small groups supported by tutors or lecturers were crucial, and much more important than support via the troubleshooting portal. Cho, Heron [3] recommended accompanying the course with opportunities for interaction on social media. In a study from 2009, learners valued blogging as an equivalent or even superior means of communication over discussion boards in a learning management system [18]. This could be a possible extension for the next iteration.

4   Conclusion

Autonomous and self-organized learning prepares students for life-long learning. This paper describes two iterations of an educational design experiment on the complex topic of business processes and their support through ERP systems. Students gained a sound understanding of business processes and business information systems. Awareness for data quality increased, aspects of integration became visible. A gamified, self-paced learning environment was presented that covers the content of the course without requiring compromises in the scope or scale of the content. Students appreciated the option to work anywhere and anytime at their own speed, and even enjoyed working within the platform. Playful elements supported associations with non-learning activities and made the learning process more relaxed.

Educational design research [16] is an experimental approach relying heavily on prototypes. Due to the urgency to react to the situation, "throw-away" prototypes were not an option. An "all-in" approach was decided on: The prototype was rolled out immediately, to prove itself within real life learning environments. Whether there would be another iteration depended on how the students perceived the self-paced learning environment. As their feedback was encouraging, the experiences from the first iteration were gathered to feed into the next iteration. As only participants of the course were invited, the results won't generalize well. Further research is recommended to explore on this on a broader scale.

Within the first iteration (autumn semester 2020/21), a prototype was developed to convert a hands-on-training on SAP ERP systems into a gamified, self-paced digital distant learning course. Students were allowed to make mistakes during the case study, to keep their attention level high and to make achievement within the case study more rewarding. Within the first iteration, two hypotheses were evaluated: Self-paced learning has positive impact on learning efficiency (H_1) and learning from mistakes has a positive impact on learning efficiency (H_2). Smart PLS was used to analyse the data. The relevance of self-paced learning for learning efficiency could be confirmed, but we were not able to confirm a positive impact of leaning from mistakes on learning efficiency. Comments and statements pointed towards a beneficial effect worth further exploration. As there is a paucity of research on learning from mistakes in digital distant learning environments, further research is recommended.

The students successfully participating in the course were an encouraging sign of the benefits of this approach. Further improvements to the design and functionality led to the second iteration. A change to S/4 HANA let to a relaunch in which every single component had to be exchanged. Lessons learned from the first iteration led to improvements in user interactions. We were able to test this second iteration in a hybrid learning situation, allowing students to choose between online courses or courses located at the department. To empower students to fix problems themselves, the first iteration of the self-paced learning environment contained troubleshooting files, one for each process domain. Within this second iteration a troubleshooting portal was established in the form of a pin-board. This troubleshooting pin-board followed the structure of the layout, taking up the three process domains: source, make and deliver, plus service.

The self-paced e-learning environment is mostly self-explanatory, but as the topic is rather complex, we opted against an unaccompanied asynchronous self-learning option and kept the traditional course concept. Tutors and lecturers each guided a small group of students (30 max.) through the scenarios. The small size of the groups led to close contact between lecturers and students, thus lowering barriers to ask for assistance should problems occur. The fact that tutors and lecturers were the first points of contact when problems did come up underscores the importance of contact persons and interacting with them.

Gamified elements were combined to enrich students' learning experience. The students could work with the learning environment at their own pace, completing missions that are rewarded with badges in the learning management system. We confirmed that this hands-on-training on ERP systems could be transformed into a gamified, self-paced learning platform without compromising the scope or scale of the content. Students can learn and understand the content at their own individual speed. They are in control of their learning progress and need to take initative. Some felt challenged, but kept on working, understood the process logic and even reported that the tasks were fun. However, it became evident that support by tutors and lecturers was crucial. Therefore, we recommend that asyncronous learning platforms be accompanied by regular meetings.

The use of playful elements to raise students' interest and to keep them motivated could be a promising approach even in the aftermath of the pandemic. As the experiment took place under the influence of the pandemic, a tendency towards digital distant learning could be circumstantial. Further research would be necessary to validate if students would opt for digital distant learning voluntarily.

Some improvement in the storytelling could be worth further consideration, to make the story more intriguing within the limits of the topic. Adding smaller videos to the environment, in order to explain single steps for those who forgot how to work with the system, could be another extension.

Even though not representative on a large scale, the participants are representative of the target audience. This helped to avoid bias resulting from a mismatch of sample group with the target audience, but without a control group the results cannot be compared, thus limiting the options for interpretation. There is also another limitation that needs to be addressed, since the evaluation in both iterations was placed at the end of the leaning platform, close to the finish. Students' who gave up never made it that far: As only students who successfully mastered the course participated in the evaluation, the evaluations will be overly positive.

The evaluations presented in this publication focused mainly on the learning process as perceived by students, not on learning outcomes. We suggest further evaluations on the impact of gamified e-learning environments on learning outcomes.

References

1. Anthonysamy, L., Koo, A.-C., Hew, S.-H.: Self-regulated learning strat-egies and non-academic outcomes in higher education blended learning environments: a one decade review. Educ. Inf. Technol. **25**, 3677–3704 (2020). https://doi.org/10.1007/s10639-020-10134-2

2. Bernik, A., Bubas, G., Radosevic, D.: Measurement of the effects of e-learning courses gamification on motivation and satisfaction of students. In: 2018 41st International Convention on Information and Communication Technology, Electronics and Microelectronics (MIPRO). IEEE, pp. 806–811 (2018)
3. Cho, M.-H., Heron, M.L.: Self-regulated learning: the role of motivation, emotion, and use of learning strategies in students' learning experiences in a self-paced online mathematics course. Distance Educ. **36**, 80–99 (2015). https://doi.org/10.1080/01587919.2015.1019963
4. Comrey, A.L., Lee, H.B.: A First Course in Factor Analysis. Psychology Press, New York, Second edition (2016)
5. Dicheva, D., Dichev, C., Agre, G., et al.: Gamification in education: a systematic mapping study. Educ. Technol. Soc. **18**, 75–88 (2015)
6. Dicheva, D., Irwin, K., Dichev, C.: OneUp: supporting practical and experimental gamification of learning. IJSG **5**, 5–21 (2018). https://doi.org/10.17083/ijsg.v5i3.236
7. Flynn, C., Olson, J., Reinhardt, M.: Self-regulated learning in online graduate business communication courses: a qualitative inquiry. Bus. Prof. Communi. Quarterly **83**, 80–95 (2020). https://doi.org/10.1177/2329490619885904
8. Hamari, J.: Do badges increase user activity? a field experiment on the effects of gamification. Comput. Hum. Behav. **71**, 469–478 (2017). https://doi.org/10.1016/j.chb.2015.03.036
9. Iverson, K., Colky, D.: Scenario-based e-learning design. nonprofit management. Leadership **43**, 16–22 (2004). https://doi.org/10.1002/pfi.4140430105
10. Kartika, H.: Instructional design in mathematics for undergraduate students based on learning by mistakes approach utilizing scilab assis-tance. J Phys.: Conf. Ser. **983**, 12082 (2018). https://doi.org/10.1088/1742-6596/983/1/012082
11. Mathan, S.A., Koedinger, K.R.: Fostering the intelligent novice: learning from errors with metacognitive tutoring. Educ. Psychologist **40**, 257–265 (2005). https://doi.org/10.1207/s15326985ep4004_7
12. McKenney, S., Reeves, T.C.: Educational design research. In: Spector, J.M., Merrill, M.D., Elen, J., et al. (eds): Handbook of Research on Educational Communications and Technology, vol 13. Springer New York, New York, NY, pp. 131–140 (2014). https://doi.org/10.1007/978-1-4614-3185-5_11
13. McKenney, S., Reeves, T.C.: Educational design research: portraying, conducting, and enhancing productive scholarship. Med. Educ. **55**, 82–92 (2021). https://doi.org/10.1111/medu.14280
14. Metcalfe, J.: Learning from errors. Annu. Rev. Psychol. **68**, 465–489 (2017). https://doi.org/10.1146/annurev-psych-010416-044022
15. Nejabati, N.: The effects of teaching self-regulated learning strategies on EFL students' reading comprehension. JLTR **6**, 1343 (2015). https://doi.org/10.17507/jltr.0606.23
16. Nieveen, N., Folmer, E.: Formative evaluation in educational design research. Design Res. **153**, 152–169 (2013)
17. Ranieri, M., Raffaghelli, J.E., Pezzati, F.: Digital resources for faculty development in e-learning: a self-paced approach for professional learning. Italian J. Educ. Technol. **26**, 104–118 (2018)
18. Rhode, J.: Interaction equivalency in self-paced online learning environments: an exploration of learner preferences. IRRODL **10** (2009). https://doi.org/10.19173/irrodl.v10i1.603
19. Ringle, C.M., Wende, S., Becker, J.-M.: SmartPLS 3 (2015)
20. Schüll, A., Brocksieper, L., Rössel, J.: Fehler oder Chance? - Lernen aus Fehlern in einer spielerischen e-Learning Umgebung zu integrierten Geschäftsprozessen der Global Bike Inc. Proceedings of the SAP Academic Community Conference D-A-CH, pp. 9–18 (2020)
21. Schüll, A., Brocksieper, L., Safontschik, A.: Fehlerbasiertes Lernen in einer spielerischen Selbstlernumgebung zu integrierten Geschäftsprozessen in S/4 HANA. Proceedings of the SAP Academic Community Conference D-A-CH, pp. 76–81 (2021)

22. Schüll, A., Brocksieper, L., Rössel, J.: Gamified hands-on-training in business information systems: an educational design experiment. In: Proceedings of the 18th International Conference on e-Business. SCITEPRESS - Science and Technology Publications, pp. 165–171 (2021)

23. Shapiro, R., White, S.A., Bock, C., et al.: BPMN 2.0 Handbook Second Edition: Methods, Concepts, Case Studies and Standards in Business Process Modeling Notation (BPMN). Future Strategies, Inc., Lighthouse Point, Florida (USA) (2011)

24. Tulis, M., Steuer, G., Dresel, M.: Learning from errors: a model of individual processes. FLR **4**, 12–26 (2016). https://doi.org/10.14786/flr.v4i2.168

25. Türk, Y., Gören, S.: Gamified self-paced e-learning platform for computer science courses. In: ICT Innovations, Web Proceedings ISSN 1865-0937, pp. 95–104 (2017)

26. Webster, J., Hackley, P.: Teaching effectiveness in technology-mediated distance learning. Acad. Manag. J. **40**, 1282–1309 (1997). https://doi.org/10.2307/257034

27. Wilson, R.L., Weiser, M.: Adoption of asynchronous learning tools by traditional full-time students: a pilot study. Inf. Technol. Manage. **2**, 363–375 (2001). https://doi.org/10.1023/A:1011446516889

28. Zimmerman, B.J.: Self-regulated learning and academic achievement: an overview. Educ. Psychol. **25**, 3–17 (1990)

Digital Transformation and Management of Transfer in University Platforms

Claudia Doering(✉) ⓘD, Finn Reiche ⓘD, and Holger Timinger ⓘD

Institute of Data and Process Science, University of Applied Sciences, Landshut, Germany
{claudia.doering,finn.reiche,holger.timinger}@haw-landshut.de

Abstract. Teaching and research have been the core activities of universities since ages. Nowadays, the topic of transfer is increasingly coming into focus, as universities are no longer seen as "ivory towers" in which research is cut off from the rest of the society, but rather as establishments with a profound knowledge and technology transfer. However, transfer often still occurs in an uncoordinated manner without distinct processes or coordination. A digital transformation of transfer activities could support and make universities fit for the future of transfer. Therefore, this paper does not only propose a framework for digital transformation of transfer, but also points out the importance of platforms and collaboration of universities.

Keywords: Transfer · Platform · Business process management · Digital Transformation · Digitalization · Inter-organizational workflows · University Collaboration

1 Introduction

Digitalization is an essential and cutting-edge topic, which has reached universities as well as the whole industry and society. Universities have embodied digital transformation in their curricula and their research activities, but often somehow lack of an understanding and application within their own structures, processes and administration. To support and learn from each other, universities are forming cooperations and alliances with each. The word "university" will be used throughout the whole text and incorporates all types of universities (e.g. universities of applied sciences and technical universities).

Being part of an alliance with other universities offers multiple benefits for universities, but also incorporates challenges, as in this situation the universities cooperate and compete with each other at the same time [1]. This state can be described as "coopetition", in which universities compete for students, projects, funds and external partners, as well as cooperate to share their knowledge and resources [2]. Coopetition was first described in the context of companies cooperating and competing against each other to for example reduce R&D expenses or gain a broader market share [3]. It is however also relevant for universities because platforms have become established in many areas to connect different players and enable joint activities. Platforms are superior to many

P. Samarati et al. (Eds.): ICETE 2021, CCIS 1795, pp. 103–117, 2023.
https://doi.org/10.1007/978-3-031-36840-0_6

other (value creation) architectures because they have the best cost-benefit relationship [4].

By now, in addition to the two existing missions of universities, teaching and research, the third mission, often called "transfer", has also become more and more established [5]. This third mission is gaining importance, also because various stakeholders such as society or business enterprises are demanding the involvement of universities in answering their questions or challenges. Transfer is gaining significance at universities, but it is still done in a widely uncoordinated process. While the first steps in the digital transformation of the areas of research and teaching are being more or less successfully completed, the transfer area is still behind. Many of the transfer processes and procedures are not defined or modeled yet, and if they are, they are usually not designed for digital usage. This situation is accompanied by strong inefficiencies, which could be remedied by digitizing the transfer area. In this context, the term digitization means that a process is transformed from analog data to digital data. Digitization, on the other hand, means using digital technologies to transform business processes and business models and create new revenue and value creation opportunities.

The context project, TRIO (Transfer and Innovation in Eastern Bavaria) is an alliance project between six universities in Bavaria, who collaborate with each other to intensify the transfer to and with the region. The focus of this project is, among others, on digitalization. During the implementation of the project, it became apparent that the collaborating universities all lack of throughout digital processes and procedures for their transfer activities and that the management of these tasks is also widely uncoordinated. Although there are various activities in the digitalization of tasks in universities it is surprising that the administrations have only partially or not at all digitized own processes, documents and procedures [6].

This paper therefore proposes a model for digital transformation of transfer within and out of universities and the management of these structures. Also die idea of university platforms and their possible benefits on transfer will be discussed in further detail. Therefore, the following research questions arise:

RQ1 How can transfer activities of universities and their management be displayed in a structured framework?
RQ2 Can university alliances or platforms support the digitalization of transfer?

This article is divided into the following sections:

The next chapter describes the methodology which was used to achieve the defined research objective. The interview design is then presented followed by the management of transfer in universities in chapter 3. Chapter 4 discusses platforms in transfer and their possible effects. This is followed by a presentation of the interview results and concludes with a discussion of the findings and an outlook on future work.

2 Research Methodology

To ensure a high quality of research, within research project, a broad and far-reaching research methodology is needed. HEVNER and CHATTERJEE describe two general methodological approaches [7]. The behavioral science approach aims at the empirical validation of a hypothesis, whereas the design science approach creates and evaluates IT artefacts. The design science approach consists of seven different guidelines and was chosen for this research project (see Fig. 1). Because this approach aims to solve business problems, a systematic literature search was conducted according to VOM BROCKE's guidelines to prove the relevance [8]. The requirement for rigorousness was thereby fulfilled as well as the requirement for research as a search process. The dissemination of the results, which HEVNER and CHATTERJEE require, is fulfilled by the publication of the results in this publication and an accompanying doctoral thesis. In order to evaluate the created artefacts, expert interviews were conducted. These semi-structured interviews were conducted according to the recommendations and guidelines of MEUSER and NAGEL [9]. These require a suitable definition and process for the selection of experts for the interviews. In this context, an expert is a person with specific expertise, which can be obtained, for example, through a specific activity in a company or organization.

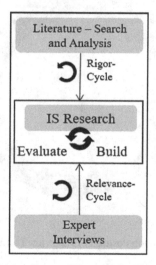

Fig. 1. Design Science Research by HEVNER et al.

Furthermore, the quality criteria of MAYER were applied in the expert interviews, which were conducted as part of the design science research [10]. The independence of the experts ensures objectivity. Therefore, the data collection was ensured by equal conditions. Reliability guarantees equivalent results at the end of the research, as the interviews were conducted under identical conditions. Validity ensures that an appropriate research design was chosen according to its specific research questions. Therefore, objectivity ensures the independence of the researchers while reliability guarantees same results under same conditions and validity secures an appropriate research design according to the specific research questions. Objectivity is the prerequisite for reliability which in turn is the prerequisite for validity.

2.1 Interview Design

To gain a better understanding of transfer management in universities and the state of being part in a university alliance, semi-structured expert interviews were conducted. This interview type was chosen, as it allows to deviate from the interview protocol, if needed. Prior to the interviews a pilot interview was conducted to check whether there were any errors or ambiguities in the interview questions. The interviews all took place in January and February 2022 and were conducted online using the platform Zoom. The duration of the interviews was 30 min and the interviews were all recorded in order to transcribe them afterwards. In total, 9 interviews were conducted with interview partners from universities, which are part of the collaboration platform TRIO [1]. The job positions of the interview partners can be seen in Fig. 2.

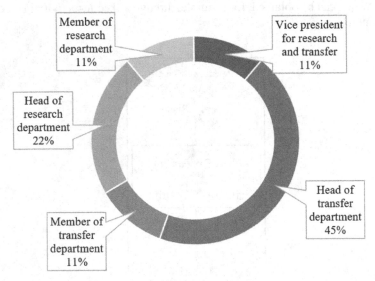

Fig. 2. Job Position of Interview Partners.

The interviews comprised eight questions were structured according to this interview guide:

Q1: What is your understanding of transfer management in a university?
Q2: In your opinion, what higher-level tasks are part of the transfer management in a university?
Q3: Who carries out these tasks?
Q4: What role does a university alliance like TRIO (Transfer and Innovation in Eastern Bavaria) play in the development of a transfer strategy?

Q5: What transfer-challenges are you trying to solve with the university alliance TRIO?

Q6: In your opinion, what are the strengths and weaknesses in the current management of transfer at your university?

Q7: In your opinion, what are the opportunities and risks in the current management of transfer at your university?

Q8: Finally, is there anything you would like to tell us about transfer management at a university?

3 Transfer Management in Universities

The management of transfer is not commonly defined and often incorporated in the idea of research management. It consists of organizing and controlling transfer processes and procedures within the administration of transfer in universities. One expert even stated *"Management and processes belong together. If there are no processes, there is nothing to manage"* (Interview 5). With an in-depth literature search and the expert interviews it was found that transfer management covers a wide range of topics, like *stakeholder management, organizational management of the transfer administration, definition of the strategic orientation, expectation management, controlling and the exploitation of research results* [11]. Especially through the expert interviews it became clear that a distinction between strategic and operative tasks cannot be clearly made in the definition of transfer management. The boundaries between these two areas often blur, mainly because of a lack of personnel within the relevant departments and in the university management. Nevertheless, it became apparent that these management tasks should be part of the task of the university management and the heads of the administrative transfer/research departments in universities.

It is also emerging that there is no shared understanding of transfer or transfer management within the universities. All experts stated that they either had just developed a transfer strategy and definition in the course of participation in the university alliance or that just the common strategic approach of the alliance was used and no own university approach was defined. Moreover, the term transfer is often not associated with the activities that are carried out by the professors in an university - even by themselves. For example, it was mentioned that professors would be doing honorary policy advice and because they would do it free of charge without a project contract, this could not be transfer. Transfer often seems to be associated only with technology transfer and not so all-encompassing as research and the Higher Education Innovation Act have defined it [12]. Since the 1980s various frameworks and definitions have been designed around the terms "transfer" and "third mission". Prominent examples are e.g. the "entrepreneurial universities" [13]. "triple helix" [14] or "mode 2" [15]. All of them incorporate the idea of universities interacting with the society. Universities interact with their environment and open up to the expectations and questions that come from society. Transfer therefore includes technology and knowledge transfer and innovation, scientific education and social commitment. According to the expert interviews these topics should be covered in the strategic management approach of universities and university management should set an example for their whole institution in not only communicating but also following these paradigms themselves.

To enable not only the digital transformation of transfer in universities, but to also give a recommendation on the management of transfer, a four-phases model was created (Fig. 3). This framework is an artefact of the Design Science Research and represents a previous development of a framework which was published earlier [6]. The framework shows the process of the digital transformation of transfer in four fundamental phases (Enabling, Development, Implementation and Sustaining & Systematic Change Phase), which universities can pass through. The axes of the model are described by a timeline and the hierarchy of meanings. The roof of the model consists of different initiation ways of the digital transformation. The incentive for digitalization can for example arise through external constraints, like changes in legislature, or internal from new strategic orientations. The arrow above the model indicates relevant management processes, which were gathered in this research through expert interviews and literature analysis. The topic of expectation management and incentives for transfer activities was pointed out by all experts in the interviews as being highly relevant. This will be further discussed in chapter 5 and is part of the stakeholder and expectation management in Fig. 3.

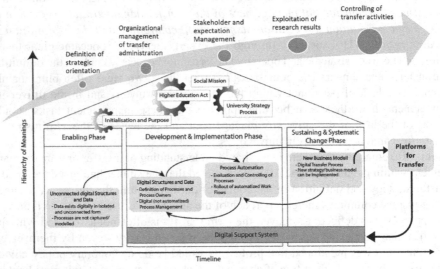

Fig. 3. Framework for Digital Transformation and Management Processes in Universities (further development of [1]).

On the right side of Fig. 3, platforms for transfer are indicated. Platforms and other forms of collaboration and alliances are a possible outcome of the digital transformation of transfer in universities. They can for example support in the implementation and usage of digital support systems, as tools and knowledge can be shared throughout the whole alliance. To support and enable the digital handling of transfer, a digital transfer platform, as a form of a digital support system, is not only advantageous, but also necessary. In the project TRIO a digital platform was developed and implemented and acts as a common mean to organize transfer activities in the alliance. Profiles of researchers from the universities within TRIO are systematically recorded on the platform, in order to bundle and offer them to the needs of business and society. This supports not only in the organization of research and transfer activities, but also helps to answer concrete cooperation requests from external partners. The main idea of the platform is that if one university cannot offer a scientific cooperation partner for the specific request from a company or a social institution, this requirement is recorded via the transfer platform and thus passed on to the other universities in the alliance. The possibility that one of the universities in the alliance will be able to provide support is therefore many times higher.

3.1 SWOT-Analysis of Transfer Management in Universities

A SWOT-analysis, which is an acronym for strengths, weaknesses, opportunities and threats-analysis, dates back to the 1960s when it was first developed by the Harvard Business School, but is still a relevant and meaningful tool for situation analysis nowadays, that can be used to obtain a systematic approach for decision-making [16]. The approach of a SWOT-analysis comprises the idea that internal (strengths, weaknesses) and external (opportunities, threats) factors influence the strategic approach of an organization. Although a SWOT-analysis also incorporates problems itself, like for example it is often hard to differentiate between an opportunity or a threat, it still gives a good starting point for decision-making [17].

In order to gain a broader understanding of the strategic approach of transfer management in universities and university alliances, a SWOT-analysis was conducted in the expert interviews. The results can be seen in Table 1.

3.2 Implications of the SWOT-Analysis

The idea of a SWOT-analysis is to maximize the benefits from strengths and opportunities and to minimize the losses from weaknesses and threats. For this purpose, the following combinations are specifically sought, after which it is asked which initiatives and measures can be derived from them:

- Strengths and opportunities: Which strengths match which opportunities? How can strengths be leveraged so that opportunity realization increases?
- Strengths and threats: Which threats can we counter with which strengths? How can existing strengths be used to avert the occurrence of certain threats?
- Weakness and opportunities: Where can opportunities arise from weaknesses? How can weaknesses be developed into strengths? Here, weaknesses are being eliminated in order to exploit new opportunities.
- Weakness and threats: Where are our weaknesses and how can we protect ourselves from threats? The idea is to develop defense strategies to prevent existing weaknesses from becoming the target of threats.

The results of this analysis are displayed in Table 2.

Concluding it can be said, that although there are weaknesses and threats for universities concerning the management of transfer and collaborating in a university alliance, there are major strengths and opportunities, which arise from this situation. The idea of being part in an alliance and forming a so-called platform with other universities, will be introduced and discussed in greater detail in the next section.

Table 1. Results from Expert Interviews for SWOT-analysis on Transfer Management and University Alliances.

Strengths	Weaknesses	Opportunities	Threats
• Established relationship with other universities in alliance and companies / institutions in the region • Through the alliance of universities, a broad portfolio of research and transfer topics can be offered • One-face-to-the-customer in the region of the alliance for external partners • Overcoming hurdles in cooperation between universities in alliance • Freedom of universities to conduct research and transfer how and with whom they like • Universities within the alliance are all rather small (up to 20.000 students), which indicates flat hierarchies and fast decision-making paths • University alliance supports the establishment of internal structures and procedures for transfer	• Still too few personnel in transfer departments • No common understanding of transfer within universities • Digitalization of processes and procedures in transfer is largely missing • On the professors' side, there are still too few personnel, as transfer often competes with teaching and research • University alliance creates needs for transfer in the region, but cannot address them because of a lack of resources • Since universities are a government agency and are bound by legal frameworks, which bundled with few staff can lead to long turnaround times. This makes it hard for universities to keep up with external competitors • Performing transfer is not attractive enough for professors (lack of support, appreciation etc.)	• University alliance is placed in an innovative region in Germany • Increasing efficiency through digitization • Support through university alliance • Research and transfer focus of university alliance on cutting-edge topics, like AI, sustainability or digital transformation • Dismantling the idea of universities as *ivory towers* and its prejudices in business and society to strengthen the connection between those • Higher Education Innovation Act in Germany forces universities to put greater focus on transfer	• Transfer activities and management can lead to work overload in the administrative departments • Transfer is often not seen as strategic task and sometimes just happens unplanned and undocumented • If universities do not continue to develop, they may be left behind and are no longer competitive in research and transfer • Competition between universities in alliance for projects, students, personnel and funding

4   Platforms for Collaboration and Digital Transformation

Before diving deeper into the topic of university alliances, a brief definition on 'platforms' need to be given, in order to create a common understanding. GAWER and CUSUMANO describe 'platforms' in the historical meaning of the term [18]. The word was already used in the Middle Ages, but the meaning has changed considerably since then. 'Platform' refers to an idea, a concept or a design that serves as a pattern or model.

Table 2. SWOT-Analysis on Transfer Management and University Alliances.

SWOT-Analysis		Internal Analysis	
		Strengths	Weaknesses
External Analysis	Opportunities	• University alliances can support in the implementation of digital transformation of transfer in the single universities, as all partners can learn from each other and share resources and best practices • Transfer projects, especially to and with the society, can dismantle the idea of universities being ivory towers, in which research is cut-off from the rest of the society • New Higher Education Innovation Act in Germany offers opportunities to enlarge and improve transfer structures and procedures in university administrations	• Support and sharing of resources to enable profound management of transfer • Implementation of common understanding of transfer can lead to a stronger anchoring and raising of awareness of the importance of transfer • Improvement of attractiveness of conducting transfer results in more transfer activities and higher quality of transfer activities, due to more personnel and resources
	Threats	• The establishment of university alliances offers the possibility to reconsider old processes and structures in transfer management. With sharing of best-practices throughout the alliance transfer can become a strategic competitive advantage for all alliance partners • Universities within an alliance are no longer mutually subject to a competitive situation with each other but can reach a state of the so-called "coopetition", in which they cooperate and compete at the same time • Strong research focus of the universities prevents them from being left behind	• To be able to persist within the university landscape in the future, universities need to intensive their transfer activities, as industry and society is highly depended on their research • Formation of committees with members of all alliance partners can support in all aspects of transfer management and therefore prevents universities from being left behind (e.g. through common definition of transfer, sharing of resources and best practices for digitalization)

The term was initially associated in academia primarily with the development of technologies and products, but has since been heavily studied in very different domains. Wheelwright and Clark have explored the term 'platform product' [19], Sawhney the term 'platform thinking' [20] and Kim and Kogut 'platform technologies' [21]. Platforms have also been studied in other domains. Pauli and Lin as well as Pauli and Marx have studied platforms in the Industrial Internet of Things [22, 23]. Zarnescu and Dunzer, on the other hand, investigate the platform ecosystem ontology while Lusch and Nambisan investigate from different perspectives value creation in platform ecosystems [24, 25]. De Reuver is dedicated to socio-technical perspectives, while Tilson investigates mainly technical perspectives [26, 27]. Rochet and Tirole focus on market-based perspectives of digital platforms and show that industrial economists subsequently adopted the term 'platform' to describe business models of companies which mediate transactions [28]. It is important to make a distinction between multi-sided markets and platforms. There is a difference between technology platforms and platforms that are mentioned in the literature to describe multi-sided markets. Many of these frequently cited examples are not platforms in the classical sense but describe multi-sided markets like shopping malls. The driving force behind multi-sided markets is the need to bring coordination between different groups of actors. The fixed point in this consideration is the architecture of the platform on which they coordinate. Platforms are characterized by the fact that components can be recycled and (thus) have the best cost-benefit ratios. Due to the direct and indirect network effects, winner-takes-it-all dynamics arise, which is why there are only very few or only one platform in each of many different business areas. Due to the chicken-and-egg problem, customer groups are usually unilaterally subsidized by platforms in order to increase their attractiveness for another customer group. This is what they have in common with multi-sided markets, which, however, have no fixed points and components are not reusable.

There are basically four different types of platforms, each of which creates value in a different way [18].

- Transaction platforms provide a technology, product or service that serves as a conduit or intermediary facilitating exchange between different actors.
- Innovation platforms are a technology, product, or service that serves as a foundation for other complementors to create value by developing complementary technologies, products or services.
- Integrated platforms combine the two previous platform types. Integrated platforms are used by companies that combine both, innovation platforms and matching platforms.
- Investment platforms consist of several companies that have developed a platform portfolio strategy and act as a holding company, active platform investor or both.

Platforms are not only digital, but the higher the degree of digitalization, the larger they become [18]. They often have physical elements integrated, but most institutions take advantage of digital connectivity through the internet, which holds billions of potential customers. With regard to platforms in the area of transfer in and out of university alliances, these findings mean above all:

- Platforms set standards: This is based on platform economies which create and combine trust, control and standardization.

- Platforms set conditions for cooperation: Platform ecosystems need platforms to be able to organize cooperation.

Transfer platforms can be assigned to the platform type 'transaction platforms' because they connect different actors, who were previously independent and organize cooperation. These platforms, such as the transfer platform TRIO, set standards that are valid across all users/universities. For example, a valid and documented transfer strategy across the alliance or identical and standardized contracts can be created and used. In this way also trust is built up within the users.

However, these theoretical classifications, as well as the consequences of the usage of platforms (like setting standards and conditions of cooperation), can be found in the application of these theories to the TRIO transfer platform, which can be shown by a statement of an interviewee:

"If a company needs help, it should get the best researcher to solve the specific need. By matching these actors via the platform, a connection function was created that mediates demand and supply in the best possible way. [...] Furthermore, the conditions of the cooperation are predefined and standardized." (Interview 9).

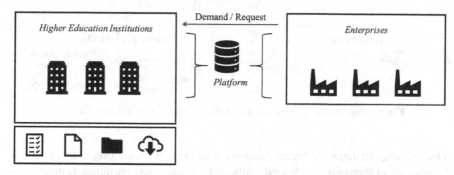

Fig. 4. Platform for transfer at Higher Education Institution.

Figure 4 shows that platforms provide an opportunity for Higher Education Institutions to organize themselves into alliances. Standards such as common contracts, common file formats, or coordinated processes and tasks can be set – this is illustrated by the common foundation across the alliance. This makes it possible for companies to submit a request to an alliance (via the platform) which is then connected to the partner best suited to the issue. The companies make a purely qualitative selection because other parameters such as the contract situation, data formats or methodologies are standardized within this network. This allows of course also for sharing knowledge and best practices and can act as a starting point for a common digitalization in the universities in an alliance.

5 Incentive Management as Part of Transfer Management

One major outcome of the expert interviews was that there are various possibilities for increasing the attractiveness of different transfer activities. The possibilities can be classified into three aspects: Finances, Expenditure and Public Relations. The triangle in Fig. 5 describes the interdependencies between these three aspects. According to the relevant literature and the expert interviews, focusing only on one aspect, which is often the expenditure, is not the best solution to make transfer and research more attractive. It is evident that a mixture of different attractiveness-enhancing measures should be chosen.

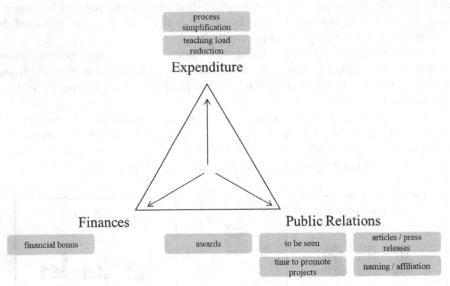

Fig. 5. Possibilities to increase the attractiveness of transfer activities.

One reward, often granted for carrying out transfer, is the reduction in teaching load or the granting of financial rewards. Nevertheless, the interview participants mentioned, several times independently of each other, that an increase in visibility of the researchers and their research would be more important. One example of the increase of visibility is the opportunity to present one's own projects and transfer activities at events. Also possible are affiliations or articles in the press - published within a university, but also beyond. In addition to increasing the visibility of projects or people, another often-mentioned way to increase transfer activities is to simplify processes in order to reduce the administrative effort. In addition to an increase in convenience, this also goes hand in hand with an increase in accessibility. Other soft factors, like the existence of an innovative or even entrepreneurial culture within a university, a profound strategic mission for transfer and an experience transfer department also have an positive impact on researchers to conduct transfer projects [29].

6   Conclusion and Outlook

Collaboration is and will never be a trivial task for all parties involved. Nevertheless, it incorporates many benefits and opportunities for all partners. As conducting transfer and its strategic management is still a frequent new task for universities, collaborations like platform-initiatives or alliances can offer a common ground for knowledge sharing and support.

This paper presented a structured approach to the management of transfer activities (**RQ1**) and the support through university alliances (**RQ2**). The target of this research was to identify relevant management tasks and processes, which influence and shape the transfer activities of universities and to put a greater importance of a strategic approach on transfer. The proposed framework acts as a means to enable the digitalization of transfer and offers possibilities, like a greater incentive management, for universities and was further enhanced by relevant management processes and the idea of platform collaborations (**RQ1**).

It was observed that platforms provide an organizational structure that can be used by university alliances to act jointly with external stakeholder groups. Through the platforms, standards can be set and a common transfer strategy can be established. In addition to a transfer strategy, common documents and a unified contract structure as well as a common database can be created commonly and shared throughout the alliance (**RQ2**).

Part of the future work will be a broader evaluation. As the current evaluation took only part within the dimensions of German universities, a more international approach should be taken into consideration to allow for a more generalist view of the model. Furthermore, a detailed investigation in the context of a case study in application of the theories of platforms and platform ecosystems to existing platforms in the area of transfer should be undertaken.

Acknowledgements. The transfer project "Transfer and Innovation East-Bavaria" is funded by the "Innovative University of Applied Sciences" East-Bavaria 2018 – 2022 (03IHS078D).

References

1. Doering, C., Reiche, F., Timinger, H.: Digital transformation of transfer in universities. In: Wijnhoven, F., van Sinderen, M. (eds.): ICE-B 2021: Proceedings of the 18th International Conference on E-Business 2021 : online streaming, July 7–9, 2021. SCITEPRESS - Science and Technology Publications Lda, Setúbal, pp. 109–115 (2021)
2. Bouncken, R.B., Gast, J., Kraus, S., Bogers, M.: Coopetition: a systematic review, synthesis, and future research directions. RMS **9**(3), 577–601 (2015)
3. Hamel, G., Doz, Y.L., Prahalad, C.K.: Collaborate with your competitors–and win. Harvard Bus. Rev. **67**, 133–139 (1989)
4. Schwab, K.: The fourth industrial revolution, First published in Great Britain by Port-folio. Portfolio Penguin, London, UK u. a. (2017)
5. Roessler, I.: Third Mission: Die ergänzende Mission neben Lehre und Forschung. wissenschaftsmanagement: 46–47 (2015)
6. Doering, C., Timinger, H.: Industry-oriented digital transformation in universities to facilitate knowledge transfer. In: International Joint Conference on Knowledge Discovery, Knowledge Engineering and Knowledge Management, pp. 212–218 (2020)
7. Hevner, A.R., Chatterjee, S.: Design research in information systems theory and practice. Integrated Series Inf. Syst. **22** (2010). https://doi.org/10.1007/978-1-4419-5653-8
8. Vom Brocke, J., Simons, A., Niehaves, B., et al.: Reconstructing the giant: On the importance of rigour in documenting the literature search process. ECIS 2009 Proceedings (2009)

9. Meuser, M., Nagel, U.: The expert interview and changes in knowledge production. In: Bogner, A., Littig, B., Menz, W. (eds): Interviewing Experts. Palgrave Macmillan UK, London, pp. 17–42 (2009)

10. Mayer, H.O.: Interview und schriftliche Befragung: Grundlagen und Methoden empirischer Sozialforschung, 6., überarb. Aufl. Sozialwissenschaften 10–2012. Oldenbourg, München (2013)

11. Aerts, G., Cauwelier, K., de Pape, S., et al.: An inside-out perspective on stakeholder management in university technology transfer offices. Technol. Forecast. Soc. Chang. **175**, 121291 (2022). https://doi.org/10.1016/j.techfore.2021.121291

12. Bavarian Ministry of Science and Art. Hochschulreform - Bayerisches Hochschulinnovationsgesetz (2021). https://www.stmwk.bayern.de/ministerium/hochschule-und-forschung/hochschulreform.html. Accessed 16 Feb 2021

13. Clark, B.R.: The Entrepreneurial University: Demand and Response. Tertiary Education and Management, pp. 5–16 (1998)

14. Etzkowitz, H., Leydesdorff, L.: The dynamics of innovation: from National Systems and "Mode 2" to a Triple Helix of university–industry–government relations (2000)

15. Gibbons, M., Limoges, C., Nowotny, H., et al.: The New Production of Knowledge: The Dynamics of Science and Research in Contemporary Societies (1994)

16. Kotler, P., Berger, R., Bickhoff, N.: The Quintessence of Strategic Management: What You Really Need to Know to Survive in Business. 2nd ed. 2016. Quintessence Series. Springer-Verlag, s.l. (2016). https://doi.org/10.1007/978-3-662-48490-6

17. Hill, T., Westbrook, R.: SWOT analysis: It's time for a product recall. Long Range Plan. **30**, 46–52 (1997). https://doi.org/10.1016/S0024-6301(96)00095-7

18. Gawer, A., Cusumano, M.A.: Industry platforms and ecosystem innovation. J. Prod. Innov. Manag. **31**, 417–433 (2014). https://doi.org/10.1111/jpim.12105

19. Wheelwright, S.C., Clark, K.B.: Creating Project Plans to Focus Product Development (1992)

20. Sawhney, M.S.: Leveraged high-variety strategies: from portfolio thinking to plat-form thinking. J. Acad. Mark Sci. **26**, 54–61 (1998). https://doi.org/10.1177/0092070398261006

21. Kim, D.-J., Kogut, B.: Technological platforms and diversification. Organization Science **7**, 283–301 (1996)

22. Pauli, T., Marx, E., Matzner, M.: Leveraging industrial IoT platform ecosystems: in-sights from the complementors' perspective. In: Proceedings of the 28th European Conference on Information Systems (ECIS) (2020)

23. Pauli, T., Lin, Y.: The Generativity of Industrial IoT Platforms: Beyond Predictive Maintenance? (2019)

24. Zarnescu, C., Dunzer, S.: A domain ontology for platform ecosystems. In: Ahlemann, F., Schütte, R., Stieglitz, S. (eds): Innovation Through Information Systems: Volume II: A Collection of Latest Research on Technology Issues, 1st ed. 2021, vol 47. Springer International Publishing; Imprint Springer, Cham, pp. 627–641 (2021). https://doi.org/10.1007/978-3-030-86797-3_41

25. Lusch, R.F., Nambisan, S.: Service innovation: a service-dominant logic perspective. MIS Q **39**, 155–175 (2015). https://doi.org/10.25300/MISQ/2015/39.1.07

26. de Reuver, M., Sørensen, C., Basole, R.C.: The digital platform: a research agenda. J. Inf. Technol. **33**, 124–135 (2018). https://doi.org/10.1057/s41265-016-0033-3

27. Tilson, D., Lyytinen, K., Sørensen, C.: Research commentary —digital infrastructures: the missing IS research agenda. Inf. Syst. Res. **21**, 748–759 (2010). https://doi.org/10.1287/isre. 1100.0318

28. Rochet, J.-C., Tirole, J.: Platform competition in two-sided markets. J. European Econ. Association **1**, 990–1029 (2003). https://doi.org/10.1162/154247603322493212

29. Friedmann, J., Silberman, J.: University technology transfer: do incentives, manage-ment, and location matter? J. Technol. Transfer **28**(1), 17–30 (2003). https://doi.org/10.1023/A:102 1674618658

A Method for Bottleneck Detection, Prediction, and Recommendation Using Process Mining Techniques

Jean Paul Sebastian Piest[1] ⓘ, Rob Henk Bemthuis[1(✉)] ⓘ, Jennifer Alice Cutinha[1] ⓘ,
Jeewanie Jayasinghe Arachchige[2] ⓘ, and Faiza Allah Bukhsh[1] ⓘ

[1] University of Twente, Drienerlolaan 5, 7522 Enschede, NB, The Netherlands
{j.p.s.piest,r.h.bemthuis}@utwente.nl
[2] University of Ruhuna, Matara 81000, Sri Lanka

Abstract. Bottlenecks arise in many processes, often negatively impacting performance. Process mining can facilitate bottleneck analysis, but research has primarily focused on bottleneck detection and resolution, with limited attention given to the prediction of bottlenecks and recommendations for improving process performance. As a result, operational support for bottleneck resolution is often partially or not realized. The aim of this paper is to propose a method for Bottleneck Detection, Prediction, and Recommendation (BDPR) using process mining techniques to achieve operational support. A design science research methodology is adopted to design, develop, and demonstrate the BDPR method. A systematic literature review and a developed classification model provide theoretical support for the BDPR method and offer scholarly in the field of process mining a starting point for research. The BDPR method extends the utility of the classification model and aims to provide guidance to scholars and practitioners for assessing, selecting, evaluating, and implementing process mining techniques to realize operational support. A case study at a logistics service provider demonstrates the use of the proposed BDPR method.

Keywords: Bottlenecks · Detection · Prediction · Recommendation · Process mining · Logistics

1 Introduction

This paper extends earlier work related to bottleneck classification using process mining [7] and interoperability challenges [23]. Bottlenecks can occur in many processes and disrupt their functioning. The effects vary per process and bottleneck, but in general bottlenecks tend to have a negative impact on process performance, especially as they may cause the depletion of valuable resources. Bottlenecks require action to mitigate their negative impact. To this end, process mining can support the analysis (e.g., detection and prediction) of bottlenecks and offer solutions for bottleneck resolution [2]. Bottlenecks can be quantified and visualized by, e.g., replaying the event log data [1].

Process mining enables process discovery from event logs and offers techniques for conformance checking and process enhancement [1]. Earlier work reveals that bottleneck analysis is applied in various domains, but mainly focused on bottleneck detection

ⓒ The Author(s), under exclusive license to Springer Nature Switzerland AG 2023
P. Samarati et al. (Eds.): ICETE 2021, CCIS 1795, pp. 118–136, 2023.
https://doi.org/10.1007/978-3-031-36840-0_7

[7] (see Sect. 4). Limited attention is given to the prediction of bottlenecks and recommendations to improve process performance. Furthermore, achieving operational support in inter-organizational processes, involving different actors and information systems, requires aggregation and harmonization of event data. Consequently, interoperability challenges can arise and operational support for bottleneck resolution may be partially or not realized at all. Process mining provides a wealth of techniques for applying bottleneck analysis, which is yet to be further developed and exploited.

Extending earlier and related work, this research paper aims to introduce, demonstrate and discuss both a theoretical and practical approach and method for Bottleneck Detection, Prediction, and Recommendation (hereafter called BDPR) using process mining techniques to achieve operational support.

The Design Science Research Methodology (DSRM) of Peffers et al. [22] is adopted to design, develop, demonstrate, and validate a classification model and the BDPR method in two iterations using its iterative development process. Both contributions are based on a Systematic Literature Review (SLR) using the methodology and guidelines of Kitchenham [14] and Kitchenham et al. [15]. In the first design iteration, the classification model is developed and presented in earlier work [7]. This classification model aims to aid scholars in assessing the state-of-the-art of BDPR-related literature and identifying future research directions. Case-based research and technical action research are conducted to demonstrate the use of the classification model. The second design iteration, which is communicated through the present paper, extends the utility of the classification model by proposing a BDPR method that practitioners can use to achieve operational support. We demonstrate the BDPR method presented in this paper through case study research and technical action research at a Logistics Service Provider (LSP). The PM^2 framework by van Ech et al. [9] has been used to guide the validation as part of the DSRM.

This section established the context, problem statement, and objective of this paper. The remainder of this paper is structured as follows. Section 2 discusses related work. Section 3 is concerned with the methodological approach. Section 4 presents the SLR and corresponding findings. Section 5 describes the BDPR method for achieving operational support and the LSP case study demonstration. Section 6 discusses the results and findings. Section 7 concludes the paper and outlines future work.

2   Related and Earlier Work

This section discusses related and earlier work regarding BDPR using process mining techniques. Subsection 2.1 introduces bottlenecks and our classification model to achieve operational support. Subsequently, Subsect. 2.2 describes process mining applications in various industries related to bottlenecks. Finally, Subsect. 2.3 summarizes earlier work regarding interoperability challenges.

2.1   Bottleneck Classification

Multiple definitions exist to describe bottlenecks. Given the fact that processes and their context vary between organizations and industries, it is difficult to generalize bottlenecks and their effects. Roser et al. [26] emphasize the influence and significance of bottlenecks regarding the throughput as part of a larger system. Bottlenecks can be linked to constraints that limit a system to achieve the desired process performance goals [11]. Based on earlier work, we define a bottleneck as a subprocess within a system that hinders the entire process [7]. Earlier work also proposes a classification model to assess the state-of-the-art of bottleneck analysis and resolution using process mining techniques [7]. We build further on this work and use their categorization in three phases (i.e., detect, predict, and recommend) as a classification means.

2.2 Process Mining

The process mining discipline attempts to bridge the gap between data mining and process modeling [2]. In process mining, event logs originating from information systems are the starting point to extract knowledge from event data. Consequently, process mining aims to utilize this data by applying process mining techniques, such as process discovery, conformance checking, and process enhancement [2].

A systematic mapping study by dos Santos Garcia et al. [28] illustrates the variety of process mining techniques and applications per domain including algorithms used. Jacobi et al. [12] propose a maturity model for applying process mining in supply chains, especially in the transport and logistic domain. Some related work exists about bottleneck analysis using process mining, however, the majority of research papers contain specific case studies (e.g., [29, 36]). To our knowledge, no method exists to classify bottlenecks and provide insights into operational support using process mining techniques.

2.3 Interoperability Challenges

Earlier work addresses challenges related to process mining and interoperability [23]. Data loss and quality issues can arise when extracting and aggregating event data from multiple data sources and actors. Existing approaches focus on dealing with noisy data instead of solving the underlying interoperability issues [23]. To this end, they introduce an approach for process mining based on the Open Trip Model (OTM), which comprises a standardized data model used to exchange logistic trip data. An informal mapping study evaluated and demonstrated the use of the OTM for process mining applications. In the present paper, we connect to future research directions posed in that paper. More specifically, we consider a baseline measurement for a comparison-based study utilizing an LSP case study demonstration. This case study is also chosen because (1) bottlenecks are omnipresent in logistics processes, causing hurdles that waste lead time, energy, costs, etc., which links to our bottleneck classification means (see Subsect. 2.2), (2) the data set concerns real-life data, which enhances this research's validity, and (3) earlier work [23] demonstrated the feasibility regarding applying process mining techniques.

3 Methodology

This section discusses the methodological approach used. Subsection 3.1 provides an overview of the DSRM and how it is applied. Subsection 3.2 describes the SLR process. Subsection 3.3 discusses the application of the PM^2 methodology for case study research.

3.1   DSRM: Overview and Application

The established DSRM by Peffers et al. (2007) [22] is adopted to conduct research, develop the classification model, and apply the BDPR method in two design iterations. Figure 1 presents how the DSRM and its steps are applied.

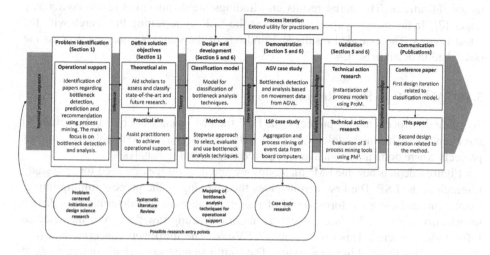

Fig. 1. Research methodology, adapted based on Peffers et al. [22].

The first design iteration relates to the design and development of the classification model for bottleneck analysis techniques, as discussed in earlier work [7]. The second design iteration concerns the BDPR method proposed in the present work, aiming to support practitioners in selecting, evaluating, and using bottleneck analysis techniques to achieve operational support.

The first design iteration identified the problem and defined solution objectives for the artifacts to be designed and developed. An SLR provided the theoretical foundation for the classification model. The three phases of operational support, as discussed by [2], were used to design a classification model and map bottleneck analysis techniques. The developed classification model was demonstrated using case study research with a process mining tool (ProM). The application of the DSRM is documented and communicated through a published paper [7].

The second design iteration is based on a process iteration prescribed by the DSRM. The main aim of this second design iteration is to extend the utility of the classification model for practical use in a real-life case study. This paper presents additional results and findings by updating the previous SLR with new research and proposing a method to achieve operational support for practitioners. The method is demonstrated in a case study with operational conditions of practice. Using a technical action research-based approach, three process mining tools (Apromore, Disco, and ProM) are implemented and compared. The application of the DSRM is documented and communicated in this paper.

3.2   SLR Methodology and Revision

The guidelines for performing an SLR as proposed by Kitchenham [14] and Kitchenham et al. [15] are used to identify papers regarding bottleneck detection, prediction, and recommendation. The initial SLR as conducted by Bemthuis et al. [7] resulted in 111 articles on Scopus and 67 articles on Web of Science. Their final sample set contained 44 articles. The initial results and findings are documented in the conference paper [7]. In the present paper, we updated the SLR by repeating the search with the latest finding. The extended results and findings of the search and review process are described in detail in Sect. 4.

3.3   PM^2 for Case Study Research

To guide the process mining project at the LSP, the PM^2 framework by van Ech et al. [9] has been used. This methodology supports iterative analysis and is suitable for complex projects where domain knowledge is required throughout the analysis.

   Figure 2 depicts how the PM^2 methodology and its six stages are used for case study research at the LSP. The first step involves the planning of the process mining implementation, including the formulation of research questions and determining relevant information systems. The second step is about extracting raw data from the selected information systems. This resulted in a CSV-file. The third step concerns data processing, which resulted in an event log. The fourth step covers mining and analysis of the event log. We considered process discovery, conformance checking, and bottleneck analysis. The fifth step evaluates the compliance of the process model and its performance. Based on a comparison of three process mining tools and iterations with stakeholders, steps three to five are repeated several times. The sixth step evaluates the use of process mining for operational support. This involves discussing the results, ideas for improvement, and recommendations. The results and findings of the case study are presented in Sect. 6.

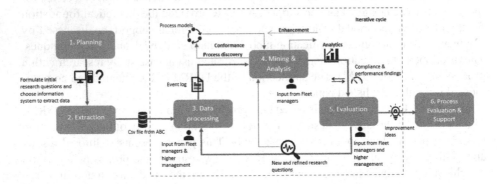

Fig. 2. An adapted version of the PM^2 framework by van Ech et al. [9].

4 Literature Review

In this section, we present the results and findings of the SLR. Subsection 4.1 describes the methodology used to find relevant papers. Subsequently, Subsect. 4.2 reports on the search results and findings of the revised search.

4.1 SLR Method

We used the SLR procedure as described in earlier work [7] and updated the results accordingly. After executing the same search string on the 25th of January 2022, the electronic search engine Scopus yielded 144 results and Web of Science yielded 90 results. Compared to the SLR conducted in 2020, this already shows an increase in the number of papers (back then, Scopus yielded 111 papers and Web of Science yielded 67 papers).

When narrowing down the literature results to the years 2020, 2021, and 2022, Scopus yielded 35 papers and Web of Science yielded 15. Similar to [7], we include only papers that are in English and we exclude papers based on screening of title, abstract and keywords as well as duplicates. As an inclusion criterion, the paper should address a process mining-related topic. All papers were screened by two authors and in case of a conflict, a third author was included to reach a consensus. In addition, we include additional papers found in the year 2020 following the previous SLR [7]. This resulted in a sample set of 37 papers.

Identical to the steps described in [7], we assessed the articles based on a full-text screening. Two authors independently assessed each paper based on its relevance by assigning it a score:

- A score of 0: the document does not mention concepts related to bottleneck analysis using process mining.
- A score of 1: the document describes concepts related to bottleneck analysis using process mining. As concept studies we considered perspective or position studies (e.g., mentioning new ideas/directions) or ongoing studies (e.g., preliminary findings that require more exhaustive validation).
- A score of 2: the document describes a complete study related to bottleneck analysis using process mining. As a complete study we refer to validated research (e.g., case study research).

Likewise, when the independent scores were conflicting, a third author was involved to reach a consensus. Papers evaluated with a 0 (8 papers) were removed from the paper sample, leaving a final set of 29 articles. Next, the findings are discussed.

4.2 Results

Similar to the work presented in [7], all the papers were assessed on whether bottleneck detection, prediction, and/or recommendation techniques were carried out. Papers that address bottleneck detection techniques primarily identify bottleneck. Articles that cover the prediction of bottlenecks consider when or that a bottleneck will happen in the future. When a paper suggests that a particular action should be carried out to manage (e.g., mitigate) a bottleneck we consider that as a recommendation technique. An example is to change an organizational resource (e.g., someone else will carry out an activity) or the sequence of activities. Assessment of all papers was done by two authors and in the case no consensus was reached, a third one was involved.

We first address literature findings for the years 2020, 2021, and 2022 in more detail, after which we address yearly trends concerning literature results (complementary to [7]). Table 1 shows the results after classifying the papers on maturity and bottleneck technique. Only 11 unique papers were identified as complete studies related to bottleneck analysis using process mining. Most of the papers only describe concepts related to bottleneck analysis. The vast majority of them focus solely on detecting bottlenecks in processes. Regarding findings of previous years, we kindly refer the interested reader to the work described in [7].

Table 1. Papers addressing concepts or a complete study related to bottlenecks.

Year	Concept papers (score = 1)			Complete papers (score = 2)		
	Detect	Predict	Recommend	Detect	Predict	Recommend
2020	[3,6,10,17,18,31,34,37,39]	[37]	[6,18,27]	[5,16,27,40]	[35]	n/a
2021	[4,21,24,25,30,32,33]	n/a	[33]	[7,13,19,20,38,41]	[7]	[19]
2022	[8]	n/a	n/a	n/a	n/a	n/a

Figures 3, 4, and 5 show the yearly numbers of articles published addressing respectively bottleneck detection, prediction, and recommendation techniques.

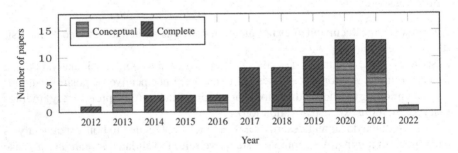

Fig. 3. Number of papers including bottleneck detection techniques.

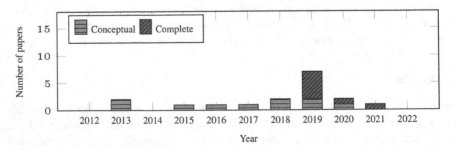

Fig. 4. Number of papers including bottleneck prediction techniques.

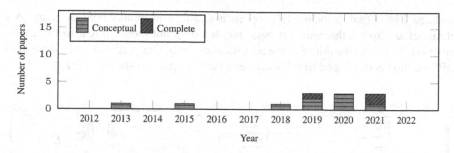

Fig. 5. Number of papers including bottleneck recommendation techniques.

The results presented in [7] were used to obtain the numbers for the years 2012–2019. In addition to the findings previously addressed (see [7]), an influx of papers is observed in the years 2020 and 2021, covering mainly detection techniques. Only a small proportion addresses bottleneck prediction techniques (3 unique articles) and recommendation techniques (5 unique articles) in the years 2020–2021. Although we only complemented our previous literature study with recent findings of a few years, we may draw a similar conclusion that prediction and recommendation techniques using process mining are marginally addressed in literature compared to bottleneck detection techniques using process mining.

5 Method for Achieving Operational Support

This section introduces the proposed BDPR method for achieving operational support and a case study demonstration at the LSP. Subsection 5.1 discusses the application of the classification model. Subsection 5.2 presents the BDPR method for achieving operational support. Finally, Subsect. 5.3 presents the results and findings of the LSP case study.

5.1 Applying the Classification Model

In earlier work, the application of the classification model is described as a three-step approach [7]. The first step identifies the bottleneck(s) in a process. This step relates to the detection of bottlenecks and provides the foundation for bottleneck analysis and possible improvement paths for resolving bottlenecks and achieving operational support. The second step concerns the prediction of bottlenecks, which is defined as the process of estimating whether a bottleneck will occur in the future, including also the anticipated effect. The third step relates to the recommendations and involves suggesting measures. This can include monitoring or managing the bottleneck (e.g., mitigating), or suggesting actions to resolve bottlenecks.

5.2 Extending the Classification Model to a Method for BDPR

The developed classification model [7] aims to aid scholars in determining the state-of-the-art literature regarding bottleneck analysis techniques and determine future research directions. The classification model supports assessing how mature bottleneck analysis techniques are from a theoretical perspective, but does not focus on real-world implementation. To extend the utility of the classification model for practitioners, a three-step BDPR method is developed to achieve operational support, as shown in Fig. 6.

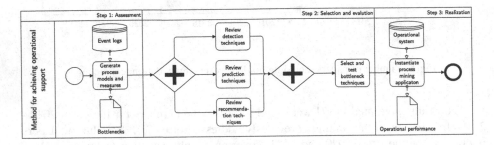

Fig. 6. BDPR method for achieving operational support.

In the next part, the application of the BDPR method is discussed. The BDPR method is designed to be methodology-independent and technology-agnostic. Thus, practitioners should be able to incorporate the BDPR method in their way of working and tool of choice. Furthermore, the presence of a process mining project (e.g., scope, skilled team, budget, tool) and event logs are assumed to be present.

Step 1: Assessment. The first step is an assessment of required and available event logs, (business) process models, and known or potential bottlenecks (e.g., through discussions with stakeholders). Event logs are used to generate process models using process discovery and/or modeling (e.g., BPMN). Inspecting the event logs and (business) process model artifacts results in a list of (candidate) bottlenecks. This list can be complemented with known bottlenecks that are not represented in the event logs and (business) process model artifacts.

Step 2: Selection and Evaluation. The next step is to select and evaluate process mining techniques for BDPR. Based on the classification model, process mining techniques can be selected and evaluated before actual implementation and use in an operational environment. Table 2 presents a overview of candidate process mining techniques per phase. This list is based on a selection of papers from the conducted SLR.

Based on the goal(s) of the process mining project, this overview can be used as a starting point to select relevant process mining techniques for achieving operational support and evaluate the feasibility of specific techniques and tools to detect bottlenecks, and predict their occurrence and recommend actions. The overview presents an initial list of candidate process mining techniques that can be considered to test and implement. It should be noted that each technique results in specific requirements and performance measures. Established process mining methodologies and business process management frameworks can support adequate selection and evaluation of techniques and test/compare features of process mining tools. From a practical perspective, an iterative development process can be applied. This will be demonstrated in the LSP case study in the next subsection.

Table 2. An overview of candidate process mining techniques per phase.

Phase	Application area	Candidate process mining technique	Source
Detect	Healthcare	Beta algorithm framework	[18]
	Online Education	Dotted chart analysis algorithm, Fuzzy Miner algorithm, and Social network miner	[4]
	Manufacturing	Visual analytics approach that facilitates interpretability and explainability of process models and bottlenecks	[13]
	Automotive industry	Inductive miner and Fuzzy miner with statistical evaluation measures	[31]
	Bank and real state	Fuzzy model algorithm	[40]
Predict	Services company	Gradual and Recurrent Adaptive Hoeffding Option Forest (GRAHOF) approach	[35]
	Logistics	Inductive miner	[7]
Recommend	Building construction	Inductive miner and Fuzzy miner	[19]

Step 3: Realization. After the selection and evaluation of process mining techniques, operational support can be realized by instantiation and systems integration. Depending on the process characteristics, dynamics, and desired level of decision support, this requires interoperability to connect one or multiple information systems. Depending on the selected process mining techniques and tool support, an artifact can be designed and developed to achieve operational support. This can be an analytical application based on batch processing, but might also be a real-time exception handling service or a recommender system.

5.3   LSP Case Study

In this subsection, the results of case study research at an LSP are presented based on the PM^2 methodology as introduced in Subsect. 3.3. In this case study, shipment and board computer event data were aggregated for process mining and BDPR.

Step 1: Planning. In the planning stage, the project scope was defined, planned, and executed within a timeframe of 10 weeks and in collaboration with different stakeholders at the LSP. The case study involves monitoring the activities of drivers, which is a major part of the fleet management process. Only fleet managers know the whereabouts of drivers. At the LSP, the drivers and fleet managers are located in four different countries - the Netherlands (NL), Germany (D), the Czech Republic (CZ), and Poland (PL). The management of the LSP aims to obtain an aggregated view of drivers' activities, evaluate drivers' performance, and compare performance across the four countries. The BDPR method was applied to detect bottlenecks and gain insights for process improvements.

Step 2: Extraction. In the extraction stage, the required data was extracted by a business intelligence expert at the LSP. The obtained CSV-file contained a total of 359,604 events relating to shipments carried out in a period of four months. An illustration of the structure of the source file is depicted in Table 3. In process mining terms, the ShipmentID, Activity, Start/End, DriverID represent respectively the case identifier, event, timestamp, and resource.

Table 3. Excerpt of the source data set.

ShipmentID	Activity	Start	End	DriverID	CorrectionUser
SHP1234	Arrival loading	7/4/2018	7/4/2018	345	Switt
SHP4536	Refueling	8:51:00	13:31:00	543	Rdul
SHP1234	Loading	7/15/2018	7/15/2018	345	Switt

Step 3: Data Processing. In the data processing stage, the CSV-file was validated and transformed to create an event log. For several events in the original file, the ShipmentID was null. These events were filtered out, reducing the event log to 153,878 events (roughly 45% of the original data set). Based on the input of fleet managers and management, a set of 6 mandatory activities was determined to form an event trace. Any shipment that did not contain these activities would impose missing information. This further reduced the event log to 43,544 events (12% of the data set). Then, the data set was divided into four subsets, representing the 4 countries for performance and bottleneck analysis.

Step 4: Mining and Analysis. In the mining and analysis stage, process mining techniques are applied using process mining tools. The first dimension in process mining is aimed at process discovery and results in process models and case statistics. Figure 7 shows a selection of process models for Poland generated by the process mining tools Disco (top left), Apromore (bottom left), and ProM (right), using the following process mining algorithms: Heuristics Miner, Inductive Miner, Fodina, ILP Miner, and the Alpha algorithm. Similar models are created for other countries. Table 4 summarizes the case statistics per country.

Table 4. Case Statistics per country.

Statistics	NL	D	CZ	PL
Number of cases or shipments	67	258	512	927
Total number of events	1,006	6,358	10,388	21,398
Total number of activities	12	12	12	12

Based on the mined event logs, it can be observed that each country has a total of 12 activities including connect, arrival loading, loading, waiting, traffic jam, refueling, driving, rest, arrival unloading, unloading, standstill, and disconnect. These can reveal the effects of bottlenecks, e.g. shipment delays as a result of a traffic jam. Arrival loading/arrival unloading is the time spent at the loading/unloading location but does not include actual loading/unloading. The waiting time can be indicated by the driver.

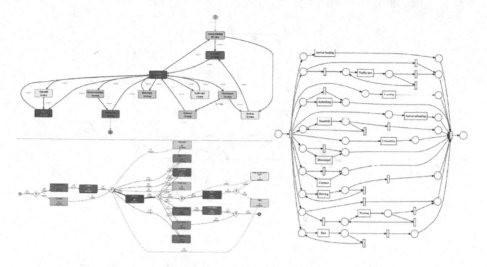

Fig. 7. Discovered process models for Poland (illustrative).

Standstill indicates periods of vehicle inactivity. Both waiting time and standstill can be the result of a bottleneck. Rest refers to the rest periods according to the EU regulation that the driver is obligated to take in between continuous driving and at the end of work. Sometimes, the logistics activities are carried out by two or more drivers. These activities are represented by connected and disconnected events. Activities are linked to shipments and resources: drivers, fleet planners, trucks, and trailers.

The second dimension of process mining is conformance checking, where a predefined process model is compared to the event log to check if the modeled behavior reflects the behavior of the event log. We created a BPMN model in Apromore in Apromore to check the flow of logistics activities in the Netherlands, as shown in Fig. 8.

To perform conformance checking, the ProM plugin 'replay log on Petri net' was used to determine the fitness. Fitness is a quality dimension that determines how well the event log can be replayed on the model. This revealed a rather low fitness metric of 0.39. During the development and testing of process mining models some activities that initially seem to be sequential turned out to be non-sequential in the control-flow perspective.

Table 5. Advised duration and actual duration of logistics activities per country.

Activity	Advised duration	NL	D	CZ	PL
Arrival loading	5 mins	45 mins	14 mins	21 mins	23 mins
Loading	45 mins	4 mins	39 mins	43.5 mins	41 mins
Arrival unloading	5 mins	55 mins	19 mins	21 mins	19 mins
Unloading	45 mins	3 mins	39 mins	36.5 mins	39 mins
Refueling	10 mins	15 mins	15 mins	45 mins	15 mins
Waiting	5 mins	35 mins	7 mins	18 mins	10 mins

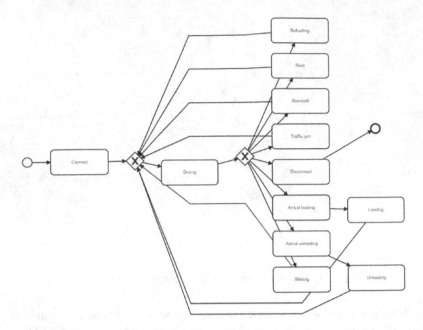

Fig. 8. Created BPMN model for conformance checking.

The performance of drivers per country can be measured by comparing the amount of time that drivers take to perform logistics activities. The LSP has determined a set of advised times for logistic activities. Table 5 shows the advised times as well as the median duration of the main logistics activities performed by drivers per country.

Another approach is to use the compliance checking plugins in ProM 6, for example, the 'elicit compliance rule and configure compliance rule' plugins. This can determine the number of cases where the drivers did not meet the requirements mentioned in Table 3. However, these plugins were still in the experimental phase and have led to errors that (with assistance on the ProM forum) could not be resolved.

The third dimension of process mining is model enhancement. Enhancements can be made for prediction and/or recommendation. Due to limited tool support and a large amount of missing data and results, no model enhancements were made.

Step 5: Evaluation. In the evaluation stage, the intermediate results were shown to various stakeholders at the LSP through bi-weekly meetings ranging from 30–60 min. The feedback resulted in incremental refinement and improvement of the produced process models. Furthermore, the three process mining tools were tested based on the four data sets. The final results were validated and discussed with three stakeholders. Table 6 contains their feedback.

Step 6: Process Improvement and Support. In the process improvement and support stage, the process mining project was evaluated, and recommendations were given to the LSP. The research project was able to provide the stakeholders at the LSP insight into how process mining techniques can be utilized to visualize and analyze driver behavior, measure the performance of operational processes and support fleet management

Table 6. Feedback received from stakeholders at LSP.

Stakeholder	Feedback
Quality manager	A loading activity should follow an arrival loading activity. The difference in the number of arrival loading and loading activities could indicate data loss or lack of board computer reporting or recording
Fleet manager Poland	Longer durations for arrival loading and arrival unloading could indicate that, in reality, a loading or unloading event must have taken place
Group supervisor	There is no centralized standard of what should and should not be reported on the board computer by the driver. So, countries perform tasks differently

processes. Additionally, the project contributed to a better understanding of how to practically implement process mining techniques and mining and intruiges the curiousity to apply process mining to other business functions as well. The main issues that restrain performance and bottleneck analysis are related to data recording, storage, and interoperability of supporting information systems. Furthermore, drivers are trained to record events on the board computer so that fleet managers can monitor their whereabouts. Due to the lack of a centralized standard procedure for what should and should not be recorded, this is done differently across countries. The produced BPMN and mined process models provide a starting point for developing such a standard procedure. Additionally, drivers and fleet managers need to be made aware of the importance of recording data and the underlying information systems need to be able to store data accordingly.

6 Discussion

In line with the findings of the previously conducted SLR, the updated SLR discussed in the present paper indicates that the use of process mining techniques for detecting bottlenecks has reached a relative mature stage. Furthermore, it indicates that most papers deal with detecting bottlenecks, while limited research is carrried out concerning the prediction and recommendation phases. The classification model developed in earlier work addressed this limitation by providing a theoretical demonstration of how bottleneck analysis can be applied to detect, predict, and recommend bottlenecks. The LSP case study introduced in the present paper complements the previous theoretical demonstration with a real-life case study, addressing, enhancing the validation of the previously proposed model.

In this paper, the classification model is extended to a BDPR method to further assist practitioners in achieving operational support which is demonstrated in the LSP case study. In addition to addressing bottlenecks, the results from this case study also highlight interoperability challenges of process mining in practice related to, e.g., poor data quality, which data quality which resonates with findings from existing studies. Consequently, various tools and algorithms have been built into process mining tools to eliminate the effect of noisy data and determine the actual control-flow of a process. However, the LSP case study investigates a process whose activities are not sequential, and therefore, tries to focus on the performance perspective rather than the control-flow perspective. Related work (e.g., [23]) shows that existing studies focus on increasing the accuracy of process mining techniques rather than addressing the causes of noisy data. In this study, an experimental approach is applied to address some interoperability issues by positioning process mining on top of a unified data model (i.e., OTM).

It is important to note that the process mining tools implemented in this case study deal, to a limited degree, with prediction and recommendation. Therefore, a potential avenue for research could be investigating the use of process mining tools to carry out these phases in a more sophisticated manner. In this paper, several process mining tools were used in the case study, namely Disco, Apromore, and ProM 6. For process discovery, Disco's interface was perceived as intuitive and easy to understand, especially by business professionals at LSP. Apromore is comparable to Disco, however, it has a feature to also view models in BPMN. An attempt was also made to produce models in ProM 6 using the inductive miner. However, no 'flow' could be identified. The PM^2 methodology has proven to be useful in the stepwise execution of the process mining project.

7 Conclusion and Future Work

This section first summarizes the main results and implications of this study. Next, we discuss the significance of the study, followed by addressing limitations. Lastly, we outline directions for future work.

7.1 Main Results and Findings

Building on previous research, this paper presents an updated overview of literature related to BDPR using process mining techniques. An SLR was previously conducted to identify papers and categorize them according to bottleneck "maturity" phases. This led to the development of a classification model with three phases: detect, predict, and recommend. The SLR has been repeated and serves as the theoretical foundation for further development of the classification model. In the present paper, a BDPR method is introduced and discussed for achieving operational support. The use of the proposed method is demonstrated through an LSP case study, using the PM^2 methodology. The LSP case study concerned aggregated shipment and board computer event data.

Event data originating from the board computers provides a rich source for conducting process mining, but it requires data aggregation from multiple sources to be linked to higher-order activities. Process discovery resulted in the visualization and comparison of the 12 main activities and behaviors of drivers and fleet planners in 4 countries, revealing different bottlenecks and process mining-related challenges. For example, missing data significantly affects performance, as the results of the data reflect only 12% of reality, resulting in a fitness metric of 0.39. These two main issues, along with differences in reporting behavior constrained further analysis in this case study, including compliance checking and model enhancements. Furthermore, the LSP case study revealed that all three of the implemented process mining tools have limited capabilities for bottleneck prediction and recommendation.

7.2 Implications for Process Mining Discipline

The BDPR method and underlying classification model provide a starting point for scholars persuing to work on process mining projects. The SLR provides insight into the state-of-the-art literature related to BDPR using process mining techniques. The vast majority of the papers focus on detecting bottlenecks, while limited research has been conducted on predicting and recommending activities.

The BDPR method aims to extend the classification model for practitioners. The demonstrations illustrate how the identified and classified process mining techniques can be applied in practice. However, it is important to note that the process mining tools used in this case study only deal with bottleneck prediction and recommendation to a limited extent. Therefore, a direction for further research could develop process mining tools that support bottleneck prediction and recommendation techniques.

7.3 Significance of the Study

The main contribution of this paper is a BDPR method that uses process mining techniques to achieve operational support. An updated SLR confirms that the focus of state-of-the-art literature regarding BDPR is on detection and analysis rather than prediction and recommendation. The case study, which involves three process mining tools, also revealed limited support for prediction and recommendation. The demonstration provides direction on how bottlenecks can be detected and predicted, as well as what the next steps could be to mitigate their impact or prevent their occurrence. Despite its exploratory nature, this study offers insight into how bottlenecks could be classified, the maturity of related literature, and potential directions for further research.

7.4 Limitations of the Study

There are limitations to this research. One limitation is that the BDPR method was demonstrated and validated using a single-case mechanism experiment. In earlier work [7], an initial demonstration illustrated how a bottleneck classification model can be applied, but that research provided limited depth in terms of actual implementation. In constrast, the LSP case study was based on real-life data, but data quality issues limited validation. Ideally, the BDPR method would be tested in cases with similar conditions to compare and contrast the findings.

7.5 Future Work

In current industrial research, the logistics domain is being explored to map use cases for process mining and further validate the BDPR method. Further research can also be conducted by implementing the OTM for a comparison study. Additionally, domain mapping could be applied to assess the BDPR method for other use cases beyond the logistics domain.

A possible direction for future research, resulting from our literature study, is to focus more on prediction and making recommendations on bottlenecks using process mining. For example, a taxonomy could be developed to classify process mining techniques and provide detailed guidance for researchers and practitioners. Research could also focus on assessing process mining tools to support practitioners in applying the BDPR method and related process mining techniques.

Acknowledgements. This research is funded by the Dutch Research Council (NWO) (grant 628.009.015, project DataRel), and the Dutch Institute for National Advanced Logistics (DINA-LOG) (grant nr. 2018-2-169 TKI, project ICCOS). The authors would also like to thank Niels van Slooten for his contribution to this work.

References

1. van der Aalst, W.M.P.: Process mining in the large: a tutorial. In: Zimányi, E. (ed.) eBISS 2013. LNBIP, vol. 172, pp. 33–76. Springer, Cham (2014). https://doi.org/10.1007/978-3-319-05461-2_2
2. van der Aalst, W.M.P.: Process mining: data science in action. Springer (2016). https://doi.org/10.1007/978-3-662-49851-4
3. Agostinelli, S., Covino, F., D'Agnese, G., De Crea, C., Leotta, F., Marrella, A.: Supporting governance in healthcare through process mining: a case study. IEEE Access **8**, 186012–186025 (2020). https://doi.org/10.1109/ACCESS.2020.3030318
4. Arpasat, P., Premchaiswadi, N., Porouhan, P., Premchaiswadi, W.: Applying process mining to analyze the behavior of learners in online courses. Int. J. Inf. Educ. Technol. **11**(10) (2021). https://doi.org/10.18178/ijiet.2021.11.10.1547
5. Badakhshan, P., Alibabaei, A.: Using process mining for process analysis improvement in pre-hospital emergency. In: Baghdadi, Y., Harfouche, A., Musso, M. (eds.) ICT for an Inclusive World. LNISO, vol. 35, pp. 567–580. Springer, Cham (2020). https://doi.org/10.1007/978-3-030-34269-2_39
6. Bemthuis, R., Mes, M., Iacob, M.E., Havinga, P.: Using agent-based simulation for emergent behavior detection in cyber-physical systems. In: Proceedings of the 2020 Winter Simulation Conference, pp. 230–241. IEEE (2020). https://doi.org/10.1109/WSC48552.2020.9383956
7. Bemthuis, R.H., van Slooten, N., Arachchige, J.J., Piest, J.P.S., Bukhsh, F.A.: A classification of process mining bottleneck analysis techniques for operational support. In: Proceedings of the 18th International Conference on e-Business, pp. 127–135 (2021)
8. Bloemen, V., van Zelst, S., van der Aalst, W., van Dongen, B., van de Pol, J.: Aligning observed and modelled behaviour by maximizing synchronous moves and using milestones. Inf. Syst. **103**, 101456 (2022). https://doi.org/10.1016/j.is.2019.101456
9. van Eck, M.L., Lu, X., Leemans, S.J.J., van der Aalst, W.M.P.: PM^2: a process mining project methodology. In: International Conference on Advanced Information Systems Engineering, pp. 297–313 (2015). https://doi.org/10.1007/978-3-319-19069-3_19
10. Hakim, A.: Improving healthcare systems through process mining. In: 2020 IEEE 23rd International Multitopic Conference, pp. 1–4 (2020). https://doi.org/10.1109/INMIC50486.2020.9318159
11. Heo, G., Lee, J., Jung, J.Y.: Analyzing bottleneck resource pools of operational process using process mining. ICIC express letters. Part B, Applications: an international journal of research and surveys **9**(5), 437–441 (2018)

12. Jacobi, C., Meier, M., Herborn, L., Furmans, K.: Maturity model for applying process mining in supply chains: Literature overview and practical implications. Logistics J. Proc. **2020**(12) (2020). https://doi.org/10.2195/lj_Proc_jacobi_en_202012_01

13. Kaouni, A., Theodoropoulou, G., Bousdekis, A., Voulodimos, A., Miaoulis, G.: Visual analytics in process mining for supporting business process improvement. In: Novelties in Intelligent Digital Systems, pp. 166–175 (2021). https://doi.org/10.3233/FAIA210089

14. Kitchenham, B.: Procedures for performing systematic reviews. Keele, UK, Keele University **33**(2004), 1–26 (2004)

15. Kitchenham, B., Brereton, O.P., Budgen, D., Turner, M., Bailey, J., Linkman, S.: Systematic literature reviews in software engineering-a systematic literature review. Inf. Softw. Technol. **51**(1), 7–15 (2009). https://doi.org/10.1016/j.infsof.2008.09.009

16. Kouhestani, S., Nik-Bakht, M.: IFC-based process mining for design authoring. Autom. Constr. **112**, 103069 (2020). https://doi.org/10.1016/j.autcon.2019.103069

17. Markovska, V., Kabaivanov, S.: Process mining in support of technological readiness level assessment. IOP Conf. Ser. Mater. Sci. Eng. **878**(1), 012080 (2020). https://doi.org/10.1088/1757-899X/878/1/012080

18. Oueida, S., Kotb, Y.: Healthcare emergency room optimization using a process learning algorithm. In: Proceedings of the Future Technologies Conference. pp. 46–63 (2020). https://doi.org/10.1007/978-3-030-63092-8_4

19. Pan, Y., Zhang, L.: Automated process discovery from event logs in bim construction projects. Autom. Constr. **127**, 103713 (2021). https://doi.org/10.1016/j.autcon.2021.103713

20. Pan, Y., Zhang, L.: A BIM-data mining integrated digital twin framework for advanced project management. Autom. Constr. **124**, 103564 (2021). https://doi.org/10.1016/j.autcon.2021.103564

21. Pang, J., Xu, H., Ren, J., Yang, J., Li, M., Lu, D., Zhao, D.: Process mining framework with time perspective for understanding acute care: a case study of AIS in hospitals. BMC Med. Inform. Decis. Mak. **21**(1), 1–10 (2021). https://doi.org/10.1186/s12911-021-01725-1

22. Peffers, K., Tuunanen, T., Rothenberger, M.A., Chatterjee, S.: A design science research methodology for information systems research. J. Manag. Inf. Syst. **24**(3), 45–77 (2007). https://doi.org/10.2753/MIS0742-1222240302

23. Piest, J.P.S., Cutinha, J.A., Bemthuis, R.H., Bukhsh, F.A.: Evaluating the use of the open trip model for process mining: An informal conceptual mapping study in logistics. In: Proceedings of the 23rd International Conference on Enterprise Information Systems. pp. 290–296 (2021). https://doi.org/10.5220/0010477702900296

24. Prasetyo, H.N., Sarno, R., Budiraharjo, R., Sungkono, K.R.: The effect of duration heteroscedasticity to the bottleneck in business process discovered by inductive miner algorithm. In: 2021 IEEE Asia Pacific Conference on Wireless and Mobile. pp. 52–58 (2021). https://doi.org/10.1109/APWiMob51111.2021.9435199

25. Rojas-Candio, P., Villantoy-Pasapera, A., Armas-Aguirre, J., Aguirre-Mayorga, S.: Evaluation method of variables and indicators for surgery block using process mining and data visualization. In: Proceedings of the 5th Brazilian Technology Symposium. pp. 159–168 (2021). https://doi.org/10.1007/978-3-030-57566-3_16

26. Roser, C., Lorentzen, K., Deuse, J.: Reliable shop floor bottleneck detection for flow lines through process and inventory observations: the bottleneck walk. Logist. Res. **8**(1), 1–9 (2015). https://doi.org/10.1016/j.procir.2014.05.020

27. dos Santos, G.A., Southier, L.F.P., Scalabrin, E.E.: Method to reduce lead-time of business process discovered. In: 13th International Congress on Image and Signal Processing, BioMedical Engineering and Informatics. pp. 840–845 (2020). https://doi.org/10.1109/CISP-BMEI51763.2020.9263520

28. dos Santos Garcia, C., et al.: Process mining techniques and applications-a systematic mapping study. Expert Syst. Appl. **133**, 260–295 (2019). https://doi.org/10.1016/j.eswa.2019.05. 003

29. Seara, L.G., De Carvalho, R.M.: An approach for workflow improvement based on outcome and time remaining prediction. In: Proceedings of the 7th International Conference on Model-Driven Engineering and Software Development, pp. 473–480 (2019). https://doi.org/ 10.5220/0007577504730480

30. Siek, M., Mukti, R.M.G.: Business process mining from e-commerce event web logs: conformance checking and bottleneck identification. IOP Conf. Ser. Earth Environ. Sci. **729**, 012133 (2021). https://doi.org/10.1088/1755-1315/729/1/012133

31. Siek, M., Mukti, R.M.G.: Process mining with applications to automotive industry. IOP Conf. Ser. Mater. Sci. Eng. **924**, 012033 (2020). https://doi.org/10.1088/1757-899X/924/1/012033

32. Singh, S., Verma, R., Koul, S.: A collaborative method for simultaneous operations: case of an eye clinic. OPSEARCH, pp. 1–21 (2021). https://doi.org/10.1007/s12597-021-00513-9

33. Singh, S., Verma, R., Koul, S.: A data-driven approach to shared decision-making in a healthcare environment. OPSEARCH, pp. 1–15 (2021). https://doi.org/10.1007/s12597-021-00543-3

34. Sitova, I., Pecerska, J.: Process data analysis using visual analytics and process mining techniques. In: 61st International Scientific Conference on Information Technology and Management Science of Riga Technical University, pp. 1–6 (2020). https://doi.org/10.1109/ ITMS51158.2020.9259296

35. Spenrath, Y., Hassani, M.: Predicting business process bottlenecks in online events streams under concept drifts. In: Proceedings of European Council for Modelling and Simulation, pp. 190–196 (2020). https://doi.org/10.7148/2020-0190

36. Stefanini, A., Aloini, D., Benevento, E., Dulmin, R., Mininno, V.: Performance analysis in emergency departments: a data-driven approach. Measuring Business Excellence (2018). https://doi.org/10.1108/MBE-07-2017-0040

37. Toosinezhad, Z., Fahland, D., Köroğlu, Ö., van der Aalst, W.M.P.: Detecting system-level behavior leading to dynamic bottlenecks. In: 2nd International Conference on Process Mining, pp. 17–24 (2020). https://doi.org/10.1109/ICPM49681.2020.00014

38. Unger, A.J., Neto, J.F.d.S., Fantinato, M., Peres, S.M., Trecenti, J., Hirota, R.: Process mining-enabled jurimetrics: analysis of a Brazilian court's judicial performance in the business law processing. In: Proceedings of the Eighteenth International Conference on Artificial Intelligence and Law, pp. 240–244 (2021). https://doi.org/10.1145/3462757.3466137

39. Yazdi, M.A., Politze, M.: Reverse engineering: the university distributed services. In: Proceedings of the Future Technologies Conference, pp. 223–238 (2020). https://doi.org/10. 1007/978-3-030-63089-8_14

40. Yazici, I.E., Engin, O.: Use of process mining in bank real estate transactions and visualization with fuzzy models. In: Intelligent and Fuzzy Techniques in Big Data Analytics and Decision Making (2020). https://doi.org/10.1007/978-3-030-23756-1_33

41. Zisimou, A., Kalaitzoglou, I., Theodoropoulou, G., Bousdekis, A., Miaoulis, G.: Evaluation of public funding processes by mining event logs. In: 2021 12th International Conference on Information, Intelligence, Systems & Applications, pp. 1–7 (2021). https://doi.org/10.1109/ IISA52424.2021.9555573

Security and Cryptography

A Classification of Software-Architectural Uncertainty Regarding Confidentiality

Sebastian Hahner[✉], Stephan Seifermann, Robert Heinrich, and Ralf Reussner

KASTEL – Institute of Information Security and Dependability,
Karlsruhe Institute of Technology (KIT), Karlsruhe, Germany
{sebastian.hahner,robert.heinrich,ralf.reussner}@kit.edu,
stephan.seifermann@alumni.kit.edu

Abstract. In our connected world, ensuring and demonstrating the confidentiality of exchanged data becomes increasingly critical for software systems. However, especially in early system design, uncertainty exists about the software architecture itself and the software's execution environment. This does not only impede early confidentiality analysis but can also cause data breaches due to the lack of awareness of the impact of uncertainty. Classifying uncertainty helps in understanding its impact and in choosing proper analysis and mitigation strategies. There already exist multiple taxonomies, e.g., from the domain of self-adaptive systems. However, they do not fit the abstraction of software architecture and do not focus on security-related quality properties like confidentiality.

To address this, we present a classification of architectural uncertainty regarding confidentiality. It enables precise statements about uncertain influences and their impact on confidentiality. It raises awareness of uncertainty properties, enables knowledge transfer to non-experts, and serves as a baseline for discussion. Also, it can be directly integrated into existing notions of data flow diagrams for uncertainty-aware confidentiality analysis. We evaluate the structural suitability, applicability, and purpose of the classification based on a real-world case study and a user study. The results show increased significance compared to existing taxonomies and raised awareness of the impact of uncertainty on confidentiality.

Keywords: Software architecture · Uncertainty · Confidentiality

1 Introduction

Today's software systems become increasingly complex. With growing size and connections, ensuring software quality becomes a major challenge. This is especially true for security-related quality properties like confidentiality. Confidentiality demands that "information is not made available or disclosed to unauthorized individuals, entities, or processes" [17]. Violations of confidentiality cannot only harm user acceptance [45] but also have legal consequences [16]. To identify flaws early and to avoid costly repairs of running systems [4], design-time confidentiality analyses have been proposed [39,42]. Based on analyzing the software architecture and its data against confidentiality requirements [15], the software design can be enhanced and statements about potential

P. Samarati et al. (Eds.): ICETE 2021, CCIS 1795, pp. 139–160, 2023.
https://doi.org/10.1007/978-3-031-36840-0_8

violations can be made. Here, data flow-oriented analyses became common because "problems tend to follow the data flow, not the control flow" [40].

However, especially in early development and in complex systems of systems, the software architecture is subject to uncertainty. Uncertainty describes "any departure from the unachievable ideal of complete determinism" [43]. This does not only affect decision making—also known as the *cone of uncertainty* [28]—but even blurs which decisions should be prioritized. When not managed properly, the lack of awareness of uncertainty can void a system's confidentiality. Also, the OWASP Top 10 [29] lists issues like *insecure design* as top security risks.

Multiple taxonomies were defined to better understand the nature of uncertainty [31,32,43]. However, they mostly originate from the domain of self-adaptive systems and do not focus on confidentiality. Consequences are the lack of applicability and an increase of ambiguity. The relation of software architecture, confidentiality and uncertainty remains unclear [13]. And while "there is growing consensus on the importance of uncertainty" [27], much is yet unknown regarding the impact of uncertainty on software systems [10]. Hezavehi et al. [27] conducted a survey on uncertainty. They find a "lack of systematic approaches for managing uncertainty" [27] and that uncertainty should already be addressed at design time. This statement is supported by the work of Troya et al. [41]. They conducted a Systematic Literature Review (SLR) and analyzed 123 papers. They state that software engineers require more help "to identify the types of uncertainty that can affect their application domains" [41].

In previous work [38], we presented a unified model to express data flows and analyze confidentiality violations in software architectures. We mined modeling primitives from existing approaches [37,42], defined a meta model and an analysis using label propagation. We also showed its integration into existing Architectural Description Languages (ADLs) like Palladio [33]. The underlying goal of a data-centered approach without predefined analysis goals or data flow constraints is the possibility of user-defined confidentiality analyses [39]. However, the previous approach was only able to analyze confidentiality with perfect knowledge, i.e., by excluding uncertainty about software systems and its data.

In this paper, we present a classification scheme of architectural uncertainty. This classification is specifically designed to express uncertainty on the architectural abstraction level regarding confidentiality. We build on the existing data flow model [38] and consider the impact of uncertainty on the software architecture's confidentiality. Here, we focus on *known unknowns*, i.e., uncertainty that can be identified but not always resolved immediately. The classification shall help architects to describe uncertain influences more precisely, find mitigation and analysis strategies, raise awareness of relevant uncertainty attributes, enable the reuse of knowledge, and serve as a baseline for discussion. We argue that making uncertainty explicit enhances the overall design and simplifies phase containment, i.e., fixing defects in the same phase as they appear. Here, uncertainty should not be avoided but become a source for improvement [11].

We start by discussing the state of the art in Sect. 2 and present the contributions of this paper (**C1** and **C2**) thereafter.

C1. First, we define *architectural uncertainty* and relate uncertainty to Architectural Design Decisions (ADDs) and confidentiality in Sect. 3. We extract relevant classification categories and discuss their applicability to describe the impact of uncertainty on confidentiality. Based on this, we present an uncertainty classification scheme in Sect. 4.

C2. Second, we show how the classification helps identifying the impact of uncertainty on confidentiality in Sect. 5. We demonstrate how the classified impact of uncertainty maps can be modeled using the unified modeling primitives [38]. We also provide a reference set of classified uncertainties.

The evaluation of the classification in Sect. 6 is based on the guidelines of Kaplan et al. [19]. The authors propose to evaluate the structure's suitability, the applicability, and the purpose. This enables us to make statements not only about the appropriateness and the quality of the classification as such, but also consider its reliability and ease of use, as required by *usable security* [36]. The evaluation also includes the metrics-based comparison to the state of the art, i.e., existing taxonomies of uncertainty. We conducted a user study with researchers from the software architecture domain and a real-world case study based on the German open-source contact-tracing app *Corona Warn App* [34].

The results show increased significance compared to existing taxonomies, i.e., better applicability and more precise classification. The user study shows that the classification scheme helps in understanding and analyzing uncertainty and is a satisfying base for discussions. This cannot only be seen in the gathered data but has also been independently reported by multiple study participants. Section 7 concludes this paper and gives an outlook on future application areas.

2 State of the Art

In this section, we give an overview of the state of the art based on three categories: Uncertainty taxonomies, uncertainty in software architecture, and ADDs.

Uncertainty Taxonomies. To better understand uncertainty, researchers created several taxonomies [5,8,26,31,32,43]. Walker et al. [43] present a taxonomy of uncertainty using three dimensions. The *location* describes where the uncertainty can be found, e.g., in the model input or context. The *nature* distinguishes between epistemic (i.e., lack of knowledge) and aleatory (i.e., natural variability) uncertainty. Last, the *level* describes how much is known about the uncertain influence. Although this taxonomy has been the baseline for many others, it does not specifically aim to describe software-related uncertainty. Perez-Palacin and Mirandola [31] build upon this classification in the context of self-adaptive systems. They adjust the dimension *location* to better fit software models. Bures et al. [5] adapt this taxonomy again to "fit the needs of uncertainty in access control" [5]. Although this work only considers access control in Industry 4.0 scenarios, it is also a good foundation for our classification. Esfahani and Malek [8] describe characteristics of uncertainty and hereby focus on the variability and reducibility of different sources of uncertainty. Mahdavi-Hezavehi et al. [26] propose a classification framework of uncertainty. They aim at architecture-based, self-adaptive system but do also not consider security, privacy, or confidentiality. Also related is the uncertainty template by Ramirez et al. [32]. They present a scheme to describe uncertainty sources for dynamically adaptive systems in requirements, design, and runtime. Due to the different scope, they describe uncertainty in software architecture as *inadequate design* which is not precise enough to identify the impact of architectural uncertainty on confidentiality.

Uncertainty in Software Architecture. Numerous approaches exist to handle uncertainty in software architecture [7,22,25]. For the sake of brevity, we only summarize to work related most. For an in-depth analysis, refer to the previously mentioned surveys [27,41]. GuideArch [7] and PerOpteryx [22] are approaches to explore the architectural solution space under uncertainty. Both approaches try to achieve optimal architectures under given constraints and degrees of freedom but do not aim at security-related properties like confidentiality. Lytra and Zdun [25] propose an approach to combine ADDs under uncertainty by utilizing fuzzy logic. Although this approach considers the software design, the representation of uncertainty as fuzzy values alone is not suitable to analyze confidentiality.

Architectural Design Decisions. The relation between design decisions and uncertainty has already been described more than two decades ago [28]. Kruchten [23] presents an ontology of ADDs. The author distinguishes between existence, property and executive decisions and provides an overview of ADDs attributes. This is especially relevant when considering uncertainty that can void existing decisions and require software architects to backtrack. Jansen and Bosch [18] see software architecture as a composition of ADDs. This shows how uncertainty, e.g., about the system context, can hinder good software design as the *best* decision might not be found. Although both approaches do not focus on uncertainty, they inspired our classification which is strongly coupled to architectural design.

3   Uncertainty, Confidentiality, and Software Architecture

In this section, we give an overview of uncertainty in software architecture. We propose the term *architectural uncertainty* and describe the relation of uncertainty, ADDs and confidentiality based on an exemplary architecture model. Afterwards, we discuss existing classifications of uncertainty and their applicability to describe the relation of architectural uncertainty and confidentiality.

When speaking about uncertainty in software architecture, we propose speaking in terms of *impact* rather than only considering the uncertainty's type or source. This enables software architects to focus on its mitigation during design, e.g., to enhance confidentiality. Also, when interpreting an architecture as set of ADDs [18], the impact is one of the most important properties to consider [28].

We understand *architectural uncertainty* as uncertainty, that can be described on architectural abstraction and where (early) awareness enables considering its impact on quality attributes like confidentiality. We do not use the term *design time*, as the real impact of the uncertainty might happen later, e.g., at runtime. We also do not only refer to *known unknowns*, as this only implicates awareness which is too imprecise. We refine this term by requiring the architectural abstraction, e.g., as part of an architectural model with specified impact on software-architectural elements, e.g., software components, interfaces, or hardware resources. Here, we also exclude higher orders of uncertainty [31] as their impact cannot immediately be expressed due to the lack of awareness. However, awareness can be raised with increasing knowledge, e.g., by asking a domain expert [30] or by using a classification scheme for systematic treatment [43].

Figure 1 shows an example of two architectural uncertainties and their impact on confidentiality [12]. The diagram represents a simplified *Online Shop* that consists of two components and two hardware resources. The first uncertainty **U1** is the allocation of the *Database Service* that stores the *Online Shop* data. The second uncertainty **U2** is the trustworthiness of the provider of the cloud service, a potential deployment location of the *Database Service*. Both uncertainties can be annotated in the architectural model and have a potential impact on confidentiality, e.g., due to legal requirements like the GDPR [6]. However, this example also shows the difference between awareness and mitigation: While deciding the allocation could resolve Uncertainty **U1**, Uncertainty **U2** potentially remains and requires further ADDs, e.g., the encryption of data.

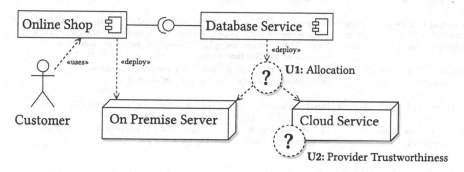

Fig. 1. Combined component and deployment architecture model with uncertainty.

When dealing with architectural uncertainty, considering ADDs helps to structure the design process. In the beginning of this process, much is yet unknown or imprecise and ADDs are made under assumptions [28], e.g., that the provider is trustworthy in Uncertainty **U2**. Making this uncertainty explicit can help to mark decisions as challenged [23] and consider backtracking. While some uncertainty only exists due to not yet decided ADDs (e.g., Uncertainty **U1**), other cannot be reduced immediately [31] (e.g., Uncertainty **U2**). Still, creating awareness of the impact of uncertainty can help refining the architecture and making more informed statements about confidentiality. This impact can be understood, modeled, simulated, analyzed, measured and—eventually—managed.

There are multiple relevant properties of ADDs that help in the mitigation of uncertainty. The number of solutions of related ADDs [18] can help to estimate whether the uncertainty can already be fully reduced at design time. We distinguish between closed sets that could at least partially be analyzed and open sets with a potentially infinite number of solutions or configurations. In our example, Uncertainty **U1** relates to the ADD of the allocation and represents a closed set. This can be analyzed, e.g., by combining design space exploration with dataflow analysis [44]. But even with a closed

Table 1. Available categories and options to classify uncertainty used in related work.

Available Categories	Available Options
Location: Describes where uncertainty originates from or where it manifests itself within the system or model [5,26,31,41,43]	**Context**: system boundaries [31,43], user input [5], execution context [26]; **Model structural**: existence of elements [41], elements and their relationship [31,43], structural differences [26], components and their properties [5]; **Model technical**: software and hardware [43]; **Input**: input types [43], input values [31], measurement deviation [41]; **Parameters**: parameter calibration [31,43]; **System behavior**: actual behavior [5], including parameters and actions [41]; **Belief**: uncertain statements about system and environment [41];
Level: Describes how much is known about the uncertain influence and how the uncertainty can be described [1,5,26,31,43]	**Statistical**: Statistical data available [26,43]; **Scenario**: Possible scenarios available without statistical data [1,26,43]; **Recognized ignorance**: Awareness of uncertainty, but cannot be further described [43]; **Total ignorance**: Lack of awareness of uncertainty [43]; **Orders of Uncertainty**: No uncertainty (0th), known uncertainty (1st), lack of awareness, i.e., unknown unknowns (2nd), lack of awareness and process (3rd), meta-uncertainty (4th) [1,5,31];
Nature: Describes the essence and character of the uncertainty [5,26,31,41,43]	**Aleatory**: Uncertainty due to inherent variability or randomness [5,26,31,41,43]; **Epistemic**: Uncertainty due to a lack of knowledge [5,26,31,41,43];
Manageability: Describes whether the uncertainty can be reduced [8,43]	**Reducible**: Uncertainty can be fully reduced after acknowledgement [8,43]; **Irreducible**: Uncertainty cannot be further reduced at this point in time [8,43];
Emerging time: Describes at which state of the software development uncertainty arises [26,27,31,32,41]	**Requirements time**: As requirements are defined [32,41]; **Design time**: As the software system is designed [26,27,32,41]; **Verification**: At verification of software models [41]; **Testing**: During software testing [27,41]; **Implementation**: As the software gets implemented [41]; **Run time**: During software execution [26,27,31,32,41];
Impact on Quality: Describes how uncertainty affects quality properties [27]	**Performance**: Impact on performance [27]; **Resources**: Impact on resource consumption [27]; **Safety**: Impact on a system's safety [27];
Relationship: The relation between uncertainties [32]	**Directed**: Directed relationship or influences between uncertainties [32]; **Related**: Unspecified relationship between uncertainties [32];
Source: Potential sources of uncertainty [8,26,31,32]	Several publications list sources of uncertainty, e.g., human in the loop, abstraction, missing requirements, inadequate design, …

set of alternatives, one cannot guarantee that a given ADD might not be challenged in the future [23] due to changes in requirements or the system's execution context. Thus, when speaking about decisions under uncertainty, considering the probability, possibility and costs of revisions can help to quantify the risk. This awareness also helps in the prioritization of ADDs and deciding whether existing mitigation is sufficient.

However, only considering ADDs to understand the impact of uncertainty is not enough because uncertainty might not be directly connected to a single decision (e.g., resolving Uncertainty **U2**). Thus, we argue to also consider which architectural elements are affected, rather than only considering this transitively via the impact of ADDs. This does not only help understanding the consequences of uncertain influences but also helps to connect these to architecture-based analyses. In our example, modeling and analyzing the data flows [38,39] between the *Online Shop* component and the *Database Service* component helps determining whether the impact of Uncertainty **U2** is a problem for confidentiality.

To choose proper decision, mitigation, and analysis strategies, software architects need to be aware of the impact of uncertainty and be able to describe this impact precisely. To support this activity, we analyzed existing taxonomies and classifications of uncertainty. We gathered, assessed and adapted categories (i.e., dimensions, or characteristics) and options with the purpose of more precisely classifying uncertainty in relation to confidentiality. The following discussion is based on existing taxonomies [5,8,26,31,32,43] as well as recent systematic literature reviews and surveys on uncertainty [27,41]. Table 1 gives an overview of available categories and options derived from related work.

Uncertainty is often described with its *location*. However, there is no common distinction between the source and the impact of an uncertain influence. Also, there is no common understanding of the term *model* and its boundaries as the taxonomies originate from different research areas. Thus, uncertainty **U1** could be classified as *context*, *model structural*, *model technical*, and *belief uncertainty*. Such ambiguity can invalidate the purpose of a taxonomy. Regarding the *level*, two different approaches exist. Some classifications define the level based on the description of uncertainty, e.g., by using statistical means or scenarios. Others refer to the orders of uncertainty [1]. As already discussed, we focus on *known unknowns*, i.e., the first order of uncertainty. However, even in this order exist different nuances, e.g., recognized ignorance compared with statistical data.

Many classifications refer to the *nature* of uncertainty. However, this category is questioned [8,20] as it depends on the point of view and is often not clearly distinguishable. Thus, we prefer the category *manageability* since it focuses on the reducibility. Besides the category *emerging time*, we propose to also consider the resolution of uncertainty, i.e., at which time the impact of uncertainty can be understood and managed. Regarding design-time confidentiality analyses, it is valuable to know whether uncertainty can be directly analyzed (e.g., Uncertainty **U1**) or must be mitigated in later phases (e.g., Uncertainty **U2**).

The *impact on quality* is an important as not all uncertainties affect a system's confidentiality. To focus analysis capabilities, software architects must know about potential impacts and their severity. Although we focus on confidentiality, the analysis of multiple properties is possible, e.g., by using design space exploration combined with dataflow analysis, as demonstrated by Walter et al. [44]. The remaining categories are only defined for sources of uncertainty. Still, such information can be valuable, e.g., to describe the relation of uncertainty to ADDs like the allocation to Uncertainty **U1**.

4   Classification of Architectural Uncertainty

In this section, we present a classification scheme to aid software architects in understanding the impact of *architectural uncertainty* on confidentiality. This shall raise awareness of properties of uncertainty and their relevance for choosing appropriate ADDs and mitigation strategies. We intentionally speak of a classification rather than a taxonomy because we focus on a subset of uncertainty, i.e., known unknowns on architectural abstraction.

The classification scheme consists of 8 categories with a total of 27 options and is shown in Table 2. The categories are partially based on taxonomies of uncertainty [5,8,26,31,32,43], related work on ADDs [18,23] and ADLs like Palladio [33]. A category-based classification helps to group uncertainties and identify similar characteristics and mitigation approaches. Once classified, the information can be reused across different software architectures. This is possible due to the connection between architectural uncertainty and reusable ADDs. To create this classification, we assessed and adapted existing categories and combined or refined their options (see Sect. 3). We repeated this process until each category fulfilled its purpose, i.e., being able to describe and partition the impact of uncertainty on confidentiality in software architectures.

In this work, we focus on confidentiality requirements in the design time. Thus, the categories should be interpreted from an architectural viewpoint, e.g., while modeling a software system. In the following, we explain each category. We provide information about the rationale and possible benefits of applying each category. We also define whether the options are unordered (i.e., nominal) or ordered without defined distance (i.e., ordinal), and single or multiple choice. Last, we specify if the gained knowledge by classification can be reused, i.e., if it is specific for the uncertainty type, or the software architecture under investigation.

Location and Architectural Element Type. The first two categories are concerned with the location of the uncertainty impact. Previous taxonomies [5,26,31,43] already considered "where the uncertainty manifests itself within the model" [31] but did not explicitly relate to an ADL. Since the location of the impact is one of the most important properties for design-time confidentiality analysis, we connect this category with the viewpoints and element types of Palladio [33]. Compared to existing taxonomies, this enables more precise description and mitigation planning because we can model uncertainty and its relation to existing architecture elements. While *Location* is on the abstraction of the viewpoint (e.g., structure, or behavior), the *Architecture Element Type* describes the concrete elements (e.g., components, or hardware resources) affected by the uncertainty. Because this—especially regarding confidentiality—may affect multiple elements at once, both categories are multiple choice. Also, both categories are nominal as there is no order between location or element types. By understanding which elements and viewpoints are affected, software architects can assess responsibilities and evaluate mitigation methods. The knowledge gained about the location is uncertainty-specific and can thus be reused across architectural models.

Type and Manageability. The next two categories specify how much is known about the uncertain influence and whether the uncertainty can be reduced. Other taxonomies [5,31] only specify this in terms of levels on a scale from knowledge to ignorance [1] which is too imprecise to classify uncertainty for mitigation. With the *Type*, we describe how much is known about the uncertainty, based on the definitions by Walker et al. [43]. All options represent *known unknowns* [31] but also specify how this knowledge can be represented for mitigation, e.g., if there is statistical data available. *Manageability* states whether we can control or reduce the impact of the uncertainty at design time (see *Data Protection by Design* [6]) or are only aware of it [8]. We do not consider the nature of the uncertainty [43] because the manageability is closer to the uncertainty's impact [8]. Both categories are ordinal and single choice. By understanding how much is known about an uncertain influence beyond awareness, one can choose appropriate mitigation methods or choose to gather specific knowledge. The classification depends on the context of the architecture under investigation. However, many uncertainty types tend to be categorized similarly across architectures. For instance, the allocation (see

Table 2. Categories and options of the architectural uncertainty classification.

Location: Describes where uncertainty manifests itself within the architecture	
System Structure	Structure, e.g., components, their static wiring, assembly, and allocation
System Behavior	Behavior of the system and its components as well as their communication
System Environment	System's context, including hardware resources and the external situation
System Input	Inputs provided by external actors, e.g., people using the software system
Architectural Element Type: Elements to which an uncertainty can be assigned	
Component	Assignable to software components, e.g., related to their allocation
Connector	Assignable to, e.g., wires between components, or communication
Interface	Assignable to interfaces, e.g., signatures, parameters, and return values
Hardware Resource	Assignable to hardware resources, e.g., servers, and external actors
Behavior Description	Assignable to behavior descriptions, e.g., algorithms or user input
Type: How much is known about the uncertainty and how can it be described	
Statistical Uncertainty	Uncertainty describable with statistical means, e.g., stochastic expressions
Scenario Uncertainty	Distinct scenarios depending on the uncertain outcome, no statistical means
Recognized Ignorance	Awareness of the uncertainty but no mitigation or description strategy
Manageability: Can more knowledge or appropriate means reduce the uncertainty	
Fully Reducible	Reducible, e.g., by acquiring more knowledge, or comprehensive simulation
Partial Reducible	At least partially reducible, e.g., by applying scenario-based mitigation
Irreducible	Uncertainty cannot be further reduced, e.g., due to its aleatory nature
Resolution Time: Time at which the uncertainty is expected to be fully resolved	
Requirements Time	As soon as requirements are defined, e.g., confidentiality requirements
Design Time	As soon as the systems is designed, e.g., its structure, or components
Realization Time	As soon as the system or parts of it are implemented and deployed
Runtime	As knowledge is gained from testing and system operations, e.g., monitoring
Reducible by ADD: Uncertainty resolvable by an architectural design decision	
Yes	Uncertainty can be reduced by taking an ADD, i.e., by designing the system in a way that the impact of the uncertainty is (partially) mitigated
No	Uncertainty is not resolvable or treatable by taking an ADD
Impact on Confidentiality: Potential impact on confidentiality requirements	
Direct	Direct impact on confidentiality, e.g., by directly affecting personal user data
Indirect	Impact only in conjunction with contextual factors, ADDs or uncertainties
None	No impact on confidentiality, e.g., if only publicly available data is affected
Severity of the Impact: Describes the severity if uncertainty is not mitigated	
High	Total loss of confidentiality, or sensitive data, e.g., an admin's password
Low	Access to restricted information could be obtained but the damage is limited
None	No loss of confidentiality expected at all

Uncertainty U1 in Sect. 3) can usually be described *scenario-based* and be reduced in the design or realization time.

Resolution Time and Reducible by ADD. These categories relate uncertainty to the architectural design using ADDs. The *Resolution Time* is based on the phases of software development and can help to narrow down sources and responsibilities. Since we focus on the impact of uncertainty on confidentiality, we consider the expected full resolution time rather than the emerging time [27,31,32,41]. Also, we only include phases that are relevant from the point of view of design time analyses. The category *Reducible by ADD* specifies whether the impact of the classified uncertainty can at least be partially mitigated by a design decision. Making the connection between ADDs and uncertainty explicit [25] helps to prioritize, e.g., check whether multiple or critical uncertainty impacts can be tackled by a single decision. Both options are single choice, the options of the *Resolution Time* are ordinal, reducibility is considered to be nominal. Also, both categories are only uncertainty-specific and thus reusable.

Impact on Confidentiality and Severity of the Impact. The last two categories are used to quantify the impact of uncertainty on confidentiality requirements. To prioritize uncertainty with a critical impact, we combine the impact type with its severity. A direct *Impact on Confidentiality* can void confidentiality even without taking other factors, decisions, or uncertainties into account. Indirect impact relates to such contextual properties. *Severity of the Impact* is based on the confidentiality impact metrics of the open industry standard Common Vulnerability Scoring System (CVSS) [9]. They refer to a high impact if a total loss of confidential data or access to restricted information is expected. An impact that is rated low implies that data can be stolen, but the information could not be used directly or is limited. Both categories are single choice and ordinal. The knowledge gained by classification can help in clustering and prioritizing uncertainty and related ADDs but is specific for the architecture and its context.

5 Applying the Classification for Confidentiality Analysis

In this section, we apply the previously defined classification to analyze the impact of uncertainty on confidentiality. Confidentiality requirements are manifold. They include the legal restriction of data processing, e.g., personal data being regulated in the GDPR [6] but also organizational protection policies of restricted data like an administrator's password or encryption keys [9]. Thus, when speaking about the impact of uncertainty on confidentiality, one has to consider all relevant data in a software architecture. We achieve this by first classifying uncertainty and then considering the impact of this uncertainty in data flow-based confidentiality analysis [38,39].

Table 3 shows an exemplary classification based on the *online shop* in Sect. 3. While the allocation (**U1**) represents uncertainty in the structure of the architecture and can be annotated to the deployable component, trustworthiness (**U2**) of a resource provider affects the behavior and is located in the environment of the system. Making the location explicit already helps in understanding the impact in terms of architecture models, e.g., describable as possible scenarios or model variations [30]. The allocation refers to the ADD of the same name and can thus be fully resolved at realization time, e.g., by limiting possible deployment locations. The trustworthiness remains unclear even at runtime, but can be partially mitigated, e.g., by enforcing encryption of data that flows to the

Table 3. Exemplary classification of the uncertainty in the online shop example.

	U1: Allocation	U2: Provider Trustworthiness
Location	System Structure	System Behavior/Environment
Architectural Element Type	Component	Behavior/Hardware Resource
Type	Scenario Uncertainty	Scenario Uncertainty
Manageability	Fully Reducible	Partial Reducible
Resolution Time	Realization Time	Runtime
Reducible by ADD	Yes	Yes
Impact on Confidentiality	Direct	Indirect
Severity of the Impact	High	Low

Database service. Regarding legal confidentiality requirements [6], the allocation represents a serious and direct impact and can be prioritized over the trustworthiness which also depends on the allocation. Here, the classification helps to connect uncertainties and ADDs and also helps to prioritize. If a decision is revoked later, e.g., the deployment is changed to the *Cloud Service*, documenting classified uncertainties, assumptions and risk helps in reevaluation [23] and potential backtracking. Note, this classification is only exemplary and also allows to draw other conclusions due to the lack of contextual information in our simplified example. A comprehensive reference set of architectural uncertainties and their impact on confidentiality can be found in our data set [14].

Besides documentation and design, classifying uncertainty also helps in analysis and mitigation. Here, several approaches have been proposed (see Sect. 2). Perez-Palacin and Mirandola [30] distinguish between two mitigation paths: modifying the model (i.e., making the required ADD) and managing a model with uncertainty. These paths are a good fit to the previous discussion about manageability and reducibility. However, to choose one of these paths, software architects must be aware of the uncertain influence and require knowledge about its potential impact and related ADDs and elements of the software architecture.

To analyze confidentiality under uncertainty, we demonstrate how to manage a model with uncertainty and integrate the classification results into the previously presented data flow meta model [38]. This is possible because our classification has been designed for confidentiality and both—the classification scheme and the data flow meta model—relate to Palladio [33] as common ADL.

The unified modeling primitives [38] consist of *nodes, pins, flows, behavior* and *label assignments*. Nodes represent structural elements of software systems, e.g., processes, stores, or external entities. Pins represent their interfaces and flows are used to connect multiple nodes through their pins. Nodes have a defined behavior that assigns labels, e.g., based on labels at the node's input pins, constants, logical expressions or a combination of the above. We can follow the data flow by propagating the assigned labels through the system and applying the propagation function at each node. By comparing the labels at each node to defined requirements that are formulated as data flow constraints [15, 39], we can analyze confidentiality.

Table 4. Mapping of architectural element types to data flow modeling primitives.

Architectural Element	Data Flow Modeling Primitive	Impact of Uncertainty
Component	Node (process or store)	Existence and use of nodes
Connector	Flow	Existence of flows to nodes
Interface	Pin (input or output)	Existence and form of pins
Hardware Resource	Label assignment	Values of node assignments
Behavior Description	Behavior (label propagation)	Propagation function output

The modeling primitives are integrated into the control flow modeling of Palladio [33, 38]. Table 4 shows the mapping of Palladio elements used in our classification to the meta model of the unified modeling primitives. It also shows how the impact of uncertainty on these elements can be transformed and represented in data flow models. As explained in Sect. 4, describing affected elements can be used for mitigation planning and analysis. Regarding the data flow modeling primitives, structural uncertainty can alter the existence of nodes, pins, and flows. Exemplary uncertain influences are component choices, interface definitions, or system configuration. Uncertainty can also arise from the context of a system, which is expressed by label assignments on nodes. Last, behavioral uncertainty could alter the output of affected label propagation functions.

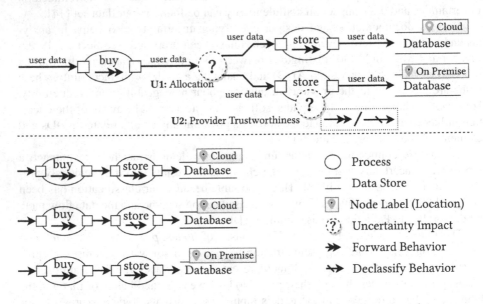

Fig. 2. Data flow diagrams of the running example with and without uncertainty.

We demonstrate this mapping based on the *Online Shop* example whose uncertainties (**U1** and **U2**) have been classified in Table 3. Here, we are interested in the confidentiality of user data that is processed in the *Online Shop* component and then stored in a database. Figure 2 shows the resulting data flow diagrams, following the adapted notation presented in [38]. In the upper part, we show a non-deterministic data flow diagram under uncertainty (**U1** and **U2**). In the lower part, we show the impact of those uncertainties by rolling out the upper diagram and listing all resulting, deterministic diagrams. This is possible because both uncertainties represent *Scenario Uncertainty*, and we are also aware of all possible cases. Uncertainty **U1** is caused by an unknown allocation and represented by the two alternative label assignments *Cloud* and *On Promise*. Uncertainty **U2** is caused by the unknown provider trustworthiness that is represented by two alternative label propagation functions. While the *Forward behavior* passes incoming labels without modification, unauthorized behavior is represented as *Declassify Behavior* that changes propagated labels.

By defining constraints on these labels, we can analyze the resulting data flow diagrams on confidentiality violations. An exemplary constraint could prohibit unencrypted user data to be declassified. Although this is only the case in one of the possible data flows, to completely mitigate this issue, the *On Premise* allocation has to be chosen. Alternatively, user data can be encrypted. By altering propagation functions and data flow constraints, multiple scenarios under different uncertainties can be analyzed. This can be automated with tool support by combining the presented approach [37–39] with data flow constraints [15] and design space exploration. An initial approach has been realized by using PerOpteryx [22] to analyze confidentiality under structural uncertainty [44].

6 Evaluation

In this section, we present the evaluation of our classification. First, we define goals, questions and metrics and present the evaluation design. Afterwards, we discuss the evaluation results as well as threats to validity and known limitations.

6.1 Goals, Questions, and Metrics

Konersmann et al. [21] state the lack of guideline-based evaluation in current software engineering research. Especially taxonomies of uncertainty are often only evaluated based on application examples [5,31] or not evaluated at all [32,43]. To prevent this, we structure our evaluation according to the taxonomy evaluation method of Kaplan et al. [19]. The authors propose to use a *Goal-Question-Metrics*-plan [2] to evaluate the structure's suitability, the applicability, and the purpose of a classification. Table 5 summarizes the evaluation plan together with the evaluation results. In the following, we give an overview.

We evaluate the structure's suitability (**G1**), i.e., whether it permits the appropriate classification of objects under study by having the right scope and granularity. This includes the *generality* (**Q1.1**), where we measure if the classification is not too general but also not to specific. Here, low laconicity (**M1.1.1**) indicates a too fine-grained and low lucidity (**M1.1.2**) indicates a too coarse-grained classification. A good trade-off regarding the granularity is important because we want to be able to differentiate between uncertainties without assigning a separate class to every instance. Also, the granularity must fit to the purpose of classifying architectural uncertainty regarding confidentiality. The *appropriateness* (**Q1.2**) asks whether the classification is complete (**M1.2.1**), i.e., has enough categories, and whether it is sound (**M1.2.2**), i.e., has no unnecessary categories. On the one hand, we shall be able to classify every architectural uncertainty that can have an impact on confidentiality. On the other hand, categories and options that are never used, should not be maintained. Last, the *orthogonality* (**Q1.3**) evaluates whether the taxonomy has overlapping categories (**M1.3**). A lack in orthogonality implicates that options depend on each other and can be removed to increase preciseness. Overall, a classification with bad structural quality yield ambiguous results and shall be adapted.

We evaluate the applicability (**G2**), i.e., whether the classification is understandable and usable (see *Usable Security* [36]) by conducting a user study. Here, we consider the *reliability* (**Q2.1**), i.e., whether participants have consistent results (**M2.1**). An ambiguous classification with inconsistent results indicates a lack of preciseness. We evaluate the *correctness* (**Q2.2**) by comparing the classification results to a predefined gold standard and calculating the recall (**M2.2**) based on classification hits and misses. A lack in correctness indicates that users could not benefit from applying the classification. Last, we evaluate the *ease of use* (**Q2.3**) based on the System Usability Scale (SUS) [24] (**M2.3**). Additionally, we ask participants if they understand the categories and find them helpful and whether they experienced a knowledge gain by participating in the user study. A taxonomy has to yield consistent results to be usable.

We evaluate the purpose (**G3**), i.e., the classification's quality compared to existing taxonomies based on case study. We consider the *relevance* (**Q3.1**), i.e., whether each category helps the purpose of the classification (**M3.1**). In our case, the purpose is understanding the impact of uncertainty on confidentiality. The *novelty* (**Q3.2**) asks how many categories and options are new (**M3.2.1**) or adapted (**M3.2.2**). Here, the sum of both metrics indicates the strength of the relation of the classification to other taxonomies. Last, we consider the *significance* (**Q3.3**) by measuring the classification delta (**M3.3**) of our classification to other taxonomies. A positive delta indicates an increase in preciseness for which we aim. If the classification fails the evaluation of purpose, it represents no significant improvement over the state of the art.

6.2   Evaluation Design

Our validation comprises three properties. We evaluate the structural quality (**G1**) by analyzing the classification and we perform a user study to evaluate its applicability (**G2**). Our evaluation of purpose (**G3**) compared to the state of the art is based on the real-world case study of the *Corona Warn App* [34]. In the following, we describe the evaluation design in detail. Additional information such as raw evaluation data and questionnaires can be found in our data set [14].

Structural Evaluation. We start the evaluation by considering generality (**Q1.1**) and appropriateness (**Q1.2**). The calculation of the related metrics is based on the guidelines of Kaplan et al. [19]. The authors also provide tool support. For the metrics laconicity, lucidity, completeness, and soundness *1* represents the best and *0* the worst result. Besides the categories and options of our classification, this evaluation requires terms that describe uncertainties. We extracted a total of 38 terms of existing taxonomies (see Sect. 3). Examples are *Uncertainty fully reducible by acquiring enough knowledge* or *Uncertainty refers to user input*. The full list of terms can be found in our data set [14]. To evaluate the orthogonality (**Q1.3**) we construct a self-referencing orthogonality matrix based on our classification's categories and options. A category or option that is implied by another is not orthogonal and thus overlapping. Based on the 27 options of our classification, we evaluate all $27 * 27 - 27 = 702$ combinations.

User Study. We conduct a user study with ten researchers from the domain of software architecture. First, they complete a self-assessment, where they describe their prior knowledge related to the task, e.g., uncertainty, and software architecture. Then, we provide them with a one-page summary of our classification (cf. Sect. 4) with all categories and options and also an application example (cf. Sect. 5) that demonstrates how to use it. During the study, the participants have to classify two different tasks within 15 min time, respectively. Each task consists of an architecture diagram, a short description (cf. Sect. 3), and four uncertainty impacts to classify using our classification. We counterbalance the task order to mitigate learning effects and anonymize the participants' results. Last, they fill out a SUS (**Q2.3**) and a questionnaire related to their understanding of our classification. No session takes longer than one hour to mitigate fatigue effects. After gathering all results, we measure the reliability (**Q2.1**) by calculating the percentage of agreement and the correctness (**Q2.2**) by comparing them to a predefined gold standard and calculating the recall.

Case Study. The *Corona Warn App* [34] is a German digital contact tracing app. It is publicly founded and open source. The source code of the app and the server, as well as comprehensive documentation can be found on GitHub[1]. This does not only include architecture documentation but also security analysis and risk assessment. By rolling back design decisions and considering solutions for problems and risks that are related to confidentiality, realistic uncertainties can be analyzed. We created a collection of 28 uncertainties that are possible during the design process based on the available documentation and ADDs. We use this collection as baseline for the evaluation of the purpose. For each category, we argue whether it helps to understand the impact of the uncertainties and is thus relevant (**Q3.1**). This extends the evaluation of generality (**Q1.1**) and appropriateness (**Q1.2**) based on our case study. We compare all categories to other taxonomies [5,8,26,31,32,43] of uncertainty to evaluate the classification's novelty (**Q3.2**). Here, we discuss the origin and adaption compared to the state of the art. We evaluate the significance (**Q3.3**) by classifying all 28 uncertainties with our classification and with other taxonomies [5,26,31] with a related purpose. As our goal is a higher precision for the impact of uncertainty, we aim for a positive classification delta, i.e., a higher number of uncertainty classes.

6.3 Evaluation Results and Discussion

In the following, we present and discuss the evaluation results for each question individually. Table 5 summarizes all goals, questions, and metrics as well as the evaluation results.

---

[1] https://github.com/corona-warn-app/.

Table 5. Evaluation plan with goals, questions, metrics, and evaluation results.

Goal	Questions	Metrics	Results
Structure's Suitability	Generality	Laconicity, Lucidity	0.95, 0.70
	Appropriateness	Completeness, Soundness	0.97, 1.00
	Orthogonality	Orthogonality Matrix	695 of 702
Applicability	Reliability	Inter-Annotator Agreement	0.69
	Correctness	Recall	0.73
	Ease of Use	Usability Score	68.25
Purpose	Relevance	Fraction of Relevant Classes	1.00
	Novelty	Innovation, Adaptation	0.49, 0.51
	Significance	Classification Delta	0.54

Structure's Suitability. To evaluate the structure's suitability (**G1**) of the classification, we consider generality (**Q1.1**) and appropriateness (**Q1.2**) and we measured laconicity, lucidity, completeness, and soundness. These metrics are defined for the leaves of a taxonomy, i.e., the 27 options of our classification. We gathered a collection of 38 terms R that describe the object under study, i.e., architectural uncertainties. In a laconic (**M1.1.1**) and thus non-redundant classification C, each term can be described using exactly one option. The *laconicity* is the fraction of terms that is uniquely describable: $laconicity(C, R) = \frac{36}{38} = 0.95$. We argue that the remaining two redundant terms are totally acceptable and originate due to the increased precision regarding confidentiality: User input can be classified as *Input* and *Environment* and uncertainty about non-confidentiality data has both *no impact* and *no severity*. In a lucid (**M1.1.2**) classification, each option describes no more than one term. *Lucidity* is the fraction of options that describe exactly one term: $lucidity(C, R) = \frac{19}{27} = 0.70$. Several terms are described by the same option, e.g., *Structure* describes both uncertainty in components and assembly. Another example is the *realization time* that includes implementation and deployment as this can be simplified from a design time perspective. Here, we decided that more fine-grained options would only harm the purpose of classifying and clustering uncertainties for understanding their impact and mitigation. In a complete (**M1.2.1**) classification, there is no term than cannot be described by at least one option. The completeness is thus calculated as fraction of terms that can be described: $completeness(C, R) = \frac{37}{38} = 0.97$. The completeness is reduced because we do not explicitly handle *known unknowns* that never resolve. From a design time point of view, it does not matter whether an uncertainty resolves at run time or never. In a sound (**M1.2.2**) classification, there are no unnecessary options that are not required to describe at least one term. $soundness(C, R) = \frac{27}{27} = 1.0$. The perfect result is expected, as we intentionally build the classification to fit our purpose. To evaluate the orthogonality (**Q1.3**), we constructed an orthogonality matrix (**M1.3**) and searched for implications between options. We found overlapping only in *7 of 702 cases*, e.g., uncertainty about the system's input implies a behavioral description and there exists the already discussed relation between *no impact* and *no severity*. However, none of the overlaps where comprehensive enough to justify the removal of a category or an option. All results were satisfying, so we continued with the second evaluation step as proposed by Kaplan et al. [19].

Applicability. To evaluate the applicability (**G2**), we conducted a user study with researchers with knowledge about software architecture but no or only little knowledge about uncertainty (for detailed results, please see our data set [14]). Ten participants classified two architecture models with four uncertainties each which yields a set of 80 classified uncertainties and 640 selected options [14]. To evaluate the reliability (**Q2.1**), we calculated the inner-annotator agreement (**M2.1**) by finding the largest consensus for each uncertainty and each category. The overall agreement is *69* percent. High agreement was measured in the categories *Location, Impact on Confidentiality, Severity*, and *Reducible by ADD*. The lowest agreement was measured in the category *Resolution Time*. One explanation is the earlier description of the category, which was ambiguous and has thus been refined. To evaluate correctness (**Q2.2**), we compared the classifications to our gold standard and calculated a recall (**M2.2**) of *0.73*. Based on the participants' feedback, we find that the result can be explained with the short case descriptions of about the quarter of a page and the hard timing constraints. As also shown in Sect. 5, short descriptions of fictional architectures can leave a large room for interpretation. In view of the fact that the participants had no prior experience in classifying uncertainty, this result still is satisfying. Last, we evaluated the ease of use (**Q2.3**) with an average SUS (**M2.3**) score of *68.25*. In the questionnaire, most of the categories were considered understandable and helpful to describe the impact of uncertainty. The only outlier is the category *Type*. However, the value of this category has already been discussed in multiple publications [26,43]. Additionally, we demonstrated in Sect. 5 that this category helps in design-time confidentiality analysis. Also based on the participants' feedback, we summarize that our classification is a sufficiently useful tool to understand the impact of uncertainty but requires some familiarization. Most of the participants welcomed a lively debate about their classifications after the study sessions which is what we aimed for.

Purpose. To evaluate the purpose (**G3**), we first argue for the relevance (**Q3.1**) based on the fraction of relevant classes (**M3.1**). The purpose of our classification is to describe the impact of architectural uncertainty on confidentiality. The *Location* has already been discussed in other work [5,31]. We use *Architectural Element Type* because this enables the connection to architectural modeling and analysis. We demonstrated this in Sect. 5 with analyzing data flow models under uncertainty. We argue that *Type* and *Manageability* are better to describe uncertainty than only to refer to its level because this helps in choosing appropriate mitigation strategies. E.g., a scenario-based, reducible uncertainty can be handled different to a recognized, irreducible uncertainty. This has also been discussed in Sect. 5. *Resolution Time, Reducible by ADD* and both impact-related categories can be used in prioritization together with connected ADDs. This prioritization and connection to ADDs is important because it helps structuring the software design and also helps focusing modeling and analysis capabilities. We close that no category can omitted without significantly reducing the expressiveness and thus the fraction of relevant classes is *1.0*. For the novelty (**Q3.2**), we counted new (**M3.2.1**) and adapted (**M3.2.2**) categories and options. A category or option is adapted if it is adopted or derived from another classification. Examples for adopted categories are the *Resolution Time* or *Severity of the Impact*. Examples for new options are the *partial reducibility*. We find the hard distinction between manageable and irreducible not precise enough for design time mitigation. Also in our running example, we were able to better understand and partially reduce the impact of uncertainty. A full discussion of all 8 categories and 27 options can also be found in our data set [14]. We are right in the middle between innovation ($\frac{17}{35} = 0.49$) and adaption ($\frac{18}{35} = 0.51$). This is expected as we build upon existing taxonomies but extended them to fit our purpose. Last, we evaluate the significance (**Q3.3**) by calculating the classification delta (**M3.3**). Our classification is able to distinguish the 28 uncertainties of the case study into 21 classes. Other taxonomies yield between 4 and 8 classes. Thus, the classification delta is $\frac{21-8}{28} = 0.54$. As we aimed for higher precision, a value higher than 0 is sufficient. We conclude that the metrics indicate that our classification fits its purpose, also compared to the state of the art.

6.4   Threats to Validity

We discuss threats to validity based on the guidelines by Runeson and Höst [35]. Regarding *internal validity*, the biggest threat is the evaluation of structure's suitability that has only been performed by the authors and is thus based on their limited experience. However, we adhered to the metrics and guidelines of Kaplan et al. [19]. The *external validity* and generalizability of our results is threatened by the number of participants in our user study and the selection of the case study. Still, we argue that both were large enough to identify a general trend of applicability and purpose. The participating researchers deal with software architecture in their daily work and the *Corona Warn App* is a large open-source system that is actively observed by the community. Additional information on the construction of the case study can be found here [3]. To face threats to *construct validity*, we applied a GQM-based evaluation plan [19]. Additionally, the SUS provides a standardized format, which might not fit the evaluation of classifications. We mitigated this using a questionnaire which yields similar results regarding the usability. To enhance *reliability* and replicability by other researchers, we publish all evaluation data [14].

6.5   Limitations

We are aware of three limitations of our classification. First, we only focus on confidentiality as central quality attribute. While this reduces the applicability, we did this intentionally to obtain more precise results for mitigation. For example, the focus on confidentiality at design time enables the connection to a data flow meta model [38] for design time confidentiality analysis. Second, the classification is focused on Component Based Software Engineering (CBSE) and works best based on architectural modeling. This was also an explicit design decision due to fit existing modeling [33,38] and analysis [37,39,42] approaches for confidentiality. Still, most categories are general enough to be used even without explicit models, e.g., *Type*, *Manageability*, or *Resolution Time*.

Last, the classification provides no assistance for the transitive impact of uncertainty. The direct impact is often not the location where the uncertainty affects confidentiality and where it can be mitigated. In our exemplary application in Sect. 5, the uncertain provider's trustworthiness could not only directly affect the data base but indirectly other parts of the system. However, to face such propagation effects, a precise description of uncertainty—such as our classification—is required in the first place. Additionally, the propagation, mapping, and analysis of uncertainty for design-time confidentiality analysis requires tool-support as "detecting confidentiality issues manually is not feasible" [37].

7 Conclusion

In this paper, we presented a classification of architectural uncertainty to describe its impact on confidentiality. We explained the relation of software architecture, uncertainty, and confidentiality based on existing classifications. Then, we defined our uncertainty classification and showed how the gained knowledge can be used for mitigation. We demonstrated the mapping of classified uncertainties to an existing data flow model for design time confidentiality analysis. This shall help software architects to better understand the different uncertainty types and analyze their impact. The evaluation showed satisfying results regarding the structural quality, the applicability, and the significance of our classification compared to the state of the art.

Our work benefits software architects in terms of more precise statements about architectural uncertainty and awareness of its different types. As several categories are reusable, this also enables knowledge transfer and reduces the required expertise for mitigating uncertainty. It is also a good baseline for discussion and assessment of uncertainty impacts. This has also been confirmed by our user study. Our classification helps to understand uncertainties and also to document and to prioritize ADDs. This can shorten the span of required backtracking in case of challenged decisions. By making design time confidentiality analyses uncertainty-aware, more comprehensive statements about confidentiality are possible. This shall also help in building more resilient software systems.

In future work, we want to tackle the limitation of manual annotation and analysis of the impact of uncertainty. Based on the presented classification, we want to create assistance for modeling and propagating uncertainty through the software architecture. We also want to create guidelines for better understanding different types of uncertainty and their potential impact on confidentiality. This shall not only enhance reliability and correctness of uncertainty classification, but also enable software architects to identify and mitigate the transitive impact of uncertainty and to make statements about confidentiality under uncertainty.

Acknowledgments. This work was supported by the German Research Foundation (DFG) under project number 432576552, HE8596/1-1 (FluidTrust), as well as by funding from the topic Engineering Secure Systems (46.23.03) of the Helmholtz Association (HGF) and by KASTEL Security Research Labs. We like to thank Niko Benkler, who helped in developing this classification during his Master's thesis. We also like to thank all participants of the user study.

References

1. Armour, P.G.: The five orders of ignorance. Commun. ACM **43**(10) (2000)
2. Basili, V.R., Weiss, D.M.: A Methodology for Collecting Valid Software Engineering Data. TSE, pp. 728–738 (1984). https://doi.org/10.1109/TSE.1984.5010301
3. Benkler, N.: Architecture-based Uncertainty Impact Analysis for Confidentiality. Master's thesis, Karlsruhe Institute of Technology (KIT) (2022)
4. Boehm, B., Basili, V.: Defect reduction top 10 list. Computer **34**(1), 135–137 (2001)
5. Bures, T., Hnetynka, P., Heinrich, R., Seifermann, S., Walter, M.: Capturing dynamicity and uncertainty in security and trust via situational patterns. In: Margaria, T., Steffen, B. (eds.) ISoLA 2020. LNCS, vol. 12477, pp. 295–310. Springer, Cham (2020). https://doi.org/10.1007/978-3-030-61470-6_18
6. Council of European Union: REGULATION (EU) 2016/679 (General Data Protection Regulation) (2016). https://eur-lex.europa.eu/eli/reg/2016/679/2016-05-04. Accessed 05/11/2022
7. Esfahani, N., et al.: GuideArch. In: ICSE, pp. 43–52 (2013). https://doi.org/10.1109/ICSE.2013.6606550
8. Esfahani, N., Malek, S.: Uncertainty in self-adaptive software systems. In: de Lemos, R., Giese, H., Müller, H.A., Shaw, M. (eds.) Software Engineering for Self-Adaptive Systems II. LNCS, vol. 7475, pp. 214–238. Springer, Heidelberg (2013). https://doi.org/10.1007/978-3-642-35813-5_9
9. FIRST: CVSS v3.1 specification document. https://www.first.org/cvss/v3.1/specification-document#2-3-Impact-Metrics. Accessed 05/11/2022
10. Garlan, D.: Software engineering in an uncertain world. In: Proceedings of the FSE/SDP Workshop on Future of Software Engineering Research - FoSER 2010, p. 125. ACM Press (2010). https://doi.org/10.1145/1882362.1882389
11. Grassi, V., Mirandola, R.: The Tao way to anti-fragile software architectures: the case of mobile applications. In: ICSA-C, pp. 86–89. IEEE (2021). https://doi.org/10.1109/ICSA-C52384.2021.00021
12. Hahner, S.: Architectural access control policy refinement and verification under uncertainty. In: ECSA-C (2021)
13. Hahner, S.: Dealing with uncertainty in architectural confidentiality analysis. In: Proceedings of the Software Engineering 2021 Satellite Events, pp. 1–6. GI (2021)
14. Hahner, S., et al.: Companion data set. https://doi.org/10.5281/zenodo.6814107
15. Hahner, S., et al.: Modeling data flow constraints for design-time confidentiality analyses. In: ICSA-C, pp. 15–21. IEEE (2021). https://doi.org/10.1109/ICSA-C52384.2021.00009
16. Isaak, J., Hanna, M.J.: User Data Privacy. Computer **51**(8), 56–59 (2018). https://doi.org/10.1109/MC.2018.3191268
17. ISO: ISO/IEC 27000:2018(E) Information technology – Security techniques – Information security management systems – Overview and vocabulary. Standard (2018)
18. Jansen, A., Bosch, J.: Software architecture as a set of architectural design decisions. In: WICSA, pp. 109–120 (2005). https://doi.org/10.1109/WICSA.2005.61
19. Kaplan, A., et al.: Introducing an evaluation method for taxonomies. In: EASE. ACM (2022). https://doi.org/10.5445/IR/1000145968, accepted, to appear
20. Kiureghian, A.D., Ditlevsen, O.: Aleatory or epistemic? does it matter? Struct. Saf. **31**, 105–112 (2009). https://doi.org/10.1016/j.strusafe.2008.06.020
21. Konersmann, M., et al.: Evaluation methods and replicability of software architecture research objects. In: ICSA. IEEE (2022), accepted, to appear
22. Koziolek, A., et al.: PerOpteryx: automated application of tactics in multi-objective software architecture optimization. In: QoSA-ISARCS, pp. 33–42. ACM (2011). https://doi.org/10.1145/2000259.2000267

23. Kruchten, P.: An Ontology of Architectural Design Decisions in Software-Intensive Systems. In: 2nd Groningen Workshop on Software Variability, pp. 54–61 (2004)
24. Lewis, J.R.: The system usability scale: past, present, and future. Int. J. Hum.-Comput. Interact. **34**(7), 577–590 (2018). https://doi.org/10.1080/10447318.2018.1455307
25. Lytra, I., Zdun, U.: Supporting architectural decision making for systems-of-systems design under uncertainty. In: SESoS, pp. 43–46. ACM (2013). https://doi.org/10.1145/2489850.2489859
26. Mahdavi-Hezavehi, S., et al.: A Classification Framework of Uncertainty in Architecture-Based Self-Adaptive Systems with Multiple Quality Requirements. Managing Trade-Offs in Adaptable Software Architectures, p. 33 (2017). https://doi.org/10.1016/B978-0-12-802855-1.00003-4
27. Mahdavi-Hezavehi, S., et al.: Uncertainty in Self-Adaptive Systems: A Research Community Perspective. ACM TAAS (2021)
28. McConnell, S.: Software Project Survey Guide. Microsoft Press, Redmond, Wash (1998)
29. OWASP Foundation: Owasp top 10:2021 (2021). https://owasp.org/Top10/. Accessed 05/11/2022
30. Perez-Palacin, D., Mirandola, R.: Dealing with uncertainties in the performance modelling of software systems. In: QoSA, pp. 33–42. ACM (2014). https://doi.org/10.1145/2602576.2602582
31. Perez-Palacin, D., Mirandola, R.: Uncertainties in the modeling of self-adaptive systems. In: ICPE, pp. 3–14. ACM (2014). https://doi.org/10.1145/2568088.2568095
32. Ramirez, A.J., et al.: A taxonomy of uncertainty for dynamically adaptive systems. In: SEAMS, pp. 99–108 (2012). https://doi.org/10.1109/SEAMS.2012.6224396
33. Reussner, R.H., et al.: Modeling and Simulating Software Architectures: The Palladio Approach. The MIT Press (2016)
34. Robert Koch Institute: Open-Source Project Corona-Warn-App (2020). https://www.coronawarn.app/en/. Accessed 05/11/2022
35. Runeson, P., Höst, M.: Guidelines for conducting and reporting case study research in software engineering. Empir. Softw. Eng. **14**, 131 (2009). https://doi.org/10.1007/s10664-008-9102-8
36. Sasse, M.A., Flechais, I.: Usable security: Why do we need it? how do we get it? O'Reilly (2005)
37. Seifermann, S., Heinrich, R., Reussner, R.: Data-driven software architecture for analyzing confidentiality. In: ICSA, p. 1–10. IEEE (2019). https://doi.org/10.1109/ICSA.2019.00009
38. Seifermann, S., Heinrich, R., Werle, D., Reussner, R.: A unified model to detect information flow and access control violations in software architectures. In: SECRYPT, pp. 26–37. SCITEPRESS (2021). https://doi.org/10.5220/0010515300260037
39. Seifermann, S., et al.: Detecting violations of access control and information flow policies in data flow diagrams. JSS (2022). https://doi.org/10.1016/j.jss.2021.111138
40. Shostack, A.: Threat Modeling: Designing for Security. John Wiley & Sons (2014)
41. Troya, J., Moreno, N., Bertoa, M.F., Vallecillo, A.: Uncertainty representation in software models: a survey. Softw. Syst. Model. **20**(4), 1183–1213 (2021). https://doi.org/10.1007/s10270-020-00842-1
42. Tuma, K., et al.: Flaws in flows. In: ICSA, pp. 191–200. IEEE (2019). https://doi.org/10.1109/ICSA.2019.00028
43. Walker, W.E., et al.: Defining uncertainty: a conceptual basis for uncertainty management in model-based decision support. Integr. Assess. **4**(1), 5–17 (2003). https://doi.org/10.1076/iaij.4.1.5.16466

44. Walter, M., et al.: Architectural optimization for confidentiality under structural uncertainty. In: ECSA'21 Post-Proceedings. Springer (2022), accepted, to appear
45. Weisbaum, H.: Trust in facebook has dropped by 66 percent since the cambridge analytica scandal (2018). https://www.nbcnews.com/business/consumer/trust-facebook-has-dropped-51-percent-cambridge-analytica-scandal-n867011. Accessed 05/11/2022

Zero-Knowledge Predicates for Hashing to Prime: Theory and Applications

Thomas Groß[✉]

School of Computing, Newcastle University, Newcastle upon Tyne, UK
thomas.gross@newcastle.ac.uk

Abstract. Hashing to prime in zero-knowledge takes as input a committed secret a-bit input x and outputs a committed secret $(k + 1)$-bit prime number p_x. In this work we are considering zero-knowledge arguments that establish that the corresponding computations are done correctly and that the resulting commitment is indeed on the prime number derived from x. Depending on the number of zero-knowledge argument rounds k and the number of primality bases t used to establish primality, we obtain a soundness error probability of at most $2^{-k} + 2^{-t}$. While the corresponding ZK arguments have already been established in earlier work [22], we explore the use of hash-to-prime ZK arguments to enable dynamic encodings for a selection of cryptographic schemes, namely prime-based accumulator [2,10], attribute-based credential [7], and graph signature schemes [19,21].

Keywords: Primality testing · Prime hashing · RSA · Prime encoding · Zero-knowledge argument

1 Introduction

Prime numbers are a common ingredient for the encoding of data. Schemes that rely on prime or division-intractable encoding include credential schemes [8], special-purpose and graph signature schemes [21], and dynamic accumulators and related revocation systems [2,10]. These schemes typically select prime numbers randomly or from a predefined fixed alphabet, rendering it challenging to extend them to full-domain message spaces. At the same time, it is often crucial to convince verifiers in zero-knowledge of their faithful protocol execution.

This is where hashing-to-prime zero-knowledge predicates [22] come into play. Hashing to prime enables the computation of a $(k + 1)$-bit prime number p_x from an a-bit input x. The primitive is already regularly applied in schemes that rely on division-intractable encoding, such as in private information retrieval [6], verifiable random functions [28] or verifiable computing [30]. Schemes that not only rely on prime or division-intractable encoding but also aim at proving in zero-knowledge of their faithful protocol execution require the use of hash-to-prime zero-knowledge predicates to fulfil the latter requirement.

In this work, we explore hashing-to-prime zero-knowledge predicates proving that a committed secret a-bit input x was deterministically hashed to a committed secret $(k + 1)$-bit prime number p_x. Therein, we are especially interested in practical constructions in the discrete-log based zero-knowledge proof paradigm, that is, Σ-proofs

© The Author(s), under exclusive license to Springer Nature Switzerland AG 2023
P. Samarati et al. (Eds.): ICETE 2021, CCIS 1795, pp. 161–194, 2023.
https://doi.org/10.1007/978-3-031-36840-0_9

and the Camenisch-Stadler [14] and the UC ZK framework [9]. Clearly, this aim is doable in general as all NP-languages are provable in zero-knowledge [18].

Hashing to prime can operate in different ways. First, one may generate a sequence of pseudo-random numbers from the input and eliminate all candidates that are not prime. This is called hash-to-prime by elimination. Second, one generates a sequence of prime number recursively in a Pocklington sequence. This is called hash-to-prime by recursive construction. The corresponding zero-knowledge predicates follow the same principles while establishing that a hidden integer p_x is a prime derived from input x. The prover establishes a zero-knowledge predicate $p_x = \mathsf{hashToPrime}(x)$ between two commitments C_x and C_{p_x} on input x and output prime p_x, respectively.

Hash-to-Prime by Elimination. On input of a a-bit bitstring x, the prover computes a sequence of $(k+1)$-bit pseudo-random numbers $y_i = \mathsf{PRG}_{\mathcal{H}(x)}(i)$, iterating over i starting from 1 until y_u is tests positive as a probable prime. The prover commits to input x and the sequence $(y_i)_{i=1}^u$. He proves to a verifier in a zero-knowledge argument:

1. that all computations were executed correctly,
2. that the final committed output $p_x := y_u$ passes a primality test.
3. that all committed intermediate candidates $(y_i)_{i=1}^{u-1}$ are composites.

The number of eliminated composites u is public knowledge.

Hash-to-Prime by Recursive Construction. On input of a a-bit bitstring x, the prover establishes a first prime number p_0 as $2^{\ell_{n_0}} h_0 + n_0$ where $h_0 := \mathcal{H}_{Q_0, z_0}(x)$ and n_0 is number of iterations till the first prime is found. Then, the prover builds a Pocklington sequence (p_{j-1}, a_j, r_j) where each r_j is given by $r_j := 2^{\ell_{n_j}} \cdot \mathcal{H}_{Q_j, z_j}(x) + n_j$ for the current Pocklington step j. The prover tests in the sequence of integers $y_{j,i} := p_{j-1} \cdot r_{j,i} + 1$ for primality, till one is found to be a probable prime. Then, the prover commits to input x, the sequence $(y_{j,i})$, r_j, a_j. The prover makes the integers $n_{j,i}$ public. The prover communicates with the verifier in a zero-knowledge argument yielding that the base value is prime and the preceding candidates composite, followed by a zero-knowledge argument that for each Pocklington step holds:

1. the prover knows a Pocklington witness (p_{j-1}, a_j, r_j),
2. the Pocklington criterion is fulfilled such that the subsequent number p_j is prime,
3. the intermediate candidates $(y_{j,i})$ leading up to p_j are composites.

The integer n_j of each step is public knowledge.

Contributions. In this work, we are discussing zero-knowledge predicates and arguments for hashing-to-prime by (i) elimination and (ii) recursive construction. While these predicates have been proposed earlier [22], we complement them with new protocol constructions and proofs. Section 5 offers new applications in terms of certifying (x, p_x) associations, of identity-based prime-based accumulators [10] and dynamic encoding for the Camenisch-Groß anonymous credential scheme [8] and the SRSA graph signature scheme [21].

2   Preliminaries

We assume a group $\mathbb{G}$ with prime order Q and two generators g and h, $\langle g \rangle = \langle h \rangle = \mathbb{G}$, for which the discrete logarithm $\log_g h$ is not known. We assume a commitment scheme in group $\mathbb{G}$ which commits messages m with commitments of the structure $C_m := g^m h^{r_m}$, where r_m is chosen uniformly at random, $r_m \in_R \mathbb{Z}_Q$.

We assume the setup for a *Square Hash* (SQH/U) [17] family of functions from $\mathbb{Z}_Q$ to $\mathbb{Z}_Q$ as: $\{\mathcal{H}_{Q,z} : \mathbb{Z}_Q \longrightarrow \mathbb{Z}_Q | z \in \mathbb{Z}_Q\}$ and $\{\mathcal{H}_{Q,z,b} : \mathbb{Z}_Q \longrightarrow \mathbb{Z}_Q | z, b \in \mathbb{Z}_Q\}$ where the functions $\mathcal{H}_{Q,z}$ and $\mathcal{H}_{Q,z,b}$ are defined as:

$$\text{SQH:}\quad \mathcal{H}_{Q,z}(x) \qquad\qquad \equiv (x+z)^2 \quad (\text{mod } Q)$$

$$\text{SQHU:}\quad \mathcal{H}_{Q,z,b}(x) \qquad\qquad \equiv (x+z)^2 + b \quad (\text{mod } Q)$$

Theorem 1 (Square Hash [17]). *The family SQH is Δ-universal. The family SQHU is strongly universal.*

We assume a setup for the Naor-Reingold PRG [29]. An instance is generated with a key $\langle Q, P, \mathfrak{g}, \vec{a} \rangle$ with prime Q, prime P dividing $Q - 1$, $\mathfrak{g}$ a generator of order P, $\mathfrak{G} := \langle \mathfrak{g} \rangle \subset \mathbb{Z}_Q$, and $\vec{a}$ a sequence of $k + 1$ elements of $\mathbb{Z}_P$. For an a-bit input x with bits $x_1, \ldots, x_n$, $\text{PRG}_{a_0}(x) := f_{Q,P,\mathfrak{g},\vec{a}}$ is defined as:

$$f_{Q,P,\mathfrak{g},\vec{a}} := (\mathfrak{g}^{a_0})^{\prod_{x_i=1} a_i} \quad (\text{mod } Q).$$

2.1   Known Primality Criteria

We introduce in turn primality criteria related to (i) Lehmann's and Solovay-Strassen's tests, (ii) Miller's test, and (iii) Pocklington's test.

Theorem 2 ([25]). *An odd integer $n > 1$ is prime if and only if*

$$\forall a \in \mathbb{Z}_n^* : \quad a^{(n-1)/2} \equiv \pm 1 \quad (\text{mod } n) \text{ and} \tag{1}$$

$$\exists a \in \mathbb{Z}_n^* : \quad a^{(n-1)/2} \equiv -1 \quad (\text{mod } n). \tag{2}$$

Theorem 3 (Miller, Adapted from [25]). *For any odd integer $n > 1$ write $n - 1 = 2^e u$, with u odd. Then, n is prime if and only if*

$$(\forall a \in \mathbb{Z}_n^*) : \quad a^u \not\equiv 1 \quad (\text{mod } n) \Longrightarrow$$

$$\exists k < e : \left(a^{2^k u} \equiv -1 \quad (\text{mod } n) \right).$$

Definition 1. *We call an odd integer $n > 1$ in Theorem 3 which fulfills both clauses with respect to base a, a strong probable prime to base a. We call a composite n fulfilling those clauses a strong pseudoprime to base a, extending naturally to the case of pseudoprimes to several bases $(a_j)_{j=1}^t$. [23,31] We write:*

$$\text{spsp}\left((a_j)_{j=1}^t, n\right).$$

Theorem 4 (Pocklington, in an Adaptation by [5,30]). *Let p be a prime, and $r < p$ and a be positive integers. Define $p' := p \cdot r + 1$. Pocklington's criterion states that if $a^{pr} \equiv 1 \pmod{p'}$ and $\gcd(a^r - 1, p') = 1$, then p' is prime. In this case, we say that (p, r, a) is a Pocklington witness for p'.*

Definition 2 (Pocklington Witness Sequence). We call a Pocklington witness sequence *a sequence* $(p_{j-1}, r_j, a_j)_{i=j}^{t}$ *attesting to primes* p_j *with* $j = 1, \ldots, t$ *such that* $a_j^{p_{j-1} r_j} \equiv 1 \pmod{p_j}$ *and* $\gcd(a_j^{r_j} - 1, p_j) = 1$.

2.2 Known Zero-Knowledge Proofs

In the following, we introduce a selection of zero-knowledge proof predicates that are well known in the community. We are starting with simple statements, e.g., that a number is not ± 1 or that two numbers are coprime. We include a range of secret computations under a secret modulus as well as a primality zero-knowledge argument, both proposed by Camenisch and Michels [13]. Tables 1 and 2 summarize the computation and communication complexity of these known zero-knowledge predicates. In parts the protocols require bitlength restrictions to be maintained. For these purposes we employ range-bounded commitments introduced by Chan et al. [15] and summarized in Appendix A of Camenisch and Michels [12] with a length parameter ℓ and a security parameter $\epsilon > 1$.

$(\mu \not\equiv \pm 1)$: Shows that given committed value is neither one nor minus one [7,8].

$$S_{\neg \pm 1} := PK\{(\alpha, \rho, \sigma, \psi, \varsigma, \varpi) :$$
$$D = g^\mu h^\rho \wedge$$
$$g = (D/g)^\sigma h^\psi \wedge g = (gD)^\varsigma h^\varpi$$
$$\}.$$

Together, the clauses prove that the committed value of D is neither ± 1. The first line establishes the proof of knowledge of the representation of D. For the first clause of the second line, assuming the hardness of the finding the discrete logarithm $\log_g h$ holds, $(D/g)^\sigma h^\psi$ is equivalent to $1 \equiv (\alpha - 1)\sigma \pmod{q}$, which in turn implies that $\alpha \not\equiv 1 \pmod{q}$. For the second clause, we have that $1 \equiv (\alpha + 1)\varsigma$, which in turn implies that $\alpha \not\equiv -1 \pmod{q}$.

$(\gcd(\mu, \nu) = 1)$: Showing coprimality is a vital part of the Camenisch-Groß anonymous credential scheme [7,8] and the SRSA graph signature scheme [21]. To show that two values μ and ν are coprime, we show that $(\gcd(\mu, \nu) = 1)$, which is true if and only if there exist integers α and β such that Bézout's identity is $\gcd(\mu, \nu) = 1 = \alpha\mu + \beta\nu$:

$$S_{\gcd} := PK\{(\mu, \nu, \rho_\mu, \rho_\nu, \alpha, \beta, \rho) :$$
$$C_\mu = g^\mu h^{\rho_\mu} \wedge C_\nu = g^\nu h^{\rho_\nu} \wedge$$
$$g = C_\mu^\alpha C_\nu^\beta h^\rho$$
$$\}.$$

$(\mu > 0)$: Following a method used in Boudot's interval proofs [4], we can show with a predicate $(\mu > 0)$ that an integer μ is greater than zero, proving knowledge of four integers $\chi_1, \chi_2, \chi_3, \chi_4$ such that $\mu = \sum_{i=1}^{4} \chi_i^2$:

$$S_{>0} := PK\{ \left((\chi_i, \rho_{\chi_i})_{i=1}^{4}, \rho \right) :$$

$$(C_{\chi_i} = g^{\chi_i} h^{\rho_{\chi_i}})_{i=1}^{4} \wedge \qquad C_\mu = \prod_{i=1}^{4} (C_{\chi_i}^{\chi_i}) h^\rho$$

$$\}.$$

$\underline{(a^b \equiv d \pmod{n})}$: Camenisch and Michels [13] introduced statistical zero-knowledge arguments for (i) secret modular addition with PK predicate S_+, (ii) secret modular multiplication with PK predicate S_*, (iii) secret modular exponentiation with PK predicate $S_\uparrow$, and (iv) secret evaluation of general multivariate polynomials with PK predicate S_f. The proof of secret exponentiation we will adapt in two forms:

$(a^b \equiv d \pmod{n})$: signifies a secret modular exponentiation with secrets a, b, d, and n, realized with computing a committed square-and-multiply $\pmod{n}$ with respect to the committed bit-representation of b.

$(a^b = d)$: means a secret exponentiation over the integers with secrets a, b, and d, which can be easily adapted from the former, but needs to maintain a small enough size for the group setup.

Both forms have in common that they produce intermediary commitments C_{v_i} to either $a^{2^i} \pmod{n}$ in the former case or C_{v_i} to a^{2^i} over the integers in the latter case. We note that while a proof exponentiation can also be implemented by cumulative squared commitments or by Wesolowski's proof of exponentiation [33], those methods would disclose the exponent b.

Theorem 5 (Secret ModExp [13, **p. 114]).** *Let c_a, c_b, c_d, and c_n be commitments on integers a, b, d, and n and let $c_{b_0}, \ldots, c_{b_{\ell-1}}, c_{v_1}, \ldots, c_{v_{\ell_b}-1}, c_{u_0}, \ldots, c_{u_{\ell_b}-2}$ be auxiliary commitments. Then assuming computing discrete logarithms in G is infeasible, the protocol $S_\uparrow$ is a statistical zero-knowledge argument that the equation $a^b \equiv d \pmod{n}$ holds. The soundness error probability is 2^{-k}.*

Corollary 1 (Secret Exponentiation). *Let c_a, c_b, and c_d be commitments on integers a, b, and d and let $c_{b_0}, \ldots, c_{b_{\ell-1}}, c_{v_1}, \ldots, c_{v_{\ell_b}-1}, c_{u_0}, \ldots, c_{u_{\ell_b}-2}$ be auxiliary commitments. Then assuming computing discrete logarithms in G is infeasible, the protocol $S_\uparrow'$ is a statistical zero-knowledge argument that the equation $a^b = d$ over the integers holds. The soundness error probability is 2^{-k}.*

$\underline{(a_i \in \mathbb{Z}_n)_{i=1}^{k}}$: This proof predicate governs the joint generation of group elements $a_i \in \mathbb{Z}_n$, where the verifier may not be privy of n, showing that the bases were generated correctly with randomness from both prover and verifier. This predicate is part of the primality protocol [13]. The full version contains a modular construction. We present it in Fig. 6 as a reusable shorthand in the Appendix.

Table 1. Computation complexity of known PK predicates for k rounds (cf. [22]).

Predicate	Computations (mexp)	
	Prover	Verifier
$(\mu \not\equiv \pm 1)$	$1 + 3k$	$3k$
$(\gcd(\mu, \nu) = 1)$	$2 + 3k$	$3k$
$(\mu > 0)$	$5 + 5k$	$5k$
$\begin{pmatrix} a^b \equiv d \pmod{n} \\ a^b = d \end{pmatrix}$	$3\ell_b + (7\ell_b)k$	$(7\ell_b)k$
$(\mu \in \mathsf{primes}_\mathsf{L}(t))$	$2t \log n + (7t \log n)k$	$(7t \log n)k$
$(\mu \in \mathsf{composites}_\mathsf{L}())$	$2 \log n + (11 + 7 \log n)k$	$(11 + 7 \log n)k$
$(\mu = \mathcal{H}_\varsigma(\nu))$	$4 + 6k$	$6k$
$(\mu = \mathcal{H}_{\varsigma,\beta}(\nu))$	$4 + 8k$	$8k$
$(\mu = \mathsf{PRG}_\varepsilon(\nu))$	$2n + 4 + (4 + 2n)k$	$(4 + 2n)k$

Note: mexp = multi-base exponentiations; k = number of PK rounds; ℓ_b = bitlength of the exponent b; in primes and composites n refers to the integer under consideration

Table 2. Communication complexity of known PK predicates for k rounds (cf. [22]).

Predicate	Communication (ge/bits)
$(\mu \not\equiv \pm 1)$	$1 + 3k$ ge $+ 6k \log Q$ bits
$(\gcd(\mu, \nu) = 1)$	$2 + 3k$ ge $+ 7k \log Q$ bits
$(\mu > 0)$	$5 + 5k$ ge $+ 5k \log Q$ bits
$\begin{pmatrix} a^b \equiv d \pmod{n} \\ a^b = d \end{pmatrix}$	$3\ell_b$ ge $+ (14\ell_b \log Q + 4\ell_b \epsilon \ell)k$ bits
$(\mu \in \mathsf{primes}_\mathsf{L}(t))$	$2t \log n$ ge $+ (14t \log n \log Q + 4t \log n\epsilon\ell)k$ bits
$(\mu \in \mathsf{composites}_\mathsf{L}())$	$2 \log n$ ge $+ (14 \log n \log Q + 4 \log n\ell_b\epsilon\ell)k$ bits
$(\mu = \mathcal{H}_\varsigma(\nu))$	$4 + 6k$ ge $+ 10k \log Q$ bits
$(\mu = \mathcal{H}_{\varsigma,\beta}(\nu))$	$5 + 8k$ ge $+ 13k \log Q$ bits
$(\mu = \mathsf{PRG}_\varepsilon(\nu))$	$2n + 4$ ge $+ (4 + 2n)k$ ge $+ (7 + 3n)k \log Q$ bits

Note: ge = group elements from $\mathbb{G}$; k = number of PK rounds; ℓ_b = bitlength of the exponent b; ℓ = bitlength restriction; ϵ = security parameter; in primes and composites n refers to the integer under consideration

$(\mu \in \mathsf{primes}_\mathsf{L}(t))$: Camenisch and Michels offered a PK predicate we call $\mathsf{primes}_\mathsf{L}(t)$ proving that a committed number is prime using a predicate S_p for a secret execution of Lehmann's primality test [26]. The realization of this predicate is included in Fig. 7 in the appendix. To render this paper self-contained, we include a compact reformulation of Camenisch and Michels [13] PK predicate $(\mu \in \mathsf{primes}_\mathsf{L}(t))$ realized with $\left((a_i)_{i=1}^t \in_R \mathbb{Z}_n^k\right)$ in Fig. 7 in the Appendix.

Theorem 6 (Primality [13, p. 118]). *Assume computing discrete logarithms in G is infeasible. Then, the protocol $\mathsf{primes}_\mathsf{L}(t)$ on a commitment c_n is a statistical zero-knowledge argument that the integer committed to by c_n is a prime. The soundness error probability is at most $2^{-k} + 2^{-t}$.*

$(\mu \in \mathsf{composites}(t))$: We include a statistical zero-knowledge argument that a committed value is a composite without knowledge of its factors. While this is easy to achieve when the factors of x are known to the prover, we show the *compositeness of* a committed value x without knowledge of the factors of x. As such, our PK predicate composites(t) is the proper complement of Camenisch and Michels' PK predicate primes(t) [13].

Theorem 2 entails in Clause 1 that if there exists an $\bar{a} \in \mathbb{Z}_n^*$ such that $\bar{a}^{(n-1)/2} \not\equiv \pm 1$ (mod n), then n cannot be a prime. Hence, to prove a committed value n a composite, we prove $\exists \bar{a} \in \{a_i | i = 1, \ldots, t, a_i \in_R \mathbb{Z}_n^*\} : \bar{a}^{(n-1)/2} \not\equiv \pm 1$ (mod n) in a statistical zero-knowledge argument. For a non-empty random selection $(a_i)_{i=1}^t$ from $\mathbb{Z}_n^*$ such an $\bar{a}$ will exist with overwhelming probability.

The setup of the protocol proceeds as in Camenisch and Michels' [13] secret primality test, for which we assume a group G with large prime order Q and two generators g and h for which $\log_g h$ is not known.

1. The prover picks random $\hat{a} \in \mathbb{Z}_n$ for $i = 1, \ldots, t$ and commits to them as $C_{\hat{a}_i} := g^{\hat{a}_i} h^{r_{\hat{a}_i}}$, where $r_{\hat{a}_i} \in_R \mathbb{Z}_Q$ are chosen uniformly at random.
2. The prover sends the commitments $C_{\hat{a}_1}, \ldots, C_{\hat{a}_t}$ to the verifier.
3. The verifier chooses uniformly at random integers $-2^{(k+1)} < \check{a}_i < 2^{(k+1)}$ for $i = 1, \ldots, t$ and sends them to the prover.
4. The prover computes (a) $C_n := C^n h^{r_n}$ with $r_n \in_R \mathbb{Z}_Q$, (b) $a_i := \hat{a}_i \check{a}_i$ (mod n) for $i = 1, \ldots, t$, and (c) $d_i := a_i^{(n-1)/2}$ (mod n) for $i = 1, \ldots, t$.
5. The prover commits to $(n-1)/2$ in the form of $C_b := g^{(n-1)/2} h^{r_b}$ with $r_b \in_R \mathbb{Z}_Q$.
6. The prover searches for a base $\bar{a} \in (a_i)_{i=1}^t$ such that $\bar{a}^{(n-1)/2} \not\equiv \pm 1$ (mod n). We call the corresponding congruence result $\bar{d}$ and the corresponding random base components $\hat{a}$ and $\check{a}$.
7. The prover computes the commitment on the result $C_{\bar{d}}$ as $C_{\bar{d}} := g^{\bar{d}} h^{r_{\bar{d}}}$ with $r_{\bar{d}} \subset_R \mathbb{Z}_Q$.
8. Then, the Prover and the Verifier engage in the following interactive sub-protocol proving sequentially k times.

$$S_{\neg p} := PK\{(\alpha, \beta, \nu, \xi, \gamma, \delta, \varepsilon, \zeta, \varrho, \omega, \mu, \psi, \sigma, \pi, \varsigma, \varpi) :$$

$$C_b = g^\alpha h^\beta \wedge \mathsf{size}(\alpha) \wedge \tag{3}$$

$$C_n = g^\nu h^\xi \wedge \mathsf{size}(\nu) \wedge \tag{4}$$

$$C_b^2 g / C_n = h^\gamma \wedge \tag{5}$$

$$C_{\hat{a}} = g^\delta h^\varepsilon \wedge \mathsf{size}(\delta) \wedge \tag{6}$$

$$C_{\bar{a}}/g^{\check{a}} = g^\delta C_n^\zeta h^\nu \wedge \mathsf{size}(\zeta) \wedge \tag{7}$$

$$C_{\bar{a}} = g^\varrho h^\omega \wedge \tag{8}$$

$$C_{\bar{d}} = g^\mu h^\psi \wedge \tag{9}$$

$$(\varrho^\alpha \equiv \mu \pmod{\nu}) \wedge \tag{10}$$

$$g = (C_{\bar{d}}/g)^\sigma h^\pi \wedge g = (gC_{\bar{d}})^\varsigma h^\varpi \tag{11}$$

$$\}.$$

Clauses 3 and 4 prove the knowledge of the representations of the commitments to $(n-1)/2$ and of candidate n itself. Clause 5 proves that the committed value in C_b has the correct structure $(n-1)/2$.

Clause 6 establishes the knowledge of the representation of the commitment on the prover's input to the random base, while Clause 7 shows that the joint random base $\bar{a}$ is correctly constructed with the verifiers randomness. Then, Clause 8 proves the knowledge of the representation of $C_{\bar{a}}$ as commitment on base $\bar{a}$, itself.

Finally, Clause 9 proves the knowledges of the representation of the commitment on the result $\bar{d}$. Together, the clauses in line 11 prove that the result committed in $C_{\bar{d}}$ is neither ± 1. This line of reasoning is completed by Clause 10 proving that the secret modular exponentiation of Lehmann's primality test $\bar{a}^{(n-1)/2} \equiv \bar{d} \pmod{n}$ holds.

Theorem 7. *If the discrete-logarithm problem is hard in group G, then the protocol* composite(t) *on commitment C_n is a statistical zero-knowledge argument that the integer n committed to by C_n is a composite. The soundness error probability is at most* 2^{-k}.

Proof. That n cannot be a prime given a suitable $\bar{d}$ with follows from the negation of the all-quantified first clause of Theorem 2. Hence, it remains to show that $\bar{a}^{(n-1)/2} \not\equiv \pm 1 \pmod{n}$. Together, the clauses in line 11 prove that $\bar{d} \neq \pm 1$. For the first clause of this line, assuming the hardness of the finding the discrete logarithm $\log_g h$ holds, $(C_{\bar{d}}/g)^{\sigma} h^{\psi}$ is equivalent to $1 \equiv (\mu - 1)\sigma \pmod{q}$, which in turn implies that $\mu \not\equiv 1 \pmod{q}$. The second clause, likewise, yields under the intractability of the discrete-logarithm problem that $(gC_{\bar{d}})^{\varsigma} h^{\varpi}$ is equivalent to $1 \equiv (\mu + 1)\varsigma \pmod{q}$, which implies that $\mu \not\equiv -1 \pmod{q}$. The final Clause 10 then shows that $\bar{a}^{(n-1)/2} \equiv \bar{d}$ with respect to the hidden modulus n. (Cf. Theorem 5 proven by Camenisch and Michels [13]).

$(C = \mathsf{GCCommit}(f(\mu), \rho))$: This PK predicate is a special case of the elegant construction of Jawurek, Kerschbaum, Orlandi [24] to prove non-algebraic statements in zero-knowledge with garbled circuits. It is especially useful in the context of discrete-logarithm based zero-knowledge proofs of knowledge and signature schemes, which often operate on committed, hidden values.

Here, the public input is a commitment C to the result of a non-algebraic computation f on a secret witness x. The PK predicate is written as follows:

$$(C = \mathsf{GCCommit}(f(\mu), \rho)),$$

where the function f is publicly known, μ represents the secret witness x in the zero-knowledge proof and ρ the randomness of commitment C. Figure 8 illustrates the implementation of this predicate in the Appendix.

$(\mu = \mathcal{H}_{\varsigma, \beta}(\nu))$: We are using the square-hash function proposed by Etzel, Patel, and Ramzan [17]. This predicate proves that a committed value μ is the output of a square hash SQHU $\mathcal{H}_{Q,z,b}$ with key (ς, β) on committed input ν. A corresponding predicate $(\mu = \mathcal{H}_{\varsigma}(\nu))$ for SQH $\mathcal{H}_{Q,z}$ follows trivially. When evaluated in $\mathbb{Z}_Q$, we omit parameter Q.

$$S_{SQH} := PK\{ \, (\mu, \rho_\mu, \nu, \rho_\nu, \zeta, \rho_\zeta, \bar{\mu}, \rho_{\bar{\mu}}, \gamma, \delta) : $$
$$C_\mu = g^\mu h^{\rho_\mu} \wedge C_\nu = g^\nu h^{\rho_\nu} \wedge $$
$$C_\zeta = g^\zeta h^{\rho_\zeta} \wedge C_{\bar{\mu}} = g^{\bar{\mu}} h^{\rho_{\bar{\mu}}} \wedge $$
$$C_{\bar{\mu}} = C_\zeta C_\nu h^\gamma \wedge C_\mu = C_{\bar{\mu}}^{\bar{\mu}} h^\delta $$
$$\}.$$

$$S_{SQHU} := PK\{ \, (\mu, \rho_\mu, \nu, \rho_\nu, \zeta, \rho_\zeta, \bar{\mu}, \rho_{\bar{\mu}}, \beta, \rho_\beta, \gamma, \delta, \eta) : $$
$$C_\mu = g^\mu h^{\rho_\mu} \wedge C_\nu = g^\nu h^{\rho_\nu} \wedge $$
$$C_\zeta = g^\zeta h^{\rho_\zeta} \wedge C_{\bar{\mu}} = g^{\bar{\mu}} h^{\rho_{\bar{\mu}}} \wedge $$
$$C_{\bar{\mu}} = C_\zeta C_\nu h^\gamma \wedge C_{\hat{\mu}} = C_{\bar{\mu}}^{\bar{\mu}} h^\delta \wedge $$
$$C_\beta = g^\beta h^{\rho_\beta} \wedge C_\mu = C_{\hat{\mu}} C_\beta h^\eta $$
$$\}.$$

Remark 1. For algebraic hash functions such as the *square hash* proposed by Etzel, Patel, and Ramzan [17] this is facilitated with a discrete-logarithm based zero-knowledge proof of knowledge. For non-algebraic hash functions, we can use the predicate GCCommit($f(\mu), \rho$) based on zero-knowledge proofs with garbled circuits [24] to show that a commitment contains the output of function $\mathcal{H}()$.

$(\mu = \mathsf{PRG}_\xi(\nu))$: This predicate proves that μ is the output of pseudo-random generator PRG on seed ξ and input ν. We can prove predicate of the Naor-Reingold PRG in discrete-logarithm-based zero-knowledge proofs efficiently that the relation $\mu = f_{Q,P,\mathfrak{g},\vec{a}}(\nu)$ is fulfilled in $\mathfrak{G}$.

We consider a Naor-Reingold PRG [29] instance as introduced in the beginning of Sect. 2. For an a-bit input x with bits $x_1, \ldots, x_n$, $\mathsf{PRG}_{a_0}(x) := f_{Q,P,\mathfrak{g},\vec{a}}$ is defined as:

$$f_{Q,P,\mathfrak{g},\vec{a}} := (\mathfrak{g}^{a_0})^{\Pi_{x_i=1} a_i} \pmod{Q}$$

To prove the ZK predicate $\mu = f_{Q,P,\mathfrak{g},\vec{a}}(\nu)$, holding commitments C_x on n-bit input x and C_y on the pseudo-random output y, the prover proceeds as follows:

1. The prover computes bit commitments C_{x_i} on the bits x_i of input x.
2. The prover sends the commitments C_x, C_y and $C_{x_i}, i = 0, \ldots, n$ to the verifier.
3. The prover computes a series of cumulative commitments, starting from $C_{a_0} := \mathfrak{g}^{a_0} \mathfrak{h}^{r_{a_0}} \pmod{Q}$ for $i = 1, \ldots, n$:

$$C_{a_i} := C_{a_{i-1}}^{x_i a_i} h^{r_{a_i}} \pmod{Q}$$

4. The prover engages with the verifier in an interactive zero-knowledge protocol:

$$S_{PRG} := PK\{ (\mu, \rho_\mu, \nu, \rho_\nu, (\nu_i, \rho_i, \rho_{a_i})_0^n) :$$
$$C_\mu = g^\mu h^{\rho_\mu} \wedge C_\nu = g^\nu h^{\rho_\nu} \wedge$$
$$(C_{x_i} = g^{\nu_i} h^{\rho_i})_0^n \wedge C_\nu = g^{(2^i \nu_i)_{i=1}^n} h^{\rho_\nu} \wedge$$
$$C_{a_0} = \mathfrak{g}^{a_0} \mathfrak{h}^{\rho_{a_0}} \wedge$$
$$\left(C_{a_i} = C_{a_{i-1}}^{\nu_i a_i} \mathfrak{h}^{\rho_{a_i}} \right)_{i=1}^{n-1} \wedge$$
$$C_\mu = C_{a_{n-1}}^{\nu_n a_n} \mathfrak{h}^{\rho_{a_n}}$$
$$\}.$$

Remark 2. There are two avenues to pursue: For an algebraic PRG, such as one proposed by Naor and Reingold [29], we can use discrete-log zero-knowledge proofs to show the correct computation efficiently. For non-algebraic PRG such as the PRG over bitstrings in a Galois Field over a polynomial proposed as part PrimeSeq by Cachin, Micali, and Stadler [6] and used in the first VRF construction [28], we employ MPC ZK with the predicate $\mathsf{GCCommit}(f(\mu), \rho)$.

3 Security Requirements

Definition 3 (Requirements [27]**).** *We expect the following properties of our interactive proof systems.*

Completeness: *An interactive proof system is* complete *if, given an honest prover and an honest verifier, the protocol succeeds with overwhelming probability.*

Soundness: *An interactive proof system is* sound *if there exists an exists an expected polynomial-time algorithm M with the following property: if a dishonest prover can with non-negligible probability successfully execute the protocol with the verifier, then M can be used to extract from this prover knowledge which with overwhelming probability allows successful future protocol executions.*

Zero-Knowledge: *A proof of knowledge has the* zero-knowledge *property if there exists an expected polynomial-time algorithm* (simulator) *which can produce, upon input of the assertions to be proven but without interacting with the real prover, transcripts indistinguishable from those resulting from interaction with the real prover.*

We will specify the protocols in the Camenisch-Stadler framework [14], which naturally extends to UC proofs in the Camenisch, Krenn and Shoup's corresponding UC framework [9]. We take natural composition of discrete-logarithm based zero-knowledge proofs including their completeness and zero-knowledge properties for granted and focus on the soundness property and soundness error probability quantification.

Table 3. Overview of ZK primality arguments. [22].

Name	Th	Src	Type	Form p_x	t	Witnesses
Lehmann	2	[13]	Monte-Carlo	n/a	$-\log_2 \varepsilon_S$	$(a_j)_{j=1}^t$
Det. Miller	3	Sect. 4.1	Deterministic	$< \dot{\ell}_n$	fixed t for $\dot{\ell}_n$	fixed $(a_j)_{j=1}^t$
Pocklington	4	Sect. 4.2	Recursive	$p \cdot r + i$	$\approx \log_2(k+1)$	(p_{i-1}, r_i, a_i)

ε_S: Soundness error

4 Constructions of ZK Predicates

4.1 ZK Predicate for Miller Primality

The Monte-Carlo Miller-Rabin primality test operates on positive odd integers n unrestricted in bitlength, has t rounds for a soundness error $\varepsilon_S = 4^{-t}$ and uses a random collection of bases $(a_j)_{j=1}^t \in_R \mathbb{Z}_n^*$. We can execute a deterministic Miller test on a careful selection of bases $(a_j)_{j=1}^t \in \mathbb{Z}_n^*$ to enable a deterministic primality test for small positive integers n, with fixed bitlength $\dot{\ell}_n$ and a soundness error of $\varepsilon_S = 0$. The latter is based on research on strong pseudoprimes to several bases [23,31].

Prover and Verifier agree on the variant of test to run by establishing the parameters $\dot{\ell}_n$, t, and $(a_j)_{j=1}^t$ as follows:

- Monte-Carlo Miller-Rabin ($\mu \in \text{primes}_{MR}(t)$): Prover and Verifier determine $t := -\log_4 \varepsilon_S$ dependent on the desired soundness error. They jointly choose random bases $\left((a_j)_{j=1}^t \in_R \mathbb{Z}_n^*\right)$ following the protocol described in the Appendix.
- Deterministic Miller $\left(\mu \in \text{primes}_M(\dot{\ell}_n, (a_j)_{j=1}^t)\right)$: Prover and Verifier agree on bitlength $\dot{\ell}_n$. t is set dependent on a fixed base set $(a_j)_{j=1}^t$ such that the least n^* with spsp $\left((a_j)_{j=1}^t, n^*\right)$ is greater than $2^{\dot{\ell}_n}$.

To establish PK predicate $\text{primes}_M(t)$, let us begin by proving that an odd integer $n > 1$ has the form $n = 2^e u + 1$, with u odd.

1. The prover efficiently finds e such that $n - 1 = 2^e u$ with u odd.
2. The prover commits to n in the form of $C_n := g^n h^{r_n}$, to u in the form $C_u := g^u h^{r_u}$, and to constant 2 in the form $C_2 := g^2 h^{r_2}$.
3. The prover computes the strong pseudo-prime equation for the selected bases $(a_j)_{j=1}^t$:
   (a) $d_j := a_j^u \pmod{n}$.
   (b) If $d_j \not\equiv 1 \pmod{n}$, the prover finds the $k < e$ such that

   $$d_j' := a_j^{2^k u} \pmod{n} \wedge d_j' \equiv -1 \pmod{n}.$$

4. The prover commits to d_j and d_j' in the form of $C_{d_j} := g^{d_j} h^{r_{d_j}}$ and $C_{d_j'} := g^{d_j'} h^{r_{d_j'}}$.
5. The prover sends all commitments to the verifier. Then the prover runs the following protocol with the verifier sequentially for k times:

$$PK\{\,(\nu,\alpha,\beta,\mu,\gamma,\upsilon,\varepsilon,$$
$$(\varrho_j,\psi_j,\varpi_j,\upsilon_j,\xi_j,\kappa_j,\eta_j,\Delta_j,\zeta_j,\tau_j,\varsigma_j,\delta_j,$$
$$\pi_j,\delta_j',\pi_j',\vartheta_j,\vartheta_j')_{j=1}^{t},\chi,\Big)\;:$$

$$C_n = g^\nu h^\alpha \wedge (\nu > 0) - 2^{\ell_n} < \nu < 2^{\ell_n} \wedge \tag{12}$$

$$C_2 = g^2\,h^\beta \wedge C_u = g^\mu h^\gamma \wedge \tag{13}$$

$$\left(C_{a_j} = g^{\varrho_j} h^{\varpi_j}\right)_{j=1}^{t} \wedge \tag{14}$$

$$C_{2^\varepsilon} = g^\upsilon h^{\psi_j} \wedge (2^\varepsilon = \upsilon) \wedge \tag{15}$$

$$C_n/g = C_{2^\varepsilon}^\mu h^\chi \wedge (\gcd(\mu,2) = 1) \wedge \tag{16}$$

$$\left(C_{2^{k_j}} = g^{\upsilon_j} h^{\xi_j} \wedge (2^{\kappa_j} = \upsilon_j)\right)_{j=1}^{t} \wedge \tag{17}$$

$$\left(C_{\Delta_j} = g^{\Delta_j} h^{\zeta_j}\right)_{j=1}^{t} \wedge \tag{18}$$

$$\left(C_{\Delta_j} = g^\varepsilon/g^{\kappa_j} h^{\eta_j} \wedge (\Delta_j > 0)\right)_{j=1}^{t} \wedge \tag{19}$$

$$\left(C_{2^{k_j}u} = g^{\mu_j} h^{\tau_j}\right)_{j=1}^{t} \wedge \tag{20}$$

$$\left(C_{2^{k_j}u} = C_{2^{k_j}}^\mu h^{\varsigma_j}\right)_{j=1}^{t} \wedge \tag{21}$$

$$\left(C_{d_j} = g^{\delta_j} h^{\pi_j} \wedge C_{d_j'} = g^{\delta_j'} h^{\pi_j'}\right)_{j=1}^{t} \wedge \tag{22}$$

$$\left(\varrho_j^\mu \equiv \delta_j \pmod{\nu}\right)_{j=1}^{t} \wedge \tag{23}$$

$$\left(\varrho_j^{\mu_j} \equiv \delta_j' \pmod{\nu}\right)_{j=1}^{t} \wedge \tag{24}$$

$$\left(C_{d_j}/g = h^{\vartheta_j} \vee C_{d_j'}g = h^{\vartheta_j'}\right)_{j=1}^{t} \tag{25}$$

$$\}.$$

Clause 12 establishes the knowledge of candidate n, that n is positive and fulfills the length restriction to ℓ_n. Clause 14 proves knowledge of the bases $(a_j)_{j=1}^{t}$ committed to in C_{a_j} for $j = 1, \ldots, t$; in the deterministic case, these bases are known publicly. Clause 13 shows the representation to commitments to 2 and u as foundation for the decomposition of $n - 1 = 2^e u$. The following clauses 15 thru 16 establish the composition of $n - 1 = 2^e u$, where the second clause of Line 16 yields that u is odd.

Subsequent clauses establish the deterministic Miller test for fixed known bases $(a_j)_{j=1}^{t}$. First, we prove the correct representation of $C_{2^{k_j}}$, which proceeds similarly to the proof for C_{2^e} in Line 15. Secondly, we establish the difference between 2^e and 2^{k_j} and prove that this difference is greater than zero in Clause 15. The clauses on Line 21 establish the knowledge and structure of commitment $C_{2^{k_j}u}$. The clauses on Line 22 establish the knowledge of the results of the Miller test d_j and d_j'. Clauses 23 and 24 establish the relations of the Miller test $a_j^u \equiv d_j \pmod{n}$ and $a_j^{2^{k_j}u} \equiv d_j' \pmod{n}$, where secret μ_j represents $2^{k_j}u$. The final clauses on Line 25 establish the different cases of strong probable prime test, that is, either $d_j = 1$, entailing $a_j^u \equiv 1 \pmod{n}$, or $d'_j = -1$, entailing $a_j^{2^{k_j}u} \equiv -1 \pmod{n}$.

Theorem 8. *Assuming that the discrete logarithm problem is hard in $\mathbb{G}$ and that the least n^* with $\mathsf{spsp}((a_j)_{j=1}^t, n^*)$ is greater than 2^{ℓ_n}, then the protocol $\left(\mu \in \mathsf{primes_M}(\dot{\ell}_n, (a_j)_{j=1}^t)\right)$ is a zero-knowledge argument that the committed integer μ is prime. The soundness error probability is 2^{-k}.*

Proof. The proof is based on the zero-knowledge properties of the underlying predicates. Using standard techniques a knowledge extractor can extract integers for the secrets in the protocol. Given that the discrete-logarithm problem in $\mathbb{G}$ is assumed hard and provided that the $\log_g h$ is unknown, then the equations encoded on generator g hold in the exponent $\pmod{Q}$. The knowledge extractor gains the integer $\hat{n}$ and integers $\hat{u}$ and $\hat{e}$ for which it establishes the relation $\hat{n} - 1 = 2^{\hat{e}}\hat{u}$ and that $\hat{u}$ is odd. The knowledge extractor gains bases $(\hat{a}_j)_{j=1}^t$. We are interested which relations hold for these extracted secrets, especially the Miller primality relations $\hat{a}_j^{\hat{u}} \equiv \hat{d}_j \pmod{\hat{n}}$ and $\hat{a}_j^{2^{k_j}\hat{u}} \equiv \hat{d}'_j \pmod{\hat{n}}$. That these relations hold in zero-knowledge follows from Theorem 5. $\hat{d}_j = 1$ and $\hat{d}'_j = -1$ is established with standard techniques. Finally, we have that $\hat{n} < 2^{\ell_n} < n^*$, where n^* is the least integer such that $\mathsf{spsp}\left((\hat{a}_j)_{j=1}^t, n^*\right)$. Therefore, $\hat{n}$ fulfilling the established relations must be prime. The primality relation established by the extracted secrets are deterministic. Therefore the soundness error probability is 2^{-k}, gained from the number of zero-knowledge proof rounds k.

Table 4 tabulates example instances for the deterministic Miller primality test by their upper bound, that is, the first strong pseudoprime n^* to all selected bases $(a_j)_{j=1}^t$.

Table 4. Deterministic Miller primality instances.

Upper Bound	$\dot{\ell}_n$	t	$(a_j)_{j=1}^t$
$2,047$	10	1	(2)
$1,373,653$	20	2	$(2,3)$
$4,759,123,141$	32	3	$(2,7,61)$

Note: Upper bound is the least $n^* > 0 \in \mathbb{Z}$ s.t. $\mathsf{spsp}\left((a_j)_{j=1}^t, n^*\right)$

4.2 ZK Predicate for Pocklington Primality Witness

The predicate $\nu_j \in \mathsf{primes_P}(\nu_{j-1}, \varrho_j, \chi_j)$ convinces a verifier that Pocklington's criterion is fulfilled for p_j based on a secret Pocklington witness (p_{j-1}, r_j, a_j) such that:

$$a_j^{p_j-1 r_j} \equiv 1 \pmod{p_j} \wedge \gcd(a_j^{r_j} - 1, p_j) = 1.$$

We assume that a commitment to p_{j-1} is given as $C_{p_{j-1}} = g^{p_{j-1}}h^{r_{p_{j-1}}}$ and a commitment to r_j is given as $C_{r_j} = g^{r_j}h^{r_{r_j}}$ where $r_{p_{j-1}}, r_{r_j} \in_R \mathbb{Z}_Q$.

Table 5. Secrets allocation for primes$_M(t)$.

Secret	Description
ν	Prime number candidate n
μ	Greatest odd factor u of $n-1$
δ_j	Result d_j of j-th Miller test: $d_j := a_j^u \pmod{n}$
υ	Greatest power-of-2 factor of $n-1$, 2^e
ε	Exponent e of 2^e
α, β	Factors of Bézout's identity proving coprimality
μ_j	Exponent $2^k u$ in the second clause of j-th Miller's test
δ'_j	Result d'_j of the j-th Miller test: $d'_j := a_j^{2^k u} \pmod{n}$

1. The prover searches for a positive integer a_j such that Pocklington's criterion mentioned above is fulfilled for p_{j-1}, r_j, a_j and p_j. If p_j is prime, such an a_j will exist.
2. The prover commits to a_j with the structure $C_{a_j} = g^{a_j} h^{r_{a_j}}$ with $r_{a_j} \in_R \mathbb{Z}_Q$.
3. Then the prover engages with the verifier in the following zero-knowledge proof k times:

$$PK\{\, (\nu_j, \nu_{j-1}, \varrho_j, \chi_j, \delta_j, \Delta_j, \alpha, \beta, \gamma, \varepsilon, \zeta, \eta, \kappa, \xi, \tau, \pi, \psi) :$$

$$C_{p_{j-1}} = g^{\nu_{j-1}} h^{\alpha} \wedge C_{p_j} = g^{\nu_j} h^{\beta} \wedge \tag{26}$$

$$C_{a_j} = g^{\varrho_j} h^{\gamma} \wedge C_{r_j} = d^{\chi_j} h^{\varepsilon} \wedge \tag{27}$$

$$-2^{\ell} < \varrho_j, \chi_j, \nu_j < 2^{\ell} \wedge \tag{28}$$

$$C_{\Delta_j} = g^{\Delta_j} h^{\zeta} \wedge C_{\Delta_j} = g^{\nu_{j-1}}/g^{\chi_j} h^{\eta} \wedge \tag{29}$$

$$(\varrho_j > 0) \wedge (\chi_j > 0) \wedge (\Delta_j > 0) \wedge \tag{30}$$

$$C_{p_j}/g = C_{p_{j-1}}^{\chi_j} h^{\kappa} \wedge \tag{31}$$

$$C_{d_j} = g^{\delta_j} h^{\xi} \wedge \tag{32}$$

$$(\varrho_j^{\nu_{j-1}\chi_j} \equiv \delta_j \pmod{\nu_j}) \wedge \tag{33}$$

$$C_{d_j}/g = h^{\tau} \wedge \tag{34}$$

$$C_{\lambda_j} = d^{\lambda_j} h^{\pi} \wedge C_{\lambda_j} g = C_{a_j}^{\chi_j} h^{\psi} \wedge \tag{35}$$

$$(\gcd(\lambda_j, \nu_j) = 1) \tag{36}$$

$$\}.$$

We assume that the length of p_{j-1} has been established by the corresponding primality zero-knowledge argument. Clauses 26 establish the knowledge of the successive Pocklington primes p_{j-1} and p_j. Clauses 27 proves the knowledge of the remainder of the Pocklington witness a_j and r_j. The clauses 28 thru 30 prove the length restrictions on p_j, r_j, and a_j, where Clause 30 ensures that a_j and r_j are indeed positive integers and that $r < p_{j-1}$ as required by Theorem 4.

Clauses 32 thru 36 prove the Pocklington criterion itself. Clause 32 proves knowledge of the committed result d_j of the Pocklington congruence. Clause 33 shows the structure of the key Pocklington congruence: $a_j^{p_j-1^r} \equiv 1 \pmod{p_j}$. Subsequently, Clause 34 shows that the result is indeed congruent to 1. Clause 35 shows the commitment to the term $a_j^{r_j} - 1$ and the subsequent Clause 36 yields the coprimality with p_j.

Theorem 9. *Assuming that ν_{j-1} has been established to be prime and assuming that the discrete logarithm problem is hard in $\mathbb{G}$, then the protocol $(\nu_j \in \mathsf{primes_P}(\nu_{j-1}, \varrho_j, \chi_j))$ is a zero-knowledge argument that the committed integer ν_j is prime. The soundness error probability is 2^{-k}.*

Proof. With standard techniques the knowledge extractor extracts integers for the secrets in the protocol. Assuming the hardness of the discrete logarithm and that $\log_g h$ is unknown, equations encoded on g hold in the exponent $\pmod Q$. Especially, it gains $\hat{p}_{j-1}, \hat{r}_j, \hat{p}_j$, and $\hat{a}_j$. In the relations it is assured that $\hat{r}_j$ and $\hat{a}_j$ are positive and that $\hat{r}_j < \hat{p}_j$. Thereby, the conditions for the Pocklington criterion named in Theorem 4 are fulfilled. Two aspects remain to show: First, $\hat{a}^{\hat{p}\cdot\hat{r}} \equiv 1 \pmod{\hat{p}'_j}$, which follows from Theorem 5 and the standard comparison of $\hat{d}$ with 1. Second, $\gcd(\hat{a}^{\hat{r}_i} - 1, \hat{p}_i)$ is shown with the predicate $(\gcd(x, y) = 1)$. Provided that $\hat{p}_{j-1}$ is prime and that these two relations have been established, by $\hat{p}_j$ is prime by Theorem 4. The soundness error probability of 2^{-k} stems from the k rounds of the zero-knowledge proof. $\square$

4.3   ZK Predicate Showing Special RSA Modulus

In this section, we discuss how the Pocklington Witness predicate from Sect. 4.2 offers a more efficient zero-knowledge argument that a number n is a product of two safe primes. By proving knowledge of a Pocklington witness we can assert the structure of the constituent safe primes, improving on computational and communication complexity as well as soundness error probability of earlier methods [13].

1. The Prover computes two safe primes $p := 2\tilde{p} + 1$ and $q := 2\tilde{q} + 1$, creating the RSA modulus $n := pq$.
2. The prover searches for two bases a_p and a_q that complete Pocklington witnesses for the primality of p and q such that

$$a_p^{2\tilde{p}} \equiv 1 \pmod p \text{ and } \gcd(a_p^2 - 1, p) = 1$$
$$a_q^{2\tilde{q}} \equiv 1 \pmod q \text{ and } \gcd(a_q^2 - 1, q) = 1$$

3. We assume a commitment on integer n be given as $C_n = g^n h^{r_n}$. The prover commits to p, q as well as a_p and a_q with $C_p := g^p h^{r_p}$, $C_q := g^q h^{r_q}$, $C_{\tilde{p}} := g^{(p-1)/2} h^{r_{\tilde{p}}}$, $C_{\tilde{q}} := g^{(q-1)/2} h^{r_{\tilde{q}}}$, $C_{a_p} := g^{a_p} h^{r_{a_p}}$, $C_{a_q} := g^{a_q} h^{r_{a_q}}$, where the corresponding randomnesses $r_p, r_q, r_{\tilde{p}}, r_{\tilde{q}}, r_{a_p}$, and $r_{a_q} \in_R \mathbb{Z}_Q$. Furthermore, the prover computes all commitments prescribed by $\tilde{p} \in \mathsf{primes_L}(t)$, $\tilde{q} \in \mathsf{primes_L}(t)$, $p \in \mathsf{primes_P}(\tilde{p}, 2, a_p)$, $q \in \mathsf{primes_P}(\tilde{q}, 2, a_q)$.
4. Then the prover and the verifier engage in the following zero-knowledge protocol k times.

$$PK\{\,(\mu, \nu, \tilde{\mu}, \tilde{\nu}, \varrho_p, \varrho_q, \alpha, \beta, \gamma, \varepsilon, \zeta, \eta, \kappa, \xi)\,:$$

$$C_p = g^\mu h^\alpha \wedge C_q = g^\nu h^\beta \wedge \tag{37}$$

$$C_{\tilde{p}} = g^{\tilde{\mu}} h^\gamma \wedge C_{\tilde{q}} = g^{\tilde{\nu}} h^\delta \wedge \tag{38}$$

$$C_n = C_p^\nu h^\varepsilon \wedge \tag{39}$$

$$C_p/(C_{\tilde{p}}^2 \, g) = h^\zeta \wedge C_q/(C_{\tilde{q}}^2 \, g) = h^\eta \wedge \tag{40}$$

$$C_{a_p} = g^{\varrho_p} h^\kappa \wedge C_{a_q} = g^{\varrho_q} h^\xi \wedge \tag{41}$$

$$(\tilde{\mu} \in \mathsf{primes_L}(t)) \wedge \tag{42}$$

$$(\tilde{\nu} \in \mathsf{primes_L}(t)) \wedge \tag{43}$$

$$(\mu \in \mathsf{primes_P}(\tilde{\mu}, 2, \varrho_p)) \wedge \tag{44}$$

$$(\nu \in \mathsf{primes_P}(\tilde{\nu}, 2, \varrho_q)) \tag{45}$$

$$\}.$$

The length of μ, ν, $\tilde{\mu}$, $\tilde{\nu}$, ϱ_p and ϱ_q is constrained by the corresponding $\mathsf{primes_L}(t)$ and $\mathsf{primes_P}(n, r, a)$ protocols. While the primality of $(p-1)/2$ and $(q-1)/2$ is proven by secret Lehmann primality tests in clauses 42 and 43. We proceed with proving the primality of the p and q with a Pocklington witness.

Theorem 10 ([22]). *Assuming that the discrete logarithm problem is hard in $\mathbb{G}$, then the protocol is a zero-knowledge argument that the integer n committed to in C_n is the product of two safe primes p and q, for which $(p-1)/2$ and $(q-1)/2$ are prime as well. The soundness error probability is at most $2^{-k} + 2^{-t}$.*

Proof. It is standard to construct knowledge extractors for the given protocol and to establish the relation between the secrets showing that the following relations between extracted integers hold hold:

$$\hat{p} = 2\tilde{\hat{p}} + 1, \hat{q} = 2\tilde{\hat{q}} + 1, \text{ and } \hat{n} = \hat{p}\hat{q}.$$

The primality of $(\hat{p} - 1)/2$ and $(\hat{q} - 1)/2$ is established as a zero-knowledge argument governed by Theorem 6, yielding a soundness error probability of $2^{-k} + 2^{-t}$ with t being the number of Lehmann primality bases employed. The primality of $\hat{p}$ and $\hat{q}$ is given by the Pocklington witness zero-knowledge argument established in Theorem 9. The latter proven with one base only per predicate and has a soundness error probability of 2^k.

4.4 ZK Predicate for Hash-to-Prime

Definition 4 (Hash-to-Prime [22]).
$(\mu \in \mathsf{hashToPrime}_{\mathcal{F}}(\nu, t))$ *is a zero-knowledge predicate stating that committed secret μ an element of the set of prime numbers derived according to a specified procedure $\mathcal{F}$ from committed secret input ν, using t steps.*

$\left(\mu = \mathsf{hashToPrime}_{\mathcal{F}}^{\Upsilon}(\nu, t, u)\right)$ *is a zero-knowledge proof predicate stating that committed secret μ is exactly the first prime number in sequence derived according to a* *specified procedure $\mathcal{F}$ from committed secret input ν, using t steps and having eliminated u composite candidates in sequence. The parameters t and u are public knowledge.*

We offer two constructions for proving in a zero-knowledge argument that a committed $(k+1)$-bit prime p_x was generated via hashing from an a-bit input x: (i) by elimination (E) and (ii) by recursive construction (R). Both variants of the predicate $\left(\mu = \mathsf{hashToPrime}_{\mathcal{F}}^{\Upsilon}(\nu, t, u)\right)$ have in common that the prover is required to prove the compositeness of u eliminated candidates in a fixed order, enforcing that the first prime in sequence must be used.

Hash-to-Prime by Elimination. The idea of hashing-to-prime by elimination is that the prover hashes the input x which then seeds a PRG, evaluated in a deterministic sequence with known indices $i = 1, \ldots, u$ until the outcome y_u passes a test as a probable prime. To establish the predicates

$$(\mu \in \mathsf{hashToPrime}_E(\nu, t)) \text{ and } \left(\mu = \mathsf{hashToPrime}_E^{\Upsilon}(\nu, t, u)\right),$$

the prover runs a protocol with the verifier to establish a zero-knowledge argument (i) that the hash- and PRG-computations are executed correctly, (ii) that all committed eliminated candidates $(y_i)_{i=1}^{u-1}$ are composites ($*$), and (iii) that the final committed value $p_x := y_u$ is prime, where ($*$) is only executed for predicate $\left(\mu = \mathsf{hashToPrime}_E^{\Upsilon}(\nu, t, u)\right)$.

Given pseudo-random number generator PRG(), a hash function $\mathcal{H}_{Q,z,b}()$ and corresponding ZK predicates $(\mu = \mathsf{PRG}_{\chi}(\nu))$ and $(\mu = \mathcal{H}_{\varsigma,\beta}(\nu))$, we establish the ZK predicates

$$(\mu \in \mathsf{hashToPrime}_E(\nu, t)) \text{ and } \left(\mu = \mathsf{hashToPrime}_E^{\Upsilon}(\nu, t, u)\right)$$

as follows, where ($*$) marks the steps transforming the former to the latter:

1. The prover computes $y_i := \mathsf{PRG}_{\mathcal{H}_{z,b}(x)}(i)$ for $i = 1, \ldots, u$ testing each y_i with a Miller-Rabin test till y_u passes the primality test as a probable prime. The prover calls this y_u the outcome p_x.
2. the prover commits to the intermediary output of the hash function $\mathcal{H}_{z,b}()$ as $\bar{y}$, in the form of $C_{\bar{y}} = g^{\bar{y}} h^{r_{\bar{y}}}$ and $r_{\bar{y}} \in_R \mathbb{Z}_Q$.
3. The prover computes commitments on all eliminated composite values y_i as $C_{y_i} := g^{y_i} h^{r_{y_i}}$ with $i = 1, \ldots, u-1$ and r_{y_i} is $\in_R \mathbb{Z}_Q$. ($*$) The prover commits to the determined prime $p_x = y_u$ in the form of $C_{p_x} := g^{p_x} h^{r_{p_x}}$, where $r_{p_x} \in_R \mathbb{Z}_Q$.
4. The prover sends all commitments, including ones of sub-ordinate predicates to the verifier.
5. Finally, the prover engages with the verifier in a zero-knowledge argument sequentially for k times:

$$PK\{ \left(\nu, \zeta, \beta, \mu, \rho, \rho', \bar{\mu}, \bar{\rho}, (\mu_i)_{i=1}^{u-1} \right) :$$

$$C_x = g^\nu g^\rho \wedge C_{p_x} = g^\mu h^{\rho'} \wedge \tag{46}$$

$$\left(C_{y_i} = g^{\mu_i} h^{\rho_i} \right)_{i=1}^{u-1} \wedge \tag{47}$$

$$\left(C_{\bar{y}_i} = g^{\bar{\mu}_i} h^{\bar{\rho}_i} \right)_{i=1}^{u} \wedge \tag{48}$$

$$(\bar{\mu} = \mathcal{H}_{\zeta,\beta}(\nu)) \wedge \tag{49}$$

$$(\mu = \mathsf{PRG}_{\bar{\mu}}(u)) \wedge \tag{50}$$

$$(\mu \in \mathsf{primes_L}(t)) \wedge \tag{51}$$

$$(\mu_i = \mathsf{PRG}_{\bar{\mu}}(i))_{i=1}^{u-1} (*) \wedge \tag{52}$$

$$(\mu_i \in \mathsf{composites}())_{i=1}^{u-1} (*) \tag{53}$$

$$\}.$$

The first three clauses 46 thru 48 establish the representation of the commitments. Clause 49 yields the correct computation of the hash function $\mathcal{H}_{Q,z,b}()$ with respect to the secret input x, while the following two clauses 52 and 50 give the correct computation of the PRG. Clause 51 shows the primality of the resulting output p_x. Clause 53 establishes the elimination of intermediary composites $(*)$. The size constraints are governed in the corresponding subordinate ZK predicates.

Theorem 11 ([22]). *Assuming that the discrete logarithm and the decisional Diffie-Hellman problems are hard in $\mathbb{G}$. Then $(\mu \in \mathsf{hashToPrime_E}(\nu, t))$ is a zero-knowledge argument that the committed integer μ is prime and was derived as hash-to-prime from committed integer ν. The protocol $\left(\mu = \mathsf{hashToPrime_E^\Upsilon}(\nu, t, u) \right)$ is a zero-knowledge argument that the committed integer μ is exactly the first prime in sequence succeding u eliminated candidates derived as hash-to-prime from committed integer ν, where the integer u is publicly known. The soundness error probability is at most $2^{-k} + 2^{-t}$.*

Hash-to-Prime by Recursion. For a recursive construction, we draw inspiration from Ozdemir et al.'s approach to hashing to primes [30] to establish predicates

$$(\mu \in \mathsf{hashToPrime_R}(\nu, t)) \quad \text{and} \quad \left(\mu = \mathsf{hashToPrime_R^\Upsilon}(\nu, t, (n_j)_{j=0}^t) \right),$$

$(*)$ marking the steps to transform the former to the latter. The recursion has has t steps, each doubling the size of the prime established, using a setup of collection of SQHUs $\left(\mathcal{H}_{Q_j, z_j, b_j}(\cdot) \right)_{j=0}^t$.

We start with establishing a first small prime p_0 based on the result of $\mathcal{H}_{Q_0, z_0, b_0}(x)$. From this first prime, we recursively establish Pocklington steps with their proofs with predicate $\nu_j \in \mathsf{primes_P}(\nu_{j-1}, \varrho_j, \chi_j)$, while each step roughly doubles the bitlength of the prime p_j. Finally, the prover convinces the verifier (i) that the initial value p_0 is prime with a deterministic Miller predicate, while showing that intermediate candidates were composite $(*)$, (ii) that, for each subsequent value p_j, it is prime with a Pocklington primality witness predicate $\nu_j \in \mathsf{primes_P}(\nu_{j-1}, \varrho_j, \chi_j)$ relating it to the previous prime p_{j-1}, (iii) that, for each primes p_j, the candidates eliminated in finding r_j to complete p_j are composite (*). For clarity, we shall explain the base case and the recursion step separately, even if the protocol is executed as one compound zero-knowledge argument.

Base Case ($j = 0$). We establish the first prime p_0 with a bitlength arbitrarily set to 32 bits. This prime will be derived from input secret x as $p_0 := 2^{\ell_{n_0}} h_0 + n_0$ with $h_0 := \mathcal{H}_{Q_0, z_0, b_0}(x)$ and an integer counter n_0. The primality is established with a deterministic Miller primality predicate (cf. Sect. 4.1) and constant 3 bases.

1. The prover computes $\mathcal{H}_{Q_0, z_0, b_0}(x)$ and establishes the first integer n_0 in the sequence $1, \ldots, n_0$ such that $p_0 = 2^{\ell_{n_0}} \cdot h_0 + n_0$ is probable prime. The prover stores all intermediate values $y_{0,i} = 2^{\ell_{n_0}} h_0 + i$ for $1, \ldots, n_0 - 1$ that are composites. (*)
2. The prover commits to p_0 as $C_{p_0} = g^{p_0} h^{r_{p_1}}$ with $r_{p_0} \in_R \mathbb{Z}_Q$ and to the eliminated composites as $C_{y_{0,i}} = g^{y_{0,i}} h^{r_{y_{0,i}}}$ for $i = 1, \ldots, n_0 - 1$ and with $r_{y_{0,i}} \in_R \mathbb{Z}_Q$ (*) and sends the commitments to the verifier.
3. Then the prover runs the following protocol with the verifier sequentially k times:

$$PK\{ \left(\mu, \alpha, \beta_0, \bar{\mu}, \bar{\alpha}, \nu_0, \rho_0, (\nu_{0,i}, \rho_{0,i} \gamma_{0,i},)_{i=1}^u, \gamma\right) :$$

$$C_x = g^\mu h^\alpha \wedge C_{\bar{\mu}} = g^{\bar{\mu}} h^{\bar{\alpha}} \wedge \tag{54}$$

$$C_{p_0} = g^{\nu_0} h^{\rho_0} \wedge \tag{55}$$

$$\left(C_{y_{0,i}} = g^{\nu_{0,i}} h^{\rho_{0,i}}\right)_{i=1}^{n_0-1} \wedge \tag{56}$$

$$(\bar{\mu} = \mathcal{H}_{\zeta_0, \beta_0}(\mu)) \wedge \tag{57}$$

$$C_{p_0} = C_{\bar{\mu}}^{2^{\ell_{n_0}}} g^{n_0} h^\gamma \wedge \tag{58}$$

$$\nu_0 \in \mathsf{primes}_\mathsf{M}(t) \wedge \tag{59}$$

$$\left(C_{y_{0,i}} = C_{\bar{\mu}}^{2^{\ell_{n_0}}} g^i h^{\gamma_{0,i}}\right)_{i=1}^{n_0-1} (*) \wedge \tag{60}$$

$$(\nu_i \in \mathsf{composites}())_{i=1}^{n_0-1} (*) \tag{61}$$

$$\}.$$

Recursion Step ($j - 1 \rightarrow j$). The prover constructs the subsequent prime p_j of the form $p_{j-1} \cdot r_{j,i} + 1$ and established a Pocklington Witness zero-knowledge argument on is primality.

1. Given p_{j-1} and input x committed in C_x, the prover computes $y_{j,i} := p_{j-1} \cdot r_{j,i} + 1$ where the positive integer $r_{j,i} := 2^{\ell_{n_j}} \cdot \mathcal{H}_{Q_j, z_j, b_j}(x) + i$, iterating over $i = 1, \ldots, u$ till $p_j := y_{j,u}$ is a probably prime. The integer u is stored as n_j, the corresponding $r_{j,u}$ is called r_j.
2. The prover searches for a positive integer a_j such that Pocklington's criterion is fulfilled for p_{j-1}, r_j, a_j and p_j:

$$a_j^{p_{j-1} r} \equiv 1 \pmod{p_j} \wedge \gcd(a_j^{r_j} - 1, p_j) = 1.$$

If p_j is prime, such an a_j exists.

3. The prover commits to p_j, a_j, r_j as well as all intermediate values $y_{j,i}$ for $i = 1, \ldots, u-1$ (*). The commitments have the forms $C_{p_j} := g^{p_j} h^{r_{p_j}}$, $C_{a_j} := g^{a_j} h^{r_{a_j}}$, $C_{r_j} := g^{r_j} h^{r_{r_j}}$, $C_{y_{j,i}} := g^{y_{j,i}} h^{r_{y_{j,i}}}$, where r_{p_j}, r_{a_j}, r_{r_j}, and $(r_{y_{j,i}})_{i=1}^{u-1}$ are all $\in_R \mathbb{Z}_Q$.
4. The prover sends commitments to the verifier.
5. Then the prover engages with the verifier in the following protocol sequentially k times:

$$PK\{ \left(\bar{\mu}, \bar{\alpha}, \beta_j \left(\chi_{j,i}, \beta_{j,i}, \gamma_{j,i}, \psi_{j,i}, \varphi_{j,i}, \varepsilon_{j,i} \right)_{i=1}^{u}, \varrho_j, \delta_j \right) :$$

$$C_{\bar{\mu}} = g^{\bar{\mu}} h^{\bar{\alpha}} \wedge \left(\bar{\mu} = \mathcal{H}_{\zeta_j, \beta_j}(\mu) \right) \wedge \tag{62}$$

$$\left(C_{r_{j,i}} = g^{\chi_{j,i}} h^{\beta_{j,i}} \right)_{i=1}^{u} \wedge \tag{63}$$

$$\left(C_{r_{j,i}} = C_{\bar{\mu}}^{2^{\ell_{n_j}}} g^i h^{\gamma_{j,i}} \right)_{i=1}^{u} \wedge \tag{64}$$

$$\left(C_{y_{j,i}} = g^{\psi_{j,i}} h^{\varphi_{j,i}} \right)_{i=1}^{u} \wedge \tag{65}$$

$$C_{a_j} = g^{\varrho_j} h^{\delta_j} \wedge \tag{66}$$

$$(\nu_j \in \mathsf{primes_P}(\nu_{j-1}, \varrho_j, \chi_{j,i})) \wedge \tag{67}$$

$$\left(C_{y_{j,i}}/g = C_{p_{j-1}}^{\chi_{j,i}} h^{\varepsilon_{j,i}} \right)_{i=1}^{u} (*) \wedge \tag{68}$$

$$(\psi_{j,i} \in \mathsf{composites}(t))_{i=1}^{u-1} (*) \tag{69}$$

$$\}.$$

Theorem 12 ([22]). *Assuming that the discrete logarithm problem is hard in $\mathbb{G}$. Then the protocol ($\mu \in \mathsf{hashToPrime_R}(\nu, t)$) is a zero-knowledge argument that the committed integer μ is prime and was derived as hash-to-prime from committed integer ν. $\left(\mu = \mathsf{hashToPrime_R^{\Upsilon}}(\nu, t, (n_j)_{j=0}^{t}) \right)$ is a zero-knowledge argument that the committed integer μ is the prime created by choosing the first prime in sequence in each of the t steps succeeding $(n_j)_{j=0}^{t}$ eliminated candidates, derived as hash-to-prime from committed integer ν, where the integers $(n_j)_{j=0}^{t}$ are publicly known. The soundness error probability is 2^{-k}.*

The following proof covers Theorems 11 and 12.

Proof. For the secrets derived by the knowledge extractor, the Theorems 6, 8, and 9 govern that the committed integer $\hat{p}_x$ is indeed prime with a primality soundness error probability of at most 2^{-t}. Furthermore, proof predicates ($\mu = \mathcal{H}_{\zeta,\beta}(\nu)$) and ($\mu = \mathsf{PRG}_{\xi}(\nu)$) govern that the outputs of hash function and PRG were computed correctly. It remains to show that the prime $\hat{p}_x$ is indeed the first prime in the sequence $\hat{y}_i$ established by the known indices $i = 1, \ldots, u$. For each $\hat{y}_i$ with $i = 1, \ldots, u-1$, the predicate ($\mu \in \mathsf{composites}()$) establishes that $\hat{y}_i$ is composite by Theorem 7. By contradiction, if $\hat{y}_i$ were prime, it holds by Theorem 2, Clause 1, that $\forall a \in \mathbb{Z}_n^* : a^{(n-1)/2} \equiv \pm 1 \pmod{n}$. Hence, an extracted base $\hat{a} \in \mathbb{Z}_Q^*$ such that $\hat{a}^{(\hat{n}-1)/2} \not\equiv \pm 1 \pmod{\hat{n}}$ does not exist. Consequently, the sequence $(\hat{y}_i)_{i=1}^{u-1}$ does not contain a prime. Therefore, the overall soundness error probability of ($\mu = \mathsf{hashToPrime_E}(\nu, t)$) is at most $2^{-k} + 2^{-t}$ and of ($\mu = \mathsf{hashToPrime_R}(\nu, t)$) is 2^{-k}. We note that the predicates

$\left(\mu = \mathsf{hashToPrime}_{\mathsf{E}}^{\Upsilon}(\nu, t, u)\right)$ and $\left(\mu = \mathsf{hashToPrime}_{\mathsf{R}}^{\Upsilon}(\nu, t, (n_j)_{j=0}^{t})\right)$ declare as public knowledge the number of eliminated prime candidates u and $(n_j)_{j=0}^{t}$, respectively, in the predicate specification.

Remark 3 (**Relaxation**). Whereas the hashToPrime() enforces that the *first prime* in sequence be chosen by proving compositeness of all preceding candidates, this requirement can be relaxed when it is only relevant that the prover choses *an prime* derived from the hash of x. Then, the prover can eliminate all intermediate compositeness proofs, by which the complexity is dominated by the primality predicate employed.

5 Applications

In this section, we are discussing natural extensions and applications of hashing-to-prime, while also considering the design decisions in the use of these zero-knowledge predicates. First, we consider a natural extension, which allows for the blind signature of a hidden pair (x, p_x) as follow-up for a hash-to-prime execution. Second, we consider the creation of identity-based prime accumulators [10]. Third, we discuss how the hash-to-prime schemes can extend the Camenisch-Groß [8] anonymous credential scheme and the SRSA graph signature scheme [21]. Finally, we discuss the design decisions for choosing a hash-to-prime PK predicate.

5.1 Value-Prime Association

Hashing-to-prime zero-knowledge predicates are expensive. Hence, it is natural to store the pairing of an input x and the corresponding prime p_x in a digital certificate.

We employ the SRSA Camenisch-Lysyanskaya signature scheme [11] to obtain a confidentiality-preserving blind signature on an association between an input x and a prime p_x. Given two integer commitments $C_x := R_x^x S^{v_x}$ and $C_{p_x} := R_{p_x}^{p_x} S^{v_{p_x}}$ in a Special RSA group $\mathbb{QR}_N$ under modulus N, a signature requestor can prove the knowledge of x and p_x as well as their relation $(p_x = \mathsf{hashToPrime}(x, t))$ to obtain a special Camenisch-Lysyanskaja (CL) signature σ_{x, p_x} on the association.

As SRSA-CL setup, we assume that a group of the quadratic residues $\mathbb{QR}_N$ under a special RSA modulus N is given, for which the group order is not known. We assume the discrete logarithm and the strong RSA problem to be hard in this group. We assume that an Integer commitment scheme [16] is set up in $\mathbb{QR}_N$ with bases R_x, R_{p_x} and S, for which the pair-wise discrete logarithms are not known.

Assuming the computation of the commitments C_x and C_{p_x} is included in hashToPrime(x, t), this protocol has a constant computational complexity overhead of 8 modular exponentiations for the requestor and 6 modular exponentiations for the signer.

Theorem 13 ([11]). *The signature scheme secure against adaptive chosen message attacks under the strong RSA assumption.*

Subsequently, the requestor now in the role of prover can convince a verifier that value p_x is a prime deterministically determined by an input x by proving knowledge of the signature σ_{x, p_x}. For multi-use unlinkability, the prover can create a new random

Signer	Requestor

$$C_x, C_{p_x}, (p_x = \mathsf{hashToPrime}(x, t)) \quad\longleftarrow$$

$$C_x = R_x^x S^{v_x},$$
$$C_{p_x} = R_{p_x}^{p_x} S^{v_{p_x}}$$

$v' \in_R \{0,1\}^{\ell_v}$

$e \in_R \mathcal{P}^{\ell_e}$

$$A := \left(\frac{Z}{C_x C_{p_x} S^{v'}} \right)^{1/e} \qquad \sigma'_{x,p_x} := (A, e, v') \longrightarrow$$

$$v := v' + v_x + v_{p_x}$$

$$\sigma_{x,p_x} := (A, e, v)$$

$$Z \stackrel{?}{\equiv} A^e R_x^x R_{p_x}^{p_x} S^v$$

Note: Main equations in $\mathbb{Z}_N^*$

Fig. 1. Creating a blind CL-signature on a proven (x, p_x) association.

signature (A', e, v') with $A' := AS^{-r} \pmod{N}$ and $v' = v + er$ for $r \in_R \{0,1\}^{\ell_N + \ell_\emptyset}$. The prover reveals group element A' and engages with the verifier in the following proof:

$$PK\{(\varepsilon, \nu', \mu, \varpi) :$$

$$Z \equiv \pm A'^\varepsilon R_x^\mu R_{p_x}^\varpi S^{\nu'} \pmod{N} \wedge \tag{70}$$

$$- 2^{\ell_M} < \mu < 2^{\ell_M} \wedge -2^{\ell_M} < \varpi < 2^{\ell_M} \wedge \tag{71}$$

$$- 2^{\ell_e - 1} + 1 < \varepsilon 2^{\ell_e} - 1 \tag{72}$$

$$\}.$$

This proof has a constant computational complexity of 4 modular exponentiations for both prover and verifier.

5.2 Identity-Based Accumulators

Dynamic accumulators have been introduced by Camenisch and Lysyanskaya [10] based on an earlier construction by Barić and Pfitzmann [2]. They are a foundational primitive to establish privacy-preserving revocation in anonymous credential schemes.

The Camenisch-Lysyanskaya scheme is based on a Quadratic-Residues group $\mathbb{QR}_n$ under a special RSA modulus n with p' and q' as Sophie-Germain primes. It chooses values from a bounded domain of primes:

$$\chi_{A,B} = \{e \in \mathcal{P} : e \neq p', q' \wedge A \leq e \leq B\}.$$

Values $\tilde{x}$ from $\chi_{A,B}$ are added to the accumulator v by exponentiation, deleted from it by exponentiation with its multiplicative inverse wrt. the group order. The scheme is rounded out protocols for updating the accumulator witnesses as well as zero-knowledge proofs of knowledge showing that a committed value $\tilde{x}$ is part of the accumulator v.

This construction can be extended to include identity-based elements $\tilde{x}$ derived from an input x into the accumulator and the revocation scheme. This is facilitated by establishing a hash-to-prime setup that hashes into the range $\chi_{A,B}$ of the accumulator setup.

Consequently, the prover can show with ZK predicate $\left(\mu = \mathsf{hashToPrime}_{\mathcal{F}}^{\Upsilon}(\nu, t, u)\right)$ that the corresponding prime was generated correctly. This enables parties (issuers and users) to have primes p_x derived from identity strings x incorporated in the dynamic accumulator. The Camenisch-Lysyanskaya accumulators can, thereby, be extended to a full-domain group elements.

5.3   Dynamic Prime Encoding

Camensich and Groß [7,8] proposed an anonymous credential scheme incorporating efficient prime-encodings for binary and finite-set attributes. That encoding scheme is the foundation of the enumeration data type of the IBM Identity Mixer system [3]. While the scheme offers highly efficient AND, OR and NOT proofs on prime-encoded attributes, the scheme is limited by the issuer needing to pre-define an alphabet of prime numbers along with their meaning. Hence, the scheme cannot easily accommodate dynamically changing attribute values from a full-domain message space.

The SRSA graph signature scheme proposed by Groß [21] faces a similar problem: The scheme requires that the signer pre-establishes and certifies a graph alphabet, that is, an enumeration of prime representatives for vertex identifiers and labels. Thereby, the SRSA graph signature scheme is limited to a fixed size of graphs and a fixed selection of labels. This constitutes a limitation for proposed use cases, such as topology certification [20], which are normally operating on dynamically changing graphs with full-domain identifiers for different entities (machines, network and storage devices, etc.) While this limitation was lifted in the q-SDH version of the graph signature scheme [32], hashing to prime can offer an alternative route to a solution.

Using the hash-to-prime predicates shown in this paper, we can extend both the Camenisch-Groß anonymous credential scheme and the SRSA graph signature scheme as follows. We are considering the case of a user-known hidden value x. Let us assume that a commitment C_x on a value x is available and established that said commitment includes the relevant value (e.g., by equality proof with another credential). The user wants the issuer to sign a corresponding prime p_x as representation of x in a graph or in a finite-set attribute.

The user computes p_x from x with the chosen hash-to-prime algorithm and commits to p_x in commitment C_{p_x}. The user, acting as the requestor of a signature, interacts with the issuer, sending C_x, C_{p_x} over the wire. The user engages with the issuer in a zero-knowledge argument that $\left(\mu = \mathsf{hashToPrime}_{\mathcal{F}}^{\Upsilon}(\nu, t, u)\right)$ holds for x and p_x. The issuer can then be convinced that p_x was computed correctly and, without being privy to the value itself, create a blind signature on it. This technique can easily be used for multiple finite-set attributes and complex graph element, incl. multiple labels.

6   Evaluation

We have analyzed the computation complexity of proving the primality of a secret integer n in number of multi-base exponentiations by the bitlength of n and the maximum soundness error probability ε_S allowed, which in turn determines the number of

Table 6. Computation complexity of constituent predicates for k rounds (cf. [22]).

	Computations (mexp)
$(\mu \in \mathrm{primes}_L(t))$	$2t \log n + (7t \log n)k$
$(\mu \in \mathrm{primes}_M(t))$	$4 + 6 \log n + (13 + 12t + (3t + 1)(7 \log n))k$
$(\nu_j \in \mathrm{primes}_P(\nu_{j-1}, \varrho_j, \chi_j))$	$18 + 3 \log n + (29 + 7 \log n)k$

Note: mexp = multi-base exponentiations; k = number of PK rounds; t = number of primality-test rounds; n = candidate integer

Table 7. Communication complexity of primality zero-knowledge arguments for k rounds.

Predicate	Communication (ge/bits)
$(\mu \in \mathrm{primes}_L(t))$	$2t \log n$ ge $+(14t \log n \log Q + 4t \log n 2\epsilon\ell)k$ bits
$(\mu \in \mathrm{primes}_M(t))$	$9t\ell_b + 7t + 3\ell_b + 5$ ge +
	$(14t + 8)k$ ge + $(42\ell_b \log Q + 14\ell_b \log Q)k$ bits +
	$(22t + 14)k \log Q + 12t\ell_b\epsilon\ell k + 4\ell_b\epsilon\ell k$ bits
$(\nu_j \in \mathrm{primes}_P(\nu_{j-1}, \varrho_j, \chi_j))$	$3\ell_b + 18$ ge +
	$29k$ ge + $(14\ell_b \log Q)k$ bits +
	$39k \log Q + (4\ell_b\epsilon\ell)k$ bits

Note: ge = group elements from $\mathbb{G}$; k = number of PK rounds; n = candidate integer; Q = group order of $\mathbb{G}$; ℓ = length restriction; ϵ = security parameter

primality-test bases used t and the number of ZKP rounds k executed. All simulations are computed in the statistics software R. Tables 6 and 7 summarize the corresponding complexities numerically as function of those variables.

6.1 Primality ZK Arguments

We have computed an simulation in R pitting the growth of the number of multi-base exponentiations for different primality predicates by bitlength of n against each other. Figure 2 displays this complexity analysis graphically for small primes; Fig. 3 shows the secret primality proof for primes n up to a bitlength of $\ell_n = 1024$. Therein, we notice that the secret primality test with probabilistic Lehmann and Miller-Rabin tests $((\mu \in \mathrm{primes}_L(t))$ and $(\mu \in \mathrm{primes}_{MR}(t)))$ dominate the complexity, where the Lehmann test proposed by Camenisch and Michels [13] is the more efficient of the two for equal soundness error probabilities. Their complexity is largely dictated by the number of rounds t.

For the new primality predicates proposed in this work, we find that they excel at proving the primality of small primes. While the deterministic Miller test $((\mu \in \mathrm{primes}_M(t)))$ realized here only allows proving the primality of primes of a max bitlength of 81, it can be computed with a small number of fixed based for each bitlength. The Pocklington witness sequence employs $(\nu_j \in \mathrm{primes}_P(\nu_{j-1}, \varrho_j, \chi_j))$ recursively from a threshold bitlength of 32 bits yielding the recursion base with a deterministic Miller test $(\mu \in \mathrm{primes}_M(t))$. Each recursion step doubles the bitlength of the intermediate prime, which leads to a logarithmic growth of the length t of the Pocklington sequence in the bitlength of n.

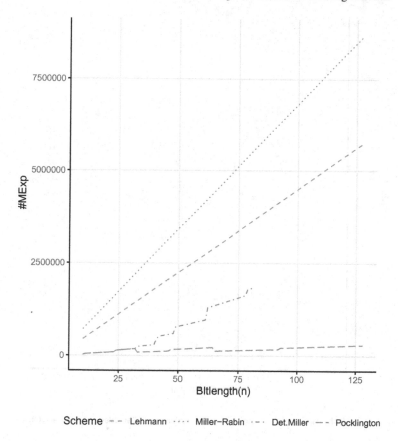

Fig. 2. Number of multi-base exponentiations by bitlength of n for a primality ZK argument on small primes $n, |n| \leq 128$, with a fixed number of rounds $k = 80$ and a soundness error probability of at most $2^{-80} + 2^{-80}$ [22].

To put the recursive Pocklington sequence simulation on even footing with the other primality predicates, we included an estimate of the cost that each Pocklington step j needs to find by trial-and-error a new integer r_j to construct the subsequent prime p_j. Given ℓ as bitlength of that prime, we use as expected number of intermediary Miller-Rabin (MR) tests computed per recursion step $\frac{1-1/(\ln(2)\ell)}{1/(\ln(2)\ell)}$. We account for two multi-base exponentiations per MR trial.

6.2 SRSA ZK Arguments

We simulated the zero-knowledge argument that a number n is product of two safe primes, comparing Camenisch and Michels' method based on the Lehmann primality criterion and our new construction using a Pocklington witness from Sect. 4.3. Figure 4 shows the comparison in number of multi-base exponentiations by bitlength of the product n. In the figure, we can clearly see that new Pocklington-Lehmann ZK argument is more efficient and its complexity in mexp growing more slowly that the ZK argument

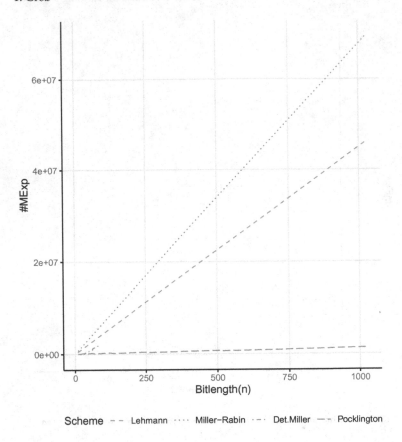

Fig. 3. Number of multi-base exponentiations by bitlength of n for a primality ZK argument on primes n, with a fixed number of rounds $k = 80$ and a soundness error probability of at most $2^{-80} + 2^{-80}$ [22].

by Camenisch and Michels. It is, thereby, more suitable to compute large special RSA moduli for strong key strengths. For instance, the number of mexp the CM-algorithm uses to establish a ZK argument that a 2048-bit number is a special RSA modulus is roughly the same as to make an equivalent ZK argument for a 4096-bit number with our new method, maximum soundness error probabilities being equal.

6.3   Hash-to-Prime ZK Arguments

We simulated the expected computational complexity of the hash-to-prime zero-knowledge arguments. We computed the expected number of multi-base exponentiations for making a zero-knowledge argument that a committed prime p_x is the outcome of a hash-to-prime operation on a committed input x. We evaluate that based on the bitlength of the output prime p_x. The simulation takes into account the expected number of eliminated prime candidates at each stage and thereby the expected number of

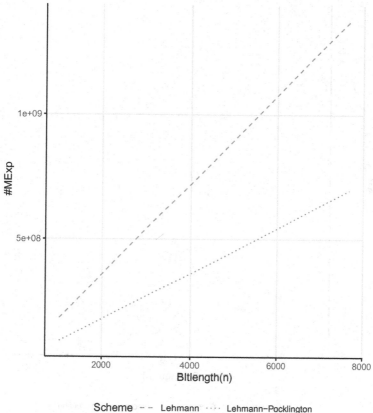

Scheme – – Lehmann ···· Lehmann–Pocklington

Fig. 4. Number of multi-base exponentiations by bitlength of n for the proof that a number n is the product of two safe primes, with a fixed number of rounds $k = 80$ and a soundness error probability of at most $2^{-80} + 2^{-80}$ [22].

calls to the composite() predicate. Figure 5 illustrates the outcome of the complexity simulation.

We observe in this analysis that the predicate $\left(\mu = \mathsf{hashToPrime}_{\mathcal{F}}^{\Upsilon}(\nu, t, u) \right)$ is considerably more efficient when realized by recursive construction (R) than by elimination (E). This efficiency comes with a trade-off in prime distribution. Whereas the elimination method yields primes that are statistically closely distributed to uniform at random, the recursive construction method yields primes with less entropy and not uniformly distributed. We note that the recursive construction method is quite efficient for hashing to primes with less than 256 bits. For this reason, the scheme is very promising for applications that encode into a message space of primes with limited bitlength. For instance, the Camenisch-Groß encoding [8] is typically constrained to messages with a bitlength of 256 bits. Similarly, the SRSA graph signature scheme of Groß [21] encodes vertex and edge labels with small primes (e.g., 16 bits) and vertex identifiers with primes

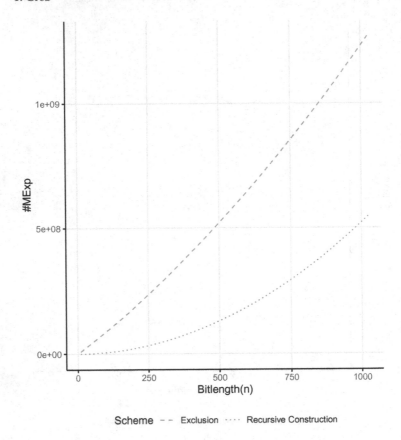

Fig. 5. Expected number of multi-base exponentiations for prove predicate ($\mu = \text{hashToPrime}$ (ν)) by bitlength of the output prime p_x [22].

smaller than 128 bits. Consequently, the scheme yields an efficient embedding of arbitrary bitstrings into the respective prime encodings.

7   Related Work

The computation of hash-to-prime functions is part of a range of known constructions. When it comes to hash-to-prime by elimination, Cachin, Micali, and Stadler [6] created a function PrimeSeq, which produces a prime p_x from an input x with a deterministic algorithm. Micali, Rabin, and Vadhan [28] used an adaptation of that construction in their construction of a verifiable random function.

For hash-to-prime by recursive construction, Ozdemir et al. [30] offered construction for division-intractable encoding. They chose a recursive, constructive method by establishing a sequence of primes and Pocklington witnesses. They do this in the context of SNARKs and verifiable computing. These approaches are not applicable as zero-knowledge arguments discrete-log based signature and zero-knowledge proof systems.

The contributions of this work are related to Camenisch and Michels' general zero-knowledge arguments on the primality of a secret integer and the composition of a special RSA modulus from two safe primes [13]. This work improved upon by Algesheimer, Camenisch, and Shoup [1] in the distributed setting.

8 Conclusion

In this paper, we discussed different variants of hash-to-prime zero-knowledge predicates and their corresponding zero-knowledge arguments. We show how these primitives can be used to create identity-based prime accumulators. These constructions can also be applied to prime-encoding in anonymous credential schemes and graph signature schemes to enable a dynamic encoding of full-domain inputs.

Acknowledgment. The author is grateful for the discussions with Ioannis Sfyrakis and Syh-Yuan Tan on hashing-to-prime zero-knowledge arguments. This work was funded by the ERC Starting Grant CASCAde (GA n°716980).

Appendix

In the following, we include detailed constructions for protocols used in the paper. Figure 6 shows the joint generation of random group elements as used by Camenisch and Michels [13]. Figure 7 outlines the protocol for the zero-knowledge argument that a number is a prime [13].

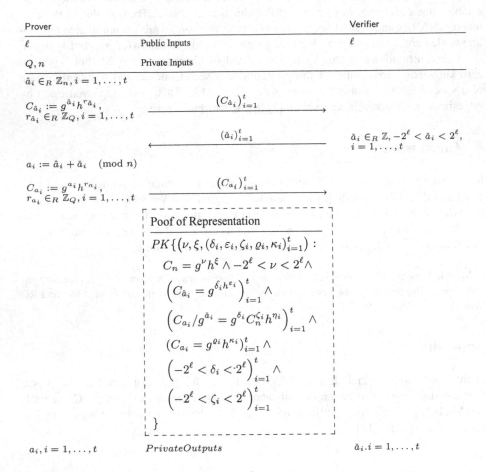

Prover		Verifier
ℓ	Public Inputs	ℓ
Q, n	Private Inputs	

$\hat{a}_i \in_R \mathbb{Z}_n, i = 1, \ldots, t$

$C_{\hat{a}_i} := g^{\hat{a}_i} h^{r_{\hat{a}_i}},$
$r_{\hat{a}_i} \in_R \mathbb{Z}_Q, i = 1, \ldots, t$
$\xrightarrow{\quad (C_{\hat{a}_i})_{i=1}^t \quad}$

$\xleftarrow{\quad (\breve{a}_i)_{i=1}^t \quad}$ $\breve{a}_i \in_R \mathbb{Z}, -2^\ell < \breve{a}_i < 2^\ell,$
$i = 1, \ldots, t$

$a_i := \hat{a}_i + \breve{a}_i \pmod{n}$

$C_{a_i} := g^{a_i} h^{r_{a_i}},$
$r_{a_i} \in_R \mathbb{Z}_Q, i = 1, \ldots, t$
$\xrightarrow{\quad (C_{a_i})_{i=1}^t \quad}$

Poof of Representation

$PK\{ \left(\nu, \xi, (\delta_i, \varepsilon_i, \zeta_i, \varrho_i, \kappa_i)_{i=1}^t \right) :$
$\quad C_n = g^\nu h^\xi \wedge -2^\ell < \nu < 2^\ell \wedge$
$\quad \left(C_{\hat{a}_i} = g^{\delta_i} h^{\varepsilon_i} \right)_{i=1}^t \wedge$
$\quad \left(C_{a_i}/g^{\breve{a}_i} = g^{\delta_i} C_n^{\zeta_i} h^{\eta_i} \right)_{i=1}^t \wedge$
$\quad (C_{a_i} = g^{\varrho_i} h^{\kappa_i})_{i=1}^t \wedge$
$\quad \left(-2^\ell < \delta_i < \cdot 2^\ell \right)_{i=1}^t \wedge$
$\quad \left(-2^\ell < \zeta_i < 2^\ell \right)_{i=1}^t$
$\}$

| $a_i, i = 1, \ldots, t$ | $PrivateOutputs$ | $\breve{a}_i . i = 1, \ldots, t$ |

Fig. 6. PK Predicate $\left((a_i)_{i=1}^t \in_R \mathbb{Z}_n^k \right)$ for secret n (adapted from [13]).

Prover		Verifier
ℓ	Public Inputs	ℓ
Q, n	Private Inputs	

> Establish random bases $(a_i)_{i=1}^t$
>
> $$\left((a_i)_{i=1}^t \in_R \mathbb{Z}_n^k \right)$$

$d_i := a_i^{(n-1)/2} \pmod{n}, i = 1, \ldots, t$

$C_{d_i} := g^{g_i} h^{r_{d_i}}, r_{d_i} \in_R \mathbb{Z}_Q, , i = 1, \ldots, t$

$C_b := g^{(n-1)/2} h^{r_b}, r_b \in_R \mathbb{Z}_Q$

Find $\tilde{a} : \tilde{a}^{(n-1)/2} \equiv -1 \pmod{n}$

$C_{\tilde{a}} := g^{\tilde{a}} h^{r_{\tilde{a}}}, r_{\tilde{a}} \in_R \mathbb{Z}_Q$ $\xrightarrow{\quad C_b, C_{\tilde{a}}, (C_{d_i})_{i=1}^t \quad}$

> Poof of Representation
>
> $PK\{(\alpha, \beta, \nu, \xi, \gamma, \varrho, \varepsilon,$
>
> $(\varrho_i, \kappa_i, \vartheta_i, \mu_i, \psi_i)_{i=1}^t) :$
>
> $C_b = g^\alpha h^\beta \wedge -2^\ell < \alpha < 2^\ell \wedge$
>
> $\underline{C_n = g^\nu h^\xi} \wedge (\underline{C_{a_i} = g^{\varrho_i} h^{\kappa_i}})_{i=1}^t \wedge$
>
> $C_b^2 g / C_n = h^\gamma \wedge$
>
> $C_{\tilde{a}} = g^\varrho h^\varepsilon \wedge$
>
> $(\varrho^\alpha \equiv -1 \pmod{n}) \wedge$
>
> $\left(C_{d_i}/g = h^{\vartheta_i} \vee C_{d_i} g = h^{\vartheta_i} \right)_{i=1}^t \wedge$
>
> $\left(C_{d_i} = g^{\mu_i} h^{\psi_i} \right)_{i=1}^t \wedge$
>
> $(\varrho_i^\alpha \equiv m u_i \pmod{\nu})_{i=1}^t$
>
> $\}$

Note: The underlined clauses form the bridge to $\left((a_i)_{i=1}^t \in_R \mathbb{Z}_n^k \right)$; proof overhead can be avoided if the PKs of both predicates are combined into one.

Fig. 7. PK Predicate $(\mu \in \text{primes}_\mathsf{L}(t))$ (adapted from [13]).

Prover		Verifier
(C, g, h, f, a, ℓ_r)	Public Inputs	(C, g, h, f, a, ℓ_r)
x, r	Private Inputs	

$$f_{\mathsf{C}} := (C \stackrel{?}{=} g^{f(x)} h^r)$$

$$\xrightarrow{\mathsf{OTChoose}(\{x_i\}_{i=0}^a, \{r_i\}_{i=0}^{\ell_r})}$$

$$f_{\mathsf{C}} := (C \stackrel{?}{=} g^{f(x)} h^r)$$

$$\begin{pmatrix} GC, \{K_i^0, K_i^1\}_i, Z \end{pmatrix} \\ \leftarrow \mathsf{Gb}(1^\kappa, f_{\mathsf{C}})$$

$$\xleftarrow{\mathsf{OTTransfer}(\{K_i^0, K_i^1\}_i, GC)}$$

$$Z' \leftarrow \mathsf{Ev}(GC, \{K_i^{w_i}\}_i)$$

$$\xrightarrow{C := \mathsf{Commit}(Z')}$$

$$\xleftarrow{\{K_i^0, K_i^1\}_i := \mathsf{OTOpenAll}()}$$

$$v \leftarrow \mathsf{Ve}\left(f', GC, \{K_i^0, K_i^1\}_i\right)$$

$$\xrightarrow{\text{if } v \text{ then } Z' \text{ else reject}}$$

$$\text{Output} \left(Z' \stackrel{?}{=} Z\right)$$

Fig. 8. PK Predicate $(C = \mathsf{GCCommit}(f(\mu), \rho))$.

References

1. Algesheimer, J., Camenisch, J., Shoup, V.: Efficient computation modulo a shared secret with application to the generation of shared safe-prime products. In: Yung, M. (ed.) CRYPTO 2002. LNCS, vol. 2442, pp. 417–432. Springer, Heidelberg (2002). https://doi.org/10.1007/3-540-45708-9_27

2. Barić, N., Pfitzmann, B.: Collision-free accumulators and fail-stop signature schemes without trees. In: Fumy, W. (ed.) EUROCRYPT 1997. LNCS, vol. 1233, pp. 480–494. Springer, Heidelberg (1997). https://doi.org/10.1007/3-540-69053-0_33

3. Bichsel, P., Binding, C., Camenisch, J., Groß, T., Heydt-Benjamin, T., Sommer, D., Zaverucha, G.: Cryptographic protocols of the identity mixer library. Research Report RZ 3730, IBM Research Division (2009)

4. Boudot, F.: Efficient proofs that a committed number lies in an interval. In: Preneel, B. (ed.) EUROCRYPT 2000. LNCS, vol. 1807, pp. 431–444. Springer, Heidelberg (2000). https://doi.org/10.1007/3-540-45539-6_31

5. Brillhart, J., Lehmer, D.H., Selfridge, J.L.: New primality criteria and factorizations of $2^{m} \pm 1$. Math. Comput. **29**(130), 620–647 (1975)

6. Cachin, C., Micali, S., Stadler, M.: Computationally private information retrieval with polylogarithmic communication. In: Stern, J. (ed.) EUROCRYPT 1999. LNCS, vol. 1592, pp. 402–414. Springer, Heidelberg (1999). https://doi.org/10.1007/3-540-48910-X_28

7. Camenisch, J., Groß, T.: Efficient attributes for anonymous credentials. In: Proceedings of the 15th ACM Conference on Computer and Communications Security (CCS 2008), pp. 345–356. ACM Press (2008)

8. Camenisch, J., Groß, T.: Efficient attributes for anonymous credentials. ACM Trans. Inf. Syst. Secur. (TISSEC) **15**(1), 1–30 (2012)

9. Camenisch, J., Krenn, S., Shoup, V.: A framework for practical universally composable zero-knowledge protocols. In: Lee, D.H., Wang, X. (eds.) ASIACRYPT 2011. LNCS, vol. 7073, pp. 449–467. Springer, Heidelberg (2011). https://doi.org/10.1007/978-3-642-25385-0_24

10. Camenisch, J., Lysyanskaya, A.: Dynamic accumulators and application to efficient revocation of anonymous credentials. In: Yung, M. (ed.) CRYPTO 2002. LNCS, vol. 2442, pp. 61–76. Springer, Heidelberg (2002). https://doi.org/10.1007/3-540-45708-9_5

11. Camenisch, J., Lysyanskaya, A.: A signature scheme with efficient protocols. In: Cimato, S., Persiano, G., Galdi, C. (eds.) SCN 2002. LNCS, vol. 2576, pp. 268–289. Springer, Heidelberg (2003). https://doi.org/10.1007/3-540-36413-7_20

12. Camenisch, J., Michels, M.: Proving in zero-knowledge that a number is the product of two safe primes. Tech. Rep. RS-98-29, BRICS (1998)

13. Camenisch, J., Michels, M.: Proving in zero-knowledge that a number is the product of two safe primes. In: Stern, J. (ed.) EUROCRYPT 1999. LNCS, vol. 1592, pp. 107–122. Springer, Heidelberg (1999). https://doi.org/10.1007/3-540-48910-X_8

14. Camenisch, J., Stadler, M.: Efficient group signature schemes for large groups. In: Kaliski, B.S. (ed.) CRYPTO 1997. LNCS, vol. 1294, pp. 410–424. Springer, Heidelberg (1997). https://doi.org/10.1007/BFb0052252

15. Chan, A., Frankel, Y., Tsiounis, Y.: Easy come — easy go divisible cash. In: Nyberg, K. (ed.) EUROCRYPT 1998. LNCS, vol. 1403, pp. 561–575. Springer, Heidelberg (1998). https://doi.org/10.1007/BFb0054154

16. Damgård, I., Fujisaki, E.: A statistically-hiding integer commitment scheme based on groups with hidden order. In: Zheng, Y. (ed.) ASIACRYPT 2002. LNCS, vol. 2501, pp. 125–142. Springer, Heidelberg (2002). https://doi.org/10.1007/3-540-36178-2_8

17. Etzel, M., Patel, S., Ramzan, Z.: Square Hash: fast message authentication via optimized universal hash functions. In: Wiener, M. (ed.) CRYPTO 1999. LNCS, vol. 1666, pp. 234–251. Springer, Heidelberg (1999). https://doi.org/10.1007/3-540-48405-1_15

18. Goldreich, O., Micali, S., Wigderson, A.: Proofs that yield nothing but their validity or all languages in NP have zero-knowledge proof systems. J. ACM (JACM) 38(3), 690–728 (1991)

19. Groß, T.: Certification and efficient proofs of committed topology graphs. Cryptology ePrint Archive Report 2014/255, IACR (2014). http://eprint.iacr.org/

20. Groß, T.: Efficient certification and zero-knowledge proofs of knowledge on infrastructure topology graphs. In: Proceedings of the 6th edition of the ACM Workshop on Cloud Computing Security (CCSW 2014), pp. 69–80. ACM (2014)

21. Groß, T.: Signatures and efficient proofs on committed graphs and NP-statements. In: Böhme, R., Okamoto, T. (eds.) FC 2015. LNCS, vol. 8975, pp. 293–314. Springer, Heidelberg (2015). https://doi.org/10.1007/978-3-662-47854-7_18

22. Groß, T.: Hashing to prime in zero-knowledge. In: In proceedings of the 18th International Conference on Security and Cryptography (SECRYPT'2021), pp. 62–74 (2021)

23. Jaeschke, G.: On strong pseudoprimes to several bases. Math. Comput. 61(204), 915–926 (1993)

24. Jawurek, M., Kerschbaum, F., Orlandi, C.: Zero-knowledge using garbled circuits: how to prove non-algebraic statements efficiently. In: Proceedings of the 2013 ACM SIGSAC Conference on Computer & Communications Security, pp. 955–966. ACM (2013)

25. Kranakis, E.: Primality and cryptography. Springer-Verlag (2013). https://doi.org/10.1007/978-3-322-96647-6

26. Lehmann, D.J.: On primality tests. SIAM J. Comput. 11(2), 374–375 (1982)

27. Menezes, A.J., Van Oorschot, P.C., Vanstone, S.A.: Handbook of applied cryptography. CRC Press (2018)

28. Micali, S., Rabin, M., Vadhan, S.: Verifiable random functions. In: 40th Annual Symposium on Foundations of Computer Science (cat. No. 99CB37039), pp. 120–130. IEEE (1999)

29. Naor, M., Reingold, O.: Number-theoretic constructions of efficient pseudo-random functions. In: Proceedings 38th Annual Symposium on Foundations of Computer Science, pp. 458–467. IEEE (1997)

30. Ozdemir, A., Wahby, R., Whitehat, B., Boneh, D.: Scaling verifiable computation using efficient set accumulators. In: 29th USENIX Security Symposium (USENIX Security 20), pp. 2075–2092 (2020)
31. Pomerance, C., Selfridge, J.L., Wagstaff, S.S.: The pseudoprimes to $25 \cdot 10^9$. Math. Comput. **35**(151), 1003–1026 (1980)
32. Tan, S.Y., Sfyrakis, I., Groß, T.: A q-sdh-based graph signature scheme on full-domain messages with efficient protocols. Cryptology ePrint Archive Report 2020/1403, IACR (2020)
33. Wesolowski, B.: Efficient Verifiable Delay Functions. In: Ishai, Y., Rijmen, V. (eds.) EUROCRYPT 2019. LNCS, vol. 11478, pp. 379–407. Springer, Cham (2019). https://doi.org/10.1007/978-3-030-17659-4_13

Improving Time Complexity and Utility of k-anonymous Microaggregation

Florian Thaeter and Rüdiger Reischuk[✉]

Institut für Theoretische Informatik, Universität zu Lübeck, Lübeck, Germany
{thaeter,reischuk}@tcs.uni-luebeck.de

Abstract. For research in medicine, economics and social sciences specific data of individuals is needed. Thus it should be publicly available, but this should not offend the privacy of each individual. Microaggregation applied to databases is a standard technique to protect privacy. It clusters similar people in larger groups to achieve so called k-anonymity – every individual is hidden in a cluster of size at least k. Then the data can be made public for all kinds of analysis, whereas other concepts like differential privacy keep the database secret and allow only specific questions about the data to be asked by outsiders.

The modification of a database to achieve anonymity should be as small as possible to keep its utility – that means the loss of information should be minimized. In this respect microaggregation typically performs much better than other anonymization techniques like generalization or suppression. However, minimizing the information loss by k-anonymous microaggregation is an NP-hard optimization problem for $k \geq 3$. Not only computing optimal solutions efficiently is unlikely, nontrivial approximations are lacking, too. Therefore, a bunch of heuristics all with at least quadratic time complexity have been developed.

This paper improves microaggregation significantly and provides a tradeoff between computational effort and utility. First, we make a detailed analysis and tuning of the maximum distance methodology – the common approach to generate a clustering that provides k-anonymity. We review the methods proposed so far and design a new algorithm $\texttt{MDAV}_\gamma^*$ that gives better utility on standard benchmarks.

A different approach of quadratic time complexity based on Lloyd's algorithm has been proposed and named ONA, but not completely analysed. This paper fills this gap and improves several steps resulting in a new algorithm $\texttt{ONA}^*$ with better utility.

Mondrian is a another approach for clustering data that can be adopted for microaggregation. It is quite fast, but typically achieves very pure utility. We improve on this and design an almost linear time algorithm that gives acceptable utility, however worse than the quadratic time algorithms.

Finally, we combine both techniques, ONA and Mondrian, to construct a new class of parameterized algorithms called $\texttt{MONA}$. They are quite fast with time complexity between almost linear and quadratic, and deliver competitive utility compared to the MDAV approach.

Keywords: Microaggregation · k-anonymity · Data clustering · Maximum distance heuristic

© The Author(s), under exclusive license to Springer Nature Switzerland AG 2023
P. Samarati et al. (Eds.): ICETE 2021, CCIS 1795, pp. 195–223, 2023.
https://doi.org/10.1007/978-3-031-36840-0_10

1 Introduction

k-anonymous microaggregation is a technique designed to improve privacy of individual-related data, still keeping the data useful for research. It has been introduced by Anwar, Defays and Nanopoulus [1,4] in 1993. Higher dimensional numerical data is clustered into groups of size at least k. We will call the result a *k-member clustering* in contrast to a *k-clustering* where the number of clusters is bounded by k. As final output each data point is represented by the centroid of its cluster and thus the modified database is k-anonymous [19,23].

While k-anonymity is quite a simple condition, other more complex properties have been considered to guarantee privacy like ℓ-diversity [15], t-closeness [11] or ε-differential privacy [9]. ℓ-diversity and t-closeness may sound theoretically more appealing, but it is unclear whether and how efficiently these properties can be achieved in practice. In addition, they require a strict separation of attributes into so-called *quasi-identifiers (QI)* and *confidential attributes (CA)* which decreases the flexibility when using the anonymized data. On the other hand, differential privacy is restricted to a setting where instead of anonymizing the database and making it publicly known, only a predefined type of questions can be sent to the owner of the database. The answers protect private information by adding a suitable amount of noise depending on the diversity of the data and the type of questions. The usability is therefore limited and highly diverse data may yield quite useless answers because of larger deviations. For a more detailed discussion why these measures cannot replace k-anonymity entirely see [12].

Minimizing the information loss in k-anonymous microaggregation is an NP-hard optimization problem for $k \geq 3$ [17,26]. Even more, no efficient approximation algorithms with a nontrivial approximation ratio are known. Several heuristics with quadratic time complexity in the number of individuals have been developed to achieve k-anonymity (see e.g. [8,21,25]). Quadratic time may be acceptable for small databases, but large ones with millions of individuals cannot be handled in reasonable time. This paper tries to mitigate this problem.

Most competitive k-anonymous microaggregation algorithms are based on the MDAV (maximum distance to average vector) principle initially formulated by Domingo-Ferrer et al. in [8]. The idea is to start with an element $\bar{x}$ of greatest distance to the centroid $c(X)$ of the whole database X and to form clusters by grouping $\bar{x}$ with its $k-1$ nearest neighbours. If less than k elements are left, the remaining elements are assigned to their closest cluster. Since the distance of many pairs of elements has to be computed this results in quadratic time complexity. While no approximation guarantees have been shown for this strategy and further improvements, these algorithms seem to perform well on benchmark databases.

In [25] we have proposed an extension called MDAV*. Instead of creating a new group in every step, one is given the additional option to add the current most distant element $\bar{x}$ to the closest cluster already created. The decision is made by comparing the impact on cluster cost in the local area. Without increasing the time complexity significantly the results in [25] show that MDAV* outperforms MDAV and other MDAV variants. In this paper we present a further improvement of this algorithm by adding a parameter that controls this decision. The new algorithm is called MDAV$_\gamma^*$ and will be presented in Sect. 3.

Another approach named PCL was published in [18] using clustering techniques for the case that an upper bound is given on the number of clusters – the k-means problem – instead of a lower bound on the size. However, no analysis of its computational complexity has been made which seems to be difficult.

In 2019 Soria-Comas et al. presented an algorithm named ONA (Near-Optimal microaggregation Algorithm) [21]. It is based on the Lloyd algorithm for efficiently clustering high dimensional data that starts with a random clustering and then iteratively improves the clustering by reassigning data points to closer clusters until a stopping condition holds [14]. As the Lloyd algorithm is not tailored to guarantee a lower bound on cluster sizes it has to be modified. ONA starts with a randomly created k-member clustering and repeats the following steps for several rounds. Iterate over all elements x and consider their cluster C_x. If C_x has more than k elements try to lower the information loss by reassigning x to another cluster. If $|C_x| = k$ try to improve the clustering by dissolving C_x and redistribute its elements to other clusters nearby. Finally, split all clusters that have grown to size at least $2k$ by applying ONA recursively. This rearrangement of elements is stopped when within a round no change has occurred or a preset number of rounds has been reached.

Regarding information loss ONA seems to be comparable to previous quadratic time heuristics on real and synthetic benchmark databases. However, it was not possible for us to reproduce the excellent results claimed in [21]. We have investigated how the strategy of rearranging clusters can be improved. It turned out that iterating over data points in an arbitrary order, which seems to be a good strategy for k-clustering, is not as good for k-member clustering. Instead iterating over clusters in a well chosen order is computationally more efficient and according to the benchmarks applied gives better utility. This new strategy called ONA* will be presented in Sect. 4.

In 2006 LeFevre et al. introduced MONDRIAN, a clustering algorithm that achieves k-anonymity in $O(n \log n)$ time [10]. The optimization goal of the MONDRIAN algorithm are clusters with sizes as close to k as possible. This algorithm has not been developed for microaggregation, still it creates clusterings with cluster size at least k. Hence, this strategy can be used to perform k-anonymous microaggregation by calculating and reporting centroids for each cluster created. However, the question arises whether the resulting information loss is comparable to state-of-the-art heuristics designed to minimize information loss. Our investigations have shown that this is not the case. Therefore we modify and improve this strategy to design two new algorithms MONDRIAN_V and MONDRIAN_V2D that have the same time complexity as the original one, but achieve reasonable utility. The information loss occurring is larger than that of the best quadratic time algorithms, but still on the same order. These results will be discussed in Sect. 5.

Finally, by combining both methods – almost linear time complexity with a larger information loss and quadratic time with better utility – we design two new classes of algorithms called $MONA_\rho$ and $MONA\_2D_\rho$ that are scalable by the parameter ρ between almost linear and quadratic time. They deliver competitive utility shown by benchmark tests in Sect. 6.

Summarizing the results of this paper, the performance of state-of-the-art quasi-linear, resp. quadratic time heuristics for k-anonymity are significantly improved. Furthermore, we have exploited the tradeoff between computational effort and data quality providing a whole range of algorithms that suit different demands in practice.

This paper contains results of the first author's dissertation [24]. It extends our paper presented at the conference SECRYPT 2021 [27] by a detailed analysis of maximum distance heuristics and a further improved algorithm named $\mathtt{MDAV}_\gamma^*$. In addition, we have added a number of experimental results of all algorithms discussed on standard benchmarks. The class of $\mathtt{MONA}$-algorithms is extended by a 2-dimensional variant $\mathtt{MONA\_2D}$ that is based on the 2-dimensional version of $\mathtt{MONDRIAN}$.

In the discussion of our experimental results, due to space limitations we provide data for illustration often only for some of the benchmarks. Data for other standard benchmarks and randomly generated problem instances can be found in [24].

2   Problem Setting

Let us start with a formal definition of the problem and relevant notation.

Definition 1 (Database). *A **data point, element or individual** is a d-dimensional vector $x_i = (x_i^1, \ldots, x_i^d) \in \mathbb{R}^d$ of numerical attributes. A **database** $X = x_1, \ldots, x_n$ is a sequence of data points, potentially including duplicates. X is k-**anonymous** if each data point occurring in X has a multiplicity of at least k.*

The common property of all microaggregation algorithms is the use of a k-member clustering to generate a partition of the data. Once clusters are defined, elements of the database are replaced by the centroid of their cluster. As a result one obtains a k-anonymous database which protects privacy of its individuals by the principle *hiding in a group of k*.

Definition 2 (k-member Clustering). *A k-**member clustering** of a database X is a partition C of its members into clusters $C_1, \ldots, C_m$ such that each cluster contains at least k elements.*
Let $\delta(x, x')$ denote the Euclidean distance between two elements $x, x' \in \mathbb{R}^d$. Then $\delta(\cdot, \cdot)^2$ is the distance measure used for clusterings.

*The **centroid of a cluster** C_j is given by* $c(C_j) = \dfrac{1}{|C_j|} \sum_{x \in C_j} x$.

*The **diversity of a cluster** C_j is defined as* $Cost(C_j) := \sum_{x \in C_j} \delta(x, c(C_j))^2$

*and the **cost of a clustering** C by* $Cost(C) := \sum_{C_j \in C} Cost(C_j)$.

Note that δ^2 is additive with respect to the individual attributes and implies the following well known property of the centroid.

Fact 1. *For a cluster C_j its centroid $c(C_j)$ minimizes the sum of the distances to its elements, that means the function $\sum_{x \in C_j} \delta(x, y)^2$ is minimized by $y = c(C_j)$.*
The diversity $Cost(C_j)$ equals $\frac{1}{2|C_j|} \sum_{x \in C_j} \sum_{y \in C_j} \delta(x, y)^2$, that is half the average sum of distances of an element x to all other members of C_j.

Hence, $Cost(C_j)$ measures the closeness of elements within C_j. Replacing an element x put into cluster C_j by the centroid of its cluster minimizes the total amount of deviations of all elements in C_j. Once the clusters are established, creating a k-anonymous database is straight-forward by selecting the centroid as the anonymous version of each data point. Thus the data disturbance of such a procedure is related to $Cost(C)$ and should be as small as possible. Let us note

Fact 2. *Given a clustering C, for each cluster C_j the centroid $c(C_j)$ and $Cost(C_j)$ can be computed with $O(d\,|C_j|)$ arithmetic operations, hence $Cost(C)$ in $O(d\,n)$ many steps.*

Note that the input size is $N = d\,n$ real numbers, thus this computation takes only linear time.

Definition 3 (k-anonymous Microaggregation). *Given a database X he k-anonymous microaggregation problem is to find a k-member clustering C with minimum cost.*

It has been shown that this is an NP-hard optimization problem for $k \geq 3$ [17,26]. Even approximation algorithms with a nontrivial approximation ratio are not known. Hence, several heuristics have been developed.

To compare the data disturbance between several databases of different sizes and dimensionality, the notion *information loss* has been introduced. By dividing cost by the worst possible clustering (cluster all elements in one big cluster), one obtains a utility measure ranging from 0 for perfect utility and 1 for worst possible utility. Typically, information loss is stated as percentages, see e.g. [21].

Definition 4 (Information Loss). *The diversity $\Delta(X)$ of a database X is the sum of squared distances of its elements to the global centroid:* $\Delta(X) := \sum_{i=1}^{n} \delta(x_i, c(X))^2$.

The information loss of a clustering C of X is defined as $L(C,X) := \dfrac{Cost(C)}{\Delta(X)}$.

Thus, for a given database X minimizing $Cost(C)$ minimizes the information loss, too. For a meaningful measurement of the information loss the attributes of the databases should be standardized – typically to mean value 0 and variance 1 – prior to anonymization to exclude scaling effects. More general, if one does not want all attributes to have the same impact on the loss a linear transformation of the standardized attribute values could be applied to weight each attribute individually. As microaggregation is dimension and order conserving, such a transformation can be reversed after anonymization.

3 Maximum Distance Heuristics

Univariate k-anonymous microaggregation ($d = 1$) can be solved efficiently in time $O(n\log n + n\,k^2)$. However, multidimensional k-anonymous microaggregation is NP-hard for $k \geq 3$ and $d \geq 2$ [17,26]. Early microaggregation heuristics used univariate approaches to solve the microaggregation problem for higher dimensional data as well. By assuming the dimensions are statistically independent, d instances of univariate microaggregation approaches can anonymize d-dimensional databases (see e.g. [3]).

As a result one obtains d univariate, k-anonymous clusterings. Obviously, this approach has its limits, as in most cases multidimensional data is compiled *because* of potential dependencies between attribute dimensions. Hence, utility of the anonymized data for statistical analysis is severely impaired. Another primitive method proposed in [16] is to project multidimensional data onto a single dimension by using principal component analysis or other projection techniques. While this procedure might preserve some global dependencies between attributes, diverse local clusters with few elements can hardly be preserved by such representations.

Definition 5 (Neighborhood and Closest Clusters). *Let X be a database and C a (potentially incomplete) clustering of X.*

- *The* nearest neighbor *of an element $x \in X$ according to $\delta(\cdot,\cdot)^2$ within a set of elements S is denoted as $\nu(x,S)$.*
- *The ℓ-neighborhood of an element $x \in X$ within a set of elements S, noted as $N_\ell(x,S)$, is a cluster of size $\ell+1$ including x and its ℓ nearest-neighbors within S according to $\delta(\cdot,\cdot)^2$.*
- *An* unassigned element *is an element $x \in X$ that has not jet been assigned to a cluster $C \in C$ during a clustering process. Let U denote the set of such elements.*
- *The* closest cluster *of an element $x \in X$ is the cluster*

$$clos(x) := \arg\min_{C \in C} \delta(x, c(C))^2.$$

In the following we assume that nearest elements are unique. Otherwise, such an element may be selected arbitrarily, for example randomly or according to the ordering in the database.

3.1   MD

In 1998 Mateo-Sanz and Domingo-Ferrer introduced the first truly multivariate microaggregation heuristic called MD (Maximum Distance) [7, 16]. When there are at least $2k$ elements, find the two elements x_r and x_s in greatest distance to each other and build clusters C_r and C_s out of x_r and x_s by clustering them with their respective $k-1$ nearest neighbors. Repeat until there are less than $2k$ elements. If between k and $2k-1$ elements are remaining, create an additional cluster with all remaining elements, otherwise assign all remaining elements x to their closest existing cluster $clos(x)$.

Any cluster in the resulting clustering has between k and $2k-1$ elements. Further, for large databases most clusters would be of size exactly k, as the algorithm performs a strict k-member clustering until the last $2k-1$ elements. However, as several elements might be added to the same cluster in the last step, the result might contain several clusters of more than k elements, which prevents the algorithm from being categorized as *fixed-size*.

Let us take a closer look at the computational effort of this procedure. For all common microaggregation algorithms, $O(d\,n)$ arithmetic operations are needed to compute cluster centroids and to create an anonymized database given a k-member clustering. All pairwise distances can be computed in $O(d\,n^2)$ time and stored in a matrix. MD makes $n/2k$ Iterations. Each time a pair of maximal distance can be found in the sub-matrix of unassigned elements by a linear scan. In the final phase the closest clusters can be determined in linear time. This results in time complexity $O(d\,n^2 + n^3/k)$ and space complexity $O(n^2)$.

Over the years, MD received several incremental updates, resulting in the algorithms MDAV (Maximum Distance to Average Vector) [8], MDAV$^+$ [20], V-MDAV [20], and MDAV* [25] which achieved competitive information losses and time complexities compared to other microaggregation algorithms. As all these algorithms are based on MD and use distance computations to find cluster-generating elements, we refer to them as the class of *maximum distance heuristics* from now on.

3.2 MDAV

A core idea behind MD is to create clusters in greatest distance to each other. As outliers need to be included in some clusters, it might be better to include them right away to avoid a large sparely populated (and hard to cluster) domain of elements later on. However, selecting the two elements with maximum distance between each other is computationally expensive and ineffective when looking for outliers in more than one dimension. As the name suggests, in each round MDAV calculates the centroid $c(U)$ of all remaining unassigned elements $x \in U$ and selects the element x_r in greatest distance to $c(U)$. As for MD, MDAV chooses x_s as the element in greatest distance to x_r and clusters x_r as well as x_s with their $k - 1$ nearest neighbors.

Another difference between MD and MDAV is the handling of the last elements. MDAV stops its initial behavior when less than $3k$ elements remain unassigned. If there are between $3k - 1$ and $2k$ elements left, their centroid and its most distant element x_r are determined. Now, two clusters are created: One including x_r and its $k - 1$ nearest neighbors and another one with all other elements remaining. However, if there are less than $2k$ elements left all remaining elements are clustered together in a single new cluster. In contrast to MD, the resulting clustering is fixed-size, as only one cluster might have more than k elements.

In the first round, $O(d\,n)$ time is needed to compute the centroid of the database. With the same effort the most distant elements x_r and x_s can be found and using linear select the $k - 1$ nearest neighbors to x_r and x_s, too. This gives a total time complexity $O(d\,n^2/k)$ for MDAV.

3.3 MDAV+

Another variation of MD is a nameless simplified version of MDAV used as a building block for the V-MDAV algorithm by Solanas and Martínez-Ballesté in [20]. Let us call it MDAV$^+$. n each round only one cluster is created around the element x_r in greatest distance to the global centroid $- x_s$ is not needed. Furthermore, the global centroid is not updated throughout the algorithm. The clustering loop is stopped when there are less than k elements, which are assigned to their closest cluster.

Our experiments have shown that these changes deliver equivalent or slightly lower information loss than MDAV, but speed-up the computation. However, the asymptotic complexity remains unchanged.

3.4 V-MDAV

The algorithm V-MDAV (Variable-sized MDAV) proposed by Solanas and Martínez-Ballesté in [20] combines variable-sized clustering with the maximum distance principle for the first time. As in MDAV$^+$, a persistant global centroid $c(X)$ is used to find elements x_r in greatest distance to it. After x_r is clustered with its $k-1$ nearest neighbors, a process called *extend* is used to decide whether additional unassigned elements should be clustered with x_r. This way, a cluster including x_r may grow to up to $2k-1$ elements before the process is stopped. Using a *gain factor* γ, a cluster C is extended by the element x_I that is the unassigned element closest to any element $x \in C$ if $\delta(x,x_I)^2 < \gamma \cdot \delta(x_I,x_O)^2$ for the element x_O being the unassigned element closest to x_I. If x_I is included, the process repeats, otherwise it is halted.

γ determines how aggressively the extend process tries to include additional elements. In case $\gamma = 1$, x_I is included in C if x_I is strictly closer to an element in C than to any unassigned neighbor. For $\gamma < 1$ the extension process is less aggressive – an element must be much closer to an element inside C than to its closest unassigned neighbor. In an extreme case $\gamma = 0$ no extension is possible at all and V-MDAV generates clusterings identical to MDAV$^+$.

How to determine an optimal γ for a given database is not known. Solanas and Martínez-Ballesté proposed to use $\gamma = 0.2$ for so-called *scattered* databases and $\gamma = 1.1$ for *clustered* databases. However, no criterion is disclosed on how to decide whether a database is scattered or clustered.

The additional extension mechanism of V-MDAV comes at the cost of higher computational complexity. Assume that distances are computed on-the-fly, as in MDAV$^+$. It takes $O(d\,n\,k)$ to find x_I and x_O as well as to decide whether to include x_I in a cluster C. As any cluster might be extended up to $k-1$ times, the extension process may cost $O(d\,n\,k^2)$ operations. However, at least $n/2k$ clustering rounds are still needed. Hence, the worst case time complexity goes up to $O(d\,n^2\,k)$.

3.5 MDAV*

The extension problem is addressed by another modification called MDAV* [26]. The greedy nature of the extend process used by V-MDAV ignores the effect of the inclusion of an additional element on clusters to be created later. Even though an element x_I might be closer to the edge of a cluster than to its closet unassigned neighbor x_O, it might still be a bad idea to include x_I because x_O might need to substitute x_I by worse options if it becomes assigned elsewhere. Another major problem is that V-MDAV is not able to detect natural clusters of size less than k.

The main novelty of the heuristic MDAV* is to take into account the effects on nearby elements when the extension of a cluster has to be decided and to handle cluster extension before creating a new cluster instead of after the creation. When assigning elements to existing clusters MDAV* considers the additional cost per element (marginal cost) a decision would cause and greedily selects an optimal one.

Let U denote the currently unassigned elements. After the choice of a new origin $x_r \in U$, MDAV* considers two options. The first one is to build a new cluster $N_{k-1}(x_r,U)$ as usual. The second one is to extend the cluster $clos(x_r)$ by x_r in which case the cluster

$N_{k-1}(x_r, U)$ cannot be built. Instead, the neighbors of x_r have to be assigned differently. For this, we take the nearest neighbor $v(x_r, U)$ of x_r and consider establishing a new cluster around it. The underlying decision rule considers the marginal cost in both cases and chooses the option of lower cost. If marginal cost is equal, a new cluster is created. Still, this is only an estimate of the best possible usage of x_r because we do not know whether $v(x_r, U)$ is ever chosen as the origin of a new cluster. For the same reason the cluster around $v(x_r, U)$ is not actually created at this time, even if $clos(x_r)$ is extended by x_r.

The cost divided by the number of elements k for creating a new cluster $N_{k-1}(x_r, U)$ out of the element x_r is calculated as

$$cost_N(x_r) := \frac{cost(N_{k-1}(x_r, U))}{k}$$

while the cost per element of extending the cluster $clos(x_r)$ by x_r and establishing a new cluster around $v(x_r, U)$ (now assigning $k+1$ elements) is defined as

$$cost_E(x_r) := \frac{cost(clos(x_r) \cup x_r) - cost(clos(x_r)) + cost(N_{k-1}(v(x_r, U), U \setminus \{x_r\}))}{k+1}.$$

When there are exactly k elements left, $cost_E(x_r)$ cannot be computed. In this case $cost_E(x_r)$ is thought to be infinity so a new cluster $N_{k-1}(x_r, U)$ is created.

As before, closest clusters and neighborhoods can be computed in time $O(d\,n)$. Hence, a single execution of the clustering loop of MDAV* takes $O(d\,n)$ time. However, in contrast to MDAV$^+$, we cannot guarantee a worst case limit of $O(n/k)$ clustering rounds, as the inclusion of an x_r-element into an existing cluster reduces the size of U by one element only. Thus, there might be up to $O(n)$ clustering rounds and the worst case time complexity of MDAV* becomes $O(d\,n^2)$.

3.6   MDAV$^*_\gamma$

After this overview of the development of MD-heuristics we present a further improvement combining a gain factor γ with a local optimization of marginal costs. $\gamma = 0$ causes the algorithm to behave like MDAV$^+$, whereas for $\gamma = 1$ the algorithm behaves like MDAV*. Again, values in between or above 1 are possible as well. Now the extension criterion allows to enlarge a cluster C by an element x_r even if $v(x_r, U)$ cannot be clustered cost effectively without x_r. The additional criterion checks whether marginal cost of x_r and $v(x_r)$ when clustered with C are lower than the marginal cost of elements in the original cluster C:

$$cost_{E2}(x_r) := \frac{cost(clos(x_r) \cup \{x_r, v(x_r, U)\}) - cost(clos(x_r))}{2}$$

This check is applied when the extension rule of MDAV* opts for the creation of a new cluster and is especially beneficial in situations in which either both x_r and $v(x_r, U)$ or none of them should be included in C to minimize cost. As before, when there are exactly k elements unassigned at the time of choosing x_r, a new cluster will be created. Note that even in the case $cost_{E2}(x_r) < cost_N(x_r)$ the cluster $clos(x_r)$ is extended by

x_r only. This approach is aimed at considering uncertainty about future clusters. Not including $v(x_r, U)$ right away allows it to be clustered somewhere else, when it is indeed not chosen as a new x_r element later on. However, if it is chosen as x_r element, a new decision with more accurate data can be done. In general, it is save to assume that delaying any extension decisions as long as possible is safer, as these decisions relay on assumptions on the future clustering process, which might not be accurate.

Another design decision is the application of the gain factor only for the original extension check. As the original and new extension check consider different scenarios, different gain factors will be optimal for each of them on a given database. However, introducing a second gain factor γ' would increase the amount of work to be done to tune parameters disproportionately.

There is no difference in time or space complexity between MDAV^* and MDAV^*_γ besides the extra time needed to find a suitable γ for the database given. A pseudocode of MDAV^*_γ is given as Algorithm 1.

Algorithm 1. MDAV^*_γ.

---

input : database X and minimal cluster size k and gain factor γ
output: k-member clustering $C = \{C_1, \ldots, C_m\}$

1 Let $U \leftarrow X$
2 Let $C \leftarrow \emptyset$
3 Let $c(X)$ be the global centroid
4 **repeat**
5 $\quad$ Let $x_r \leftarrow \arg\max_{x \in U} \delta(x, c(X))^2$
6 $\quad$ Calculate $cost_N(x_r)$
7 $\quad$ Calculate $cost_E(x_r)$
8 $\quad$ Calculate $cost_{E2}(x_r)$
9 $\quad$ **if** $cost_E(x_r) < \gamma \cdot cost_N(x_r)$ **or** $cost_{E2}(x_r) < cost_N(x_r)$ **then**
10 $\quad\quad$ $clos(x_r) \leftarrow clos(x_r) \cup x_r$
11 $\quad\quad$ $U \leftarrow U \setminus \{x_r\}$
12 $\quad$ **else**
13 $\quad\quad$ $C \leftarrow C \cup \{N_{k-1}(x_r, U)\}$
14 $\quad\quad$ $U \leftarrow U \setminus N_{k-1}(x_r, U)$
15 **until** $|U| < k$
16 **foreach** $x \in U$ **do**
17 $\quad$ $clos(x) \leftarrow clos(x) \cup \{x\}$

When considering the possibility of cluster extension by two elements at once, one might be tempted to generalize this behavior to consider the extension of up to $k - 1$ elements at once, depending on the size of $clos(x_r)$. Despite the obvious increase in time complexity there is another good reason not to pursue this approach: Deciding for a cluster extension or cluster generation inherently uses assumptions about future clustering processes. When more and more elements are included in this decisions, we also need to assume more about their ideal clustering, all without being able to see the big picture of clustering opportunities much later during the run of the algorithm.

Hence, there is not only diminishing return in including more elements in our extension check, but also a negative impact of a decision based on weak data preventing a simple design of even smarter extension rules.

Table 1. Key properties of the maximum distance heuristics discussed in this section.

	Time	Space	Variable size	Gain factor	Introduced	Reference
MD	$O(d\,n^2 + n^3/k)$	$O(n^2)$	yes	no	1998	[16]
MDAV	$O(d\,n^2/k)$	$O(d\,n)$	no	no	2005	[8]
MDAV$^+$	$O(d\,n^2/k)$	$O(d\,n)$	yes	no	2006 (2018)	[20,25]
V-MDAV	$O(d\,n^2 k)$	$O(d\,n)$	yes	yes	2006	[20]
MDAV*	$O(d\,n^2)$	$O(d\,n)$	yes	no	2018	[25]
MDAV$^*_\gamma$	$O(d\,n^2)$	$O(d\,n)$	yes	yes	this	paper

3.7 Finding the Closest Cluster

As discussed in the introduction of this chapter, the closest cluster C to an element x is assumed to be

$$clos(x) := \arg\min_{C\in\mathcal{C}} \delta(x, c(C))^2$$

for all heuristics so far. Another solution to this problem would be to consider cluster C which contains the clustered element y closest to x, i.e.

$$clos'(x) := \arg\min_{C\in\mathcal{C}} \min_{y\in C} \delta(x, y)^2.$$

This operation would be similar to the computation of x_I in V-MDAV. A third option proposed in [25] is to choose the cluster C which has the minimal cost increase, when extended with x among all current clusters, i.e.

$$clos''(x) := \arg\min_{C\in\mathcal{C}} cost(C\cup x) - cost(C).$$

As $clos(\cdot)$ is used to extend clusters and our main goal is to minimize information loss, the third option seems to be the obvious choice. However, selecting the closest cluster according to the first two measures can lead to a larger increase than $clos''(x)$.

Fact 3. *For the extension by an element x, the closest cluster to x according to $clos(x)$ or $clos'(x)$ may not minimze the real extension cost, that is $clos''(x)$. A smaller cluster with center little further away can be a better choice.*

Proof. Consider a cluster C containing κ identical elements y_i with $\delta(x, c(C)) = \lambda$. When including x in C, the centroid shifts towards x and yields

$$\delta(y_i, c(C\cup x))^2 = \left(\frac{\lambda}{\kappa+1}\right)^2 \quad \text{and} \quad \delta(x, c(C\cup x))^2 = \left(\lambda - \frac{\lambda}{\kappa+1}\right)^2,$$

which adds up to $cost(C\cup x) = \lambda^2 \dfrac{\kappa}{\kappa+1}$.

Now for $k \leq \kappa_1 < \kappa_2 < 2k$ one can always find values $\lambda_1 > \lambda_2$ such that

$$\lambda_1^2 \frac{\kappa_1}{\kappa_1 + 1} < \lambda_2^2 \frac{\kappa_2}{\kappa_2 + 1} \, ,$$

that means the cluster C_1 with parameters κ_1, λ_1 increases the extension cost less than the cluster C_2 with corresponding parameters, although x is closer to C_2.

However, our experiments have indicated that replacing $clos(\cdot)$ by $clos''(\cdot)$ a significant time increase occurs without an adequate information loss reduction. Hence, we have made no further effort to use $clos''(\cdot)$ instead.

3.8 Experimental Evaluation

To compare these heuristics we have made implementations as discussed above and tests with several real and synthetic benchmark databases. These are *Census*, *Tarragona* and *EIA* from the CASC project [6], *Cloud1*, *Cloud2*, the *Adult data set* and the *credit card clients data set* from the UCI Machine Learning Repository [13] as well as uniformly distributed synthetic databases *SimU* and clustered synthetic databases *SimC* created as proposed in [5]. Here we state results of these many experiments that are described in [24] in more detail for some benchmarks only; more data can be found in this dissertation. Always a fixed set of values for the anonymization parameter k has been used, namely $K = \{2, 3, 4, 5, 7, 10\}$.

The EIA (Energy Information Authority) data set consists of $n = 4092$ elements with 15 attributes. As in previous works (see e.g. [5]) only $d = 11$ numerical attributes precisely 1 and 6 to 15 have been used of this benchmark. For a meaningful test, the attributes of the databases are standardized to mean value 0 and variance 1 prior to anonymization. In the following we provide results for this data set to compare the different MD heuristics. Information losses are always stated in percentages.

Computations have been performed based on single-threaded Java implementations on a PC equipped with an AMD Ryzen 9 5900X with 4.8 GHz turbo frequency and 32 GB of DDR4-3200 MHz MHz RAM.

Table 2. Runtimes in sec of the different MD heuristics on the benchmark EIA with $n = 4092$ and $d = 11$ [24].

k	2	3	4	5	7	10
MD	2.38	1.58	1.15	0.91	0.67	0.49
MDAV	0.23	0.15	0.10	0.09	0.07	0.06
MDAV$^+$	0.11	0.06	0.05	0.04	0.03	0.02
V-MDAV	0.15	0.13	0.10	0.11	0.08	0.13
MDAV*	0.37	0.24	0.18	0.14	0.10	0.09
MDAV$^*_\gamma$	0.30	0.22	0.18	0.18	0.18	0.14

All algorithms are benchmarked against each other with respect to runtime (Table 2) and information loss (Table 3).

Information loss obviously increases with the security parameter k since an optimal k-member clustering is a k'-member clustering for $k' < k$, too. The same holds for the maximum distance heuristics. However, the relative performance of each algorithm in this group of algorithms seems to be quite independent of k. The same holds for the different benchmarks. No algorithm was consistently better than another algorithm on one particular database, but consistently worse on another. Comparing the different benchmarks, however, some are more resistant to utility preserving anonymization than others.

Table 3. Information losses in percentage of the MD heuristics on EIA [24].

k	2	3	4	5	7	10
MD	0.27	0.47	0.77	1.67	2.28	3.71
MDAV	0.31	0.48	0.67	1.67	2.17	3.84
MDAV$^+$	0.32	0.49	0.67	1.78	2.21	3.55
V-MDAV	0.23	0.46	0.67	1.06	2.21	2.79
MDAV*	0.22	0.45	0.62	0.91	2.03	2.63
MDAV$^*_\gamma$	0.20	0.39	0.54	0.82	1.66	2.18

Surprisingly, neither MDAV nor MDAV$^+$ are able to beat MD for all values of k on EIA. Further, note the big jump between $k = 4$ and $k = 5$ for all three. The relation becomes even worse when taking the average over all benchmarks. In Table 4 the result of a pairwise comparison between all algorithms discussed in this section is listed. Here the average is taken over all benchmarks and values in the set K. The average information loss of the algorithm labelling a row is scaled to the value 100 and compared with that of the algorithm labelling a column. A valued below 100 means that the second algorithm causes less information loss, where above 100 the information loss is worse.

Table 4. Comparing average information loss of MD heuristics over all benchmarks and values for k [24].

from\to	MD	MDAV	MDAV$^+$	V-MDAV	MDAV*	MDAV$^*_\gamma$
	Comparison of Information Loss					
MD	100	100.3	100.2	96.6	93.9	91.8
MDAV		100	99.9	96.2	92.6	89.8
MDAV$^+$			100	96.3	92.7	89.9
V-MDAV				100	96.2	93.1
MDAV*					100	96.7
MDAV$^*_\gamma$						100

With respect to average information loss the results show a clear ordering. MDAV and MDAV$^+$ behave almost identical with highest losses. The variable size relaxation of

V-MDAV yields a significant improvement. The information loss is further reduced by the more detailed local investigations of MDAV*. Adding a gain factor on top gives the new algorithm MDAV$_\gamma^*$ that outperforms all previous heuristics.

We have also measured average cluster sizes for the three variable-size algorithms (Table 5). It shows that MDAV$_\gamma^*$ takes maximum profit of this option.

Table 5. Average cluster sizes of variable-size MD heuristics on EIA [24].

k	2	3	4	5	7	10
V-MDAV	2.17	3.61	4.00	5.54	7.01	11.46
MDAV*	2.24	3.38	4.24	5.62	7.56	10.88
MDAV$_\gamma^*$	2.19	3.37	4.60	6.14	9.39	12.00

Because no simple and reliable way to determine a good value of the gain γ for V-MDAV or MDAV$_\gamma^*$ is known, we have tested values from 0 to 2 in steps of 0.1. Information loss and time consumption is reported above only for the best value found. The results of this optimization are given in Table 6.

Table 6. Gain factors γ used for V-MDAV and MDAV$_\gamma^*$ on EIA to achieve minimal information losses [24].

k	2	3	4	5	7	10
V-MDAV	0.2	0.6	0.0	0.4	0.0	1.3
MDAV$_\gamma^*$	0.8	0.7	0.8	1.2	1.1	1.2

Despite the fact that V-MDAV levitates variable-size mechanisms, has higher time complexity and is evaluated for the best out of 21 gain factors γ, it delivers only a slight reduction in information loss compared to MDAV$^+$ on average. This slight reduction is indeed remarkable low as we allow $\gamma = 0$ for our test, so V-MDAV can by design never be worse than MDAV$^+$. In 11 out of the 54 tests (combinations of different databases and anonymity parameters k) V-MDAV is not able to use cluster extension at all, to reduce information loss. Hence, in these cases $\gamma = 0$ is chosen. As our experiments show, MDAV* is able to outperform MDAV even without the use of gain factors adjusted to a particular database. On average it achieves about 7% and 4% lower information loss compared to MDAV$^+$ and V-MDAV respectively. Adding an adjustable gain factor and improved cluster extension mechanisms further improves MDAV* significantly. By allowing $\gamma = 0$ as well as $\gamma = 1$ it is further guaranteed that the algorithm can never introduce information losses above those of MDAV$^+$ or MDAV*. In none of the tests performed, a gain factor of $\gamma = 0$ resulted in best information loss for MDAV$_\gamma^*$. Furthermore, optimal gain factors for MDAV$_\gamma^*$ are quite consistent, ranging from 0.6 to 1.1 over all test cases compared to a range of 0 to 1 for V-MDAV. This shows that the cluster extension mechanism of MDAV* and MDAV$_\gamma^*$ is superior and easier to tune than that of V-MDAV.

The high time consumption of MD in these experiments can be expected from the worst case analysis. Between MDAV and MDAV$^+$, which have the same asymptotic time complexity, MDAV$^+$ seems to profit more from larger values of d as e.g. found in Credit

Card. There it needs less than half the time of MDAV. The variable-size mechanics of V-MDAV and MDAV* come at the cost of higher runtimes. However, the performance of V-MDAV in practice does not seem to match its theoretical worst case time complexity of $O(d\, n^2\, k)$. Instead of a linear increase in time consumption with increased k, the algorithm becomes slightly faster for greater values of k. This behavior can be explained by looking at the average cluster size and γ used (Table 6) to achieve optimal results in our experiments. It can be observed, that only very few cluster extensions are made, given they are profitable at all. As extending clusters is, per element, much more time consuming than creating new clusters, the average case complexity of V-MDAV is significantly lower.

A similar, although weaker form of this behavior can be observed for MDAV* and MDAV^*_γ that are slower than MDAV^+ by at most a factor k. Unlike implied by the asymptotic worst case time complexity of $O(d\, n^2)$ the heuristics are getting faster with larger values of k. Both can be explained by the unusual high amount of cluster extension assumed for computing the worst case complexity. However, as the average cluster sizes and gain factors used are higher than those of V-MDAV these algorithms are typically a little bit slower than V-MDAV.

Comparing not only information loss or performance isolated from each other but general overall behavior instead, there is no clear *best* algorithm. When time is critical, MDAV^+ should be considered, as it is the fastest of these algorithms while delivering results comparable to MD and MDAV which are much slower. When an increase of the runtime by the factor 2 is acceptable, but there is no time to evaluate good gain factors, MDAV* is a good choice. However, if time consumption is secondary, the preferred choice should be MDAV^*_γ as it is guaranteed to produce lower or equal information losses than MDAV^+ and MDAV*. Moreover, as our experiments show, is not likely to perform worse than MD, MDAV or V-MDAV on any real world databases. Applying the original MD or MDAV heuristics should be avoided as there seems to be no situation in which their increased time and space requirements result in any meaningful advantage over newer maximum distance heuristics.

4 ONA

The ONA algorithm [21] uses a different approach for k-anonymous microaggregation. Its strategy has already been explained in the introduction: start with a random k-member clustering and then improve it iteratively by reassigning elements to closer clusters. While for large values of k the algorithm delivers slightly lower information loss than MDAV variants on benchmark databases, there are some open issues. It is unclear when to stop the iteration – the convergence criteria. An obvious condition is that nothing has changed within a round, but it is not clear how many rounds this may require, even more whether this situation will always be reached. In the implementation to generate the benchmark results presented below we have stopped the iteration when this condition has not been fulfilled within 30 rounds. This has happened very rarely in our tests.

Another problem is caused by the probabilistic initialization with a randomly generated k-member clustering. As for the Lloyd algorithm, a bad initialization inevitably leads to a bad output. Hence, the results may differ quite a lot and indeed, they range

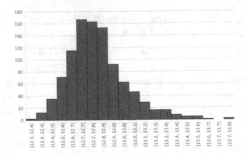

Fig. 1. Histogram of the information losses of 1000 ONA runs on the Census database for $k = 10$ [24].

Table 7. Statistics of the information loss (IL) in percentages for 1000 ONA executions on the Census benchmark database for different k. The information loss of MDAV* is included for reference [27].

	ONA on Census					MDAV* on Census
	lowest IL	highest IL	median	mean	variance	IL
$k = 2$	3.43	3.90	3.63	3.63	0.01	3.17
$k = 3$	5.42	6.24	5.70	5.71	0.01	5.78
$k = 4$	6.94	7.74	7.25	7.25	0.02	7.44
$k = 5$	8.12	9.10	8.47	8.48	0.02	8.81
$k = 7$	10.04	11.11	10.43	10.44	0.03	11.37
$k = 10$	12.36	13.66	12.77	12.80	0.04	14.01

from better to worse than those of MDAV algorithms. In Fig. 1 and Table 7 this behavior is shown on the benchmark database *Census*.

While the authors do not provide any guidelines on how to tackle this problem, the standard approach would be to repeat the algorithm several times, let this number be μ, and output the clustering with the best solution found. As can be seen in Table 8, there is some improvement to be gained by increasing μ. But when a good confidence is aimed at, this increases the runtime significantly.

Table 8. Statistics of the information loss on different numbers of ONA executions on the Census benchmark database for $k = 10$ and runtimes in sec (rounded); in comparison the deterministic MDAV* run only once [27].

	ONA on Census for $k = 10$						MDAV* on Census	
	lowest IL	highest IL	median	mean	variance	runtime	IL	runtime
10 runs	12.54	13.00	12.74	12.76	0.02	1	14.01	0
100 runs	12.41	13.39	12.79	12.80	0.04	9		
1000 runs	12.36	13.66	12.77	12.80	0.04	100		

We have analyzed the methodology of generating and rearranging clusters in detail and propose a new algorithm, subsequently called ONA* that uses better selection strategies. In Table 9 ONA and ONA* are compared with a previous state-of-the-art heuristic based on the MDAV principle.

Replacing the random initial clustering by a good deterministic process increases the performance significantly. Our experiments have shown that using an optimized variant of MDAV like MDAV* gives better results typically with lower information loss compared to the original ONA algorithm with $\mu = 100$ repetitions.

MDAV* does not guarantee a limit on the maximum cluster size, however a split is guaranteed if $2k$ or more elements are given. As a result, inputs of $3k - 1$ or less elements cannot result in a cluster of size $2k$ or more. To guarantee a maximum cluster size throughout the ONA* algorithm, after initialization with MDAV* we apply the variant MDAV$^+$ (see [25]) to all clusters of size $2k$ or more. MDAV$^+$ delivers slightly worse information loss in general, but guarantees a maximum cluster size of $2k - 1$ within the same time frame. In practice, the influence of MDAV$^+$ on ONA* is very limited, as situations in which MDAV* returns large clusters are very rare.

Concerning reassignment, ONA* makes a more precise estimation (line 22). Whereas ONA bases its decision, whether and where to move an element x, on the distances to centroids, ONA* compares the actual costs before and after a change.

A final modification simplifies matters substantially. Every cluster in step 21 of ONA has between $2k$ and $3k - 1$ elements and should be divided into 2 parts. For this task ONA is not likely to find better solutions than MDAV algorithms, but requires more time and works probabilistically. Hence, we have replaced the recursive execution of ONA by a call to MDAV* which first creates 2 clusters with exactly k elements on opposite sides of the global centroid and afterwards assigns remaining elements to their closest cluster which is likely to yield an optimal solution in this special case. A complete description of ONA* is given as Algorithm 2.

We have further tried to improve ONA* by replacing the first phase based on MDAV* by the superior heuristic MDAV$^*_\gamma$. This new version ONA$^*_\gamma$ requires additional work to determine the optimal gain factor γ for each database. It turned out that this overhead hardly pays, the information loss gets only marginally better.

To evaluate the improvements by replacing ONA with ONA*, we have performed several tests on established benchmark sets (see Table 9 and Table 10). The best out of 100 ONA runs is able to outperform MDAV* in most of the tests. With bigger k, the difference between MDAV* and ONA becomes larger. Compared to MDAV*, ONA* is able to lower the information loss in all test cases with improvements ranging from 2% for Cloud1 and $k = 2$ to 31% for EIA and $k = 10$. The average improvement from MDAV* to ONA* is 11% over all experiments. While the average improvement from ONA to ONA* is just 3% over all experiments, its deterministic behaviour takes much lower runtime.

To determine the time complexity of ONA* consider its basic building blocks and let ζ be the number of repetitions until convergence. There are at most n/k clusters C_i of size k which might be dissolved in phase 1. For each element s of such a cluster its closest centroid $j(s)$ can be found in time $O(d\,n/k)$. For each cluster C_i evaluating the cost function for it and the at most k neighbours $C_{j(s)}$ takes time $O(d\,k^2)$.

Splitting a cluster C_ℓ by MDAV* requires $O(d\,|C_\ell|^2)$ time. Each cluster C_i can give rise to at most k splits of a cluster C_ℓ of size less than $3k$, which adds up to $O(d\,k^3)$ computational effort. Thus the total time of phase 1 can be bounded by $n/k \cdot (k \cdot O(d\,n/k) + O(d\,k^2 + d\,k^3)) = O(d\,(n^2/k + n\,k^2))$.

Algorithm 2. ONA*.

> **input** : database X and min cluster size k
> **output:** k-member clustering C

1 Let $C = \{C_1, \ldots, C_m\} \leftarrow \text{MDAV}^*(X, k)$
    // Split large clusters
2 **foreach** $C \in C$ **do**
3   **if** $|C| \geq 2k$ **then**
4        $C \leftarrow C \setminus \{C\}; \; C \leftarrow C \cup \text{MDAV}^+(C, k)$

5 **repeat**
    // Phase 1: dissolving clusters
6   **foreach** $C_i \in C$ *with* $|C_i| = k$ **do**
7   For $s \in C_i$ let $C_{j(s)}$ be the cluster with the closest centroid to s in $C \setminus \{C_i\}$
8   Let $L \leftarrow \{j(s) : s \in C_i\}$
9   Let $C'_\ell \leftarrow C_\ell \cup \{s \in C_i : j(s) = \ell\}$, for each $\ell \in L$
10   Let $Cost_1 \leftarrow Cost(C_i) + \sum_{\ell \in L} Cost(C_\ell)$
11   Let $Cost_2 \leftarrow \sum_{\ell \in L} Cost(C'_\ell)$
12   **if** $Cost_1 > Cost_2$ **then**
13        $C \leftarrow \{C'_\ell : \ell \in L\} \cup \{C_\ell : \ell \notin (L \cup \{i\})\}$
         // Split large clusters
14   **foreach** $\ell \in L$ **do**
15   **if** $|C_\ell| \geq 2k$ **then**
16            $C \leftarrow C \setminus \{C_\ell\}$
17            $C \leftarrow C \cup \text{MDAV}^*(C_\ell, k)$

    // Phase 2: reassigning elements
18   **foreach** $C_i \in C$ *with* $|C_i| > k$ **do**
19   **repeat**
20   **foreach** $s \in C_i$ **do**
21   Let $C_{j(s)}$ be the cluster with the closest centroid to s among those in $C \setminus C_i$
22   Let $improvement(s) \leftarrow$
             $(Cost(C_i) - Cost(C_i \setminus \{s\})) - (Cost(C_{j(s)} \cup \{s\}) - Cost(C_{j(s)}))$
23   Let $s' \leftarrow \arg\max_{s \in C_i} improvement(s)$
24   **if** $improvement(s') \leq 0$ **then**
25   **break**
26   **else**
27            $C_i \leftarrow C_i \setminus \{s'\}$
28            $C_{j(s')} \leftarrow C_{j(s')} \cup \{s'\}$
             // Split large clusters
29   **if** $|C_{j(s')}| \geq 2k$ **then**
30              $C \leftarrow C \setminus \{C_{j(s')}\}$
31              $C \leftarrow C \cup \text{MDAV}^*(C_{j(s')}, k)$

32   **until** $|C_i| = k$
33 **until** *convergence_condition*

Table 9. Comparison of quadratic time microaggregation algorithms on the benchmark databases for different values of k. For ONA the best result out of 100 runs is stated, ONA*, MDAV and MDAV* are run only once as they are deterministic [27].

	Information Loss in % on Census					
	$k=2$	$k=3$	$k=4$	$k=5$	$k=7$	$k=10$
MDAV	3.18	5.69	7.49	9.09	11.60	14.16
MDAV*	3.17	5.78	7.44	8.81	11.37	14.01
ONA	3.44	5.47	6.92	8.16	10.08	12.45
ONA*	3.06	5.26	6.81	7.99	10.07	12.46

	Information Loss in % on Tarragona					
	$k=2$	$k=3$	$k=4$	$k=5$	$k=7$	$k=10$
MDAV	9.33	16.93	19.55	22.46	27.52	33.19
MDAV*	9.44	16.14	19.19	22.25	28.40	34.75
ONA	9.19	15.01	17.66	20.88	26.50	30.95
ONA*	9.06	15.11	17.79	20.69	26.34	31.15

	Information Loss in % on EIA					
	$k=2$	$k=3$	$k=4$	$k=5$	$k=7$	$k=10$
MDAV	0.31	0.48	0.67	1.67	2.17	3.84
MDAV*	0.22	0.45	0.62	0.91	2.03	2.63
ONA	0.21	0.40	0.59	0.81	1.60	2.01
ONA*	0.20	0.37	0.52	0.79	1.63	1.99

	Information Loss in % on Cloud1					
	$k=2$	$k=3$	$k=4$	$k=5$	$k=7$	$k=10$
MDAV	1.21	2.22	3.74	4.31	5.70	7.05
MDAV*	1.16	2.11	3.65	4.09	5.54	6.70
ONA	1.21	2.16	3.18	3.82	4.97	6.35
ONA*	1.15	2.02	3.25	3.92	5.07	6.28

	Information Loss in % on Cloud2					
	$k=2$	$k=3$	$k=4$	$k=5$	$k=7$	$k=10$
MDAV	0.68	1.21	1.70	2.03	2.69	3.40
MDAV*	0.64	1.10	1.52	1.87	2.51	3.28
ONA	0.67	1.08	1.46	1.73	2.28	2.96
ONA*	0.60	1.04	1.40	1.70	2.22	2.92

For phase 2 one has to consider less than n/k clusters of size between $k+1$ and $2k-1$. The loop starting in line 19 is executed less than k times. In each execution, again for each element s of a cluster to compute its closest centroid and its improvement takes time $O(d\,n/k)$ and $O(d\,k)$ respectively. Now there can be at most one split adding time $O(d\,k^2)$. Hence, per cluster $O(d\,n\,k) + O(d\,k^3)$ time is needed. All together this gives an upper bound

$$n/k \cdot (O(d\,n\,k) + O(d\,k^3)) = O(d\,(n^2 + n\,k^2))$$

for phase 2. If the time $O(d\,n^2)$ for the initialization by MDAV* is added we finally get

Table 10. Comparison of quadratic time microaggregation algorithms on the EIA benchmark database for different values of k. For ONA the total runtime for 100 runs is stated, ONA* and MDAV* are run only once as they are deterministic [27].

	Runtime on EIA in sec (rounded)					
	$k=2$	$k=3$	$k=4$	$k=5$	$k=7$	$k=10$
MDAV*	2	1	1	0	0	0
ONA	162	255	138	327	41	36
ONA*	2	1	1	1	0	0

Lemma 1. *If* ONA* *needs* ζ *iterations till convergence its runtime is bounded by* $O(d\,(n^2 + \zeta\,(n^2 + n\,k^2)))$.

To establish a time bound for ONA, which is missing in [21], seems to be more difficult. The time used for random initialization can be considered linear in n, a reassignment check takes time $O(d\,n/k$ and a dissolve check $O(d\,(n+k^2))$. Iterating over n elements this already adds up to $O(d\,(n^2 + nk^2))$. This has to be multiplied by the number ζ of executions of the main loop till convergence and furthermore by the number μ of probabilistic repetitions The correct time bound may even be larger because in this calculation the recursive splitting has been ignored, for which an analysis does not seem to be obvious.

5   Microaggregation in Almost Linear Time

In 2006 LeFevre et al. introduced MONDRIAN, an anonymization algorithm which achieves k-anonymity in $O(n\log n)$ time [10]. The optimization goal of MONDRIAN is to create clusters with cluster sizes as close to k as possible.

MONDRIAN is not defined as a microaggregation algorithm, but it creates a k-member clustering in the process of anonymization. Hence, this strategy can be used to perform k-anonymous microaggregation by calculating and reporting centroids for each cluster created. However, the question arises, whether the resulting information loss is comparable to state-of-the-art heuristics designed to minimize information loss. We have developed extensions of MONDRIAN and compared the resulting runtimes and information losses to those of the original MONDRIAN algorithm as well as to MDAV* and ONA*.

The lower time complexity of MONDRIAN s caused by the fact that no distances between elements are computed. Instead, MONDRIAN resembles the process of subdividing a d-dimensional space by d-dimensional trees. A database is interpreted as a d-dimensional space with the elements being points in that space. In the first step, MONDRIAN splits the database into two clusters by projecting it onto one of its d dimensions and dividing elements at the median. Subsequently clusters are divided further, potentially using different *splitting dimensions* for different (sub)clusters. A cluster is no longer split and considered final, if a split at the median would result in at least one new cluster having less than k elements. Thus, in the final clustering the size of each cluster is between k and $2k - 1$.

Algorithm 3. MONDRIAN [10].

---

   input : database X and min cluster size k
   output: k-member clustering C

1 **if** $|X| < 2k$ **then**
2 | **return** X

3 Let $dim \leftarrow \arg\max_{j \in \{1,\dots,d\}} \left(\max_{x_i \in X} x_i^j - \min_{x_i \in X} x_i^j \right)$
4 Let $median \leftarrow median(\{x_i^{dim} \mid x_i \in X\})$
5 Let $lhs \leftarrow \emptyset$; Let $rhs \leftarrow \emptyset$
6 **foreach** $x_i \in X$ **do**
7 | **if** $x_i^{dim} \leq median$ **then**
8 | | $lhs \leftarrow lhs \cup \{x_i\}$
9 | **else**
10 | | $rhs \leftarrow rhs \cup \{x_i\}$

11 **return** MONDRIAN(lhs, k) $\cup$ MONDRIAN(rhs, k)

Choosing a good splitting dimension for each cluster is a crucial part of the algorithm. Especially for higher-dimensional data, choosing a less optimal splitting dimension might result in big and sparsely populated clusters, resulting in high information loss. MONDRIAN chooses the splitting dimension for any cluster as the attribute dimension with widest range of values in that cluster, a strategy aimed at reducing the area of clusters as far as possible. A pseudo code of MONDRIAN is given as Algorithm 3.

As can be seen in Table 12, MONDRIAN is not able to deliver information loss as low as ONA or MDAV variants. However, its computation takes far less time. Its strategy can be interpreted as acting in rounds of cutting every existing cluster of size at least $2k$ into two smaller clusters. There are $O(\log n)$ cutting rounds where every element is assigned to a new, smaller cluster. Computation of the splitting dimension is linear in d and n and computation of the median is linear in n. Hence, the total time complexity of MONDRIAN is $O(d\, n \log n)$.

Choosing splitting dimensions according to the *widest range* rule might be problematic as information loss is defined by cluster density rather than cluster area. We have investigated several alternative splitting criteria with the same asymptotic time complexity and come to the conclusion that a significant improvement could be achieved by choosing the splitting dimension as the dimension with the largest variance of values. Our resulting algorithm called MONDRIAN_V achieves 20% lower information loss on average over MONDRIAN in the test cases provided in Table 12. The splitting rule of MONDRIAN_V has the same time complexity of $O(nd)$ and can be formalized as

$$dim = \arg\max_{j \in \{1,\ldots,d\}} \left(\sum_{x_i \in X} \left(x_i^j - c(X)^j \right)^2 \right).$$

The improvement going from MONDRIAN to MONDRIAN_V shows that even for low-dimensional data, the choice of the right way to cut is quite important. A natural next step is to increase the number of options for splits. Up to this point we have considered cuts according to attribute values in a single dimension only. The largest possible set of cuts would be the set of all hyperplanes dividing the database into two parts with a varying amount of elements on each side. However, deciding which splitting hyperplane to choose is a time consuming process, eliminating the performance gains made by MONDRIAN_V over ONA*.

Algorithm 4. MONDRIAN_V2D.

---

    input : database X and min cluster size k
    output: k-member clustering C

1   **if** $|X| < 2k$ **then**
2       $\lfloor$ **return** X
3   Let $(dim1, dim2, o) \leftarrow \arg\max_{j_1, j_2 \in \{1,\ldots,d\}, o \in \{-1,1\}}$
       $\left(\sum_{x_i \in X} \left(\frac{1}{\sqrt{2}} \cdot \left(x_i^{j_1} + o \cdot x_i^{j_2} \right) \right) \right)$
4   Let $median \leftarrow median(\{ x_i^{dim1} + o \cdot x_i^{dim2} \mid x_i \in X \})$
5   Let $lhs \leftarrow \emptyset$; Let $rhs \leftarrow \emptyset$
6   **foreach** $x_i \in X$ **do**
7   **if** $x_i^{dim} \leq median$ **then**
8          $\lfloor$ $lhs \leftarrow lhs \cup \{x_i\}$
9   **else**
10         $\lfloor$ $rhs \leftarrow rhs \cup \{x_i\}$

11 **return** MONDRIAN_V2D(lhs, k) $\cup$ MONDRIAN_V2D(rhs, k)

In MONDRIAN_V splits can be interpreted as hyperplanes perpendicular to one of the unit vectors $e_1, \ldots, e_d$ of the data space $\mathbb{R}^d$ dividing the elements into two clusters. The second algorithm called MONDRIAN_V2D considers additional splits. We now also allow hyperplanes that are perpendicular to a combination $e_{j_1 j_2}$ of a pair of unit vectors $e_{j_1 j_2}^+ = \frac{1}{\sqrt{2}} \cdot (e_{j_1} + e_{j_2})$ and $e_{j_1 j_2}^- = \frac{1}{\sqrt{2}} \cdot (e_{j_1} - e_{j_2})$. In other words, we expand the set of possible splits by hyperplanes which are 45° and 315° between any two unit vectors. As before, splits are made at the median of the dimension (or combination of dimensions) with largest variance. Note that, by the prefactor $\frac{1}{\sqrt{2}}$ we ensure measuring variances in an orthonormal basis resulting in values comparable to those measured along original dimensions.

The number of possible splits for a cluster increases from d to $2 \cdot \binom{d}{2} + d = d^2$ since there are $\binom{d}{2}$ pairs of dimensions to choose from and two orientations for each pair together with the d options to cut along a single dimension as before. The time complexity of MONDRIAN_V2D increases to $O(d^2 \, n \log n)$, but information loss further decreases by 6% on average on the Adult data set (low-dimensional data) and by 25% on average on the Credit Card data set (higher-dimensional data). A pseudo code for MONDRIAN_V2D is given as Algorithm 4.

Of course, one could extend this further and take combinations of 3 or more unit vectors increasing the time bound by additional factors of d. However, the largest gain seems to be the step from 1 to 2 dimensions.

6   Combining ONA* and MONDRIAN_v

As can be seen in Table 12, no MONDRIAN variant can compete with MDAV* or ONA* with respect to information loss. How can one still get the best of both worlds? We propose to combine both methods, the fast one at the beginning to split large clusters and the one of better quality for a fine grained clustering of small clusters, and name this MONA. The combination is flexible governed by a parameter ρ that can be chosen between 0 and 1. It defines the switch from MONDRIAN_V to ONA*: clusters of size larger than n^ρ are iteratively split by MONDRIAN_V, smaller ones are then handled by ONA*. Thus, we get a family of algorithms MONA$_\rho$, where MONA$_0$ equals MONDRIAN_V and MONA$_1$ is identical to ONA*. The code of MONA$_\rho$ is described in Algorithm 5. Analogously the algorithm MONA_2D$_\rho$ combines MONDRIAN_V2D and ONA*.

Algorithm 5. MONA$_\rho$ (MONDRIAN_V combined with ONA*, split limit n^ρ).

---

    input : database X, min cluster size k and split limit n^ρ
    output: k-member clustering C

1 **if** $|X| < n^\rho$ **then**
2      $\lfloor$ **return** ONA*(X,k)

3 Let $dim \leftarrow \arg\max_{j \in \{1,\dots,d\}} \left(\sum_{x_i \in X} \left(x_i^j - c(X)^j \right)^2 \right)$
4 Let $median \leftarrow median(\{x_i^{dim} \mid x_i \in X\})$
5 Let $lhs \leftarrow \emptyset$; Let $rhs \leftarrow \emptyset$
6 **foreach** $x_i \in X$ **do**
7   **if** $x_i^{dim} \leq median$ **then**
8         $\lfloor$ $lhs \leftarrow lhs \cup \{x_i\}$

9   **else**
10       $\lfloor$ $rhs \leftarrow rhs \cup \{x_i\}$

11 **return** MONA$(lhs, k, n^\rho) \cup$ MONA(rhs, k, n^ρ)

Since ONA* has quadratic time complexity, but is only applied to a bunch of smaller datasets, the total runtime in the ONA*-phase is reduced. Furthermore, most computation of MDAV or ONA variants is due to distance calculations between far apart elements. But this has little influence on the local arrangements of elements. Thus, saving these estimations in the MONDRIAN_V-phase does not increase the information loss much. Still, there might occur a decrease of data quality in the MONDRIAN_V-phase if ONA* would have clustered elements together that lie on both sides of the median of a splitting dimension used by MONDRIAN_V and now are assigned to different subproblems. However, for larger datasets such cases can be expected to have only a small influence.

In the ONA*-phase $MONA_\rho$ has to manage $O(n/n^\rho) = O(n^{1-\rho})$ instances with input size n^ρ at most. The runtime of the MONDRIAN_V-phase is obviously not larger than a complete run of this algorithm. Hence, the total time complexity of $MONA_\rho$ can be bounded by

$$O(d\,n\log n) + O\left(n^{1-\rho}\right) \cdot O(d\,(n^{2\rho} + \zeta(n^{2\rho} + n^\rho k^2)))$$
$$= O(d\,n\log n) + O(d\,(n^{1+\rho} + \zeta(n^{1+\rho} + nk^2)))\,.$$

For MONA_2D$_\rho$ the first term gets an additional factor d. For $\rho > 0$ the first term is majorized by the second. If k is small compared to n, which for larger databases typically holds, and ζ is considered as a constant we get

Lemma 2. *For* $0 < \rho \leq 1$ *the runtime of* MONA$_\rho$ *and* MONA_2D$_\rho$ *is bounded by* $O(d\,n^{1+\rho})$.

The information loss of both algorithms for different ρ are shown in Fig. 2. Additionally, runtimes for MONA and MONA_2D on Credit Card are listed in Table 11.

To give an overview of the performance of the MONA variants, in Table 12 MONA$_{0.5}$ and MONA_2D$_{0.5}$ are compared to MONDRIAN_V and ONA* on Adult and Credit Card. It can be observed that both deliver better results than pure MONDRIAN_V approaches. On the low-dimensional database Adult, MONA$_{0.5}$ is in reach of quadratic time algorithms like ONA* whereas MONA_2D$_{0.5}$ is not able to improve much compared to MONA$_{0.5}$. On the higher dimensional database Credit Card, MONA_2D$_{0.5}$ achieves a notable improvement to MONA$_{0.5}$. However, both have higher information loss than the quadratic time algorithms. But compared to MONDRIAN_V the improvement is significant.

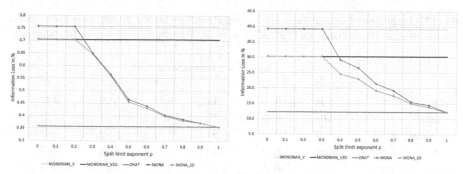

(a) Adult database: $n = 48842, d = 3, k = 10$.

(b) Credit Card database: $n = 30000$, $d = 24$, $k = 10$.

Fig. 2. Information Losses of MONA and MONA_2D for different split limits compared to MONDRIAN_V variants and ONA* on two different databases. As $n^\rho < 2k$ for small values of ρ, both MONA and MONA_2D behave like their MONDRIAN_V counterparts [27].

Table 11. Runtimes of $MONA_\rho$ and $MONA\_2D_\rho$ for different ρ and k on Credit Card. Compare with information losses stated in Fig. 2b [27].

	Runtime on Credit Card in sec (rounded)					
	$k=2$	$k=3$	$k=4$	$k=5$	$k=7$	$k=10$
$MONA_{0.3}$	0	0	0	0	0	0
$MONA_{0.4}$	0	0	0	0	0	0
$MONA_{0.5}$	1	0	0	0	0	0
$MONA_{0.6}$	4	2	2	2	1	1
$MONA_{0.7}$	8	5	4	4	3	3
$MONA_{0.8}$	33	24	19	16	13	11
$MONA_{0.9}$	67	48	39	37	30	25
$MONA_1$	306	226	174	146	123	101
$MONA\_2D_{0.3}$	2	1	1	1	1	1
$MONA\_2D_{0.4}$	2	1	1	1	1	1
$MONA\_2D_{0.5}$	2	2	2	1	1	2
$MONA\_2D_{0.6}$	5	3	3	2	2	2
$MONA\_2D_{0.7}$	8	6	5	4	4	4
$MONA\_2D_{0.8}$	34	24	20	18	14	12
$MONA\_2D_{0.9}$	70	49	42	37	31	25
$MONA\_2D_1$	309	216	176	146	124	98

Table 12. Comparison of several microaggregation algorithms on benchmarks Adult ($n = 48842$ elements) using $d = 3$ attributes and Credit Card ($n = 30000$ elements) with $d = 24$ attributes [27].

	Information Loss in % on Adult					
	$k = 2$	$k = 3$	$k = 4$	$k = 5$	$k = 7$	$k = 10$
MDAV*	0.04	0.09	0.14	0.18	0.28	0.42
ONA*	0.04	0.08	0.12	0.16	0.24	0.36
MONDRIAN	0.25	0.51	0.51	0.51	0.92	0.92
MONDRIAN_V	0.21	0.41	0.41	0.41	0.76	0.76
MONDRIAN_V2D	0.19	0.38	0.38	0.38	0.71	0.71
MONA$_{0.5}$	0.05	0.11	0.16	0.21	0.32	0.46
MONA_2D$_{0.5}$	0.05	0.10	0.16	0.21	0.30	0.46

	Information Loss in % on Credit Card					
	$k = 2$	$k = 3$	$k = 4$	$k = 5$	$k = 7$	$k = 10$
MDAV*	3.65	6.44	8.48	10.21	12.36	14.68
ONA*	3.50	5.86	7.53	8.64	10.23	12.24
MONDRIAN	30.33	30.33	41.47	41.47	43.75	50.71
MONDRIAN_V	24.05	24.05	32.54	32.54	34.12	39.27
MONDRIAN_V2D	15.81	15.81	21.93	21.93	23.23	27.34
MONA$_{0.5}$	7.74	12.56	15.99	18.53	22.45	26.59
MONA_2D$_{0.5}$	6.87	10.96	13.89	16.16	19.50	22.95

	Runtime on Adult in sec (rounded)					
	$k = 2$	$k = 3$	$k = 4$	$k = 5$	$k = 7$	$k = 10$
MDAV*	211	141	89	77	50	40
ONA*	538	358	267	218	163	116
MONDRIAN	0	0	0	0	0	0
MONDRIAN_V	0	0	0	0	0	0
MONDRIAN_V2D	0	0	0	0	0	0
MONA$_{0.5}$	1	0	0	0	0	0
MONA_2D$_{0.5}$	1	0	0	0	0	0

	Runtime on Credit Card in sec (rounded)					
	$k = 2$	$k = 3$	$k = 4$	$k = 5$	$k = 7$	$k = 10$
MDAV*	223	158	120	95	78	61
ONA*	292	209	174	145	123	106
MONDRIAN	0	0	0	0	0	0
MONDRIAN_V	0	0	0	0	0	0
MONDRIAN_V2D	1	1	1	1	1	1
MONA$_{0.5}$	1	0	0	0	0	0
MONA_2D$_{0.5}$	2	2	2	1	1	2

7   Conclusion

Databases with personal data of specific groups of individuals are needed for new research insights. Before making such data public, the individual values of confidential attributes have to be modified if privacy is a concern. But these disturbances of the real data should be as small as possible such that the modified database is still useful. Some people have claimed that microaggregation combined with the concept of k-anonymity is outdated for this purpose, that there are much better techniques like generating synthetic data from the original database by machine learning. A recent extensive experimental evaluation indicates that this is not the case [22]. Thus, it still makes sense to analyse and improve microaggregation techniques.

In this paper, the maximum distance heuristic is further optimized resulting in a new algorithm MDAV$_\gamma^*$ that generates significantly lower information loss as Table 4 shows.

Next, the ONA-approach is improved and transformed into a deterministic variant that works considerably faster with an information loss at least as good.

Further, the clustering algorithm MONDRIAN is adapted to perform better in microaggregation applications. Two variants, MONDRIAN_V and MONDRIAN_V2D, are presented, both delivering superior information loss compared to MONDRIAN. For lower-dimensional data the MONDRIAN technique can achieve almost the same data quality as significantly slower algorithms known.

Combining both advantages, the performance of MONDRIAN_V and the data quality of ONA*, we design new classes of algorithms MONA$_\rho$ and MONA_2D$_\rho$ that achieve high quality data anonymization even for huge databases where quadratic time would be far too expensive. These results are summarized in Table 12.

What could be the next steps in further improving microaggregation techniques? An obvious question is whether there are even better splitting rules for MONDRIAN? On the other hand, is it possible to decrease the information loss further by spending more than quadratic time? By design, any improvement here could be applied to the MONA$_\rho$ approach to get fast solutions with better quality.

Finally, how well k-anonymous microaggregation can be approximated is still wide open. There is hope to achieve approximation guarantees for ONA* by carefully designing an initial clustering similar to the k-means++ algorithm [2]. We plan to investigate this issue in more detail.

References

1. Anwar, N.: Micro-aggregation-the small aggregates method. Technical report, Internal report. Luxembourg: Eurostat (1993)
2. Arthur, D., Vassilvitskii, S.: k-means++: the advantages of careful seeding. In Proceedings of the eighteenth annual ACM-SIAM Symposium on Discrete Algorithms, pp. 1027–1035. Society for Industrial and Applied Mathematics (2007)
3. Defays, D., Anwar, M.N.: Masking microdata using micro-aggregation. J. Offic. Stat. **14**(4), 449 (1998)

4. Defays, D., Nanopoulos, Ph.: Panels of enterprises and confidentiality: the small aggregates method. In: Proceedings of the 1992 Symposium on Design and Analysis of Longitudinal Surveys, pp. 195–204 (1993)

5. Domingo-Ferrer, J., Martínez-Ballesté, A., Mateo-Sanz, J.M., Sebé, F.: Efficient multivariate data-oriented microaggregation. VLDB J. Int. J. Very Large Data Bases 15(4), 355–369 (2006)

6. Domingo-Ferrer, J., Mateo-Sanz, J.M.: Reference data sets to test and compare sdc methods for protection of numerical microdata (2002). https://web.archive.org/web/20190412063606/http://neon.vb.cbs.nl/casc/CASCtestsets.htm

7. Josep Domingo-Ferrer and Josep Maria Mateo-Sanz: Practical data-oriented microaggregation for statistical disclosure control. IEEE Trans. Knowl. Data Eng. 14(1), 189–201 (2002)

8. Domingo-Ferrer, J., Torra, V.: Ordinal, continuous and heterogeneous k-anonymity through microaggregation. Data Min. Knowl. Disc. 11(2), 195–212 (2005)

9. Dwork, C., McSherry, F., Nissim, K., Smith, A.: Calibrating noise to sensitivity in private data analysis. In: Halevi, S., Rabin, T. (eds.) TCC 2006. LNCS, vol. 3876, pp. 265–284. Springer, Heidelberg (2006). https://doi.org/10.1007/11681878_14

10. LeFevre, K., DeWitt, D.J., Ramakrishnan, R.: Mondrian multidimensional k-anonymity. In: 22nd International Conference on Data Engineering (ICDE'06), pp. 25–25. IEEE (2006)

11. Li, N., Li, T., Venkatasubramanian, S.: t-closeness: Privacy beyond k-anonymity and l-diversity. In: 2007 IEEE 23rd International Conference on Data Engineering, pp. 106–115. IEEE (2007)

12. Li, N., Qardaji, W., Su, D.: On sampling, anonymization, and differential privacy or, k-anonymization meets differential privacy. In: Proceedings of the 7th ACM Symposium on Information, Computer and Communications Security, pp. 32–33. ACM (2012)

13. Lichman, M.: UCI machine learning repository (2013). http://archive.ics.uci.edu/ml

14. Lloyd, S.P.: Least squares quantization in PCM. IEEE Trans. Inf. Theory 28(2), 129–137 (1982)

15. Machanavajjhala, A., Kifer, D., Gehrke, J., Venkitasubramaniam, M.: l-diversity: Privacy beyond k-anonymity. ACM Trans. Knowl. Discovery Data (TKDD) 1(1), 3 (2007)

16. Sanz, J.M.M., Ferrer, J.D.: A comparative study of microaggregation methods. Qüestiió 22(3) (1998)

17. Oganian, A., Domingo-Ferrer, J.: On the complexity of optimal microaggregation for statistical disclosure control. Stat. J. U. N. Econ. Comm. Eur. 18(4), 345–353 (2001)

18. Rebollo-Monedero, D., Forné, J., Pallarès, E., Parra-Arnau, J.: A modification of the lloyd algorithm for k-anonymous quantization. Inf. Sci. 222, 185–202 (2013)

19. Samarati, P.: Protecting respondents identities in microdata release. IEEE Trans. Knowl. Data Eng. 13(6), 1010–1027 (2001)

20. Solanas, A., Martinez-Balleste, A., Domingo-Ferrer, J.: V-mdav: a multivariate microaggregation with variable group size. In: 17th COMPSTAT Symposium of the IASC, Rome, pp. 917–925 (2006)

21. Soria-Comas, J., Domingo-Ferrer, J., Mulero, R.: Efficient near-optimal variable-size microaggregation. In: Torra, V., Narukawa, Y., Pasi, G., Viviani, M. (eds.) MDAI 2019. LNCS (LNAI), vol. 11676, pp. 333–345. Springer, Cham (2019). https://doi.org/10.1007/978-3-030-26773-5_29

22. Stadler, T., Oprisanu, B., Troncoso, C.: Synthetic data - anonymisation groundhog day. In: USENIX 2022, to appear

23. Sweeney, L.: k-anonymity: a model for protecting privacy. Internat. J. Uncertain. Fuzziness Knowl.-Based Syst. 10(05), 557–570 (2002)

24. Thaeter, F.: k-anonymous microaggregation. Dissertation, Universität zu Lübeck (2021)

25. Thaeter, F., Reischuk, R.: Improving anonymization clustering. In: Langweg, H., Meier, M., Witt, B.C., Reinhardt, D. (eds.) SICHERHEIT 2018, pp. 69–82, Bonn (2018). Gesellschaft für Informatik e.V

26. Thaeter, F., Reischuk, R.: Hardness of k-anonymous microaggregation. Discret. Appl. Math. **303**, 149–158 (2021)

27. Thaeter, F., Reischuk, R.: Scalable k-anonymous microaggregation: Exploiting the tradeoff between computational complexity and information loss. In: 18th International Conference on Security and Cryptography (SECRYPT), pp. 87–98 (2021)

Extended Formal Analysis of the EDHOC Protocol in Tamarin

Karl Norrman[1,2](✉) (iD), Vaishnavi Sundararajan[3] (iD), and Alessandro Bruni[4]

[1] KTH Royal Institute of Technology, Stockholm, Sweden
[2] Ericsson Research, Security, Stockholm, Sweden
karl.norrman@ericsson.com
[3] Indian Institute of Technology Delhi, New Delhi, India
vaishnavi@cse.iitd.ac.in
[4] IT University of Copenhagen, Copenhagen, Denmark
brun@itu.dk

Abstract. Given how common IoT devices that use constrained resources are becoming today, the need of the hour is communication protocols which can operate securely under such limitations. For a few years, the Internet Engineering Task Force (IETF) has been working to standardize EDHOC, an authenticated key establishment protocol for such constrained IoT devices. The first version of EDHOC was proposed in 2016. In 2018, Bruni et al. [3] used the ProVerif tool [2] to formally analyze an early version of EDHOC, which had only two key establishment methods. By 2021, the protocol had been fleshed out much more, with multiple new key establishment methods, and this version was formally analyzed using the Tamarin prover [15] in [17]. In this paper, we build on that work, by modifying the model, analyzing some new properties, and discussing some aspects of the latest EDHOC specification. In particular, we extend the modeling in [17] with trusted execution environments (TEEs), modify the way we model XOR encryption, and in addition to the properties verified in [17], we verify weak post-compromise security (PCS) as well as the secrecy and integrity of some additional data used as part of the protocol.

Keywords: Formal verification · Symbolic dolev-yao model · Authenticated key establishment · Protocols · IoT · Tamarin

1 Introduction

IoT protocols are often run on devices which operate under severe restrictions on resources like bandwidth and energy consumption. These constrained devices are often simple in their operation, but need to communicate and function without human interference or maintenance for extended periods of time. The Internet Engineering Task Force (IETF) is standardizing new protocols to secure communications between devices that operate under such restrictions. One such is the Object Security for Constrained RESTful Environments (OSCORE) protocol. However, OSCORE requires the pre-establishment of a security context. To this end, a key exchange protocol named Ephemeral Diffie-Hellman Over COSE (EDHOC) is being discussed in the IETF. Since

© The Author(s), under exclusive license to Springer Nature Switzerland AG 2023
P. Samarati et al. (Eds.): ICETE 2021, CCIS 1795, pp. 224–248, 2023.
https://doi.org/10.1007/978-3-031-36840-0_11

EDHOC will establish security contexts for OSCORE, the same resource constraints (especially those pertaining to message size) apply to the former as for the latter. While establishing security contexts for OSCORE is the primary goal for the EDHOC protocol, there might well be other use cases which have not been explored in depth yet. It is therefore important to ensure that fundamental properties expected of key exchange protocols as established in the literature are satisfied by EDHOC as well.

1.1 Evolution of EDHOC

The first EDHOC framework was introduced in March 2016. It allowed two different key establishment methods – one involved a pre-shared Diffie-Hellman (DH) *cryptographic core*, and the other was a variation on challenge-response signatures, à la OPTLS [13].

A *cryptographic core*, often just called a core, is an academic protocol, i.e., with no encodings or application-specific details as needed for an industrial protocol. Once these ingredients are added to a cryptographic core, we obtain a key-establishment method. Since then, the protocol has seen multiple changes. In May 2018, the designers replaced the challenge-response signature core with one based on SIGMA (SIGn-and-MAc) [10,21], and in 2020, three new cores, which mixed challenge-response signatures and regular signatures were added as well [22]. While this is the version we base our formal analysis on, there have been later versions. See Sect. 7.1 for a more detailed discussion.

1.2 Related Work and Contributions

The earliest related work is [3], which formally analyzes the May 2018 version of EDHOC using the ProVerif tool [2]. In this paper, the authors analyze two key establishment methods – one built on a pre-shared key authentication core, and one based on SIGMA. The authors check the following properties: secrecy, identity protection, strong authentication, perfect forward secrecy (PFS), and integrity of application data. Later work [17] analyzes the July 2020 version of EDHOC in the Tamarin prover [15]. This version of the protocol has four key establishment methods. In [17], the properties checked for are injective agreement, implicit agreement, and perfect forward secrecy for the session key material. That work also includes a discussion about the various design choices made as part of EDHOC, and the impact of EDHOC in multiple use-case scenarios.

1.3 Contributions

In this paper, we extend the work presented in [17]. We formally analyze the EDHOC specification as of July 2020 [22], but our formal analysis applies as far as the version of the specification from February 2021. We extend the adversary model and Tamarin system models to capture weak post-compromise security (PCS) and model Trusted Execution Environments (TEE). We also alter the formal modeling used for encryption under XOR. We formally verify the following properties:

- Injective agreement
- Implicit agreement
- Perfect Forward Secrecy (PFS) for the session-key material
- Weak post-compromise security for the session-key material
- Secrecy and integrity of ad_3

We follow the definition of weak PCS by [4], which subsumes PFS. Since EDHOC is still a protocol under development, the latest version of EDHOC is the one from July 2022 [23], which contains details which are not covered by our formal model. We do, however, refer to various aspects (error handling, denial of service etc.) of the July 2022 version of the specification, namely in Sects. 5 and 6. We also discuss various issues arising due to the use of trusted execution environments (TEEs), denial of service (DoS) attacks, error handling, the negotiation of parameters (which the formal model abstracts away) for establishing the protocol, and other potential attacks and concerns. We have communicated these issues to the developers of the protocol.

2   The EDHOC Protocol

In this section, we describe the various key establishment methods of the EDHOC protocol. Following [17], we refer to the two roles executing the protocol as the initiator I and the responder R. We annotate values with I and R to make explicit which role they belong to.

2.1   Notation

We denote by $\langle d_{t,id}, Q_{t,id} \rangle$ public-private key pairs, where d is the private key, Q is the public key, $t \in \{e, s\}$ indicates whether the key is ephemeral or static, and id indicates the party to whom the key pair belongs. When clear from context, we will often drop some (or all) of the subscripts. Static key pairs (suitable for regular or challenge-response signatures) are long-term authentication credentials, whereas ephemeral key pairs are those generated afresh for each execution of the protocol.

Parties can authenticate using regular signatures or challenge-response signatures. In the former case, we say that they use the *signature-based authentication method* (SIG). In the latter case, we say, following the terminology in the specification, that they use the *static key authentication method* (STAT). We adopt the challenge-response terminology from [11].

EDHOC fundamentally uses elliptic curves and associated Diffie-Hellman operations. Signatures using a party A's keys are denoted by $sign_A(\cdot)$, while the verification thereof is denoted by $vf_A(\cdot)$. A Diffie-Hellman operation which combines a private key d and a point P on the elliptic curve is represented as $dh(d, P)$. We will often overload notation to let P stand for both the point on the elliptic curve as well as the corresponding bitstring encoding.

2.2 Overall Description

EDHOC is designed to establish a security context for the OSCORE protocol. This context, in particular, includes the session-key material (we denote this by Z). The generalized abstract protocol as given in the specification [22] consists of three messages, and is shown in Fig. 1. The abstract structure is the same across methods. However, the authentication mechanisms and key derivation procedures differ between methods. EDHOC may also transfer application data ad_1, ad_2, and ad_3 in addition to establishing the OSCORE security context.

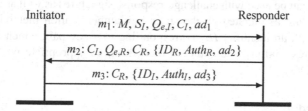

Fig. 1. Structure of EDHOC: $\{t\}$ means t is encrypted and integrity protected [17].

Of the three messages m_1, m_2, and m_3, the first two, among other things, establish a common authentication method M and ciphersuite S_I. The party playing the initiator role uses M to propose which authentication methods the two parties shall use, and in S_I, proposes an ordered list of choices for the ciphersuite. The chosen authentication methods may differ for the two roles, yielding four possible combinations: SIG-SIG, SIG-STAT, STAT-SIG, and STAT-STAT, where the first authentication method in each combination is used by the initiator, and the second by the responder.[1] The party executing the responder role may choose to reject the method and/or ciphersuite chosen by the initiator by sending an error message. This results in abandoning this session and renegotiating, as the initiator goes down their list of choices for ciphersuites, and picks the next option for a next execution of the protocol. Our analysis does not cover such renegotiation which requires maintaining state between executions to remember the rejected ciphersuites. However, we will discuss the ramifications of such a renegotiation procedure and the error messages later, in Sect. 5.

In addition to negotiating the method and ciphersuite, the first two messages are also instrumental for the exchange of public ephemeral keys $Q_{e,I}$ and $Q_{e,R}$, and connection identifiers C_I and C_R, for the initiator and responder roles respectively. The specification states that the connection identifiers serve only to route messages to the correct party executing EDHOC, but also claims that they may be used in turn by protocols (like OSCORE) which use the security context established by EDHOC. While the specification does not require any explicit security guarantees to be satisfied by these connection identifiers, it does, however, require that the identifiers be unique, i.e., in any session, $C_I \neq C_R$, and that the parties involved in the session can verify this uniqueness. More precisely, the specification states that OSCORE should be able to use these identifiers to retrieve any particular security context. In this work, as in [17], we verify that the

---

[1] As in the specification, we will from now on overload notation and refer to the combinations of authentication methods as methods as well.

parties agree on the values of C_I and C_R. The second and third messages also serve to identify and authenticate each party to the other. These messages contain long-term key identifiers (ID_I and ID_R). Additionally, the messages contain authenticating information ($Auth_I$ and $Auth_R$), which lets each party know that the other party does indeed control the long-term key associated with these identifiers. The authentication information is structured differently for each authentication method.

Consider the following scenario. The initiator I chooses the method SIG-STAT, and sends this via M to the responder R. R now has the option to reject this choice of method. However, if R chooses to accept this method, they need to provide an identifier ID_R for a key pair which can be used with challenge-response signatures as well as authenticating information $Auth_R$, as dictated by the static key authentication method STAT. I will then respond with an identifier ID_I corresponding to a key pair, which is suitable for regular signatures, and provide authentication $Auth_I$ as appropriate for the signature-based method SIG.

2.3   Key Schedule

The second and third messages of EDHOC contain authenticating information. This information is either a signature or a message authentication code (MAC), as we will describe in more detail in Sect. 2.4. The keys for these are generated using a key schedule which is intrinsic to the functioning of EDHOC. The key schedule takes a DH key P_e as basic input and builds upon it, as shown in Fig. 2.

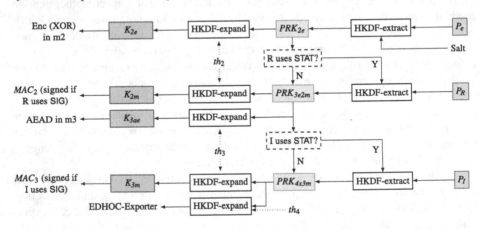

Fig. 2. Key schedule for [22]: P_e, P_I, P_R are the DH keys, PRK_{2e}, PRK_{3e2m}, PRK_{4x3m} are the intermediate key material, and $K_{2e}, K_{2m}, K_{3ae}, K_{3m}$ are the encryption keys for AEAD or XOR. Dashed boxes are conditionals [17].

To derive keys, EDHOC uses two functions from the HKDF interface [12], HKDF-extract and HKDF-expand. Both functions take as argument two values – an input and a salt. For HKDF-extract, the input is a DH key, while for HKDF-expand, it is intermediate key material.

As mentioned earlier, the fundamental building block for the key schedule is the ephemeral DH key P_e, which is computed in two different ways by I (as $dh(d_{e,I}, Q_{e,R})$)

and R (as $dh(d_{e,R}, Q_{e,I})$). This key gives rise to intermediate keys PRK_{2e}, PRK_{3e2m} and PRK_{4x3m}, which can be derived as part of protocol execution. Each intermediate key gives rise to encryption and integrity keys (K_{2e}, K_{2m}, K_{3ae}, and K_{3m}) corresponding to each message in the protocol.

In order to generate the final keys, the two HKDF algorithms use various values for salt. PRK_{2e} is generated by the HKDF-extract algorithm while using the empty string as the salt. PRK_{3e2m} and PRK_{4x3m} are separately generated if R or I uses the STAT method, using the corresponding DH key as input and the previous intermediate key as salt. The key P_R, which is computed as $dh(d_{e,I}, Q_{s,R}) = dh(d_{s,R}, Q_{e,I})$, is used if the responder uses the STAT authentication method. Similarly, the key P_I is used if the initiator uses STAT, and is computed as $dh(d_{e,R}, Q_{s,I}) = dh(d_{s,I}, Q_{e,R})$.

These intermediate keys are fed into HKDF-expand, which uses as salt a value th, which is a running hash of the information transmitted thus far as part of the protocol. By th_i, we denote the hash corresponding to the ith message.

At the end of a successful run of the protocol, the session-key material is established as Z, which we define as a set of various keys. This set always includes P_e, and if the initiator (resp. the responder) uses the STAT authentication method, then it also includes P_I (resp. P_R). We discuss which material should be included in Z in more detail in Sect. 4, and the consequences of various choices in Sect. 6.3. Once Z has been established, an HKDF-based key exporter named EDHOC-Exporter extracts the keys required by the security protocol.

2.4 About Authentication in EDHOC

We now describe how the authentication information is constructed, depending on whether the SIG or STAT method is used. For both methods, the following information is used to compute $Auth_R$: ID_R, $Q_{s,R}$, a transcript hash of all the communicated information thus far in the protocol, and ad_2, if included. $Auth_I$ uses the same pieces of information, but corresponding to the initiator role. A MAC is obtained by feeding this material as additional data and the empty string as input to the Authenticated Encryption with Additional Data (AEAD) algorithm as indicated in the established ciphersuite S_I. The encryption key for the AEAD algorithm is constructed, for both roles, using the ephemeral key material $Q_{e,I}$, $Q_{e,R}$, $d_{e,I}$, and $d_{e,R}$. The initiator computes $dh(d_{e,I}, Q_{e,R})$ while the responder computes $dh(d_{e,R}, Q_{e,I})$, and DH operations give rise to the same key under both these computations.

When I uses the SIG authentication method, $Auth_I$ is I's signature over the MAC computed as above, along with the data covered by the MAC. However, when I uses the STAT method, $Auth_I$ is just the MAC, with one difference: the MAC key is derived using both the ephemeral key material P_e as well as the long-term key for the initiator $\langle d_{s,I}, Q_{s,I} \rangle$. This is similar to the 1-RTT semi-static pattern in OPTLS which computes the MAC key sfk for the message sfin [13]. The same procedures works for R as well (with the values corresponding to R). The abstract calculation for the authentication information values is as shown in Table 1 [17]. We use MAC_R (resp. MAC_I) to denote a MAC which uses an encryption key constructed using $\langle d_{s,R}, Q_{s,R} \rangle$ and $\langle d_{e,I}, Q_{e,I} \rangle$ (resp. using $\langle d_{s,I}, Q_{s,I} \rangle$ and $\langle d_{e,R}, Q_{e,R} \rangle$).

In addition to this, the second and third messages have provisions for transferring application messages which are encrypted and integrity protected, as can be seen in 1.

Table 1. The outer functions for each method M [17].

M	$Auth_I$	$Auth_R$
SIG-SIG	$sign_I(\cdot)$	$sign_R(\cdot)$
SIG-STAT	$sign_I(\cdot)$	$MAC_R(\cdot)$
STAT-SIG	$MAC_I(\cdot)$	$sign_R(\cdot)$
STAT-STAT	$MAC_I(\cdot)$	$MAC_R(\cdot)$

The second message is encrypted by performing a bit-wise XOR between the plaintext and the output of the key derivation function HKDF, as in Sect. 2.3. For the third message, encryption and integrity protection is assured by the AEAD algorithm.

In Fig. 3 we show an example of protocol execution under the SIG-STAT method. The figure describes in detail the various message patterns, operations and key derivations used to construct these messages.

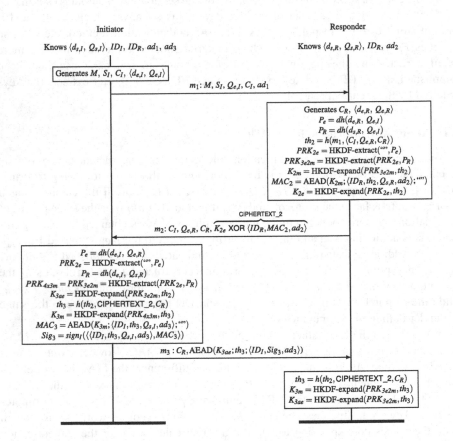

Fig. 3. The SIG-STAT method for EDHOC. $\langle \cdot \rangle$ denotes a tuple, and the hash function h is as established in the ciphersuite S_I [17].

3 Implementation Aspects and Key Protection

Authentication of a specific IoT device assumes that the device is the only entity with access to the long-term key associated with its identity. Since IoT devices may be accessible to adversaries, e.g., an insider cloning a key card, long-term keys must be appropriately protected. A state-of-the-art approach is to use a trusted execution environment (TEE), which holds the key and provides an API for operations using the key. This is the approach taken by the TrustZone-based μEDHOC [9] implementation, for example. Typical operations include signatures using the long-term private key of a party.

TEEs can be of differing complexity. Some, like ARM TrustZone and Intel SGX, are general-purpose execution environments, which can be programmed in many different ways. Others, like the Universal Subscriber Identity Modules (USIM) used for authentication to 3GPP mobile networks, have application-specific interfaces for authentication, key agreement protocols etc.

A fundamental aspect of TEEs is how much of the application is placed in the TEE. For larger devices that include general-purpose processors with TrustZone or SGX, entire EDHOC and OSCORE implementations may reside inside the TEE. For constrained IoT devices on the lower end of the scale, a TEE might have to be implemented using a special-purpose integrated circuit. In the latter case, it may be beneficial to follow a minimalistic approach, and only store in the TEE the long-term key and operations that need access to it, to reduce cost.

In general, it might appear more secure to implement as much as possible inside the TEE, but there is a security trade-off. Because security-critical code runs in the same area as where long-term keys reside, an implementation error here risks leaking information of the key to the adversary. From this perspective, it might be beneficial to follow the minimalistic approach even when having access to TrustZone or SGX.

A slightly more secure division of functionality is to keep both the long-term key and the session key inside the TEE and extend the interface to accept messages and return the (en/de)crypted counterpart, i.e. the interface exposes AEAD functions.

4 Formalization and Results

The EDHOC specification [22] claims that EDHOC satisfies many security properties, but these are imprecisely expressed and motivated. In particular, there is no coherent adversary model. It is therefore not clear in which context properties should be verified. We resolve this by clearly specifying an adversary model, in which we can verify properties.

4.1 Formal Model

As in [17], we verify EDHOC in an extended Dolev-Yao model [6]. The Dolev-Yao model is well established for the symbolic verification of security protocols. Messages are modelled as terms in an algebra, and the various cryptographic operations are assumed to be perfect, e.g., encrypted messages can only be decrypted with the correct key, there are no hash collisions etc.

The adversary is assumed to be in control of the communication channel and can see all messages being communicated as part of the protocol. In addition, they can interact with an unbounded number of protocol sessions, and drop, inject and modify messages at will.

On top of the standard Dolev-Yao model, [17] allows the adversary to access long-term and ephemeral keys via specific events. Long-term key reveal, denoted by $\mathbf{A}_{\mathsf{LTK}}^t(A)$, stands for the adversary gaining access to a party A's long-term private key $d_{s,A}$ at a time point t. Ephemeral key reveal, denoted by $\mathbf{A}_{\mathsf{Eph}}^t(A, k)$, stands for the adversary obtaining, at time t, the ephemeral private key $d_{e,A}$ used by party A in a session where they establish a session key k. Formalizing these two capabilities allows more fine-grained control over the access that an adversary has to these fundamentally different kinds of keys. Furthermore, we modify the model from [17] by strengthening the adversary capabilities, as detailed next.

System and Adversary Model Extensions Supporting TEE. We extend the adversary model of [17] by allowing the adversary to use the long term key of any party via an interface, without directly accessing the key itself. This allows us to model the scenario where the adversary has gained access to a device, but the long-term key is protected by a trusted execution environment (TEE), and thus only accessible via the TEE interface. According to the terminology of [4], a protocol is considered to enjoy *weak post-compromise security* (Weak-PCS) if it achieves its security goals for a specific session even when the following hold:

- Before the session starts, the adversary has limited access to the long-term keys of the parties involved, through an interface that securely maintains the keys but allows principals to run cryptographic operations using them, and
- The adversary has full access to the keys of the parties involved after the end of the session, as well as access to the keys of all other parties.

As in the framework of [24], we add adversary capabilities corresponding to a server adversary, i.e., upon compromising a party, the adversary learns their ephemeral keys and may temporarily access their TEE, but does not learn their long-term key. This extension to the model of [17] thus allows us to verify all the previous security properties under a "Weak-PCS model". Note that this attacker model is strictly more powerful than that of [17], as it subsumes the previous attacker capabilities.

We split the functionality of EDHOC as follows. The TEE contains the long-term key and allows the non-TEE parts of the application to perform the operations using it via an interface. More precisely, parties using the SIG authentication method use a TEE interface which accepts a message and returns the signature of that message using the party's private long-term key. A party U using the STAT authentication method uses a TEE with an interface accepting a point P on the curve and returning $dh(d_{s,U}, P)$.

This interface requires the least functionality from the TEE, reducing the TEE's complexity and (possibly) its cost. This functional split is suitable even when a constrained device has implemented the storage of only the long-term key in a special purpose circuit with minimal processing functionality. Since EDHOC focuses on constrained IoT devices, it seems appropriate to cater for this setting.

Extended Formalism and Security Properties. Formally, we model the TEE interface by adding two new rewrite rules:

```
rule forge_SIG:
    [!LTK_SIG($A, ~ltk), In(xx)] --[TEE($A)]-> [Out(sign(xx, ~ltk))]

rule exp_STAT:
    [!LTK_STAT($A, ~ltk), In('g'^~xx)] --[TEE($A)]-> [Out(('g'^~xx)^~ltk)]
```

These rules allow the adversary to obtain terms representing signatures on a value of their choice (`forge_SIG`), or to obtain terms representing a curve point of their choice raised to the power of the long-term key (`exp_STAT`).

Because it is a trivial attack when the adversary accesses these rules with values from a session in progress, we must disqualify those rule applications. We do so by creating an action fact `TEE($A)`, where `$A` is the identity corresponding to the private key used, and then augmenting the properties with a condition that no such action fact exists from the start of the protocol execution till its end. Care must be taken when specifying the start and the end: specifically, the start and end of the execution must be viewed with respect to the current role. For example, the injective agreement property for the initiator in the SIG-SIG method requires that the adversary does not have access to the TEE of the responder from the time that the first message is transmitted till the second message is received by the initiator (or equivalently, till the third message is transmitted by the initiator, since reception of a message and transmission of the next one by a party is one atomic operation). Thus, these timepoints represent the start and end of the protocol run from the perspective of the initiator.

The second message encrypts two values: the responder's identity R and the authentication information authR. We model XOR encryption by XOR-ing each term with their own key-stream term. However for some problematic methods[2] we XOR the entire tuple <R, authR> with a single key-stream term. This simplification is likely to miss an attack on implicit authentication which occurs due to the combination of a malleable XOR encryption and access to the TEE interface. However, given that no attacks were identified due to the use of XOR in our original modeling, nor in the current modeling for all other authentication methods, we believe that this is not a severe restriction.

Next we provide a quick overview of the Tamarin tool, and describe our modeling of EDHOC in it.

4.2 Tamarin

We extend the formal model of [17], using the tool Tamarin [15], which is an interactive tool for the symbolic verification of security protocols. Protocols are modelled in Tamarin as multiset rewrite rules which encode a transition relation. The elements of these multisets, called facts, contribute to the global system state. For syntactic sugar, Tamarin also allows the use of let-bindings and tuples. For ease of presentation, we will present the model and properties in a slightly different syntax in this paper, but this syntax can be directly mapped to that of Tamarin.

---

[2] See Table 2 for all verification results and computation times.

Rewrite rules can be annotated with events, called actions in Tamarin. Communicated messages in the protocol are modelled as terms in an algebra, which specifies sets of names, variables, and allowable function symbols. Facts and actions are modelled as n-ary predicates in the term algebra, and actions can be parametrized using terms.

An annotated multiset-rewrite rule is represented as $l\ -\!\![e]\!\!\rightarrow r$, where l and r are multisets, and e is a multiset of actions. A sequence of actions yields a protocol execution trace. Properties are defined as formulas in a fragment of temporal first order logic, and these formulas can be verified over execution traces. Event types are predicates over global states generated during protocol execution. Consider an event type E and a timestamp t as part of a trace. By $E^t(p_i)_{i\in\mathbb{N}}$, we represent an event of type E occurring at time t in a trace, parametrized by the sequence of values $(p_i)_{i\in\mathbb{N}}$ (corresponding to the action fact $E(p_i)_{i\in\mathbb{N}}@t$ in Tamarin). Thus, the time points form a quasi order, and we denote the fact that t_1 comes before t_2 in a protocol trace by $t_1 \lessdot t_2$, and that t_1 and t_2 stand for the same time point in a trace by $t_1 \doteq t_2$. Tamarin allows events to occur at the same time point, with one restriction: multiple events of the same type cannot occur simultaneously, so if $t_1 \doteq t_2$, then $E^{t_1} = E^{t_2}$.

Protocol verification in Tamarin happens under an equational theory E. For example, to represent the fact that E satisfies the reversal of symmetric encryption by using a decryption operation with the key, one can write $dec(enc(x,y),y) =_E x$. The equational theory E is fixed upfront to handle the functions supported by the term algebra, so we will omit the subscript for the rest of this paper.

Users can extend the default term algebra and equational theory in Tamarin with new function symbols and unification rules (if any) for these new symbols. For example, EDHOC requires authenticated encryption, which we model using the symbol aeadEncrypt. We augment Tamarin with the following rule for this operation, which represents the fact that if the adversary knows a key k, a message m, and authenticated data ad, and has access to an encryption algorithm ai, then they can obtain the message corresponding to the authenticated encryption of m with k [17].

```
[!KU(k), !KU(m), !KU(ad), !KU(ai)] --[]-> [!KU(aeadEncrypt(k, m, ad, ai))]
```

Other than modeling authenticated encryption, we use Tamarin's built-in equational theories for signing, Diffie-Hellman, hashing and XOR.

Tamarin has also built-in rules for modeling a Dolev-Yao adversary and the evolution of their knowledge as the protocol executes. We extend the Dolev-Yao adversary model by adding other rules that increase the capabilities of the attacker. To denote that the adversary has access to a message p at time t, we use $\mathcal{K}^t(p)$. As an example, the following implication

$$\forall t,k,k' . \mathcal{K}^t(\langle k,k'\rangle) \rightarrow \mathcal{K}^t(k) \wedge \mathcal{K}^t(k'),$$

models the fact that if the adversary gets to know the pair of keys $\langle k,k'\rangle$ at a time point t, then the adversary knows each of those keys k and k' at time point t as well. For more details about how Tamarin manages adversary knowledge, see [15].

4.3 Model and Desired Properties

In this section, we describe our modeling of EDHOC and its desired security properties.

The party I executing the initiator role considers a run of the protocol begun as soon as it sends the first message m_1 with event type $\mathbf{I_S}$, and considers the run ended once it has sent the third message m_3 with event type $\mathbf{I_C}$. Similarly, the responder R considers a run started upon receiving m_1 with event type $\mathbf{R_S}$, and finished upon receiving m_3 with type $\mathbf{R_C}$.

In this work we consider the following properties: secrecy of the session key, injective agreement and implicit agreement on the session-key material for both initiator and responder, and secrecy and integrity of the application data sent as part of message 3 (ad_3). Agreement is considered on a set of parameters S which also contains the session-key material Z. We will first describe in detail all these properties, and then describe the contents of the set S. We formalize these properties as shown in Fig. 4, which is a modified version of a figure in [17].

Secrecy of the Session-Key Material. We show that the adversary cannot gain access to the session-key material Z, even under the weak post-compromise security model which allows the adversary limited access to the long-term keys of the involved parties via a secure interface before the session starts, and unrestricted access to the long-term keys of all parties as well as access to all other session keys after the session ends. This property is formalized as **PCS** in Fig. 4.

In the $\mathbf{I_C}$ event, *tid* represents a "thread identifier" which uniquely identifies the current session, I represents the identity of the initiator, and R represents the identity of the party who the initiator believes is playing the responder role, while Z stands for the established session-key material. $\mathbf{R_C}$ has analogous parameters; in particular, the responder R believes I is the party playing the initiator role. Intuitively, the PCS property states that an adversary obtains Z only if one of the following conditions hold: either a party's long-term key is compromised before their run ends, or the TEE interface for the responder is used during the current session for the initiator, i.e., after the initiator starts and before it completes, or, similarly, the TEE interface for the initiator is used during the current session for the responder. Note that the properties in Fig. 4 are unlike the actual Tamarin lemma in one minor way: Tamarin's logic does not allow disjunctions to appear on the left-hand side of an implication inside a universally-quantified formula. Therefore, in the Tamarin code, instead of using the disjunction $\mathbf{I_C^{t2}}(tid, I, R, Z) \vee \mathbf{R_C^{t2}}(tid, I, R, Z)$ to model the fact that either party may have completed their execution, we use a single action parametrized by the terms tid, I, R, and Z.

Authentication Properties. Following [17], we prove two different kinds of authentication properties, namely *injective agreement* in the style of [14], and implicit agreement. Injective agreement can be guaranteed to either party running the protocol. For the initiator I, it guarantees to I that whenever I believes that they have completed a run with R as responder, then the party R has indeed executed the protocol in the role of a responder, and that this run of I uniquely corresponds to one of R where the set of parameters is S and includes, in particular, the session-key material Z. It can be defined for R in a similar manner.

We formalize injective agreement for the initiator role as **InjAgree**$_I$ and for the responder role as **InjAgree**$_R$ in Fig. 4. For the initiator I, this property represents the fact that either injective agreement (as described above) holds, or the long-term key of

$$\mathbf{PCS} \triangleq \forall tid, I, R, Z, t_2, t_3 \,.\, \mathcal{K}^{t_3}(Z) \wedge (\mathbf{I}^{t_2}_\mathsf{C}(tid, I, R, Z) \vee \mathbf{R}^{t_2}_\mathsf{C}(tid, I, R, Z)) \rightarrow$$

$$(\exists t_1 \,.\, \mathbf{A}^{t_1}_\mathsf{LTK}(I) \wedge t_1 \lessdot t_2) \vee (\exists t_1 \,.\, \mathbf{A}^{t_1}_\mathsf{LTK}(R) \wedge t_1 \lessdot t_2)$$

$$\vee\ (\exists t_1 \,.\, \mathbf{A}^{t_1}_\mathsf{Eph}(R, Z)) \vee (\exists t_1 \,.\, \mathbf{A}^{t_1}_\mathsf{Eph}(I, Z))$$

$$\vee\ (\exists t_0, t_1, Z' \,.\, \mathbf{I}^{t_0}_\mathsf{S}(tid, I, R, Z') \wedge \mathbf{A}^{t_1}_\mathsf{TEE}(R) \wedge (t_0 \lessdot t_1 \wedge t_1 \lessdot t_2))$$

$$\vee\ (\exists t_0, t_1, Z' \,.\, \mathbf{R}^{t_0}_\mathsf{S}(tid, I, R, Z') \wedge \mathbf{A}^{t_1}_\mathsf{TEE}(I) \wedge (t_0 \lessdot t_1 \wedge t_1 \lessdot t_2))$$

$$\mathbf{InjAgree}_I \triangleq \forall tid_I, I, R, Z, S, t_2 \,.\, \mathbf{I}^{t_2}_\mathsf{C}(tid_I, I, R, Z, S) \rightarrow$$

$$(\exists tid_R, t_1 \,.\, \mathbf{R}^{t_1}_\mathsf{S}(tid_R, R, Z, S) \wedge t_1 \lessdot t_2 \wedge (\forall tid'_I, I', R', t'_1 \,.\, \mathbf{I}^{t'_1}_\mathsf{C}(tid'_I, I', R', Z, S) \rightarrow t'_1 \doteq t_2))$$

$$\vee\ (\exists t_1 \,.\, \mathbf{A}^{t_1}_\mathsf{LTK}(R) \wedge t_1 \lessdot t_2)$$

$$\vee\ (\exists t_0, t_1, Z' \,.\, \mathbf{I}^{t_0}_\mathsf{S}(tid_I, I, R, Z') \wedge \mathbf{A}^{t_1}_\mathsf{TEE}(R) \wedge (t_0 \lessdot t_1 \wedge t_1 \lessdot t_2))$$

$$\mathbf{InjAgree}_R \triangleq \forall tid_R, I, R, Z, S, t_2 \,.\, \mathbf{R}^{t_2}_\mathsf{C}(tid_R, I, R, Z, S) \rightarrow$$

$$(\exists tid_I, t_1 \,.\, \mathbf{I}^{t_1}_\mathsf{S}(tid_I, I, R, Z, S) \wedge t_1 \lessdot t_2 \wedge (\forall tid'_R, I'R't'_1 \,.\, \mathbf{R}^{t'_1}_\mathsf{C}(tid'_R, I', R', Z, S) \rightarrow t'_1 \doteq t_2))$$

$$\vee\ (\exists t_1 \,.\, \mathbf{A}^{t_1}_\mathsf{LTK}(I) \wedge t_1 \lessdot t_2)$$

$$\vee\ (\exists t_0, t_1, Z', S' \,.\, \mathbf{R}^{t_0}_\mathsf{S}(tid_R, R, Z', S') \wedge \mathbf{A}^{t_1}_\mathsf{TEE}(I) \wedge (t_0 \lessdot t_1 \wedge t_1 \lessdot t_2))$$

$$\mathbf{ImpAgree}_I \triangleq \forall tid_I, I, R, Z, S, t_1 \,.\, \mathbf{I}^{t_1}_\mathsf{C}(tid_I, I, R, Z, S) \rightarrow$$

$$(\forall tid_R, I', R', S', t_2 \,.\, \mathbf{R}^{t_2}_\mathsf{C}(tid_R, I', R', Z, S') \rightarrow (I = I' \wedge R = R' \wedge S = S')$$

$$\wedge (\forall tid'_I, I', R', Z, S') \,.\, \mathbf{I}^{t'_1}_\mathsf{C}(tid'_I, I', R', Z, S') \rightarrow t'_1 \doteq t_1))$$

$$\vee\ (\exists t_0 \,.\, \mathbf{A}^{t_0}_\mathsf{LTK}(R) \wedge t_0 \lessdot t_1) \vee (\exists t_0 \,.\, \mathbf{A}^{t_0}_\mathsf{Eph}(R, Z)) \vee (\exists t_0 \,.\, \mathbf{A}^{t_0}_\mathsf{Eph}(I, Z))$$

$$\vee\ (\exists t_0, t_1, Z' \,.\, \mathbf{I}^{t_0}_\mathsf{S}(tid_I, I, R, Z') \wedge \mathbf{A}^{t_1}_\mathsf{TEE}(R) \wedge (t_0 \lessdot t_1 \wedge t_1 \lessdot t_2))$$

$$\mathbf{Secad}_3 \triangleq \forall ad_3, I, R, Z, tid_I, t_3, t_2 \,.\, \mathcal{K}^{t_3}(ad_3) \wedge \mathbf{I}^{t_2}_\mathsf{SEND}(I, R, Z, ad_3, tid_I) \rightarrow$$

$$((\exists t_1 \,.\, \mathbf{A}^{t_1}_\mathsf{LTK}(I) \wedge t_1 \lessdot t_2) \vee (\exists t_1 \,.\, \mathbf{A}^{t_1}_\mathsf{LTK}(R) \wedge t_1 \lessdot t_2)$$

$$\vee\ (\exists t_0 \,.\, \mathbf{A}^{t_0}_\mathsf{Eph}(R, Z)) \vee (\exists t_0 \,.\, \mathbf{A}^{t_0}_\mathsf{Eph}(I, Z))$$

$$\vee\ (\exists t_0, t_1, Z' \,.\, \mathbf{I}^{t_0}_\mathsf{S}(tid_I, I, R, Z') \wedge \mathbf{A}^{t_1}_\mathsf{TEE}(R) \wedge t_0 \lessdot t_1)$$

$$\vee\ (\exists t_0, t_1, t_4, tid_R, Z', S' \,.\, \mathbf{A}^{t_1}_\mathsf{TEE}(I) \wedge \mathbf{R}^{t_4}_\mathsf{Recv}(I, R, Z, ad_3, tid_R) \wedge \mathbf{R}^{t_0}_\mathsf{S}(tid_R, R, Z', S') \wedge t_0 \lessdot t_1))$$

$$\mathbf{Integad}_3 \triangleq \forall ad_3, I, R, Z, tid_R, t_3 \,.\, \mathbf{R}^{t_3}_\mathsf{Recv}(I, R, Z, ad_3, tid_R) \rightarrow$$

$$((\exists tid_I, t_2 \,.\, \mathbf{I}^{t_2}_\mathsf{SEND}(I, R, Z, ad_3, tid_I) \wedge t_2 \lessdot t_3)$$

$$\vee\ (\exists t_2 \,.\, \mathbf{A}^{t_2}_\mathsf{LTK}(I) \wedge t_2 \lessdot t_3) \vee (\exists t_2 \,.\, \mathbf{A}^{t_2}_\mathsf{LTK}(R) \wedge t_2 \lessdot t_3)$$

$$\vee\ (\exists t_0 \,.\, \mathbf{A}^{t_0}_\mathsf{Eph}(R, Z)) \vee (\exists t_0 \,.\, \mathbf{A}^{t_0}_\mathsf{Eph}(I, Z))$$

$$\vee\ (\exists t_0, t_1, t_2, tid_I, Z' \,.\, \mathbf{A}^{t_1}_\mathsf{TEE}(R) \wedge \mathbf{I}^{t_2}_\mathsf{SEND}(I, R, Z, ad_3, tid_I) \wedge \mathbf{I}^{t_0}_\mathsf{S}(tid_I, I, R, Z') \wedge t_0 \lessdot t_1)$$

$$\vee\ (\exists t_0, t_1, Z', S' \,.\, \mathbf{A}^{t_1}_\mathsf{TEE}(I) \wedge \mathbf{R}^{t_0}_\mathsf{S}(tid_R, R, Z', S') \wedge t_0 \lessdot t_1))$$

Fig. 4. Formalization of security properties.

the party R assumed to be playing the responder role has been compromised before I's role finished. The property should hold even if the adversary has access to the TEE of party R before and after the protocol execution. An analogous definition holds for the responder R.

As part of our analysis, we found that all the EDHOC methods satisfy weak post-compromise security. However, this is not the case for the injective agreement property as stated above. Thus, we show a different property, a form of implicit agreement on the same set of parameters, which is guaranteed for all methods. This modification is inspired by the definitions of implicit authentication in the computational model [5]. While that paper focuses on authenticating just a key and related identities, our definition encompasses a general set of parameters, as in the notion of injective agreement proposed by Lowe [14].

The "implicit" in the name of the property stands for the fact that a party A assumes that any party B who has access to the session-key material Z must, in fact, be the intended party, and that if B is honest, B will agree on a set S of parameters which includes Z. Implicit agreement for both roles guarantees to A that A is or has been involved in exactly one protocol execution with B, and that B agrees or will agree with A on S. This property diverges from injective agreement in that upon sending the last message, A concludes that if this message reaches B, then A and B agree on each other's identities and roles, as well as the set S.

Note that for implicit agreement to hold for I, the ephemeral keys must not be revealed since the property relies on the fact that the intended responder is the only one who knows the session-key material. If the adversary has access to the ephemeral keys, they can use them along with the public keys of I and R to compute the session-key material. However, either party's long-term key can be revealed after the other party has finished their execution, since this still leaves the adversary unable to compute P_e.

Since Tamarin runs out of memory to verify this property as is, we split it into two lemmas – **ImpAgree$_I$** for I for one **ImpAgree$_R$** for R. Figure 4 contains the definition for **ImpAgree$_I$**. **ImpAgree$_R$** is formalized similarly, so we omit it.

Set S of Agreed Parameters. We now describe the set S of parameters upon which the two parties obtain guarantees via the above properties. The initiator I gets injective and implicit agreement guarantees on the following partial set S_P of parameters [17]:

- the roles played by itself and its peer,
- responder identity,
- session-key material (which varies depending on the EDHOC method),
- context identifiers C_I and C_R, and
- cipher suites S_I.

Due to the initiator being guaranteed identity protection under EDHOC, I cannot get explicit agreement with R on the initiator's identity. Similarly, when using the STAT authentication method, I does not get any such guarantees about P_I. However, I does get implicit agreement with R about I's identity and the full set S_F of agreed parameters. In contrast, since R's run finishes after that of I, R can get explicit injective agreement assurances on the full set S_F of agreed parameters. The full set of agreed parameters S_F is $S_P \cup \{I, P_I\}$ when P_I is part of the session-key material, and $S_P \cup \{I\}$ otherwise.

In addition to these properties, a couple of properties can be inferred without being explicitly modelled and verified. One such property is Key-Compromise Impersonation (KCI) [1]. A KCI attack occurs when an adversary who has access to A's long-term private key to make A believe that they completed an execution with a peer B, while B did not participate in said execution at all. This is in particular relevant when STAT authentication methods are used. Our above notions of agreement ensure that both parties agree on each other's identity, role, and session-key material. Therefore, all EDHOC methods that satisfy these agreement properties also avoid KCI attacks.

Another kind of attack is Unknown Key Share attacks (UKS) [1]. As part of a UKS attack, a party A can be made to believe that it finished an execution with a party B, but where the session-key material is actually shared between A and C instead. Again, due to the agreement on identities and session-key material, any method that satisfies the above agreement properties also resists UKS attacks. Overall, the agreement properties capture entity authentication, and satisfy any properties based on that notion. However, see Sect. 6.1 for a discussion on the interaction between EDHOC and the application leading to similar issues.

4.4   Encoding EDHOC in Tamarin

In this section, we describe how we model the SIG-SIG, SIG-STAT, STAT-SIG, and STAT-STAT methods of EDHOC in Tamarin. As in [17], we construct the Tamarin model by utilizing the fact that all methods of EDHOC share a common underlying structure (as shown in Fig. 1). We do so by using a single specification file in the M4 macro language, which generates all the methods. As in [17], we only present the STAT-SIG method which illustrates the use of two different authentication methods. The full Tamarin code for all models can be found at [18].

As mentioned in Sect. 4.2, we extend the default equational theory of Tamarin to handle various operations used in EDHOC. Of the built-in theories, we use the ones for exclusive-or (XOR), Diffie-Hellman operations, signatures (sign and verify operations), and hashing [7, 20].

In addition to these default operations, EDHOC is built over the following functions: HKDF-expand, HKDF-extract, and AEAD. We represent HKDF-expand by expa and HKDF-extract by extr. AEAD operations need us to add extra equations to the underlying theory. A term encrypted using the AEAD algorithm is represented by aeadEncrypt(m, k, ad, ai), where m is the underlying message, k is the encrypting key, ad is the additional data, and ai is the identifier for the encryption algorithm. Decryption of such a term is defined via two equations that we add to Tamarin's theory. The following equation requires the decrypting party to know the additional data ad to decrypt this encrypted term with verification of its integrity.

```
aeadDecrypt(aeadEncrypt(m, k, ad, ai), k, ad, ai) = m.
```

Only the above equation is used by honest parties, but the adversary should also be able to decrypt without having to go through the additional step of identity verification. To this end, we also add the following equation, where the adversary does not need access to the additional data ad in order to decrypt.

```
decrypt(aeadEncrypt(m, k, ad, ai), k, ai) = m.
```

Having described how we adapt the equational theory to model EDHOC, we now move on to the modeling of the adversary model and the environment in which the protocol is executed. We extend the built-in Dolev-Yao adversary rules which are part of Tamarin.

We use the following rules to capture the link between a party's identity and their long-term key pairs, in the SIG- and in the STAT-based methods respectively.

```
1 rule registerLTK_SIG:                    1 rule registerLTK_STAT:
2   [Fr(~ltk)] --[UniqLTK($A, ~ltk)]->     2   [Fr(~ltk)] --[UniqLTK($A, ~ltk)]->
3     [!LTK_SIG($A, ~ltk),                 3     [!LTK_STAT($A, ~ltk),
4      !PK_SIG($A, pk(~ltk)),              4      !PK_STAT($A, 'g'^~ltk),
5      Out(<$A, pk(~ltk)>)]                5      Out(<$A, 'g'^~ltk>)]
```

Using the fact `Fr(~ltk)`, Tamarin creates a new term `ltk` and uses it to represent a secret long-term key. Via the `Out(<$A, pk(~ltk)>)` fact, Tamarin puts out onto the communication channel the identity of the party to whom this long-term key belongs, along with their public key. Since the adversary has access to the communication channel, they can pick up all of this information. The event `UniqLTK` parametrized by a party's identity and their long-term key models the unique correspondence between those two values. As a result, this rules out a party owning multiple long-term keys – in particular, it keeps the adversary from registering long-term keys in some honest party's name. This aligns well with an external mechanism such as a certificate authority ensuring that long-term keys are uniquely assigned to the corresponding identities, which is ensured by the specification.

To model the reveal of long-term keys and ephemeral keys to an adversary, we use standard reveal rules and events of type A_{LTK} and A_{Eph}, respectively. It is also important to keep track of the time points at which these events occur. Long-term keys can be revealed on registration, even before the protocol begins. Ephemeral keys in our model can only be revealed when a party completes their role, i.e., simultaneously with events of type I_C and R_C. Having set out the capabilities of the adversary, we now model the execution of the honest agents' roles.

For each protocol method, we use two rules apiece for the initiator and responder – I1, R2, I3, R4. Each of these stand for one step of the protocol as executed by either party. To disambiguate, we will attach the method to the rule name. These four rules directly map to the event types I_S, R_S, I_C, and R_C, respectively. We show the R2_STAT_SIG rule below to illustrate the various aspects of the Tamarin modeling we are describing here.

In order to keep track of the initiator's state, we use facts prefixed with StI, which carry information between the I1 and I3 rules. Similarly, for the responder's state, we have StR to carry state data between R2 and R4. In order to link two rules to a state fact, we use tid, which is unique to the current session. The use of these state facts can be seen in line 28 in the R2_STAT_SIG rule.

Note that we do not model any error message that R might send in response to message m_1 rejecting I's choice of ciphersuite and/or method.

As in [17], we model the XOR encryption of CIPHERTEXT_2 with the key K_2e by allowing each part of the encrypted term to be separately attacked. This means that we first expand K_2e to the same number of key terms as subterms in the plaintext tuple. This is done by applying HKDF-expand to unique inputs per subterm. After this, we XOR each subterm with its own key term. This is more faithful to the specification than XOR-ing K_2e on its own with the plaintext tuple. This can be seen in lines 18–21 in the code for R2_STAT_SIG.

As we extended the model with TEEs and augmented the adversary's capabilities with access to them, Tamarin failed to complete in a reasonable time for some combination of authentication methods and security properties (see Sect. 7 for a detailed discussion). To circumvent the problem, we simplified the XOR encryption to XOR-ing a single term on the entire tuple for these cases.

```
1  rule R2_STAT_SIG:
2  let
3     agreed = <CS0, CI, ~CR>
4     gx = 'g'^xx
5     data_2 = <'g'^~yy, CI, ~CR>
6     m1 = <'STAT', 'SIG', CS0, CI, gx>
7     TH_2 = h(<$H0, m1, data_2>)
8     prk_2e = extr('e', gx^~yy)
9     prk_3e2m = prk_2e
10    K_2m = expa(<$cAEAD0, TH_2, 'K_2m'>, prk_3e2m)
12    protected2 = $V // ID_CRED_V
13    CRED_V = pkV
14    extAad2 = <TH_2, CRED_V>
15    assocData2 = <protected2, extAad2>
16    MAC_2 = aead('e', K_2m, assocData2, $cAEAD0)
17    authV = sign(<assocData2, MAC_2>, ~ltk)
18    plainText2 = <$V, authV>
19    K_2e = expa(<$cAEAD0, TH_2, 'K_2e'>, prk_2e)
20    K_2e_1 = expa(<$cAEAD0, TH_2, 'K_2e', '1'>, prk_2e)
21    K_2e_2 = expa(<$cAEAD0, TH_2, 'K_2e', '2'>, prk_2e)
22    CIPHERTEXT_2 = <$V XOR K_2e_1, authV XOR K_2e_2>
23    m2 = <data_2, CIPHERTEXT_2>
24    exp_sk = <gx^~yy>
25 in
26    [!LTK_SIG($V, ~ltk), !PK_SIG($V, pkV), In(m1), Fr(~CR), Fr(~yy), Fr(~tid)]
27    --[ExpRunningR(~tid, $V, exp_sk, agreed), R2(~tid, $V, m1, m2)]->
28    [StR2_STAT_SIG($V, ~ltk, ~yy, prk_3e2m, TH_2, CIPHERTEXT_2, gx^~yy, ~tid, m1, m2, agreed),
29    Out(m2)]
```

As mentioned earlier, we use actions to represent parametrized events. For example, in line 27 above, the action ExpRunningR(~tid, $V, exp_sk, agreed) represents an event of type R_S parametrized by the session id, the responder's identity, and the session-key material exp_sk. The exp in the name of the variable for session-key material represents the fact that the agreement property satisfied by this key is explicit, i.e., it includes P_I, as in Sect. 4.3. We use imp_sk for the corresponding session-key material which does not include P_I. For the SIG-SIG and SIG-STAT methods, therefore, the two values are the same.

The properties we listed in Sect. 4.3 translate directly into Tamarin's logic. We show the Tamarin lemma which encodes the **PCS** property. Other properties are formalized similarly.

```
1  lemma secrecyPCS:
2     all-traces
3     "All u v sk tid #t3 #t2.
4        (K(sk)@t3 & CompletedRun(u, v, sk, tid)@t2) ==>
5        ( (Ex #t1. LTKRev(u)@t1 & #t1 < #t2)
6        | (Ex #t1. LTKRev(v)@t1 & #t1 < #t2)
7        | (Ex #t1. EphKeyRev(sk)@t1)
8        | (Ex m1 #t0 #k. I1(tid, u, v, m1)@t0 & TEE(v)@k & (t0 < k | k < t2))
9        | (Ex m1 m2 #t0 #k. R2(tid, v, m1, m2)@t0 & TEE(u)@k & (t0 < k | k < t2))
10       )"
```

In this formalization, we use the action CompletedRun(u, v, sk) (in line 4) to represent the disjunction of the events $\mathbf{I}_C^{t2}$ and $\mathbf{R}_C^{t2}$. As expected, this action is emitted by both I3 and R4. Similarly, the action EphKeyRev(sk) in line 7 stands for the reveal of the ephemeral key for I or R or both. Lines 8 and 9 captures that the parties TEEs must be inaccessible to the adversary between the start and end of the execution as seen by each party respectively. The entire code can be found at [18].

5   Error Handling

Section 6 of the current EDHOC specification [23] states that error messages can be sent at any time and by any party. There are three types of error messages: type 0 is used to represent success, type 1 represents a generic error message used for debugging purposes, and type 2 represents the failure to negotiate a common ciphersuite. Type 2 messages carry a list of supported ciphersuites by the responder. The contents and semantics of type 1 messages are dependent on the implementation. Consequently, type 1 error messages provide a generic message passing mechanism, albeit without a predefined semantics. We now discuss some issues with this specification of error messages. In this section, we use "specification" to mean the latest specification, as in [23].

5.1   Lack of Connection Identifiers

Error messages do not include the optional connection identifiers C_I or C_R. This is potentially problematic for connection-less transport layers, where these identifiers may be used to correlate messages.

5.2   Proper Reception Handling

EDHOC provides an error message mechanism, but little to no guidance on how it should be used safely. For example, assume that an application using EDHOC logs error messages on a finite log with rotation. If the log is used for anomaly detection or detection of sensitive events, then an adversary can simply inject error messages and fill the log until the sensitive event is overwritten. In such situations, implementers should do proper log-separation and log management.

5.3   Unspecified Semantics for Debugging Messages

Sect. 6.2 gives an example of sending a type 1 error message with the information string "Method not supported". Note that EDHOC does not include a mechanism to support the negotiating of the connection method. The initiator selects the method as part of the first message, and if the responder replies with a type 1 error message along with the information string "Method not supported", the standard does not tell an implementation how to act upon this information string for negotiation purposes. An adversary can fake an error message, and there is no algorithm that is specified to ensure that a common available authentication mechanism is always selected. In particular, note that

Sect. 5.1 in the specification states that if processing fails for some reason, then "typically" an error message is sent, processing is terminated, and protocol state is discarded. But negotiation needs us to remember state.

With respect to ciphersuite negotiation, Sect. 5.2.2 of the specification also states "The Initiator MUST NOT change the supported cipher suites and the order of preference in SUITES_I based on previous error messages." However, S_I is sent in the clear, and therefore can be modified by the adversary. It is important to consider what happens if the order of preference in S_I is changed either by the adversary, or by the initiator themselves for some other reason. It might be helpful to include a flag in m_1 to indicate to the responder that a (modified) ciphersuite ordering depends on that from a previous execution.

6   Improvements to the Specification

The EDHOC specification has many points where it can be improved. We discovered a few of these issues in [17], but in this work, we also discuss a couple of new issues. We communicated the points discussed in [17] to the authors of the specification. Here, we also list the protocol developers' response (if any) to being told of these ambiguities in the specification.

6.1   Unclear Intended Use

There are several security goals listed in the specification. However, these goals are informal and imprecisely specified, and the lack of intended usage makes them difficult to interpret. Since we have little indication about use case restrictions, it is also hard to evaluate whether the security goals are the most relevant ones.

In order to identify security goals that might be relevant we made up some user stories corresponding to typical use cases, which helped us identify some subtle points of concern in EDHOC. We communicated these points to the authors of EDHOC.

Non-Repudiation. Access control mechanisms can vary depending on what the underlying application is. A nuclear power-plant might need to keep track of who enters and leaves, but a coffee machine that logs every user and their coffee preference might lead to a privacy concern. This simple thought experiment allowed us to identify that the EDHOC specification did not even consider non-repudiation. When we pointed this out to the authors of the specification, they recognized this concern, and added a discussion about how the various EDHOC methods satisfy (or not) non-repudiation.

Unintended Peer Authentication. In Sect. 3.2 in the specification, the authors state that parties executing EDHOC must be configured such that they only run EDHOC with a restricted (according to some reasonable policy) set of peers. However, the responsibilities of verifying which identity was authenticated is not clearly split between the application and EDHOC and therefore an attack similar in effect to UKS is possible.

Suppose a person configures the restriction policy such that every device in their home is allowed to set up an EDHOC session with any other device in the home. However, the adversary has managed to gain control of one of these devices (say A). Device A is part of the allowed group of devices, so B will accept an EDHOC run with A, even though A is now compromised. If the application in B tasks the EDHOC implementation to establish a security context with C, B will send an initial message to C. However, if A responds to the initial message before C can, the specification does not require B to verify that ID_R matches what is expected for C. A valid EDHOC implementation may then look up the appropriate credentials for A, complete the execution and deliver the security context to the application. The application gets no indication of that the security context is shared with A rather that C as intended.

A straight forward check that the received ID_R matches the expected identity thwarts the problem. We included this check in our model. We communicated this to the authors of EDHOC, who in the latest version of the specification, added that EDHOC makes ID_R available to the application, and added an appendix D listing credential validations that the application must take care of.

Denial of Service. Denial of Service (DoS) attacks for IoT protocols are well-studied, but DoS aspects particular to EDHOC is not. The specification does not include any specific measures countering such attacks, but assumes the application takes care of it.

Section 8.7 of the latest version of the EDHOC specification [23] gives two recommendations for countering DoS attacks. First, EDHOC relies on lower layers to mitigate DoS, and an example of DoS countermeasures is given: checking the return address upon receipt of the first message. Second, a recommendation is given that applications may try to determine (in some way) that a seemingly valid message is in fact probably a forgery and should be ignored or cause the protocol to abort.

No recommendation is given on how to minimize DoS effects stemming from the use of error messages, which can be used in a relatively arbitrary way in EDHOC (see Sect. 5). We now elaborate on some considerations that the application developers need to take into account.

As in the IKEv2 DDoS analysis by [16], the responder in EDHOC is more vulnerable than the initiator. The key similarity is that the initiator enjoys identity protection in the first message. None of the elements in the first EDHOC message can be proved by the responder to be invalid, as long as the format is correct and the chosen elliptic curve points lie on the chosen curve. Additionally, execution may require the responder to obtain and verify certificate chains. For example, the content of the ad_1 information element may need the responder to take further action. Since EDHOC is designed for constrained devices, this asymmetry needs to be considered even more carefully than for IKEv2 [16].

The asymmetry between the adversary's effort towards the first message and that of the responder may hence be significant and the possibility for applications to select which entity acts as initiator and which acts as responder may important. EDHOC is profiled to work in conjunction with CoAP and OSCORE [19]. The profiling locks the EDHOC initiator role to the CoAP client role and hence reduces the possibilities to change the EDHOC roles according to DoS vulnerability preferences.

Reflection attacks are another risk. These are attacks where an adversary spoofs the source address of a victim in a message and thereby tricks the responder into sending a message to the victim. EDHOC suggests using a return path reachability method similar to IKEv2. Note that even such reachability mechanisms can easily be used to make a responder send reachability requests to arbitrary addressable targets. However, such mechanisms might require that unsolicited reachability requests be discarded, limiting the effects of anonymous DoS attacks. In situations where the responder does not need to perform additional communications to verify certificates etc, a reachability mechanism may be more expensive in terms of time and storage compared to continuing with the protocol while keeping a half-open state for a period of time. However, if round-trip times are large, and half-open states hence are kept by the receiver for a long time, a reachability mechanism can trade communication for storage.

EDHOC responders querying external servers for certificate revocation checks or lookups may cause systems-level issues if many distributed EDHOC responders frequently queries such servers when DoSed by clients.

An adversary may also send forged error messages (see Sect. 5), and specifically reject proposed ciphersuites. The EDHOC specification recommends the initiator to not try that ciphersuite with the responder again in a new session. If the adversary rejects all options for an initiator this way, it can prevent communication between the initiator and that responder until the initiator's cache is cleared. Potentially, an adversary could lock a party of a group out of communication altogether this way.

6.2 Unclear Security Model

In addition to unclear contexts in which EDHOC can be used, the specification also does not provide enough detail about adversary capabilities. The four different cryptographic cores included in EDHOC are based on academic protocols which are designed to work with highly specific but potentially different adversary models. Since SIGMA cannot protect against compromised ephemeral keys, the authors of EDHOC felt that considering the compromise of ephemeral keys separately from that of long-term keys was not required [8]. The reason was presumably based on the fact that the SIG-SIG method was modeled closely on the SIGMA-I variant of SIGMA, and that it would be preferable to obtain a homogeneous security level among the EDHOC methods [17]. However, this only holds true for situations where one is only interested in the session key confidentiality for an ongoing session. Secure modules, in addition to being able to store long-term keys, are useful in other ways too. They also provide weak Post-Compromise Security (PCS) guarantees as discussed above. Upon discussion with the authors, they included recommendations on storing long-term keys, and how to perform operations on these keys inside a secure module.

6.3 Session Key Material

As we have seen, EDHOC establishes some session-key material, which can be fed into the EDHOC-Exporter to derive session keys. This key material is directly influenced by P_e and a party's secret static long-term key, if they use STAT. As mentioned earlier, mutual explicit injective agreement cannot be obtained for P_I. This might prove to be a problem, and we proposed three potential alternatives for addressing this to the EDHOC authors.

- Include ID_I or a hash thereof in the first and second messages: This increases message size and also leaks the initiator's identity.
- Derive session-key material without using P_I: This deviates from the structure of protocols like OPTLS from which the STAT-based methods draw heavy inspiration. In those protocols, including P_I while computing session-key material is crucial to obtaining resistance against the compromise of the initiator's ephemeral key.
- Include a fourth message from the responder to the initiator which contains a MAC based on information obtained using P_I:

While the last option increases the number of messages in the protocol, the EDHOC authors decided to go with this option for situations where it is necessary to provide explicit injective agreement on P_I.

7   Conclusions and Future Work

As part of this paper, we modeled all four authentication methods of the EDHOC protocol using the Tamarin verification tool. We extended the protocol model by [17] to include a TEE that performs operations using the long-term key of a party. Additionally, we strengthened their adversary model by granting the adversary access to all parties' TEEs prior to the protocol execution (and also afterwards). This allowed us to model weak PCS properties.

We used a server with 2 Intel(R) Xeon(R) Gold 6242 CPU @ 2.80GHz, which had a total of 32 cores / 64 threads, and of the total 384GiB, the server allotted 256GiB of memory for the Tamarin job. We report both the time taken to complete the task ("real time") and the CPU time spent on the task ("user time"). Time measurements are rounded to the nearest second. We formulated and verified the following properties in a precise adversary model with controlled access to TEEs and a precise modeling of XOR.

- Injective agreement for both I and R
- Implicit agreement for both I and R
- Secrecy (PFS and weak PCS) for the session-key material
- Secrecy and integrity of ad_3

Different EDHOC methods provide different degrees of agreement. Therefore, we differentiate between agreement on a full set of parameters S_F, and a partial set of parameters S_P. The set S_P consists of the following pieces of information: the identity of the responder, roles, context identifiers C_I and C_R, cipher suites S_I, and session-key material excluding P_I. For injective agreement, when the initiator uses a STAT method, they are ensured agreement only on this above set of parameters. The set S_F is the set S_P along with the initiator's identity and P_I. The responder is guaranteed injective agreement on the parameters S_F, irrespective of what method they run, while the initiator is guaranteed injective agreement on S_F as long as they run a SIG method. Implicit agreement can be reached for both parties on the set S_F. In addition, mutual entity authentication,

UKS- and KCI-resistance can be inferred from the verified properties. We present the results in Table 2.

Mutual entity authentication, UKS- and KCI-resistance can be inferred from the verified properties.

Table 2. Verified properties. S_P contains roles, responder identity, session-key material (excluding P_I), C_I, C_R, and S_I. S_F is S_P, the initiator identity, and P_I. †: For SIG-STAT and STAT-STAT implicit authentication using the full XOR model the verification had to be abandoned at 14246m43s and 2057m47s of computation time, respectively. The time reported is for verification under the simplified XOR modeling of message 2. ‡: When the initiator is using STAT mode we cannot get explicit agreement on the initiator's own key material, therefore in these two cases we check injective agreement for all key material except P_I.

Lemma \ Method	SIG-SIG	SIG-STAT	STAT-SIG	STAT-STAT
Injective agreement / I	S_F	S_F	S_P‡	S_P‡
Injective agreement / R	S_F	S_F	S_F	S_F
Time (real/user)	3m10.782s / 76m23.828s	52m57.153s / 1909m1.455s†	5m32.432s / 139m36.018s	30m54.891s / 848m36.833s
Implicit agreement / I	S_F	S_F	S_F	S_F
Implicit agreement / R	S_F	S_F	S_F	S_F
Time (real/user)	3m34.222s / 89m41.770s	6m46.187s / 180m6.615s	10m34.228s / 253m22.845s	1m32.187s / 67m2.723s †
Session key secrecy	✓	✓	✓	✓
Time (real/user)	1m23.317s / 52m16.347s	3m54.009s / 155m54.834s	12m33.884s / 457m32.698s	20m40.391s / 915m15.590s
Secrecy of AD3	✓	✓	✓	✓
Integrity of AD3	✓	✓	✓	✓
Time (real/user)	2m39.727s / 101m2.371s	5m51.728s / 223m59.728s	5m51.728s / 223m59.728s	46m0.643s / 1786m3.825s

We identified an attack where an adversary can force initiators to establish an OSCORE security context with a different party than the application using EDHOC intended, and proposed a simple mitigation. We discussed how the IETF may extract and better define security properties to enable easier verification. We also discussed some aspects of the protocol with respect to error handling and denial of service attacks.

We verified each method in isolation, and leave as future work to verify whether the methods are secure under composition.

7.1 A Note About the Version of EDHOC

In this work, we have analyzed the EDHOC specification as of July 2020 [22]. Our analysis also applies to v5 of the specification (February 2021), but newer versions exist. The latest version at the time of writing is v15 (July 2022) [23], which, among other things, differ from v5 in terms of some inputs to the key derivations. Modeling the new key derivation function would have needed sweeping changes across our entire formal model, and due to paucity of time, we could not modify the Tamarin model to be up to date with the current version. However, we do refer to various aspects (error handling, denial of service etc.) of this latest version, in Sects. 5 and 6. Modeling the latest version of the protocol is also left as future work.

Acknowledgements. This work was partially supported by the Wallenberg AI, Autonomous Systems and Software Program (WASP) funded by the Knut and Alice Wallenberg Foundation. We are grateful to Göran Selander, John Mattsson and Francesca Palombini for clarifications regarding the specification.

References

1. Blake-Wilson, S., Johnson, D., Menezes, A.: Key agreement protocols and their security analysis. In: Darnell, M. (ed.) Cryptography and Coding 1997. LNCS, vol. 1355, pp. 30–45. Springer, Heidelberg (1997). https://doi.org/10.1007/BFb0024447
2. Blanchet, B.: An efficient cryptographic protocol verifier based on prolog rules. In: Proceedings of IEEE CSFW-14, pp. 82–96 (2001)
3. Bruni, A., Jørgensen, T.S., Petersen, T.G., Schürmann, C.: Formal verification of ephemeral Diffie-Hellman over COSE (EDHOC). In: Proceedings of SSR, pp. 21–36 (2018)
4. Cohn-Gordon, K., Cremers, C., Garratt, L.: On post-compromise security. In: IEEE 29th Computer Security Foundations Symposium, CSF 2016, Lisbon, Portugal, 27 June - 1 July 2016. pp. 164–178. IEEE Computer Society (2016). https://doi.org/10.1109/CSF.2016.19
5. de Saint Guilhem, C.D., Fischlin, M., Warinschi, B.: Authentication in key-exchange: definitions, relations and composition. In: Proceedings of IEEE CSF, pp. 288–303 (2020). https://doi.org/10.1109/CSF49147.2020.00028
6. Dolev, D., Yao, A.: On the security of public key protocols. IEEE Trans. Inf. Theory **29**(2), 198–208 (1983)
7. Dreier, J., Hirschi, L., Radomirovic, S., Sasse, R.: Automated unbounded verification of stateful cryptographic protocols with exclusive OR. In: Proceedings of IEEE CSF, pp. 359–373 (2018)
8. EDHOC authors: Personal communication (2020)
9. Hristozov, S., Huber, M., Xu, L., Fietz, J., Liess, M., Sigl, G.: The cost of OSCORE and EDHOC for constrained devices. In: Joshi, A., Carminati, B., Verma, R.M. (eds.) CODASPY 2021: Eleventh ACM Conference on Data and Application Security and Privacy, Virtual Event, USA, 26–28 April 2021, pp. 245–250. ACM (2021). https://doi.org/10.1145/3422337.3447834
10. Krawczyk, H.: SIGMA: The 'SIGn-and-MAc' approach to authenticated Diffie-Hellman and its use in IKE protocols. In: Proceedings of CRYPTO, pp. 400–425 (2003)
11. Krawczyk, H.: HMQV: a high-performance secure Diffie-Hellman protocol. In: Shoup, V. (ed.) CRYPTO 2005. LNCS, vol. 3621, pp. 546–566. Springer, Heidelberg (2005). https://doi.org/10.1007/11535218_33
12. Krawczyk, H., Eronen, P.: HMAC-based extract-and-expand key derivation function (HKDF). RFC 5869 (May 2010). https://rfc-editor.org/rfc/rfc5869.txt
13. Krawczyk, H., Wee, H.: The OPTLS protocol and TLS 1.3. In: Proceedings of IEEE EuroS&P 2016, pp. 81–96 (2016)
14. Lowe, G.: A hierarchy of authentication specification. In: Proceedings of IEEE CSFW-10, pp. 31–44 (1997)
15. Meier, S., Schmidt, B., Cremers, C., Basin, D.A.: The TAMARIN prover for the symbolic analysis of security protocols. In: Proceedings of CAV, pp. 696–701 (2013)
16. Nir, Y., Smyslov, V.: Protecting internet key exchange protocol version 2 (IKEv2) implementations from distributed denial-of-service attacks. RFC 8019 (2016). https://doi.org/10.17487/RFC8019. https://www.rfc-editor.org/info/rfc8019

17. Norrman, K., Sundararajan, V., Bruni, A.: Formal analysis of EDHOC key establishment for constrained iot devices. In: di Vimercati, S.D.C., Samarati, P. (eds.) Proceedings of the 18th International Conference on Security and Cryptography, SECRYPT 2021, 6–8 July 2021, pp. 210–221. SCITEPRESS (2021). https://doi.org/10.5220/0010554002100221

18. Norrman, K., Sundararajan, V., Bruni, A.: Code repository. https://www.dropbox.com/sh/y3dk6t421040mq9/AADct4SSGOhOlbx6mFszvq-da?dl=0 (2022)

19. Palombini, F., Tiloca, M., Höglund, R., Hristozov, S., Selander, G.: Profiling EDHOC for CoAP and OSCORE. Internet-Draft draft-ietf-core-oscore-edhoc-03, Internet Engineering Task Force (2022). https://datatracker.ietf.org/doc/draft-ietf-core-oscore-edhoc/03/

20. Schmidt, B., Meier, S., Cremers, C.J.F., Basin, D.A.: Automated analysis of Diffie-Hellman protocols and advanced security properties. In: Proceedings of IEEE CSF, pp. 78–94 (2012)

21. Selander, G., Mattsson, J.P., Palombini, F.: Ephemeral Diffie-Hellman Over COSE (EDHOC) (2018). https://datatracker.ietf.org/doc/html/draft-selander-ace-cose-ecdhe-08. iETF Internet-Draft

22. Selander, G., Mattsson, J.P., Palombini, F.: Ephemeral Diffie-Hellman Over COSE (EDHOC). Internet-Draft draft-ietf-lake-edhoc-00, Internet Engineering Task Force (2020). https://datatracker.ietf.org/doc/draft-ietf-lake-edhoc/00/

23. Selander, G., Mattsson, J.P., Palombini, F.: Ephemeral Diffie-Hellman Over COSE (EDHOC). Internet-Draft draft-ietf-lake-edhoc-15, Internet Engineering Task Force (Jul 2022). https://datatracker.ietf.org/doc/draft-ietf-lake-edhoc/15/

24. Xu, S., Zhao, Y., Ren, Z., Wu, L., Tong, Y., Zhang, H.: A symbolic model for systematically analyzing TEE-based protocols. In: Meng, W., Gollmann, D., Jensen, C.D., Zhou, J. (eds.) ICICS 2020. LNCS, vol. 12282, pp. 126–144. Springer, Cham (2020). https://doi.org/10.1007/978-3-030-61078-4_8

Putting the Pieces Together: Model-Based Engineering Workflows for Attribute-Based Access Control Policies

Marius Schlegel$^{(\boxtimes)}$ and Peter Amthor

TU Ilmenau, Ilmenau, Germany
{marius.schlegel,peter.amthor}@tu-ilmenau.de

Abstract. Although being well-adopted and in widespread use, attribute-based access control (ABAC) remains a hard-to-master security paradigm in application software development. Despite considerable research towards ABAC policy engineering and ABAC policy correctness, this mainly is because there is still no unified workflow to encompass both the versatility of application domains and the strong guarantees promised by formal modeling methods. This work contributes to improving this situation. By presenting a flexible, yet highly formalized modeling scheme for designing and analyzing ABAC policies (DABAC), a reference implementation in Rust (dabac-rs), and a reference architecture for its integration into applications (APPSPEAR) including developer support (appspear-rs), we put together loose pieces of a tool-supported model-based security engineering workflow. The effectiveness of our approach is demonstrated based on a real-world engineering scenario.

Keywords: Model-based security engineering · Security policies · ABAC · Access control models · Formal methods · Rust

1 Introduction

Security policies implement the security properties of IT systems and are highly critical system and application components. As a consequence, their development must meet paramount correctness requirements, which in turn mandates highly efficient engineering based on formal methods for modeling and analysis. A unified workflow for engineering security policies using standardized formalized artifacts is *model-based security policy engineering* (MSPE) [12,42,44]. As a generalization of traditional software engineering, MSPE comprises four steps (see Fig. 1): Model Engineering, Model Analysis, Model Implementation, and Model Integration.

First, in the Model Engineering step, the informal policy representation is formalized (*model*) and its correctness conditions (*model properties*) are defined. Second, during the Model Analysis step, formal methods are applied to verify a *model instance* (initialized model components according to the policy) against the latter. Third, in the Model Implementation step, the model instance verified so far is translated into *(model) source code* for implementation. Forth and finally, in the Model Integration step, the model code is integrated into the *runtime environment (RTE)* of the respective system or application security architecture.

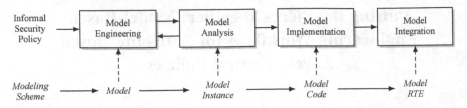

Fig. 1. The workflow of model-based security policy engineering (MSPE). Formal and coding artifacts are printed italic, dashed arrows denote "used-in".

The choice of formal model semantics is crucial because the security policy rules must be adequately formalizable. Attribute-based access control (ABAC) has become the de facto semantical paradigm for access control (AC) models [17,18,21,24] since it suits a broad range of application scenarios, such as grid computing [26], IoT [14], and large, distributed information systems [28]. In comparison to previously popular models, ABAC solves several issues regarding expressiveness, granularity, scalability, and context-awareness. Authorizations depend on the user, object, and environment attributes involved in access requests. Access decisions may change if attribute values change.

Due to the broad application range, ABAC models have specialized and diversified. Adapting MSPE to ABAC is not trivial, as each of the MSPE steps requires certain distinguished, reusable artifacts and tool support. In recent years, the AC community contributed many important pieces to this comprehensive puzzle: specialized policy engineering and mining approaches [29,47], the NIST ABAC standardization [21], numerous application-specific ABAC models, as well as implementation support and enforcement environments [18].

Modeling schemes [13,17,24] are an important building block for unifying the individual solutions: By providing formal toolboxes of predicates, set-theoretical expressions, automata theory, etc., modeling schemes support engineers in choosing model formalisms suitable for policy specification, the analysis of correctness properties, and implementation. In [38], we introduce DABAC: a novel modeling scheme that (1.) models protection state dynamics in an automaton calculus enabling analyses of undecidable model properties (e. g. state reachability properties used to foresee privilege escalation vulnerabilities) and unlocking ABAC models for a broad range of automaton-based model analysis approaches while (2.) preserving the expressiveness of state-of-the-art ABAC models.

This paper is a revised and extended version of [38]. We aim to put together the pieces to complete the overall puzzle: The goal of this paper is to tailor the entire MSPE workflow to ABAC policies. In detail, we made the following changes and extensions to achieve this goal:

- The problem of model engineering is introduced from a process-oriented point of view, highlighting the importance of tool-based integration and interoperation of formal methods (Sect. 1).
- The definition and discussion of DABAC as a core contribution is retained (Sect. 2), but we reduced a discussion of formal methods for model safety analysis (Sect. 2.3), which can be found in specialized publications ([7,39]).

- In an additional section (Sect. 3), the latest research in putting the modeling-scheme approach of DABAC into practice is presented: We describe a prototypical implementation of a policy logic evaluator in the Rust programming language (Sects. 3.1 and 3.2) as well as the design and implementation of a reference monitor framework for the architectural integration of DABAC policies (Sect. 3.3).
- Beyond a practical application scenario for DABAC (Sects. 4.1 and 4.2), which is retained from the original paper, we went beyond the theory by showcasing this scenario's policy implementation through the tools and architecture introduced (Sect. 4.3).
- In addition, we have expanded the discussion of related work (Sect. 5) to reflect the new focus of the paper.

The paper is organized as follows: In Sect. 2, we present the DABAC modeling scheme, ready-made patterns for defining privilege escalation (safety) properties, and an analysis approach. Subsequently, we describe the implementation of DABAC models, the specification of DABAC policies, and their integration into the APPSPEAR security architecture framework [35, 36] (Sect. 3). In Sect. 4, we demonstrate the ABAC-tailored MSPE workflow for an IoT healthcare scenario. Finally, Sect. 5 gives an overview of related work and Sect. 6 concludes the paper.

2   Model Engineering and Analysis

The formal basis of MSPE is a flexible modeling scheme as a calculus that (1.) remains close to the informal policy in its semantics and (2.) allows formal analyses regarding application-relevant security properties at the same time. To address these goals this section introduces DABAC: Sect. 2.1 details its requirements in light of the MSPE workflow; more precisely, how it should support simulative, dynamic analyses and iterative model refinement. Sect. 2.2 then defines its formalisms on three levels of abstraction: primitive model components, model dynamics, and model safety. Sect. 2.3 finally discusses its integration in model analyses.

2.1   Requirements

ABAC Expressiveness. To support the broad range of real-world ABAC applications, a modeling scheme must be sufficiently expressive and streamlined to use. As a few examples, this includes application domains such as vehicular networks [19], cloud and edge computing [14], or hospital information systems [28, 32]. For the design of DABAC, this means that an ABAC feature typical for such distributed application scenarios has to be supported: to consider both the internal state of the AC system as well as its external context for making an access decision. Examples of the latter, also called *environmental information* [11, 17], are notifications from third-party systems, sensor values that depend on physical conditions, or threat information for risk management. Such information is observed from external sources, but has an impact on the internal logic of the AC system; thus, context needs to be modeled as distinct entities, attributes, and attribute values, respectively. Consequently, though it is used in access decision-making, an AC system has no influence on possible context changes.

Model Engineering. A core concept of MSPE is reiterative model refinement: a necessary result of both refined policy requirements (as part of Model Engineering) and revised policy rules (as an outcome of Model Analysis). Thus, a key requirement for modeling ABAC policies is the flexibility of modeling abstractions, which primarily means formal artifacts for attribution and attribute evaluation. We therefore require DABAC to support (1.) indirect attribution (attributes which are attributed themselves, e. g. role attributes in parameterized RBAC models [41]), and (2.) both enumeration-based and formula-based attribute evaluation [15].

Model Analysis. As with any AC model class, dynamic properties of ABAC models are undecidable in the most general case (commonly called *safety* properties [6]). To allow reasoning about instances of this problem class, even without a priori knowledge about their particular decidability class, we settle for heuristic algorithms that simulate dynamic model behavior. In previous work, we have described a specialized automaton calculus (*dynamic model core* [3,5,39]), which serves as the formal basis of such analyses. Therefore, we require DABAC to enable (1.) the definition of core-based model instances by design, and (2.) the definition of application-specific safety definitions based on the model's abstractions. This enables the reuse of safety analysis methods for dynamic RBAC models [37].

Model Implementation. For the integration into AC systems, we require DABAC's syntax to be reusable as a functional model specification. This includes (1.) specification of administrative and non-administrative policy interface, (2.) data structure specification for internal state, and (3.) interface specification of external state, if required by the application. As a goal of ongoing research, these are also prerequisites of semi-automatic policy logic implementation and runtime monitoring of policy invariants (cf. Sect. 6).

2.2 DABAC

Any DABAC model instance is defined on three semantical abstraction levels:

First, *primitive model components* are artifacts used to formally structure a policy. DABAC distinguishes them into *families* for (1.) sets of elementary identifiers that express entities and attribute values; (2.) relations, mappings, or boolean expressions that express attribution and authorization rules.

Second, *model dynamics* are expressed as a deterministic automaton $\langle \Gamma, \Sigma, \Delta, Perm \rangle$ consisting of

1. the *state space* Γ: a set of protection states;
2. the *input set* Σ: a set of possible inputs that may trigger state transitions, based on parameterized operations made available by the AC system;
3. the *state transition scheme (STS)* $\Delta \subseteq \Sigma \times \mathscr{P}(Perm) \times \Phi$: state transition pre- and post-conditions for any input $\sigma \in \Sigma$;[1]
4. the *permissions set Perm*: a set of identifiers for fine-grained access conditions.

---

[1] Φ denotes the set of expressions in first-order logic.

Table 1. Summary of DABAC families [38]. For each row, $n, m \in \mathbb{N}$ are independent.

	Internal	External
EN	$EN = \{E_1, \ldots, E_n\}$, where $E_{1,\ldots,n}$ are policy-specific sets of internal entities	$EN^{\text{ext}} = \{E_{n+1}, \ldots, E_{n+m}\}$, where $E_{n+1,\ldots,n+m}$ are policy-specific sets of external entities
AV	$AV_i = \{V_1, \ldots, V_n\}$, where $V_{1,\ldots,n}$ are policy-specific sets of internal attribute values of indirection degree $0 \leq i \leq i_{\max}$	$AV_i^{\text{ext}} = \{V_{n+1}, \ldots, V_{n+m}\}$, where $V_{n+1,\ldots,n+m}$ are policy-specific sets of internal attribute values of indirection degree $0 \leq i \leq i_{\max}$
AA	$AA_0 = \{att : E \to V \mid E \in EN \wedge (\exists V' \in AV_0 : V = V' \vee V = \mathscr{P}(V'))\}$, where att are internal direct attribute mappings; $AA_i = \{att : V_{i-1} \to V_i \mid V_{i-1} \in AV_{i-1} \wedge (\exists V_i' \in AV_i : V_i = V_i' \vee V_i = \mathscr{P}(V_i'))\}$, where att are internal attribute mappings of indirection degree $1 \leq i \leq i_{\max}$	AA_i^{ext} are external attribute mappings analogous to $AA_i, 0 \leq i \leq i_{\max}$
AR	$AR = \{auth_p : [v_1, \ldots, v_{n_p}] \to \mathbb{B}, n_p \in \mathbb{N} \mid p \in Perm \wedge (\exists V_k \in AV \cup AV^{\text{ext}} : v_k \in V_k \vee v_k \in \mathscr{P}(V_k), 1 \leq k \leq n_p)\}$, where $auth_p$ are authorization functions for each permission p, which map a vector of (internal or external) AV elements to a boolean decision value	*not applicable*

Third, a *safety property* expresses the analysis question that the model should be checked against.

Practical model engineering may not iterate through these levels of abstractions in a sequential manner. Due to their heavy interrelations (e. g. a safety property depends on both primitive model components and state definition), they are inherently subject to refinement and reiteration. In favor of a concise discussion, we will now address these three levels in sequence.

Primitive Model Components. Any ABAC decision is based on three variables: which entities are involved, which attributes are associated with them, and is there an access rule for authorizing the requested operation. In DABAC, these information are reflected in four families that subdivide primitive model components (see Table 1 for their formal definitions):

Entities (*EN*) is a set of atomic entity identifiers. In DABAC, an entity is any abstraction immediately involved in an access, both actively or passively (such as users, principals, applications, sessions, devices);

Attribute Values (*AV*) is a set of values that are subject to access rules evaluation (such as user age, login time of a session, numerical sensor value);

Attribute Association (*AA*) is a mapping from an EN or AV component to an AV component (attribution with a single value) or its power set (attribution with multiple values);

Access Rule (*AR*) is a set of logical formulas over primitive model components.[2] For each permission in *Perm*, an AR component contains at least one formula which evaluates to a boolean value for a vector of AV elements as arguments.

We allow for any set of identifiers to be countable but possibly infinite. In the subsequent discussion, the following notation conventions apply: In a formal context, we denote sets representing these families by their italic symbol. When part of prose, we use upright abbreviations as follows: "an EN" stands for "a component from the entities family", "element of an EN" stands for "an element in a set which is an EN", and so on for the other families.

The modeling scheme regards these families as sets of primitive model components, each a formal artifact of a DABAC model instance. The choice of families explicitly aims at fundamental ABAC policy semantics, enabling to involve both MSPE and application domain experts in reiterative model engineering.

Note that the definition of AV and AA not only allows for direct attribution, but also to use AV elements as arguments for AA (indirect attribution requirement). Based on [4], each attribute association AV_i is parameterized by an *indirection degree i*, which denotes if the domain of the respective mappings is from *EN* (direct attribution) iff $i = 0$, or from AV_i (indirect attribution) iff $0 < i \leq i_{max}$ (where i_{max} denotes the maximum indirection degree in a model). When used without an index, the respective set symbol denotes any possible indirection degree, i. e. $AV = \bigcup_{0 \leq i \leq i_{max}} AV_i$ and similar for *AA*.

Another requirement not addressed so far relates to the requirement of environmental information used for access decision-making. For any DABAC instance, we explicit distinguish between internal and external domain: the internal domain (also called authorization domain) contains any local information and any authorization rules of the modeled AC system. The external domain (information domain) contains observable, external information, which cannot be controlled by the AC system: it cannot effect, anticipate, or causally explain any changes in the external domain. A primitive model component is exclusively part of either the internal or the external domain, which results in a refinement of the semantical families introduced so far: *EN* denote internal entities (creation, destruction, and modification solely occurs within the domain of the AC system), EN^{ext} external entities (observable at the modeled system's interface, while another system controls their observability), *AV* internal attribute values (assigned through mechanisms implemented in the modeled system), AV^{ext} external attribute values (assignment is observable by the modeled system), and finally, AA/AA^{ext} denote attribution mappings for internal/external attribute associations analogous to AV/AV^{ext}. AR describe functionality rather than information. To this end, a distinction based on controllability vs. observability is not applicable. Still, however, since authorization is internal functionality of the modeled system, we will technically treat them as part of the internal domain.

---

[2] For DABAC, we assume these might consist of predicate logic and attribute value enumerations, which might be further restricted by a policy specification language.

Model Dynamics. While primitive model components are used to model the information a policy is based on, we will now detail the automaton calculus used to model its dynamic behavior.

In any DABAC instance, the automaton's state space Γ describes mutable model components. This results in a number of (possibly infinite) state-specific instances of primitive model components from the families EN and AA:

$$\Gamma = \underset{k \in K}{\times} \mathscr{P}(E_k) \times \underset{l \in L}{\times} \{att_{l\gamma} : X \to V \mid att_l : X' \to V \wedge X \subseteq X'\}$$

where $E_k \in EN$ and $K \subseteq \{1, \ldots, |EN|\}$ is an index enumeration of dynamic internal entities sets; $att_l \in AA$ and $L \subseteq \{1, \ldots, |AA|\}$ is an index enumeration of dynamic internal attribute mappings. For addressing model components in a state $\gamma \in \Gamma$, we will use γ as a subscript, i. e. $\gamma = \langle E_{1\gamma}, \ldots, E_{|K|\gamma}, att_{1\gamma}, \ldots, att_{|L|\gamma} \rangle$. Similarly, we will use the regular expression $[\gamma^*]$ as a subscript of dynamics-agnostic model components, such that $E_{k[\gamma^*]} = E_{k\gamma}$ in a DABAC model where $k \in K$, but $E_{k[\gamma^*]} = E_k$ otherwise.

The specific choice of these two families is based on the following considerations. First, we exclude AV from model dynamics since their values are relevant for access decisions only as far as they are assigned to entities – which implies that both EN and AA should be dynamic to enable AC system reconfiguration, whereas adding to or removing from AV does not enable any security-relevant use cases. Second, AR are excluded to prevent a dynamically self-modifying *policy* (in contrast to a dynamically modifiable model state). Since $auth_p \in AR$ are defined based on AV elements (for both enumerated and formula-based ABAC), the immutable nature of the latter requires the former to be immutable as well. Third, any model components in the external domain cannot be modeled dynamic by their nature – simply because any possible changes of these are not controlled by the system itself (formalized as post-conditions in Δ). Nevertheless, since external information might still impact authorization decisions (pre-conditions in Δ), they must not be ignored. Semantically, we call them *transient* w. r. t. dynamics; from an automaton point of view, however, they are treated similar to static internal components (whose actual mutability is unknown).

For model engineering, we can summarize the instantiation of a DABAC model as a definition of formal artifacts for primitive model components, which are categorized in three dimensions: (1.) one of the DABAC family, (2.) internal or external, (3.) static, dynamic, or transient. Tool support for this process as well as model implementation semantics should then support the engineer by enforcing the semantic constraints between these dimensions.

Both the process of access-decision-making and dynamic mutation of model components is formalized through the automaton's interface Σ (parameterized input operations), STS Δ (state-change rules) and permissions set *Perm*. *Perm* is a set of atomic identifiers. We then define Σ as $\Sigma = \{\langle op, [a_1, \ldots, a_{n_{op}}] \rangle \mid op \in OP \wedge (\exists A_k \in EN \cup EN^{ext} \cup AV \cup AV^{ext} : a_k \in A_k, 1 \leq k \leq n_{op})\}$, where OP is a set of atomic identifiers for access operations and $[a_k]$ is a vector of operation-specific argument values from either EN or AV.

Finally, a model's STS is expressed through pre-conditions (access decision rules) and post-conditions (model component mutations) for each state transition to be authorized via an operation op. We formalize it as a set of tuples $\Delta \subseteq \Sigma \times \mathscr{P}(Perm) \times \Phi$, where each $\langle \sigma = \langle op, [a_k]_{k=1}^{n_{op}} \rangle, Perm_{op}, \phi_{op} \rangle$ is written as:

$$\blacktriangleright op(a_1, \ldots, a_{n_{op}}) ::=$$
$$\text{VAR: } v_1 = \phi_1, \ldots, v_{m_{op}} = \phi_{m_{op}}$$
$$\text{PRE: } \bigwedge_{p \in Perm_{op}} auth_p([v_{pk}]_{k=1}^{n_p})$$
$$\text{POST: } \phi_{op}$$

In this notation, any operation's pre-condition is a CNF of AR (abbreviated op.PRE) and any post-conditions is a boolean expression ϕ_{op} (abbrev. op.POST). When applied to the automaton calculus, op.PRE describes any state γ to legally transition from, while op.POST describes how γ and any γ' reachable by input word σ differ. For the latter, ϕ_{op} requires redefinition of one or more mutable model components, where $\phi_{op} = $ true for not state-modifying operations (i. e. $\gamma = \gamma'$). For easier readability we allow alias definitions $v_{1,\ldots,m_{op}}$ ($\phi_{1,\ldots,m_{op}} \in \Phi$) which can be used in op.PRE or op.POST. See Fig. 5 for some examples.

Model Safety. For its use in model analysis, a security model needs to be annotated with formal properties that define the actual criteria of model correctness. DABAC aims at a generalized family of dynamic properties: the question of reachability of some defined (here, unintended) protection state. Amongst others, these properties allow reasoning about potential privilege escalation.

In DABAC, authorization functions in AR encode the rules base for any access decision. A potential privilege escalation is characterized by a decision change, based on the same automaton input, after a sequence of protection state transitions. We formalize this as a *permission leak*.

Definition 1 (Permission Leak). *For two states γ and γ' of a DABAC model, γ' leaks a permission $p \in Perm$ w. r. t. γ iff there is either (1.) an $X \in EN$ and an $att \in AA_0$ (direct leakage) or (2.) an $X \in AV$ and an $att \in AA_i, i > 0$ (indirect leakage), such that $\exists \{x_1, \ldots, x_{n_p}\} \subseteq X_{[\gamma]^*} \cap X_{[\gamma']^*}$:*

$$auth_p([att_{[\gamma]^*}(x_h)]_{h=1}^{n_p}) = \text{false} \wedge auth_p([att_{[\gamma']^*}(x_h)]_{h=1}^{n_p}) = \text{true}.$$

Some observations towards this definition should be discussed first. (1.) Potentially, both static and dynamic model components could be subject to a privilege escalation since even a static entity set might be subject to changing attribution. The only exception is a model in which an attribute mapping in AA_0 is static, which formally requires its domain set E to be static as well. Consequently, we use the dynamics-agnostic notation $[\gamma^*]$ as introduced before. (2.) Likewise, both direct and indirect attribute mappings must be taken into account since $auth_p$ definitions are not restricted to require only direct attribute values. (3.) Since privilege escalation is only relevant (and fixable) for the internal domain of our modeled system, safety definitions only include internal model components for the violating state γ'. External components could still contribute to a path in the model's state space for γ' to be reachable, though. (4.) We deliberately ask for leaks affected by such model component values x_h that are already present in γ. The reason for this is practical rather than technical: We agree with [43] that a meaningful safety analysis result should expose entities or indirect attribute values that a model analyst can identify in γ and therefore relate to some actual vulnerability in terms of her policy.

We use Definition 1 to define DABAC safety as follows.

Definition 2 ($\langle p \rangle$**-Safety**). *For a state γ of a DABAC model and a permission $p \in Perm$, is there an input sequence $\sigma_1, \ldots, \sigma_n \in \Sigma^*$ that leads from γ to γ' via Δ such that γ' leaks p w. r. t. γ? If no such sequence exists, γ is called $\langle p \rangle$-safe.*

For any concrete DABAC model, the final step of model engineering is to adapt Definitions 1 and 2 to model-specific EN and AA. By doing so, more practical instances of *safety* (e. g. related to a specific input operation) might be devised. This paves the way for subsequent, tool-based analysis.

Apart from model-adaption, safety definitions also need to be tailored to a particular analysis problem (cf. [43]). The idea here is to add, additionally to p, problem-specific parameters that confine analysis cases to relevant model component values (called analysis *targets*) x_h. These could be security-critical objects, untrusted users, and the like; again, we support iterative MSPE by allowing for a step-by-step increase of granularity here – starting from Definition 2, which only relates to state γ and a permission p as a parameter.

Problem-specific safety analyses are formally based on an analysis *query*, which amends the model-specific safety definition as follows.

Definition 3 (Safety Analysis Query). *A DABAC safety analysis query is a tuple $\langle \gamma_0, p, [\tau_1, \ldots, \tau_n] \rangle$, where $\gamma_0 \in \Gamma$ is a model state to analyze, p is the target permission, and $[\tau_k]_{k=1}^n, \tau_k \in EN \cup AV$ is a vector of additional analysis targets.*

Composed Safety. Apart from spreading singular permissions, authorizing a whole particular operation is an even more interesting analysis use case in practice. To this end, even problem-specific analysis queries can be subject to further refinement, which also requires a corresponding *composed safety* definition. Composed safety can be regarded as a conjoining macro over multiple, operation-specific instances of $\langle p \rangle$-safety for a specific policy. Definitions 4 and 5 give examples for this approach w. r. t. spreading authorization for a particular operation.

Definition 4 ($\langle op \rangle$**-Safety Analysis Query**). *An $\langle op \rangle$-safety analysis query is a tuple $\langle \gamma_0, op, [x_1, \ldots, x_{n_{op}}] \rangle$, where $\gamma_0 \in \Gamma$ is a model state to analyze, op is the target operation to analyze, and $x_{1, \ldots, n_{op}}$ are actual arguments of op.*

Definition 5 ($\langle op \rangle$**-Safety**). *Given an $\langle op \rangle$-safety analysis query $q = \langle \gamma_0, op, [x_1, \ldots, x_{n_{op}}] \rangle$ against a DABAC model such that $\langle \langle op, [a_k]_{k=1}^{n_{op}} \rangle, Perm_{op}, \phi_{op} \rangle \in \Delta$. Is there an input sequence $\sigma_1, \ldots, \sigma_n \in \Sigma^*$ that leads from γ_0 to γ' via Δ such that both of the following is true:*

- $\phi_{op} = \text{true}$ *for the input $\langle op, [x_k]_{k=1}^{n_{op}} \rangle$ in state γ' and*
- $\exists p \in Perm_{op} : \langle p \rangle$*-safety for the query $\langle \gamma_0, p, [x_k]_{k=1}^{n_{op}} \rangle$ is false?*

If no such sequence exists, $\langle op \rangle$-safety for q is true.

2.3 Model Analysis

As an insight dating back to the seminal HRU model [20], safety properties are generally undecidable. This means that without specific assumptions about a model's STS, properties such as in Definition 2 cannot be expected to be verifiable for any arbitrary DABAC model.

This yields two alternative approaches to nevertheless allow for meaningful safety analyses: (1.) to restrict a model w. r. t. its dynamics and, thus, its expressive power (cf. $ABAC_\alpha$ and Admin-CBAC, Sect. 5); (2.) to accept undecidability but aim at the semi-decidable nature of the problem instead. Since our goal is to enable a general-purpose application software MSPE process, we outline an approach that employs DABAC safety definitions for semi-deciding about safety. It leverages the fact that, given a model state γ and another state γ' reachable from γ, it is efficiently decidable whether in γ' the considered safety property is *violated*.

In our previous work we have studied model properties that allow to efficiently find such states, especially in complex and large model instances. Such properties are then exploited by heuristic strategies, one of which we have designed to extract knowledge about execution dependencies in a model's STS – accordingly named *dependency search*. Two algorithms that implement this strategy, DepSearch [5] and WSDepSearch [39], are based on an abstract (and provably terminating) pre-analysis of inter-dependencies between operations, based on the automaton-model specification of a DABAC STS: it searches for necessary pre-condition of an operation, which are established by the post-condition of another operation. Thus, in order to show the unsafety of a given model state, a privilege escalation is deliberately provoked by executing a sequence of STS operations parameterized by a heuristically guided choice of arguments. An algorithm performs the more efficient, the closer an execution sequence's length is to a minimal number of state transitions leading to safety violations. If no such violation is possible however, analysis might never terminate (so despite unprovable, model safety tends to become more likely once an experience threshold of execution steps is exceeded).

For more details on heuristic safety analysis, we refer the reader to [7] and [39]. In the context of the DABAC modeling scheme in an MSPE process, we have so far demonstrated the necessary prerequisites of this model analysis approach in terms of model components and model dynamics definitions, a model-specific safety property, and a corresponding analysis query. These pieces will be put together in an exemplary MSPE workflow in Sect. 4, including an application of the model analysis paradigm outlined here.

3 Model Implementation and Architectural Integration

We have so far discussed the DABAC modeling scheme as an artifact to bridge the semantic gap between an informal security policy and an instance of a formal model. In this section, we will address the next gap that occurs subsequently in the MSPE process: between the analyzed, possibly verified formal model instance and its implementation in software. More specifically, we address (1.) the implementation of policy logic that runs in a trusted RTE (also called *trusted policy server*, TSP) and (2.) how to embed the RTE itself in an application-level security architecture which satisfies the reference monitor principles [9].

Artifacts used for these purposes include policy specification and implementation languages as well as a security architecture framework. Thus, the remainder is structured as follows: Sect. 3.1 gives an overview of our model data structures implementation in the Rust programming language. Sect. 3.2 discusses how policy logic for a specific DABAC instance is implemented, leveraging the state-of-the-art policy specification language *Polar* [30, 31]. Sect. 3.3 finally showcases the integration of this implementation as a TSP in the APPSPEAR security architecture [35, 36].

3.1 Model Components Implementation

To implement a model that is an instance of DABAC, we provide a set of design patterns readily usable by the programmer to correctly and consistently define model data structures and their behavior. These patterns should directly reflect the structure of DABAC, as outlined in Sect. 2.2, to pave the way for an efficient and, most importantly, error-preventing implementation of the actual policy logic.

To foster a more resilient implementation also on the technical level, we opt for Rust [27] as a modern, general-purpose programming language. It explicitly targets and encourages writing correct code with an emphasis on memory safety which contributes to our requirement of a vulnerability-free policy RTE as the core part of an application's TCB. To conform with the MSPE process behind DABAC, Rust also allows for a high degree of generic programming to enable patterns that mimic those behind our formal artifacts. The long-term mindset is that once security-critical parts of an application are written in Rust, the remaining functional code might be as well (at least for applications developed from scratch).

The RTE prototype `dabac-rs`[3] provides implementation patterns on three abstraction levels matching the model abstraction levels introduced in Sect. 2.2. On each level, a Rust *trait* stipulates what the actual model implementer might (or might not) do with parts of the modeling scheme: *Superfamilies* describe capabilities of bare values in a primitive model component: either atomic identifiers or mappings between such; either mutable or immutable.[4] *Families* describe the intended usage of the semantical model component families *EN*, *AV*, or *AA*. A *model instance* stores structural information about the specific DABAC model as a whole.

Superfamilies. Superfamily traits define the exposed behavior of mathematical artifacts, more specifically of inner values wrapped in any model component. Their implementation can be based on optimized data structures by discretion of the implementer. For our prototype, we use ready-made types of `std::collections`.

Listing 1 shows the available distinction on this basic level of semantics, represented by three traits: `SuperAtomic` exposes an atomic-value behavior (e. g. for a user or role identifier). It requires one fixed, copyable identifier type `AtomicT` encapsulated by

---

[3] Ongoing work, available as a Rust crate: https://crates.io/crates/dabac-rs.

[4] Due to semantic overloading with the Rust lifetime `static`, we refrain from using the automaton-related term *static* in this section.

```
1  pub trait SuperAtomic {
2      type AtomicT: Copy;  // identifier type
3      fn get_elem(&self) -> Self::AtomicT;
4  }
5  pub trait SuperMapping<D: Hash, C: Copy> {
6      // partial mapping from D (domain) to C (Co-Domain)
7      fn map(&self, e: &D) -> Option<&C>;
8  }
9  pub trait SuperDynamic: Eq {  // comparable for duplicate checks
10     type ContainerT;  // type of enclosing container
11     // getter for enclosing container:
12     fn container_static() -> &'static Self::ContainerT;
13     // dynamic modifications:
14     fn add_elem(e: Self) -> Result<bool, DABACErr>;
15     fn rem_elem(e: &Self) -> Result<bool, DABACErr>;
16 ... }
```

Listing 1. Superfamily traits for model components (details omitted).

any type to implement such atomic values. `SuperMapping` describes semantics needed for attribute-mappings by two generic types, D and C. It allows implementing partial mappings on any model component type by returning either a wrapped reference to a co-domain value or the standard variant None. `SuperDynamic` is used to distinguish between mutable and immutable primitive model component values. To describe the behavior associated with mutability in terms of our automaton-based calculus, more declarations are needed here: as the listing shows, the trait includes associated functions for basic manipulation operations on the enclosing, static container of the respective value type. This design is necessary because of the call semantics for these methods from a Polar policy (cf. Sect. 3.2). Immutable value types are characterized simply by not implementing this trait.

Implementing these superfamily traits enables a developer to create types for the actual model component values. These do not yet relate to the specific semantic families of DABAC, however.

Families and Prototypes. The actual DABAC family traits fulfill two goals: they (1.) contribute to enforcing model engineering constraints by explicitly requiring (or denying) superfamily traits implemented for each family and (2.) encode additional, more fine-grained knowledge about security-related usage of application data (which may be evaluated during construction and operation of the model instance, see below).

Listing 2 demonstrates both aspects: while `EntityElem` and `AttrValElem` do not add any new capabilities to a type, they both require `SuperAtomic` as a supertrait. Moreover, `AttrValElem` uses a blanket implementation to prevent a developer from implementing `SuperDynamic` on the same type (details omitted here). The other two traits, both to be implemented for AA model components, demonstrate the second goal of encoding fine-grained knowledge: since the possible types for an attribute mapping's domain depend on the degree of indirection n, we provide two different traits here whose implementations are mutually exclusive. This is an example for how `dabac-rs`

```
1  pub trait EntityElem: SuperAtomic {}  // EN components trait
2  pub trait AttrValElem: SuperAtomic {} // AV components trait
3  ...
4  pub trait EntAttrAssocElem<D: EntityElem + Eq + Hash, C: Copy>:
5      SuperMapping<D, C> { ... }  // AA₀ components trait
6  pub trait AttrAttrAssocElem<D: AttrValElem + Eq + Hash, C: Copy>:
7      SuperMapping<D, C> { ... }  // AAₙ:ₙ>₀ components trait
```

Listing 2. Model component family traits (details omitted).

```
1  pub trait SuperComponent {
2      fn get_features(&self) -> Vec<DABACCompFeat>;
3  ... }
4  pub struct DABAC {
5      components: Vec<Box<dyn SuperComponent>>, // model components
6      policy: Oso,                             // policy object
7  }
```

Listing 3. The DABAC type.

leverages language mechanisms to enforce type safety, efficiently checked by the Rust compiler.

Since families traits are supposed to be used with data structures specifically designed for the respective primitive model components, we have included minimal convenience-implementations of these in dabac-rs: a tuple struct Entity<T>(T) for entities that merely encapsulate their identifier and similar types with pre-implemented behavior for AV and AA (including, amongst others, conversion functions to integrate with the Polar policy rules evaluation framework; cf. Sect. 3.2).

It should be explicitly noted that these prototypes are a limiting in a twofold sense: (1.) their minimality prevents the model implementer to (re-)use data types for entity management, e. g. a struct Record that contains function metadata such as creation time, data format, etc. beside the DABAC-related security metadata; (2.) they offer a reduced type safety: since only one single type is provided for each: entities, attribute values etc., their correct evaluation must be ensured by the programmer instead of the compiler.[5]

Model Instance. Finally, a model instance is represented by an instance of the top-level type DABAC (cf. Listing 3). It provides a concise wrapper for two fields: the collection of model components, each represented by an application-defined container type for model component family types (see above), and the rules for authorization (AR) and state transitions (STS). Listing 3 also shows the declaration of one last superfamily trait, SuperComponent: it describes the management capabilities of any model family type wrapper, most importantly their ability to return knowledge about model engineering semantics. This is encoded through an enum DABACCompFeat (cf. Listing 4), whose variants summarize all possible categories of primitive model components introduced

---

[5] At mild boilerplate costs, this last issue can be resolved through explicit type wrapping (*new-type pattern*) [25, pp. 437–438].

```
1  pub enum DABACCompFeat {
2      En,     // EN marker
3      Av(u8), // AV marker with variable indirection degree
4      Aa(u8), // AA marker with variable indirection degree
5      Ar,     // AR marker
6      Ext,    // marker for external values
7      Dyn,    // marker for dynamic components
8  }
9  pub struct DABACComp<T> {
10     pub name: String,
11     pub features: [Option<DABACCompFeat>; 6],
12     pub inner: T,
13 }
```

Listing 4. The DABACComp prototype.

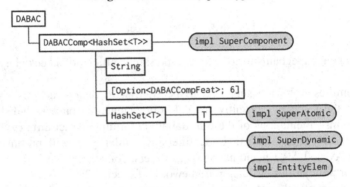

Fig. 2. Possible usage of DABAC types and traits they implement.

in Sect. 2.2, which can be used as "feature markers" for custom model component types. DABAC should always be instantiated as a static singleton.

As with the prototypes for family traits, correct usage of the DABAC singleton is also supported in two ways: (1.) a builder-pattern type DABACBuilder, which allows for both convenience and atomicity of building a sealed DABAC object, (2.) one more prototype usable for model component containers, which seamlessly interacts with DABAC. Listing 4 shows the declaration of this type, DABACComp. Figure 2 visualizes the relationships between these types for a model instantiation.

3.2   Policy Specification

We have so far discussed how programming paradigms enforce an error-preventing implementation of the formal artifacts used for any DABAC model instance. We did not cover, however, the actual policy rules that specify authorization and state-transition behavior (and which, as presented in Sect. 2.2, were subject to a formal safety analysis methodology). Therefore we discuss the implementation of a model's AR and STS in the remainder of this subsection.

```
1  auth_read(age: Integer, class: Pegi) if age >= class;
```

Listing 5. Exemplary definition of $auth_{read} : \mathbb{N}^+ \times V_{PEGI} \rightarrow \mathbb{B}, V_{PEGI} \in AV_0$.

```
1  buy_movie(u: User, o: Movie) if
2      auth_read(u.age, o.rating) and
3      auth_pay(u.balance, o.fee) and
4      UserBalance.deduct(u, o.fee);
```

Listing 6. Exemplary definition of an STS operation $buyMovie(u \in U_\gamma, o \in O_\gamma)$.

```
1  let dabac_model = DABACBuilder::new()
2      .with_comp(&user_comp)
3      ...
4      .with_policy("path/to/policy_file.polar")
5      .build();                        // initialize model
6  ...                                  // some application logic
7  // user 42 requests `read` access on object 8:
8  if dabac_model.op("read", (User(42), Object(8))) { ... }
```

Listing 7. Calling a policy operation on a DABAC instance.

The paramount goal of implementing these formal artifacts is to strictly preserve any guarantees acquired during the model analysis step of MSPE. To this end, we refrain from a semi-formalized approach of language paradigms and ready-made convenience implementations, but instead settle for a tried-and-tested programming framework for AC. Our requirements for the choice of this framework are (1.) semantical flexibility that enables the STS expressiveness required by our modeling scheme, (2.) compatibility with our Rust-implemented framework for the DABAC RTE, (3.) widespread use, maturity and support, and (4.) an open-source license that allows for error-correction and individual adaption if required. One framework that satisfies these properties is the *Oso* library for application-level AC [30]. It provides a policy evaluation machine itself implemented in Rust. For policy specification, Oso relies on the declarative policy specification language *Polar* [31], whose computational power and strong expressiveness complement our model data structures and interfaces already implemented in Rust. We therefore propose a model implementation using both dabac-rs and the oso crate.

Closely following DABAC paradigms, we have separated a model's policy into at least two sets of Polar rules: one allows for an isolated specification (and debugging) of elementary authorization functions (AR family). The other one makes use of these to define the model's STS based on the definition of Δ, where the according Polar rules are defined as logical predicates. Listings 5 and 6 show examples for both, respectively. Note that Integer is a built-in Polar type, while User (EN), Movie (EN), Pegi (AV), and UserBalance (AA) are types made available by implementing them as model components and adding them when the model instance is built. Listing 6 also demonstrates how both pre- (ll. 2–3) and post-conditions (l. 4) are merged in a conjunction (predicate body).

It should be highlighted that, despite semantically supported by Polar, this design for implementing AR and STS is not ideal: While a Polar policy specification can be generated automatically from a DABAC model specification (cf. [8]), its integration still relies on the programmer to correctly implement the manipulation of model component value types, such as in the Rust function UserBalance::deduct in the example. The problem here is that, even if a model's STS correctness could have been verified during the MSPE step of model analysis, it might still be subject to error-introducing human interpretation when implementing parts of it (i. e. those post-conditions) manually. This is subject to ongoing work.

The eventual integrating policy evaluation in dabac-rs is simple (Listing 7): To query access decisions, the DABAC type exposes a convenient interface (function op) equivalent to formal automaton input which evaluates the Oso call query_rule: self.policy.query_rule(rule, args) that again evaluates the Polar policy loaded at model initialization.

3.3   Architectural Integration

Having generated an implementation for an instance of a formally verified DABAC model is the foundation for its integration into a concrete security architecture. For more than two decades, strong approaches for policy integration and enforcement have been established in a wide range of operating systems (OSs) such as Linux, Android, and FreeBSD [46]. Unfortunately, these do not provide support for application-specific ABAC policies, which (1.) control objects at a higher, application-specific abstraction level and (2.) have application-specific AC semantics that are typically different from that at the OS level and also specific for each individual application.

While recently sprouted application-specific AC frameworks such as Casbin [16] and Oso [30] are improving the situation, they do not provide architectural support, leaving developers responsible for an application's security architecture and its implementation. This renders policy protection from unauthorized manipulation hard if not impossible and leads to large, heterogeneous application trusted computing base (TCB) implementations. The lack of a standard for flexible application policy enforcement hinders the streamlined, tool-supported architectural integration of modeling schemes such as DABAC within MSPE.

To address these issues, we propose APPSPEAR [35,36] for architectural integration: (1.) APPSPEAR provides a functional framework for implementing the reference monitor principles at the application layer. (2.) The corresponding developer framework anchors architecture implementation alternatives based on different isolation mechanisms enabling application developers to conveniently balance the rigor of policy enforcement (*effectiveness*) and isolation/communication costs (*efficiency*). (3.) APPSPEAR enables a streamlined integration of DABAC models, which we demonstrate based on the TPS interfaces.

Architecture Design. APPSPEAR satisfies two fundamental architectural requirements: (1.) the reference monitor properties requiring a security policy to be inevitably involved in any security-related action (RM 1), protected from unauthorized manipulation (RM 2), as well as small and simple (enabling verifiability) (RM 3), and (2.) policy flexibility through policy interchangeability. While RM 2 leads to a clear separation between application-related and security-related functionality, policy flexibility

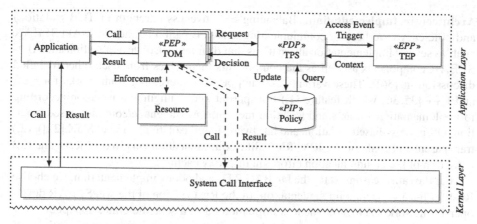

Fig. 3. APPSPEAR's functional architecture [35,36].

requires the separation of authorization logic (*policy decision point*, PDP) and enforcement mechanisms (*policy enforcement points*, PEPs). Furthermore, taking the logical and physical system context typically involved in ABAC policy decisions results in a further structuring of the PDP. The resulting functional architecture of APPSPEAR is illustrated in Fig. 3.

Trusted object managers (TOMs) are architecture components isolating trusted and non-trusted application parts and comprise the functionality for establishing confidentiality, integrity, and authenticity of application objects. Thus, a TOM provides interfaces for actions to an application (e. g. for modifying patient record objects). The interface is implemented via local or remote functions or methods depending on the isolation mechanism. Inspired by object-oriented software design and from a functional point of view, a generic TOM provides a generic object abstraction and abstract basic create, read, update and destroy object management. Concrete applications derive type-specific TOMs and implement the abstract object and functions.

When an application requests an object interaction, the corresponding policy is involved through the interface between a TOM and the TPS. This way, (1.) any interaction is inevitably controlled by the policy and (2.) decision enforcement is tamperproof. TOMs are part of the application TCB and, thus, are isolated from untrusted application logic. Depending on the decision (granted or denied), the results of the object access is returned to the calling application logic function.

The TPS represents the PDP and provides the policy RTE, where (amongst others) a DABAC model might be implemented using dabac-rs. To promote a small TCB perimeter, the TPS is always tailored to an application-specific model – it provides just enough functionality for its respective application while maintaining the interfaces for TOM-to-TPS and TPS-to-TOM communication.

The *trusted event processor* (TEP) is an add-on to provide information about the physical and logical system context. The TEP can be implemented based on asynchronous triggers, which originate from local hardware and software components, e. g. GPS, clock, or temperature sensors. Any access decision of the TPS may also trigger an event needed for logging and auditing.

Architecture Implementation. Balancing effectiveness (strength of TCB isolation) and efficiency (overhead of communicating across isolation boundaries), APPSPEAR enables several implementation alternatives that differently isolate application and APP-SPEAR components as well as the components themselves from each other (detailed discussion in [36]). These variants are supported by developer frameworks for Rust and C++ [35,36] which feature (1.) transparent and configurable isolation according to implementation variants and isolation mechanisms (language/compiler-based isolation, OS/process-based isolation, and hardware-based isolation via Intel SGX [22]), (2.) transparent and configurable RPC/RMI-alike communication via proxy objects, and (3.) reduction of the communication effort via in-proxy caching.

For the same reasons as for the DABAC RTE and policy implementation, we choose Rust for the architecture implementation. In the Rust version of the APPSPEAR developer framework, each component is implemented in a separate crate: `appspear_tom`, `appspear_tps`, and `appspear_tep` each contain the corresponding component's functionality and proxy object pairs (comparable to sockets) for isolation-transparent communication with the application or interacting APPSPEAR components. Moreover, two crates provide additional functionality: `appspear` is a dependency of the application and contains proxy objects for the communication with TOMs and initialization functionality. `appspear_types` contains constants and definitions of the message structs for the communication between application logic and TOM as well as between TOM and TPS and is therefore used by all crates as a dependency.

The choice of isolation mechanisms can be conveniently made via Cargo features which are a mechanism to express conditional compilation and optional dependencies provided by Rust's package and dependency manager.

Policy Integration. The developer framework provides patterns that are reusable and tailorable for the integration of APPSPEAR and DABAC instances into applications. In particular, the integration is achieved in three sequential steps: (1.) the implementation of application-specific TPS and TEP based on the default TPS and TEP implementations of the `appspear_tps` and `appspear_tep` crates[6], (2.) the implementation of an application-specific TOM based on the default TOM implementation of the `appspear_tom` crate, and (3.) the definition of message types for possible application-specific request/result communication patterns derived from the `appspear_types` crate.

First, the DABAC TPS implementation is created in a new crate outside the `appspear_tps` crate (e. g. `mytps`). This requires to instantiate the default DABAC-based TPS implementation (`Tps`) and initialize it with the intended policy implementation. Based on known and defined `CmdReq` and `CmdRes` types (see third step),

---

[6] Since the TEP is typically only isolated lightly (cf. [36]), the explicit consideration of the TEP will not be discussed further in this paper.

```
1  pub trait TTps {
2      fn cmd(&self, req: &CmdReq) -> CmdRes;
3  ... }
4  pub struct Tps {
5      model: dabac_rs::DABAC,
6  }
7  impl TTps for Tps {
8      fn cmd(&self, req: &CmdReq) -> CmdRes { self.model.op(...).into() }
9  ... }
```

Listing 8. TPS implementation (details omitted).

```
1  pub struct MyTps(Tps) {}
2  impl TTps for MyTps {
3      fn cmd(&self, req: &CmdReq) -> CmdRes { self.0.cmd(...) }
4  ... }
```

Listing 9. Application-specific TPS implementation (details omitted).

```
1  pub struct Proxy<T> where T: TTps {
2      tps: T,
3  }
4  impl<T> Proxy<T> where T: TTps {
5      pub fn new(tps: T) -> Proxy<T> { Proxy { tps } }
6      pub fn cmd(&self, req_srlzd: &[u8]) -> Vec<u8> { ... }
7  ... }
```

Listing 10. TPS communication proxy implementation (details omitted).

everything else is plug-and-play. The cmd method is used to execute commands[7] and is used directly by the parent communication proxy (see below).

As an alternative to the generic TPS implementation (Tps), a custom type can be created. The foreign trait TTps specifies the behavior of a TPS, in particular the execution of commands (see Listing 8). This trait cannot be implemented straight-forward for the foreign standard type Tps due to Rust preventing implementations of foreign traits on foreign types (*orphan rule*). A solution for this problem is the *newtype pattern* [25, pp. 437–438]: The wrapper MyTps around the Tps value provides a different type that can implement the trait TTps (Listing 9). The reuse of standard Tps methods is then possible via simple forwarding. Alternatively, application-specific implementations are created. More precisely, the actual policy is called within cmd according to Listing 7.

From an implementation point of view, the TPS is part of the TPS-side communication proxy (for TOM-to-TPS communication and vice versa) using a field in the struct Proxy<T> so that it can pass calls to/from commands directly. For each type of isolation mechanism, a separate communication proxy is implemented. The method cmd is thus specific for a particular isolation mechanism. Listing 10 abstracts from the latter

---

[7] "Command" is an equivalent term to "STS operation" and is used to not to have overload with other "operations" such as on TOM-controlled objects.

property, but shows that the struct (Proxy<T>) uses a generic type parameter with trait bounds to be able to use any TPS implementation that implements the TTps trait.

Essentially the implementation of an application-specific TOM is analogous to that of the TPS in the first step since the same pattern is present: The application-specific implementation TOM (e. g. MyTom) is built based on the TTom trait and then integrated by the TOM-side proxy required for the communication with the application. In addition, the definition of the Call and Result enums for application-logic-to-TOM (and vice versa) communication and the CmdReq and CmdRes enums for TOM-to-TPS (and vice versa) is done in a separate crate (e. g. mytypes) with dependency on the appspear_types crate.

In summary, although the architectural integration requires manual work, this effort is moderate due to the prepared structure of the APPSPEAR developer framework. In the future, we plan to partially automate the generation of TPSs based on the DYNAMO specification language [8] so that a corresponding code skeleton is already compiler-generated.

4   Practical Application

In this section, we demonstrate the DABAC-based MSPE workflow for a scenario of the health care domain. In this scenario, balancing security and usability is practically challenging: confidentiality and integrity of health care data and prevention of unauthorized access to sensors and actuators are critical requirements. Nevertheless, common workflows for patient treatment must be possible anytime. The following sections demonstrate the Model Engineering (Sect. 4.1), Model Analysis (Sect. 4.2), and Model Implementation and Integration (Sect. 4.3) steps of MSPE.

4.1   Model Engineering

The exemplary security policy and the corresponding DABAC model are created for a hospital information system (HIS) within a smart health care environment. The HIS aims at medical data management but also includes remote patient monitoring capabilities based on external medical IoT sensors and actuators (cf. [28, 32]).

Primitive Model Components. *Users* are primary system entities, which are either humans or smart devices. Users perform accesses on: *objects* that represent data objects (e. g. patient-specific electronic health records, EHRs), *sensors* that represent interfaces to health monitoring sensors connected to patients (e. g. clinical thermometers), and *actuators* that represent interfaces to medical actuators connected to patients (e. g. insulin pumps). In model terms, user entities (set U) and object entities (set O) are internal entities. In contrast, both sensor entities (set Sen) and actuator entities (set Act) external entities since they are separated logically and physically from the AC system of the HIS. Subsequently, O represents EHRs, Sen represents thermometers, and Act

$\triangleright$ $auth_{\text{read}}(r_u \in R) \Leftrightarrow r_u \neq \text{rPatient}$

$\triangleright$ $auth_{\text{shareCases}}(I_u \subseteq I, I_o \subseteq I) \Leftrightarrow I_u \cap I_o \neq \emptyset$

$\triangleright$ $auth_{\text{assign}}(r_u \in R) \Leftrightarrow r_u = \text{rManager} \vee r_u = \text{rPhysician}$

$\triangleright$ $auth_{\text{isAssignee}}(r_u \in R, r_{u'} \in R) \Leftrightarrow$
$((r_u = \text{rManager} \wedge r_{u'} = \text{rPhysician}) \vee r_{u'} = \text{rNurse})$

$\triangleright$ $auth_{\text{delegate}}(r_u \in R) \Leftrightarrow r_u = \text{rPhysician}$

$\triangleright$ $auth_{\text{isDelegate}}(r_u \in R) \Leftrightarrow r_u = \text{rPhysician}$

Fig. 4. Exemplary definitions of authorization functions for permissions [38].

represents insulin pumps. The individual elements of these sets are patient-specific; for each, we assume each a one-to-one mapping to patients.

The formalization of the scenario's policy is based on attributes that reflect the organizational structure and workflows of the hospital. Each user is assigned a *role* (e. g. physician, nurse, or patient) that enables accessing passive entities. Additionally, each user is assigned to a hospital *ward* (e. g. internal, ICU, or surgery). Hence, user entities are attributed by two functions att_{UR} and att_{UW} with role and ward attribute values (from R respectively W). For simplicity, we limit to one role and one ward per user.

For the treatment of a disease a user would be assigned to the corresponding ward. Thus, this would give all users who are also assigned to that ward access to their EHR. To ensure that only the doctors and nurses involved in a treatment have access, we introduce another attribute to represent treatment *cases*. Moreover, the policy does not prohibit that personnel assigned to treatments belongs to different wards. In the model, this is represented by an attribute value set I consisting of medical case identifiers (represented by indexing) and att_{UI} and att_{OI}, which attribute (1.) users related to that case (assigned physicians or nurses, patients treated) and (2.) EHR objects that represent the information about that case.

The external entities, thermometer sensors and insulin pump actuators, are attributed as follows: each temperature sensor is attributed with a temperature value from the set *Temp* by att_{ST} and each insulin pump actuator is attributed with a dose value from the set *Dose* by att_{AD}.

Following the components from EN, AV, and AA families, we conclude by defining the AR families. Generally, *AR* contains a set of attribute-checking permissions modeled as authorization functions. Figure 4 contains a selection of definitions with the following semantics:

$auth_{\text{read}}$: The permission read is granted iff r_u is any role other than rPatient.

$auth_{\text{shareCases}}$: The permission shareCases is granted iff given case attribute value sets I_u and I_o have a non-empty intersection.

$auth_{\text{assign}}$: The permission assign is granted for the roles rManager or rPhysician.

$auth_{\text{isAssignee}}$: The permission isAssignee is granted iff either a physician or a nurse is assignee, where only managers can assign cases to physicians.

$auth_{\text{delegate}}$: The permission delegate is granted for the delegator role rPhysician.

$auth_{isDelegate}$: The permission isDelegate is granted for the delegate role rPhysician.

Note that $auth_{delegate}$ and $auth_{isDelegate}$ have different semantics here, their identical definition is merely due to the simplifications of the example scenario. Although making heavy use of roles, we would like to emphasize that this is not a policy which can be immediately modeled using a standard RBAC96 [34], administrative RBAC (ARBAC97) [33], or DRBAC models [37] – $auth_{isAssignee}$, e. g., defines a logical condition on roles assignment which cannot be covered in the permission-assignment relation PA; the condition $auth_{shareCases}$ does not even relate to roles at all.

All described primitive components and their instantiations (cf. automaton's initial state) for our model are summarized in Table 2.

Model Dynamics. In DABAC, model dynamics are defined based on a specialized deterministic automaton. The model dynamics are defined as described in Sect. 2.2 and tailored model-specifically as follows:

- $\Gamma = \mathscr{P}(U) \times \mathscr{P}(O) \times \{att_{UR_\gamma} : U_\gamma \to R \mid U_\gamma \subseteq U\} \times \{att_{UW_\gamma} : U_\gamma \to W \mid U_\gamma \subseteq U\} \times \{att_{UI_\gamma} : U_\gamma \to \mathscr{P}(I) \mid U_\gamma \subseteq U\} \times \{att_{OI_\gamma} : O_\gamma \to \mathscr{P}(I) \mid O_\gamma \subseteq O\}$, where $\gamma = \langle U_\gamma, O_\gamma, att_{UR_\gamma}, att_{UW_\gamma}, att_{UI_\gamma}, att_{OI_\gamma} \rangle \in \Gamma$ is a single protection state;
- $OP = \{$readEHR, appendToEHR, createEHR, deleteEHR, fetchTemp, pushDose, addUser, removeUser, assignCase, delegateCase, revokeCase$\}$;
- Δ is defined by a set of operations according to the identifiers from OP. Generally, users may read or write objects, read but not write sensors, and write but not read actuators.[8] Figure 5 illustrates three representative examples readEHR, assignCase, and delegateCase. Their semantics are as follows:

readEHR represents an operation to read an EHR. A user $u \in U_\gamma$ is allowed to read $o \in O_\gamma$ iff (1.) u is attributed a role $r_u \in R$ other than rPatient, i. e. no patient may read[9] ($auth_{read}$), (2.) u shares cases with o ($auth_{shareCases}$), and (3.) there is at least one user, who shares cases with o and who is from the reader's own ward (last statement in VAR and $auth_{shareCases}$). Given all permission checks evaluate to true, POST does not have any effect on the model state and, thus, evaluates to true.

assignCase represents the assignment of treatment capabilities. A user $u \in U_\gamma$ is allowed to assign a case $i \in I$ to user $u' \in U_\gamma$ iff (1.) u is attributed with role rPhysician or rManager, i. e. the assigner is either a physician or manager ($auth_{assign}$), (2.) the assignee u' is attributed with rNurse or, if u is a manager, rPhysician ($auth_{isAssignee}$), and (3.) u is attributed with case i ($auth_{shareCases}$). Given all permissions are successfully evaluated to true, POST renders a new state by additionally attributing u'.

---

[8] In practice, there might be devices such as ICU bedside monitors which allow both to monitor ("fetch") real-time patient data and to store ("push") history records from newly arrived patients. These could be modeled by a common identifier, both in *Sen* and in *Act*. However, for the sake of simplicity, we assume $Sen \cap Act = \emptyset$.

[9] One might argue that a patient should be allowed to read her own EHR at any time. This could be easily achieved by just removing the $auth_{read}$ authorization clause in PRE. Note that this relaxation cannot be made for appendToEHR.

Table 2. Overview of primitive model components and their instantiation (functions written in relational style) [38].

	Symbol	Description	HIS Instantiation
EN	U	set of user identifiers	{drCox, drKelso, drJD, nurseCarla, nurseLaverne, mrsFriendly, mrBruise, msPregnant, ...}
	O	set of (data) object identifiers	{ehrMrsFriendly, ehrMrBruise, ehrMsPregnant, ...}
EN^{ext}	Sen	set of sensor identifiers	{sThermometerMsPregnant, ...}
	Act	set of actuator identifiers	{actPumpMrsFriendly, ...}
AV_0	R	set of role attribute values	{rPhysician, rPatient, rNurse, rParamedic, rManager, rClerk}
	W	set of ward attribute values	{wInternal, wICU, wSurgery, wCardiology, wMaternity}
	I	set of numerical case identifiers	$I \subseteq \mathbb{N}$
AV_0^{ext}	$Temp$	set of temperature attribute values	$Temp \subseteq \mathbb{N}$
	$Dose$	set of drug dose attribute values	$Dose \subseteq \mathbb{R}$
AA_0	$att_{UR} : U \to R$	user-role-attribution	{⟨nurseCarla, rNurse⟩, ⟨drCox, rPhysician⟩, ⟨drKelso, rPhysician⟩, ...}
	$att_{UW} : U \to W$	user-ward-attribution	{⟨nurseCarla, wInternal⟩, ⟨drCox, wInternal⟩, ⟨drKelso, wMaternity⟩, ...}
	$att_{UI} : U \to \mathscr{P}(I)$	user-cases-attribution	{⟨drKelso, {42}⟩, ...}
	$att_{OI} : O \to \mathscr{P}(I)$	EHR-cases-attribution	{⟨ehrMsPregnant, {42}⟩, ...}
AA_0^{ext}	$att_{ST} : Sen \to Temp$	sensor-temperature-attribution	*not applicable*
	$att_{AD} : Act \to Dose$	actuator-dose-attribution	*not applicable*
AR	AR	set of permission authorization functions	{$auth_{read}$, $auth_{shareCases}$, $auth_{assign}$, $auth_{isAssignee}$, $auth_{delegate}$, $auth_{isDelegate}$, ...}

delegateCase covers medical referrals and treatment delegations in the sense of "a physician assigns another physician responsibility for some case". Thus, a user $u \in U_\gamma$ is allowed to delegate a case $i \in I$ to user $u' \in U_\gamma$ iff (1.) u is attributed with role rPhysician ($auth_{delegate}$), (2.) the delegate u' is attributed with role rPhysician as well ($auth_{isDelegate}$), and (3.) u is attributed with case i ($auth_{shareCases}$). Given all checks evaluate to true, **POST** renders a subsequent state by attributing u' with i.

▶ **readEHR**$(u \in U_\gamma, o \in O_\gamma) ::=$
    VAR: $r_u = att_{UR_\gamma}(u)$, $I_u = att_{UI_\gamma}(u)$, $I_o = att_{OI_\gamma}(o)$, $w_u = att_{UW_\gamma}(u)$,
        $I' = \bigcup_{u' \in U_\gamma \setminus \{u\}, att_{UW_\gamma}(u') = w_u} att_{UI_\gamma}(u')$
    PRE: $auth_{read}(r_u) \wedge auth_{shareCases}(I_u, I_o) \wedge auth_{shareCases}(I', I_o)$
    POST: true

▶ **assignCase**$(u \in U_\gamma, u' \in U_\gamma, i \in I) ::=$
    VAR: $r_u = att_{UR_\gamma}(u)$, $r_{u'} = att_{UR_\gamma}(u')$, $I_u = att_{UI_\gamma}(u)$
    PRE: $auth_{assign}(r_u) \wedge auth_{isAssignee}(r_u, r_{u'}) \wedge auth_{shareCases}(I_u, \{i\})$
    POST: $att_{UI_{\gamma'}}(u') \leftarrow att_{UI_\gamma}(u') \cup \{i\}$

▶ **delegateCase**$(u \in U_\gamma, u' \in U_\gamma, i \in I) ::=$
    VAR: $r_u = att_{UR_\gamma}(u)$, $r_{u'} = att_{UR_\gamma}(u')$, $I_u = att_{UI_\gamma}(u)$
    PRE: $auth_{delegate}(r_u) \wedge auth_{isDelegate}(r'_u) \wedge auth_{shareCases}(I_u, \{i\})$
    POST: $att_{UI_{\gamma'}}(u') \leftarrow att_{UI_\gamma}(u') \cup \{i\}$

Fig. 5. Exemplary definitions of STS operations [38].

4.2 Model Analysis

Once a model has been designed, the model engineer is interested in whether it meets the required correctness guarantees. Such questions are asked and answered in the Model Analysis step.

We exemplarily consider the following practical analysis question in the introduced scenario: "Is nurseCarla ever able to read ehrMsPregnant?" This precisely reflects a query regarding the $\langle op \rangle$-safety (Definition 5), where op equals readEHR. Based on a given initial state γ_0, this query would be expressed by $\langle \gamma_0, readEHR, [nurseCarla, ehrMsPregnant] \rangle$.

Leveraging a heuristic safety analysis approach as outlined in Sect. 2.3, a possible sequence of operations and inputs leading to a safety-violating state can be identified in the given model instance and rendered as follows:

1. delegateCase(drKelso, drCox, 42);
2. assignCase(drCox, nurseCarla, 42);
3. readEHR(nurseCarla, ehrMsPregnant).

To enable nurseCarla to execute readEHR on ehrMsPregnant, the following pre-clauses must be met: (1.) she must be authorized to read – this is true since she is a nurse, not a patient; (2.) she must be assigned to at least one case that ehrMsPregnant is also assigned to; (3.) at least one user of the same ward must be assigned that case.

The latter two pre-clauses must have been explicitly established beforehand due to the assignments in the initial state (cf. Table 1). Being assigned to case 42 by drCox via assignCase satisfies the second pre-clauses for nurseCarla. For assignCase to be executable (1.) drCox as assigner must be either physician or manager – this is true; (2.) drCox as assigner and physician must be attributed with this case; (3.) nurseCarla must be a nurse – this is also true.

Table 3. Overview of additions to primitive model components and instantiations [38].

	Symbol	Description	HIS Instantiation
AV_0, AV_1	T	set of team attribute values	$T \subseteq \mathbb{N}$
AA_0	$att_{UT} : \{u \in U \mid att_{UR}(u) \in$ {rPhysician, rNurse, rParamedic, rManager}$\} \rightarrow T$	user-team-attribution	$\{\langle drKelso, 4242 \rangle,$ $\langle drCox, 4242 \rangle,$ $\langle nurseCarla, 4242 \rangle, ...\}$
AA_1	$att_{TI} : T \rightarrow \mathscr{P}(I)$	team-case-attribution	$\{\langle 4242, \{42\} \rangle, ...\}$

```
1  lazy_static! {
2  static ref USER_DB: MutStatic<HashMap<u32, User>> = MutStatic::new();
3  static ref OBJECT_DB: MutStatic<HashMap<u32, Object>> = MutStatic::new();
4  ... } // more for other state members
```

Listing 11. Static container definition for dynamic model components.

Both, the second pre-clauses of assignCase and third pre-clauses of readEHR, become satisfiable by the delegation of case 42 to drCox by drKelso via delegateCase: (1.) drKelso as delegator and drCox as delegate are both physicians; (2.) drKelso is assigned to this case. Consequently, privilege escalations are possible on a ward-by-ward base: If at least any member of ward x is capable of accessing cases originally treated in ward y, this also holds for any other member of x. If, then again, a different member of x is capable of accessing cases from ward z, this may spread transitively.

The model originally formalizes a policy which is based on the organizational structure of a hospital. Now, the analysis results produced a more substantial understanding of possible privilege escalation vulnerabilities that are anchored in this design. To address these design flaws, a reiteration step in the model engineering phase of MSPE is necessary to improve the model design.

One possible approach to fix the above-discussed privilege escalation phenomenon is presented in Table 3. To cover the semantics of treatment workflows across wards, the attribute *team*, the user-team-attribution att_{UT}, and the indirect team-case-attribution att_{TI} are introduced. A team consists of users, possibly from different wards, such that any team could commonly treat cases independent of their original wards.

4.3 Model Implementation and Architectural Integration

This section demonstrates the implementation of the (verified) HIS model instance based on dabac-rs. The architectural integration is performed following the approach described in Sect. 3.3 using the standard TPS implementation (and under the assumption that the HIS itself is also implemented in Rust). The remainder of this section therefore illustrates model implementation based on excerpts.

As a foundation, we define static containers for any dynamic model component which serve as basic data storage. Listing 11 shows examples for user identifiers in U

```
1  struct User(u32);   // expandable as a struct for real-world policies
2  impl SuperAtomic for User {
3      type AtomicT = u32;
4      fn get_elem(&self) -> Self::AtomicT { self.0 }
5  }
6  impl SuperDynamic for User {
7      type ContainerT = USER_DB;
8      fn add_elem(e_new: Self) -> bool {
9          if let Ok(mut guard) = Self::container_static().write() {
10             guard.insert(e_new.0, e_new);
11             true
12         } else { false }
13     }
14     ...
15     fn container_static() -> &'static Self::ContainerT { &USER_DB }
16 }
17 impl EntityElem for User {}
```

Listing 12. Type definition for dynamic model components values $u \in U_\gamma$.

```
1  struct Role(u32);   // expandable as a struct
2  impl SuperAtomic for Role {
3      type AtomicT = u32;
4      fn get_elem(&self) -> Self::AtomicT { self.0 }
5  }
6  impl AttrValElem for Role {}
```

Listing 13. Type definition for static attribute values $r \in R$.

and EHR object identifiers in O. Using the lazy_static macro, it is possible to have statics that require code for initialization to be executed at runtime, such as the used HashMap container, which requires heap allocations. Additionally, the containers are static and mutable (MutStatic) for Polar integration.

Next, the DABAC model is implemented successively. As representative examples for primitive model components, we demonstrate the realization of the user identifier set U (part of EN), the role attribute value set R (part of AV_0) and att_{UR} (part of AA_0).

Listing 12 shows the type definition of the single entity (EN) value User (l. 1). Based on this type, the superfamily traits SuperAtomic (ll. 2–5) and SuperDynamic (ll. 6–16) are implemented. Additionally, the EN components trait EntityElem is implemented for User (l. 17). As a result, the user values are (1.) atomic set members, (2.) dynamic, (3.) entities, and (4.) internal values.

In contrast, however, role values are (1.) atomic set members, (2.) *not* dynamic, (3.) attribute values, and (4.) internal values. Therefore, as Listing 13 shows, the implementation of the superfamily trait SuperDynamic is not required. In addition, the AV components trait AttrValElem is implemented for Role.

```
1  struct UserRole {
2      map: HashMap<User, Role>,
3  }
4  impl SuperMapping<User, Role> for UserRole {
5      fn map(&self, e: &User) -> Option<&Role> { self.map.get(e) }
6  }
7  impl SuperDynamic for UserRole {
8      type ContainerT = HashMap<User, Role>;
9      fn add_elem(e: Self) -> bool { ... }
10 ... }
11 impl EntAttrAssocElem<User, Role> for UserRole {}
```

Listing 14. Type definition for dynamic model components values $att_{UR_\gamma}: U_\gamma \rightarrow R$.

```
1  let user_comp = DABACComp {
2      name: "User".to_owned(),
3      features: [Some(En), None, None, None, None, Some(Dyn)],
4      inner: &USER_DB,
5  };
6  let ur_comp = DABACComp {
7      name: "att_UR".to_owned(),
8      features: [None, None, Some(Aa(0)), None, None, Some(Dyn)],
9      inner: &USER_ROLE,
10 };
```

Listing 15. Exemplary model component instantiation for U_γ and att_{UR_γ}.

```
1  auth_read(r_u: Role) if
2      r_u != Role::Patient;
3  auth_share_cases(i_u: List, i_o: List) if
4      [first, *tail] = i_o and
5      (first in i_u or auth_share_cases(i_u, tail)); # branch into recursion
6  auth_is_assignee(r_u: Role, r_u2: Role) if
7      (r_u == Role::Manager and r_u2 == Role::Physician) or
8      r_u2 == Role::Nurse;
```

Listing 16. Exemplary Polar definitions of authorization functions.

The implementation of att_{UR} is shown in Listing 14. Using Rust's standard HashMap container, the type UserRole is defined (ll. 1–3). By implementing the superfamily traits SuperMapping (ll. 4–6) and SuperDynamic (ll. 7–11) and the model component family trait EntAttrAssocElem, the implementation of att_{UR} is (1.) a mapping, (2.) dynamic, (3.) an AA_0 component, and (4.) internal.

To unify the separately defined model components into a single model instance, first, they are each instantiated as a DABACComp (see Listing 15). Then, an instance of the top-level type DABAC is created (cf. Listing 7). Alternatively, the builder-pattern type DABACBuilder can be used for this purpose, which ensures the atomicity of building a sealed DABAC object.

```
1  assign_case(user_1: User, user_2: User, ehr_id: Integer) if
2      # VAR:
3      # `att_UR` is the Polar alias for the Rust variable `ur_comp`,
4      # `map` is the Polar method alias for `get_inner().map` on `att_UR`
5      r_u1 = att_UR.map(user_1) and r_u2 = att_UR.map(user_2) and
6      I_u1 = att_UI.map(user_1) and
7      # PRE:
8      auth_assign(r_u1) and auth_is_assignee(r_u, r_u2) and
9      auth_share_cases(I_u1, [ehr_id]) and
10     # POST:
11     UserCase.assign_case_to_user(ehr_id, user_2);
```

Listing 17. Exemplary Polar definition of STS operation *assignCase*, cf. Fig. 5.

The specification of the actual policy rules that cover authorization and state-transition behavior (the model's AR and STS) is shown exemplarily in Listings 16 and 17. While the specification of $auth_{read}$ and $auth_{isAssignee}$ are straightforward, the specification of $auth_{shareCases}$ demonstrates that recursion may be required in some cases (which is supported by Polar) (see Listing 16). Listing 17 shows a peculiarity when defining STS operations: Polar requires registered names for component data types (DABACComp::get_name() is provided for this) and for their methods (omitted here). These are then used to call the corresponding Rust implementation; in the case of the *assignCase* operation (cf. Listing 6), this is UserCase.assign_case_to_user (l. 11).

5   Related Work

Related work can be classified in two categories: focused on either model engineering and model analysis, or on model implementation and integration.

Model Engineering and Analysis. Since we aim for a tight integration of formalisms into MSPE, we first discuss modeling schemes for ABAC policies that are closest to one or both of the major goals of DABAC: (1.) versatility to express and implement diverse policies and (2.) capability to analyze their dynamic security properties.

CBAC [11] is a modeling scheme based on axiomatic categories of entities and their relationships. Its high degree of abstraction imposes a significant semantics gap for both model engineering and model implementation. DABAC aims at formalizing ABAC policies closer to their functional semantics instead.

$ABAC_\alpha$ [24] aims at frugality of modeling semantics, used to demonstrate the still considerable expressive power of the ABAC paradigm. Due to its relative restrictiveness in terms of STS specification, it was also found useful as a study case for engineering practical model instances with decidable safety properties (cf. [2]).

While more versatile in terms of expressive power, AMABAC [23,40] achieves terminating reachability analyses in a way similar to $ABAC_\alpha$: a fixed pattern for STS commands is hard-wired into the model. Going beyond $ABAC_\alpha$ however, the authors introduce a complete formal analysis framework based on deductive reasoning instead of state machine simulation. Despite the formal confinement of model dynamics, AMABAC takes an approach similar to DABAC in that it seamlessly integrates dynamic analysis methods in MSPE (goal 2).

C-ABAC [17] as a modeling scheme applies CBAC abstractions to ABAC policies. It shares with DABAC the concept of *environmental information*, and moreover, both modeling schemes aim at general-purpose expressive power. Unlike DABAC however, C-ABAC explicitly refrains from modeling dynamic protection state changes, rendering it a solid foundation to verify static model properties rather than dynamic. This latter restriction is resolved by Admin-CBAC [13], which unlocks C-ABAC to state reachability analyses but only for decidable dynamic properties. Again, since DABAC should be flexible enough to allow for incomplete analysis methods toward semi-decidable properties, we opt for an automaton-based modeling scheme rather than the axiomatic approach from CBAC, C-ABAC, and Admin-CBAC.

For in-depth comparison of DABAC with $ABAC_\alpha$ and C-ABAC, refer to [38].

Model Implementation and Integration. With the increasing adoption of ABAC policies for application-level AC, a plethora of libraries that provide programming support for their effortless and correct implementation has emerged. We have already highlighted *Oso* [30], which is used in our prototypical implementation of a DABAC model RTE. Other examples range from Rust libraries such as *Casbin* [16] or *dacquiri* [1] to multi-purpose frameworks for implementing security mechanisms beyond AC, such as Spring Security [45] or Apache Shiro [10].

From a broader perspective, these programming frameworks are yet more individual pieces in the security engineering puzzle, that need to be rearranged for any application with its individual security policy. Despite using Oso in our DABAC RTE prototype, we could have opted for any other of the above-mentioned alternatives. This emphasizes the fact that the choice of a specific policy logic implementation (for some specific programming language, encapsulated in some specific library) is not where methodical integration should happen.

To this end, the DABAC modeling scheme is deliberately language-neutral and technology-agnostic – we could easily implement a database application or a web service using the same MSPE abstractions. With our focus on a sound and complete formal basis for correct ABAC enforcement, we attemt to contribute to a more homogeneous, interoperable ecosystem that allows to implement and integrate high-quality security policies yielded by a rigorous MSPE process.

6 Conclusions

In this paper, we bundle loose ends for ABAC policy design and implementation into a unified MSPE workflow that bridges typical semantic gaps by exploiting standardized formal artifacts between the MSPE steps: (1.) Model engineering and model analysis steps are both supported by DABAC – a modeling scheme for ABAC policies that enables the incremental automaton-based specification and formal analyses of ABAC policies towards runtime properties (e. g. privilege escalation). (2.) Based on the formally analyzed DABAC model instance specification, an implementation framework in

Rust (dabac-rs), which makes use of the Polar policy specification language, bridges the gap to model implementation. (3.) The model integration step is backed by the APPSPEAR security architecture and the Rust developer framework appspear-rs to enable a flexible and founded integration into application software. Based on a real-world scenario, we have highlighted how an end-to-end MSPE workflow is performed.

Ongoing and future work aims at further streamlining this workflow and thus focuses on all areas of the MSPE process: (1.) the extension and integration of the DYNAMO [8] language for tool-supported generation of model and policy implementations, including STS post-conditions which have to be manually implemented in our current framework, (2.) the generalization of the WSDepSearch algorithm [39] to foster efficient safety analyses of DABAC models, and (3.) the integration of context information to enable the enforcement of risk-based ABAC policies based on real-time threat information from external sources.

References

1. Dacquiri: An authorization framework with compile-time enforcement (2022). https://github.com/resyncgg/dacquiri
2. Ahmed, T., Sandhu, R.: Safety of $ABAC_\alpha$ Is decidable. In: NSS 2017 (2017)
3. Amthor, P.: Efficient heuristic safety analysis of core-based security policies. In: SECRYPT 2017 (2017)
4. Amthor, P.: Aspect-oriented Security Engineering. Cuvillier Verlag (2019). ISBN 978-3-7369-9980-0
5. Amthor, P., Kühnhauser, W.E., Pölck, A.: Heuristic safety analysis of access control models. In: SACMAT 2013 (2013)
6. Amthor, P., Kühnhauser, W.E., Pölck, A.: WorSE: a workbench for model-based security engineering. Elsevier COSE **42** (2014)
7. Amthor, P., Rabe, M.: Command dependencies in heuristic safety analysis of access control models. In: Benzekri, A., Barbeau, M., Gong, G., Laborde, R., Garcia-Alfaro, J. (eds.) FPS 2019. LNCS, vol. 12056, pp. 207–224. Springer, Cham (2020). https://doi.org/10.1007/978-3-030-45371-8_13
8. Amthor, P., Schlegel, M.: Towards language support for model-based security policy engineering. In: SECRYPT 2020 (2020)
9. Anderson, J.P.: Computer security technology planning study. Tech. Rep. ESD-TR-73-51, vol. II (1972)
10. Apache Software Foundation: Apache Shiro (2022). https://shiro.apache.org
11. Barker, S.: The next 700 access control models or a unifying meta-model? In: SACMAT 2009 (2009)
12. Basin, D., Clavel, M., Egea, M.: A decade of model-driven security. In: SACMAT 2011 (2011)
13. Bertolissi, C., Fernández, M., Thuraisingham, B.: Admin-CBAC: an administration model for category-based access control. In: CODASPY 2020 (2020)
14. Bhatt, S., Sandhu, R.: ABAC-CC: attribute-based access control and communication control for internet of things. In: SACMAT 2020 (2020)
15. Biswas, P., Sandhu, R., Krishnan, R.: Label-based access control: an ABAC model with enumerated authorization policy. In: ABAC 2016 (2016)
16. Casbin Organization: Casbin (2022). https://casbin.org

17. Fernández, M., Mackie, I., Thuraisingham, B.: Specification and analysis of ABAC policies via the category-based metamodel. In: CODASPY 2019 (2019)
18. Ferraiolo, D., Chandramouli, R., Kuhn, R., et al.: Extensible access control markup language (XACML) and next generation access control (NGAC). In: ABAC 2016 (2016)
19. Gupta, M., M. Awaysheh, F., Benson, J., et al.: An attribute-based access control for cloud-enabled industrial smart vehicles. TII 17(6), 4288-4297 (2020)
20. Harrison, M.A., Ruzzo, W.L., Ullman, J.D.: Protection in Operating Systems. Comm. ACM 19(8) (1976)
21. Hu, V.C., Ferraiolo, D., Kuhn, R., et al.: Guide to attribute based access control (ABAC) definition and considerations. NIST Special Publication, pp. 800–162 (2014)
22. Intel Corp.: Intel®SGX. https://software.intel.com/en-us/sgx (2022)
23. Jha, S., Sural, S., Atluri, V., et al.: Security analysis of ABAC under an administrative model. IET Inf. Secur. 13(2), 96–103 (2019)
24. Jin, X., Krishnan, R., Sandhu, R.: A unified attribute-based access control model covering DAC, MAC and RBAC. In: Cuppens-Boulahia, N., Cuppens, F., Garcia-Alfaro, J. (eds.) DBSec 2012. LNCS, vol. 7371, pp. 41–55. Springer, Heidelberg (2012). https://doi.org/10.1007/978-3-642-31540-4_4
25. Klabnik, S., Nichols, C.: The Rust Programming Language. No Starch Press (2018)
26. Lang, B., Foster, I.T., Siebenlist, F., et al.: A flexible attribute based access control method for grid computing. J. Grid Comput. 7(2), 169–180 (2009)
27. Matsakis, N.D., Klock, F.S.: The Rust language. In: HILT 2014 (2014)
28. Mukherjee, S., Ray, I., Ray, I., et al.: Attribute based access control for healthcare resources. In: ABAC 2017 (2017)
29. Narouei, M., Khanpour, H., Takabi, H., et al.: Towards a top-down policy engineering framework for attribute-based access control. In: SACMAT 2017 (2017)
30. Oso Security Inc: Oso (2022). https://www.osohq.com
31. Oso Security Inc: Polar Language Reference (2022). https://docs.osohq.com/rust/reference/polar.html
32. Ray, I., Alangot, B., Nair, S., et al.: Using attribute-based access control for remote healthcare monitoring. In: SDS 2017 (2017)
33. Sandhu, R., Bhamidipati, V., Munawer, Q.: The ARBAC97 Model for Role-based Administration of Roles. TISSEC 2(1) (1999)
34. Sandhu, R.S., Coyne, E.J., Feinstein, H.L., et al.: Role-based access control models. IEEE Comput. 29(2), 38–47 (1996)
35. Schlegel, M.: Poster: Shielding AppSPEAR - enhancing memory safety for trusted application-level security policy enforcement. In: SACMAT 2021 (2021)
36. Schlegel, M.: Trusted enforcement of application-specific security policies. In: SECRYPT 2021 (2021)
37. Schlegel, M., Amthor, P.: Beyond administration: a modeling scheme supporting the dynamic analysis of role-based access control policies. In: SECRYPT 2020 (2020)
38. Schlegel, M., Amthor, P.: The missing piece of the ABAC puzzle: a modeling scheme for dynamic analysis. In: SECRYPT 2021 (2021)
39. Schlegel, M., Kühnhauser, W.: Exploiting hot spots in heuristic safety analysis of dynamic access control models. In: SECRYPT 2020 (2020)
40. Singh, M.P., Sural, S., Atluri, V., et al.: Security analysis of unified access control policies. In: SKM 2019 (2020)
41. Stoller, S.D., Yang, P., Gofman, M., et al.: Symbolic reachability analysis for parameterized administrative role based access control. In: SACMAT 2009 (2009)
42. Tripunitara, M.V., Li, N.: A theory for comparing the expressive power of access control models. J. Comput. Secur. 15(2), 231–272 (2007)

43. Tripunitara, M.V., Li, N.: The Foundational Work of Harrison-Ruzzo-Ullman Revisited. TDSC **10**(1), 28–39 (2013)
44. De Capitani di Vimercati, S., Samarati, P., Jajodia, S.: Policies, models, and languages for access control. In: Bhalla, S. (ed.) DNIS 2005. LNCS, vol. 3433, pp. 225–237. Springer, Heidelberg (2005). https://doi.org/10.1007/978-3-540-31970-2_18
45. VMware Inc: Spring Security (2022). https://spring.io/projects/spring-security
46. Watson, R.N.M.: A decade of OS access-control extensibility. Queue **11**(1) (2013)
47. Xu, Z., Stoller, S.D.: Mining attribute-based access control policies. TDSC **12**(5) (2015)

Evaluating Defensive Countermeasures for Software-Based Hardware Abstraction

J. Todd McDonald[1]([⊠])[iD], Ramya K. Manikyam[1][iD], Sébastien Bardin[2][iD],
Richard Bonichon[3], Todd R. Andel[1], and James Carambat[1]

[1] University of South Alabama, Mobile, AL 36688, USA
{jtmcdonald,tandel}@southalabama.edu,
{rk1421,jec1623}@jagmail.southalabama.edu
[2] Université Paris-Saclay, CEA, LIST, Palaiseau, France
sebastien.bardin@cea.fr
[3] Nomadic Labs, Paris, France
richard.bonichon@nomadic-labs.com

Abstract. Protecting software from illegal reverse engineering and malicious hackers is often remedied through either legal or technical means. In the technical domain, software obfuscation provides less than perfect protection against such attacks since there is no perfect obfuscator for all classes of programs. However, semantic preserving transformations can attempt to make the cost of attacks prohibitive in either time or resources. Software-based hardware abstraction (SBHA) is a novel approach that transforms traditional software code segments into a digital logic form and thus virtualizes code into a hardware abstraction. SBHA can be used to protect embedded secrets in programs that are used to guard intellectual property (IP). Secrets such as passwords, PINs, and activation codes authorize legitimate end-users to install or activate software for use and are validated typically through point functions that check for the single unique input that is expected. In this study we extend initial analysis of SBHA against state-of-the-art dynamic symbolic execution (DSE) attacks in recovering embedded program secrets and consider the limits of an attacker that recovers the logic circuit netlist from an SBHA-protected program. We pose four approaches for hardened SBHA configurations and evaluate their effectiveness using typical analysis tools that cover synthesis, binary decision diagram recovery, and symbolic analysis. We show that such attacks can be mitigated by these countermeasures outright and discuss the trade-off in size and overhead relative to the relatively low-cost of SBHA point-functions stand alone. We conclude that for single use operations such as point function checks, the overhead is large but the execution runtime delta is negligible.

Keywords: Man-at-the-end attacks · Hardware virtualization · Dynamic symbolic execution · Software protection

This work was partly funded by a grant of high-performance computing resources and technical support from the Alabama Supercomputer Authority and by the National Science Foundation awards 1811560 and 1811578 in the NSF 17–576 Secure and Trustworthy Cyberspace (SaTC) program.

P. Samarati et al. (Eds.): ICETE 2021, CCIS 1795, pp. 281–304, 2023.
https://doi.org/10.1007/978-3-031-36840-0_13

1   Introduction

A 2018 BSA study [18] highlights intellectual property (IP) theft in the software industry and estimates $46.3 billion loss annually for unlicensed software on a global scale. Anti-piracy mitigation most often involves software licensing solutions and copy protection schemes [47], with remediation based on detection of misuse and legal means of recourse. The Man-at-the-End (MATE) attack model represents attackers in protection contexts where the adversary has full control of the execution environment, which includes code in source or binary form being executed by a legitimate end-user [2,24]. Code protection for legitimate software by technical countermeasures is typically integrated with licensing mechanisms and is based on semantic preserving transformations that make programs harder to understand and reverse engineer [45]. Traditional approaches for MATE protection are categorized as obfuscation, tamper-proofing, and watermarking [25]. MATE attacks can violate normal assumptions of program integrity and confidentiality, where licensed software typically contains assets that need to be protected such as keys, passwords, PINs, or registration codes. As Fig. 1 illustrates, various tools such as debuggers, disassemblers, decompilers, tracers, and symbolic analyzers can be used maliciously to find and leak such secrets embedded within a program.

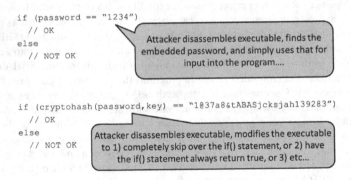

Fig. 1. MATE Attack on Password Point Function.

Software obfuscation is thus a proactive approach to deter hackers that attempt to reverse engineer programs illegally. Theoretic limits show that no general obfuscation approach can achieve information theoretic security for all programs [9], and practitioners admit that all software protection mechanisms will eventually be cracked [47]. The goal for technical approaches such as obfuscation is to drive up cost of adversarial analysis or program alteration. A worst-case bound on defeating protection schemes is termed a rewrite attack by Collberg and Nagra [25], where the adversary would expend as much time or resources as it would take to actually rewrite the target software from scratch. In recent results, semantic attacks based on advanced program analysis such as dynamic symbolic execution (DSE) [19] have been shown to be highly effective against conventional obfuscation methods [4,6,10,21,31,50].

1.1 Protecting Code with SBHA

In [39], McDonald et al. introduce a novel approach for software protection called *software-based hardware abstraction* (SBHA). SBHA leverages virtualization of software constructs into digital logic circuit forms. As Fig. 2 illustrates, an example SBHA transformation begins by first localizing a particular software code sequence that needs protection. For this work, we focus on point-functions in the form of if-statements that are typically used to verify embedded program secrets for authorization. The point-function $f : \{0,1\}^{k*8} \rightarrow \{0,1\}$ for example represents a typical k-character ASCII value of size $k * 8$ bits that is checked against a user-supplied value. For equality, only a single input will result in the function returning true (1). We can represent the Boolean function using a standard canonical method such as sum-of-products or product-of-sums equation, which is synthesized as a digital logic circuit using AND, OR, and NOT gates. Figure 2 shows the circuit in a netlist language known as BENCH format, which is the *hardware abstraction* in language form. The next step of SBHA takes the netlist format and converts it back into a code form in the native language of the original program (such as C). Inputs and outputs are treated as arrays of Boolean or character values and gate logic such as AND, OR, and NOT are represented as C function calls. Thus, the original code of interest is virtualized as a hardware-based operation in software form.

McDonald et al. [39] point out that virtualization is one of many MATE defense approaches which translates code into a random instruction set architecture (ISA) [21]

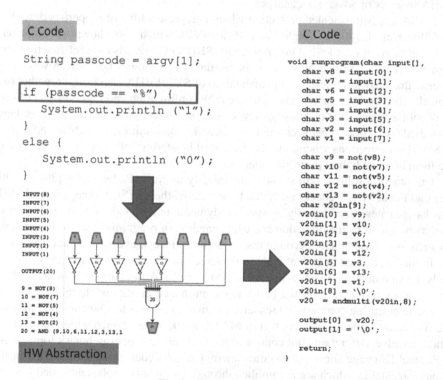

Fig. 2. SBHA Overview.

that is then interpreted at runtime. Traditionally these virtualized program segments behave as a CPU with a particular instruction set, execution stack, program counter, and code. Vahid [48] made an early observation of fluidity between logic circuits and software program representation, of which SBHA provides a suitable implementation of the idea. In MATE defense, sensitive parts of a program that contain protected assets would be the target of transformation algorithms (obfuscations) that induce higher overhead (resource/time) to reverse engineer or result in outright defeat of particular analyzers.

1.2 Preliminary SBHA Evaluation

In [39], we focus on attackers with the capacity to use dynamic symbolic execution (DSE) engines [19] to leak program secrets. Prior work [6,43,45] illustrated how DSE and concolic analysis were able to defeat entire categories of obfuscating transformations in terms of recovering embedded secrets they were meant to protect. Even though it was shown that many transformations including virtualization were effective (requiring the adversary to expend more resources than they would in analyzing the original unprotected program), all eventually leaked secrets [6]. In practical use, every discovered path by a DSE tool is actually feasible, but such tools are also *incomplete* because transformations can cause feasible paths to be skipped [55]. Our prior work in [39] considers both source-level tools and pure binary code analyzers (which are less precise) [5]. These initial experiments thus favored the attacker and strengthened the results of SBHA in terms of adversarial analysis.

SBHA is a path-oriented protection which is representative of properties described by Ollivier et al. [40] as Single-Value Path (SVP), which was shown to completely hinder effectiveness of DSE. Our preliminary SBHA evaluations of point-function program segments confirmed strengths of the similarity and showed how SBHA was a new defense that provides tractable implementation of SVP. SBHA also brings together two typically disparate research areas: software (SW) obfuscation and logic-level hardware (HW) obfuscation, thus opening up new classes of protection schemes that have been unstudied. As a bridge between the two research communities, it enables application of SW/HW protections schemes in the context of bolstering software MATE defense in the form of novel hybrid protection mechanisms.

Our studies evaluate skilled and economically motivated adversaries [20] that utilize traditional MATE attacks tools that have state-of-the-art (SOTA) capability. MATE attacks are categorized broadly as static or dynamic and include a broad spectrum of analyzers that allow manipulation and understanding of programs from the binary level up such as disassemblers, decompilers, emulators, tracers, and slicers. Such attackers are framed as limited in budget with no resource or capability to create beyond-SOTA tools. From a defensive viewpoint, we aim to use SBHA to completely break or drive up the cost considerably for the best-known automated attacks while making manual reverse engineering complex and resource intensive, and thus less desirable or impossible. We consider the general context of MATE attacks (also termed white-box attacks) where an adversary retains full control of the code environment in binary form versus high-level language form. Adversaries attempt to find code secrets embedded in the binary executable, which are exemplified through passwords, PINs, embedded keys, or other authorization data.

Our preliminary work [39] under this attack model established several foundational aspects of SBHA:

- Defining SBHA as a new and low-resource obfuscation technique for point-function transformation. Initial evaluation performed on C programs with SBHA transforms illustrated how both software and hardware obfuscation algorithms could be integrated to strengthen SBHA against more advanced attacks. SBHA thus also represents a unique transformation among others because it forces the adversary to have both software and hardware analysis expertise.
- SBHA was shown to be highly effective against SOTA DSE engines such as KLEE and Angr, where only 1 out of 320 tests resulted in adversarial leakage of an embedded secret despite a 120-hour timeout period.
- SBHA was shown to have high resilience against adversarial reverse engineering. Prior work looked at the assumption of worst-case scenarios where 1) an adversary recovers an embedded circuit netlist and then performs circuit-based attacks, 2) an adversary uses compiler optimizations which are akin to deobfuscating transformations, and 3) an adversary utilizes path merging attacks. Preliminary results considered anti-BDD and anti-SAT methods from the hardware side to strengthen conclusions about SBHA resilience.
- SBHA was shown to be a low cost virtualizing transformation with minimal overhead but medium stealth (assuming supporting obfuscations). Our results establish SBHA as a new form of software virtualization that demonstrates only 10% runtime overhead, 3.5x source code and 50% executable code overhead (for point functions) – compared to much costlier traditional virtualization.

1.3 Netlist-Based Countermeasures

In this paper, we extend our preliminary results by considering adversarial actions related to the embedded digital logic circuit netlist. In particular, we consider the limits of an adversary that successfully recovers the netlist from an SBHA protected program and the corresponding analysis done at the circuit level to recover embedded secrets. Such analysis takes on the form of three primary SOTA tool lines: 1) binary decision diagram (BDD) based analyzers, 2) hardware synthesis tools, and 3) satisfiability modulo theory (SMT)/satisfiability (SAT) solver based tools. Our contributions for the present study include:

- Proposal of four different configurations for hardening SBHA netlists against adversarial analysis, given the assumption that the adversary can recover a clean netlist from the SBHA binary program. Hardened forms use fully functional arithmetic circuit components, which induce higher overhead, but can be generalized to specific byte-length embedded secrets.
- Case study analysis of attack effectiveness using BDD, SAT, and synthesis based tools using an simple case for adversarial recovery (single character password).
- Performance and overhead comparison of proposed defensive countermeasures to characterize runtime or program size constraints.

The remainder of paper is organized as follows. Section 2 provides a brief synopsis of background concepts and related work with comparative placement of SBHA along-side other DSE protections. Section 3 provides a summary of SBHA case-study analysis against several categories of MATE attacks which is reported in [39]. Section 4 discusses enhancements to SBHA by applying circuit-level transformations at the netlist level, prior to converting the hardware abstraction back into code. Section 5 provides results and trade-off analysis of applying four different styles of SBHA defensive countermeasures. Section 6 provide conclusions and our plans for future work. We provide additional benchmark data and descriptions related to SBHA studies online[1].

2   Background and Related Work

Collberg et al. [23,25] define obfuscation as a semantic preserving transformation (or sequence of transformations) intended to change an original program (or circuit) into a form that is harder to analyze. Three layered MATE attack vectors include analyzing, altering, or pirating a program and thus obfuscation targets the initial stage of analyzing or understanding a program. A transformer O is defined functionally as $O : \mathcal{P} \to \mathcal{P}$ that takes input program P and outputs P' ($O(P) = P'$) with equivalent operational semantics ($\forall x : P(x) = P'(x)$). P' is (expected to) be harder to analyze than P and is typically in the same domain $\mathcal{P}$ as the original program (binary, IRR, HLL, etc.). Program protection normally involves the application of several different kinds of transformations, including applying the same transformation more than once. Obfuscation executives (which are generically referred to as *obfuscators*) apply transformations in some order and sequence based on an underlying algorithm [25,33]. In most cases, obfuscators use overhead (code size) or estimated performance to determine when to stop the transformation process [25].

We can thus define an obfuscator O as a program that applies an ordered sequence of transformations to a program P, choosing transformations T from a set of transformations τ. For example, given $\tau = T_1, T_2, T_3, T_4, T_5$, an obfuscator O acts like a transformer (where $O(P) = P'$) through the application of some number and order of transformations. Distribution of program variants, for example, can be produced by the application of transformations in a given sequence, for example, $O(P) = T3(T1(T4(T5(P)))) = P'$. [23,25] classify transformations as **abstract** (the core structure of a program is changed by altering original abstractions such as functions and classes), **data** (data structures and variables are renamed or replaced with encryption, mappings, or alternative data types), **control** (structures such as conditionals and loops are modified to change the original control flow), or **dynamic** (programs are transformed and change themselves dynamically at runtime).

Schrittwieser et al. [45] use three major classifications of 357 published works in obfuscation research: data obfuscation, static code rewriting (which encompasses both abstract and control transformations), and dynamic code rewriting. Their survey delineated four analyst aims (locating data, locating program functionality, extracting code fragments, and understanding the program) cross-matched against four code analysis

---

[1] http://soc.southalabama.edu/~mcdonald/SBHA/.

categories (pattern matching, automated static analysis, automated dynamic analysis, and human-assisted analysis). Given enough time, protected programs can be reverse-engineered and their secrets divulged [9,25,37]. In general, programs require protection because of the presence of some inherent secret information contained in them: we define such information as a *property* of a given program (also known as a *program asset* [11]).

2.1 Obfuscation Metrics

Collberg et al. [22] state that an obfuscated program P' should have certain properties, which form the basis of metrics for evaluating transformations. Apart from semantic equivalence, key metrics include:

1. **Effectiveness** measures how hard it is to analyze or modify the obfuscated program P', typically by manual analysis, which should require more time or resources than for the original program P. The metric embodies the notion that good transformations should increase analysis time required to leak program assets;
2. **Resilience** is a metric that accounts both for the time or resources required to reduce potency, both as *programmer effort* (PE) and *deobfuscator effort* (DE). [25] define resilience T with respect to program P as a function $T_{res}(P) = Resilience\ (T_{DE}, T_{PE})$. Thus, it measures the ability of automated tools to reverse engineer or deobfuscate the protected program P' in comparison to the original.
3. **Stealth** measures the statistical properties of P' compared to the original unprotected version, so that transformations do not induce patterns that are easy to recognize or locate;
4. **Cost** measure the increase in execution time and overhead due to obfuscation, and thus provides a minimizing goal relative to any gain in security.

In [39], we report case study results in detail for how SBHA can protect a program against automated semantic deobfuscation techniques such as DSE. In this paper we extend these results to include detailed analysis of the circuit-level abstraction of the SBHA construction.

2.2 Digital Logic Abstractions

Combinational circuits are logic networks composed of gates with specified Boolean logic functions chosen from a basis set Ω that typically includes AND, OR, XOR, NOT, $NAND$, NOR, and $XNOR$. A circuit netlist is a structural view of the logic network and can be represented in programmatic form such as BENCH format [32] or as a visual schematic. Semantically, circuits have a function that can be represented through Boolean expressions, truth tables, or in graphical forms such as binary decision diagrams (BDDs). Combinational logic derives its output only from an applied set of inputs, whose binary values are propagated through the gates of the circuit to compute the functional output. Figure 3 illustrates a small 4 input, 2 output, 8 gate combinational circuit in schematic form with corresponding BENCH netlist.

An n-input, m-output circuit function can be seen as the collection of 2^n input vectors and the corresponding set of output bits that are derived for each input in tabular

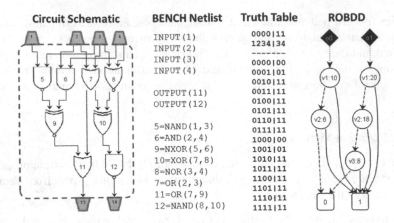

Fig. 3. Combinational Logic Structure and Semantics.

(truth table) form. The circuit embodies a set of Boolean functions $f_i : B^n \rightarrow \{0,1\}$, where $i = 1..m$ [27]. BDDs are a visual representation of the truth table in the form of a decision tree [16], and a reduced ordered binary decision diagram (ROBDD) represents a canonical form of the circuit function. Figure 3 shows the semantics of the circuit in truth table and ROBDD form.

2.3   Software to Hardware Transformation

We are not the first to propose or use software-to-hardware abstractions. To our knowledge, however, we are the first to propose the technique as a means to achieve software protection goals. Both secure multi-party computation (MPC) and hardware synthesis research areas provide many decades of prior work.

MPC: In the area of secure multi-party computation [29], cryptographers have long sought the answer to the question of how multiple parties of interest can securely compute a joint function on their private inputs, without disclosing anything more than the result of the function. Yao proposed the first seminal protocol for two-party secure function evaluation (SFE) [56], but he never published his original protocol that used the notion of garbled circuits. MPC schemes since then have expanded the idea of garbled circuits by taking the function computed by all parties in a SFE and transforming it into a Boolean or arithmetic logic circuit representation consisting of AND, OR, XOR, and NOT gates. MPC research has continued to progress and has brought about a multitude of practical applications and MPC libraries that support the translation of functions into circuits in Boolean, arithmetic, or formula form [29]. Fairplay [36] was one of the first implementations of a two-party protocol, and moving on, there are now multiple implementations of software-to-circuit compilers for MPC construction based on C and C++ which include ABY [28], EMP [51], OblivC [57,58], and PICCO [59].

Hardware Synthesis: In the domain of systems design and synthesis, the distinction between hardware and software has become less clear for some time. Vahid [48] noted in 2007 that the distinction between hardware and software is becoming fluid, with many applications that require hardware efficiency are now using some form of software/hardware co-design [53] or partitioning [49]. Almost 20 years ago, Wirth [52] pointed out traditional software constructs (sequence and choice) are easily translatable to combinational logic while looping constructs can be handled with sequential logic forms. Since then, several realizations of this concept have made their way into commercial synthesis tools and systems design thought. SystemC [14] is probably the more well known and earliest examples of this hardware/software marriage and is now an IEEE standard. Such programming environments support hardware description languages such as Verilog or VHDL and their translation to C++ [1].

2.4 Anti-DSE Research

So-called semantic or symbolic deobfuscation techniques rely on advanced (semantic) program analysis methods such as abstract interpretation [42] or symbolic execution [19] to overcome or simplify obfuscated constructs within a protected program. Several existing works have established the effectiveness of such methods against standard protection schemes [6,10,43], especially in an interactive attack scenario where the attacker launches local automated attacks on well-chosen parts of code. See [45] for a survey. In [39], we focus especially on Dynamic Symbolic Execution [19], whose ability to combine both the robustness of dynamic analysis (useful for, e.g., bypass packing or self-modifying code) and the reasoning-ability of symbolic methods (useful for, e.g., find triggering inputs and cover the path space) makes it a weapon of choice.

Study of DSE protections have grown in recent years alongside potential techniques to guard point-function statements within program code. A recent survey by Schrittweiser et al. [45] highlights the extreme effectiveness of DSE-based deobfuscation attacks in leaking secrets protected by obfuscating transformations [10,26,43,55]. Banescu et al. [6,8] provided seminal evaluation of DSE tools (KLEE, Angr) against password-based programs that were obfuscated using multiple types of transformations from the Tigress and ObfuscatorLLVM obfuscators. Results from this study showed effectiveness of certain types of transformations (virtualizing being chief), but that all combinations of transformations leaked the embedded program under analysis by DSE. Banescu et al. [7] also studied how complex constraints can affect symbolic deobfuscation by using machine learning to create predictions for which types of obfuscating transformations would increase the overhead for a DSE-based attack. Ollivier et al. [40] examined path exploration as a potential weakness in DSE tools, where their version of password-protected programs are consistent with ours in SBHA studies. In later work [41], they survey various anti-DSE protections and give comparative analysis of approaches. Biondi et al. [13] and Eyrolles et al. [30] evaluated Mixed Boolean Arithmetic expressions [60] for point-function protection in a separate study. Abstract model checking was studied by Bruni et al. [15] and they offered a formally provable obfuscation approach against these attacks. Manikyam et al. [37] evaluated commercial obfuscators including Themida, Code Virtualizer, and VMProtect to show the limits of password-protection code from human-based analysis and supporting analysis tools like IDAPro and CheatEngine.

In closely related work to the SBHA approach, Lan et al. [35] proposed a transformer that replaces program assets in conditional instructions with complex execution pathways which ultimately defeated DSE analysis under KLEE. Since SBHA can be seen as path-oriented protection with the "Single-Value Path" property identified by Ollivier et al. [40], SBHA represents a new approach of this protection class. SVP protection can make DSE search more akin to fuzzing, but only a very few tractable SVP path-oriented protection schemes have been proposed and studied. In general, SBHA causes problems for software-minded human attackers that are confronted with dual abstractions (SW and HW) that required fundamentally different skills and analysis techniques. SBHA can also be applied beyond point-function constructs to general code blocks (especially if sequential circuit designs are introduced), and can thus go beyond traditional path-oriented protections. DSE when used for automated testing is known for three weaknesses that include complex constraints, path divergence, and path explosion [3]. These weaknesses can be exploited by potential protection techniques, of which SBHA induces both divergence and explosion.

3   Initial Case Study

In [39], we introduce software-based hardware abstraction (SBHA) and evaluate its potential as a software protection technique, which we briefly summarize here. Analysis in the initial case study and results in this paper are focused on point-function protection. SBHA in its current form is a C (source) to C (source) transformation and the basic algorithm involves three steps:

1. Given a program P in source code form, first identify the relevant point function software construct.
2. Virtualize the software construct into a semantically equivalent Boolean logic form, then synthesize it into a combinational logic circuit (C).
3. Implement the hardware construct (C) into source code form and replace it in the original program, creating an SBHA variant P_{HW}.

3.1   SBHA Example

Program 1 illustrates a C program that checks for a 1-character (ASCII) password, which prints 0 and exits if a correct password is not entered by the user and runs normally otherwise (printing a 1). As an abstract example, it represents the general class of point-function checks that are associated with embedded program secrets. The Boolean function of this if-statement can be used to derive a corresponding truth-table, which has one input that produces the only true (1) result. As Fig. 2 illustrates, the single character input value for the password (%) is equivalent to 0x25 or 0b00100101. A canonical sum-of-products circuit can be thus synthesized from the Boolean equation or truth table to represent the identical equality check. Given the circuit (C) that represents the function of the software construct embodied in program P, SBHA then translates this back into software form to produce the variant P_{HW}. To accomplish this, we use a custom Boolean logic library (logiclib) that has corresponding C code for each logic gate type [39].

Program 2 shows the equivalent C code which is contained within the runcircuit function. Program 3 shows the corresponding transformation of Program 1 with the hardware-based abstraction now replacing the original if-statement.

Program 1. 1-Char Password C Program [39].

```
int main( int argc, char *argv[] )  {
  int compareResult = strncmp(argv[1], "%", 1);
  if (compareResult != 0) { printf ("0"); exit(-1); }
  else {                    printf ("1"); runprogram(); }
}
```

Because the circuit is semantically equivalent to the original if-statement, the replacement operates now by converting traditional data structures into binary (or Boolean) form. For example, input and output takes the form of bool arrays and the circuit is directly encoded by logiclib functions.

Program 2. SBHA Point Function Program [39].

```
void runcircuit(bool input[], bool out[]) {
   bool v8=input[0], v7=input[1], ... v2=input[6], v1=input[7];
   bool v9=not(v8), v10=not(v7), ... v12=not(v4), v13=not(v2);
   bool v20in[8];
   v20in[0] = v9; v20in[1] = v10; v20in[2] = v6; v20in[3] = v11;
   v20in[4] = v12; v20in[5] = v3; v20in[6] = v13; v20in[7] = v1;
   v20  = andmulti(v20in,8); out[0] = v20;
}
```

Program 3. Final SBHA Variant Code [39].

```
int main( int argc, char *argv[] )  {
  bool circuitinput[8];
  bool circuitoutput[1];
  convertString(argv[1],circuitinput,1);
  runcircuit (circuitinput, circuitoutput);
  if (circuitoutput[0]) {  printf ("0"); exit(-1); }
  else {                   printf ("1"); runprogram(); }
}
```

3.2 Methodology and Results

We examined four research questions related to obfuscation metrics in our original study [39]: effectiveness, resilience, stealth, and cost. A detailed technical report provides supporting detail for the study as well[2]. Our case study involved reproduction of prior results using benchmark programs that had embedded password and PIN code checks of varying sizes (1 to 16 characters) and fresh analysis of those programs with SBHA protection applied.

---

[2] http://soc.southalabama.edu/~mcdonald/SECRYPT_SBHA_TechReport.pdf.

Effectiveness. We repeated the experimental analysis of Holder et al. [33] on an extended benchmark set of programs that were created by applying different sequences of obfuscating transforms from the Tigress obfuscator. We then analyzed these programs using both KLEE and Angr. We demonstrated that no sequence of obfuscation types from Tigress prevented leakage of the embedded program asset (password or PIN code), but most transformation sequences increased analysis overhead (and thus were effective). We also found that some transformation sequences were ineffective, requiring roughly the same amount of analysis time on the unprotected original programs, and some even defective, actually reducing the analysis time. In testing 132 programs, KLEE and Angr ran with a max runtime of 9935 s seconds (2.75 h) for Angr and 42 s for KLEE. In all cases, KLEE and Angr revealed the embedded secrets (password and PIN) of the sample program (132/132 attack successes for each tool).

We evaluated a benchmark set of password/pin programs in 288 unprotected samples that ranged 576 experiments; for password and code only programs Angr leaked the password in 32 of 32 cases, KLEE leaked the password in 27 of 32 cases; for combined pwd/pin programs, KLEE leaked both pwd/pin in 120 of 256 cases and Angr leaked both pwd/pin in 169 of 256 cases [39]. We defined failure as exceeding the time-out of 120 h in the case of both KLEE and Angr. Angr had a maximum analysis time of 5.3 h and KLEE had a maximum analysis time of 79.3 h. We demonstrated that KLEE and Angr achieved high attack success rates (resp. 142/288 and 201/288).

To summarize, we applied SBHA in two different contexts for the study [39]:

1. We added SBHA on top of 12 out of each of 22 obfuscated variants and each original program in the original Holder benchmark set, in cases where we could still identify the point function in source code after Tigress transformations were applied. For 39 variants that were tested with both Angr and KLEE and given a timeout of 120 h for every sample file analyzed, adding SBHA to existing software obfuscations resulted in complete defeat of the DSE tools KLEE and Angr.
2. Similarly, we applied SBHA as the only obfuscating transformation to set of benchmark programs with a single password, single PIN code, and combined password/PIN. We analyzed the benchmarks with KLEE and Angr, giving them given a 120-h timeout period. Out of 288 SBHA-only protected program, the attack tools only succeeded in 1/288 cases, which was a single-password protected program with a 1-character password. Figure 4 provides a tabular summary of the study results, showing password and pin character sizes (1–16) for combined and standalone test programs. Green indicates that SBHA caused failure of the KLEE/Angr analysis whereas red indicates that the secret was leaked.

In its original (basic) version, with no other circuit-based transformations applied, SBHA is extremely effective against DSE attacks. Overall, Angr and KLEE were unable to retrieve passwords from any but one (1/327) of the protected variants including the SBHA version of the original programs (despite the generous 120 h time-out per sample), where these tools recover a significant part of the passwords without SBHA (KLEE: 181/327, Angr: 240/327).

Resilience. Since resilience measures the hardness of deobfuscating or simplifying complexity in obfuscasting transforms, in [39] we evaluated the property along three

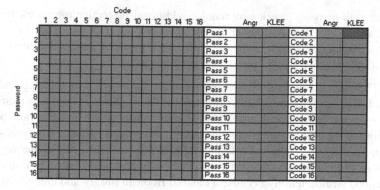

Fig. 4. SBHA Effectiveness against Angr/KLEE [39].

different lines: 1) optimizing attacks through compiler tool chain, 2) circuit (netlist) recovery attacks, and 3) path merging attacks. In this paper, we provide enhanced analysis involving netlist recovery and describe enhanced countermeasure techniques and security analysis in Sect. 4. In terms of reduction attacks, Tigress programs are C source code and we thus considered how GCC optimization levels would simplify obfuscated code. We positioned GCC as an attacker with potential to deobfuscate introduced SBHA protections. Our experiments transformed SBHA-protected benchmark programs using 6 different GCC optimization levels, and then analyzed the 36 program using Angr. With a 120 h timeout period for each variant, we found that Angr was not aided by any optimization level. This test of course gave even more power to the attacker by allowing pure source code level access, and thus strengthened the results. We concluded that optimizations refactor logic circuit abstraction code into different instructions, but do not optimize netlists enough to thwart the protection.

We also considered the impact of attackers that attempt to use path merging to reduce the impact of inherent DSE path explosion weakness. We approximated path merging attacks by replacing the standard Boolean library in the C code with Boolean operators (!, ||, &&)) instead of conditional statements. This allowed us to see what the effect of getting rid of paths taken in the code would be on the DSE analysis (thus simulating path merging in an optimizing DSE engine). This again was a worst case attack giving the adversary maximum power in the analysis and discounting the potential impact of other protections that might be geared to creating alternate Boolean logic functions in C or obfuscating the Boolean data itself. In this regard, we are experimenting with a worst case attack, where other forms of obfuscation of the Boolean library itself (many different alternate forms for each Boolean logic function in C code, obfuscating the Boolean data type itself, etc.) have failed and the reverse engineering has achieved path merging [34]. We tested an 8-character password-only program that simulates a path-merging attack using KLEE and Angr. KLEE failed to return a password in 24 h while Angr cracked the 8 character password in ≈ 1 h computation time for the same sample. Nonetheless, if we included countermeasures at the circuit-level (as discussed further in Sect. 4), path-merged 1 and 2 character password SBHA C programs resisted KLEE and Angr runs for at least 24 h. Our initial study thus showed that a worst-case path-merging attack may require additional protective measures, but when those are added, an effective counter can be produced. Overall, our study in [39] concluded that SBHA offers high resilience to the three forms of attacks that were studied (optimization, netlist recovery attacks, and path-merging).

Stealth. This metric gauges how well obfuscated code blends with existing code. Our initial study [39] utilized the MOSS program similarity checker [44] to measure similarity between the original programs and obfuscated variants. We also compute op-code distributions of the original programs versus their obfuscated variants. Analysis showed that *mov*, *movzx*, *lea*, *call*, and *add* instructions appeared at much higher rates than distributions in the original code versions. The study observed that SBHA alone does not have good stealth, mainly because a custom Boolean library and embedded circuit definition are tell-tale indicators.

Cost. Our initial study [39] considered overhead of SBHA using just the standard algorithm, with no countermeasures at the circuit-level itself. Cost was calculated in terms of source lines of code (LOC), memory, and execution time of the SBHA protected programs. Table 1 provides a summary of the key metrics (LOC, size, runtime) between original programs and SBHA variants. The study points out that standard virtualization is very expensive in terms of code size and runtime penalty [40]. Our analysis showed that standard SBHA does not suffer similar degradation and runtime difference was negligible. A maximum of 0.01 s (10%) between original and SBHA variants was observed. The source lines of code (SLOC) count provides a measure of size increase (which can affect memory, storage, and power consumption) and we reported 3.5× average overhead for SBHA transformation (min 2.02×, max 5.64x×). We observed that both SLOC and executable code size had a linear increase with unoptimized executables having ≈55% increase on average, with a minimum of 38% and maximum of 103%. We concluded that SBHA in its basic algorithm is a low-cost transformation for point-function constructs.

Table 1. Overhead Analysis: Original vs SBHA [39].

	Original			SBHA					
	LOC	Size	Runtime	LOC	xLOC	Size	xSize	Runtime	Delta
Pass6	174	12816	0.084	709	3.07	17704	38%	0.084	0.00
Pass9	113	8720	0.081	750	5.64	17704	103%	0.084	0.00
Pass 12	195	12816	0.083	938	3.81	21800	70%	0.082	0.00
Pass3Code2	256	12824	0.001	773	2.02	17784	39%	0.001	0.00
Pass3Code3	186	12824	0.091	731	2.93	17784	39%	0.083	0.01
Pass4Code4	172	12824	0.091	789	3.59	17784	39%	0.082	0.01

Avg xLOC: **3.51**   Avg Size: **55%**

4   Extended Algorithm with Enhanced Countermeasures

The initial study [39] on SBHA resilience provides initial results for attacks where we assume an adversary recovers the circuit netlist from an SBHA binary. The study showed initial positive results in this regard and posed countermeasures that could be included at the circuit level, prior to digital logic being converted back into code form. In this regard, the point-function circuit can leak the embedded secret through standard hardware analysis techniques. This paper provides a more full analysis of the potential circuit component configurations that might be utilized for enhanced countermeasures. We consider three lines of adversarial analyzers and corresponding methods for hindering or defeating their analysis outright:

1. **Anti-BDD:** Binary Decision Diagram (BDD) reduction can be used to derive semantics of a circuit in graph-based functional representations. However, we observe that BDD complexity and construction overhead [12,54] depends on the structure of an underlying circuit. We thus pose an anti-BDD technique that utilizes multiplier components which are known to have an exponential lower bound for BDD encoding [17,54] - seen in Fig. 5. For analysis, we utilize JDD[3]) to evaluate whether circuit-based analyzers can recover the embedded password from the circuit itself via BDD reduction.

2. **Anti-SAT:** Boolean-Satisfiability solvers (SAT-solvers) are often used in hardware deobfuscation and can simplify logic networks to find reduced functional expressions or solve unknown values. Our anti-SAT algorithm is based upon [46]'s, which was suggested the possible use of AND-trees as a means to improve resistance to logic encryption attacks. For analysis, we use the z3 Theorem Prover[4], created by Microsoft, which is well-known SMT solver to analyze circuit descriptions that are translated into equational form for analysis.

3. **Anti-Synthesis:** Synthesis tools can utilize a variety of methods (BDD, SAT, SMT, And-Inverter-Graph or AIG, multi-level minimization, etc.) to express the function of logic networks in canonically reduced forms (such as Programmable Logic Array/PLA or MINTERM/MAXTERM format). We utilize the well-studied open source synthesis tool ABC[5] to analyze BENCH circuit descriptions in the attempt to create PLA forms of the function.

4.1 Circuit Transformations

Once the basic point-function for an IF statement construct is derived from a protected piece of code, there are several forms of transformation that we apply. We insert a multiplier component prior to the point function circuit itself, which represents a semantically equivalent mathematical operation end-to-end. Figure 5 illustrates the concept, using as an example a single-character password (8 bit) point function circuit. For our circuit components, we utilize BENCH-transformed versions of (unsigned) multiplier and divider circuits used by Nigel Smart's research group at KU Leuven in other SMPC research[6]. Because combinational logic components are very precise in terms of input/output size, we utilize custom expanders and slicers to either extend or reduce

---

[3] https://bitbucket.org/vahidi/jdd/src/master/.

[4] https://github.com/Z3Prover.

[5] https://people.eecs.berkeley.edu/~alanmi/abc/.

[6] https://homes.esat.kuleuven.be/~nsmart/MPC/.

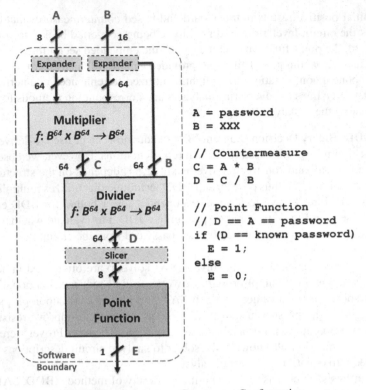

Fig. 5. Countermeasure Component Configuration.

bit size values, with guarantees that values are never truncated. In this example, the software-side which calls the "runcircuit" function (seen in Program 3 marshals data values in normal software variables into arrays of Boolean values. Likewise, the software side can be used to pass values into the circuit itself. Figure 5 depicts a circuit that expects two values: one is the password entered by the user (A) which is 8 bits and the other is a short (2-byte) value that will be used for semantic preserving mathematical computation (B) in 16 bits. Mathematically, these values are multiplied together (C) then the B value is divided out (D). The multiplier component is fixed with two 64-bit inputs, and thus software-provided values must be expanded to the correct bit size. Likewise, the divider outputs a 64-bit value, which must be reduced in size to fit the point-function circuit input size of 8-bits. Overall, the entire collection of components is functionally equivalent to the original point-function circuit.

We also consider other semantic-preserving transformations to the component circuit that is illustrated in Fig. 5. As we describe in our initial study [39] and supporting technical report 2, we utilize AND-tree constructs that hinder certain synthesis and SAT analysis methods. We add variable numbers (20–40) of AND-trees of varying input sizes (8,16,24,32,64, and 128-bit) to this component circuit, in a semantic preserving manner. We also perform polymorphic variation on the circuit using a simple obfuscation algorithm known as Iterative Selection and Replacement (ISR) [38]. There

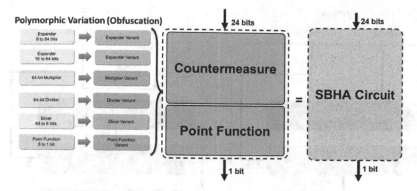

Fig. 6. Polymorphic Variation for SBHA Component Circuit.

are two methods in which ISR/AND-tree variation can be applied and Fig. 6 illustrates the basic method. In this case, each circuit component (extenders, multiplier, divider, point-function, etc.) are all transformed individually, then composed together to create the SBHA circuit. We view the circuitry added prior to the point function collectively as the "countermeasure". The other approach (which we refer to as ISR-FULL) applies an additional layer of obfuscation on the composed circuit form after the first round of obfuscations are applied at the component level. We wanted to see if polymorphic variation had any effect on the underlying analyzers that we studied (ABC, z3, and JDD).

4.2 Countermeasure Circuit Configurations

There are multiple different ways in which the software/hardware interface can be configured in terms of the countermeasure circuit itself. We derived four possibilities based on: 1) whether or not the software was responsible for expanding password and computation values to meet the expected bit-sizes of the multiplier component - called Type A (vs. the circuit itself which is called Type B), 2) whether internally the circuit would provide a value for the math computation involved in the multiplication or not (which we describe as Type C and D circuits) or whether the software provides it (type A and B do), and 3) whether the circuit only needs to receive the password/asset value (as the original point function circuit would) - Type D embodies this approach.

Figure 7 illustrates two approaches where the software side provides the value used in the mathematical computation, but Type A expects the password value to be in the correct bit-size on input. Type B will take the correctly sized input for the password and expand it to the expected size of the multiplier. Figure 8 illustrates two approaches where the hardware side provides the value used in the mathematical computation. In Type C, the circuit does receive an input for this value, but it is used to seed or trigger a constant generator circuit that is inside the component circuit itself. Even though we used a constant generating circuit (it produces the same output number on all inputs), we envision this component to be a random number generating circuit and the input

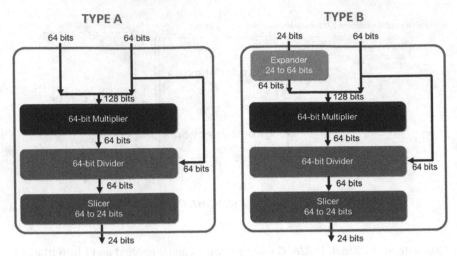

Fig. 7. Type A and B Countermeasures.

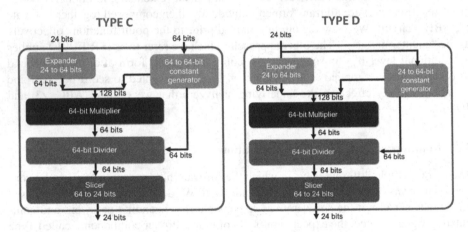

Fig. 8. Type C and D Countermeasures.

value being a seed for it. Type D component circuits actually use the password value itself as the input to the constant generator.

5   Countermeasure Evaluation

For evaluating these different component configurations (A,B,C,D) against three lines of adversarial attack, we looked at a simple 1-character password program. We chose this mainly because it represents what should be the easiest scenario for an attacker to analyze (with other than brute-force means). Of course, brute-force approaches easily leak secrets up to tractable computation limits, but it also illustrates how attack lines use other-than brute-force approaches. Table 2 provides a summary of the 12 benchmark variants we generated from the original 1-character password point-function circuit.

In this study, we only evaluate the circuit construct using hardware-based analyzers, assuming the adversary has recovered the netlist cleanly from the SBHA binary. For each configuration type (A, B, C, D), there are three versions: no obfuscation (A1, B1, etc.), component-level ISR/AND-tree insertion (A2, B2, etc.), and component-level ISR plus a final round of obfuscation on the entire circuit (A3, B3, etc.). Variants are delineated by whether the password is expanded and an input value from the software itself is required. Type C and D countermeasures have an embedded constant generator whose source is either seeded by a software-provided value or the password itself.

Table 2. Test Configuration Summary.

Type	Password Expanded	Value Required	Constant Generator	Constant Source	ISR/ AND-tree
A1	N	Y	N	N/A	N
A2	N	Y	N	N/A	Y
A3	N	Y	N	N/A	FULL
B1	Y	Y	N	N/A	N
B2	Y	Y	N	N/A	Y
B3	Y	Y	N	N/A	FULL
C1	Y	Y	Y	Value	N
C2	Y	Y	Y	Value	Y
C3	Y	Y	Y	Value	FULL
D1	Y	N	Y	Password	N
D2	Y	N	Y	Password	Y
D3	Y	N	Y	Password	FULL

After creating BENCH circuits based on the component configuration and applying obfuscations, we ran analysis tools against each variant. All experiments were conducted on a standard PC workstation with 32 GB RAM and a 2.50 GhZ Intel Core i7-4710MQ processor. Table 3 provides a summary of the results. Of note, all configurations of type A and B circuits caused complete failure of JDD, z3, and ABC in recovering the embedded secret in the test circuits. For configuration types C and D, all variants defeated ABC synthesis attempts to create a PLA of the circuit function, but only those with added polymorphic variation caused defeat of the z3 analyzer. In the case of JDD, no type C or D variant was able to prevent creation of a BDD that clearly revealed the password input required for the circuit. z3 completed execution in all cases with varying times (less than 2 min), but either returned an incorrect model (an input that did not represent the point), reported no model, or recovered the model that represented the password. The use of a constant internal to the circuit component provided more advantage to the adversarial analysis such as z3 and JDD.

Table 3. Case Study Results.

Type	Polymorphic Variation	Gate Size	JDD Recovery	JDD Time	z3 Recovery	z3 Time	ABC Recovery
A1	N	26706	N	-	incorrect model	1m:17s	N
A2	Y	33601	N	-	no model	1m:19s	N
A3	FULL	35556	N	-	no model	45s	N
B1	N	26770	N	-	incorrect model	53s	N
B2	Y	34838	N	-	no model	50s	N
B3	FULL	36863	N	-	no model	45s	N
C1	N	26834	Y	1m:48s	recovered	52s	N
C2	Y	36064	Y	1m:45s	no model	55s	N
C3	FULL	38161	Y	2m:51s	no model	1m:2s	N
D1	N	26834	Y	1m:47s	recovered	50s	N
D2	Y	35909	Y	2m:12s	no model	1m:0s	N
D3	FULL	37779	Y	2m:16s	no model	55s	N

In terms of overhead analysis, gate size increase from the original point function circuit for any of the countermeasure types was of course large. Using real circuit components (full multiplier and divider circuits) include components with over 10K gates themselves. This translates directly to linear increase (roughly one to one per gate in the circuit) in source lines of code. This in turn results in corresponding increase in executable size. Gate size increase using basic ISR resulted in 6800–9200 additional gates whereas full ISR resulted in 8800–11300 additional gates. The countermeasure circuit itself roughly adds 26K additional gates. Although execution size is greatly impacted, we translated all circuits back into C programs, compiled them with -O3 optimization, and executed them. The actual computation time from entry of the password until its evaluation was recorded for all variants. On average, response time varied from 0.14–0.17 s, representing around a 20% increase from the original execution time. In essence, from a user-experience perspective, the SBHA construct would not be perceivable. We surmise that using SBHA transformation (in general) for generic code sequences, especially those that are part of high volume computations at runtime, would cause higher impact on runtimes, which we don't study in this work. Point-function checks are typically executed a small number of times and in limited contexts, and conclude that SBHA would be ideal for such protection scenarios. In our initial study [39], we confirmed similar results, but used representative forms of multipliers and dividers based on shifters and using mathematical values that were powers of 2. Given the success of full components in the hard-case of a single-character password, we can also conclude that obfuscation is not needed for defeating automated circuit analyzers, but might be useful for deterring reverse engineering or component analysis of the netlist with a human-guided attack. The study did show that obfuscation did make a difference in defeating one type of attack analysis with the z3 solver.

6   Conclusion and Future Work

In this paper we analyze SBHA-based software transformation as a completely new approach to software protection and further initial studies provided in [39]. The starting case for using SBHA to protect point-function programs, particularly against DSE-based attacks, shows great promise since a basic (non-obfuscated or hardened) SBHA circuit is highly effective stand-alone. In this work, we evaluate resilience against SBHA circuits to attacks where the adversary fully recovers a clean netlist from an SBHA binary. Given such advantage, an attacker can employ BDD, SAT/SMT, and synthesis based tools on the circuit to discover functional forms that leak the embedded secret. We evaluate four different countermeasure configuration for the SBHA circuit using a single-character password program and show that specific configurations can defeat representative attackers beyond just driving up overhead time for computation. We further the results that show SBHA to be highly effective and resilient as an obfuscating transformation. With countermeasure configurations there is a potential large overhead in size (increase SLOC and executable size), but for point-function applications the runtime overhead and experience are essentially negligible.

SBHA is fundamentally a data obfuscation when used for point-function protection, but future work will involve evaluation in other software protection contexts. SBHA could offer new ways to achieve opaque predicate insertion (fundamentally IF-based structures), provide extended forms of mixed Boolean arithmetic, implement basic blocks at the assembly level (any straight-line piece of code can be represented directly as combinational logic), and achieve function merging or splitting depending on the content of the function. We expect as a diversifying transformation, SBHA also has promise for applications where real hardware might be integrated into software defense-circuit partitions provide a natural way to divide software/hardware interactions in a protection context.

References

1. Abrar, S.S., Jenihhin, M., Raik, J.: Extensible open-source framework for translating RTL VHDL IP cores to SystemC. In: IEEE DDECS (2013)
2. Akhunzada, A., Sookhak, M., Anuar, N.B., et al.: Man-at-the-end attacks: analysis, taxonomy, human aspects, motivation and future directions. J. Netw. Comput. Appl. **48**, 44–57 (2015). https://doi.org/10.1016/j.jnca.2014.10.009
3. Anand, S., Păsăreanu, C.S., Visser, W.: Symbolic execution with abstraction. Int. J. Softw. Tools Technol. Transf. **11**(1) (2009). https://doi.org/10.1007/s10009-008-0090-1
4. Averbuch, A., Kiperberg, M., Zaidenberg, N.J.: An efficient VM-based software protection. In: 2011 5th International Conference on Network and System Security, pp. 121–128, September 2011. https://doi.org/10.1109/ICNSS.2011.6059968
5. Balakrishnan, G., Reps, T.W.: WYSINWYX: what you see is not what you execute. ACM Trans. Program. Lang. Syst. **32**(6) (2010). https://doi.org/10.1145/1749608.1749612
6. Banescu, S., Collberg, C., Ganesh, V., Newsham, Z., Pretschner, A.: Code obfuscation against symbolic execution attacks. In: ACSAC'16 (2016). https://doi.org/10.1145/2991079. 2991114
7. Banescu, S., Collberg, C., Pretschner, A.: Predicting the resilience of obfuscated code against symbolic execution attacks via machine learning. In: USENIX SEC'17 (2017). http://dl.acm. org/citation.cfm?id=3241189.3241241

8. Banescu, S., Ochoa, M., Pretschner, A.: A framework for measuring software obfuscation resilience against automated attacks. In: SPRO'15 (2015). http://dl.acm.org/citation.cfm?id=2821429.2821442

9. Barak, B., Goldreich, O., Impagliazzo, R., Rudich, S., et al.: On the (im)possibility of obfuscating programs. J. ACM 59(2) (2012). https://doi.org/10.1145/2160158.2160159

10. Bardin, S., David, R., Marion, J.: Backward-bounded DSE: targeting infeasibility questions on obfuscated codes. In: S&P '17, May 2017. https://doi.org/10.1109/SP.2017.36

11. Basile, C., Canavese, D., Regano, L., Falcarin, P., Sutter, B.D.: A meta-model for software protections and reverse engineering attacks. J. Syst. Softw. 150 (2019). https://doi.org/10.1016/j.jss.2018.12.025

12. Beyer, D., Stahlbauer, A.: BDD-based software verification. Int. J. Softw. Tools Technol. Transf. 16(5), 507–518 (2014). https://doi.org/10.1007/s10009-014-0334-1

13. Biondi, F., Josse, S., Legay, A., Sirvent, T.: Effectiveness of synthesis in concolic deobfuscation. Comput. Secur. 70 (2017). https://doi.org/10.1016/j.cose.2017.07.006

14. Black, D.C., Donovan, J., Bunton, B., Keist, A.: SystemC: From the Ground Up, 2nd edn. Springer, New York (2009). https://doi.org/10.1007/978-0-387-69958-5

15. Bruni, R., Giacobazzi, R., Gori, R.: Code obfuscation against abstract model checking attacks. In: VMCAI 2018. LNCS, vol. 10747, pp. 94–115. Springer, Cham (2018). https://doi.org/10.1007/978-3-319-73721-8_5

16. Bryant: Graph-based algorithms for Boolean function manipulation. IEEE Trans. Comput. $C\text{-}35$(8) (1986). https://doi.org/10.1109/TC.1986.1676819

17. Bryant, R.E.: On the complexity of vlsi implementations and graph representations of boolean functions with application to integer multiplication. IEEE Trans. Comput. 40(2) (1991). https://doi.org/10.1109/12.73590

18. BSA Foundation: BSA Global Software Survey: Software management: Security imperative, business opportunity, June 2018. https://gss.bsa.org/wp-content/uploads/2018/05/2018_BSA_GSS_Report_en.pdf. Accessed 01 June 2021

19. Cadar, C., Sen, K.: Symbolic execution for software testing: three decades later. Commun. ACM 56(2) (2013). https://doi.org/10.1145/2408776.2408795

20. Ceccato, M., et al.: How professional hackers understand protected code while performing attack tasks. In: ICPC'17 (2017). https://doi.org/10.1109/ICPC.2017.2

21. Cheng, X., Lin, Y., Gao, D., Jia, C.: DynOpVm: VM-based software obfuscation with dynamic opcode mapping. In: Applied Cryptography and Network Security (2019)

22. Collberg, C., Thomborson, C., Low, D.: A taxonomy of obfuscating transformations. Technical report, Univ. of Auckland (1997)

23. Collberg, C.S., Thomborson, C.: Watermarking, tamper-proofing, and obfuscation - tools for software protection. IEEE Trans. Softw. Eng. 28(8) (2002). https://doi.org/10.1109/TSE.2002.1027797

24. Collberg, C., Davidson, J., Giacobazzi, R., Gu, Y.X., Herzberg, A., Wang, F.Y.: Toward digital asset protection. IEEE Intell. Syst. 26(6) (2011). https://doi.org/10.1109/MIS.2011.106

25. Collberg, C., Nagra, J.: Surreptitious Software: Obfuscation, Watermarking, and Tamper-proofing for Software Protection. Addison-Wesley Professional (2009)

26. Coogan, K., Lu, G., Debray, S.: Deobfuscation of virtualization-obfuscated software: a semantics-based approach. In: CCS'11 (2011). https://doi.org/10.1145/2046707.2046739

27. De Micheli, G.: Synthesis and Optimization of Digital Circuits. McGraw-Hill Higher Education (1994)

28. Demmler, D., Schneider, T., Zohner, M.: Aby - a framework for efficient mixed-protocol secure two-party computation. In: NDSS (2015)

29. Evans, D., Kolesnikov, V., Rosulek, M.: A pragmatic introduction to secure multi-party computation. Found. Trends Privacy Secur. 2(2–3), 70–246 (2018). https://doi.org/10.1561/3300000019

30. Eyrolles, N., Goubin, L., Videau, M.: Defeating MBA-based obfuscation. In: SPRO'16 (2016). https://doi.org/10.1145/2995306.2995308
31. Fang, D., Gao, L., Tang, Z., Chen, X.: A software protection framework based on thin virtual machine using distorted encryption. In: 2011 International Conference on Network Computing and Information Security, vol. 1, pp. 266–271, May 2011. https://doi.org/10.1109/NCIS.2011.60
32. Hansen, M.C., Yalcin, H., Hayes, J.P.: Unveiling the ISCAS-85 benchmarks: a case study in reverse engineering. IEEE Des. Test **16**(3) (1999). https://doi.org/10.1109/54.785838
33. Holder, W., McDonald, J.T., Andel, T.R.: Evaluating optimal phase ordering in obfuscation executives. In: 7th SSPREW (2017). https://doi.org/10.1145/3151137.3151140
34. Kuznetsov, V., Kinder, J., Bucur, S., Candea, G.: Efficient state merging in symbolic execution. In: PLDI'12 (2012). https://doi.org/10.1145/2254064.2254088
35. Lan, P., Wang, P., Wang, S., Wu, D.: Lambda obfuscation. In: SecureComm'17 (2018)
36. Malkhi, D., Nisan, N., Pinkas, B., Sella, Y.: Fairplay–a secure two-party computation system. In: Proceedings of the 13th Conference on USENIX Security Symposium. SSYM'04, vol. 13. p. 20. USENIX Association, Berkeley, CA, USA (2004). http://dl.acm.org/citation.cfm?id=1251375.1251395
37. Manikyam, R., McDonald, J.T., Mahoney, W.R., Andel, T.R., Russ, S.H.: Comparing the effectiveness of commercial obfuscators against mate attacks. In: SSPREW'16 (2016). https://doi.org/10.1145/3015135.3015143
38. McDonald, J., Kim, Y., Grimaila, M.: Protecting reprogrammable hardware with polymorphic circuit variation. In: Proceedings of the 2nd Cyberspace Research Workshop (2009)
39. McDonald, J., Manikyam, R., Bardin, S., Bonichon, R., Andel, T.R.: Program protection through software-based hardware abstraction. In: SECRYPT (2021). https://doi.org/10.5220/0010557502470258
40. Ollivier, M., Bardin, S., Bonichon, R., Marion, J.Y.: How to kill symbolic deobfuscation for free (or: unleashing the potential of path-oriented protections). In: ACSAC'19 (2019). https://doi.org/10.1145/3359789.3359812
41. Ollivier, M., Bardin, S., Bonichon, R., Marion, J.: Obfuscation: where are we in anti-DSE protections (a first attempt). In: SSPREW '19 (2019)
42. Rival, X., Yi, K.: Introduction to Static Analysis: An Abstract Interpretation Perspective. The MIT Press (2020)
43. Salwan, J., Bardin, S., Potet, M.L.: Symbolic deobfuscation: from virtualized code back to the original. In: DIMVA'18 (2018)
44. Schleimer, S., Wilkerson, D.S., Aiken, A.: Winnowing: local algorithms for document fingerprinting. In: ICMD'03 (2003). https://doi.org/10.1145/872757.872770
45. Schrittwieser, S., Katzenbeisser, S., Kinder, J., Merzdovnik, G., Weippl, E.: Protecting software through obfuscation: can it keep pace with progress in code analysis? ACM Comput. Surv. **49**(1) (2016). https://doi.org/10.1145/2886012
46. Subramanyan, P., Ray, S., Malik, S.: Evaluating the security of logic encryption algorithms. In: HOST'15, May 2015. https://doi.org/10.1109/HST.2015.7140252
47. Thales Group: Software protection & licensing solutions (2022). https://cpl.thalesgroup.com/software-monetization/software-protection-licensing. Accessed 01 June 2022
48. Vahid, F.: It's time to stop calling circuits "hardware". Computer **40**(9) (2007). https://doi.org/10.1109/MC.2007.322
49. Vahid, F.: What is hardware/software partitioning? SIGDA Newsl. **39**(6), 1–1 (2009). https://doi.org/10.1145/1862900.1862901
50. Wang, H., Fang, D., Li, G., Yin, X., Zhang, B., Gu, Y.: Nislvmp: improved virtual machine-based software protection. In: Proceedings of the 2013 Ninth International Conference on Computational Intelligence and Security. CIS '13, pp. 479–483. Washington, DC, USA (2013). https://doi.org/10.1109/CIS.2013.107

51. Wang, X., Ranellucci, S., Katz, J.: Authenticated garbling and efficient maliciously secure two-party computation. In: Proceedings of the 2017 ACM SIGSAC Conference on Computer and Communications Security. CCS '17, pp. 21–37. New York, NY, USA (2017). https://doi.org/10.1145/3133956.3134053

52. Wirth, N.: Hardware compilation: translating programs into circuits. Computer **31**(6), 25–31 (1998). https://doi.org/10.1109/2.683004

53. Wirth, N.: From Programming Language Design to Computer Construction, p. 1984. Association for Computing Machinery, New York, NY, USA (2007). https://doi.org/10.1145/1283920.1283941

54. Woelfel, P.: Bounds on the OBDD-size of integer multiplication via universal hashing. J. Comput. Syst. Sci. **71**(4) (2005). https://doi.org/10.1016/j.jcss.2005.05.004

55. Yadegari, B., Johannesmeyer, B., Whitely, B., Debray, S.: A generic approach to automatic deobfuscation of executable code. In: S&P'15 (2015). https://doi.org/10.1109/SP.2015.47

56. Yao, A.C.C.: How to generate and exchange secrets. In: Proceedings of the 27th Annual Symposium on Foundations of Computer Science. SFCS '86, pp. 162–167. Washington, DC, USA (1986). https://doi.org/10.1109/SFCS.1986.25

57. Zahur, S., Evans, D.: Obliv-c: a language for extensible data-oblivious computation. Cryptology ePrint Archive, Report 2015/1153 (2015). https://eprint.iacr.org/2015/1153

58. Zahur, S., Rosulek, M., Evans, D.: Two halves make a whole. In: Oswald, E., Fischlin, M. (eds.) EUROCRYPT 2015. LNCS, vol. 9057, pp. 220–250. Springer, Heidelberg (2015). https://doi.org/10.1007/978-3-662-46803-6_8

59. Zhang, Y., Steele, A., Blanton, M.: Picco: a general-purpose compiler for private distributed computation. In: Proceedings of the 2013 ACM SIGSAC Conference on Computer and Communications Security. CCS '13, New York, NY, USA (2013). https://doi.org/10.1145/2508859.2516752

60. Zhou, Y., Main, A., Gu, Y.X., Johnson, H.: Information hiding in software with mixed Boolean-arithmetic transforms. In: WISA'07 (2007)

Trace Recovery: Attacking and Defending the User Privacy in Smart Meter Data Analytics

Nazim Uddin Sheikh[1,2(✉)], Zhigang Lu[2], Hassan Jameel Asghar[2,3], and Mohamed Ali Kaafar[2]

[1] Australian Institute of Health Innovation, Macquarie University, Sydney, NSW 2109, Australia
nazim-uddin.sheikh@mq.edu.au
[2] Cyber Security Hub, School of Computing Macquarie University, Sydney, NSW 2109, Australia
{zhigang.lu,hassan.asghar,dali.kaafar}@mq.edu.au
[3] Data61, CSIRO, Sydney, Australia

Abstract. Energy consumption data is collected the service providers and shared with various stakeholders involved in a smart grid ecosystem. The fine-grained energy consumption data is immensely useful for maintaining and operating grid services. Further, these data can be used for future consumption prediction using machine learning and statistical models and market segmentation purposes. However, sharing and releasing fine-grained energy data or releasing predictive models trained on user-specific data induce explicit violations of private information of consumers [34,41]. Thus, the service providers may share and release aggregated statistics to protect the privacy of users aiming at mitigating the privacy risks of individual users' consumption traces. In this chapter, we show that an attacker can recover individual users' traces of energy consumption data by exploiting *regularity* and *uniqueness* properties of individual consumption load patterns. We propose an unsupervised attack framework to recover hourly energy consumption time-series of users without any background information. We construct the problem of assigning aggregated energy consumption meter readings to individual users as a mathematical assignment problem and solve it by the Hungarian algorithm [30,50]. We used two real-world datasets to demonstrate an attacker's performance in recovering private traits of users. Our results show that an attacker is capable of recovering 70% of users' energy consumption patterns with over 90% accuracy. Finally, we proposed few defense techniques, such as differential privacy and federated machine learning that may potentially help reduce an attacker's capability to infer users' private information.

Keywords: Inference Attacks · Aggregate Statistics · Differential Privacy · Energy Data Privacy · Smart Meter Privacy · Federated Learning

© The Author(s), under exclusive license to Springer Nature Switzerland AG 2023
P. Samarati et al. (Eds.): ICETE 2021, CCIS 1795, pp. 305–333, 2023.
https://doi.org/10.1007/978-3-031-36840-0_14

1   Introduction

Smart meters are integral components of smart metering infrastructure in smart grids. Recently, smart meters are widely being deployed in domestic and commercial building across the globe. Smart meter consumption measurements are used in various applications, such as monitoring, operations and management of grids [29]. A cluster (a group of) individual households' smart meter data are aggregated and communicated to the electricity providers over a secure channel for the different purposes, predictive analysis, demand forecasting and business analytics without compromising the privacy of individual households [17, 38]. Many mechanisms based on such secure aggregation have been proposed to protect the privacy of consumers [5]. Although aggregation itself is cryptographically protected, the electricity providers have access to the decrypted aggregated form of energy consumption over a cluster (group) of households [5].

There are usually two types of aggregations can be performed on smart metering readings data: temporal and/or spatial. The temporal aggregation is performed over a long period of time, for example, monthly or quarterly [8] which is required for the billing purposes. On the other hand, the spatial aggregation [8] is performed on multiple households' load patterns by combining them together into a cluster for hiding individual users' patterns [18]. Such aggregated data can be shared with the third-party stakeholders [32] as it is considered that such aggregated data do not infringe the privacy of customers. However, this assumption on aggregation providing enough privacy requires further investigation. In this chapter, we modelled an attack framework where an attacker (e.g., curious service provider, a third-party stakeholder or an external malicious entity) is capable of recovering fine-grained energy consumption traces of users through having access to the aggregated statistics of energy consumption time-series data. The essential elements of our attack are based on the attack from Xu et al. [50] on de-aggregating user location traces from aggregated mobility traces, and a similar argument is often used about privacy via aggregation.

In essence, we show that an attacker can infringe the privacy of individuals by exploiting two key attributes of their load patterns. First, the load pattern of a household is consistent, which makes their load pattern highly predictable. Second, the load pattern of each household can be uniquely distinguished from each other with high probability. Combining the two observations, we could split the aggregated energy data to different traces of energy consumption iteratively (by the first observation), then link the recovered traces to most of the individual households (by the second observation). Moreover, we propose few defense techniques that could be used to thwart such attack against energy data.

Contributions. In this chapter, we aim to quantitatively investigate the privacy implications of releasing aggregated statistics of smart meter energy consumption data of individual customers without any prior knowledge. Our contributions are as follows:

- We constructed an unsupervised adversarial model based on aggregated statistics of energy consumption data [40]. The adversarial framework does not require any background information about the individuals to reconstruct their fine-grained energy consumption records from aggregates. The adversary exploits the *regularity* and *uniqueness* property in day-to-day energy consumption load patterns. Then we present the problem as a mathematical balanced assignment problem and construct cost matrices [50] based on expected energy consumption change at each time step. Our quantitative analysis shows that the households' consumption patterns are similar over time and most of them are different from each other. We compute expected energy consumption changes from one time step to another, which help to estimate energy consumption in the next time steps and formulate a cost matrix to optimise the assignment of households to energy consumption traces (see Sect. 4) [40].

- We use two real-world smart meter reading datasets to empirically evaluate the adversary's capability to reconstruct individual users' fine-grained energy usage load patterns. We show that the adversary recovers energy consumption patterns with high accuracy (between 80% and 95%) averaged over all target households and the entire time period. We observe that 70% of households' load patterns can be inferred from aggregated statistics with an accuracy over 90%. Finally, we show that the adversary recovers 60% of households' energy consumption by incurring a 0.4 kWh or less error from the actual (ground truth) consumption traces [40].
- We provide insightful directions for future research in differential privacy and AI-enabled energy data analytics in a privacy-preserving way. We survey and analyze existing privacy preserving technologies in AI-enabled energy data analytics and identify their limitations and open research questions in the field. Some of the salient contributions, such as proposing AI-enabled energy data analytics and differentially private mechanisms.

A key feature of our attack on aggregated energy data is that it does not rely on any background knowledge of any individual household's consumption. This is unlike other attacks on smart-meter aggregation, for example, [5], as detailed in the next section.

2   Related Work

In this section, we review some related work pertaining to privacy preserving energy data analytics, issues in energy data sharing with third-parties, releasing aggregated data, adversarial models and privacy enhancing technologies that are widely used to protect the privacy of individuals while leveraging aggregated data analytics.

Privacy Preserving Data Analytics: A massive amount of energy consumption data from millions of households and generated on a daily basis is being collected and shared with third-parties and different stakeholders involved in the smart meter ecosystem [51]. Smart meter data analytics involve descriptive, predictive [22] and prescriptive analyses, it also includes many critical applications, such as load analysis, load forecasting and load management [46]. The main objective of privacy friendly data analytics is to safeguard the users (households) from private information leakage while leveraging the utility of the data [39]. Many other schemes have been proposed to facilitate privacy preserving data collection, sharing and analytics [33]. Sirojan et al. [42] envisaged an edge computing based architecture to provide a variety of energy data analytic services such as event detection, down-sampling and load identification, however, this architecture does not guarantee the privacy of user specific sensitive data. Cloud based hierarchical architectures are conceived as facilitating access control mechanisms that help manage to share and analyse data while keeping sensitive information hidden [31]. Shateri et al. [39] studied the privacy-utility tradeoff in privacy preserving energy data analytics using an information theoretic approach. Chen et al. [7] reviewed some learning based methods that leverage efficient privacy-aware energy data analytics. Wen et al. [48] proposed a privacy preserving query-based cloud server model for encrypted consumption data.

Non-intrusive Load Monitoring: A myriad of study has been conducted on how fine-grained energy consumption data can reveal an enormous amount of private information about individual households. Non-intrusive load monitoring (NILM) has been a prolific research area in the last decade. NILM has shown that the individual appliance specific energy consumption can be separated from the load pattern of a household using different statistical methods [23,52] and deep learning algorithms [28]. Therefore, information about personal activities can be discovered from their electricity consumption patterns. This constitutes a severe privacy threat to individual consumers [36]. Note that, NILM is successful only if an adversary has access to the load patterns of individual consumers. All the aforementioned studies rely on individual households' energy consumption time-series data to retrieve appliance specific consumption or to derive appliances' ON/OFF states at different point of time. However, in this chapter, we attempt to recover each individual household's fine-grained energy consumption traces from an aggregate, which is the combination of a cluster (group) of households' energy consumption time-series data without relying on any prior knowledge and/or access to individual's load patterns.

Reconstruction Attacks: In a reconstruction attack, given some aggregated statistics, an attacker aims to retrieve (or infer) private information of individuals with limited background knowledge [3,25,37,45]. This type of attack could be either partial or full. In the literature different terms have been coined to refer to this type of attack, such as *"attribute inference"* [21,27] or *"model inversion"* [19,44] attacks. The term *"attribute inference"* has been coined in other privacy related domains to describe adversarial aspects that infer sensitive attributes of individual users by exploiting publicly available databases [20,27]. In the energy data context *"attribute inference"* refers to the sensitive attributes or characteristics of a household, such as occupancy level, daily routines and appliances being used [34].

Privacy of Aggregation Models: Aggregation is widely used to safeguard the privacy of individual households by masking the individual specific consumption [18]. More generally, two types of privacy preserving aggregation methods exist in the literature: many solutions rely on trusted third-party based services using cryptographic protocols (e.g., homomorphic encryption) [2,15,43] and decentralised techniques, relying on blockchain technology [22,49]. Hong et al. [24] proposed a streaming algorithm that safeguards the implications of information leakage from the readings of a meter on the state of a specific appliance. A study by an industrial body suggests that aggregation of two load patterns of two different households is sufficient to protect the privacy of individuals in aggregated data [16]. However, this study was revisited and its findings disputed in [5], which shows that individuals in an aggregate of size two are distinguishable with high accuracy. Moreover, Buescher et al. [5] demonstrated the risk of being distinguishable for different size of aggregates. However, one of the limitations of this distinguishability attack model is that the adversary knows the load profiles contained in the aggregate and past consumption records of all aggregators [5]. The key difference between our attack model and the work in [5] is that our attack model does not rely on any prior knowledge about the individual energy consumption records.

Our work has been inspired by [50] that recovers individuals mobility data (trajectories) by exploiting *regularity* and *uniqueness* features of mobility patterns of users. Authors posed and verified that most mobile users follow explicit moving patterns, with little mobility during night time and stable (and hence predictable) mobility patterns during daytime. In [50], Xu et al. considered that during day time users' velocities are uniform which may not be a realistic assumption. While our work on Energy data consumption is different, we additionally took into consideration changes in consumption (analogous to speed or velocity in mobility data) from one time window to the next over the entire population.

3   Background and Threat Model

In this section we define the notation that will be used throughout the paper, and precisely describe the threat model behind energy consumption data recovery.

3.1   Notation

The energy reading of household i by a smart meter at time step $t \in \mathbb{N}$ is denoted by $x_i^{(t)}$.[1] Energy data of household i over horizon T (i.e., T time steps) is represented as a time-series, and denoted by the T-element vector $\mathbf{x}_i$, whose t-th element is $x_i^{(t)}$.

---

[1] In general, time steps t and $t + 1$ represent consecutive, potentially equally-spaced, times. In this chapter, they represent hours.

The aggregate (sum) consumption of n number of households over a time period T, defined as a set of one or more time steps, is given by

$$x_{agg} = \left[\sum_{i=1}^{n} x_i^{(1)}, \ \sum_{i=1}^{n} x_i^{(2)}, \ \ldots, \ \sum_{i=1}^{n} x_i^{(T)} \right] \tag{1}$$

3.2 Energy Trace Recovery: Threat Model

We now describe an adversary ($\mathcal{A}$) who wishes to reconstruct fine-grained energy consumption patterns of individual households from aggregate statistics. First, the adversary $\mathcal{A}$ accumulates aggregated statistics of n number of households in a neighbourhood over T period of time from a publicly released aggregated dataset or through querying a database via a user interface. The queries to the database may include but not be limited to the following: *(i) What are the maximum and minimum consumption in kWh in a neighbourhood at each time step t over the horizon of time T?, (ii) How many households consume x kWh of energy at a specific time of a day?, (iii) How many households' consumption is in a given range of energy (e.g., how many households' energy consumption is between 0 and 1 kWh at time t)* and *(iv) How many households' electricity usage increases or decreases at different hourly of a day and how much?*. There could be many other possible queries which are beyond the scope of this paper.

The adversary $\mathcal{A}$ then analyses the aggregated statistics to construct an attack strategy that helps reconstruct the energy consumption patterns of individual households. A key consideration here is that the adversary might not be able to reconstruct the energy consumption of each household at very fine granularity levels. This is due to the fact that even though the energy consumption of a household may show *similar* trends over time, these trends are not expected to be precisely the same due to small fluctuations in energy consumption. We therefore propose the idea of energy consumption within buckets. More precisely, given the answers to the above queries, adversary $\mathcal{A}$ divides the energy consumption at each time step into different equal sized intervals (semi-closed) which are defined as buckets throughout the paper. The idea of *bucket* describes the granularity of users in each interval of energy consumption at every time step over the horizon T. For instance, at each hour during the night-time most households consume between 0.50 kWh and 1 kWh (i.e., (0.5, 1]), so we state that most of the users' consumption is taken place from $\mathcal{B}_1$ and when households are on holidays, they do not consume any electricity, thus we state that during that period of time energy consumption took place from $\mathcal{B}_0$.

Energy Buckets. Formally, we illustrate the concept of *bucket* as follows. A *bucket* of energy consumption is denoted by $\mathcal{B}$ and value of each *bucket* represents a half-open interval (i.e., energy consumption range in kWh), where the interval size, i.e., *bucket* size, is denoted by $\Delta\mathcal{B} = e$. We denote buckets by $\mathcal{B}_0 = [0]$, $\mathcal{B}_1 = (0, e]$, $\mathcal{B}_2 = (e, 2e]$, $\mathcal{B}_3 = (2e, 3e]$ and so on, and we try different *bucket* sizes to test the attacker's accuracy. We say a household is in a *bucket* $\mathcal{B}_i$ at time t if the household's energy consumption falls into the interval of $\mathcal{B}_i$. Note that when a user does not consume any electricity at a specific time of a day this falls under *bucket* $\mathcal{B}_0$. We have considered a *bucket* with 0 consumption because an adversary could be interested to know when her target home is not occupied.

4 Dataset and Feasibility of Privacy Breach

In this section, we first explain the datasets which are used to evaluate the performance of the adversary $\mathcal{A}$, then show the key features behind the load patterns of households energy consumption.

4.1 Data

We use two real-world datasets that capture the fine-grained (i.e., "disaggregated") energy consumption (time-series) records of households: the UK Power Networks (London Dataset)[2] and Ausgrid households dataset[3]. We then aggregate these datasets to perform analyses and attacks on them. The actual-"disaggregated"-datasets serve as ground truth against the estimated consumption data.

These publicly available datasets contain different numbers of households with a variety of smart-meter reading frequencies over various periods of time. We use these datasets primarily because of their different characteristics, such as different meter-reading resolutions, geographic locations of the households, time periods and number of households. Note that the actual datasets contain more households over a greater period of time. We discarded the rest as they are inconsistent or incomplete. A brief summary of the datasets, which were used in our evaluation, is presented in Table 1.

Table 1. Some features of the datasets used in the experiments as discussed in [40]

Dataset	Number of Households	Location	Year	Meter Reading Interval
London Dataset	4681	London, UK	2013	30 min
Ausgrid Dataset	6981	NSW, Australia	2013	30 min

4.2 Regularity and Uniqueness Properties of Energy Consumption

By performing analysis on the raw (find-grained, dis-aggregated) data for both London and Ausgrid datasets, we argue that each household follows a consistent energy consumption pattern and hence the households can be uniquely distinguished with a high probability.

---

[2] https://data.london.gov.uk/dataset/smartmeter-energy-use-data-in-london-house holds.

[3] https://data.gov.au/data/dataset/smart-grid-smart-city-customer-trial-data.

To comprehensively understand the *regularity* of energy consumption patterns of all households over the entire period of time, we study the percentage of households that consume energy from Top-5 buckets over four sizes of buckets in {0.25, 0.5, 1.0, 2.0} for both datasets. Figure 1 shows the results in the Ausgrid dataset. We observe that the percentage of households that consume from the top buckets increases with the increase of *bucket* size. When the *bucket* size is 0.25, around 40% and 25% of households consumer energy from Top-1 and Top-2 buckets, respectively. Furthermore, we observed over 12% of households' consumption is from Top-3 *bucket*. Note that number of buckets and the hourly/daily/monthly maximum value of the buckets are varying over the population and the entire time period.

Doubling the *bucket* size to 0.5 and 1.0, around 60% and 70% of households' energy consumption remains in Top-1 buckets respectively. Increasing the *bucket* size to 2.0, over 90% of the households consume energy from Top-2 buckets. We also observe similar pattern in consuming energy in London dataset (see Fig. 2).

Observations from both the datasets suggest that most of the households tend to consume from the same (top) buckets consistently. Thus, the consumption patterns are highly *consistent*. Note that with the increase of *bucket* size, the top buckets are accommodating more users as the buckets include more coarse-grained meter readings within their boundaries.

To evaluate the *uniqueness* of households' energy consumption patterns, we first generate a vector containing K energy consumption buckets, then investigate the percentage of households not sharing the same given buckets vector. We use three different strategies to obtain the buckets vector, that is, selecting the Top-K frequently used buckets by the households (Top-K), randomly selecting K buckets belonging to the households' energy consumption patterns (Rand-K) and randomly selecting K consecutive buckets (Cont-K). Under these three strategies, we show the percentage of (consumption patterns of) households that can be distinguished from other households by the selected patterns in Fig. 3.

In the Ausgrid dataset (Fig. 3a), we observe that within the Top-5 buckets 80% of households have unique Top-5 energy consumption buckets. Whereas a smaller number of households (73% and 55%) can be distinguished from Rand-5 and Cont-5 buckets respectively. Further, considering the Top-15 buckets, almost all households can be distinguished. However, only 55% and 70% of households can be distinguished when we consider Rand-15 and Cont-15 buckets. Similar observations are observed in the London household dataset (Fig. 3b).

The above results quantitatively show that the energy consumption patterns of households are consistent and distinct. This finding helps us construct an attack model to reconstruct the consumption patterns of individual households.

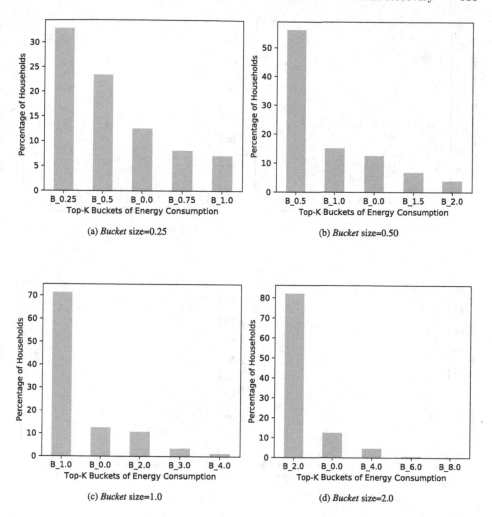

(a) *Bucket* size=0.25

(b) *Bucket* size=0.50

(c) *Bucket* size=1.0

(d) *Bucket* size=2.0

Fig. 1. The percentage of households that consume energy from top buckets for four different size of buckets over the period of one year in Ausgrid dataset [40]

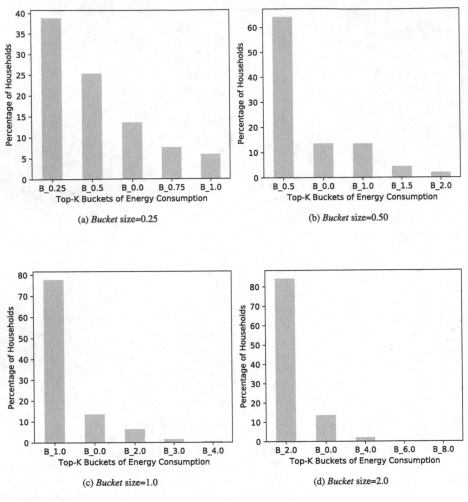

(a) *Bucket* size=0.25

(b) *Bucket* size=0.50

(c) *Bucket* size=1.0

(d) *Bucket* size=2.0

Fig. 2. The percentage of households that consume energy from top buckets for four different size of buckets over the period of one year in London dataset [40].

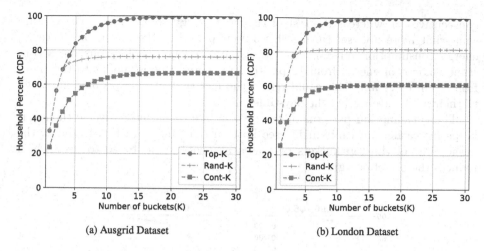

(a) Ausgrid Dataset   (b) London Dataset

Fig. 3. The percentage of households that can be distinguished by K buckets of energy consumption for the bucket size 0.25 [40].

4.3   Capturing Energy Consumption Speed

Since we know that the energy consumption of households are consistent and distinct, in this section, we study the energy consumption speed. Prior to showing the results of consumption speed, we first show that the energy consumption speed is also stable over the whole time period.

Figure 4 depicts the average percentage of time when the households consume from Top-20 buckets at different hour of a day in the Ausgrid dataset.

The top left figure in Fig. 4 reports that the percentage of time that the households consume energy from top buckets during the night-time (i.e., 12:00 am–6:00 am). We observe that over 80% and 90% of the time households consume electricity from Top-3 buckets and Top-5 buckets respectively. We also observe that almost 100% of the time Ausgrid households' consumption patterns revolve within Top-10 energy buckets. The figures show that energy consumption over six consecutive hours (from 12 am to 5 am) were quite consistent. These observations are presumably due to the natural sleeping cycles, energy consumption patterns of households remains consistent during night-time in the Ausgrid dataset.

The top right figure in Fig. 4 shows the percentage of time that the households consume energy from top buckets in the morning (i.e., 6 am–12 am). We observe that over 80% of the time households' energy consumption occurred from top-5 buckets. Moreover, over 95% of the time energy is consumed from Top-10 buckets from 7 am to 11 am. Interestingly, the consumption patterns during this time interval are quite uniform. Further, the consumption patterns in the morning are more diverse than that in the night-time.

The bottom left figure in Fig. 4 illustrates the cumulative percentage of households consumption duration from each of the frequently used buckets. Top-5 and Top-10 buckets are used by the households over 80% of the time for the first consecutive 4 h, whereas the rest of the time energy consumption patterns are somewhat more diverse. During this 3-hour period in the afternoon, however, energy consumption remains very consistent (i.e., households consume a constant amount of energy from 12 pm to 3 pm), and this is similar to the trend from 7 am to 11 am. This could reflect the fact that usually people tend to go to their workplace during the day-time.

The consumption patterns in the evening are much more diverse though it keeps increasing until mid-night (see bottom right figure in Fig. 4). Then, the usage time of the top buckets decreases as people tend to go to bed, which reduces the use of energy.

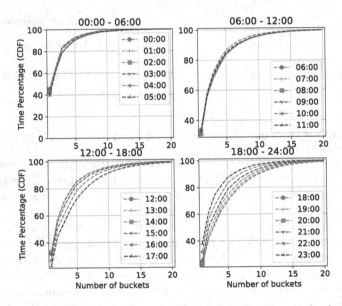

Fig. 4. Percentage of time (on an average) a household uses top buckets of energy where *bucket* size is 0.25, over the entire period of time in Ausgrid dataset [40].

Similarly, in the London dataset (see Fig. 5), the average percentages of time when the households consume the top buckets of energy also remains steady. Households usually consume from Top-5 buckets over a whole natural day. Although the specific consumption pattern is quite different than that of in the Ausgrid dataset.

We now demonstrate how different households' energy consumption varies from one time step to another. We show the results for 2 consecutive hours of a day using the London dataset. Figure 6 depicts what percentage of households fall in which range of energy consumption variation (increase or decrease) from one time step to the next. For example, we observe that at Hour-1, we see around a 10% increase in the percentage of households that showed an increase by 0–10% of their energy consumption than its previous time step. Moreover, at Hour-2, we observe that most of the households' (around 60%) energy consumption showed an increase by 0 – 10%.

Note that the negative percentage change refers to decrease in percentage. Based on such an observation, we calculate the expected energy consumption speed for each given *bucket*. The detailed calculation given in the next section.

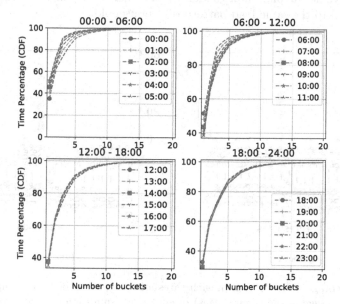

Fig. 5. Percentage of time (on an average) a household uses top buckets of energy where *bucket* size is 0.25, over the entire period of time in London dataset [40].

To conclude, all of the aforementioned observations indicate that from the aggregated dataset, we could take advantage of the consistence, *uniqueness* and expected energy consumption speed to recover the energy consumption traces of the individual households.

5   Unsupervised Attack Model

In this section, we present our unsupervised attack model for individual energy consumption recovery from an aggregated dataset.

5.1   Overview

We consider a realistic scenario [5] where a data curator releases time-series energy consumption data aggregated from a set of n households over a time period T. To recover the trace of individual energy consumption over the entire time period, we extract individual energy consumption from the aggregated data time by time. In general, once given a *bucket* size, we can assign the aggregated data to different buckets. The salient point here is that at a single moment, one *bucket* contains only one household. Formally, we can derive the energy consumption buckets $B^{(t)} = [B_1^{(t)}, B_2^{(t)}, \ldots, B_k^{(t)}]$ at time step t with k buckets. Recovering a consumer's energy usage load pattern is equivalent to associating anonymised buckets that are consumed by the same consumer across different time slots. We now explain how to identify the energy consumption buckets that can be linked to the same load pattern of a household.

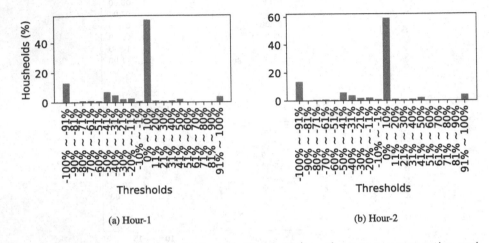

(a) Hour-1

(b) Hour-2

Fig. 6. Percentage of households in each threshold (i.e., the energy consumption variation in percentage in the given ranges) of energy consumption change at consecutive two hours of a day in London dataset [40].

To address this problem, we propose an unsupervised attack model inspired by the work in [50] that iteratively associates the same households' load patterns from its following time steps, and the adversary then recovers the entire load patterns (by linking consumption buckets). At each point in time, the adversarial method can be divided into two steps. First, we estimate the likelihood of the next energy consumption *bucket* that belongs to a given load pattern by exploiting the characteristics of household energy consumption patterns. Second, we derive an optimal solution to link households' energy consumption buckets with the next consumption bucket which maximises the overall likelihood. We first discuss how we can estimate an optimal association between recovered and actual energy consumption traces through having access to the estimated likelihood.

We define the cost matrix at time t as $C^{(t)} = \{c_{i,j}^{(t)}\}_{k \times k}$, where $c_{i,j}$ corresponds to the inverse of likelihood of connecting a load pattern of household i to the next consumption *bucket* $B_j^{(t+1)}$. The load pattern reconstruction problem is equivalent to solving an optimal match between the rows and columns, which minimises the overall cost. Let us suppose the decision matrix $X^{(t)} = \{x_{i,j}^{(t)}\}_{k \times k}$, where, $x_{i,j}^{(t)} = 1$ denotes that the load pattern gets linked with next consumption $bucket\ B_j^{(t+1)}$ and $x_{i,j}^{(t)} = 0$ otherwise. Now, we construct the energy consumption recovery problem as follows.

$$\text{minimise} \qquad \sum_{i=1}^{k} \sum_{i=1}^{k} c_{i,j}^{(t)} \cdot x_{i,j}^{(t)} \tag{2}$$

$$\text{subject to:} \qquad x_{i,j}^{(t)} = \{0, 1\} \tag{3}$$

$$\sum_{i=1}^{k} x_{i,j}^{(t)} = 1 \text{ and } \sum_{j=1}^{k} x_{i,j}^{(t)} = 1 \tag{4}$$

Such an optimisation problem could be solved by the Hungarian algorithm [30, 50].

5.2   Recovering Fine-Grained Energy Consumption Patterns

We propose a scheme inspired by the work in [50] based on our observations discussed in Sect. 4 to formulate the cost matrix over the 24 h of a day. The steps are as follows.

1) We calculate the expected changing for a given $bucket$ at time t by our observation about the energy consumption speed. We use $\Delta^{(t)} = \{\delta_1^{(t)}, \dots, \delta_k^{(t)}\}$ to indicate the matrix of such expectations for all possible buckets under given $bucket$ size. Note that, once given a $bucket$ size, all the energy consumption values can be assigned to a specific $bucket$.

According to what we have in Fig. 6, we calculate $\delta_j^{(t)} \in \Delta^{(t)}$ for $bucket\ B_j^{(t)}$ as

$$\delta_j^{(t)} = \sum_{i=1}^{20} \Pr_i \times change_i, \tag{5}$$

where $change_i$ indicates the ith changing step (x axis) shown in Fig. 6, $\Pr_i$ is the corresponding probability measured by the percentage of households (y axis) in Fig. 6, 20 is a predefined value for the steps of energy consumption changing from time t to $t + 1$. Then for a given $bucket\ j$ at time t, we estimate its value for time $t + 1$ as

$$\hat{B}_j^{(t+1)} = B_j^{(t)} \times \delta_j^{(t)} \tag{6}$$

2) We consider $\Delta^{(t)}$ at each time step t as the thresholds that have been discussed in Sect. 4.3.

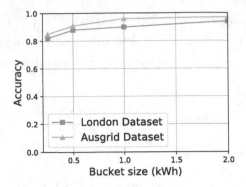

Fig. 7. Mean recovery accuracy of energy consumption buckets for different size of buckets [40].

We used the above discussed assumption to construct the cost matrix $C^{(t)}$. Thus, we use the Euclidean distance between the estimated/predicted *bucket* $\hat{B}_{u_i}^{(t+1)}$ of households i and each unassigned *bucket* $B_j^{(t+1)}$ at the next time slot to formulate the cost matrix $C^{(t)}$. The cost for each household for consuming energy from each *bucket* is illustrated in the following equation.

$$c_{ij}^{(t)} = |\hat{B}_{u_i}^{(t+1)} - B_j^{(t+1)}|. \tag{7}$$

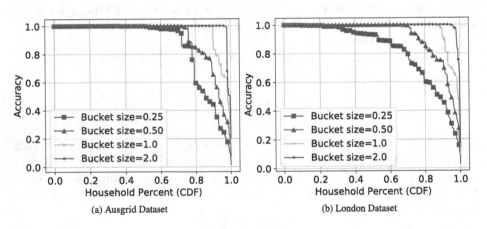

(a) Ausgrid Dataset   (b) London Dataset

Fig. 8. Adversarial performance (accuracy) of the attacker in recovering energy consumption patterns of individual households using both datasets [40]

For example, let the corresponding *bucket* of Alice's energy consumption be x at time t. We first calculate the estimated *bucket* $\hat{x}$ for time $t + 1$ based on current time t. Let the unassigned *bucket* at time $t + 1$ be y_1 and y_2. Then we have to decide whether we move Alice from *bucket* x to y_1 or y_2. We calculate the cost of such a movement by calculating the distance between $\hat{x}$ and y_1, y_2 respectively. Solving the optimisation problem in last section with the cost matrix would provide us with a decision as to whether Alice moves to *bucket* y_1 or y_2, that is, the energy consumption of Alice at time $t + 1$.

6 Experimental Evaluation

In this section, we first introduce the configurations, together with the metrics used in our experimental analysis of the attack model, then report the attack performance against two famous real-world datasets of individual's energy consumption data.

6.1 Experimental Configurations

First, we aggregate the half hourly reading to hourly readings for both datasets. We split the datasets randomly into five samples where each sample contains 1000 households over 2 months. One month of data is chosen from the beginning of the year and another month of data from the middle of the year because the households' energy consumption distribution in the middle of the year is different from that of at the beginning and end of the year for both the datasets.

This variation in energy consumption distribution could be caused by seasonal change (e.g., winter to summer) over time. We choose four values of $l = [0.25, 0.50, 1.0, 2.0]$ to check how user percentages vary from one *bucket* size to another. We then generate buckets for each value of l for each sample of the data. We also calculate the number of households in each *bucket* at each time step to observe how consistent the households are in consuming energy from different size of buckets. Then we compute the percentage of households at different ranges of energy consumption change (as a percentage) (see Fig. 6). We then convert the range of percentage changes into discrete values (e.g., if the percentage change of energy consumption remains between 0 to 10%, we map this range into 0.1, and if the range is between 11–20%, we map this into 0.2 and so on). We then compute the expected speed of energy consumption that is, expected energy consumption change over each hour of the day by multiplying the mapped value with its corresponding user percentage, as explained earlier in Sect. 4.3. This Δ helps us construct the cost matrices to reconstruct energy consumption patterns in terms of buckets. Then we apply the Hungarian algorithm to optimise the assignment problem using `linear_sum_assignment` solver imported from a python library `scipy.optimise`. The entire project is implemented in Python3.

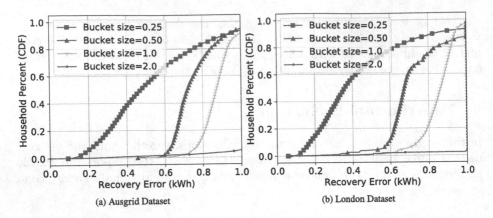

Fig. 9. Cumulative errors (recovery error) in estimating energy consumption trace of individual households using both datasets [40].

6.2 Metrics

We evaluate the attack performance of the adversary by considering the following two metrics: accuracy in recovering buckets which the households consuming the energy from and recovery error. First, we pair the recovered energy consumption patterns in terms of buckets with the most similar actual load patterns (i.e., the ground truth buckets) using a greedy approach. Let the actual load pattern buckets of ith household be $B_i = \{B_i^{(1)}, B_i^{(2)}, \ldots, B_i^{(T)}\}$ and the jth recovered load pattern buckets be $\hat{B}_i = \{\hat{B}_i^{(1)}, \hat{B}_i^{(2)}, \ldots, \hat{B}_i^{(T)}\}$ over a period of time T. Thus, the average accuracy is denoted by $\mathscr{A}$ is defined as follows.

$$\mathscr{A} = \frac{1}{n} \sum_{i,j}^{n} \frac{|\hat{B}_j \cap B_i|}{|B_i|}, \tag{8}$$

where, $\hat{B}_j \cap B_i$ refers to the common energy consumption buckets between the estimated buckets and the actual buckets, and $|*|$ refers to the total number of buckets in $*$.

Secondly, we compute the recovery error (RE) by measuring the distance between the estimated buckets and the actual energy consumption traces (not the actual buckets) of households as follows.

$$RE := \frac{1}{T} \begin{bmatrix} \sum_{t=1}^{T} |x_1^{(t)} - \hat{B}_1^{(t)}| \\ \vdots \\ \sum_{t=1}^{T} |x_n^{(t)} - \hat{B}_n^{(t)}| \end{bmatrix}, \tag{9}$$

where, $\hat{B}_i^{(t)}$ is the estimated *bucket* of a household i at time t and $x_i^{(t)}$ is the actual energy consumption trace of a household i at time t.

6.3   Adversarial Performance

We empirically quantify the performance of the adversary $\mathcal{A}$ in recovering energy consumption buckets. We first present the average recovery accuracy of reconstruction attack on the two above discussed datasets.

Figure 7 shows that the average recovery accuracy (over all target households) averaged over the entire period of time, varies between 80% and 95% for the different sized buckets. We observe that the buckets (i.e., energy consumption patterns) recovery accuracy in the Ausgrid dataset is a small amount higher than in the London dataset. The accuracy increases with the increase of the size of buckets because the top buckets are accommodating more users as the buckets include more coarse-grained meter readings within their boundaries.

We now demonstrate the cumulative accuracy (see Fig. 8) of the attacker in recovering the energy consumption patterns of households using both datasets for four different size of buckets. Figure 8a shows that over 90% of the households' consumption patterns can be recovered accurately when the *bucket* size is between 1 and 2. Reducing the size of the *bucket* to 0.50, we observe the cumulative accuracy falls, though still achieving more than 95% accuracy for around 75% of households in reconstructing their load patterns in terms of buckets. When we set *bucket* size to 0.25, we observe that the adversary is still capable of recovering over 70% of the households' energy consumption patterns with over 95% accuracy. Moreover, 80% of the households' load patterns can be inferred with at least 80% accuracy. In using the London smart meter dataset, we observe similar results for all size of buckets except the 0.25 bucket. Setting the *bucket* size to 0.25, we observe that 50% and 70% of households' load patterns can be inferred from aggregated statistics with around 90% and 80%, respectively, or higher accuracy.

Thus, our experimental evaluations show that the adversary successfully recovers most of the households' energy consumption load patterns (i.e., the quantity of households that consume from which buckets). These findings show that the privacy threat is severe and this attack paves a way for other possibilities of inferring minute private information about occupancy levels and the activities of target households.

Finally, we report how far the estimated buckets of energy consumption patterns deviate from the ground truth energy consumption traces. Figure 9 shows the recovery errors in kWh (x-axis) and the y-axis represents the households' percentage. We observe that increasing the size of the buckets, increases recovery errors, whereas a smaller *bucket* size decreases recovery errors for both smart meter energy datasets. For the smallest *bucket* the adversary recovers 60% of households' energy consumption by incurring 0.6 kWh or less error from the actual (ground truth) consumption traces in the Ausgrid dataset. The adversary **A** incurs less errors in the London dataset compared to that of in Ausgrid dataset. The attacker recovers energy consumption traces of 40% and 80% households and incurs only 0.4 kWh and 0.6 kWh or less deviation from the ground truth traces, respectively.

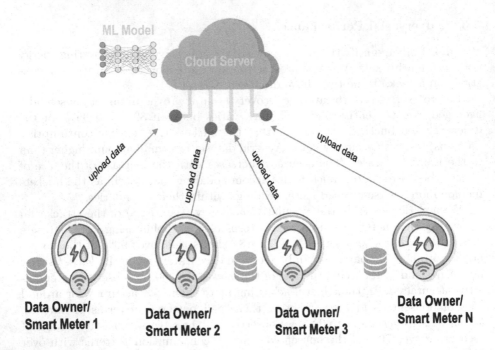

Fig. 10. Centralised ML Framework where the data owners are required to upload the energy consumption data into a remote server to train ML models on their data.

We conclude from the above discussed empirical evaluations that our adversarial strategy is effective in inferring the fine-grained energy consumption load patterns of individual households from aggregated statistics. Our study deduces that private information such as household occupancy level and home activities can be gleaned from the estimated fine-gained energy consumption data with high accuracy and low recovery errors. These findings suggest that releasing or sharing the aggregated statistics of energy consumption records of individual households, is not privacy protective. A malicious entity can infringe the privacy of individuals by exploiting the *regularity* and *uniqueness* properties of consumption patterns. Therefore, data owners must quantify the risks in aggregated statistics before releasing publicly or sharing with third party stakeholders.

7 Future Directions Towards Differential Privacy and Machine Learning Frameworks for Privacy Enhancing Smart Meter Data Analytics

In this section, we discuss various machine learning frameworks and the associated privacy risks in deploying them in a sensitive data context. First, we overview the centralised machine learning (CL) framework in energy data analytic context and how privacy of individual smart meters could be compromised.

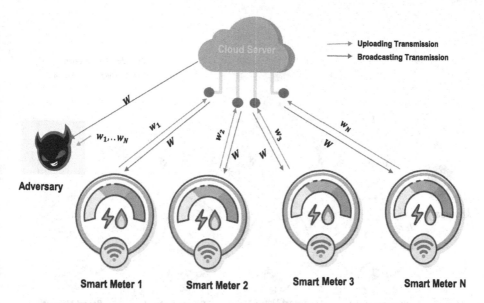

Fig. 11. Adversarial attack against a federated ML framework where the smart meters data are trained on an ML models then send it to a remote server maintained by the utility provider.

Second, we discuss how differentially private mechanisms can be deployed to curb attacks on privacy of smart meter data while leveraging intensive data analytics. Third, we describe the concept of federated (aka decentralised) machine learning (FL) framework and how it protects privacy of sensitive data by design. We also discuss how the FL framework is susceptible to some privacy attacks. Finally, we discuss how such adversarial impact can be minimised by using differential privacy.

7.1 Differential Privacy

In this section, we describe that differential privacy (DP) could be one of the most promising solutions to mitigate privacy threats in energy data analytics while keeping the utility of the data high.

Promises of Differential Privacy Differential privacy assures that the probability of harm incurred due to adversarial data analytics is negligible [12]. In the literature of privacy there are many attacks that compromise an individual's privacy, such as linkage attacks based on additional information obtained from other sources; DP counteracts such attacks automatically [9,10]. Furthermore, DP shields against arbitrary risks that would arise from the weak foundation of widely used privacy mechanisms in the past. Nevertheless, DP does not absolutely guarantee to protect an individual's sensitive data. However, its rigorous probabilistic quantification of privacy loss and data utility is a new and efficient

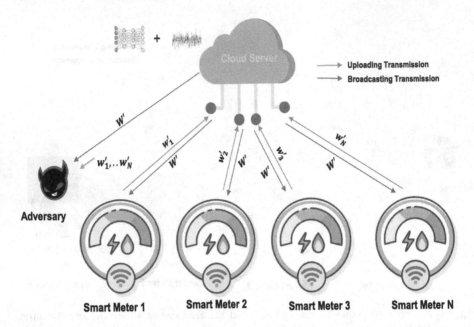

Fig. 12. Differentially private federated ML framework where the perturbed model parameters are sent to a remote server maintained by the utility provider.

approach in the privacy literature. Further, DP has many other beneficial properties, for example, composition and measure of privacy loss under compositions and a group privacy feature [1, 6, 13, 35].

Notions of Differential Privacy

Definition 1 (Differential Privacy [11]). *A randomised algorithm $\mathcal{M}$ with domain X and range Range($\mathcal{M}$) is said to be ϵ-differentially private if for all subsets S of Range($\mathcal{M}$) and for every pair of values $x, x' \in X$, we have*

$$\frac{\Pr[\mathcal{M}(x) \in S]}{\Pr[\mathcal{M}(x') \in S]} \leq e^{\epsilon},$$

where $\epsilon \geq 0$ is the privacy parameter. Let $\tilde{x}$ denote the output of $\mathcal{M}(x)$ in Definition 1. The accuracy of $\tilde{x}$, i.e., how close it is to the input x, is in part determined via a parameter called sensitivity which measures the maximum possible change in the input, defined as

$$\Delta = \max_{x, x' \in X} |x - x'| \tag{10}$$

Differential Privacy as a Defence Mechanism: There are different types of attacks such as reconstruction and tracing attacks to break aggregate statistics [14]. The reconstruction attack is used to approximately recover a sensitive attribute of

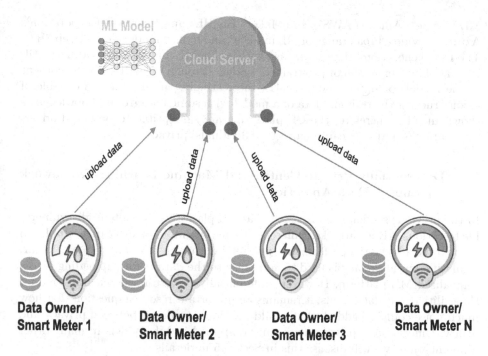

Fig. 13. Centralised ML Framework where the data owners are required to upload the energy consumption data into a remote server to train ML models on their data.

all individuals in an aggregated dataset, and the tracing is used to determine whether or not a particular individual's data are present in the dataset. Both attacks can be provably circumvented using differentially private techniques [14]. Differential privacy [12] is an effective way to protect the privacy of individuals and can also be used to attenuate the success of inference or reconstruction attacks, as discussed above.

7.2   Centralised Machine Learning Framework for Energy Data Analytics

The centralised machine learning is the traditional approach to ML architecture. The clients (e.g., energy providers) acquire the energy consumption data from the smart meters through a secure channel. First, the clients are required to upload their data to a CL server. Then, they train ML models on their uploaded data to get insights over the data (see Fig. 13). However, this induces an explicit violation of privacy as sensitive data leave clients' own devices. Further, it causes high traffics and computational overheads to the underlying network as well as the server. On the other hand, ML models can be widely shared for further prediction and extensive data analyses purposes. Similar to the use of ML as a service (MLaaS), many technology companies provide MLaaS platforms with support for ML models for commercial use. For instance, Google Inc.'s Cloud

ML Engine[4], Amazon AWS's SageMaker[5] BigML[6] and Microsoft Corporation's Azure[7] provide a broad range of ML models[8] and hybrid models (e.g., DeepAR[9]). The next generation MLaaS systems, such as BigML and Azure Learning, facilitate a white-box access of pre-trained models through an API with the consent of the models or data owners [19,41]. Interestingly, an adversary is capable of reconstructing the training data of a model with some background knowledge as shown in [41]. Therefore, the CL platforms are susceptible to potential adversarial attacks and may cause harm to individuals' privacy.

7.3 Differentially Private Centralised Machine Learning Framework for Energy Data Analytics

In the previous section, we discussed that CL platforms are potentially vulnerable to various privacy attacks. Differentially private mechanisms can be employed to curb the adversarial performance in inferring the sensitive data. In particular, local differential privacy is used to add noise to the data before uploading it to a centralised ML platform. However, differentially private noise naturally reduce the utility of the data. Thus, it remains an important research question that how much noise could be added, that would provide a trade-off between privacy and utility. Differentially private noise can be applied in ML models in many other different ways, we will discuss this in Sect. 7.5 in details.

7.4 Federated Machine Learning Framework for Energy Data Analytics

In this section, we discuss an emerging and evolving technique that can preserve the privacy of users by design. In traditional machine learning framework, data need to be shared or uploaded into a remote server (or cloud) to train a model (i.e., machine learning algorithm) to get an insight over the data. This may induce an implicit risk of privacy breach as the data leave the local devices of the owners. This type of architecture is also known as centralised machine learning framework.

On the contrary, federated learning [4] is a distributed or decentralised machine learning framework where the sensitive data such as, the energy data, do not leave local devices of customers (or clients). Rather, the models are being trained on clients' devices (e.g., smart meters) then the models are sent to a cloud server that aggregates the parameters of the models and then the aggregated model is broadcasted to all the clients (Fig. 11). This framework enables several stakeholders to collaborate on the development of ML models without

---

4 https://cloud.google.com/ai-platform.

5 https://aws.amazon.com/sagemaker/.

6 https://www.bigml.com/.

7 https://azure.microsoft.com/en-au/services/machine-learning/.

8 https://docs.aws.amazon.com/forecast/latest/dg/aws-forecast-recipe-arima.html.

9 https://docs.aws.amazon.com/sagemaker/latest/dg/deepar.html.

sharing sensitive data between them. Consequently, this approach provides a layer of privacy protection to different organisations. However, sensitive information can still be divulged by analysing the differences between the uploaded parameters from clients and the aggregated model parameters computed by the central server, such as, weights and bias in a deep neural network model [47].

Algorithm 1: Differentially Private Gradient Perturbation Process.

Input: $\mathcal{D}(X,y)$: energy dataset, X: training features (records), y: training labels.

Output: θ': differentially parameters.

Initialization: $\theta \leftarrow 0$

Noise: $\eta \sim M(\mu,0)$

Cost function: $\mathcal{J}(\theta) = \frac{1}{m}\sum_{k=1}^{m} \mathcal{L}(\theta, X_i, y_i) + \lambda R(\theta)$

Time epochs: $T = \{t_1, t_2, \ldots t_n\}$

for *each t in T* **do**

   $\quad\quad\mid\quad \theta' = \theta - \beta(\nabla \mathcal{J}(\theta)) + \eta$

end

return θ'

7.5 Differentially Private Federated Machine Learning Framework for Energy Data Analytics

Figure 11 shows that an attacker can have access to the model parameters from different client by sneaking into the networks and the aggregated model that is broadcasted by the server as demonstrated in [47]. Further, they showed how DP can be used to mitigate such attacks. DP noise can be applied in various ways [26], such as follows.

- **Input Perturbation:** noise is added to the data before training a model.
- **Objective Perturbation:** noise is added to the cost function of the model.
- **Gradient Perturbation:** noise is added to the gradient of an ML model.
- **Weight Perturbation:** noise is added to the weights in one or more hidden layers in deep learning model. **Output Perturbation:** noise is added to the final updated gradient output of an ML algorithm.

Figure 12 shows that the client devices upload the perturbed models into the server to help protect the privacy of sensitive user-centric data. However, this process could be computationally expensive as the client devices have limited hardware or software capacity. In this scenario, the cloud server could itself employ DP mechanisms to make the models differentially private by adding noise to the model parameters before or after aggregation.

Gradient Perturbation using Differential Privacy: In this section, we summarise the method to perturb the gradient descent of the ML models using differentially privacy. There are few other DP perturbation methods to make ML models private, such as adding noise to the objective function and output perturbation (i.e., adding noise to the output of the algorithm). We skip elaborating these methods as they are out of the scope of this paper. Algorithm 1 shows how gradient descent of a ML algorithm can modified and DP noise can be added to make a model differentially private.

8 Conclusion

In this chapter, we investigated the privacy implications of the aggregated energy consumption data of a cluster of households in a neighbourhood. We evaluated an attacker's performance without having any background information to recover individual users' fine-grained energy consumption at each hourly over a long period of time. We presented a real-world example of how an attacker can formulate an unsupervised attack method; we posed the problem as a balanced mathematical assignment problem and solved it using the Hungarian algorithm to find the optimal match by minimising the cost. Overall, our work presented a novel methodology to assess privacy risks in aggregated electricity consumption data. Moreover, our methodology can be used to quantify the privacy implications in other real-world settings such as transaction data, health data and web search data. Finally, we proposed few defense techniques that could be used to minimise the privacy risks in releasing aggregated energy data and predictive machine learning or statistical models which were trained on individual users' energy consumption data.

References

1. Abadi, M., et al.: Deep learning with differential privacy. In: Proceedings of the 2016 ACM SIGSAC Conference on Computer and Communications Security, pp. 308–318 (2016)
2. Abdallah, A., Shen, X.S.: A lightweight lattice-based homomorphic privacy-preserving data aggregation scheme for smart grid. IEEE Trans. Smart Grid 9(1), 396–405 (2016)
3. Barzegar, M., Shajari, M.: Attack scenario reconstruction using intrusion semantics. Expert Syst. Appl. 108, 119–133 (2018)
4. Bonawitz, K., et al.: Towards federated learning at scale: system design. arXiv preprint arXiv:1902.01046 (2019)
5. Buescher, N., Boukoros, S., Bauregger, S., Katzenbeisser, S.: Two is not enough: privacy assessment of aggregation schemes in smart metering. Proc. Privacy Enhanc. Technol. 2017(4), 198–214 (2017)

6. Bun, M., Steinke, T.: Concentrated differential privacy: simplifications, extensions, and lower bounds. In: Hirt, M., Smith, A. (eds.) TCC 2016. LNCS, vol. 9985, pp. 635–658. Springer, Heidelberg (2016). https://doi.org/10.1007/978-3-662-53641-4_24

7. Chen, K., He, Z., Wang, S.X., Hu, J., Li, L., He, J.: Learning-based data analytics: moving towards transparent power grids. CSEE J. Power Energy Syst. **4**(1), 67–82 (2018)

8. Dong, X., Zhou, J., Cao, Z.: Efficient privacy-preserving temporal and spacial data aggregation for smart grid communications. Concurr. Comput. Pract. Exp. **28**(4), 1145–1160 (2016)

9. Dwork, C.: Differential privacy: a survey of results. In: Agrawal, M., Du, D., Duan, Z., Li, A. (eds.) TAMC 2008. LNCS, vol. 4978, pp. 1–19. Springer, Heidelberg (2008). https://doi.org/10.1007/978-3-540-79228-4_1

10. Dwork, C., Kenthapadi, K., McSherry, F., Mironov, I., Naor, M.: Our data, ourselves: privacy via distributed noise generation. In: Vaudenay, S. (ed.) EUROCRYPT 2006. LNCS, vol. 4004, pp. 486–503. Springer, Heidelberg (2006). https://doi.org/10.1007/11761679_29

11. Dwork, C., McSherry, F., Nissim, K., Smith, A.: Calibrating noise to sensitivity in private data analysis. In: Halevi, S., Rabin, T. (eds.) TCC 2006. LNCS, vol. 3876, pp. 265–284. Springer, Heidelberg (2006). https://doi.org/10.1007/11681878_14

12. Dwork, C., Roth, A.: The algorithmic foundations of differential privacy. Found. Trends Theor. Comput. Sci. **9**(3–4), 211–407 (2014)

13. Dwork, C., Rothblum, G.N.: Concentrated differential privacy. arXiv preprint arXiv:1603.01887 (2016)

14. Dwork, C., Smith, A., Steinke, T., Ullman, J.: Exposed! a survey of attacks on private data. Annu. Rev. Stat. Appl. **4**, 61–84 (2017)

15. Efthymiou, C., Kalogridis, G.: Smart grid privacy via anonymization of smart metering data. In: 2010 First IEEE International Conference on Smart Grid Communications, pp. 238–243. IEEE (2010)

16. ENA-Report. Energy networks association: smart meter aggregation assessment final report (2015)

17. Erkin, Z., Tsudik, G.: Private computation of spatial and temporal power consumption with smart meters. In: Bao, F., Samarati, P., Zhou, J. (eds.) ACNS 2012. LNCS, vol. 7341, pp. 561–577. Springer, Heidelberg (2012). https://doi.org/10.1007/978-3-642-31284-7_33

18. Farokhi, F.: Review of results on smart-meter privacy by data manipulation, demand shaping, and load scheduling. IET Smart Grid (2020)

19. Fredrikson, M., Jha, S., Ristenpart, T.: Model inversion attacks that exploit confidence information and basic countermeasures. In: Proceedings of the 22nd ACM SIGSAC Conference on Computer and Communications Security, pp. 1322–1333 (2015)

20. Gong, N.Z., Liu, B.: You are who you know and how you behave: attribute inference attacks via users' social friends and behaviors. In: 25th {USENIX} Security Symposium ({USENIX} Security 16), pp. 979–995 (2016)

21. Gong, N.Z., Liu, B.: Attribute inference attacks in online social networks. ACM Trans. Privacy Secur. (TOPS) **21**(1), 1–30 (2018)

22. Habtemariam, B., Miranskyy, A., Miri, A., Samet, S., Davison, M.: Privacy preserving predictive analytics with smart meters. In: 2016 IEEE International Congress on Big Data (BigData Congress), pp. 190–197. IEEE (2016)

23. Revuelta Herrero, J., et al.: Non intrusive load monitoring (NILM): a state of the art. In: De la Prieta, F., et al. (eds.) PAAMS 2017. AISC, vol. 619, pp. 125–138. Springer, Cham (2018). https://doi.org/10.1007/978-3-319-61578-3_12

24. Hong, Y., Liu, W.M., Wang, L.: Privacy preserving smart meter streaming against information leakage of appliance status. IEEE Trans. Inf. Forensics Secur. **12**(9), 2227–2241 (2017)

25. Hossain, Md.N., et al.: {SLEUTH}: real-time attack scenario reconstruction from {COTS} audit data. In: 26th {USENIX} Security Symposium ({USENIX} Security 17), pp. 487–504 (2017)

26. Jayaraman, B., Evans, D.: Evaluating differentially private machine learning in practice. In: 28th {USENIX} Security Symposium ({USENIX} Security 19), pp. 1895–1912 (2019)

27. Jia, J., Gong, N.Z.: Attriguard: a practical defense against attribute inference attacks via adversarial machine learning. In: 27th {USENIX} Security Symposium ({USENIX} Security 18), pp. 513–529 (2018)

28. Kelly, J., Knottenbelt, W.: Neural NILM: deep neural networks applied to energy disaggregation. In: Proceedings of the 2nd ACM International Conference on Embedded Systems for Energy-Efficient Built Environments, pp. 55–64 (2015)

29. Knirsch, F., Eibl, G., Engel, D.: Error-resilient masking approaches for privacy preserving data aggregation. IEEE Trans. Smart Grid **9**(4), 3351–3361 (2016)

30. Kuhn, H.W.: The Hungarian method for the assignment problem. Naval Res. Logist. Q. **2**(1–2), 83–97 (1955)

31. Lee, Y.-T., Hsiao, W.-H., Lin, Y.-S., Chou, S.-C.T.: Privacy-preserving data analytics in cloud-based smart home with community hierarchy. IEEE Trans. Consum. Electron. **63**(2), 200–207 (2017)

32. Liu, Y., Guo, W., Fan, C.-I., Chang, L., Cheng, C.: A practical privacy-preserving data aggregation (3pda) scheme for smart grid. IEEE Trans. Industr. Inf. **15**(3), 1767–1774 (2018)

33. Makhdoom, I., Zhou, I., Abolhasan, M., Lipman, J., Ni, W.: Privysharing: a blockchain-based framework for privacy-preserving and secure data sharing in smart cities. Comput. Secur. **88**, 101653 (2020)

34. Molina-Markham, A., Shenoy, P., Fu, K., Cecchet, E., Irwin, D.: Private memoirs of a smart meter. In: Proceedings of the 2nd ACM workshop on Embedded Sensing Systems for Energy-Efficiency in Building, pp. 61–66. ACM (2010)

35. Palanisamy, B., Li, C., Krishnamurthy, P.: Group differential privacy-preserving disclosure of multi-level association graphs. In: 2017 IEEE 37th International Conference on Distributed Computing Systems (ICDCS), pp. 2587–2588. IEEE (2017)

36. Reinhardt, A., Egarter, D., Konstantinou, G., Christin, D.: Worried about privacy? Let your PV converter cover your electricity consumption fingerprints. In: 2015 IEEE International Conference on Smart Grid Communications (SmartGrid-Comm), pp. 25–30. IEEE (2015)

37. Salem, A., Bhattacharya, A., Backes, M., Fritz, M., Zhang, Y.: Updates-leak: data set inference and reconstruction attacks in online learning. In: 29th {USENIX} Security Symposium ({USENIX} Security 20), pp. 1291–1308 (2020)

38. Sankar, L., Rajagopalan, S.R., Mohajer, S., Poor, H.V.: Smart meter privacy: a theoretical framework. IEEE Trans. Smart Grid **4**(2), 837–846 (2012)

39. Shateri, M., Messina, F., Piantanida, P., Labeau, F.: Deep directed information-based learning for privacy-preserving smart meter data release. In: 2019 IEEE International Conference on Communications, Control, and Computing Technologies for Smart Grids (SmartGridComm), pp. 1–7. IEEE (2019)

40. Sheikh, N., Lu, Z., Asghar, H., Kaafar, M.: Trace recovery: inferring fine-grained trace of energy data from aggregates. In: Proceedings of the 18th International Conference on Security and Cryptography - Volume 1: SECRYPT, pp. 283–294. INSTICC, SciTePress (2021)

41. Sheikh, N.U., Asghar, H.J., Farokhi, F., Kaafar, M.A.: Do auto-regressive models protect privacy inferring fine-grained energy consumption from aggregated model parameters. IEEE Trans. Serv. Comput. (2021)

42. Sirojan, T., Lu, S., Phung, B.T., Ambikairajah, E.: Embedded edge computing for real-time smart meter data analytics. In: 2019 International Conference on Smart Energy Systems and Technologies (SEST), pp. 1–5. IEEE (2019)

43. Vahedi, E., Bayat, M., Pakravan, M.R., Aref, M.R.: A secure ECC-based privacy preserving data aggregation scheme for smart grids. Comput. Netw. **129**, 28–36 (2017)

44. Veale, M., Binns, R., Edwards, L.: Algorithms that remember: model inversion attacks and data protection law. Philos. Trans. Roy. Soc. A Math. Phys. Eng. Sci. **376**(2133), 20180083 (2018)

45. Wang, H., Wen, X., Xu, Y., Zhou, B., Peng, J.-C., Liu, W.: Operating state reconstruction in cyber physical smart grid for automatic attack filtering. IEEE Trans. Ind. Inform. (2020)

46. Wang, Y., Chen, Q., Hong, T., Kang, C.: Review of smart meter data analytics: applications, methodologies, and challenges. IEEE Trans. Smart Grid **10**(3), 3125–3148 (2018)

47. Wei, K., et al.: Federated learning with differential privacy: algorithms and performance analysis. IEEE Trans. Inf. Forensics Secur. **15**, 3454–3469 (2020)

48. Wen, M., Rongxing, L., Zhang, K., Lei, J., Liang, X., Shen, X.: Parq: a privacy-preserving range query scheme over encrypted metering data for smart grid. IEEE Trans. Emerg. Top. Comput. **1**(1), 178–191 (2013)

49. Chang, X., et al.: Aggregate in my way: privacy-preserving data aggregation without trusted authority in ICN. Futur. Gener. Comput. Syst. **111**, 107–116 (2020)

50. Xu, F., Tu, Z., Li, Y., Zhang, P., Fu, X., Jin, D.: Trajectory recovery from ash: user privacy is not preserved in aggregated mobility data. In: Proceedings of the 26th International Conference on World Wide Web, pp. 1241–1250 (2017)

51. Yang, L., Chen, X., Zhang, J., Poor, H.V.: Cost-effective and privacy-preserving energy management for smart meters. IEEE Trans. Smart Grid **6**(1), 486–495 (2014)

52. Zhang, J., Chen, X., Ng, W.W.Y., Lai, C.S., Lai, L.L.: New appliance detection for nonintrusive load monitoring. IEEE Trans. Ind. Inform. **15**(8), 4819–4829 (2019)

On Applying Boolean Masking to Exponents

Michael Tunstall[1]([✉]), Louiza Papachristodoulou[2], and Kostas Papagiannopoulos[3]

[1] Cryptography Research, 425 Market Street, 11th Floor, San Francisco, CA 94105, USA
michael.tunstall@cryptography.com
[2] ASML Semiconductors, Application Security Group, De Run 6543, 5504DR Veldhoven, The Netherlands
louiza.papachristodoulou@asml.com
[3] Faculty of Science Informatics Institute, University of Amsterdam, Science Park 904, Amsterdam, The Netherlands
k.papagiannopoulos@uva.nl

Abstract. Implementations of block ciphers typically use Boolean shares of intermediate states to prevent side-channel analysis. Implementations of public-key cryptographic algorithms are typically protected by using the algebraic properties of the algorithms. In this work, we present an exponent splitting technique with minimal impact on performance based on Boolean shares. This method can be combined with other countermeasures to make a side-channel resistant implementation with minimal increase in execution time.

Keywords: Exponent splitting · Masking · Side-channel attacks and countermeasures

1 Introduction

Side-channel analysis as a method of extracting cryptographic keys was first presented by Kocher [33], who noted that timing differences in the execution time of a modular exponentiation could be used to break instances of RSA [45]. Subsequently, Kocher et al. [34] observed that the instantaneous power consumption could reveal information on intermediate states of any cryptographic algorithm, since the instantaneous power consumption has, in many cases, been shown to be proportional to the Hamming weight of the data being manipulated [10]. Electromagnetic emanations around a device can also be exploited in the same way [20,44]. Attacks based on these observations are typically referred to as Differential Power Analysis (DPA) and Differential Electromagnetic Analysis (DEMA), respectively.

A variety of countermeasures have been proposed to prevent side-channel analysis. To protect an implementation of a block ciphers, one would typically divide intermediate states into shares that vary from one execution to another (referred to as masking). Hence, an adversary cannot predict any intermediate state to reveal information on the secret key. The most common instance of masking would be to randomly split each plaintext word, of an arbitrarily chosen bit length, into two shares, such that the XOR of the two shares gives the plaintext word [34]. The computation of a block cipher would then proceed such that the XOR difference remains constant, and the ciphertext can be produced by XORing two shares at the end.

P. Samarati et al. (Eds.): ICETE 2021, CCIS 1795, pp. 334–361, 2023.
https://doi.org/10.1007/978-3-031-36840-0_15

In public key cryptography, one typically uses countermeasures based on redundant representations to prevent side-channel leakage [16,52] (referred to as blinding). To protect an exponent used in a group exponentiation one would typically add a random multiple of the order of the group to the exponent, providing a random bitwise representation of the exponent. These countermeasures can provide a strong resistance to differential power analysis (DPA), but are not convenient in some instances. As noted by Smart et al. [48], the random value used to blind an exponent needs to have a bit length larger than the longest run of zeros or ones in the bitwise representation of the the order of the group. If we consider ECDSA [41], for example, the bitwise representations of the orders of the groups used typically contain long runs of ones making this countermeasure undesirable. That is, to provide a randomized bitwise representation the random value used would have a bit length comparable to the exponent it is protecting, leading to a prohibitive impact on performance. While alternative elliptic curves avoid this problem [36], widely used curves will continue to have long runs of zeros and ones in the bitwise representation of the order of the group, since the modulus is typically chosen with this property to allow for the rapid computation of a modular reduction. See, for example, the elliptic curves proposed by Bos et al. [9], Hamburg [24] and Bernstein [7].

This paper improves upon those exponent blinding techniques by using a two-share Boolean split of the exponent. This is very surprising at first, because the arithmetic operations involved in exponentiation algorithms do not seem to combine well with bitwise XOR operations. The trick is to use exponentiation algorithms involving several (normally two) varying group elements in their main loop, such as the Montgomery powering ladder or Joye's double-and-add-always algorithm. The choice of which group element to update at each step of the algorithm can then be somewhat decoupled from the expression assigned to it. When the exponent is split into two Boolean shares, roughly speaking, one share can be used on one side of assignments while the other share is used on the other side. It is clearly not possible to achieve such a complete decoupling, but one can come close enough that the actual bits of the exponent do not need to be computed explicitly at any step of the algorithm.

An attack applicable to exponents blinded by adding a random multiple of the group order has been proposed by Walter [51], where one seeks to determine if the input to one operation in an exponentiation is the same as the input to another operation. This is achieved by comparing traces of the instantaneous power consumption during consecutive group operations. Many analyses of how this attack could be applied to cryptographic algorithms have been described in the literature [1,5,6,14,32,42,53]. Hanley et al. [25] have also shown that these attacks could be applied to a single trace. Hence, protecting an exponent by adding a random multiple of the order of the group may not be sufficient, since the randomized exponent is still equivalent to the exponent. Furthermore, Hanley et al. further demonstrated that one can construct an attack by determining if the output of one operation in an exponentiation is the same as the input to another operation. These attack techniques can also be applied to scalar multiplication algorithms for Elliptic Curve Cryptography (ECC), for instance when additive scalar blinding is used, as shown in [19]. Furthermore, online template attacks [3] make it possible to attack implementations of a blinded scalar by using one trace from the device under attack and several template traces from a similar device running the same implementation. It is, therefore, clear that the various ways of exponent (or scalar) blinding do not provide a single, efficient countermeasure against recent attacks.

1.1 Contribution

In this paper, we present a *new countermeasure for exponent splitting*. We describe a method of splitting an exponent into *two Boolean shares*, analogous to the countermeasures that one would use for an implementation of a block cipher and similar to the countermeasures used to prevent address-bit side-channel attacks [27,37,38]. Having embedded devices as our targeted implementation, and an adversary able to get useful information from the length of the exponent or the intermediate values, we provide a number of secure algorithms against a broad range of side-channel attacks.

At the same time, the modifications that are required to a group exponentiation algorithm have negligible effect on the time required to compute the actual group exponentiation, which is a significant advantage over previous examples of exponent splitting [13,15].

In addition, our method can be efficiently combined with blinding techniques applied to the input to a group exponentiation algorithm, in order to prevent leakage of the intermediate values. We further demonstrate that the proposed algorithms can be used to compute an ECDSA signature where the nonce is generated in two shares that do not need to be combined. Hence, providing a convenient method for implementing a side-channel resistant instance of ECDSA with no significant impact on performance.

A further property that two of our algorithms have is that the exponent (or scalar) length can be hidden. The way the operations are handled by registers combining the Boolean splitting of the exponent can provide some algorithms with the useful property of tolerating leading zero bits.

Finally, the method of Boolean exponent splitting, cornerstone of the proposed algorithms, is evaluated in terms of security. An evaluation using the information-theoretic framework of Standaert et al. [49] and a Test Vector Leakage Assessement (TVLA) by Goodwill et al. [21] are performed. We investigate the usual leakage models based on data or location leakage and show that an adversary would need either a second-order data attack or a third-order location attack to successfully break the security of our algorithms. In addition, we present for the first time a hybrid model, where data leakage is combined with location leakage, offering new exploitation opportunities. The rich interactions between data and location leakage corroborates the need for holistic countermeasures that encompass a wide spectrum of side-channel attacks.

1.2 Organization of the Paper

The rest of this paper is organized as follows: In Sect. 2, we describe previously proposed exponent splitting methods, their efficiency and known attacks against these countermeasures. Section 3 presents our proposed methods of exponent splitting based on an XOR operation. More precisely, Sects. 3.1–3.2, present the splitting method on various regular exponentiation algorithms. We show that when XOR-splitting is applied, each algorithm is resistant against first-order side-channel attacks. In Sect. 3.3

we present our splitting method in the context of scalar multiplication for elliptic curves. In Sect. 4, we demonstrate how this method can be used to generate an ECDSA signature where only shares of the random nonce are manipulated. An efficient algorithm to transform the Boolean share to multiplicative is also presented and shown to be first-order secure. We further provide details on how our countermeasure can be used with ECDH. Section 5 presents an extensive security evaluation of our algorithms based on formal methods and the mutual information framework. Data and location leakage diagrams are also presented here, together with the hybrid leakage attack. Section 6 discusses implementation considerations and shows the results of TVLA of a practical implementation on a Xilinx Zynq evaluation board. Finally, we conclude in Sect. 7.

1.3   Differences with the Original Paper of SECRYPT

This section highlights the additions and differences from our original publication at SECRYPT 2021 [50]. Our introduction is extended with two subsections, clearly analyzing our contribution with comparison to related work and with the organization of the paper. In the core of our paper, after presenting our proposed algorithm 2, two new subsections are added. In Sect. 3.2 we propose two versions of our main algorithm that are more appropriate for groups where inversions can be readily computed. The variant of Algorithm 5 is thoroughly analyzed and shown to be resistant against first-order attacks in Lemma 2. Section 3.1 is also added, in order to explain better the fundamentals of elliptic curve arithmetic, before introducing how our algorithm can be securely implemented for elliptic curves. Section 4.2 is also new, explaining how our algorithm can be used for key exchange using EC Diffie-Hellman. Finally, the whole new Sect. 5 discusses the security of all the algorithms presented in the paper by a theoretical comparison with state-of-the-Art algorithms, against template attacks and using the mutual information evaluation methodology. A hybrid data and location leakage attack of second order is analyzed and the security of our scheme is evaluated.

2   Exponent Splitting Methods

The critical operation in public key cryptographic algorithms is exponentiation in a certain group $\mathbb{G}$ of order μ, where the input message $x \in \mathbb{G}$ is raised by a secret exponent κ and the result $y = x^\kappa$ is the public output of the algorithm. When implementing a group exponentiation algorithm, the exponent is typically blinded by adding some random multiple of the order of the group to the exponent. Trivially, $(r\mu) + \kappa \equiv \kappa \pmod{\mu}$ for $r, \kappa \in \mathbb{Z}$ where r is random. Hence, computing $x^{\kappa+r\mu}$ is equivalent to computing x^κ. While this randomizes the bitwise representation of an exponent, the entire exponent is still equivalent to the exponent in a given group. Examples of attacks that have been proposed include analyzing a single trace (from SPA [34] to collisions in manipulated values [25,32,53]) or attempting to find collisions in the random values used to then derive a (blinded) exponent [46].

One method that can hinder these attacks, is to split an exponent into two values whose bitwise representations are random. Then one would compute a group exponentiation, where the combined effect of the two values is equivalent to that of the desired exponent. There are several methods of exponent splitting proposed by Clavier and Joye [15]:

- **Additive Splitting.** For a random integer r with bit-length smaller or equal to the exponent κ, we can define $\kappa = r + (\kappa - r)$. The output of the modular exponentiation $y = x^\kappa$ in $\mathbb{G}$ can be computed by calculating $y = x^r \cdot x^{\kappa - r}$ in $\mathbb{G}$.
- **Multiplicative Splitting.** For some group $\mathbb{G}$ we can define $k' = k \, r^{-1} \bmod |\mathbb{G}|$ for some integer r. Then the exponentiation $y = x^k$ in $\mathbb{G}$ can be computed by using $y = (x^r)^{k'} \bmod |\mathbb{G}|$.

The same techniques can be applied to scalar multiplication algorithms for elliptic curves (ECs), in order to hide the secret scalar. The problem with these methods of exponent splitting is that one is required to know the order of the group $\mathbb{G}$, which may not be available in some instances. They will also typically double the time to compute a group exponentiation, because r is required to have a bit-length similar to the exponent. A practical attack by Feix et al. [19] demonstrates that a blinded scalar can be determined if r is too small.

A further method described by Ciet and Joye [13] is:

- **Euclidean Splitting.** By writing the exponent as $k = \lfloor k/r \rfloor r + k \bmod r$ and letting $s = x^r$ for some r, then $y = x^k$ can be computed by $y = s^{k'} \times x^{k \bmod r} = (x^r)^{k'} \times x^{k \bmod r}$, where $k' = \lfloor k/r \rfloor$.

The impact on the time required to compute an exponentiation is lower than the other splitting methods listed above. In fact, in [13] the authors evaluated this variant applied to Shamir's double ladder to have the same cost as the 'double-and-add-always' algorithm (equivalent to the 'square-and-multiply-always' for exponentiation). Precomputation of powers of s can reduce the exponentiation cost compared to additive or multiplicative splitting. However, this method has the same constraints as adding a multiple of the group order. That is, r needs to have a bit length larger than the longest run of ones and zeros in k and may have a significant impact on performance [48]. A secure division algorithm is also required, see, for example, Joye and Villegas [30].

3 Boolean Exponent Splitting Methods

In this section, we propose methods of exponent splitting based on XOR operation, and how an XOR-split exponent can be applied to the Montgomery powering ladder.

3.1 Montgomery Powering Ladder

The Montgomery Powering Ladder (MPL) was originally proposed as a means of speeding up scalar multiplication over ECs and later shown to be applicable to multiplicative written Abelian groups [31,39]. We recall the description of the MPL given by Joye and Yen [31]: We consider the problem of computing $y = x^\kappa$ in $\mathbb{G}$ for inputs x and κ. Let $\sum_{i=0}^{n-1} k_i \, 2^i$ be the binary expansion of κ with bit length n (for ease of expression we shall also denote this as $(k_{n-1}, \ldots, k_0)_2$ where convenient). Then, defining $L_j = \sum_{i=j}^{n-1} k_i \, 2^{i-j}$ and $H_j = L_j + 1$, we have

$$L_j = 2\,L_{j+1} + k_j = L_{j+1} + H_{j+1} + k_j - 1 = 2\,H_{j+1} + k_j - 2 \qquad (1)$$

and so we obtain

$$(L_j, H_j) = \begin{cases} (2\,L_{j+1}, L_{j+1} + H_{j+1}) & \text{if } k_j = 0\,, \\ (L_{j+1} + H_{j+1}, 2\,H_{j+1}) & \text{if } k_j = 1\,. \end{cases} \qquad (2)$$

If we consider one register containing x^{L_j} and another containing x^{H_j} then (2) implies that

$$(x^{L_j}, x^{H_j}) = \begin{cases} \left(\left(x^{L_{j+1}}\right)^2, x^{L_{j+1}} \cdot x^{H_{j+1}} \right) & \text{if } k_j = 0\,, \\ \left(x^{L_{j+1}} \cdot x^{H_{j+1}}, \left(x^{H_{j+1}}\right)^2 \right) & \text{if } k_j = 1\,. \end{cases}$$

Given that $L_0 = k$ one can build an exponentiation algorithm that requires two group operations per bit of the exponent. Joye and Yen give several different versions, one of which is shown in Algorithm 1. All these methods are highly regular, meaning that a deterministic sequence of operations is executed for an exponent of a given bit length.

Algorithm 1. Montgomery Ladder.

Input: $x \in \mathbb{G}$, an n-bit integer $\kappa = \sum_{i=0}^{n-1} k_i\, 2^i$
Output: x^κ

1 $R_0 \leftarrow 1_{\mathbb{G}}$; $R_1 \leftarrow x$;

2 **for** $i = n - 1$ **down to** 0 **do**

3 $\quad\Big|\quad R_{\neg k_i} \leftarrow R_{k_i} \cdot R_{\neg k_i}$;

4 $\quad\Big|\quad R_{k_i} \leftarrow (R_{k_i})^2$;

5 **end**

6 **return** R_0

In applying an XOR-split exponent to MPL we use one share to dictate the address accessed and the other to act as the exponent. That is, we consider (2), where the previous round may provide either (L_j, H_j) or (H_j, L_j) and the computation changed accordingly.

We further consider $\sum_{i=0}^{n-1} a_i\, 2^i$ and $\sum_{i=0}^{n-1} b_i\, 2^i$ be the binary expansion of A and B, respectively, where $\kappa = A \oplus B$ of bit length n. Let $S_{0,j} = L_j$ and $S_{1,j} = H_j$ and $\sum_{i=0}^{n-1} a_i\, 2^i$ be the binary expansion of A with bit length n (i.e. the same bit length as the exponent). Then we can use the values of a_i to dictate whether a pair of registers holds (L_j, H_j) or (H_j, L_j). Specifically, (2) can be rewritten as

$$(S_{a_j,j}, S_{\neg a_j,j}) = \begin{cases} (2\,S_{a_j,j+1}, S_{a_j,j+1} + S_{\neg a_j,j+1}) & \text{if } k_j = 0\,, \\ (S_{a_j,j+1} + S_{\neg a_j,j+1}, 2\,S_{\neg a_j,j+1}) & \text{if } k_j = 1\,. \end{cases} \qquad (3)$$

In (3), the values of L_j and H_j are assigned to S in an order dictated by the binary expansion of A. Generating A as a random sequence of bits could provide some side-channel resistance, but does not protect the exponent. We note that, as above,

$\sum_{i=0}^{n-1} k_i \, 2^i$ is the binary expansion of κ and $k_i = a_i \oplus b_i$ for $0 \le i < n$. Then (3) can be rewritten as

$$(S_{a_j,j}, S_{\neg a_j,j}) = \begin{cases} (2\,S_{b_j,j+1}, S_{b_j,j+1} + S_{\neg b_j,j+1}) & \text{if } k_j = 0, \\ (S_{b_j,j+1} + S_{\neg b_j,j+1}, 2\,S_{\neg b_j,j+1}) & \text{if } k_j = 1. \end{cases} \qquad (4)$$

Rather than using the same value to control which order L_j and H_j are assigned and read, we use the bits of A to determine the order L_j and H_j are assigned, and the bits of B to determine the order they are read. The combined effect is that the order the L_j and H_j are assigned and read is dictated by the bits of κ.

We note that (4) implies

$$(x^{S_{a_j,j}}, x^{S_{\neg a_j,j}}) = \begin{cases} \left(\left(x^{S_{b_j,j+1}}\right)^2, x^{S_{b_j,j+1}} \cdot x^{S_{\neg b_j,j+1}}\right) & \text{if } k_j = 0, \\ \left(x^{S_{b_j,j+1}} \cdot x^{S_{\neg b_j,j+1}}, \left(x^{S_{\neg b_j,j+1}}\right)^2\right) & \text{if } k_j = 1. \end{cases}$$

From which we can define Algorithm 2, which operates in much the same way as the MPL, as it produces a regular sequence of multiplications and squaring operations. However, one more register is required to allow the assignment in line 5 to affect R_0 or R_1. This algorithm is the basis that we use to present the essence of Boolean-split exponent. Algorithm 2 is largely equivalent to an algorithm proposed by Izumi et al. [29] where we set the multiplication in line 4 to operate in a random order as it provides a better resistance to collision attacks, as demonstrated by Kim et al. [32]. We discuss this further in Sect. 6.

Algorithm 2. Montgomery Ladder with XOR-Split Exponent I.

Input: $x \in \mathbb{G}$, n-bit integers $A = \sum_{i=0}^{n-1} a_i \, 2^i$ and $B = \sum_{i=0}^{n-1} b_i \, 2^i$
Output: x^κ where $\kappa = A \oplus B$

1   $R_0 \leftarrow 1_\mathbb{G}$; $R_1 \leftarrow 1_\mathbb{G}$; $R_2 \leftarrow 1_\mathbb{G}$;

2   $b' \xleftarrow{R} \{0,1\}$; $R_{\neg b'} \leftarrow x$;

3 **for** $i = n - 1$ **down to** 0 **do**

4      $R_2 \leftarrow R_{a_i} \cdot R_{\neg a_i}$;

5      $R_{a_i} \leftarrow \left(R_{(b_i \oplus b') \oplus a_i}\right)^2$;

6      $R_{\neg a_i} \leftarrow R_2$;

7      $b' \leftarrow b_i$;

8 **end**

9 **return** $R_{b'}$

The intermediate states of the registers are not randomized in Algorithm 2 and would require additional countermeasures to provide a secure implementation. For example, inexpensive solutions such as randomizing projective points [52] or Ebeid and Lambert's blinding method for RSA [17] can be used (see Sect. 6). Regarding the side-channel resistance of Algorithm 2, the following holds:

Lemma 1. *Assuming that the values held in registers* $\{R_0, R_1, R_2\}$ *do not leak, an implementation of Algorithm 2 is resistant to first-order side-channel analysis.*

Proof. It suffices to consider each intermediate state and verify that at least one random mask is applied. Verifying this for an entire group exponentiation would be tedious, but can be simplified if we consider two rounds of Algorithm 2. That is, if we consider round m, where $0 \leq m \leq n - 2$, then the following operations are performed:

1. $R_2 \leftarrow R_{a_m} \cdot R_{\neg a_m}$	6. $R_2 \leftarrow R_{a_{m+1}} \cdot R_{\neg a_{m+1}}$
2. $\alpha \leftarrow b_m \oplus b'$	7. $\alpha \leftarrow b_{m+1} \oplus b_m$
3. $\beta \leftarrow \alpha \oplus a_m$	8. $\beta \leftarrow \alpha \oplus a_{m+1}$
4. $R_{a_m} \leftarrow R_\beta{}^2$	9. $R_{a_{m+1}} \leftarrow R_\beta{}^2$
5. $R_{\neg a_m} \leftarrow R_2$	10. $R_{\neg a_{m+1}} \leftarrow R_2$

Let the proposition $\mathcal{P}(n)$ be that round $n > 0$ is resistant to first-order side-channel analysis for the n-th treated bit of the exponent. If we consider the first round, we wish to show $\mathcal{P}(1)$ is true and, in the above code fragment, b' is set to a random value from $\{0, 1\}$. Then, it is easy to see that:

- the results of the operations in lines 1, 4, 5, 6, 9 and 10 are dependent on the random values $\{R_0, R_1, R_2\}$.
- the results of the operations in lines 2, 3, 7 and 8 are uniformly distributed on $\{0, 1\}$.

If we assume that $\mathcal{P}(m)$ is true for all $m \in \{1, \ldots, n\}$, then we consider $\mathcal{P}(n + 1)$ where b' is set to b_n. As b_n is one share of a previously treated exponent bit, it is indistinguishable from a random value from $\{0, 1\}$. The above statements regarding the results of the operations apply. Hence, by induction we have shown $\mathcal{P}(n)$ is true for all $n > 0$. To complete the proof, we simply note that only half of the code fragment above will need to be considered in the last round. $\qquad\square$

Remark 1. In [28], the authors present the randomized addressing method (RA), in order to provide protection against ADPA and eliminate the correlation between an exponent bit and the register where the result of an operation is stored. In this work, we do not limit our countermeasure to work only against ADPA. Our goal is to perform operations on different exponent shares, in a way that an adversary would need a combination of leakages (like Higher Order DPA combined with template attacks) in order to recover the exponent.

3.2   Using Inverses

In this section we propose an algorithm more suited to groups where inversions can be readily computed. Le Duc et al. [35] propose a straightforward variant of the Montgomery powering ladder that requires the computation of inverses. They note that (2) can be rewritten as

$$(L_j, H_j) = \begin{cases} (H_j - 1, L_{j+1} + H_{j+1}) & \text{if } k_j = 0, \\ (L_{j+1} + H_{j+1}, L_j + 1) & \text{if } k_j = 1. \end{cases} \tag{5}$$

From which we can define Algorithm 3. If we let $T_{0,j} = L_j$ and $T_{1,j} = H_j$, or $T_{0,j} = H_j$ and $T_{1,j} = L_j$ and store the ordering in another variable we can rewrite (5) as

$$(T_{0,j}, T_{1,j}) = \begin{cases} (L_j, H_j) & \text{if } k_j = 0 \\ (H_j, L_j) & \text{if } k_j = 1 \end{cases} = \begin{cases} (L_{j+1} + H_{j+1}, L_j - 1) & \text{if } k_j = 0, \\ (L_{j+1} + H_{j+1}, L_j + 1) & \text{if } k_j = 1. \end{cases}$$

(6)

From which we can define Algorithm 4.

Algorithm 3. Variant with Inverses I.
Input: $x \in \mathbb{G}$, an n-bit integer $\kappa = \sum_{i=0}^{n-1} k_i \, 2^i$
Output: x^κ
1   $R_0 \leftarrow 1_{\mathbb{G}}$; $R_1 \leftarrow x$;
2   $U_0 \leftarrow x^{-1}$; $U_1 \leftarrow x$;
3   **for** $i = n - 1$ **down to** 0 **do**
4      $R_{\neg k_i} \leftarrow R_{k_i} \cdot R_{\neg k_i}$;
5      $R_{k_i} \leftarrow R_{\neg k_i} \cdot U_{k_i}$;
6   **end**
7   **return** R_0

Algorithm 4. Variant with Inverses II.
Input: $x \in \mathbb{G}$, an n-bit integer $\kappa = \sum_{i=0}^{n-1} k_i \, 2^i$
Output: x^κ
1   $R_0 \leftarrow 1_{\mathbb{G}}$; $R_1 \leftarrow x$;
2   $U_0 \leftarrow x^{-1}$; $U_1 \leftarrow x$;
3   **for** $i = n - 1$ **down to** 0 **do**
4      $R_0 \leftarrow R_0 \cdot R_1$;
5      $R_1 \leftarrow R_0 \cdot U_{k_i}$;
6   **end**
7   **return** $R_{\neg k_0}$

Following the previous notation, we notice that $T_{0,j}$ should contain the sum of the registers in the previous round[1]. Therefore, (6) can be rewritten as follows:

$$(T_{0,j}, T_{1,j}) = \begin{cases} (T_{b',j+1} + T_{\neg b',j+1}, T_{0,j} - 1) & \text{if } k_j = b' = 0, \\ (T_{b',j+1} + T_{\neg b',j+1}, T_{0,j} + 1) & \text{if } k_j = b' = 1. \end{cases}$$

(7)

We note that to treat k_{j+1}, $b' = k_j$. However, if we let $k_j = a_j \oplus b_j$, for $a_j, b_j \in \{0,1\}$ and $h = a_j \oplus b_j \oplus b_{j-1}$, we can modify (7) as follows:

$$(T_{0,j}, T_{1,j}) = \begin{cases} (T_{\neg h,j+1} + T_{h,j+1}, T_{0,j} - 1) & \text{if } a_j = b_j, \\ (T_{\neg h,j+1} + T_{h,j+1}, T_{0,j} + 1) & \text{if } a_j = \neg b_j. \end{cases}$$

(8)

By using the above equations as exponents of x, we can define Algorithm 5.

Algorithm 5 follows the same sequence of instructions with the MPL. Its correctness can be verified by the fact that at every round the difference $R_0 / R_1 = x$ or $R_1 / R_0 = x$, as for the usual ladder step. The advantage of Algorithm 5 compared to Algorithm 2, and consequently previously proposed algorithms by Izumi et al. [29], is the elimination of the auxiliary register R_2. Instead, the auxiliary registers U_0, U_1 manipulate the known fixed value x or x^{-1} for computational purposes, and they do not require additional computational power or updates when the algorithm is executed.

---

[1] The algorithms are left-to-right, so $j + 1$ indicates the round preceding j.

Algorithm 5. Montgomery Ladder with XOR-Split Exponent II.

Input: $x \in \mathbb{G}$, n-bit integers $A = \sum_{i=0}^{n-1} a_i \, 2^i$ and $B = \sum_{i=0}^{n-1} b_i \, 2^i$, $r \in_R \mathbb{Z}$
Output: x^κ where $\kappa = A \oplus B$

1   $R_0 \leftarrow 1_\mathbb{G}$; $R_1 \leftarrow 1_\mathbb{G}$; $U_0 \leftarrow x$; $U_1 \leftarrow x^{-1}$;

2   $b' \xleftarrow{R} \{0,1\}$; $R_{\neg b'} \leftarrow x$;
3   **for** $i = n - 1$ **down to** 0 **do**
4     $\big|$ $R_0 \leftarrow R_{b_i \oplus b'} \cdot R_{(b_i \oplus b') \oplus a_i}$;
5     $\big|$ $R_1 \leftarrow R_0 \cdot U_{b_i}$;
6     $\big|$ $b' \leftarrow b_i$;
7   **end**

8   **return** $R_{b'}$

As previously, if we assume that the values held in registers $\{R_0, R_1\}$ do not leak we can state the following:

Lemma 2. *Assuming that the values held in registers $\{R_0, R_1\}$ do not leak, an implementation of Algorithm 5 is resistant to first-order side-channel analysis.*

Proof. It suffices to consider each intermediate state and verify that at least one random mask is applied. Verifying this for an entire group exponentiation would be tedious, but can be simplified if we consider two rounds of Algorithm 5. That is, if we consider round m, where $0 \leq m \leq n - 2$, then the following operations are performed:

1. $\alpha \leftarrow b_m \oplus b'$	5. $\alpha \leftarrow b_{m+1} \oplus b_m$
2. $\beta \leftarrow \alpha \oplus a_m$	6. $\beta \leftarrow \alpha \oplus a_{m+1}$
3. $R_0 \leftarrow R_\alpha \cdot R_\beta$	7. $R_0 \leftarrow R_\alpha \cdot R_\beta$
4. $R_1 \leftarrow R_0 \cdot U_{b_m}$	8. $R_1 \leftarrow R_0 \cdot U_{b_{m+1}}$

Let the proposition $\mathcal{P}(n)$ be that round $n > 0$ is resistant to first-order side-channel analysis for the n-th treated bit of the exponent. If consider the first round, we wish to show $\mathcal{P}(1)$ is true and, in the above code fragment, b' is set to a random value from $\{0,1\}$. Then, it is easy to see that:

- the results of the operations in lines 3, 4, 7 and 8 are dependent on the random values $\{R_0, R_1\}$.
- the results of the operations in lines 1, 2, 5 and 6 are uniformly distributed on $\{0,1\}$.

If we assume that all $\mathcal{P}(m)$ is true for $m \in \{1, \ldots, n\}$, then we consider $\mathcal{P}(n+1)$ where b' is set to b_n. As b_n is one share of a previously treated exponent bit, it is indistinguishable from a random value from $\{0,1\}$. The above statements regarding the results of the operations apply. Hence, by induction we have shown $\mathcal{P}(n)$ is true for all $n > 0$. To complete the proof, we simply note that only half of the code fragment above will need to be considered in the last round. □

3.3   Boolean Scalar Splitting

In the above, we define group exponentiations applicable to any multiplicatively written group $\mathbb{G}$. However, specific groups may have particular characteristics that means the algorithms above are not suitable as described. In this section, we discuss the algorithms in the context of a group formed from the points on an elliptic curve (EC). We define the EC $\mathcal{E}$ over a finite field $\mathbb{F}_q$, for a large prime q. $\mathcal{E}$ consists of points (x, y), with x, y in $\mathbb{F}_q$, that satisfy, for example, the short Weierstraß equation

$$\mathcal{E} : y^2 = x^3 + a\,x + b$$

with $a, b \in \mathbb{F}_q$, and the point at infinity denoted O. The set $\mathcal{E}(\mathbb{F}_q)$ is defined as $\mathcal{E}(\mathbb{F}_q) = \{(x, y) \in \mathcal{E} \mid x, y \in \mathbb{F}_q\} \cup \{O\}$, where $\mathcal{E}(\mathbb{F}_q)$ forms an Abelian group under the chord-and-tangent rule and O is the identity element. Alternative equations with different representations of a neutral element are also used in cryptographic algorithms, such as Edwards curves [8, 18] and Montgomery curves [39]. The scalar multiplication of a given point is a group exponentiation in $\mathcal{E}$ that uses elliptic curve arithmetic, i.e. addition between points or scalar multiplication $[\kappa]\,P$ for some integer $\kappa < |\mathcal{E}|$, and is an important part of many cryptographic algorithms.

The algorithms presented above cannot be securely implemented as described because of the neutral element. In the short Weierstraß example, the neutral element $1_{\mathbb{G}}$ is represented in $\mathcal{E}$ as the point at infinity O and cannot be manipulated in a regular way. That is, one would typically be obliged to test for a numerical representation of O and conduct a different operation if it is detected. In practice, one would implement the algorithm such that the most significant bit (assumed to be set to one) is already treated by the pre-processing. For example, Algorithm 2 can be implemented as shown in Algorithm 6, and Algorithm 5 as shown in Algorithm 7.

Algorithm 6. Montgomery Ladder with XOR-Split Scalar on an EC.	**Algorithm 7.** Montgomery Ladder with XOR-Split Scalar II on an EC.
Input: $\mathcal{E}, \mathbb{F}_q, P \in \mathcal{E}$, n-bit integers $A = \sum_{i=0}^{n-1} a_i\,2^i$ and $B = \sum_{i=0}^{n-1} b_i\,2^i$ **Output:** $Q = [\kappa]P$ where $\kappa = A \oplus B$	**Input:** $\mathcal{E}, \mathbb{F}_q, P \in \mathcal{E}$, n-bit integers $A = \sum_{i=0}^{n-1} a_i\,2^i$ and $B = \sum_{i=0}^{n-1} b_i\,2^i$ **Output:** $Q = [\kappa]P$ where $\kappa = A \oplus B$
1 $R_0 \leftarrow P$; $R_1 \leftarrow P$; $R_2 \leftarrow P$; 2 $b' \xleftarrow{R} \{0,1\}$; 3 $R_{\neg b'} \leftarrow 2P$; 4 **for** $i = n - 2$ **down to** 0 **do** 5 $\quad R_2 \leftarrow R_{a_i} + R_{\neg a_i}$; 6 $\quad R_{a_i} \leftarrow 2\,R_{(b_i \oplus b') \oplus a_i}$; 7 $\quad R_{\neg a_i} \leftarrow R_2$; 8 $\quad b' \leftarrow b_i$; 9 **end** 10 **return** $R_{b'}$	1 $R_0 \leftarrow P$; $R_1 \leftarrow P$; 2 $U_0 \leftarrow P$; $U_1 \leftarrow -P$; 3 $b' \xleftarrow{R} \{0,1\}$; 4 $R_{\neg b'} \leftarrow 2P$; 5 **for** $i = n - 2$ **down to** 0 **do** 6 $\quad R_0 \leftarrow R_{b_i \oplus b'} + R_{(b_i \oplus b') \oplus a_i}$; 7 $\quad R_1 \leftarrow R_0 + U_{b_i}$; 8 $\quad b' \leftarrow b_i$; 9 **end** 10 **return** $R_{b'}$

As previously, if we assume that the values held in registers $\{R_0, R_1, R_2\}$ do not leak we can state the following:

Corollary 1. *Lemma 1 implies that an implementation of Algorithm 6 is resistant to first-order side-channel analysis.*

Corollary 2. *Lemma 2 implies that an implementation of Algorithm 7 is resistant to first-order side-channel analysis.*

4 Applying Exponent Splitting to Elliptic Curve Cryptography

In this section, we describe how one could apply the above algorithms to ECDSA and ECDH, as the particular security requirements of these algorithms merit further discussion.

4.1 Applying Exponent Splitting to ECDSA

For ECDSA, a given base point $P = (x, y)$ for an EC $\mathcal{E}$ over $\mathbb{F}_q$, with private key d and hash function h, the signer that wants to sign a message m picks a random $\kappa < |\mathcal{E}| = n$ (where $n = |\mathcal{E}|$ is the order of the curve) and computes

$$r \xleftarrow{x} [\kappa]P \text{ and } s \leftarrow \kappa^{-1}\left(h(m) + dr\right) \bmod |\mathcal{E}|.$$

We denote the extraction of the x-coordinate of a point and its assignment to a variable by $\xleftarrow{x}$. The signature of m is the pair: $\{r, s\}$. We note that the security of this signature scheme relies on the random value κ remaining unknown to an attacker. Moreover, the nonce κ should be used only once and randomly generated for every new signature, otherwise the private key d can be trivially derived [41].

Securing the Scalar Multiplication. The scalar multiplication $[\kappa]P$ during the computation of r is a critical operation in ECDSA from a side-channel point of view, because an attacker only needs to derive a small number of bits of κ to obtain the secret key d. For example, a lattice-based analysis can reveal the private key from the knowledge of some bits of the scalar κ [26]. In practice, one could use the knowledge of one bit from around 30 signatures or eleven bits from one signature [40]. Similarly, one needs to prevent an adversary from determining the bit length of the scalar used to prevent a lattice attack.

When implementing a scalar multiplication, one could use Algorithm 2 described in the previous section, with extra care required to prevent the bit length of the scalar from leaking.

In implementing Algorithm 2 on an elliptic curve, one could add a multiple of the order of the group to the scalar to hide its length [16]. While this would seem to make the algorithms redundant, one could choose a small multiple of the order of the group without considering the longest run of ones or zeros in the bitwise representation of the order. Indeed, one could multiply the order of the group by a power of two such that increasing the bit length is impossible or fixed to a one bit increase. That is, ensure that the carries produced by adding the multiple of the order of the group do not extend the bit length or always extend the bit length. Given the long runs of ones or zeros typically seen in the bitwise representation of the order of many groups formed from the points of an EC, the increase in bit length should be very small [7,9,24,41]. For example, if we consider P192 defined by NIST [41], where the elliptic curve is defined over $\mathbb{F}_p$, with $p = 2^{192} - 2^{64} - 1$, then the 128 most-significant bits of p are set to one. If twice the order is added to a nonce then a carry from the most-significant bits will be produced with an overwhelming probability, thus always producing a nonce of 194 bits. However, in some cases, one may wish to ensure that the carry has been produced to prevent a theoretical reduction in the security of a system. That is, one could design attacks around an oracle that indicated the value of the carry, but such an oracle is unlikely to exist.

Alternatively, one could add some more logical functions to allow for the most significant bit to be set to zero. In Algorithms 8 and 9 we show how this could be done for a blinded scalar multiplication on an elliptic curve. In both cases we use the variable m to be set to three while the most-significant bits of the scalar, $A \oplus B$, are set to zero, allowing the output of operations to be diverted into R_2. In Algorithm 9, we do this for both operations in the loop and keep the initial state of R_0 and R_1 until after the first bit set to one is treated. Algorithm 8 starts in the same way, using m to divert the output of the operations into R_2. When the most-significant bit of the scalar, $A \oplus B$, set to one is treated the output stored in R_2 is copied to either R_0 or R_1.

Algorithm 8. Montgomery Ladder with Fixed-Length XOR-Split Scalar on an EC.	**Algorithm 9.** Montgomery Ladder with Fixed-Length XOR-Split Scalar II on an EC.
Input: $\mathcal{E}, \mathbb{F}_q, P \in \mathcal{E}$, ℓ-bit integers $A = \sum_{i=0}^{n-1} a_i \, 2^i$ and $B = \sum_{i=0}^{n-1} b_i \, 2^i$ where $n \geq \ell$ **Output:** $Q = [\kappa]P$ where $\kappa = A \oplus B$	**Input:** $\mathcal{E}, \mathbb{F}_q, P \in \mathcal{E}$, ℓ-bit integers $A = \sum_{i=0}^{n-1} a_i \, 2^i$ and $B = \sum_{i=0}^{n-1} b_i \, 2^i$ where $n \geq \ell$ **Output:** $Q = [\kappa]P$ where $\kappa = A \oplus B$
1 $R_0 \leftarrow P$; $R_1 \leftarrow P$; $R_2 \leftarrow P$;	1 $R_0 \leftarrow P$; $R_1 \leftarrow P$; 2 $U_0 \leftarrow P$; $U_1 \leftarrow -P$;
2 $b' \xleftarrow{R} \{0,1\}$; $h \leftarrow 1$; $m \leftarrow 3$;	3 $b' \xleftarrow{R} \{0,1\}$; $h \leftarrow 1$; $m \leftarrow 3$;
3 **for** $i = n-1$ **down to** 0 **do**	4 $R_{\neg b'} \leftarrow 2P$;
4 $\quad R_2 \leftarrow R_{a_i} + R_{\neg a_i}$;	5 **for** $i = n-1$ **down to** 0 **do**
5 $\quad R_{((1+a_i)\vee m)-1} \leftarrow$ $2R_{(h \oplus b_i \oplus b') \oplus a_i}$;	6 $\quad R_{(1 \vee m)-1} \leftarrow$ $R_{b_i \oplus b'} + R_{(b_i \oplus b') \oplus a_i}$;
6 $\quad h = m \wedge 1$;	7 $\quad R_{(2 \vee m)-1} \leftarrow R_0 + U_{b_i}$;
7 $\quad m = 3\left((h \wedge \neg a_i) \oplus (h \wedge b_i)\right)$;	8 $\quad b' \leftarrow (b_i \wedge \neg n) \oplus (b' \wedge n)$;
8 $\quad R_{((1+\neg a_i)\vee m)-1} \leftarrow R_2$;	9 $\quad s = \left((m \wedge \neg a_i) \oplus (m \wedge b_i)\right)$;
9 $\quad b' \leftarrow b_i$;	10 $\quad m = 3\,s$;
10 **end**	11 **end**
11 **return** $R_{b'}$	12 **return** $R_{b'}$

As previously, if we assume that the values held in registers $\{R_0, R_1, R_2\}$ do not leak we can state the following:

Proposition 1. *An implementation of Algorithm 8 is resistant to first-order side-channel analysis.*

Proof. We note that the proof is almost identical to that given for Lemma 1. In addition, we can note that h and m are set initially and remain unchanged until the first bit set to one is encountered. Then h and m are set to zero and have no further impact on the computation. Given that h and m only change at one point that will be fixed for a given exponent it cannot be attacked via a first-order side-channel analysis. $\square$

Proposition 2. *An implementation of Algorithm 9 is resistant to first-order side-channel analysis.*

The proof of this proposition is similar to the proof of proposition 4.1.

We note that Algorithms 8 and 9 require a careful implementation. The computation of h in line 6 of Algorithm 8 and s in line 9 of Algorithm 9 combine the shares of the exponent. However, once the most-significant bit of the exponent is treated each shared is zeroed with a logical-AND operation before the shares are combined (prior to this any treated bits are always zero). A detailed discussion is beyond the scope of this paper, but one needs to ensure that an implementation does not inadvertently combine these values [2].

Using an ECDSA Nonce as Two Shares. In this section we describe how one could generate an ECDSA signature where the nonce is only present as two shares. That is, one could generate two random values to represent the two shares of the nonce, and the actual value of the nonce would never appear in the signing device.

We assume that the first half of the signature r has been generated using one of the scalar multiplication algorithms given above, using shares A and B where the nonce $\kappa = A \oplus B$. To compute the inverse of κ modulo $|\mathcal{E}|$ we need to change the way that κ is shared between two variables without revealing any information on κ.

Goubin defined a secure means of modifying two shares such that the secret value is no longer given by the XOR of the shares, but by subtracting one from the other [22]. That is, the relationship $\kappa = A \oplus B$ becomes $\kappa \equiv A' - B' \pmod{|\mathcal{E}|}$. The essential observation of Goubin was that the function

$$\Phi(a,b) : \mathbb{Z}^2 \longrightarrow \mathbb{Z} : a, b \longmapsto (a \oplus b) + b \tag{9}$$

is affine over $\mathbb{F}_2$. If we consider α, β as Boolean shares of x, where $x = \alpha \oplus \beta$, then, as defined by Goubin,

$$x + \alpha = \beta \oplus \Phi(\beta, \gamma) \oplus \Phi(\beta, \gamma \oplus \alpha), \tag{10}$$

for a random variable γ. This is not side-channel resistant in $\mathbb{Z}$ because of the carries produced by the addition operations. One needs to use a group $\mathbb{Z}_{2^k}$, for some $k \in \mathbb{Z}_+$, and have γ be a random value from $\mathbb{Z}_{2^k}$. However, we wish to change a Boolean share into an additive share in the group $\mathbb{Z}_{|\mathcal{E}|}$ where (10) is not valid.

We can modify the shares such that Goubin's mask conversion can be used adding a random multiple of the order of the group as proposed by Coron for other algorithms [16]. One can generate a random integer $\ell \in \mathbb{Z}_{2^n}$ for some convenient bit length n. The Boolean shares $(A = \kappa \oplus B, B)$ can be modified to (A', B') where

$$(A', B') = (A \oplus \ell|\mathcal{E}|, \ell|\mathcal{E}| + B) . \tag{11}$$

We note that this gives $A' = \kappa \oplus (\ell|\mathcal{E}| + B)$. If we consider the bit length of $|\mathcal{E}|$ is m then the above modified shares can be used with (10) using group $\mathbb{Z}_{2^{n+m}}$ to change the shares (A', B') to (A'', B'') where

$$(A'', B'') = (\kappa + \ell|\mathcal{E}| + B, \ell|\mathcal{E}| + B) . \tag{12}$$

Then A'' and B'' can be reduced modulo $|\mathcal{E}|$ to provide additively split shares of κ in $\mathbb{Z}_{|\mathcal{E}|}$. We can generate a random integer $\omega < |\mathcal{E}|$ and change the shares to a multiplicative split (A''', B''') where

$$(A''', B''') = (\omega A'' - \omega B'' \bmod |\mathcal{E}|, \omega) . \tag{13}$$

We note that this gives $A''' \equiv \omega\kappa \pmod{|\mathcal{E}|}$. The second part of the signature can be generated from r by computing

$$s \leftarrow B''' \left(A'''^{-1} (h(m) + dr) \right) \bmod |\mathcal{E}| .$$

Thus, using the above, one can generate an ECDSA signature where the nonce κ only exists as two shares. An explicit algorithm requiring 16 operations is given in Algorithm 10.

Algorithm 10. Secure Boolean-to-Multiplicative Masking.

Input: $A, B \in \mathbb{Z}_{2^n}$, where $\kappa = A \oplus B$, $\kappa \in \mathbb{Z}_{|\mathcal{E}|}$ and n is the bit length of $|\mathcal{E}|$, random value $\gamma \in \{0, \ldots, 2^n - 1\}$, random value $\ell \in \{0, \ldots, 2^m - 1\}$ where m is the bit length of one computer word and random value $\omega \in \{1, \ldots, |\mathcal{E}|\}$.

Output: $\kappa\omega \bmod |\mathcal{E}|$.

1 $x_1 \leftarrow \ell \times |\mathcal{E}|$;	10 $x_8 \leftarrow A' \oplus x_4$;
2 $B' \leftarrow x_1 + B$;	11 $x_9 \leftarrow x_7 \oplus x_8$;
3 $x_2 \leftarrow B' \oplus B$;	12 $B'' \leftarrow B' \bmod |\mathcal{E}|$;
4 $A' \leftarrow A \oplus x_2$;	13 $A'' \leftarrow x_9 \bmod |\mathcal{E}|$;
5 $x_3 \leftarrow A' \oplus \gamma$;	14 $x_{10} \leftarrow B'' \times \omega \bmod |\mathcal{E}|$;
6 $x_4 \leftarrow x_3 + \gamma$;	15 $x_{11} \leftarrow A'' \times \omega \bmod |\mathcal{E}|$;
7 $x_5 \leftarrow B' \oplus \gamma$;	16 $x_{12} \leftarrow x_{11} - x_{10} \bmod |\mathcal{E}|$;
8 $x_6 \leftarrow A' \oplus x_5$;	17 **return** x_{12} ;
9 $x_7 \leftarrow x_6 + x_5$;	

Lemma 3. *An implementation of Algorithm 10 is resistant to first-order side-channel analysis.*

Proof. It suffices to consider each intermediate state and verify that at least one random mask is applied. We consider the intermediate states as:

1. $\ell \times |\mathcal{E}|$
2. $\ell \times |\mathcal{E}| + B$
3. $(\ell \times |\mathcal{E}| + B) \oplus B$
4. $(\ell \times |\mathcal{E}| + B) \oplus \kappa$
5. $(\ell \times |\mathcal{E}| + B) \oplus \kappa \oplus \gamma$
6. $((\ell \times |\mathcal{E}| + B) \oplus \kappa \oplus \gamma) + \gamma$
7. $(\ell \times |\mathcal{E}| + B) \oplus \gamma$
8. $(\ell \times |\mathcal{E}| + B) \oplus \kappa \oplus (\ell \times |\mathcal{E}| + B) \oplus \gamma$
9. $((\ell \times |\mathcal{E}| + B) \oplus \kappa \oplus (\ell \times |\mathcal{E}| + B) \oplus \gamma) + ((\ell \times |\mathcal{E}| + B) \oplus \gamma)$
10. $((((\ell \times |\mathcal{E}| + B) \oplus \kappa \oplus (\ell \times |\mathcal{E}| + B) \oplus \gamma) + ((\ell \times |\mathcal{E}| + B) \oplus \gamma)) \oplus (\ell \times |\mathcal{E}| + B) \oplus \kappa$
11. $\kappa + \ell \times |\mathcal{E}| + B$
12. $B \bmod |\mathcal{E}|$
13. $\kappa + B \bmod |\mathcal{E}|$
14. $B \omega \bmod |\mathcal{E}|$
15. $\kappa \omega + B \omega \bmod |\mathcal{E}|$
16. $\kappa \omega \bmod |\mathcal{E}|$

Then, it is easy to see that:

- the results of the operations in lines 1, 2, 3, 7, 12 and 14 are not dependent on the secret κ and cannot be attacked by a first-order side-channel analysis.
- the results of the operations in lines 4, 5, 6, 8, 9, 10, 11, 13, 15 and 16 are dependent on the secret κ but are masked by at least one random value and, therefore, cannot be attacked by a first-order side-channel analysis.

Hence, Algorithm 10 is resistant to first-order side-channel analysis.   □

We note that in the above proof the security of the output of line 10 may not be immediately apparent. We refer the reader to Goubin [22] for a thorough explanation.

4.2 Applying Exponent Splitting to ECDH

For ECDH, the basic primitive is to take a public key Q and compute a scalar multiplication using a private key. This operation has different security requirements to ECDSA. The bit length of the private key does not need to be protected but the input point Q could be controlled by an adversary. The exponent splitting methods detailed in this paper do not modify the intermediate states generated and one would expect that randomizing projective points would be adequate to provide a secure solution [52]. However, such multiplicative masking can be problematic if an attacker can choose and input that could produce a point with a coordinate set to zero, which cannot be blinded using a multiplication [23]. Hence, one would need to combine our algorithms with Coron's countermeasures [16] and add a small multiple of the order of the group to the private key before it is used. The bit length of the multiplier needs to be chosen such that an attacker cannot predict the location of a zero-coordinate with sufficient reliability to make is visible in a side-channel attack. Something like 16 bit may be sufficient, depending on the signal-to-noise ratio of the platform. The advantage of combining these countermeasures is that one does not need to consider the longest runs of ones or zeros in the order of the group.

5   Security Evaluation

In this section, we discuss the security of the algorithms presented previously, first by making a comparison with the state-of-the-art algorithms and then by showing the resistance of our algorithms against template attacks. Furthermore, we provide a security evaluation of Algorithm 2, proposed in this paper, in terms of noisy leakage security and its resistance to multiple forms of side-channel attack. We note that similar analyses can be carried out for all exponent splitting variants presented in this work.

5.1   Theoretical Comparison with the State-of-the-Art Algorithms

In this subsection, we compare our proposed algorithms with a selection of algorithms discussed in the previous sections and summarize our observations in Table 1.

The first block of algorithms in Table 1, contain exponentiation algorithms using the Montgomery power ladder without splitting the exponent (Algorithm 1), with additive splitting or with variations of XOR-splitting (Algorithms 2, 3, 4). Multiplicative or Euclidean splitting are not included in this table, because in terms of security they have the same side-channel resistance as an algorithm with additive splitting. In terms of performance, the number of operations is the similar, unless the values $s^{k'}$ are precomputed and stored in memory. The second block of algorithms summarizes the behavior of the corresponding scalar multiplication algorithms[2].

Table 1. Comparison Table [50].

Algorithm	#operations	#registers	Hide length	ADPA	Interm. Values
Algorithm 1	$n \cdot M + n \cdot S$	2	✗	✗	✗
Clavier-Joye [15]	$2(n \cdot M + n \cdot S)$	2	✗	✗	✗
Algorithm 2	$n \cdot M + n \cdot S$	3	✓	✓	✗
Algorithms 3–4	$2n \cdot M$	4	✓	✓	✗
Algorithm 2	$2n \cdot M$	4	✓	✓	✗
Algorithm 6	$(n-1) \cdot A + (n-1) \cdot D$	3	✓	✓	✗
Algorithm 7	$2 \cdot (n-1) \cdot A$	4	✓	✓	✗
Itoh et al. [28] Alg. 8	$(n-1) \cdot D + (n-1) \cdot A + 1 \cdot I$	3	✗	✓	✗
Izumi et al. [29] Alg. 2	$(n-1) \cdot D + (n-1) \cdot A$	3	✗	✓	✗
Algorithm 8	$n \cdot D + n \cdot A$	3	✓	✓	✗
Algorithm 9	$2 \cdot n \cdot A$	4	✓	✓	✗

We note that none of the algorithms in their current form can prevent leakage from observing the intermediate values. However, intermediate values can be blinded with a random value at the cost of an inversion (or subtraction for elliptic curves).

---

[2] We do not count XORs, which can be implemented almost for "free" compared to the cost of multiplications (M), squaring operations (S) and modular inversions (I) in the chosen field or point additions (A) and doubling operations (D) on an elliptic curve. The subtraction of points on an elliptic curve has the same cost as an addition, so we do not count them separately.

5.2   Security Against Template Attacks

Template Attacks in general are a powerful attack technique because they take advantage of most of the information available in the traces that are measured [12]. An attacker is assumed to possess a device similar to the device under attack, and can build templates for some instructions knowing the power consumption characteristics on a device.

In a template-based DPA, an attacker matches the templates based on different key hypotheses with the recorded power traces [43]. The templates that have the best match indicate the key. This type of attack is the best attack in an information theoretic sense and, in a masking scheme like ours, it would work if one could build templates for each share a_i and b_i. Simultaneous knowledge of the two shares would be necessary because, for every possible value of the key bit, there are two different possibilities for a_i, b_i that could give the same result, as follows:

$$k_i = 1 \Rightarrow (a_i = 0 \quad \text{and} \quad b_i = 1) \quad \text{or} \quad (a_i = 1 \quad \text{and} \quad b_i = 0)$$

$$k_i = 0 \Rightarrow a_i = b_i = 0 \quad \text{or} \quad a_i = b_i = 1$$

In operations where $b\prime$ is also involved, as in line 5 of Algorithm 2, line 4 of Algorithm 5 etc., we need to store the b_{i-1} value from the templates of the previous round. This procedure seems quite complex and unlikely to succeed in devices with a small signal-to-noise ratio.

Another powerful template attack technique is Online Template Attacks (OTA) [3]. OTA uses templates of multiples of a known base point kP, for some $k \in \mathbb{Z}$, and compares them with the result of a specific operation, a doubling operation for example, for every round of the algorithm. Every unprotected implementation of scalar multiplication is vulnerable to OTA, unless the coordinates of the base point are randomized[3]. The algorithms presented in this paper are secure against OTA, because the doubling (or not) of a specific point, does not reveal the bit of the scalar k_i. We demonstrate this claim, using two algorithms as case studies, one for the case of general group exponentiation and one for elliptic curves. The extension to other algorithms presented in this paper is straightforward.

Algorithm 2. In line 4 we have

$$R_{a_i} \leftarrow \left(R_{(b_i \oplus b\prime) \oplus a_i}\right)^2 n \,,$$

where a squaring is performed and we could make templates for the potential values R_0^2 and R_1^2, in order to find out which operation is most probable. Let us assume that there is a pattern match of 99% with the value R_0^2. Even if we know with high probability which value is calculated at this step, we do not know which register is going to be used in the next step using OTA. Moreover, the index 0 can be derived from several combinations of $a_i, b_i, b\prime$. Namely, if $a_i = b_i = 0, b\prime = 0$, or $a_i = b_i = 1, b\prime = 0$ or

---

[3] Although OTA is initially presented for the case of elliptic curves, the attack can be used against any exponentiation algorithm, as long as templates for certain exponent values can be created.

$a_i = 0, b_i = 1, b' = 1$ or $a_i = 1, b_i = 0, b' = 1$. If the previous shares are known, therefore b' is known, there are still two possible values for a_i and b_i that can give the same result with equal probability. The success probability of OTA is then $1/2$ which is no better than a random guess.

Algorithm 6. Let us assume that templates on a doubling operation show that in line 6 of Algorithm 8, we have $2 R_1$. The possible values of a_i, b_i, b' that could result in 1 are: $(a_i = b_i = 0, b' = 1)$, or $(a_i = b_i = 1, b' = 1)$ or $(a_i = 0, b_i = 1, b' = 0)$ or $(a_i = 1, b_i = 0, b' = 0)$. The success probability of OTA is again $1/2$ if the previous shares are known. We note here, that in both cases, knowledge of the previous bit is not enough to give a success probability of $1/2$, but knowledge of at least one of the shares is required.

5.3   Mutual Information-Based Evaluation of Boolean Exponent Splitting

Having established that the proposed exponent splitting algorithms are probing-secure against first-order side-channel attacks, we proceed to analyze the noise amplification stage of the proposed countermeasure. Analytically, we perform an evaluation of Boolean exponent splitting (as described by Algorithm 2) using the information-theoretic framework of Standaert et al. [49]. Analogous approaches can be conducted for all exponent splitting algorithms, yielding very similar results. Our analysis considers two sources of leakage, namely data-based leakage and location-based leakage (also known as address leakage). Using these two leakage sources, we demonstrate three possible attack paths against Algorithm 5, covering all possible combinations between leakage sources. Thus we show the noise amplification stage when only data-based leakage is exploited (data attack), when only location-based leakage is exploited (location attack) and finally the noise amplification stage when the adversary combines data and location leakage (hybrid attack).

Notation & MI Metric. In this subsection, random variables are denoted with capital letters. Instances of random variables and constant values are denoted with lowercase letters. Capital bold letters are used for random variable vectors and matrices and calligraphic font denotes sets. All simulations in this section are carried out with the identity leakage function. Observable data-based leakages of a certain intermediate value v are denoted using subscript L_v. Likewise, observable location-based leakages caused by accessing register R_i (where i the index) are denoted using subscript $L_{R\text{-}i}$. To distinguish between data-based leakage and location-based leakage we use superscript L^{data} and L^{loc}. In addition, we assume that different sources of leakage (data, location) have different noise levels i.e. we assume homoscedastic data noise $N^{data} \sim \mathcal{N}(0, \sigma_{data}^2)$ and homoscedastic location noise $N^{loc} \sim \mathcal{N}(0, \sigma_{loc}^2)$. We use the following formula to compute the MI metric.

$$MI(S; \mathbf{L}) = H[S] + \sum_{s \in \mathcal{S}} Pr[s] \cdot \sum_{\mathbf{m} \in \mathcal{M}^d} Pr[\mathbf{m}] \cdot \int_{\mathbf{l} \in \mathcal{L}^{(d+1)}} Pr[\mathbf{l}|s, \mathbf{m}] \cdot log_2 Pr[s|\mathbf{l}] \; d\mathbf{l} \quad (14)$$

where $Pr[s|\mathbf{l}] = \frac{\sum_{\mathbf{m}^* \in \mathcal{R}} Pr[\mathbf{l}|s, \mathbf{m}^*]}{\sum_{s^* \in \mathcal{S}} \sum_{\mathbf{m}^* \in \mathcal{R}} Pr[\mathbf{l}|s^*, \mathbf{m}^*]}$, and random variable S denotes the secret exponent bit, $\mathbf{L}$ denotes the leakage vector and $\mathbf{M}$ is a d-dimensional randomness vector that we need to sum over when randomization is in place, i.e. d is the attack order.

Data Leakage Attack. The first obvious way to recover k_{n-1} is by observing the data leakage of the values b_{n-1} and a_{n-1} at the same time. We run the algorithm for the first two rounds and note the intermediate values that can leak information. We let b' be a random value from $R\{0, 1\}$, then:

$i = n - 1$	$i = n - 2$
1. $b_m = b_{n-1} \oplus b'$	6. $b_m = b_{n-2} \oplus b'$
2. $a_m = b_m \oplus a_{n-1}$	7. $a_m = b_m \oplus a_{n-2}$
3. $R_0 = R_{b_m} \cdot R_{a_m}$	8. $R_0 = R_{b_m} \cdot R_{a_m}$
4. $R_1 = R_0 \cdot U_{b_{n-1}}$	9. $R_1 = R_0 \cdot U_{b_{n-2}}$
5. $b' = b_{n-1}$	10. $b' = b_{n-2}$

As can be observed in above, the value b_{n-1} is accessed in the first iteration ($i = n - 1$) three times, once when b_m is calculated (line 1), once implicitly for the index of $U_{b_{n-1}}$ (line 4) and finally for b' (line 5). The value a_{n-1} is accessed once during the first iteration ($i = n - 1$) and it is not used in the second iteration ($i = n - 2$). We notice that the value b_{n-1} is used implicitly again in the second iteration, since it is equal to b'. An attacker observing the power leakage of this algorithm should be able to probe at two different points in time, in order to observe both leakages $L_{a_{n-1}}^{data}$, $L_{b_{n-1}}^{data}$ and eventually the key, i.e. we conclude that a second-order attack is possible for this scheme. Note also that the an adversary with ability to conduct horizontal side-channel attacks [4] could observe the leakage of b_{n-1} multiple times, average them by computing $\bar{L}_{b_{n-1}}^{data} = \frac{1}{4} * \sum_{j=1}^{4} L_{b_{n-1}}^{data}$ in order to reduce the noise level and finally perform a second-order attack. The results of the MI evaluation are visible in Fig. 1. As expected, the exponent splitting scheme performs noise amplification and has a different slope compared to an unprotected exponentiation (Algorithm 3.1). In addition, we observe the curve's horizontal shift to the right caused by the horizontal exploitation of the available leakage, i.e. we can quantify the effect of multiple leaky points for b_{n-1}.

Location Leakage Attack. Let us assume that the adversary can distinguish between the manipulation of registers according to which address is accessed, similar to the address-bit DPA attack described in [29]. If the adversary can distinguish between accesses to, U_0 and U_1 for example, a direct consequence is recovery of value b_{n-1}. To mount a successful attack against Algorithm 5 using solely location-based leakage, we need the simultaneous observation of the address of U_{i_1} and R_{i_2} and R_{i_3}, for indexes $i_1 = b_{n-1}$ (line 4) and $i_2 = b_m$ (line 3) and $i_3 = a_m$ (line 3). Thus, in order to recover k_{n-1}, we need to observe leakage vector $L^{loc} = [L_{U \cdot i_1}^{loc}, L_{R \cdot i_2}^{loc}, L_{R \cdot i_3}^{loc}]$, i.e.

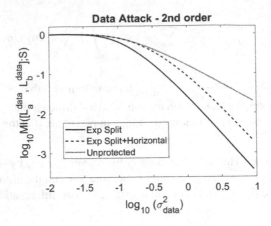

Fig. 1. MI evaluation for Algorithm 2, using a data leakage attack, with and without horizontal exploitation. Observed leakage vector $\mathbf{L} = [L_{a_{n-1}}^{data}, L_{b_{n-1}}^{data}]$ [50].

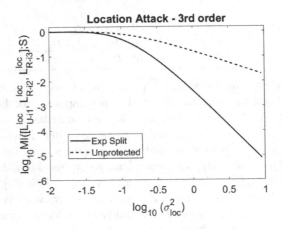

Fig. 2. MI evaluation for Algorithm 2, using a location leakage attack. Observed leakage vector $\mathbf{L} = [L_{U\text{-}i_1}^{loc}, L_{R\text{-}i_2}^{loc}, L_{R\text{-}i_3}^{loc}]$ [50].

perform a third-order attack. The results are visible in Fig. 2, where we can observe the noise amplification effect that increases the curve's slope. Naturally, a third-order attack using only location-based leakage tends to be less effective compared to a second-order attack using only data-based leakage. However, depending on the device, exploiting the address dependency may be more effective than exploiting the data dependency. That is, the third-order attack can become more efficient if $\sigma_{data} > \sigma_{loc}$.

Hybrid Leakage Attack. Lastly, we analyze the scenario in which an adversary can observe both data-based and location-based leakage. Using this information the adversary can use leakage vector

$$\mathbf{L} = [L_{a_{n-1}}^{data}, L_{U\text{-}b_{n-1}}^{loc}]$$

to carry out a second-order attack that uses data leakage to recover bit a_{n-1} and location leakage with regard to register U to recover bit b_{n-1}. Since data and location leakage imply different noise levels, i.e. ($\sigma_{data} \neq \sigma_{loc}$), we need to represent the available information as a three-dimensional plot, as in Fig. 3. The wave-like plot quantifies the attainable information with regard to a particular data and location noise level. Thus, it assists the side-channel evaluator to analyze the scheme's security in a more holistic way that factors in location leakage and demonstrates the tradeoff between data noise and location noise. If for instance $\sigma_{loc} \ll \sigma_{data}$ in the target device, the adversary can directly opt for the hybrid attack, instead of pursing a data-only attack route.

Hybrid Data+Location Attack - 2nd order

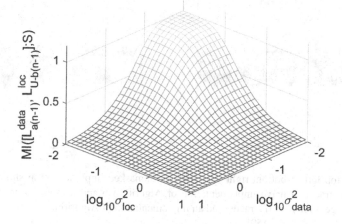

Fig. 3. MI evaluation for Algorithm 2 exponent splitting, using a hybrid leakage attack. Observed leakage vector $\mathbf{L} = [L_{a_{n-1}}^{data}, L_{U \cdot b_{n-1}}^{loc}]$ [50].

6   Implementation Considerations

In this section, we describe the results of applying Test Vector Leakage Assessment (TVLA) [21] to implementations of some of the algorithms above. We further describe modifications required to achieve a secure implementation where the hardware architecture can mean that variables that should be independent leak at the same time, potentially unmasking a secret value [2].

Our implementations were developed using Xilinx's Zynq zc702 evaluation board. The Zynq zc702 microprocessor contains two ARM7 cores and an FPGA fabric. We used one ARM7 core for our implementations, clocked at 667 MHz, and the FPGA provided a means of triggering an oscilloscope at a convenient point in our implementations. We acquired a trace of the electromagnetic emanations around one of the coupling capacitors.

The test that we used from TVLA is to determine whether there are statistically significant differences in the mean traces of two sets of traces, one acquired with a fixed scalar and the other with random scalar. One would typically randomly interleave acquisitions so that environmental effects are the same for both sets and there are no

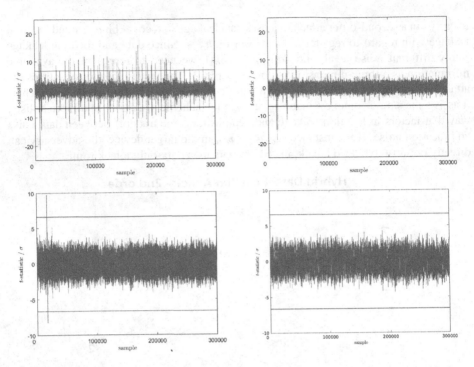

Fig. 4. From top left to bottom right we show: an unmasked implementation showing leakage after 1×10^3 traces, a naïve implementation of Algorithm 6 and a more secure variant both showing leakage after 1×10^6 traces, and an implementation of Algorithm 11 that does not show leakage after 1×10^6 traces [50].

erroneous indications of leakage, caused, for example, by the least significant bit of a variable used to count the number of acquisitions. In applying this, one would take two sets of data, and conduct Welch's t-test point-by-point to determine whether there is evidence against the null hypothesis that the sets are the same. We determine that leakage is present if we observe values above $6.63\,\sigma$ which gives the probability of indicating leakage where no leakage is present, often referred to as a Type I error, of approximately 1×10^5 when using traces containing 3×10^5 samples. The interested reader is referred to Goodwill et al. [21] and Schneider and Moradi [47] for a thorough description.

We made a straightforward implementation of Algorithm 6 using NIST's P192 curve and conducted a test where we compared a set of traces with a fixed scalar compared to a set of traces with a random scalar. The elliptic curve points were implemented as homogeneous projective points. We use the x and z-coordinates in conjunction with so-called x-only algorithms for point arithmetic [11], as one would for an implementation of ECDH. The instantaneous electromagnetic emanations around the targeted capacitor were measured during the execution of the first 20 rounds of the implementation. The top-left trace in Fig. 4 shows the result of a TVLA analysis with 1×10^3 traces where leakage can be seen in numerous places.

A straightforward implementation of Algorithm 6 was tested in the same way. The algorithm is similar to that proposed by Izumi et al. [28] but with masking conducted before the execution of the scalar multiplication, rather than on-the-fly. The resulting TVLA traces is shown in the top-right of Fig. 4, where we note that significant leakage is present with 1×10^6 traces. This is caused by the microprocessor combining values held in registers because of the architecture chosen by the designers [2].

A more secure implementation can be made by computing some of the required indices before the execution of the main loop of the scalar multiplication, as shown in Algorithm 11. We set C to $B \oplus \lfloor \frac{B}{2} \rfloor$ such that individual bits of B are masked by adjacent bits. The resulting TVLA trace is shown in the bottom-left of Fig. 4, where we observe that there is only one place where we see significant leakage with 1×10^6 traces. This leakage occurs because the initial state of $\{R_0, R_1\}$ contain $\{P, 2P\}$ in some random order. In the first loop of the scalar multiplication $\{R_0, R_1\}$ is overwritten with $\{2P, 3P\}$ or $\{3P, 4P\}$, in some random order, depending on whether the second most-significant bit of κ is set to 0 or 1, respectively. When $2P$ overwrites $2P$ the side-channel leakage will be significantly different to any other possible combination, since the Hamming distance will be zero.

Algorithm 11. Montgomery Ladder with XOR-Split Scalar on an EC.

Input: $\mathcal{E}, \mathbb{F}_q, P \in \mathcal{E}$, n-bit integers
$$A = \sum_{i=0}^{n-1} a_i\, 2^i,$$
$$B = \sum_{i=0}^{n-1} b_i\, 2^i$$
Output: $Q = [\kappa]P$ where $\kappa = A \oplus B$
Uses: $C = \sum_{i=0}^{n-1} c_i\, 2^i$

1 $R_0 \leftarrow P$; $R_1 \leftarrow P$; $R_2 \leftarrow P$;
2 $C \leftarrow B \oplus \lfloor \frac{B}{2} \rfloor$;
3 $b' \leftarrow b_{n-1}$;
4 $R_{\neg b'} \leftarrow 2P$;
5 **for** $i = n - 2$ **down to** 0 **do**
6     $R_2 \leftarrow R_{a_i} + R_{\neg a_i}$;
7     $R_{a_i} \leftarrow 2\,R_{a_i \oplus c_i}$;
8     $R_{\neg a_i} \leftarrow R_2$;
9 **end**
10 **return** R_{b_0}

Algorithm 12. Montgomery Ladder with XOR-Split Scalar II on an EC.

Input: $\mathcal{E}, \mathbb{F}_q, P \in \mathcal{E}$, n-bit integers
$$A = \sum_{i=0}^{n-1} a_i\, 2^i,$$
$$B = \sum_{i=0}^{n-1} b_i\, 2^i$$
Output: $Q = [\kappa]P$ where $\kappa = A \oplus B$
Uses: $C = \sum_{i=0}^{n-1} c_i\, 2^i$ and
$$D = \sum_{i=0}^{n-1} d_i\, 2^i$$

1 $R_0 \leftarrow P$; $R_1 \leftarrow P$;
2 $U_0 \leftarrow P$; $U_1 \leftarrow -P$;
3 $C \leftarrow B \oplus \lfloor \frac{B}{2} \rfloor$; $D \leftarrow C \oplus A$;
4 $b' \leftarrow b_{n-1}$;
5 $R_{\neg b'} \leftarrow 2P$;
6 **for** $i = n - 2$ **down to** 0 **do**
7     $R_0 \leftarrow R_{c_i} + R_{d_i}$;
8     $R_1 \leftarrow R_0 + U_{b_i}$;
9     $b' \leftarrow b_i$;
10 **end**
11 **return** R_{b_0}

A fully secure implementation can be achieved by randomizing the point produced by the doubling operation, by multiplying the x and z-coordinate of the resulting point by a random value. In implementing Algorithm 11, this was achieved by randomizing R_0 and R_1 before the main loop of the scalar multiplication. The resulting TVLA trace is shown in the bottom-right of Fig. 4, where we observe that there is no significant leakage with 1×10^6 traces. An alternative would be to set the coordinates of R_{a_i} to zero before setting R_{a_i} to R_2.

Algorithm 12 shows the same arguments applied to Algorithm 7. However there is no need to randomize any points during the loops of scalar multiplication. If the redundant representation of the point assigned to R_0 and R_1 is randomized separately to that applied to U_0 an overwrite with a Hamming distance of zero cannot occur.

7 Conclusion

Countermeasures to side-channel analysis typically significantly increase the execution time of public-key algorithms. In [50] we described a method for dividing an exponent into Boolean shares to mask the exponent value, and we expand on this work in the above. This work can be combined with inexpensive solutions such as randomizing projective points [52] or Ebeid and Lambert's blinding method for RSA [17] can be combined with out methods to provide a high level of side-channel resistance.

Acknowledgments. The authors would like to thank Lauren De Meyer and Michael Hamburg for their helpful comments.

References

1. Amiel, F., Feix, B.: On the BRIP Algorithms Security for RSA. In: Onieva, J.A., Sauveron, D., Chaumette, S., Gollmann, D., Markantonakis, K. (eds.) WISTP 2008. LNCS, vol. 5019, pp. 136–149. Springer, Heidelberg (2008). https://doi.org/10.1007/978-3-540-79966-5_10

2. Balasch, J., Gierlichs, B., Grosso, V., Reparaz, O., Standaert, F.-X.: On the Cost of Lazy Engineering for Masked Software Implementations. In: Joye, M., Moradi, A. (eds.) CARDIS 2014. LNCS, vol. 8968, pp. 64–81. Springer, Cham (2015). https://doi.org/10.1007/978-3-319-16763-3_5

3. Batina, L., Chmielewski, Ł, Papachristodoulou, L., Schwabe, P., Tunstall, M.: Online Template Attacks. In: Meier, W., Mukhopadhyay, D. (eds.) INDOCRYPT 2014. LNCS, vol. 8885, pp. 21–36. Springer, Cham (2014). https://doi.org/10.1007/978-3-319-13039-2_2

4. Battistello, A., Coron, J.-S., Prouff, E., Zeitoun, R.: Horizontal Side-Channel Attacks and Countermeasures on the ISW Masking Scheme. In: Gierlichs, B., Poschmann, A.Y. (eds.) CHES 2016. LNCS, vol. 9813, pp. 23–39. Springer, Heidelberg (2016). https://doi.org/10.1007/978-3-662-53140-2_2

5. Bauer, A., Jaulmes, É.: Correlation Analysis against Protected SFM Implementations of RSA. In: Paul, G., Vaudenay, S. (eds.) INDOCRYPT 2013. LNCS, vol. 8250, pp. 98–115. Springer, Cham (2013). https://doi.org/10.1007/978-3-319-03515-4_7

6. Bauer, A., Jaulmes, E., Prouff, E., Wild, J.: Horizontal Collision Correlation Attack on Elliptic Curves. In: Lange, T., Lauter, K., Lisoněk, P. (eds.) SAC 2013. LNCS, vol. 8282, pp. 553–570. Springer, Heidelberg (2014). https://doi.org/10.1007/978-3-662-43414-7_28

7. Bernstein, D.J.: Curve25519: New Diffie-Hellman Speed Records. In: Yung, M., Dodis, Y., Kiayias, A., Malkin, T. (eds.) PKC 2006. LNCS, vol. 3958, pp. 207–228. Springer, Heidelberg (2006). https://doi.org/10.1007/11745853_14

8. Bernstein, D.J., Lange, T.: A complete set of addition laws for incomplete edwards curves. Cryptology ePrint Archive, Report 2009/580 (2009), https://eprint.iacr.org/2009/580

9. Bos, J.W., Costello, C., Longa, P., Naehrig, M.: Selecting elliptic curves for cryptography: an efficiency and security analysis. J. Cryptographic Eng. **6**(4), 259–286 (2016)
10. Brier, E., Clavier, C., Olivier, F.: Correlation Power Analysis with a Leakage Model. In: Joye, M., Quisquater, J.-J. (eds.) CHES 2004. LNCS, vol. 3156, pp. 16–29. Springer, Heidelberg (2004). https://doi.org/10.1007/978-3-540-28632-5_2
11. Brier, É., Joye, M.: Weierstraß Elliptic Curves and Side-Channel Attacks. In: Naccache, D., Paillier, P. (eds.) PKC 2002. LNCS, vol. 2274, pp. 335–345. Springer, Heidelberg (2002). https://doi.org/10.1007/3-540-45664-3_24
12. Chari, S., Rao, J.R., Rohatgi, P.: Template Attacks. In: Kaliski, B.S., Koç, K., Paar, C. (eds.) CHES 2002. LNCS, vol. 2523, pp. 13–28. Springer, Heidelberg (2003). https://doi.org/10.1007/3-540-36400-5_3
13. Ciet, M., Joye, M.: (Virtually) Free Randomization Techniques for Elliptic Curve Cryptography. In: Qing, S., Gollmann, D., Zhou, J. (eds.) ICICS 2003. LNCS, vol. 2836, pp. 348–359. Springer, Heidelberg (2003). https://doi.org/10.1007/978-3-540-39927-8_32
14. Clavier, C., Feix, B., Gagnerot, G., Giraud, C., Roussellet, M., Verneuil, V.: ROSETTA for Single Trace Analysis. In: Galbraith, S., Nandi, M. (eds.) INDOCRYPT 2012. LNCS, vol. 7668, pp. 140–155. Springer, Heidelberg (2012). https://doi.org/10.1007/978-3-642-34931-7_9
15. Clavier, C., Joye, M.: Universal Exponentiation Algorithm A First Step towards *Provable* SPA-Resistance. In: Koç, Ç.K., Naccache, D., Paar, C. (eds.) CHES 2001. LNCS, vol. 2162, pp. 300–308. Springer, Heidelberg (2001). https://doi.org/10.1007/3-540-44709-1_25
16. Coron, J.-S.: Resistance Against Differential Power Analysis For Elliptic Curve Cryptosystems. In: Koç, Ç.K., Paar, C. (eds.) CHES 1999. LNCS, vol. 1717, pp. 292–302. Springer, Heidelberg (1999). https://doi.org/10.1007/3-540-48059-5_25
17. Ebeid, N.M., Lambert, R.: A new CRT-RSA algorithm resistant to powerful fault attacks. In: WESS 2010. p. 8. ACM (2010)
18. Edwards, H.M.: A normal form for elliptic curves. In: Çetin.K. Koç, Paar, C. (eds.) Bulletin of the American Mathematical Society. vol. 44, pp. 393–422 (2007)
19. Feix, B., Roussellet, M., Venelli, A.: Side-Channel Analysis on Blinded Regular Scalar Multiplications. In: Meier, W., Mukhopadhyay, D. (eds.) INDOCRYPT 2014. LNCS, vol. 8885, pp. 3–20. Springer, Cham (2014). https://doi.org/10.1007/978-3-319-13039-2_1
20. Gandolfi, K., Mourtel, C., Olivier, F.: Electromagnetic Analysis: Concrete Results. In: Koç, Ç.K., Naccache, D., Paar, C. (eds.) CHES 2001. LNCS, vol. 2162, pp. 251–261. Springer, Heidelberg (2001). https://doi.org/10.1007/3-540-44709-1_21
21. Goodwill, G., Jun, B., Jaffe, J., Rohatgi, P.: A testing methodology for side channel resistance validation NIST non-invasive attack testing workshop (2011)
22. Goubin, L.: A Sound Method for Switching between Boolean and Arithmetic Masking. In: Koç, Ç.K., Naccache, D., Paar, C. (eds.) CHES 2001. LNCS, vol. 2162, pp. 3–15. Springer, Heidelberg (2001). https://doi.org/10.1007/3-540-44709-1_2
23. Goubin, L.: A Refined Power-Analysis Attack on Elliptic Curve Cryptosystems. In: Desmedt, Y.G. (ed.) PKC 2003. LNCS, vol. 2567, pp. 199–211. Springer, Heidelberg (2003). https://doi.org/10.1007/3-540-36288-6_15
24. Hamburg, M.: Ed448-Goldilocks, a new elliptic curve. Cryptology ePrint Archive, Report 2015/625 (2015). http://eprint.iacr.org/2015/625
25. Hanley, N., Kim, H.S., Tunstall, M.: Exploiting Collisions in Addition Chain-Based Exponentiation Algorithms Using a Single Trace. In: Nyberg, K. (ed.) CT-RSA 2015. LNCS, vol. 9048, pp. 431–448. Springer, Cham (2015). https://doi.org/10.1007/978-3-319-16715-2_23
26. Howgrave-Graham, N., Smart, N.P.: Lattice attacks on digital signature schemes. Des. Codes Cryptography **23**(3), 283–290 (2001)

27. Itoh, K., Izu, T., Takenada, M.: Address-bit differential power analysis of cryptographic schemes OK-ECDH and OK-ECDSA. In: Jr., B.S.K., Ç. K. Koç, Paar, C. (eds.) CHES 2002. LNCS, vol. 2523, pp. 129–143. Springer (2002)
28. Itoh, K., Izu, T., Takenaka, M.: A Practical Countermeasure against Address-Bit Differential Power Analysis. In: Walter, C.D., Koç, Ç.K., Paar, C. (eds.) CHES 2003. LNCS, vol. 2779, pp. 382–396. Springer, Heidelberg (2003). https://doi.org/10.1007/978-3-540-45238-6_30
29. Izumi, M., Ikegami, J., Sakiyama, K., Ohta, K.: Improved countermeasures against address-bit DPA for ECC scalar multiplication. In: Michell, G.D., Al-Hashimi, B.M., Müller, W., Macii, E. (eds.) DATE 2010. pp. 981–984. IEEE (2010)
30. Joye, M., Villegas, K.: A protected division algorithm. In: Honeyman, P. (ed.) CARDIS 2002. USENIX (2002)
31. Joye, M., Yen, S.-M.: The Montgomery Powering Ladder. In: Kaliski, B.S., Koç, K., Paar, C. (eds.) CHES 2002. LNCS, vol. 2523, pp. 291–302. Springer, Heidelberg (2003). https://doi.org/10.1007/3-540-36400-5_22
32. Kim, H., Kim, T.H., Yoon, J.C., Hong, S.: Practical second-order correlation power analysis on the message blinding method and its novel countermeasure for RSA. ETRI J. 32(1), 102–111 (2010)
33. Kocher, P.C.: Timing Attacks on Implementations of Diffie-Hellman, RSA, DSS, and Other Systems. In: Koblitz, N. (ed.) CRYPTO 1996. LNCS, vol. 1109, pp. 104–113. Springer, Heidelberg (1996). https://doi.org/10.1007/3-540-68697-5_9
34. Kocher, P., Jaffe, J., Jun, B.: Differential Power Analysis. In: Wiener, M. (ed.) CRYPTO 1999. LNCS, vol. 1666, pp. 388–397. Springer, Heidelberg (1999). https://doi.org/10.1007/3-540-48405-1_25
35. Le, D.-P., Tan, C.H., Tunstall, M.: Randomizing the Montgomery Powering Ladder. In: Akram, R.N., Jajodia, S. (eds.) WISTP 2015. LNCS, vol. 9311, pp. 169–184. Springer, Cham (2015). https://doi.org/10.1007/978-3-319-24018-3_11
36. Lochter, M., Merkle, J., Schmidt, J.M., Schütze, T.: Requirements for standard elliptic curves. Cryptology ePrint Archive, Report 2014/832 (2014), https://eprint.iacr.org/2014/832
37. Messerges, T.S., Dabbish, E.A.: Investigations of power analysis attacks on smartcards. In: Guthery, S.B., Honeyman, P. (eds.) Smartcard 1999. USENIX Association (1999)
38. Messerges, T.S., Dabbish, E.A., Sloan, R.H.: Power Analysis Attacks of Modular Exponentiation in Smartcards. In: Koç, Ç.K., Paar, C. (eds.) CHES 1999. LNCS, vol. 1717, pp. 144–157. Springer, Heidelberg (1999). https://doi.org/10.1007/3-540-48059-5_14
39. Montgomery, P.L.: Speeding the Pollard and elliptic curve methods of factorization. Math. Comput. 48(177), 243–264 (1987)
40. Naccache, D., Nguyên, P.Q., Tunstall, M., Whelan, C.: Experimenting with Faults, Lattices and the DSA. In: Vaudenay, S. (ed.) PKC 2005. LNCS, vol. 3386, pp. 16–28. Springer, Heidelberg (2005). https://doi.org/10.1007/978-3-540-30580-4_3
41. National Institute of Standards and Technology (NIST): Recommended elliptic curves for federal government use. In the appendix of FIPS 186-3. (2009) http://csrc.nist.gov/publications/fips/fips186-3/fips_186-3.pdf
42. Okeya, K., Sakurai, K.: A Second-Order DPA Attack Breaks a Window-Method Based Countermeasure against Side Channel Attacks. In: Chan, A.H., Gligor, V. (eds.) ISC 2002. LNCS, vol. 2433, pp. 389–401. Springer, Heidelberg (2002). https://doi.org/10.1007/3-540-45811-5_30
43. Oswald, E., Mangard, S.: Template Attacks on Masking—Resistance Is Futile. In: Abe, M. (ed.) CT-RSA 2007. LNCS, vol. 4377, pp. 243–256. Springer, Heidelberg (2006). https://doi.org/10.1007/11967668_16
44. Quisquater, J.-J., Samyde, D.: ElectroMagnetic Analysis (EMA): Measures and Countermeasures for Smart Cards. In: Attali, I., Jensen, T. (eds.) E-smart 2001. LNCS, vol. 2140, pp. 200–210. Springer, Heidelberg (2001). https://doi.org/10.1007/3-540-45418-7_17

45. Rivest, R., Shamir, A., Adleman, L.M.: Method for obtaining digital signatures and public-key cryptosystems. Commun. ACM **21**(2), 120–126 (1978)
46. Schindler, W., Itoh, K.: Exponent Blinding Does Not Always Lift (Partial) Spa Resistance to Higher-Level Security. In: Lopez, J., Tsudik, G. (eds.) ACNS 2011. LNCS, vol. 6715, pp. 73–90. Springer, Heidelberg (2011). https://doi.org/10.1007/978-3-642-21554-4_5
47. Schneider, T., Moradi, A.: Leakage Assessment Methodology. In: Güneysu, T., Handschuh, H. (eds.) CHES 2015. LNCS, vol. 9293, pp. 495–513. Springer, Heidelberg (2015). https://doi.org/10.1007/978-3-662-48324-4_25
48. Smart, N., Oswald, E., Page, D.: Randomised representations. IET Proc. Inf. Secur. **2**(2), 19–27 (2008)
49. Standaert, F.-X., Malkin, T.G., Yung, M.: A Unified Framework for the Analysis of Side-Channel Key Recovery Attacks. In: Joux, A. (ed.) EUROCRYPT 2009. LNCS, vol. 5479, pp. 443–461. Springer, Heidelberg (2009). https://doi.org/10.1007/978-3-642-01001-9_26
50. Tunstall, M., Papachristodoulou, L., Papagiannopoulos, K.: Boolean exponent splitting. In: di Vimercati, S.D.C., Samarati, P. (eds.) Proceedings of the 18th International Conference on Security and Cryptography, SECRYPT 2021. pp. 321–332. SCITEPRESS (2021)
51. Walter, C.D.: Sliding Windows Succumbs to Big Mac Attack. In: Koç, Ç.K., Naccache, D., Paar, C. (eds.) CHES 2001. LNCS, vol. 2162, pp. 286–299. Springer, Heidelberg (2001). https://doi.org/10.1007/3-540-44709-1_24
52. De Win, E., Mister, S., Preneel, B., Wiener, M.: On the performance of signature schemes based on elliptic curves. In: Buhler, J.P. (ed.) ANTS 1998. LNCS, vol. 1423, pp. 252–266. Springer, Heidelberg (1998). https://doi.org/10.1007/BFb0054867
53. Witteman, M.F., van Woudenberg, J.G.J., Menarini, F.: Defeating RSA Multiply-Always and Message Blinding Countermeasures. In: Kiayias, A. (ed.) CT-RSA 2011. LNCS, vol. 6558, pp. 77–88. Springer, Heidelberg (2011). https://doi.org/10.1007/978-3-642-19074-2_6

Trusted Implementation and Enforcement of Application Security Policies

Marius Schlegel(✉)

TU Ilmenau, Ilmenau, Germany
marius.schlegel@tu-ilmenau.de

Abstract. Although system-level security policies are enforced directly in many modern operating systems, they do not provide adequate support for application-level security policies. Application software uses objects of higher abstraction requiring individual security policies with application-specific semantics. While frameworks assist in application policy implementation, developers are still responsible for their application's security architecture which often leads to large and heterogeneous application trusted computing bases rendering protection from unauthorized manipulation hard to achieve. This work contributes to improving this situation. We present APPSPEAR – an application-level security policy enforcement architecture tailorable to application requirements. To foster streamlined and tool-supported security engineering workflows, we moreover present a policy specification language (DYNAMO), a corresponding Rust source code generation approach, and a developer framework leveraging Rust and Intel SGX for trusted and memory-safe APPSPEAR implementation and policy integration.

Keywords: Security engineering · Application software security · Security architecture · Security policies · Specification language · Security policy enforcement · Trusted execution · Intel SGX · Rust

1 Introduction

For the specification and rigorous enforcement of application-specific security goals, modern software systems rely on security policies. As an automatically enforced set of rules, a security policy controls and restricts access to security-critical resources. For almost two decades, it has become a common practice to integrate security policies directly into operating systems (OSs) such as Linux, Unix/BSD, and Android [58]. Hence, OS-level security policies control objects described by abstractions such as files, processes, or sockets.

Application software typically uses objects that are subject to security policies on a higher, application-specific abstraction level: For instance, enterprise resource planning systems typically use role-based access control (AC) policies that reflect a company's organizational structure [1,6], database systems use label-based AC policies to control access to relations and views [22,35], (social) information systems use relationship-based AC policies on user data [18,37], and Big Data and IoT platforms rely on attribute-based AC policies [5,19]. Thus, policy rules require application-specific semantics, which differ from OS-level policy semantics and are specific for each individual application.

ⓒ The Author(s), under exclusive license to Springer Nature Switzerland AG 2023
P. Samarati et al. (Eds.): ICETE 2021, CCIS 1795, pp. 362–388, 2023.
https://doi.org/10.1007/978-3-031-36840-0_16

Contemporary OSs do not provide adequate support for application security policies. While application AC frameworks such as Casbin [10] and Oso [36] are improving the situation, they do not provide architectural support, leaving developers responsible for an application's security architecture and its implementation which typically results in the interweaving of application logic and security-related functionality. This approach renders the protection from unauthorized manipulation of application security policies difficult, if not impossible, and results in large, heterogeneous application trusted computing base (TCB) implementations.

We argue for an alternative approach: By separating security-related functionality from potentially untrusted application logic, the functional perimeter of an application TCB can be precisely defined. Then, this separation is enforced by leveraging isolation mechanisms [46]. In particular, trusted execution technologies are a strong alternative, e. g. Intel SGX provides enclaves that isolate security-sensitive parts of application code and data from the OS, hypervisor, BIOS, and other applications using a hardware-protected memory region [25].

Following this approach, in [40], we introduce APPSPEAR – a security architecture framework for the trusted enforcement of application-specific security policies at the application level. The implementation alternatives anchored in APPSPEAR enable balancing the rigor of policy enforcement (effectiveness) as well as the costs for isolation and communication (efficiency). The performance evaluation of different APPSPEAR implementation alternatives has shown that using SGX-based isolation with optimizations can achieve an overhead on par with conventional OS-based isolation while having higher effectiveness.

Security policies are highly critical software components and also demand careful development themselves. A modern approach is model-based security policy engineering (MSPE) [4,43,55]: First, the informal policy representation is formalized as a model and its correctness conditions are defined (Model Engineering). Second, formal methods are applied to verify an instance of the former against the latter (Model Analysis). Third, the verified model is translated into source code (Model Implementation). Finally, the model code is integrated into the runtime environment (RTE) of the respective security architecture (Model Integration).

This paper is a revised and extended version of [40]. Since a model's implementation, its RTE, and the security architecture have to integrate perfectly, we aim to make the integration of APPSPEAR into MSPE even more streamlined and convenient. Specifically, we contribute with (1.) the policy specification language DYNAMO and a Rust source code generation approach enabling convenient, memory-safe application policy and RTE implementations, and (2.) memory-safe reference implementations of APPSPEAR in Rust and corresponding evaluation results.

The paper is organized as follows: In Sect. 2, we discuss the specification of application security policies with DYNAMO and a corresponding source code generation approach for convenient policy implementations in the Rust programming language. Subsequently, in Sect. 3, we present the APPSPEAR architecture framework, in particular, its design, various implementation alternatives, and an evaluation of their runtime performance. In Sect. 4, we describe the APPSPEAR developer framework for the Rust programming language, which enables a convenient APPSPEAR implementation and application policy integration. Moreover, we demonstrate these features for a medical information management application. Finally, Sect. 5 gives an overview of related work and Sect. 6 concludes the paper.

2 Application Policy Specification and Implementation

Given the critical importance of correct security policy implementations, our high-level goal is to make the MSPE process more convenient and streamlined to avoid manual and potentially error-prone translations of model specifications in transitions between MSPE steps. Having engineered a formal model for a security policy in the Model Engineering step, both subsequent steps, Model Analysis and Model Implementation require a machine-readable model specification as input. Consequently, model specifications can and should be based on a uniform textual specification language usable across the MSPE process steps.

Towards this goal, we discuss DYNAMO – a specification language for dynamic security models based on deterministic automatons [2]. DYNAMO is designed to share goals of three major MSPE steps. Hence, a specification in DYNAMO is (1.) close to formal model abstractions (Model Engineering step), (2.) semantically expressive to capture policy dynamics enabling analyses of dynamic model properties (e. g. model safety) and machine-interpretable by analysis tools (Model Analysis step), as well as (3.) translatable into source code which can be integrated into security architecture implementations (Model Implementation step).

In the following, we will detail these goals to describe language requirements (Sect. 2.1), then explain and demonstrate actual design decisions and language paradigms (Sect. 2.2), and discuss a corresponding approach policy and RTE source code generation in Rust (Sect. 2.3).

2.1 Language Requirements

MSPE involves qualified security engineers which are familiar with mathematical notations of model abstractions. Consequently, a specification language facilitating cross-step support in MSPE should generally support these notations. AC policies are one of the most prominent policy classes in practice. DYNAMO focuses on language support for dynamic AC models which basically require three abstract data types (ADTs) as formal building blocks: set, relation, and mapping, each representing its mathematical counterpart. Since we strive for supporting a broad range of dynamic security models, the extension regarding further common mathematical model abstractions, such as matrices[1].

The Model Analysis step may not only aim at analyzing static model properties (e. g. model consistency) but also dynamic model properties (e. g. model safety) regarding the temporal changes an AC system may undergo. In previous work [41,42], we propose an approach that allows security engineers to configure modeling schemes to application-specific analysis goals. Hence, we require DYNAMO to be able to specify

---

[1] Note that for AC matrices (ACMs) mathematically formalized by mappings, a convenience matrix ADT would just ease access to ACM columns and rows.

security models with configurable dynamics, which we define based on deterministic automatons (according to the idea of [20]).

Definition 1 (Dynamic Security Model). *A dynamic security model is a deterministic automaton defined by a tuple* $\langle \Gamma, \Sigma, \Delta, \gamma_0, E \rangle$, *where*

- *the state space* Γ *is a set of states defined as a cartesian product of dynamic model components;*
- *the input set* $\Sigma = \Sigma_C \times \Sigma_Y^*$ *defines possible inputs that may trigger state transitions, where* Σ_C *is a set of* command *identifiers used to represent operations a policy may authorize and* Σ_Y *is a set of* values *usable as actual parameters of commands;*[2]
- *the state transition scheme (STS)* $\Delta \subseteq \Sigma_C \times \Sigma_X^* \times \Phi \times \Phi$ *defines state transition pre- and post-conditions for any input of a command and formal parameters, where* Σ_X *denotes a set of* variables *to identify such parameters, and* Φ *represents a set of boolean expressions in first-order logic;*
- *the initial state* γ_0;
- *the extension tuple* E *is a tuple of static model components which are not part of* Γ.

For defining each $\langle c, x, \phi, \phi' \rangle \in \Delta$, the notation $c(x) :: = \mathsf{PRE} : \phi \,;\, \mathsf{POST} : \phi'$ is used. We call the term ϕ the pre-condition and ϕ' the post-condition of any state transition to be authorized via command c. On an automaton level, this means that ϕ restricts which states γ to legally transition from, while ϕ' defines any differences between γ and the state γ' reachable by any input word $\langle c, x \rangle$. To distinguish between the value domains of individual variables in x, we use a refined definition of Σ_X to reflect distinct namespaces of variable identifiers for each model component.

In the model analysis step, our goal is to reason about possible state transitions. Hence, we require that only such commands are modeled in Δ that modify their successor state. Additionally, the model implementation step requires a complete model specification also incorporating policy authorization rules which do not necessarily modify a current protection state. We assume such rules to be modeled as STS commands with an empty post-condition.

A core motivation for DYNAMO is to prevent and respectively reduce potential errors in transitions between MSPE steps. Hence, we require our language to encompass two well-known concepts of established programming languages. First, by dividing a model specification into two parts, DYNAMO enables reusability of specifications through inheritance: The *model* part describes a certain model class defining policy abstractions through model components as well as macros for pre- and post-condition of STS commands; the *model instance* part describes a concrete initialization of a dynamic model's automaton by using parts of a derived model. Second, by encompassing a strong typing of model components, which is enforced and checked by DYNAMO compilers, security engineers are supported in finding invalid assignments or relations between common model component types.

Model engineering is an iterative approach, model analysis results often have to be incorporated manually. Therefore, DYNAMO must be ergonomic, especially for qualified security engineers, and provide language elements in a way such that specifications are as simple, concise, and unambiguous as possible.

---

[2] We use the Kleene operator to indicate that multiple parameters may be passed.

```
model_spec =
"begin" "model" string ":"
    "begin" "inheritance" ":"
        inheritance_section
    "end" "inheritance" "; "
    "begin" "components" ":"
        components_section
    "end" "components" ";"
    "begin" "pre-clauses" ":"
        pre_clauses_section
    "end" "pre-clauses" ";"
    "begin" "post-clauses" ":"
        post_clauses_section
    "end" "post-clauses" ";"
"end" "model" ";" ;
```

Listing 1. EBNF for model specifications.

```
set U, R, P, S;
relation UA(U, R), PA(P, R);
mapping user(S : U), roles(S : 2^R);
```

Listing 2. Example of a components section.

2.2 Language Design

The size and complexity of application security policies require model specifications that are as small and simple as possible. Therefore, DYNAMO supports a simple flavor of inheritance enabling hierarchical model specifications. From a high-level perspective, each DYNAMO specification consists of two parts: a model and a model-instance. A concrete model instance is then always derived from an abstract model.

Generally in DYNAMO, every statement and every block of statements encapsulated by begin and end is trailed by a semicolon. The remainder of this section details DYNAMO's language features divided into the two parts of a specification (Sect. 2.2 and Sect. 2.2) and extracts of the EBNF notations, which are demonstrated stepwise based on a *dynamic RBAC* (DRBAC) modeling scheme [41] for a simplified version of a security policy for a healthcare information system [2].

Model Specification. In general, a model specification defines the abstractions in form of all dynamic and static model components (components section) and reusable macros for pre- and post-clauses as building blocks for STS commands (pre-clauses and post-clauses sections). Listing 1 shows the structure of a model specification.

The components section defines a model's components which are, later on (in a model-instance), divided into dynamic components, belonging to the state space Γ, and static components, belonging to the extension tuple E. Each model component

```
check_acf(S s, P p):
exists r in roles(s): [p, r] in PA;
can_activate_role(S s, R r):
exists u in U: ( u == user(s) and [u, r] in UA );
```

Listing 3. Example of a pre-clauses section.

```
begin activate_role(S s, R r):
rs = roles(s);
rs = rs + { r };
roles = roles + { (s : rs) };
end;
```

Listing 4. Example of a post-clauses section.

```
begin inherited_model_1:
all;
end;
begin inherited_model_2:
components: {U, R as R_NEW};
pre-conditions: { };                              /* inherit none */
post-conditions: all;
end;
```

Listing 5. Example of an inheritance section.

has a type declared by the ADTs set, relation, or mapping, and a string identifier; parametrized types require additional parameters. Listing 2 shows an example for the DRBAC model.

As required for the specification of pre-clauses, which are used in a model-instance to specify STS command pre-conditions, DYNAMO defines the intuitive logical operators ==, !=, in, not in, not, forall, exists, and, and or, optionally grouped by parentheses ( ). Listing 3 shows two pre-clauses: First, check_acf specifies an *access control function* (ACF) $acf_{RBAC} : S \times P \rightarrow \{\text{true}, \text{false}\}$ which allows expressing whether a permission $p \in P$ may be used in a certain session $s \in S$. Second, can_activate_role checks whether a role $r \in R$ may be activated in a certain session $s \in S$ by requiring that r is associated with the s's corresponding user u in *UA*.

Post-clauses are specified as blocks of statements. Each statement modifies a model component by adding or removing elements. To ease the specification, elements of model components may be also assigned temporarily to identifiers, which are local within a clause's scope. Listing 4 exemplarily demonstrates this for the post-clause activate_role. Furthermore, it is possible to iteratively execute statements for each element a component contains by using a for statement known from common programming languages.

To further improve the reusability of specifications and to reduce the specification effort, a model specification can be inherited (inheritance section): By using all,

```
model_instance_spec =
"begin" "model-instance" string ":" string ":"
    "state-space" ":"
        "{" state_space "}" ";"
    "input-vector" ":"
        "{" input_vector "}" ";"
    "begin" "state-transition-scheme" ":"
        state_transition_scheme_section
    "end" "state-transition-scheme" ";"
    "begin" "initial-state" ":"
        inital_state_section
    "end" "initial-state" ";"
    "begin" "extension-tuple" ":"
        extension_tuple_section
    "end" "extension-tuple" ";"
"end" "model-instance" ";" ;
```

Listing 6. EBNF for model-instance specifications.

```
state-space: { U, S, UA, user, roles };
input-vector: { U, S, R };
```

Listing 7. Example of state-space and input-vector statements.

a given model specification is inherited completely. Parts of a specification can be inherited list-based under indication of the corresponding section. It is also possible to rename inherited components using the keyword as. Listing 5 shows two examples.

Model Instance Specification. A model-instance specification defines the automaton components of a dynamic model according to Definition 1. Listing 6 shows its structure.

For a concrete model-instance, the model components derived from an abstract model specification are divided into dynamic and static components. Consequently, the state-space statement defines a set of all dynamic model components (see Listing 7).

The input vector of a dynamic model defines what parameters can be used for STS commands. Accordingly, the input-vector section specifies a subset of model components and corresponding power sets (e. g. user set U or power set of user set 2^U).

The state-transition-scheme is a list of command specifications where each one either has a pre-condition part (pre: ...;) consisting of logically connected clauses and derived clause macros, a post-condition part (begin post: ... end post;) consisting of one or more clauses and clause macros, or both parts. Constants in pre- and post-conditions can be specified by using single quotes. Listing 8 shows an exemplary specification of a command delegate_treatment_doc_card.

In the initial-state, all dynamic model components are assigned their initial values. Listing 9 exemplarily shows assignments of initial values to model components of types set, relation and mapping.

```
delegate_treatment_doc_card(S s_caller, S s_deleg):
    pre: check_acf(s_caller, 'p_deleg_treatment') and
         is_activated(s_caller, 'r_doc_card') and
         can_activate_role(s_deleg, 'r_doc_card');
    begin post: activate_role(s_deleg, 'r_doc_card');
    end post;
```

Listing 8. Example of a state-transition-scheme command specification.

```
S = { s1, s2 };
UA = { [u1, r1], [u1, r2], [u2, r1] };
user = { s1 : u1, s2 : u2 };
```

Listing 9. Examples of set, relation and mapping component value assigments used in initial-state and extension-tuple sections.

Complementary to the state-space and initial-state, in the extension-tuple section, all static model components are listed and initialized.

2.3 Policy and RTE Code Generation

With the DYNAMO specification language, we aim for uniform language support across the MSPE steps Model Engineering, Model Analysis, and Model Implementation. In order that a specification in DYNAMO is effectively usable, tool support in form of compilers is required, which automate (1.) plausibility and type checking to detect specification errors, (2.) generation of an intermediate language representation for existing model analysis tools, and (3.) source code generation for machine-executable model implementations.

As a first proof-of-concept, we implemented two compilers [2]. First, a DYNAMO-to-XML compiler is able to generate an intermediate XML-based model representation which is compatible with our dynamic model analysis tool [44]. Second, a DYNAMO-to-C++ compiler enables an automated generation of algorithmic model representations in C++ and all functionality necessary for its runtime based on a layered approach.

In the next step, we aim to generate memory-safe policy and policy RTE implementations from DYNAMO specifications. A modern programming language to balance the goals of memory safety and runtime performance is Rust which is why Rust is an optimal target language for our purpose. Rust has a static type system that is safe and expressive and provides strong guarantees about isolation, concurrency, and memory safety explicitly guaranteeing the absence of data races, buffer overflows, stack overflows, and accesses to uninitialized or deallocated memory [31].

Our approach for generating Rust code is as follows: (1.) The mathematical primitive data types are implemented based on Rust's standard collection library (std::collection) which provides, for example, efficient set and map implementations. (2.) A DYNAMO model specification defines the functionality of the policy RTE and a DYNAMO model-instance specification the functionality of the policy. We maintain this logical separation in the corresponding implementations. Consequently, the data structures and functions of the RTE are included in the policy implementation. However, inheritance relationships between models are resolved instead and consequently not explicitly represented in the source code.

3 Application-level Security Policy Enforcement

This section introduces the APPSPEAR security architecture [39,40], which provides a functional framework for enforcing application software security policies. We first discuss fundamental security architecture design principles as a foundation (Sect. 3.1). Subsequently, we present the APPSPEAR architecture comprising the components, their tasks, and their interrelationships (Sect. 3.2). Balancing rigor of policy enforcement (*effectiveness*) and isolation/communication costs (*efficiency*), we discuss implementation alternatives for APPSPEAR as well as the consequences of using different isolation mechanisms (Sect. 3.3). Finally, we present an extensive evaluation of the APPSPEAR framework regarding the practical runtime costs imposed by various C++ and Rust implementation alternatives using isolation mechanisms on different abstraction levels (Sect. 3.4).

3.1 Design Principles

Security policies are part of a system's TCB. We consider an application TCB from a functional point of view as the set of all functions that are necessary and sufficient for implementing an application's security properties. The part of a software architecture that implements the TCB forms the *security architecture*. The reference monitor principles [3] provide fundamental guidelines for the design and implementation of security architectures. These principles include three rules requiring a security architecture core, a *reference monitor*, that is (1.) involved in any security-relevant interaction (RM 1, *total mediation*), (2.) protected from unauthorized manipulation (RM 2, *tamperproofness*), and (3.) as small and simple as possible in terms of functional complexity and amount of code (RM 3, *verifiability*).

According to RM 1, it must be guaranteed that any security-relevant actions on objects are inevitably controlled by the policy. In OSs, this is typically achieved by calling the policy within the kernel services, such as process management, filesystem, or I/O subsystem, before the actual execution of an action on an OS object, such as *fork* on a process, *read* of a file, or *send* on a socket [47]. At the application level, RM 1 can be achieved by separating any functionality relevant for policy enforcement and application object management, on the one hand, from functions responsible for the application logic, on the other hand. Hence, any object and any security-relevant function for accessing such an object belong to the TCB. When an application object is accessed through the application logic, an immediate entry into the TCB takes place. Accordingly, by calling the policy before any security-relevant object access, the policy cannot be bypassed.

The precise identification of the TCB also enables the protection of its application security policy from unauthorized manipulation (cf. RM 2). The functional separation can be implemented with isolation mechanisms [46], which, depending on the assumed adversary's capabilities and the required strength of tamperproofness, range

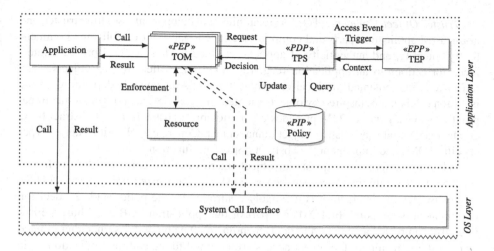

Fig. 1. AppSPEAR's functional architecture [39,40].

from language-based isolation (e. g. policy execution in a class instance separated by type-safety-checking compilers) to OS-based isolation (e. g. policy execution in a separate virtual address space) and virtualization techniques (e. g. policy execution in a virtual machine), as well as hardware-based isolation (e. g. policy execution in a trusted execution environment) to total physical separation (e. g. policy execution on a dedicated server).

With regard to RM 3, it generally holds that the smaller the size and complexity of a TCB are, the better a TCB is analyzable regarding correctness properties. A precise functional perimeter reduces TCB size and complexity because the functions solely associated with the application logic are not part of the TCB. To facilitate the verifiability of specific parts of the TCB, in particular security policies, w. r. t. model properties such as dynamic state reachability in dynamic AC models [41,42,48,53], an additional separation of policy-specific from policy-independent TCB functions can be anchored within the architecture.

3.2   Architecture Design

AppSPEAR satisfies two fundamental architectural requirements: (1.) the reference monitor properties and (2.) policy flexibility through policy interchangeability.

While RM 2 leads to a clear separation between application-related and security-related functionality, policy flexibility requires the separation of authorization logic (*policy decision point*, PDP) and enforcement mechanisms (*policy enforcement points*, PEPs).[3] Furthermore, taking into account the logical and physical system context typically involved in ABAC policy decisions results in a further structuring of the PDP. The functional architecture of AppSPEAR is illustrated in Fig. 1.[4]

---

[3] In particular, RM 1 and RM 3 are ensured by a suitable implementation.

[4] Since we focus on policy enforcement, we omit a *policy administration point* (PAP).

Trusted Object Managers (TOMs) are architecture components isolating trusted and non-trusted application parts and comprise the functionality for establishing confidentiality, integrity, and authenticity of application objects. Thus, a TOM provides interfaces for actions to an application (e. g. for modifying patient record objects). The interface is implemented via local or remote functions or methods depending on the isolation mechanism. Inspired by object-oriented software design and from a functional point of view, a generic TOM provides a generic object abstraction and abstract basic create, read, update and destroy object management. Concrete applications derive type-specific TOMs and implement the abstract object and functions.

When an application requests an object interaction, the corresponding policy is involved through the interface between a TOM and the *trusted policy server* (TPS). This way, (1.) any interaction is inevitably controlled by the policy and (2.) decision enforcement is tamperproof.TOMs are part of the application TCB and, thus, are isolated from untrusted application logic. Depending on the policy decision, either granted or denied, the results of the object access are returned to the calling application logic function.

The TPS represents APPSPEAR's PDP. Its main task is to provide the policy RTE which comprises data structures that represent any policy abstractions and components. To promote a small TCB perimeter, the TPS is always tailored to an application-specific model – it provides just enough functionality for its respective application while maintaining the interfaces for TOM-to-TPS and TPS-to-TOM communication.

In order to deal with application and system failures, crashes, or reboots, the TPS also comprises functions for the persistent and secure storage of the policy's state. Depending on the required guarantees, different strategies (e. g. logging diffs, complete state backups, etc.) are applied at different points in time (e. g. fixed times, after each state change, etc.).

The *trusted event processor* (TEP) is an add-on to provide information about the physical and logical system context. The TEP can be implemented based on asynchronous triggers, which originate from local hardware and software components, e. g. GPS, clock, or temperature sensors. Any access decision of the TPS may also trigger an event needed for logging and auditing.

3.3   Architecture Implementation

APPSPEAR's design enables the separation of its architecture components and their implementation by means of isolation mechanisms in many ways. In the following, we discuss a reasonable selection of alternatives and their individual characteristics regarding application TCB size. Each variant has, on the one hand, a certain degree of possible rigor in terms of TCB isolation (*effectiveness*) and, on the other hand, certain costs in terms of required resources and communication effort for crossing isolation boundaries (*efficiency*). To implement these instantiation alternatives, we also consider a selection of isolation mechanisms.

Implementation Alternatives. Figure 2 shows reasonable variants illustrating the boundaries at which the architecture components may be isolated from one another. Since the TEP realizes parts of the implementation of context-based security policies such as risk analysis and estimation, TPS and TEP are explicitly not isolated from each other.

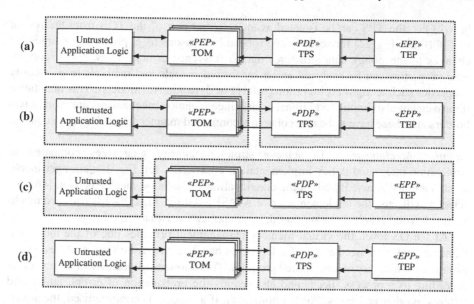

Fig. 2. APPSPEAR instantiations with different separation/isolation of the architecture components [40].

If a large application TCB comprising the potentially untrusted application logic and all APPSPEAR components can be accepted (see Fig. 2a), then the implementation is both in terms of strictness and costs at the level of application-integrated security policies. From a qualitative point of view, APPSPEAR enables a structured software engineering of a policy-controlled application.

Beyond this simple low-cost but low-quality implementation, APPSPEAR supports several alternatives with higher effectiveness. Taking advantage of the functional encapsulation of the TPS and the TEP, the security policy and its RTE can be implemented isolated from the rest of the application (see Fig. 2b). This paves the way for a tamper-proof and analyzable policy implementation. In quantitative terms, compared with the previous alternative, the application TCB comprises still the same set of functions, but here, the policy integrity is protected by more effective isolation.

Higher effectiveness can be achieved by moving the isolation boundary between the TOMs and the TPS/TEP in between the untrusted application logic and the TOMs (see Fig. 2c). This results in a smaller application TCB perimeter because only security-relevant functions are part of the TCB. From a conceptual perspective, the costs are comparable to the second variant (see Fig. 2b) due to a single isolation border and an equally frequent crossing of the TCB boundary. Nevertheless, the software engineering effort that is required for existing software architectures to create the technical prerequisites such as a well-defined interface between untrusted application logic and TOMs, is also relevant when considering the isolation of TOMs. Since many applications rely on a database storing object data, there is often already a functionally separated object management as intended by TOMs, which puts the costs into perspective.

The example of an application utilizing a database shows that due to the size and complexity, typical application TCBs cannot always be proven entirely to be correctly implemented. Analogous to the principle of separate server processes in microkernel-based OSs, the TPS can be isolated as an essential part of the TCB from the rest of the TCB (see Fig. 2d) for security and robustness reasons (e. g. preventing unintended changes to the policy data structures due to reference errors). Thus, policy correctness properties can be analyzed easier by formal models and methods (e. g. security properties such as right proliferation (safety) in dynamic AC models). This qualitative improvement also implies additional costs, since isolation mechanisms are used at two borders and these have to be overcome in a controlled manner for each policy request.

Isolation Mechanisms.   To achieve stronger security guarantees compared to application-integrated policy implementation approaches (cf. Fig. 2a), stronger mechanisms are necessary. Based on the classification of isolation mechanisms in [46], we select and discuss the implementation of APPSPEAR (cf. Figs. 2b–2d) with two mechanisms beyond purely software-based, intra-application isolation.

At the OS level, the virtual memory management provides one of the most fundamental isolation mechanisms. Each process has its own private virtual address space isolating the memory of an executed program. This allows to allocate memory resources according to a process' needs and also avoids the propagation of errors, faults, and failures to other processes. Furthermore, even if a process is compromised, the adversary cannot breach the security of other processes without extensive effort. By isolating the APPSPEAR components from the potentially untrusted application logic and each other using virtual address spaces via processes as in Figs. 2b–2d, vulnerabilities of the untrusted application part can no longer affect the trusted parts. To enable communication across process boundaries, communication mechanisms controlled by the OS are necessary (e. g. local domain sockets, messages queues, or pipes).

Beyond that, Intel SGX enables applications to protect private code and data from privileged system software such as the OS kernel, hypervisor, and BIOS as well as other applications. SGX uses protected TEEs called enclaves, which are protected areas within an application process' address space. To meet integrity and confidentiality requirements, protected application code is loaded into an enclave after hardware-based attestation and enclave data is automatically encrypted when leaving the CPU package into memory. This design significantly reduces the TCB to only code executed inside the enclave (as well as the CPU, which must always be trusted).

Since enclave memory cannot be read directly from outside an enclave, data passed between trusted and untrusted application parts has to be copied explicitly from and to an enclave. The SGX SDK provides mechanisms to create bridge functions, *ecalls*, which dispatch enclave entry calls to corresponding functions inside the enclave defining an enclave's interface. Functions that reside in the untrusted application part are called *ocalls* and invoked inside the enclave to request services outside the enclave (e. g. system calls).

3.4 Evaluation

The evaluation addresses the practical feasibility of our trusted application security policy enforcement approach. More specifically, we aim at evaluating (1.) the runtime performance overhead of different APPSPEAR implementation alternatives and

(2.) the runtime performance overhead of memory-safety-enhancing Rust implementations compared to conventional C++ implementations. For the boundaries between application logic and TOMs as well as TOMs and TPS (including TEP), we use pairwise combinations of the following isolation mechanisms: (a.) language/compiler-based isolation serving as a baseline, (b.) process-based isolation as a basic OS-level mechanism, and (c.) SGX/enclave-based isolation as a widely available trusted execution mechanism. This results in the following 7 implementation variants: (1.) LPC/LPC, (2.) LPC/IPC, (3.) LPC/SGX, (4.) IPC/LPC, (5.) IPC/IPC, (6.) IPC/SGX, and (7.) SGX/LPC. Subsequently, we first describe the evaluation methodology and then discuss the evaluation results.

Evaluation Methodology. We study two test cases from which we derive six benchmarks. First, a synthetic application with an always-allow AC policy highlights the baseline runtime for isolation and communication in each APPSPEAR implementation variant (baseline microbenchmark). The application only comprises a synthetic operation passing an identifier.

Second, a prototypical reimplementation of OpenMRS with an RBAC policy serves as a real-world use case [42]. In particular, the layered software architecture and the usage of a database are representative for a multitude of applications and yield an impression of potential costs also relevant for other scenarios. The database comprises an anonymized data set of 5,000 patients and 500,000 observations [33]. We run two types of benchmarks: four microbenchmarks show efforts for create, read, update, and destroy operations, whereas a macrobenchmark based on a real-world workload extracted from logs [11] puts the CRUD operations into a bigger context. The workload assumes the following occurrences of patient service operations: 25% of create patient, 38% of read patient diagnosis, 12% of update patient diagnosis, and 25% of delete patient. For comparison, the measured runtimes are divided by 100 (number of executed operations).

Enclave-based isolation with Intel SGX typically involves high communication costs. Thus, we consider two techniques for decreasing runtime overhead: (1.) caching of policy decisions in TPS proxies located in the TOMs and (2.) asynchronous enclave calls [60] which are provided by the SGX SDK as *switchless calls* because they do not involve costly enclave switches.

The runtimes are measured in CPU clock cycles using the RDTSCP instruction. To avoid the typical behavior of "cold" CPU caches, each measurement is preceded by a warm-up phase consisting of 1,000,000 iterations. To filter outliers, we additionally perform 1,000,000 iterations for each measurement and calculate medians. All measurements were performed on desktop hardware with an Intel Core i7-7700K CPU at 4.2 GHz and 32 GiB DDR4 RAM at 2,400 MHz. The machine runs Ubuntu 18.04.5 LTS with Linux kernel version 5.4.0 including mitigations for critical Meltdown, Spectre, L1TF/Foreshadow, and MDS class vulnerabilities [8,27,28,38,45,54] which have shown a runtime of over 2.2 times more than without patches [59]. We use the SGX driver, SDK and platform software in version 2.9.1 [23]. For the Rust implementations, we use the Apache Teaclave SGX SDK (also known as Rust SGX SDK) [14,15,57], which builds on top of the official SGX SDK. We compile using Rust nightly-2020-04-07, GCC 10.1, SGX hardware mode, and SGX SDK Prerelease configuration known to have production enclave performance [24]. The Enclave Page Cache (EPC) size is set to the maximum of 128 MiB of which ca. 93 MiB are effectively usable. We disable dynamic CPU frequency scaling, Turbo Boost, and Hyper-Threading to avoid erratic runtime behavior and reduce potential outliers by adjusting scheduling priorities and interrupt affinities.

Results. By targeting both evaluation goals, Figs. 3 and 4 show the measurement results of the 7 considered APPSPEAR implementations, each in a separate subfigure: LPC/LPC, LPC/IPC, LPC/SGX, IPC/LPC, IPC/IPC, IPC/SGX, and SGX/LPC. Each subfigure shows the absolute runtimes (unit 10^3 clock cycles on the left y-axis, unit microseconds calculated for the Intel i7 CPU with 4.2 GHz on the right y-axis) of the six micro- and macrobenchmarks, which were measured for (a.) unoptimized, (b.) cache-optimized, (c.) switchless-call-optimized ("swl"), and (d.) cache- and switchless-call-optimized implementations in C++ and Rust.

As an intra-application implementation using only language/compiler-based isolation, the LPC/LPC variant forms the baseline in terms of runtime costs for the executed benchmarks (see Fig. 3a). The runtimes of the C++ variants for the R(ead) microbenchmark are more than half as low as the runtimes for the C(reate), U(pdate), and D(elete) microbenchmarks (ca. 10,5k cycles vs. 21,5k, 22,5k, and 25,3k cycles). The benchmark runtimes for the Rust implementations are consistently higher than those of the C++ implementations. In detail, the runtimes for the R benchmark (ca. 32,8k cycles) are lower than for the U and D microbenchmarks (ca. 50k and 36,5k cycles) but also slightly higher than for the C microbenchmark (ca. 30k cycles). Detailed measurements on the composition of the runtimes have shown that the cause of this phenomenon is the database access of the SQLite wrapper `rust-sqlite`. The mixed macrobenchmark proportionally contains read operations such that their normalized runtimes are slightly lower than those of the CUD microbenchmarks for both C++ (ca. 18,7k cycles) and Rust implementations (ca. 18k cycles).

The optimizations introduced by caching, switchless calls, or both do not yield significant advantages for the LPC/LPC variant. In some cases, there is even a small additional overhead since the costs for the communication across language isolation boundaries are not high and therefore only offer a small optimization potential. Furthermore, a comparison of the C++ and Rust implementations shows that the Rust implementations consistently have higher runtime costs (ca. 20k more cycles on average); exceptions are all implementation alternatives in the macrobenchmark (advantage ranges from ca. 300 to 2,5k cycles).

By using process-based isolation between the TOMs and TPS/TEP, the LPC/IPC variant introduces higher benchmark runtimes compared to the previous LPC/LPC variant (see Fig. 3b): The unoptimized C++ implementations require more than twice the runtime for all benchmarks, the same Rust implementations require at least 1.5 times more runtime. Using enclave-based isolation at the same boundary (LPC/SGX variant, see Fig. 3c) yields runtimes at almost the same level. The optimization by in-proxy caching results in significantly lower runtimes for both LPC/IPC and LPC/SGX variants (in C++ and Rust implementations) at the level of the intra-application implementation (LPC/LPC variant). While the usage of switchless calls trivially does not affect the LPC/IPC implementations, the LPC/SGX implementations benefit, although caching

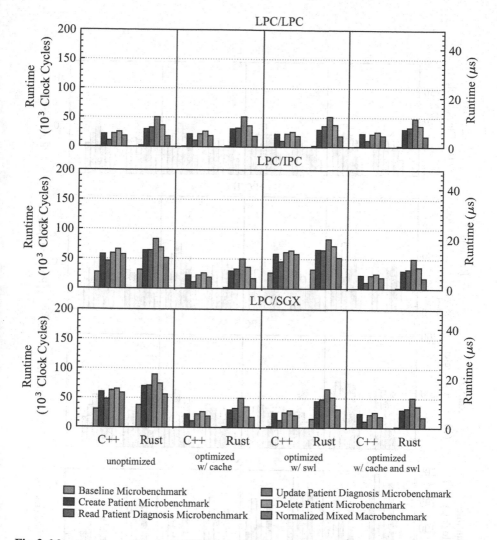

Fig. 3. Measurement results for LPC/LPC, LPC/IPC, and LPC/SGX APPSPEAR implementations.

has a higher effectiveness. Combining caching with switchless calls also reduces runtimes for cache misses.

The IPC/LPC variant is at a similar runtime level as the unoptimized LPC/IPC and LPC/SGX implementations (see Fig. 4a). Taking the optimizations into account, caching and switchless calls show no effect so that the runtimes are on par with those of the unoptimized implementations. Due to the more strict isolation and the higher communication effort occurring twice in the IPC/IPC and IPC/SGX variants (see Figs. 4b and 4c), the costs are also about twice as high compared to the single process- and SGX-isolated variants. For these implementation variants, a cache hit effectively results in a

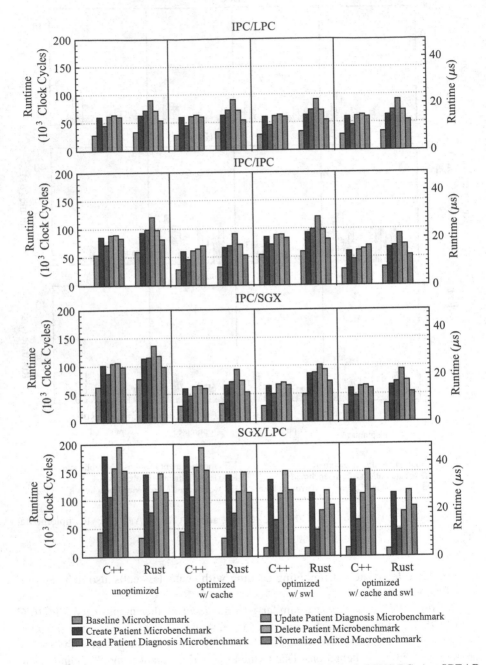

Fig. 4. Measurement results for IPC/LPC, IPC/IPC, IPC/SGX, and SGX/LPC AppSPEAR implementations.

significant reduction of the runtime overhead by eliminating IPC- or enclave-boundary-crossing. Thus, for both IPC/SGX and IPC/IPC variants the runtime is reduced to the cost level of IPC/LPC.

For the SGX/LPC variant (see Fig. 4d), it is noticeable that the Rust implementations even perform consistently better than the corresponding C++ implementations. The reason is that the C++ implementations have a higher copy overhead: Data passed at enclave entry is only available via pointer access, so copying is required. In Rust, slices can be used, which provide secure access to a memory area without requiring copying. C++20 introduced the data type $std::span$, which has comparable capabilities but cannot be used in enclaves because of the restriction to C++11. Moreover, this variant highlights that the joint isolation of TOMs and TPS/TEP and the resulting in-enclave code execution can lead to a considerable additional overhead beyond pure isolation/communication costs: The high runtime effort (for C++ about twice as high) results from the execution of SQLite within the isolated enclave, since temporary enclave exits (ocalls) may occur several times.

4 Architectural Integration

For the architectural integration of security policy implementations into applications, this section addresses two sequential steps: (1.) the integration of a security policy enforcement architecture implementation into applications and (2.) the integration of the policy implementation and its RTE into the policy enforcement environment. For integrating APPSPEAR implementations into applications, in Sect. 4.1 we present programming support provided by the APPSPEAR developer framework. Subsequently, in Sect. 4.2 we explain the integration of policy implementation based on the DABAC modeling scheme into APPSPEAR implementations. Finally, in Sect. 4.3, we demonstrate the effort required for architectural integration in the context of a case study of a medical information management application.

4.1 Developer Framework

Balancing effectiveness (i.e. the strength of TCB isolation) and efficiency (i.e. the overhead of communication across isolation boundaries), APPSPEAR enables several implementation alternatives that differently isolate application and APPSPEAR components as well as the components themselves from each other (see also detailed discussion in Sect. 3.3). These variants are supported by developer frameworks for Rust and C++ [39,40] which both feature

1. transparent and configurable isolation according to the implementation variants and possible isolation mechanisms, such as language/compiler-based isolation, OS/process-based isolation, and enclave-based isolation via Intel SGX,[5]
2. transparent RPC/RMI-alike communication via proxy objects,
3. reduction of the communication effort via in-proxy caching.

---

[5] Note that the framework implementation is conceptually not limited to this selection and can be easily extended.

The key idea for implementing these features lies in an RPC/RMI-alike communication model: Any communication between the components of a policy-controlled application is handled via pairs of proxy objects, similar to stubs known from RPC/RMI implementations. Those proxies act as intermediaries representing the callee on the caller side and the caller on the callee side. Consequently, any communication handled by these proxies is performed *transparently* so that isolation-mechanism-specific properties and their handling is not required to be considered by developers, such as the serialization of application-specific data structures and, accordingly, their deserialization. In addition, techniques for securing communication, such as encryption, hashing, or integrity certificates, and reducing communication costs, such as caching of access requests and corresponding decisions, are transparently integrated into the proxies.

To reduce communication effort and multiple processing of the same inputs, caching mechanisms are used. In principle, caching is possible for (1.) application-logic-to-TOM communication and (2.) TOM-to-TPS communication.[6] Since the application logic is assumed to be untrusted, caching of TOM calls and results on the application logic side counteracts our goals for rigorous and trustworthy application policy enforcement. Nevertheless, as argued in Sect. 3.3, many applications use databases to store application objects such that DBMS caches can achieve an overhead reduction when retrieving application object data.

Caching TPS requests and decisions on the TOM side avoids multiple identical requests (if the policy state has not changed compared to the initial request) and reduces the runtime overhead to the level of local function/method calls – especially for implementation variants with stricter TPS/TEP isolation (see Figs. 2b and 2d). To also keep access times to cache entries as low as possible, the cache is implemented using a container based on a hash table. In the case of a stateful policy, if the execution of an operation results in the modification of the policy state [41,42], it may be necessary to invalidate corresponding cache entries.

For the same reasons as for the RTE and policy implementations, we choose Rust for the APPSPEAR implementation. In the Rust version of the APPSPEAR developer framework, each component is implemented in a separate crate: appspear_tom, appspear_tps, and appspear_tep each contain the corresponding component's functionality and proxy object pairs (comparable to sockets) for isolation-transparent communication with the application or APPSPEAR components. Moreover, two crates provide additional functionality: appspear is a dependency of the application and contains proxy objects for the communication with TOMs and initialization functionality. appspear_types contains constants and definitions of the message structs for the communication between application logic and TOM as well as between TOM and TPS and is therefore used by all crates as a dependency.

The choice of isolation mechanisms to be used can be conveniently made via Cargo features which are a mechanism to express conditional compilation and optional dependencies provided by Rust's package and dependency manager Cargo.

---

[6] The communication between the TPS and the TEP is asynchronous based on callbacks or periodic updates (see Sect. 3.2). Since received context values are temporarily stored anyway, a separate cache is not useful here.

```
1  pub trait TTps {
2      fn cmd(&self, req: &CmdReq) -> CmdRes;
3      ...
4  }
5  pub struct Tps {
6      model: DMODEL,
7  }
8  impl TTps for Tps {
9      fn cmd(&self, req: &CmdReq) -> CmdRes { ... }
10     ...
11 }
```

Listing 10. Generic TPS implementation (details omitted).

```
1  pub struct MyTps(Tps) {}
2  impl TTps for MyTps {
3      fn cmd(&self, req: &CmdReq) -> CmdRes { ... }
4      ...
5  }
```

Listing 11. Application-specifc TPS implementation (details omitted).

4.2 Security Architecture and Policy Integration

The developer framework provides patterns that are reusable and tailorable for the integration of application policies into APPSPEAR-backed applications. In particular, the integration is achieved in three sequential steps: (1.) the implementation of application-specific TPS and TEP based on the default TPS and TEP implementations of the appspear_tps and appspear_tep crates[7], (2.) the implementation of an application-specific TOM based on the default TOM implementation of the appspear_tom crate, and (3.) the definition of message types for application-specific request/result communication patterns derived from the appspear_types crate.

First, the application-specifc TPS implementation is created in a new crate outside the appspear_tps crate (mytps in our example). This requires instantiating the default TPS implementation (Tps) and initializing it with the intended policy implementation. Based on known and defined CmdReq and CmdRes types (see also third step), everything else is plug-and-play. The cmd method executes commands[8] and is used directly by the corresponding communication proxy (see below and Listing 12).

As an alternative to the generic TPS implementation (Tps), a custom type can be created. The foreign trait TTps specifies the behavior of a TPS, in particular the execution of commands (see Listing 10). This trait cannot be implemented straight-forward for the foreign standard type Tps due to Rust preventing implementations of foreign traits on foreign types (*orphan rule*). A solution for this problem is the application of the *newtype*

---

[7] Since the TEP is typically only isolated in a lightweight manner (cf. [40]), the explicit consideration of the TEP will not be discussed further in this paper.

[8] "Command" is an equivalent term to "STS operation" and is used to not have overload with other "operations" such as on TOM-controlled objects.

```
1  pub struct Proxy<T> where T: TTps {
2      tps: T,
3  }
4  impl<T> Proxy<T> where T: TTps {
5      pub fn new(tps: T) -> Proxy<T> { Proxy { tps } }
6      pub fn cmd(&self, req_srlzd: &[u8]) -> Vec<u8> { ... }
7      ...
8  }
```

Listing 12. TPS communication proxy implementation (details omitted).

pattern [26, pp. 437–438]: The wrapper MyTps around the Tps value provides a different type that can implement the trait TTps (Listing 11). The reuse of standard Tps methods is then possible via simple forwarding. Alternatively, application-specific implementations are provided. More precisely, the actual policy is called within cmd.

From an implementation point of view, the TPS is part of the TPS-side communication proxy (for TOM-to-TPS communication and vice versa) using a field in the struct Proxy<T> so that it can pass calls to/from commands directly. For each type of isolation mechanism, a separate communication proxy is implemented. The method cmd is thus specific for a particular isolation mechanism. Listing reflst:archint:proxy abstracts from the latter property but shows that the struct Proxy<T> uses a generic type parameter with trait bounds to be able to use any TPS implementation that implements the TTps trait.

Essentially the implementation of an application-specific TOM is analogous to that of the TPS in the first step since the same pattern is present: The application-specific TOM implementation (e. g. MyTom) is built based on the TTom trait and then integrated by the TOM-side proxy required for the communication with the application. In addition, the definition of the Call and Result enums for application-logic-to-TOM communication (and vice versa) and the CmdReq and CmdRes enums for TOM-to-TPS communication (and vice versa) is done in a separate crate (e. g. mytypes) with dependency on the appspear_types crate.

In summary, although the architectural integration requires manual work, this effort is moderate due to the prepared structure of the APPSPEAR developer framework. Additionally, the partial automation of the generation of model-specific RTEs based on the DYNAMO specification language enables a complementary compiler-generated code skeleton.

4.3   Case Study: Medical Information Management Application

This section describes a case study in which we apply APPSPEAR to an existing database-backed application. The studied subject is OpenMRS, an electronic medical record (EMR) and medical information management system [34]. OpenMRS is an optimal representative for a policy-controlled application since the AC policy is part of its architecture and directly visible in the source code.

OpenMRS Software and Security Architecture. OpenMRS aims at being adaptable to resource-constrained environments such as healthcare facilities of low-income countries [50,51,61]. This motivation is reflected in the web application architecture consisting of three logical layers: (1.) the *UI layer*, providing the user interface which comprises input and query forms, (2.) the *service layer*, implementing the basic functionality, data model interaction, and a corresponding API, and (3.) the *database layer*, realizing the data model.

A tightly integrated role-based AC (RBAC) policy is responsible for controlling access to application objects such as EMRs or medication plans. The policy semantics are similar to the RBAC model family [17]: a logged-in user's accesses to objects are controlled according to her assigned and activated roles (e. g. physician or nurse), to which certain permissions for actions are assigned (e. g. *read/modify EMR* or *create/delete patient*).

The RBAC policy and its enforcement are implemented through an AOP mechanism (`AuthorizationAdvice`) that wraps each service layer method call with a policy call, and custom Java annotations ("`@Authorized`") which initiate checking the privileges of the currently authenticated user. Since required permissions are directly attached to each service layer method, the policy is hard-coded and distributed over 635 points (OpenMRS core, version 2.3.1). That renders the policy as well as its underlying model static, contradicting the goal of simple adaptability and flexible configurability. Beyond that, policy decision and enforcement functionality are isolated from application logic only through language-based mechanisms, missing the opportunity for stronger isolation.

Policy Enforcement Architecture Integration. While OpenMRS is implemented in Java, the APPSPEAR developer framework is implemented in Rust. Therefore, we decided to prototype OpenMRS in Rust.

Despite the software architecture being basically the same, a few functional differences exist. On the UI layer, we have only implemented a minimal command line interface for requesting service layer functionality. On the service layer, we have implemented a selection of core services for data model interaction: the (system) user service (*login, activate/deactivate role, logout*), the person service (*create/delete person object, get/set address*), and the patient (EMR) service (*create/delete patient object, get/set patient diagnosis*). On the database layer, SQLite [21] is used as relational DBMS because of its ability to fully store a database in-memory enabling its trusted execution within an SGX enclave. Based on the `rust-sqlite` crate [12], we modified SQLite version 3.32.3 for in-enclave execution by wrapping system calls through trampoline functions that temporarily exit an enclave (*ocalls*) or, where possible, by an SGX-compatible variant provided by the SDK.

Each service forms a TOM and manages its own objects (users, patients, EMRs, etc.) stored in the database and provides corresponding operations on them (generally such as *create/destroy object* and *read/modify object attribute*). When using the communication proxies provided by the developer framework, operations on TOM-managed objects called within the UI layer are transparently forwarded to the proxy counterpart of the respective TOM; depending on the isolation mechanism used, either via function/method calls, local domain socket send/receive (IPC) or SGX enclave calls. An analogous pattern applied for the TOM-to-TPS communication initiates requests to the RBAC policy regarding access permission or denial for each TOM operation to be executed. The TPS realizes the security policy using either a database or, leading to a smaller TCB, model-tailored data structures.

5 Related Work

Related work can be classified into two categories: (1.) focused on application policy specification and implementation, or (2.) on security architectures for application security policy enforcement.

Application Security Policy Specification and Implementation. In recent years several specification languages have emerged that describe security policies formalized as mathematical models in a machine-readable representation. Often these representations are tailored to a specific purpose and task within the MSPE process: as input for semi-automated model checkers [13,49] (model analysis), for translation into a functional software specification [16,32], or for direct translation into a programming language [10,36] (model implementation). These translations are required to preserve relevant knowledge from the previous process step. However, different languages often do not integrate well with each other and, therefore, still require manual work, which in turn is error-prone.

We instead take a holistic approach: our interoperating DSL approach (DYNA-MO) provides syntax and semantics tailored to streamline the above translations and is thus suitable for model engineering, model analysis (through capturing dynamic model behavior [41,42]), and model implementation (through automated source code generation [2]). This way, and by enabling automation of these tasks, large parts of the MSPE process can be covered (except for architectural/model integration).

Application-Level Security Policy Enforcement. For the specification and implementation of application security policies, the above-mentioned approaches require application developers to be responsible for implementing the policy RTE and the corresponding security architecture. However, this often results in application TCBs being large and heterogeneous, which makes protection against unauthorized manipulation hard to achieve.

A step towards more precisely identifiable application TCB perimeters can be observed in SELinux [29]: *User-space Object Managers* (USOMs) provide auxiliary functionality for managing application objects. While USOMs and their associated caching components (Access Vector Caches, AVCs) are located at the application level, the OS policy RTE (SELinux Security Server) is still embedded in the kernel. Since an application's policy rules are loaded into the SELinux Security Server and thus complement the system-wide security policy, it requires the adoption of OS-specific policy semantics [9,56]. Although collecting and locating all policy rules in the OS's policy RTE is effective in terms of policy protection and analyzability, this approach increases an application's TCB by the OS policy and its runtime functionality, giving up any policy individuality.

An approach designed to eliminate these drawbacks is the *SELinux Policy Server Architecture* [30,52]. Aiming at a clear separation of OS and application security policies, the User-space Security Server (USSS) provides a separate policy RTE at the application level. Although the USSS has a similar objective to APPSPEAR TPSs, a single instance of the USSS is intended for all applications as opposed to an individual instance of the APPSPEAR TPS for each application. That leads to considerably larger application TCBs and, in addition, challenges known from multi- and meta-policy systems [7]. Moreover, from an implementation perspective, a weaker attacker model is assumed than in APPSPEAR, as application policies are isolated from potentially untrusted application logic only based on OS mechanisms.

6 Conclusion

In this paper, we aim to foster tool-supported MSPE workflows in terms of the memory-safe implementation and the trusted enforcement of application security policies. The foundation of our approach lies in APPSPEAR – an application-level security policy enforcement architecture framework. By isolating APPSPEAR components from untrusted application logic and by applying isolation between APPSPEAR components using mechanisms on different hardware/software levels, various implementation variants enable a fine-grained balancing of rigor regarding the reference monitor principles as well as isolation/communication costs, and thus, adjustment to application-specific requirements. Moreover, we provide developer support for (1.) the specification and memory-safe implementation of application security policies based on the DYNAMO policy specification language and a Rust code generation approach, and (2.) the convenient APPSPEAR implementation and application policy integration based on a software framework for the Rust programming language.

References

1. Alam, M., Zhang, X., Khan, K., Ali, G.: xDAuth: a scalable and lightweight framework for cross domain access control and delegation. In: SACMAT '11, pp. 31–40. ACM (2011)
2. Amthor, P., Schlegel, M.: Towards language support for model-based security policy engineering. In: SECRYPT '20, pp. 513–521. SCITEPRESS (2020)
3. Anderson, J.P.: Computer security technology planning study. Technical report ESD-TR-73-51, Vol. II, U.S. Air Force Electronic Systems Division (1972)
4. Basin, D., Clavel, M., Egea, M.: A decade of model-driven security. In: SACMAT '11, pp. 1–10. ACM (2011)
5. Bezawada, B., Haefner, K., Ray, I.: Securing home IoT environments with attribute-based access control. In: ABAC '18, pp. 43–53. ACM (2018)
6. Bhatti, R., Ghafoor, A., Bertino, E., Joshi, J.B.D.: X-GTRBAC: an XML-based policy specification framework and architecture for enterprise-wide access control. ACM TISSEC 8(2), 187–227 (2005)
7. Bonatti, P.A., De Capitani di Vimercati, S., Pierangela, S.: An algebra for composing access control policies. ACM TISSEC 5(1), 1–35 (2002)
8. Canella, C., et al.: Fallout: leaking data on meltdown-resistant CPUs. In: CCS '19, pp. 769–784. ACM (2019)
9. Carter, J.: Using GConf as an example of how to create an userspace object manager. In: SEinux Symposium '07 (2007)
10. Casbin Organization: Casbin (2022). https://casbin.org

11. Chen, J., Shang, W., Hassan, A.E., Wang, Y., Lin, J.: An experience report of generating load tests using log-recovered workloads at varying granularities of user behaviour. In: ASE '19, pp. 669–681. IEEE (2019)
12. Connolly, D.: Rust-SQLite3: rustic bindings for SQLite3 (2022). https://crates.io/crates/rust-sqlite
13. Crampton, J., Morisset, C.: PTaCL: a language for attribute-based access control in open systems. In: Degano, P., Guttman, J.D. (eds.) POST 2012. LNCS, vol. 7215, pp. 390–409. Springer, Heidelberg (2012). https://doi.org/10.1007/978-3-642-28641-4_21
14. Ding, Y., et al.: POSTER: Rust SGX SDK: towards memory safety in Intel SGX enclave. In: CCS' 17, pp. 2491–2493. ACM (2017)
15. Ding, Y., et al.: apache/incubator-teaclave-sgx-sdk: Apache Teaclave (incubating) SGX SDK helps developers to write Intel SGX applications in the Rust programming language, and also known as Rust SGX SDK (2022). https://github.com/apache/incubator-teaclave-sgx-sdk
16. Fadhel, A.B., Bianculli, D., Briand, L.C.: GemRBAC-DSL: a high-level specification language for role-based access control policies. In: SACMAT '16, pp. 179–190. ACM (2016)
17. Ferraiolo, D., Kuhn, D.R., Chandramouli, R.: Role-Based Access Control, 2nd edn. Artech House (2007)
18. Fong, P.W.L.: Relationship-based access control: protection model and policy language. In: CODASPY '11, pp. 191–202. ACM (2011)
19. Gupta, M., Patwa, F., Sandhu, R.: An attribute-based access control model for secure big data processing in hadoop ecosystem. In: ABAC '18, pp. 13–24. ACM (2018)
20. Harrison, M.A., Ruzzo, W.L., Ullman, J.D.: Protection in operating systems. Commun. ACM 19(8), 461–471 (1976)
21. Hipp, D.R., Kennedy, D., Mistachkin, J.: SQLite Version 3.32.3 (2020). https://www.sqlite.org/src/info/7ebdfa80be8e8e73
22. IBM: Db2 11.1 – Label-based Access Control Overview (2016). https://www.ibm.com/support/knowledgecenter/en/SSEPGG_11.1.0/com.ibm.db2.luw.admin.sec.doc/doc/c0021114.html
23. Intel Corporation: Intel®SGX SDK for Linux* OS – Developer Reference (2020). https://download.01.org/intel-sgx/sgx-linux/2.9.1/docs/Intel_SGX_Developer_Reference_Linux_2.9.1_Open_Source.pdf
24. Intel Corporation: Intel® Software Guard Extensions (Intel®SGX) Debug and Build Configurations (2020). https://www.intel.com/content/dam/develop/external/us/en/documents/intel-sgx-build-configuration-737361.pdf
25. Intel Corporation: Intel®Software Guard Extensions (2022). https://www.intel.com/content/www/us/en/architecture-and-technology/software-guard-extensions.html
26. Klabnik, S., Nichols, C.: The Rust Programming Language. No Starch Press (2018)
27. Kocher, P., et al.: Spectre attacks: exploiting speculative execution. In: S&P '19, pp. 1–19. IEEE (2019)
28. Lipp, M., et al.: Meltdown: reading kernel memory from user space. In: Secur. '18, pp. 973–990. USENIX (2018)
29. Loscocco, P.A., Smalley, S.D.: Integrating flexible support for security policies into the Linux operating system. In: ATC '01, pp. 29–42. USENIX (2001)
30. MacMillan, K., Brindle, J., Mayer, F., Caplan, D., Tang, J.: Design and implementation of the SELinux policy management server. In: SELinux Symposium '06 (2006)
31. Matsakis, N.D., Klock, F.S.: The Rust language. In: HILT '14, pp. 103–104. ACM (2014)
32. OASIS: eXtensible Access Control Markup Language (XACML) Version 3.0. OASIS Standard 499–2013, Organization for the Advancement of Structured Information Standards (2013)
33. OpenMRS Inc.: OpenMRS Demo Data (2021). https://wiki.openmrs.org/display/RES/Demo+Data

34. OpenMRS Inc.: OpenMRS (2022). https://openmrs.org
35. Oracle: Oracle Label Security Administrator's Guide, 18c (2018). https://docs.oracle.com/en/database/oracle/oracle-database/18/olsag/index.html
36. Oso Security, Inc.: Oso (2022). https://www.osohq.com
37. Rizvi, S.Z.R., Fong, P.W., Crampton, J., Sellwood, J.: Relationship-based access control for an open-source medical records system. In: SACMAT '15, pp. 113–124. ACM (2015)
38. van Schaik, S., et al.: RIDL: rogue in-flight data load. In: S&P '19, pp. 88–105. IEEE (2019)
39. Schlegel, M.: Poster: Shielding AppSPEAR - enhancing memory safety for trusted application-level security policy enforcement. In: SACMAT '21, pp. 99–101. ACM (2021)
40. Schlegel, M.: Trusted enforcement of application-specific security policies. In: SECRYPT '21, pp. 343–355. SCITEPRESS (2021)
41. Schlegel, M., Amthor, P.: Beyond administration: a modeling scheme supporting the dynamic analysis of role-based access control policies. In: SECRYPT '20, pp. 431–442. SCITEPRESS (2020)
42. Schlegel, M., Amthor, P.: The missing piece of the ABAC puzzle: a modeling scheme for dynamic analysis. In: SECRYPT '21, pp. 234–246. SCITEPRESS (2021)
43. Schlegel, M., Amthor, P.: Putting the pieces together: model-based engineering workflows for attribute-based access control policies. In: SECRYPT 2021 Revised Selected Papers. CCIS. Springer, Cham (2022, submitted)
44. Schlegel, M., Kühnhauser, W.E.: Exploiting hot spots in heuristic safety analysis of dynamic access control models. In: SECRYPT '20, pp. 522–532. SCITEPRESS (2020)
45. Schwarz, M., et al.: ZombieLoad: cross-privilege-boundary data sampling. In: CCS '19, pp. 753–768. ACM (2019)
46. Shu, R., et al.: A study of security isolation techniques. ACM Comput. Surv. 49(3), 50:1–50:37 (2016)
47. Smalley, S.D., Vance, C., Salamon, W.: Implementing SELinux as a Linux security module. NAI Labs Rep. 01-043, NAI Labs (2001)
48. Stoller, S.D., Yang, P., Gofman, M.I., Ramakrishnan, C.R.: Symbolic reachability analysis for parameterized role-based access control. Elsevier Comput. Secur. 30(2–3), 148–164 (2011)
49. Stoller, S.D., Yang, P., Ramakrishnan, C.R., Gofman, M.I.: Efficient policy analysis for administrative role based access control. In: CCS '07, pp. 445–455. ACM (2007)
50. Thompson, A., Castle, E., Lubeck, P., Makarfi, P.S.: Experience implementing OpenMRS to support maternal and reproductive health in Northern Nigeria. In: MedInfo '10, pp. 332–336. IOS Press (2010)
51. Tierney, W.M., et al.: Experience implementing electronic health records in three East African countries. In: MedInfo '10, pp. 371–375. IOS Press (2010)
52. Tresys Technology: SELinux Policy Server (2014). http://oss.tresys.com/archive/policy-server.php
53. Tripunitara, M.V., Li, N.: The foundational work of Harrison-Ruzzo-Ullman revisited. IEEE TDSC 10(1), 28–39 (2013)
54. Van Bulck, J., et al.: Foreshadow: extracting the keys to the Intel SGX kingdom with transient out-of-order execution. In: Secur. '18, pp. 991–1008. USENIX (2018)
55. De Capitani di Vimercati, S., Samarati, P., Jajodia, S.: Policies, models, and languages for access control. In: Bhalla, S. (ed.) DNIS 2005. LNCS, vol. 3433, pp. 225–237. Springer, Heidelberg (2005). https://doi.org/10.1007/978-3-540-31970-2_18
56. Walsh, E.F.: Application of the Flask architecture to the X window system server. In: SELinux Symposium '07 (2007)
57. Wang, H., et al.: Towards memory safe enclave programming with Rust-SGX. In: CCS '19, pp. 2333–2350. ACM (2019)

58. Watson, R.N.M.: A decade of os access-control extensibility. ACM Queue **11**(1), 20:20–20:41 (2013)
59. Weichbrodt, N., Aublin, P.L., Kapitza, R.: SGX-PERF: a performance analysis tool for Intel SGX enclaves. In: Middleware '18, pp. 201–213. ACM (2018)
60. Weisse, O., Bertacco, V., Austin, T.: Regaining lost cycles with HotCalls: a fast interface for SGX secure enclaves. In: ISCA '17, pp. 81–93. ACM (2017)
61. Wolfe, B.A., et al.: The OpenMRS system: collaborating toward an open source EMR for developing countries. In: AMIA Annual Symposium '06, p. 1146 (AMIA) (2006)

Selective Encryption for Owners' Control in Digital Data Markets

Sara Foresti[ID] and Giovanni Livraga[✉][ID]

Università degli Studi di Milano, Milan, Italy
{sara.foresti,giovanni.livraga}@unimi.it

Abstract. A recent solution for permitting data owners to make their data selectively available on digital market platforms combines the adoption of selective owner-side encryption and smart contracts deployed on blockchains. Selective encryption, coupled with key derivation techniques to reduce key management burden, guarantees that only subjects who are authorized for a resource can read its content. Smart contracts permit to regulate the interactions among the interested subjects, the possible economic incentives to be paid to the owners as expected in markets, and the information needed to decrypt resource (i.e., the updates to the structure used for managing key derivation) upon payment. In this paper, we investigate different approaches for managing and updating the key derivation structure to enable selective data sharing on digital data markets, while limiting access times to resources and the cost of operations on the blockchain.

Keywords: Digital data market · Selective encryption · Key derivation

1 Introduction

An ever-increasing deal of interest focuses nowadays towards the development and adoption of platforms where data can be easily shared and/or traded among interested subjects. Such platforms, typically called digital data markets, represent virtual places where data owners (acting as data producers) offer datasets, and data consumers can access (parts of) them. The creation of these platforms, enabling data sharing among different subjects, can have a positive impact on the creation of knowledge based on the analysis of heterogeneous data, with clear societal benefits.

One of the main concerns that can hinder the adoption of digital data markets is the (perceived) lack of control owners can suffer resorting to these platforms. Some concerns naturally arise in any scenario in which a data owner wishes to delegate storage and management of data to an external third party that can be considered honest-but-curious (i.e., trusted for correctly managing the data, but not trusted for accessing their content) or, more in general, not fully trusted (e.g., it can be considered lazy). In addition, the scenario of digital data markets complicates the picture with peculiarities that require careful consideration, such as the possibility of providing owners with payments when consumers access their data as a reward for contributing their data. Clearly, ensuring proper protection to the data managed and shared in digital data markets, and ensuring owners remain in control over their data, obtaining rewards when it is the case, are key requirements for enabling a wide adoption of such markets.

© The Author(s), under exclusive license to Springer Nature Switzerland AG 2023
P. Samarati et al. (Eds.): ICETE 2021, CCIS 1795, pp. 389–409, 2023.
https://doi.org/10.1007/978-3-031-36840-0_17

To permit the adoption of digital data markets to trade data while ensuring data are protected and under the control of their owner, without the need of completely trusting the market provider, a recent proposal combines selective owner-side encryption and blockchain [6]. With selective owner-side encryption, data are published on the market only after being encrypted by their owner. Encryption is performed using different encryption keys, so that different data items are encrypted with different keys. Encryption keys are distributed to consumers according to the restrictions set by the owners, including the fact of having received a reward. In this way, encrypted data can be possibly stored directly on the premises of the data market, if available, or more generally of economically-convenient cloud platforms with the guarantee that unauthorized subjects (including the market/cloud provider itself) cannot access their plaintext content. When an interested consumer requests access to a certain dataset, the owner/consumer interaction and the possible economic transaction for the incentives are managed via smart contracts deployed on a blockchain. In this way the request, the payment, and the willingness of the owner to grant access to such data to the consumer remains logged in the immutable ledger of the blockchain, ensuring therefore transparency and accountability.

The combined adoption of blockchain and selective owner-side encryption should however be carefully regulated. To ensure a reasonable key management burden for consumers, selective owner-side encryption is typically complemented by key derivation techniques, which define key derivation structures that represent sets of tokens enabling the derivation (i.e., the computation) of one encryption key starting from another one. The catalog of the tokens is publicly stored on the blockchain so that key derivation can be executed in accordance with the restrictions imposed by the owners. Every time an owner grants access to a new data item, or set thereof, the key derivation structure (and hence the entailed token catalog) needs to be restructured to reflect and enforce the new granted access. Different optimization strategies can be pursued when updating a key derivation structure. We investigate this issue and propose two different strategies: while the first aims at maintaining a slim token catalog, trying to minimize the overall number of tokens inserted in the catalog to ensure fast retrieval of tokens, the second strategy aims at reducing the modifications to the catalog, trying to reduce the costs entailed by updating the catalog on-chain. The remainder of this paper is organized as follows. Section 2 illustrates our reference scenario and introduces the general problem of maintaining owners in control in digital data markets. Section 3 provides some preliminaries on the building blocks that our solution adopts. Section 4 discusses how access restrictions specified by the owner can be self-enforced by the data stored on the market through selective encryption and key derivation. Section 5 illustrates how to selectively encrypt data for being securely stored and traded on data markets. Section 6 illustrates our approach for selectively granting access to data by updating the key derivation structure and token catalog according to our optimization strategies. Section 7 illustrates related work. Finally, Sect. 8 concludes the paper.

2   Scenario and Problem Statement

We are concerned with the problem of permitting a secure adoption of digital data markets permitting owners to publish data, and interested consumers to access (some of) them provided that an adequate reward is paid, by the consumers, to the owner. The general reference scenario is then characterized by two sets of subjects: a set $\mathcal{O}$ of data owners on one side, and a set $\mathcal{C}$ of consumers on the other side, who leverage the availability of the a data market to sell and buy data, which for generality we model as a set $\mathcal{R}$ of resources. Formally, our problem can be formulated as follows.

Problem 1. Let $\mathcal{R}$ be a set of resources published on a data market platform, and $\mathcal{C}$ be a set of consumers. $\forall r \in \mathcal{R}, \forall c \in \mathcal{C} : c$ can access r iff c is authorized by o and paid $\mathrm{cost}(r)$ to o, with o the owner of r and $\mathrm{cost}(r)$ the reward for r.

This problem entails a number of challenges and issues that need to be carefully addressed. A first issue concerns the definition of the rewards to be paid for accessing resources. As it is to be expected in real-world scenarios, we assume such rewards to be defined by the owners of the resources, such that each owner sets the rewards that need to be paid for accessing her resources. For simplicity but without loss of generality, given a resource r published by owner o, we assume the reward $\mathrm{cost}(r)$ to be paid for accessing r to be fixed and equal for each consumer, while we note that our solution is general and is not impacted by different definitions of rewards.

A second issue that characterizes our problem concerns the processing of the payment of the rewards to the owners. In particular, considering the digital nature of data markets and the fact that owners, consumers, and the market provider may not fully trust each other, a key requirement demands payments must be correctly executed: a consumer cannot claim to have paid for a resource while she has not and, conversely, an owner cannot claim a payment by a consumer has not been received while it has. A recent solution [6] has put forward the idea of leveraging blockchain and smart contracts to execute payments and have a verifiable log of the accesses requested and granted. We build on this strategy and leverage blockchain and smart contracts to guarantee that *i)* after a consumer c purchases access to a resource r, by paying $\mathrm{cost}(r)$ to r's owner o, then o cannot claim that payment has not been received and refuse to grant access to c; and *ii)* after an owner o has granted to a consumer c access to a resource r, then c cannot claim that access has not been granted (and ask to be refunded $\mathrm{cost}(r)$).

A third issue that characterizes our problem, and which represents the main focus of this paper, concerns ensuring adequate data protection, meaning that only authorized consumers who have paid adequate rewards to the owners can access resources. A complicating factor in this regard is that the market provider may not be fully trusted to enforce access restrictions (i.e., to prevent unauthorized accesses to resources that have not been paid). The provider may in fact be lazy (and not enforce access control, partially or entirely) and/or not completely trusted to act as a reference monitor. The solution in [6] protects resources with owner-side encryption, so that resources are outsourced to the market in an encrypted form that makes them unintelligible to any subject who does not possess the correct encryption keys, and in providing authorized consumers with the correct encryption keys. In our work, we leverage selective owner-side encryption (for supporting fine-grained access restrictions) and key derivation (to ease key management to consumers) to ensure that only authorized consumers can access a resource, without relying on the active involvement of the market provider.

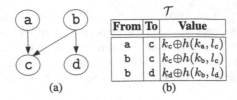

Fig. 1. An example of key derivation structure (a) and token catalog (b).

Example 1. We refer our discussion to the data generated by a smart fitness device that measures different parameters (e.g., heart rate, steps and movements, sleep, oxygen saturation levels). Such measurements are collected throughout the whole day, and the owner of the device and of the measured data can download them. Since these data can be of interest to a multitude of subjects (e.g., researchers), the owner decides to monetize them and, at regular time intervals, publishes them on a data market platform. In our examples, we consider the release of five sets of measurements $\mathcal{R}=\{a, b, c, d, e\}$. We consider four consumers $\mathcal{C} = \{\alpha, \beta, \gamma, \delta\}$, which over time require access to resources and hence pay rewards to the owner.

3   Preliminaries and Sketch of the Approach

The solution studied in this paper combines *selective encryption* (for protecting resources) and *key derivation* (for permitting efficient management), with *blockchain* and *smart contracts* (for managing the payments among possibly distrusting parties). In this section, we provide preliminaries on these building blocks.

3.1   Selective Encryption and Key Derivation

Encrypting the resources to be stored at an external platform is an effective approach for protecting their confidentiality, since the encryption layer (set by the data owner) makes resources unintelligible to subjects who do not know the encryption key, possibly including the provider itself. The enforcement of fine-grained access restrictions can be effectively managed through selective encryption [1,4] whenever the storage platform is not considered trusted to mediate access requests. Selective encryption consists in wrapping each resource with an encryption layer (set by the owner) using different keys for different resources, and in distributing keys to users in such a way that each user can decrypt all and only the resources she is authorized to access. To mitigate the burden of key management, selective encryption is usually coupled with key derivation [1]. Given two keys k_x and k_y, the derivation of k_y from k_x is enabled by a public token $t_{x,y}$ computed as $k_y \oplus h(k_x, l_y)$, with l_y a public label associated with k_y, $\oplus$ the bitwise xor operator, and h a deterministic non-invertible cryptographic function. The derivation relationship between keys can be *direct*, via a single token, or *indirect*, through a chain of tokens. Key derivation structures can be graphically represented as DAGs (directed acyclic graphs), where vertices represent encryption keys and their labels (e.g., vertex

v_x represents key k_x and its label l_x), and edges represent tokens (i.e., edge (v_x, v_y) represents token $t_{x,y}$ enabling the derivation of k_y from k_x). Tokens are physically stored in a public catalog $\mathcal{T}$ (similarly, labels are stored in a public catalog $\mathcal{L}$). Key derivation allows each user to manage a single key, from which she can compute all the keys for the resources for which she is authorized. In the following, when clear from the context, we will use the terms keys and vertices (tokens and edges, respectively) interchangeably. Figure 1 illustrates an example of a key derivation structure and of the corresponding token catalog, regulating the derivation relationships among four encryption keys k_a, k_b, k_c, and k_d. For readability, we denote the label of an encryption key k_x with x, and use the label to denote its corresponding vertex v_x in the structure (e.g., vertex a in Fig. 1 represents key k_a and its label l_a). For example, the tokens in the structure permit the derivation of k_c from key k_a and k_b, and the derivation of k_d from k_b only.

3.2 Blockchain and Smart Contracts

A blockchain is a shared and trusted public ledger of transactions, maintained in a distributed way by a decentralized network of peers. Transactions are organized in a list of blocks, linked in chronological order, and each block b_i contains a number of transaction records along with a cryptographic hash of the previous one b_{i-1}. Each transaction is validated by the network of peers, and is included in a block through a consensus protocol. The state of a blockchain is then continuously agreed upon by the network of peers: everyone can inspect a blockchain, but no single user can control it, or tamper with it, since modifications to the content of a blockchain require mutual agreement. Once a block is committed, nobody can modify it: updates are reflected in a new block containing the modified information. This permits to trust the content and the status of a blockchain, while not trusting the specific underlying peers. Blockchain is probably best known to be the core component of Bitcoin for allowing secure value transfer between two parties (through their digital wallets) without the need of a trusted central authority, such as a bank. The cryptographic primitives and digital signatures used for value transfer certify that the value is deducted from the payee's wallet, and that the receiver is indeed the party who now holds the value. Since then, blockchain technology has evolved to the aim of allowing transactions over virtually *any* value, be it material or immaterial. This has been achieved by introducing the concept of smart contract, a powerful tool for establishing contracts among multiple, possibly distrusting, parties. A smart contract is a software running on top of a blockchain defining a set of rules, on which the interacting parties agree. It can be seen as a set of 'if-then' instructions, defining triggering conditions (the 'if' part) and subsequent actions (the 'then' part). These conditions capture and model in a machine-readable format the clauses of a contract that is to be signed by the parties. The execution of a smart contact can be trusted for correctness thanks to the underlying blockchain consensus protocols, meaning that all the conditions of the agreement modeled by the contract are certainly met and validated by the network. However, smart contracts and their execution lack confidentiality and privacy, as plain visibility over the content of a contract and over the data it manipulates is necessary for contract validation [3].

3.3   Sketch of the Approach

Access restrictions to resources, ensuring their owners remain always in control of who can access them, are enforced with owner-side encryption, so that resources are stored in encrypted form, hence being protected also from the eyes of the market provider. Key management burden is reduced for consumers through key derivation, so that each consumer has to manage a single key per owner, starting from which she can derive all the keys needed to decrypt and access all authorized resources. To ensure that key derivation reflects the payments of the rewards by consumers, and to counteract possible misbehaviors by the interacting parties, we follow the proposal in [6] and assume *i)* reward payments to occur leveraging a blockchain, and *ii)* the token catalog enabling key derivation to be stored on-chain. As illustrated in the remainder of this paper, the key derivation structure (and hence the token catalog) needs to be updated whenever a consumer requests (and pays the reward for) a new resource, so to maintain correctness of the enabled key derivations. Different strategies may be adopted for enforcing such updates, which may have different costs that can be considered more or less important depending on the pursued objective. A first and natural objective is to keep the token catalog small in size, so to ensure fast retrieval by consumers when in need of deriving keys. With this strategy, possibly extensive restructuring operations to the key derivation structure and token catalog may be performed to the aim of reducing the overall number of tokens. Considering that writing on a blockchain has a cost, a second objective is to keep the number of modified tokens small, so to ensure a reduction in the costs entailed by the on-chain storage of the token catalog. In the following sections, we illustrate approaches for enforcing selective encryption and key derivation to protect resources in data markets pursuing these two objectives.

4   Authorizations and Key Derivation

We illustrate how to guarantee that the content of each resource published on the data market is visible only to authorized consumers who paid the reward to the owners of the resources. For simplicity, but without loss of generality, we refer our discussion to the set of resources published by one owner o, with the note that the same reasonings apply to all data owners operating on the data market. We illustrate how authorizations can be modeled in Sect. 4.1, and how they can be enforced through the definition of a key derivation structure in Sect. 4.2.

4.1   Authorizations

In line with the goal of monetizing data, we assume that a resource r can be accessed by any consumer who paid $\text{cost}(r)$ to the owner. For this reason, the authorization policy regulating which consumer can access which resources reflects the payments made by the consumers themselves, but we note that our approach can also manage additional access conditions that a specific owner may wish to impose.

We represent the authorization policy granting access to resources to authorized consumers through the *capability lists* of the consumers in $\mathcal{C}$. Given a consumer $c \in \mathcal{C}$,

Consumer	Capability List
α	abc
β	cde
γ	a
δ	d

Fig. 2. An example of authorizations for Example 1.

her capability list $\mathsf{cap}(c)$ includes all the resources in $\mathcal{R}$ that c can access (i.e., in our scenario, for which c paid $\mathsf{cost}(r)$ to the owner). Capability lists are by definition dynamic, and reflect the updates to the authorization policy. In particular, whenever a consumer c purchases access to a new resource r, r will be added to $\mathsf{cap}(c)$. In principle, an access (say, to resource r) that has been previously granted to c may also be revoked, resulting in r to be removed from $\mathsf{cap}(c)$. We however note that such access revocation is not in line with the peculiarities of the data market platforms, also considering the fact that our reference scenario is characterized by consumers purchasing (and not, for example, renting) access to a resources. For this reason, we do not consider access revocation and, as a consequence, capability lists of consumers never lose elements in the course of time. Figure 2 illustrates an example of authorizations for the consumers and resources of our running example (Example 1). For readability, we represent sets omitting commas and curly brackets (e.g., abc stands for $\{\mathsf{a}, \mathsf{b}, \mathsf{c}\}$). For example, $\mathsf{cap}(\alpha) = \mathsf{abc}$, meaning that consumer α is authorized (and hence has paid the reward to the owner) for resources a, b, and c.

As introduced in Sect. 3, we protect the confidentiality of the resources and enforce access restrictions through selective encryption (performed at the owner side) [4]. There are different approaches for using selective owner-side encryption for enforcing access restrictions, depending on how encryption keys are managed and distributed to consumers. A naive approach consists in encrypting each resource $r \in \mathcal{R}$ with a different key k_r, and in distributing to each consumer c the keys used to encrypt all the resources in her capability list $\mathsf{cap}(c)$. While this approach can correctly enforce an authorization policy, it would place upon consumers the burden of storing and managing a number of keys linear in the number of resources they can access (i.e., each consumer c would need to manage one key k_r for each resource $r \in \mathsf{cap}(c)$). Key management however causes a high burden for the consumer. Key derivation (Sect. 3.1) can be effectively employed for reducing such key management burden: the possibility of deriving (computing) an unlimited number of encryption keys starting from the knowledge of a single encryption key allows each consumer c to agree with the data owner a single key k_c, and the owner can define and publish a set of $|\mathsf{cap}(c)|$ tokens, each one allowing the computation of the encryption key used for a resource in $\mathsf{cap}(c)$. This way, since tokens can be publicly stored, each consumer c will have to manage a single key k_c only and compute, when needed for accessing a resource $r \in \mathsf{cap}(c)$, the corresponding encryption key k_r.

While effective, this simple solution might create more tokens than necessary. Consider two consumers ε and ζ such that $\mathsf{cap}(\varepsilon) = \mathsf{cap}(\zeta) = \mathsf{fgh}$. To permit both consumers to access the three resources, six tokens (three for permitting derivation of k_{f}, k_{g}, and k_{h} starting from k_{ε}, and three for permitting the same derivation starting from

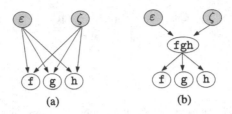

Fig. 3. Two examples of a key derivation structure enforcing $\mathsf{cap}(\varepsilon) = \mathsf{cap}(\zeta) = \mathtt{fgh}$, enabling key derivation through six tokens (a), and five tokens (b).

k_ζ) would be needed, as illustrated in Fig. 3(a). The insertion of an intermediate vertex (i.e., key) in the DAG modeling key derivation would still permit the same derivations, while saving a token, as illustrated in Fig. 3(b): it is easy to see that both ε and ζ are still able to derive all (and only) the keys they are entitled to with the creation of five (rather than six) tokens. Such additional keys are used for derivation purposes only, and are not used to encrypt any resource (nor are they assigned to any consumer). They can be defined according to different criteria: in traditional cloud-based scenarios they are typically associated with sets of users [5]. Considering the peculiarities of the market scenario, and the fact that consumers dynamically join and leave the market to acquire sets of resources, it is natural to associate them with sets of resources. We illustrate our key derivation structure in the remainder of this section.

4.2   Key Derivation Structure and Correctness

A *key derivation structure* for our problem is formally defined as follows [6].

Definition 1 (Key Derivation Structure). *Let* $\mathcal{R} = \{r_1, \ldots, r_n\}$ *be a set of resources and* $\mathcal{C} = \{c_1, \ldots, c_m\}$ *be a set of consumers. A* key derivation structure *over* $\mathcal{R}$ *and* $\mathcal{C}$ *is a DAG* $G(V, E)$ *such that:*

1. $\forall v_x \in V, (x \in \mathcal{C}) \vee (x \subseteq \mathcal{R})$;
2. $\forall c \in \mathcal{C}, v_c \in V$;
3. $\forall r \in \mathcal{R}, v_r \in V$;
4. $\forall (v_x, v_y) \in E : (y \subset x) \vee (x \in \mathcal{C} \wedge y \subseteq \mathcal{R})$.

The definition above formally characterizes a generic key derivation structure for a data market over a set of resources and a set of consumers. Condition 1 states that a key derivation structure includes a set of vertices representing consumers or sets of resources. Condition 2 demands that, for each consumer c, a key derivation structure includes a vertex v_c for c. Similarly, Condition 3 demands that, for each resource r, a key derivation structure includes a vertex v_r for r. Lastly, Condition 4 states that the (directed) edges of a key derivation structure connect either a consumer to a set of resources ($x \in \mathcal{C} \wedge y \subseteq \mathcal{R}$), or a set of resources to a subset of the same ($y \subset x$). Recall (Sect. 3.1) that vertices in a key derivation structure represent encryption keys. In our approach, each consumer $c \in \mathcal{C}$ knows the encryption key k_c represented by vertex v_c. Also, each resource $r \in \mathcal{R}$ is encrypted with the key k_r represented by vertex v_r.

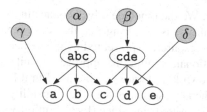

Fig. 4. An example of a key derivation structure enforcing the authorizations in Fig. 2.

Example 2. Figure 4 illustrates an example of key derivation structure defined over the four consumers $\alpha, \beta, \gamma, \delta$ and five resources a, b, c, d, e of our running example (Example 1). The structure includes a vertex for each consumer (denoted, for readability, with a colored background), a vertex for each resource, and two additional vertices defined over sets of resources. As already noted, for simplicity in the figures we denote each vertex v_x with x (e.g., a is the vertex for resource a representing the encryption key k_a used to encrypt it and, similarly, α is the vertex for consumer α representing her encryption key k_α).

The definition of a key derivation structure creates (direct and/or indirect) derivation relationships among encryption keys (be them assigned to consumers, to resources, or to groups of resources). Clearly, such derivation relationships must correctly enforce the authorization policy so to ensure that each consumer can derive all and only the encryption keys used for encrypting the resources she can access. This requires to guarantee that each consumer c can reach, starting from the vertex v_c representing her encryption key k_c, all and only the vertices representing the encryption keys k_r used to encrypt the resources in her capability list cap(c). Formally, given an authorization policy $\mathcal{A}$ over a set $\mathcal{R}$ of resources and a set $\mathcal{C}$ of consumers, a key derivation structure *correctly enforces* $\mathcal{A}$ iff $\forall r \in \mathcal{R}, \forall c \in \mathcal{C}$ it holds that $r \in$ cap(c) $\Leftrightarrow \exists$ a path in G from v_c to v_r.

Example 3. Consider the authorization policy expressed by the capability lists reported in Fig. 2. The key derivation structure in Fig. 4 correctly enforces the policy. The structure includes one vertex for each resource, one vertex for each consumer, and two additional vertices representing the non-singleton capability lists of consumers α (cap(α) = abc) and β (cap(β) = cde). The edges in the structure connect, linking their vertices, each consumer to her capability list, and sets of resources respecting subset containment relationship. It is easy to see that each consumer can reach through a path all and only the resources in her capability list (meaning she can derive the corresponding encryption keys). For example, consumer α can, from her key k_α and with token $t_{\alpha,abc}$, derive k_{abc}, from which she can use tokens $t_{abc,a}$ $t_{abc,b}$, and $t_{abc,c}$ to derive k_a, k_b, and k_c.

Given an authorization policy, a correct key derivation structure can be defined in different ways, depending on how the additional vertices (i.e., those not corresponding to consumers nor to resources, and used for derivation purposes only) and edges are defined. Our approach consists in including in the structure a vertex for each capability list of consumers in $\mathcal{C}$, and an edge $(v_c, v_{cap(c)})$ connecting each consumer c to her capability list $\mathsf{cap}(c)$. We then include edges connecting vertices representing sets of resources (e.g., capability lists) ensuring that the set R represented by vertex v_R is *covered*, that is, the set of resources represented by the vertices directly reachable from v_R is equal to R. The rationale behind this approach is quite intuitive: each consumer c can, starting from her own key (vertex v_c, included in the structure by Condition 2 in Definition 1), derive the key associated with her capability list (vertex $v_{\mathsf{cap}(c)}$ in the structure). Since $\mathsf{cap}(c)$ is covered, and since (by Condition 3 in Definition 1) the structure includes a vertex for each resource in $\mathsf{cap}(c)$, c can derive (directly and/or indirectly) all and only the keys for all resources in $\mathsf{cap}(c)$. For example, the key derivation structure in Fig. 4 is built following this approach, and correctly enforces the authorizations in Fig. 2. In the following sections, we illustrate our approach for managing the publication of resources on the market, and for enforcing access restrictions through the definition and maintenance of a key derivation structure.

5   Resource Management

An empty key derivation structure $G(V,E)$ is created whenever an owner interacts for the first time with the data market. Such key derivation is then updated whenever a resource is published by the owner on the market, as well as whenever consumers are granted access to resources, to guarantee its correctness and the correctness of the enabled key derivations. In this section, we illustrate our approach for managing the publication of a resource. We will discuss the management of the purchase of a resource by a consumer in Sect. 6.

PUBLISH_RESOURCE(r,$G(V,E)$)

1:   generate key k_r for r
2:   generate label l_r for r
3:   generate vertex v_r for r
4:   $V := V \cup \{v_r\}$
5:   $enc\_r := \mathbf{encrypt}(r,k_r)$
6:   $\mathbf{publish}(enc\_r)$

Fig. 5. Management of the publication of a resource r.

Figure 5 illustrates the pseudocode of procedure **Publish_Resouce**, managing the publication of a new resource on the market. The procedure takes as input a resource r and an existing key derivation structure $G(V, E)$, possibly empty if r is the first resource to be published by the owner. The procedure generates an encryption key k_r, which will be used for encrypting r, and the corresponding label l_r, used for enabling derivation (lines 1–2). It then creates the corresponding vertex v_r, and inserts v_r into V (lines 3–4). Resource r is encrypted with key k_r (line 5), and the resulting encrypted version enc_r is published on the market (line 6).

Fig. 6. An example of a key derivation structure after publishing the five resources of Example 1.

Example 4. Consider the publication of the five resources of our running example (Example 1). Figure 6 illustrates an example of a key derivation structure after the publication on the market of the resources. Since no authorizations have been granted yet, the structure includes only one vertex for each resource, and no vertex for consumers nor sets of resources.

6   Access Control Enforcement

The key derivation structure is updated to reflect purchases by consumers, to ensure that the key derivation enabled by the tokens represented by edges in the structure correctly enforces the granted authorizations. As mentioned in Sect. 4, we recall that revocation of an access already granted is not in line with the peculiarities of the considered market scenario. Clearly, this does not imply that once an owner has published a resource on the market she cannot remove it: as a matter of fact, owners remain in full control of their resources and, should they wish so, they can always remove resources from the market. Issues that may arise if owners remove resources for which consumers have paid are beyond the scope of this paper. We illustrate in Sect. 6.1 how to update a key derivation structure aiming at minimizing the size of the entailed token catalog (thus ensuring fast access to tokens by consumers). In Sect. 6.2, we describe an alternative strategy aiming at minimizing the number of additional tokens (thus reducing the costs entailed by updating the catalog stored on-chain).

6.1   Reducing Token Catalog Size

Figure 7 illustrates the pseudocode of procedure **Min_Token_Catalog**, updating a key derivation structure to accommodate –and reflect in the enabled key derivations– the purchase of a set R of resources by a consumer c, aiming at minimizing the overall number of tokens. The procedure takes as input the consumer c, her current capability list $cap(c)$, the set R of resources for which c has paid a reward to the owner and for which the owner grants access, and the key derivation structure $G(V,E)$ to be updated. It updates the structure to enable c to derive the keys needed to decrypt the resources in $cap(c) \cup R$.

The procedure first checks whether the structure already contains a vertex for c, meaning that c has already interacted with the market and the owner, and has already shared a key k_c with the owner. If this is not the case, the procedure generates a key k_c, a corresponding vertex v_c, and adds v_c to the structure (lines 1–4). If c has already a key in the structure, the procedure removes the edge connecting v_c to vertex $v_{cap(c)}$, representing her current (meaning before the purchase of R) capability list, and the corresponding token from the catalog (lines 5–7). The procedure then checks whether it is possible to remove from the structure $v_{cap(c)}$ and, if so, whether removing its incident edges and directly connecting its ancestors to its descendants can reduce the number of tokens in the catalog (edges in the structure, lines 8–18). To do so, it checks whether other consumers have the same current capability list as, clearly, if this is the case, then the vertex could not be removed (line 8). Otherwise, it determines the sets *Anc* and *Desc* of ancestors and descendants of $v_{cap(c)}$ (lines 9–10). If $(|Anc| \times |Desc|) < (|Anc| + |Desc|)$

MIN_TOKEN_CATALOG$(c, \text{cap}(c), R, G(V, E))$

1: **if** $v_c \notin V$ **then**
2:      generate key k_c for c
3:      generate vertex v_c for c
4:      $V := V \cup \{v_c\}$
5: **else**
6:      $E := E \setminus \{(v_c, v_{\text{cap}(c)})\}$
7:      $\mathcal{T} := \mathcal{T} \setminus \{t_{c, \text{cap}(c)}\}$
8: **if** $\nexists c' \neq c$ s.t. $\text{cap}(c) = \text{cap}(c')$ **then**
9:      let Anc be the ancestors of $v_{\text{cap}(c)}$
10:     let $Desc$ be the descendants of $v_{\text{cap}(c)}$
11:     **if** $(|Anc| \times |Desc|) < (|Anc| + |Desc|)$ **then**
            /* removing $v_{\text{cap}(c)}$ and its incident edges reduces the number of tokens */
12:         **for each** $v_a \in Anc$ **do**
13:             $E := E \setminus \{(v_a, v_{\text{cap}(c)})\}$
14:             $\mathcal{T} := \mathcal{T} \setminus \{t_{a, \text{cap}(c)}\}$
15:             **for each** $v_d \in Desc$ **do**
16:                 $E := E \setminus \{(v_{\text{cap}(c)}, v_d)\} \cup \{(v_a, v_d)\}$
17:                 $\mathcal{T} := \mathcal{T} \setminus \{t_{\text{cap}(c), d}\} \cup \{t_{a, d}\}$
18:         $V := V \setminus \{v_{\text{cap}(c)}\}$
19: $\text{cap}(c) := \text{cap}(c) \cup R$
20: **if** $v_{\text{cap}(c)} \in V$ **then**
21:     $E := E \cup \{(v_c, v_{\text{cap}(c)})\}$
22:     $\mathcal{T} := \mathcal{T} \cup \{t_{c, \text{cap}(c)}\}$
23: **else**
24:     generate key $k_{\text{cap}(c)}$ for $\text{cap}(c)$
25:     generate label $l_{\text{cap}(c)}$ for $\text{cap}(c)$
26:     generate vertex $v_{\text{cap}(c)}$ for $\text{cap}(c)$
27:     $V := V \cup \{v_{\text{cap}(c)}\}$
28:     $E := E \cup \{(v_c, v_{\text{cap}(c)})\}$
29:     $\mathcal{T} := \mathcal{T} \cup \{t_{c, \text{cap}(c)}\}$
        /* connect $v_{\text{cap}(c)}$ ensuring that $\text{cap}(c)$ is covered */
30:     $CandCover := \{v_X \in V : X \subseteq \text{cap}(c)\}$
31:     $Cover := \emptyset$
32:     $ToCover := \text{cap}(c)$
33:     **while** $ToCover \neq \emptyset$ **do**
34:         let $v_Y \in CandCover$ be the vertex s.t. $Y \cap ToCover$ is largest
35:         $Cover := Cover \cup \{v_Y\}$
36:         $CandCover := CandCover \setminus \{v_Y\}$
37:         $ToCover := ToCover \setminus Y$
38:         $E := E \cup \{(v_{\text{cap}(c)}, v_Y)\}$
39:         $\mathcal{T} := \mathcal{T} \cup \{t_{\text{cap}(c), Y}\}$
        /* check if inserting $v_{\text{cap}(c)}$ as an intermediate vertex can reduce the number of tokens */
40:     let $Par \subseteq V$ be the set of vertices over supersets of $\text{cap}(c)$
41:     let $ReachCover$ be the set of vertices directly reachable from vertices in $Cover$
42:     **for each** $v_{par} \in Par$ **do**
43:         $ToRemove := \emptyset$
44:         **for each** $v \in ReachCover \cup Cover$ **do**
45:             **if** $(v_{par}, v) \in E$ **then**
46:                 $ToRemove := ToRemove \cup \{(v_{par}, v)\}$
47:         **if** $|ToRemove| \geq 2$ **then**
48:             $E := E \cup \{(v_{par}, v_{\text{cap}(c)})\}$
49:             $\mathcal{T} := \mathcal{T} \cup \{t_{par, \text{cap}(c)}\}$
50:             **for each** $(v_{par}, v_z) \in ToRemove$ **do**
51:                 $E := E \setminus \{(v_{par}, v_z)\}$
52:                 $\mathcal{T} := \mathcal{T} \setminus \{t_{par, z}\}$

Fig. 7. Management of purchases reducing the size of the token catalog.

the procedure removes all $v_{\text{cap}(c)}$'s incident edges and connects all $v_{\text{cap}(c)}$'s ancestors to $v_{\text{cap}(c)}$'s descendants, removing also the corresponding tokens from the catalog (lines 11–17). The procedure removes $v_{\text{cap}(c)}$ from the structure (line 18) and updates c's capability list to $\text{cap}(c) \cup R$ (line 19). If the structure already includes a vertex for the updated capability list, the procedure simply adds an edge (and the corresponding token) connecting v_c to the vertex, and terminates (lines 20–22). Otherwise (line 23), it generates a key for $\mathsf{cap}(c)$, the corresponding label and vertex, and inserts the vertex in the structure (lines 24–27), also connecting v_c to it through an edge, and adding the corresponding token to the catalog (lines 28–29). To guarantee correctness of key derivation, the procedure then connects the newly created vertex $v_{\mathsf{cap}(c)}$ to other vertices of the structure, ensuring coverage (i.e., ensuring that the vertex is connected to other vertices so that the union of the resources of the vertices directly reachable from $v_{\mathsf{cap}(c)}$ is equal to $\mathsf{cap}(c)$, lines 30–39). It does so defining three sets *CandCover*, *Cover*, and *ToCover*, modeling respectively the vertices that are candidate for coverage (i.e., for becoming direct descendants of $v_{\mathsf{cap}(c)}$), the vertices that have been selected for coverage, and the resources to be covered. Such sets are initialized, respectively, to the set of vertices in the structure defined over a subset of $\mathsf{cap}(c)$ (line 30), to an empty set (line 31), and to $\mathsf{cap}(c)$ (line 32), respectively. The procedure heuristically selects, among the candidates in *CandCover*, the vertex v_Y that covers the largest number of the resources to be covered in *ToCover* (i.e., such that $Y \cap ToCover$ is largest, lines 34–35), removes it from the candidates (line 36), removes the set Y of resources from *ToCover* (line 37), and connects $v_{\mathsf{cap}(c)}$ to v_Y adding the corresponding token to the catalog (lines 38–39). These operations are repeated until all resources in $\mathsf{cap}(c)$ have been covered (i.e., *ToCover* is empty, line 33). Finally, the procedure checks whether the overall number of tokens can be further reduced thanks to the creation of $v_{\mathsf{cap}(c)}$ [4]. The procedure first identifies a set *Par* of vertices representing supersets of $\mathsf{cap}(c)$, and a set *ReachCover* of vertices reachable from the vertices used for coverage (i.e., those in *Cover*) (lines 40–41). To this aim, if a vertex v_{par} in *Par* is directly connected to more than one vertex in *Cover* and/or in *ReachCover*, the procedure inserts $v_{\mathsf{cap}(c)}$ as an intermediate vertex, and removes the edges from v_{par} to the vertices in $Cover \cup ReachCover$ (lines 42–52), reducing the number of edges (and of corresponding tokens).

Example 5. Consider the key derivation structure in Fig. 4. Figure 8 illustrates the evolution of the structure to enforce a sequence of requests. The structure in Fig. 8(a) grants γ access to b and c: the token enabling the derivation of k_a from k_γ (modeled by edge (v_γ, v_a)) is replaced with a token enabling the derivation of k_{abc} from k_γ (modeled by edge (v_γ, v_{abc})). Similarly, the structure in Fig. 8(b) grants β access to a and b, starting from the structure in Fig. 8(a): vertex v_{abcde}, representing $\mathsf{cap}(\beta) = abcde$, is inserted in the structure and is connected to vertices v_{abc} and v_{cde} (left-hand-side structure). Following this purchase, vertex v_{cde} becomes redundant, and is removed, saving two tokens while permitting the same derivations (right-hand-side structure). Finally, Fig. 8(c) grants α access to e, starting from the structure in Fig. 8(b): vertex v_{abce} is inserted in the structure, v_α is connected to it, and our approach places it also as direct descendant of v_{abcde}, saving one token in the catalog.

6.2 Reducing Token Catalog Updates

The approach illustrated in the previous section aims to limit the size of the token catalog by deleting the tokens that become unnecessary after accommodating the purchase of R by a consumer c (e.g., the token represented by the edge connecting v_c to $v_{\mathsf{cap}(c)}$,

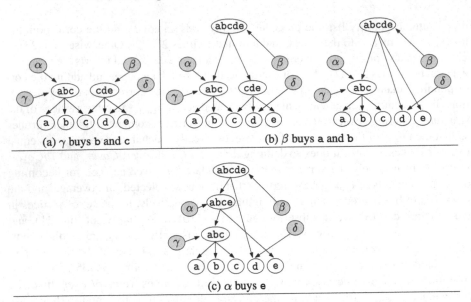

(a) γ buys b and c

(b) β buys a and b

(c) α buys e

Fig. 8. Evolution of the key derivation structure in Fig. 4 to enforce a sequence of purchases minimizing the overall number of tokens.

with $cap(c)$ the previous capability list of c, which becomes redundant due to the fact that v_c will be connected to vertex $v_{cap(c) \cup R}$ and thanks to the coverage of $cap(c) \cup R$), and by re-organizing the key derivation structure, possibly deleting unnecessary vertices (e.g., $v_{cap(c)}$) and the incident tokens, and adding new tokens leveraging the deletion of $v_{cap(c)}$ and the inclusion of $v_{cap(c) \cup R}$. All these operations have clearly a cost, and can represent an issue when reflected on the blockchain, since token catalog is stored on-chain [6]. To limit the update (write) operations on the blockchain, we propose an alternative approach that: *i)* does not require token deletion; and *ii)* tries to re-use as much as possible keys and tokens already included in the key derivation structure.

This approach follows the observation that token deletion is not necessary for enforcing new access grants, and re-using elements already existing in the structure limits the number of the tokens added to accommodate the policy update. To illustrate, consider the purchase of a set R of resources by consumer c. Indeed, the capability list of c needs to be updated to include the resources in R (i.e., it is to be updated to $cap(c) \cup R$) and, to ensure correctness of key derivation, v_c must be connected with a vertex in the structure representing $cap(c) \cup R$. If such a vertex already belongs to the hierarchy, it is possible to add to the structure an edge $(v_c, v_{cap(c) \cup R})$, representing the token enabling the derivation of $k_{cap(c) \cup R}$ from k_c, without deleting the (now redundant, but not incorrect) edge $(v_c, v_{cap(c)})$ and the corresponding token. This increases the overall number of tokens, but reduces the operations performed to accommodate the purchase. If, otherwise, $v_{cap(c) \cup R}$ does not belong to the hierarchy, two different approaches can be adopted.

- *Insertion of a new vertex*: insert vertex $v_{\text{cap}(c) \cup R}$ in the structure, and connect it to $v_{\text{cap}(c)}$ (and hence indirectly to the corresponding resources) and, directly or indirectly, to the vertices of the resources in R;
- *Relabeling of an existing vertex*: connect (directly or indirectly) vertex $v_{\text{cap}(c)}$ to the vertices of the resources in R, relabeling $v_{\text{cap}(c)}$ to represent $\text{cap}(c) \cup R$. Compared to the previous strategy, this strategy saves the insertion and deletion of one token (the one from v_c to $v_{\text{cap}(c) \cup R}$, as it already exists), but it is not always viable. In particular, relabeling $v_{\text{cap}(c)}$ to $v_{\text{cap}(c) \cup R}$ is possible only if: *i)* no other consumer c' has a capability list equal to the (previous) list of c (i.e., $\text{cap}(c')=\text{cap}(c)$), as otherwise c' would gain access to R without being authorized; and *ii)* all the ancestors of the relabeled vertex represent a superset of $\text{cap}(c) \cup R$, since otherwise consumers who can derive such vertices would be granted access to R.

Independently from the strategy chosen for including vertex $v_{\text{cap}(c) \cup R}$ in the structure, such vertex needs to be connected to the resources in R (as it is clearly already connected to those in $\text{cap}(c)$). If the structure already contains a vertex v_R, it is sufficient to add to the structure edge $(v_{\text{cap}(c) \cup R}, v_R)$ and define the corresponding token. If this is not the case, a possible solution (always available) can consist in adding $|R|$ edges, one for each resource in R. However, if the structure already includes a set K of less than $|R|$ vertices representing subsets of $\text{cap}(c) \cup R$ that completely cover R, the number of additional edges (and hence of tokens to be added) can be reduced to $|K|$ by connecting $\text{cap}(c) \cup R$ with the vertices in K.

Figure 9 illustrates the pseudocode of procedure **Min_Additional_Tokens**, updating a key derivation structure to accommodate –and reflect in the key derivations enabled– the purchase of a set R of resources by a consumer c, aiming at minimizing the number of additional tokens. The procedure takes as input the consumer c, her current capability list $\text{cap}(c)$, the set R of resources for which c has paid a reward to the owner and for which the owner grants access, and the key derivation structure $G(V,E)$ to be updated. It updates the structure to enable c to derive the keys needed to decrypt the resources in $\text{cap}(c) \cup R$.

The procedure first checks whether the structure already contains a vertex for c, meaning that c has already interacted with the market and the owner, and has already shared a key k_c with the owner. If this is not the case, the procedure generates a key k_c, a corresponding vertex v_c, and adds v_c to the structure (lines 1–4). The procedure then checks whether the structure already includes a vertex for $\text{cap}(c) \cup R$ (line 5). If this is the case, the procedure simply adds an edge connecting v_c to $v_{\text{cap}(c) \cup R}$, creates the corresponding token, and terminates (lines 5–7). Otherwise, it checks whether it is possible to relabel vertex $v_{\text{cap}(c)}$: to this end, it checks if no consumer c' has capability list equal to $\text{cap}(c)$ (line 9), and if all ancestors of $v_{\text{cap}(c)}$ are defined over supersets of $\text{cap}(c) \cup R$ (lines 10-11). If both conditions are satisfied, the procedure relabels $v_{\text{cap}(c)}$ into $v_{\text{cap}(c) \cup R}$ (line 12), resulting in the structure to include a vertex for $\text{cap}(c) \cup R$. Otherwise, the procedure generates an encryption key and a label for $\text{cap}(c) \cup R$, creates the corresponding vertex, adds it to the structure (lines 13–17), and connects it to $v_{\text{cap}(c)}$ (lines 18–19). The procedure then covers the resources in R starting from the vertices already included in the structure that have the largest intersection with R, to reduce the number of needed connections (i.e., of added edges, hence of additional

MIN_ADDITIONAL_TOKENS(c,cap(c),R,$G(V,E)$)

1: **if** $v_c \notin V$ **then**
2:      generate key k_c for c
3:      generate vertex v_c for c
4:      $V := V \cup \{v_c\}$
5: **if** $v_{\mathsf{cap}(c) \cup R} \in V$ **then**
6:      $E := E \cup \{(v_c, v_{\mathsf{cap}(c) \cup R})\}$
7:      $\mathcal{T} := \mathcal{T} \cup \{t_{c,\mathsf{cap}(c) \cup R}\}$
8: **else**
9:      **if** $\nexists c' \neq c \in C : \mathsf{cap}(c') = \mathsf{cap}(c)$ **then**
10:         let Anc be the ancestors of $v_{\mathsf{cap}(c)}$
11:         **if** $\forall v_X \in Anc : X \supset (\mathsf{cap}(c) \cup R)$ **then**
12:             relabel $v_{\mathsf{cap}(c)}$ into $v_{\mathsf{cap}(c) \cup R}$
13:     **else**
14:         generate key $k_{\mathsf{cap}(c) \cup R}$
15:         generate label $l_{\mathsf{cap}(c) \cup R}$
16:         generate vertex $v_{\mathsf{cap}(c) \cup R}$
17:         $V := V \cup \{v_{\mathsf{cap}(c) \cup R}\}$
18:         $E := E \cup \{(v_{\mathsf{cap}(c) \cup R}, v_{\mathsf{cap}(c)})\}$ /* cover cap(c) */
19:         $\mathcal{T} := \mathcal{T} \cup \{t_{\mathsf{cap}(c) \cup R, \mathsf{cap}(c)}\}$
        /* connect $v_{\mathsf{cap}(c) \cup R}$ ensuring that R is covered */
20:         $CandCover := \{v_X \in V : X \subseteq \mathsf{cap}(c) \cup R\}$
21:         $ToCover := R$
22:         **while** $ToCover \neq \emptyset$ **do**
23:             let $v_Y \in CandCover$ be the vertex s.t. $Y \cap ToCover$ is largest
24:             $CandCover := CandCover \setminus \{v_Y\}$
25:             $ToCover := ToCover \setminus Y$
26:             $E := E \cup \{(v_{\mathsf{cap}(c) \cup R}, v_Y)\}$
27:             $\mathcal{T} := \mathcal{T} \cup \{t_{\mathsf{cap}(c) \cup R, Y}\}$
28:     $E := E \cup \{(v_c, v_{\mathsf{cap}(c) \cup R})\}$
29:     $\mathcal{T} := \mathcal{T} \cup \{t_{c,\mathsf{cap}(c) \cup R}\}$

Fig. 9. Management of purchases reducing the number of additional tokens.

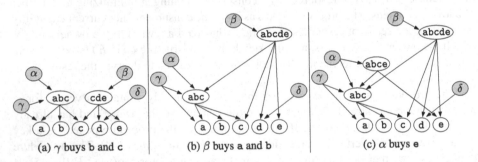

(a) γ buys b and c   (b) β buys a and b   (c) α buys e

Fig. 10. Evolution of the key derivation structure in Fig. 4 to enforce a sequence of purchases minimizing the number of additional tokens.

tokens, lines 20–27). Finally, the procedure connects v_c to $v_{\mathsf{cap}(c) \cup R}$, creating the corresponding token (lines 28–29).

Example 6. Consider the key derivation structure in Fig. 4. Figure 10 illustrates the evolution of the structure to enforce the same sequence of requests as in Fig. 8, but minimizing the number of additional tokens. The structure in Fig. 10(a) grants γ access to b and c: since the structure already includes a vertex v_{abc} for the updated capability list of γ, the structure is updated simply adding a token enabling the derivation of k_{abc} from k_γ (modeled by edge (v_γ, v_{abc})): the (now redundant) edge (v_γ, v_a) is left untouched, saving on its deletion. The structure in Fig. 10(b) grants β access to a and b, starting from the structure in Fig. 10(a): vertex v_{cde} is relabeled as v_{abcde}, and is covered by connecting it to v_{abc}, which completely covers resources ab purchased by β. Note that this approach implies the simple insertion of one token (modeled by edge (v_{abcde}, v_{abc})), in contrast to the insertion of 4 tokens and the removal of 4 tokens paid by the solution minimizing the token catalog size in Fig. 8(b). Finally, Fig. 10(c) grants α access to e, starting from the structure in Fig. 10(b): in this case it would not be possible to relabel v_{abc} as v_{abce}, as this would also allow γ to access e. In this case, it is then necessary to insert a new vertex v_{abce}, connected to v_{abc} and v_e. Again, the (now redundant) edge (v_α, v_{abc}) is left untouched, avoiding its deletion.

6.3 Further Optimizations

The reduction of the additional tokens introduced to accommodate resource purchase could leverage further optimizations, which we illustrate in the remainder of this section.

– **Remove the assumption of having a vertex representing the capability list of each customer.** The two strategies we have illustrated build on the inclusion in the hierarchy of a vertex representing the capability list of the consumers. This requires the creation of a new vertex, or the relabeling of an existing one, at each purchase of a resource. Removing this assumption may reduce the number of tokens that need to be created to manage a purchase operation. To illustrate, consider a consumer c who had purchased a set of resources, and suppose she is now purchasing a set R of resources. Suppose that the key derivation structure already includes a vertex for R. In principle, to enforce such purchase, it could be sufficient add an edge to the structure linking v_c to v_R, hence requiring the insertion of a single token in the catalog. Requiring to have, in the structure, vertex $v_{cap(c) \cup R}$ would instead imply the insertion of at least two edges (hence two tokens): one connecting v_c to

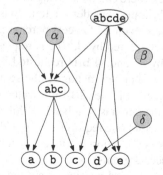

Fig. 11. Evolution of the key derivation hierarchy in Fig. 4 removing the assumption of having all capability vertices.

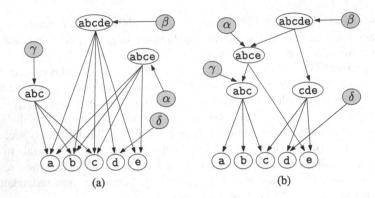

Fig. 12. Evolution of the key derivation hierarchy in Fig. 4 managing purchases in order (a) and in batch (b).

$v_{\mathsf{cap}(c)\cup R}$, one connecting $v_{\mathsf{cap}(c)\cup R}$ to v_R. Figure 11 illustrates the key derivation structure obtained, starting from the structure in Fig. 4 and managing the purchases in Fig. 10, according to this optimization strategy. In particular, the purchase of e by α is enforced by connecting v_α directly to v_e, saving 3 tokens w.r.t. Figure 10. Note that we did not manage the purchase of a and b by β and of b and c by γ connecting directly their vertices to the resources' vertices, since this would not provide any cost reduction.

- **Manage purchases in batch.** The two strategies we have illustrated assume that the owner manages each request, independently from other ones, as soon as it is submitted by a consumer. However, it can be noted that the combined management of multiple requests may enable considerable benefits. A first intuitive advantage relates to allowing the owner to be not available all the times for managing resource purchase: in agreement with the consumers (and possibly with adjustments to the reward to be paid for the resources), the owner may opt for a periodic (e.g., daily, or after a certain number of requests have been submitted) re-organization of the key derivation structure. Also, when some requests by different consumers in a batch relate to the same resources, there can be a saving in the number of tokens needed to accommodate them. To illustrate, consider the four consumers and five resources of our running example, and a sequence of access purchases, starting from the structure in Fig. 4, such that: *i)* a is requested by β, *ii)* c is requested by γ, *iii)* b is requested by β, *iv)* e is requested by α, and *v)* b is requested by γ. Figure 12(a) illustrates the key derivation structure obtained managing the sequence in the order, updating the structure at every request. Figure 12(b) illustrates the key derivation structure obtained managing the same purchases in batch. While the first strategy implies the addition of 8 tokens, the second one requires only 6 additional tokens (note that, for readability, in Fig. 12 we did not report the tokens that became redundant due to the enforcement of the new access grants).
- **Insert additional vertices.** A third possibility aiming at further reducing the number of additional tokens can leverage the observation that the insertion of additional vertices referring to sets of resources at a certain point in time may reduce the num-

ber of tokens that will be needed in the future, to accommodate future requests. The presence of a vertex in the structure representing a set R of resources could be profitably used for accommodating another purchase for a superset of R, with a saving in the number of tokens. Intuitively, if a set $R' \supset R$ of resources is acquired by at least two different consumers, the presence of R in the structure can reduce the number of tokens needed to accommodate such requests. A possible strategy following this intuition is to materialize (i.e., create and insert into the structure) the vertex representing the set R of resources acquired by a consumer. The data owner clearly pays an additional token for inserting R, but she may experience a saving in the future. To illustrate, consider the key derivation structure in Fig. 4. To enforce the purchase of resources a and b by β, the owner might materialize a vertex v_{ab} (though it does not correspond to any capability list). Suppose that, after some time, also consumers δ and ε request access to these resources. Having v_{ab} in the structure, it is sufficient to insert a token from v_{abd} to v_{ab} for δ, and from v_ε to v_{ab} for ε, saving on the number of tokens inserted to manage the three purchases (7 tokens instead of 9 tokens). Figure 13 illustrates the key derivation structure after the accommodation of purchases of a and b by β, δ, and ε, materializing vertex v_{ab} with the purchase by β.

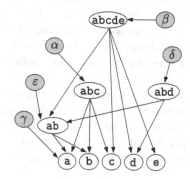

Fig. 13. Evolution of the key derivation hierarchy in Fig. 4 inserting additional vertices.

The optimizations illustrated above, while helping in further reducing the number of additional tokens, require analysis to balance the benefits against some complications they entail. In particular, for the first strategy, we note that the availability of vertices representing groups of resources in the structure can be beneficial to accommodate future requests (possibly by other consumers) which can be enforced leveraging such vertices. This reasoning clearly applies also to vertices for capability lists. Removing the assumption of having them in the hierarchy can be beneficial to enforce a specific purchase, but may result –in the long run– in additional tokens to be added to accommodate future requests. Also, if adopted from initialization time (i.e., from the very first request), it creates a structure with vertices for consumers and for single resources, resulting in a bipartite graph where each consumer c is directly connected by $|\mathsf{cap}(c)|$

edges (with an equal number of tokens in the catalog) to each resource in her capability list. For the second strategy (managing purchases in batches), it can clearly help in optimizing the key derivation structure, but brings the inevitable drawback of introducing delays in making resources available to consumers. As for the last strategy, additional vertices can be beneficial if they can be used to accommodate future requests, which requires some analysis by the owner to forecast, in a reliable way, future requests.

7 Related Work

The adoption of selective encryption for enforcing access restrictions in digital data markets, coupled with smart contracts deployed on a blockchain, has first been proposed in [6]. Our solution builds on this proposal and on the use of selective encryption and key derivation for enabling data owners to maintain control over their resources in the data market to propose different optimization strategies for effectively updating the key derivation structure enforcing new access restrictions. A preliminary version of this work appeared in [8], which is here extended with more complete and revised algorithms, and enhanced discussions on the possible strategies that can be adopted along with their pros and cons.

The adoption of selective encryption, possibly combined with key derivation, has been widely adopted as a means for protecting data in outsourcing scenarios, which are characterized by data owners storing their resources on the premises of non fully trusted (cloud) providers (e.g., [2,4,5]), and which would benefit from data self-enforcing access restrictions through an encryption layer. These approaches however operate in a different scenario and aim at enforcing a (quite static) authorization policy defined by the data owner. The key derivation hierarchy is organized to model the access control lists of resources (i.e., vertices represent groups of users), in contrast to capability lists. Changes in the authorization policy can imply both grant and revoke of privileges as decided by the data owner, who is interested in limiting her intervention to enforce policy updates. Also, they do not consider the peculiarities of digital data markets, such as the payment of rewards to the owner, nor the integration with blockchain and smart contracts.

Other lines of work close to ours are related to the adoption of blockchain and smart contracts for data management and access control (e.g., [7,9–17]). These approaches are however complementary to ours, as they do not consider selective encryption and key derivation for enforcing access restrictions to traded resources or do not consider the peculiarities of data markets.

8 Conclusions

We investigated the problem of maintaining owners in control over their data when shared and traded in digital data markets through selective owner-side encryption and smart contracts on a blockchain. We proposed different approaches for enforcing selective access restrictions by properly modifying the key derivation structure and the catalog of tokens used to distribute keys to authorized subjects. Our strategies pursue different optimization criteria that suit the peculiarities of the digital data market scenario, and aim at reducing the size of the token catalog (to ensure fast token retrieval) or the tokens to be updated for enforcing new access requests (to reduce the costs caused by update operations on the blockchain). We also presented additional considerations that may be employed for further reducing the number of tokens necessary to enforce access restrictions.

Acknowledgements. This work was supported in part by the EC within the H2020 Program under projects MOSAICrOWN, MARSAL, and GLACIATION, and by the Italian Ministry of Research within the PRIN program under project HOPE.

References

1. Atallah, M., Blanton, M., Fazio, N., Frikken, K.: Dynamic and efficient key management for access hierarchies. ACM TISSEC **12**(3), 1–43 (2009)
2. Bacis, E., De Capitani di Vimercati, S., Foresti, S., Paraboschi, S., Rosa, M., Samarati, P.: Mix&Slice: efficient access revocation in the cloud. In: Proceedings of ACM CCS 2016. Vienna, Austria (2016)
3. Cheng, R., et al.: Ekiden: a platform for confidentiality-preserving, trustworthy, and performant smart contract execution. In: Proceedings of EuroS&P 2019. Stockholm, Sweden (2019)
4. De Capitani di Vimercati, S., Foresti, S., Jajodia, S., Paraboschi, S., Samarati, P.: Encryption policies for regulating access to outsourced data. ACM TODS **35**(2), 1–46 (2010)
5. De Capitani di Vimercati, S., Foresti, S., Livraga, G., Samarati, P.: Practical techniques building on encryption for protecting and managing data in the cloud. In: Ryan, P.Y.A., Naccache, D., Quisquater, J.-J. (eds.) The New Codebreakers. LNCS, vol. 9100, pp. 205–239. Springer, Heidelberg (2016). https://doi.org/10.1007/978-3-662-49301-4_15
6. De Capitani di Vimercati, S., Foresti, S., Livraga, G., Samarati, P.: Empowering owners with control in digital data markets. In: Proceedings of IEEE CLOUD 2019. Milan, Italy (2019)
7. Di Francesco Maesa, D., Mori, P., Ricci, L.: Blockchain based access control. In: Proceedings of DAIS 2017. Neuchâtel, Switzerland (2017)
8. Foresti, S., Livraga, G.: Selective owner-side encryption in digital data markets: strategies for key derivation. In: Proceedings of SECRYPT 2021 (2021)
9. Kokoris-Kogias, E., Alp, E.C., Gasser, L., Jovanovic, P., Syta, E., Ford, B.: CALYPSO: private data management for decentralized ledgers. PVLDB **14**(4), 586–599 (2020)
10. Liang, J., Li, S., Jiang, W., Cao, B., He, C.: OmniLytics: a blockchain-based secure data market for decentralized machine learning. In: Proceedings of FL-ICML 2021 (2021)
11. Liu, K., Qiu, X., Chen, W., Chen, X., Zheng, Z.: Optimal pricing mechanism for data market in blockchain-enhanced Internet of Things. IEEE IoT-J **6**(6), 9748–9761 (2019)
12. Nguyen, D.C., Pathirana, P.N., Ding, M., Seneviratne, A.: Blockchain for secure EHRs sharing of mobile cloud based E-health systems. IEEE Access **7**, 66792–66806 (2019)
13. Nguyen, L.D., Leyva-Mayorga, I., Lewis, A.N., Popovski, P.: Modeling and analysis of data trading on blockchain-based market in IoT networks. IEEE IoT-J **8**(8), 6487–6497 (2021)
14. Shafagh, H., Burkhalter, L., Hithnawi, A., Duquennoy, S.: Towards blockchain-based auditable storage and sharing of IoT data. In: Proceedings of CCSW 2017. Dallas, TX, USA (2017)
15. Zhou, Y., Chen, J., He, B., Lv, L.: Data trading for blockchain-based data market in cyber-physical-social smart systems. In: Proceedings of IEEE PIMRC 2021 (2021)
16. Zichichi, M., Ferretti, S., D'Angelo, G.: A framework based on distributed ledger technologies for data management and services in intelligent transportation systems. IEEE Access **8**, 100384–100402 (2020)
17. Zyskind, G., Nathan, O., Pentland, A.: Decentralizing privacy: using blockchain to protect personal data. In: Proceedings of IEEE SPW 2015. San Jose, CA, USA (2015)

Author Index

P. Samarati et al. (Eds.): ICETE 2021, CCIS 1795, pp. 411–412, 2023.
https://doi.org/10.1007/978-3-031-36840-0

Printed in the United States
by Baker & Taylor Publisher Services